DEATH:

Current Perspectives

DEATH:

Current Perspectives

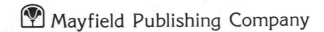 Mayfield Publishing Company

Edited by

Edwin S. Shneidman, Ph.D.

Professor of Thanatology,
Director, Laboratory for the Study of Life-Threatening Behavior,
University of California at Los Angeles

ʃʃʃ

Library of Congress Catalog Card Number: 75-21075
International Standard Book Number: 0-87484-332-4

Manufactured in the United States of America
Mayfield Publishing Company
285 Hamilton Avenue, Palo Alto, California 94301

This book was set in Zenith and Elegante by Applied
Typographic Systems and was printed and bound by
the George Banta Company. Sponsoring editor was
Alden C. Paine, Carole Norton supervised editing, and
manuscript editors were Bengt Ljunggren and Fiorella
Ljunggren. Michelle Hogan supervised production, and
the book was designed by Nancy Sears. Cover and part
title page artwork is by Patrick Korch. Mezzotint on
facing page is from an original work by Judith Malkin
Watkyns.

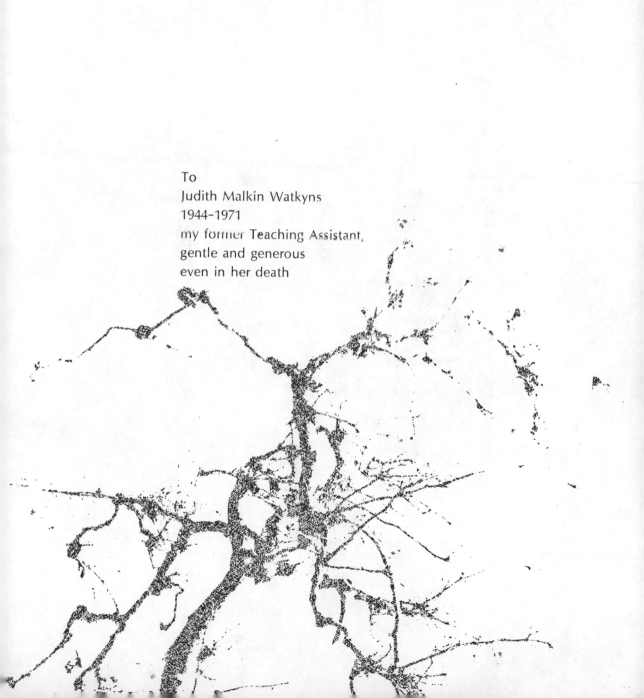

To
Judith Malkin Watkyns
1944–1971
my former Teaching Assistant,
gentle and generous
even in her death

CONTENTS

PREFACE

In a now-famous letter to his distinguished friend and fellow author Nathaniel Hawthorne, Herman Melville, ruminating about *Moby Dick,* wrote in June of 1851 these intimate lines: "Dollars damn me; and the malicious Devil is forever grinning in upon me, holding the door ajar. . . . What I feel most moved to write, this is banned—it will not pay. Yet, altogether, write the *other* way, I cannot." And elsewhere (that same year), in his flawed masterpiece *Pierre,* Melville exclaimed, "Oh, what quenchless feud is this, that Time hath with the sons of Men!"

My purpose in quoting these two diverse statements from Melville is not to make the point that either money or time were *my* antagonists; rather, my enemy and foe was *space.* The first draft of this book had over three times its present content—much too bulky and thus potentially far too expensive to be practical. To excise fully eligible articles in order to reduce this volume to any manageable size meant to give up many favorites—clear favorites of mine and possible favorites of yours.

One decision of mine—to limit the selections entirely to those written in the last decade, 1965–1975—helped in the process of selection. This was an especially difficult decision to hold to because it meant eliminating some obvious choices—such as Freud's papers on death and mourning and several worthwhile books completed before 1965, including those by Feifel, Fulton, Choron, and many other worthies—but I needed some criterion for restraint, and *recency* seemed to be an especially relevant one. Also, I chose mostly from books rather than items from the periodical literature, believing that the latter, in general, tend to be more ephemeral and to become dated more quickly.

My essential aim in assembling this volume was to provide a representative sample of recent and contemporary writings on the myriad aspects of death and dying. My principal goal was to create a set of materials which would serve as either a primary or a supplementary text for a college undergraduate course relating to death. I have sought to achieve this goal in two ways: first, by structuring the book according to a logic that offers the reader a series of pertinent perspectives with which to build up an understanding of death—death as it relates to our culture and society; death as it relates to our understanding of each other and of ourselves. Secondly, in the interstitial materials (the Introduction and the prefatory comments to each chapter) I have attempted to guide the reader—especially the reader who may be relatively unsophisticated about the contemporary literature on death—to a wider understanding of the field-as-a-whole and to provide him with some conceptual cement to pull together the disparate bricks of concept, opinion, and fact. I trust that some sense of the continuity and interrelatedness will be apparent and that the active reader will be able to sense that the selections do indeed complement one another much as there is a mysterious, complementary relationship between the complexities of human death and the complications of human life.

Though it is intended for use as a college text, I would hope that this book will also be useful to professionals in medicine, nursing, theology, law, public health and mortuary science, in police academies, and in the social and behavioral sciences in general, especially in the disciplines of psychology and sociology.

A number of people helped me personally, especially three lovely young ladies, Annita Borodin and Ann Scambler, who are as unfailingly efficient as they are gracious, and Melinda Bertolet whose cheerful efficiency was indispensable; and one gentleman, Bengt Ljunggren, whose editorial suggestions were invariably helpful. Elayne Jovicic and Larry P. Smith cheerfully prepared the Name Index and the Subject Index, respectively. I am indebted to them all.

In addition, I wish to thank Ralph B. Hupka, California State University, Long Beach; Harold A. Widdison, Northern Arizona University; Tony Bell, California State University, Fullerton; Kent Bennington, University of California, Davis; June O'Conner, University of California, Riverside; and Robert Hunt, University of Redlands, who reviewed the manuscript in its developmental stages and made valuable comments and suggestions.

Below, I happily acknowledge the several publishers from whom permission was obtained to reproduce the selections in this volume. I am grateful to them. Detailed acknowledgement notes are given on the initial page of each selection.

Aldine Publishing Co. for *Awareness of Dying* by Barney G. Glaser and Anselm L. Strauss.

George Allen & Unwin Ltd. for *Why I Am Not a Christian* by Bertrand Russell.

American Psychological Association for "Attitudes toward Death" by Herman Feifel, from the *Journal of Consulting and Clinical Psychology.*

Associated Book Publishers Ltd. for *Bereavement* by C. M. Parkes.

Basic Books for "When, Why, and Where People Die" by Monroe Lerner from *The Dying Patient* edited by Orville G. Brim, Jr. et al.

Behavioral Publications, Inc. for "The Funeral Industry in Boston" by Jonathan Baird and "Combat Death" by Joel W. Baruch from *Death and the College Student* edited by Edwin S. Shneidman; for *On Dying and Denying* by Avery D. Weisman; and for "A Psychiatrist's Response to a Life-Threatening Illness" by Eugene Trombley from *Life-Threatening Behavior.*

George Braziller, Inc. for *How Could I Not Be Among You?* by Ted Rosenthal.

Doubleday & Company, Inc. for *Death, Grief and Mourning* by Geoffrey Gorer.

Dunellen Publishing Co., Inc. for *Death, Property, and Lawyers* by Thomas L. Shaffer.

Group for the Advancement of Psychiatry, Inc. for "Attitudes of Patients with Advanced Malignancy" by Samuel L. Feder from *Death and Dying: Attitudes of Patient and Doctor.*

Hodder and Stoughton Ltd. for "The Medical Definition of Death" by A. Keith Mant, "Death and Psychical Research" by Rosalind Heywood, and "Traditional Attitudes towards Death" and "The Relation between

Life and Death, Living and Dying" by Arnold Toynbee from *Man's Concern with Death* by Arnold Toynbee and others.

The Johns Hopkins University Press for *Western Attitudes toward Death* by Philippe Ariès.

Institute of Society, Ethics and the Life Sciences for "Brain Death" by Robert M. Veatch, from the *Hastings Center Report*.

International Universities Press for *Bereavement* by C. M. Parkes.

Little, Brown and Company, Inc., for the *Aristos* by John Fowles; and for *Population, Modernization and Social Structure* by Calvin Goldscheider.

McGraw-Hill Book Co. for "The Medical Definition of Death" by A. Keith Mant; "Death and Psychical Research" by Rosalind Heywood; and "Traditional Attitudes towards Death" and "The Relation between Life and Death, Living and Dying" by Arnold Toynbee from *Man's Concern with Death* by Arnold Toynbee and others.

Macmillan Publishing Co., Inc. for *On Death and Dying* by Elisabeth Kübler-Ross.

Mental Hygiene for "The Widow-to-Widow Program" by Phyllis R. Silverman.

Nash Publishing Co. for "Prolonging Life: Some Legal Considerations" by George P. Fletcher and "Voluntary Euthanasia: The Ethical Aspect" by W. R. Matthews from *Euthanasia and the Right to Death* edited by A. B. Downing.

Harold Ober Associates, Inc. for *Death, Grief and Mourning* by Geoffrey Gorer.

Penguin Books Ltd. for *Dying* by John Hinton, and for *The Twentieth Century Book of the Dead* by Gil Elliot.

Praeger Publishing Co. for *Living and Dying* by Robert Jay Lifton and Eric Olson.

Prentice-Hall, Inc. for *Passing On* by David Sudnow.

G. P. Putnam's Sons for *A Very Easy Death* by Simone de Beauvoir.

Quadrangle/The New York Times Book Co. for *Deaths of Man* by Edwin S. Shneidman.

Random House, Inc. (Ballantine Books) for *The Twentieth Century Book of the Dead* by Gil Elliot.

St. Christopher's Hospice (London) for *Annual Report* by Cicely Saunders.

The Seabury Press for *Death: Meaning and Mortality in Christian Thought and Contemporary Culture* by Milton McC. Gatch.

Anthony Sheil Associates Ltd. for *The Aristos* by John Fowles.

Simon & Schuster, Inc. for *Why I Am Not a Christian* by Bertrand Russell.

Springer Publishing Co., Inc. for *The Psychology of Death* by Robert Kastenbaum and Ruth Aisenberg.

University of California Press for *Cancer, The Wayward Cell* by Victor Richards.

George Weidenfeld and Nicolson, Arthur Barker, Ltd. for *A Very Easy Death* by Simone de Beauvoir.

INTRODUCTION

Perhaps the single most impressive fact about death today—independent of the intransigent truth that death can never be circumvented—is how much (and in how many different ways) various aspects of death and dying are currently undergoing dramatic changes. Nowadays, there are many breezes in the thanatological wind.[1] We are experiencing a cultural revolution in many areas of our living. In the last short generation, scores of our folkways (in dress, deportment, civility, morality, sexuality) and even some of our mores have been transmuted, often in breathtaking ways. The ethics and sociology and psychology and morality of death have not been exempted from these culture-wide changes. This book attempts to reflect these changes in relation to death—changes, for example, that have led us to new, sometimes startling insights into the very process of dying; into the intricate interactions between the dying and those who care for the dying; into the impact of death on those left behind; even into the need for reexamining such fundamental questions as: When *does* death occur? When *should* death occur?

---

[1]Thanatology is the study of death and dying, after Thanatos, the mythological Greek god of death, who was a twin of Hypnus, the god of sleep.

To give the current trends in thanatology a contexture, this volume examines death from many perspectives ranging from explication of cultural strategies for dealing with death as a philosophical concept to an investigation of individual tactics for dealing with death as an inevitable reality.

What will be discussed here are the threads of change that weave through the various chapters and which constitute some of the more important developments in the current thanatological scene.

Please read this paragraph aloud, slowly, word by word:[2]

"Haul in the chains! Let the carcass go astern!" The vast tackles have done their duty. The peeled white body of the beheaded whale flashes like a marble sepulchre; though changed in hue, it has not perceptibly lost anything in bulk. It is still colossal. Slowly it floats more and more away, the water round it torn and splashed by the insatiate sharks, and the air above vexed with rapacious flights of screaming fowls, whose beaks are like so many insulting poniards in the whale. The vast white headless phantom floats further and further from the ship, and every rod that it so floats, what seem square roods of sharks and cubic roods of fowls, augment the murderous din. For hours and hours from the almost stationary ship that hideous sight is seen. Beneath the unclouded and mild azure sky, upon the fair face of the pleasant sea, wafted by the joyous breezes, the great mass of death floats on and on, till lost in infinite perspectives.

What is to be especially noted in this superlative passage is the breathtaking shift in mood between the first eight lugubrious sentences and the last lilting sentence—from horror and rapaciousness to the most pacific calm. Indeed, the last sentence itself contains this same dramatic contrast as seen in the shift in tone between the first three phrases and the last two. A combination of opposites, as in that paragraph, is called an *oxymoron*. The best known examples of oxymorons in the English language are from *Romeo and Juliet:* ". . . Feather of lead, bright smoke, cold fire, sick health" and, of course, ". . . Parting is such sweet sorrow." I have dwelled on the subject of oxymorons because it is a term that so aptly describes death in our time. Death today is oxymoronic, a paradox made up of contrasting values, opposite trends, and even contradictory facts.

We live in an oxymoronic century. At the same time we have created the most exquisitely sophisticated technological procedures for saving one individ-

---

[2]This passage is from the chapter "The Funeral" in Herman Melville's masterpiece, *Moby Dick.*

ual's life, we have also created lethal technological devices, of at least equal sophistication, with the capacity of exterminating millions, of expunging cultures, of jeopardizing time itself by not only erasing the present but threatening the future—what Melville, in *White Jacket,* called ". . . the terrible combustion of the entire planet." On the one hand, marvelous devices for emergency surgery, kidney dialysis, and organ transplantations promise life; on the other hand, megadeath bombs constantly aimed from above the clouds and beneath the waves promise death. No person in any city or any plain is safe; there is no place to hide (see Kahn's *On Thermonuclear War* [1960] and Lifton's *Death in Life* [1967]).

We live in a paradoxical century. On the one hand, there has been more killing by the state than ever before: over 110 million deaths since 1900 in brutish wars, deliberate famines, planned starvations, police and government executions (see Elliot's *Twentieth Century Book of the Dead* [1972]); on the other hand, there has been no other century where so much effort has been put into saving individual lives and into increasing the general span of life.

The oxymoronic character of our age has made death a complicated subject; but it was not always so. In the middle of the fourteenth century, for example, death seemed rather simple: it was everywhere. It struck simultaneously at everyone; no one was safe. Those days were an unmitigated time of death. From about 1347 to the end of that century, a plague, known as the Black Death, ravaged Europe, killing off as much as one-third of the population, claiming victims at every social level, destroying entire families, virtually wiping out whole communities. The topic on everyone's mind was death; and historically, because of its massive disruption of humanpower, that plague changed the social, political, agricultural, technological, and economic structure of the Western world forever (see Gasquet, *The Great Pestilence* [1893], Boccaccio's *Decameron* [1349–51], Zinsser's *Rats, Lice and History* [1935], and Ziegler's *The Black Death* [1969].

Even the scientific marvels of our age for saving individual lives are, themselves, part of the oxymoronic nature of death in our times for they exist side by side with the frustrating and unfulfilled promises of medicine to save us from the dread maladies of heart disease and cancer. Dubos has referred to this failure of medicine in his book *The Mirage of Health* (1971), and others have called it "the mythology of American medicine." We have been overpromised in part because we have oversought. But great strides have been made: in the United States, life expectancy has been extended 28 years in the last 75 years, from 47 years in 1900 to 75 years in 1975 (see Dublin's *After Eighty Years* [1966]). However it is important to note that this remarkable increase has been due not so much to medicine's miracles for adults, but·rather to work-a-day public health practices in the areas of infant mortality (reduced from 150 to 25 per 1,000 births in this century) to sanitation, immunization, and environmental control—unpretentious activities when compared with the dramatic surgical and medical cures that can increase the life span of the middle-aged and elderly, those very people who tend to be most concerned about death and wish to cling to life.

The elimination of diphtheria, scarlet fever, and typhoid fever and the reduction of mortality from tuberculosis were a million times more effective in increasing general longevity than heart transplants. Conquering the causes of death over 40—cancer, cardio-vascular diseases, and accidents—will do an incalculable amount of psychological good for those people and their children, but will not have enormous impact on the total duration of life for the populace as a whole, adding perhaps five or six years (to the 75) at a maximum (Dublin, 1966). Probably the most significant changes in mortality are to be found less in medical and hospital care than they are in health education: simply in voluntary and controllable changes in our routine daily patterns of eating, exercising, and smoking.

Nowadays the great challenge would seem to lie in our improving the kind of lives we lead. More important than extending life by a year or two would seem to be enhancing the quality of those seventy or eighty years by elevating the current level of our common courtesy, moral rights, education, employment, and contentment. This refocusing on the quality, rather than the quantity of life has profound implications for our changing views on death and for our treatment of the dying.

Certainly one of the most refreshing currents in the changing thanatological wind is the increasing emphasis on a "humanistic" approach to death—an approach which seems to be paralleling the humanistic trends in other sectors of society today. This new approach is seen, for example, in an increasing concern that the dying individual live as fully and as richly as possible until his death and that communication with the dying be tailored to specific human needs, and in the recognition of a need for special therapies to help those who have suffered the loss of someone close. Indeed, this humanistic trend in the treatment of the dying and those immediately affected by death is causing a complete reexamination of the premises on which we have, traditionally, based our views on death and dying.

There is a universal and timeless distinction—often confused in discussion of death—which is implied or made explicit in several selections in this book: it is the vital difference between *my* death and *your* death, between what I call in *Deaths of Man* (1974) the individual as he experiences himself (I_s) and the individual as he experiences others (I_o).

A very impressive aspect of thanatology in the current scene is the dynamic and changing nature of its vital issues. Consider, for example, the swirl of debate around organ transplantation, tied directly to the definition of "death"—does death occur when the heart stops? When the vital signs are gone? Or when the cradle of consciousness, the brain, ceases to generate electrical energy? (That last-named criterion is the one emphasized in the famous Harvard report on "brain death" [Beecher *et al.*, 1968]). One expert (Glaser, 1970) summed it up this way: "The brain is our master control; the heart is just a pump." Or, to put it another way: "No brain, no personality," (Murray, 1951).

And if there is controversy over the definition of "death"—or "How does one take a live heart from a dead person?"—there is a potential moral and legal storm over the issue of voluntary euthanasia. If, as has been said, war is too important to be left to generals, then is life too precious (or too miserable) to be left solely to the judgment of doctors? Can a weakened citizen, too ill to kill himself, have the right to say "Enough!" And, considering what we read and know of occasional heinous derelictions in some nursing homes, what are the chances, without any opportunity for redress, of abuses in the practice of voluntary euthanasia? For young readers especially, these questions may become real issues before their time to die.

One additional current trend can be mentioned. Today there is a new permissiveness regarding death, almost an urgency to speak and think about it. In this century death has become, as Gorer (1965) says, the new pornography—a subject banned from polite society and social discourse. Yet, in the last very few years there has been a spate of books on death; death has become a respectable field of inquiry, particularly in the social and behavioral sciences; and death has become an acceptable topic of study in the college curriculum.

The cultural revolution that we are experiencing today is effecting sweeping changes in the pattern and texture of our lives, changes that are now reaching to the very threshold of our deaths. It is the scope and impact of these changes concerning death that are the concern of this book.

REFERENCES

Beecher, Henry K., *et al.* A Definition of Irreversible Coma. *Journal of the American Medical Association*, 1968, *205*, 85–88.

Dublin, Louis I. *After Eighty Years.* Gainesville: University of Florida Press, 1966.

Dubos, Rene. *The Mirage of Health.* New York: Harper, 1971.

Elliot, Gil. *The Twentieth Century Book of the Dead.* New York: Ballantine Books, 1972.

Gasquet, F. A. *The Great Pestilence.* London: Marshall, Hamilton, Kent & Co., 1893.

Glaser, Robert J. Innovations and Heroic Acts in Prolonging Life. In Orville G. Brim, Jr. et al. (Eds.), *The Dying Patient.* New York: Russell Sage Foundation, 1970.

Gorer, Geoffrey. *Death, Grief and Mourning.* New York: Anchor Books, 1965.

Kahn, Herman. *On Thermonuclear War.* Princeton: Princeton University Press, 1960.

Lifton, Robert Jay. *Death in Life: Survivors of Hiroshima.* New York: Vantage Books, 1967.

Murray, Henry A. Some Basic Psychological Assumptions and Conceptions. *Dialectica,* 1951, *5,* 266-292.

Shneidman, Edwin S. *Deaths of Man.* New York: Penguin Books, 1974.

Ziegler, Philip. *The Black Death.* Harmondsworth, Middlesex, England: Pelican Books, 1969.

Zinsser, Hans. *Rats, Lice and History.* London: G. Routledge & Sons, 1935.

EPIGRAMMATIC
PROLOGUE

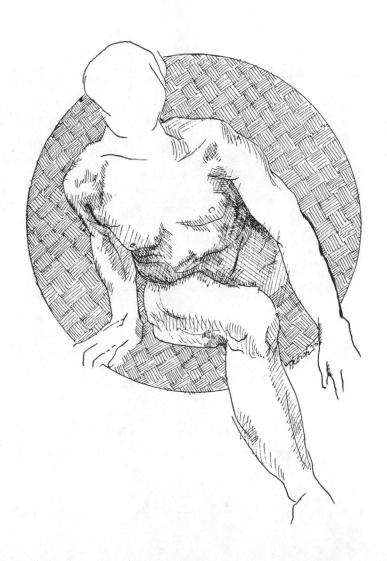

EPIGRAMMATIC PROLOGUE

Among the handful of extraordinary contemporary American and English writers—Anthony Burgess, Saul Bellow, Kurt Vonnegut, John Barth, Christopher Isherwood, Robert Graves, Norman Mailer, John Updike, Peter DeVries, J. D. Salinger—John Fowles must be mentioned quickly and near the top of any list. He is one of the most interesting and vibrant writers alive with four novels to his credit: *The Collector* (1963), an original tour de force concerning desperate evil and ineffectual innocence; *The Magus* (1966), an absolutely swooping book that, in its very own pages, creates a new genre which blurs the lines between the reality of the author's fiction and the latent psychosis in every reader's mind; *The French Lieutenant's Woman* (1969), an authentic classic, a breathtaking book about the deepest ambivalences between sacred and profane love; and *The Ebony Tower* (1974) a set of psychologically laden stories. That pervasive theme—sacred and profane love—either touches or permeates all of Fowles' work. He explores and turns this theme in each of his works, each time with an original twist, exposing a hitherto unexplored facet of the dualities, ambivalences, ambiguities, and duplicities of human life. In spirit (although surely not in style), he is the most Melvillean of our current writers—and for that reason, perhaps the greatest.

Fowles has written a fourth book, *The Aristos* (1968; revised 1970). It is not a work of fiction, but a collection of 761 aphorisms and notes subsumed under twelve chapters. Each pronouncement runs from two brief lines to almost a full page. It is a veritable tractatus of wisdom, and harkens back to Pascal's *Pensées*. The word *aristos*, from the ancient Greek, means roughly "the best for a given situation." *The Aristos* deals with those kinds of topics where the choices are, at best, often between miserable alternatives: aspects of isolation, anxiety, envy, tension, nationalism, culpability, and death.

A not insignificant number of Fowles's thoughts relate to death. Fowles tells us that the original impetus and many of the ideas for these notes came to him from Heraclitus (500 B.C.); he reprints one fragment of Heraclitus's teaching: "All that we see is death." Fowles himself is not totally focused on this thanatological topic but he is keenly invested, almost to the point of obsession, with the dark side of life. His short section on Death—only twenty-eight aphorisms subsumed under the more general topic of "Human Dissatisfactions"—provides us with some of the flavor of his work. The reader may wish to look again at Heraclitus's pithy sayings and at Pascal's *Pensées* for other sets of mind-stretching aphorisms from previous centuries.

Human Dissatisfactions

John Fowles

1   Why do we think this is not the best of all possible worlds for mankind? Why are we unhappy in it?

2 What follow are the great dissatisfactions. I maintain that they are all essential to our happiness since they provide the soil from which it grows.

DEATH

3 We hate death for two reasons. It ends life prematurely; and we do not know what lies beyond it.

4 A very large majority of educated mankind now doubts the existence of an

afterlife. It is clear that the only scientific attitude is that of agnosticism: we simply do not know. We are in the Bet Situation.

5 The Bet Situation is one in which we cannot have certainty about some future event; and yet in which it is vital that we come to a decision about its nature. This situation faces us at the beginning of a horse race, when we want to know the name of the winner. . . .

6 To Pascal, who first made this analogy with the bet, the answer was clear: one must put one's money on the Christian belief that a recompensatory afterlife exists. If it is not true, he argued, then one has lost nothing but one's stake. If it is true, one has gained all.

7 Now even an atheist contemporary with Pascal might have agreed that nothing but good could ensue, in an unjust society where the majority conveniently believed in hellfire, from supporting the idea, false or true, of an afterlife. But today the concept of hellfire has been discarded by the theologians, let alone the rest of us. Hell could be just only in a world where all were equally persuaded that it exists; just only in a world that allowed a total freedom of will—and therefore a total biographical and biological similarity—to every man and woman in it. . . .

8 The idea of an afterlife has persistently haunted man because inequality has persistently tyrannized him. It is only to the poor, the sick, the unfortunate underdogs of history, that the idea appeals; it has appealed to all honest men's sense of justice, and very often at the same time as the use of the idea to maintain an unequal *status quo* in society has revolted them. Somewhere, this belief proposes, there is a system of absolute justice and a day of absolute judgment by and on which we are all to be rewarded according to our desserts.

9 But the true longing of humanity is not for an afterlife; it is for the establishment of a justice here and now that will make an afterlife unnecessary. This myth was a compensatory fantasy, a psychological safety-valve for the frustrations of existential reality.

10 We are ourselves to establish justice in our world: and the more we allow the belief in an afterlife to dwindle away, and yet still do so little to correct the flagrant inequalities of our world, then the more danger we run.

11 Our world has a badly designed engine. By using the oil of this myth it did not for many centuries heat up. But now the oil level is dropping ominously low. For this reason, it is not enough to remain agnostic. We *must* bet on the other horse: we have one life, and it is ended by a total extinction of consciousness as well as body.

12 What matters is not our personal damnation or salvation in the world to come, but that of our fellow men in the world that is.

13 Our second hatred of death is that it almost always comes too soon. We suffer from an illusion, akin to that of the desirability of an afterlife, that we should be happier if we lived for ever. Animal desires are always for an extension of what satisfies them. Only two hundred years ago a man who reached the age of forty was exceeding the average life span; and perhaps two hundred years from now centenarians will be as common as septuagenarians today. But they will still crave a longer life.

14 The function of death is to put tension into life; and the more we increase the length and the security of individual existence then the more tension we remove from it. All our pleasurable experiences contain a faint yet terrible element of the condemned man's last breakfast, an echo of the intensity of feeling of the poet who knows he is going to die, of the young soldier going doomed into battle.

ↄↄ

Pleasure is a product of death; not an escape from it.

ↄↄↄ

15 Each pleasure we feel is a pleasure less; each day a stroke on a calendar. What we will not accept is that the joy in the day and the passing of the day are inseparable. What makes our existence worthwhile is precisely that its worth and its while—its quality and duration—are as impossible to unravel as time and space in the mathematics of relativity.

16 *Pleasure is a product of death; not an escape from it.*

17 If it were proved that there is an afterlife, life would be irretrievably spoilt. It would be pointless; and suicide, a virtue. The only possible paradise is one in which I cannot know I did once exist.

18 There are two tendencies in the twentieth century; one, a misguided one, is to domesticate death, to pretend that death is like life; the other is to look death in the face. The tamers of death believe in life after death; they indulge in elaborate after-death ceremonial. Their attitude to death is euphemistic; it is "passing on" and "going to a better place." The actual process

of death and decomposition is censored. Such people are in the same mental condition as the ancient Egyptians.

19 "Passing on": the visual false analogy. We know that passing objects, such as we see repeatedly every day, exist both before and after the passage that we see; and so we come, illogically and wrongly, to treat life as such a passage.

20 Death is in us and outside us; beside us in every room, in every street, in every field, in every car, in every plane. Death is what we are not every moment that we are, and every moment that we are is the moment when the dice comes to rest. We are always playing Russian roulette.

21 Being dead is nothingness, not-being. When we die we constitute "God."* Our relics, our monuments, the memories retained by those who survive us, these still exist; do not constitute "God," still constitute the process. But these relics are the fossilized traces of our having been, not our being. All the great religions try to make out that death is nothing. There is another life to come. . . .

22 As one social current has tried to hide death, to euphemize it out of existence, so another has thrust death forward as a chief element in entertainment: in the murder story, the war story, the spy story, the western. But increasingly, as our century grows old, these fictive deaths become more fictitious, and fulfil the function of concealed euphemism. The real death of a pet kitten affects a child far more deeply than the "deaths" of all the television gangsters, cowboys, and Red Indians.

23 By death we think characteristically of the disappearance of individuals; it does not console us to know that matter is not disappearing, but is simply being metamorphosed. We mourn the individualizing form, not the generalized content. But everything we see is a metaphor of death. Every limit, every dimension, every end of every road, is a death. Even seeing is a death, for there is a point beyond which we cannot see, and our seeing dies; wherever our capacity ends, we die.

24 Time is the flesh and blood of death; death is not a skull, a skeleton, but a clock face, a sun hurtling through a sea of thin gas. A part of you has died since you began to read this sentence.

---

*Elsewhere in The Aristos, *under "God," Fowles says: "'God' is a situation. Not a power, or a being, or an influence. Not a 'he' or a 'she' but an 'it'. Not an entity or non-entity, but the situation in which there can be both entity and non-entity."—*ED.

25 Death itself dies. Every moment you live, it dies. *O Death where is thy sting, Death I will be thy death.* The living prove this; not the dead.

26 In all the countries living above a bare subsistence level, the twentieth century has seen a sharp increase in awareness of the pleasures of life. This is not only because of the end of belief in an afterlife, but because death is more real today, more probable, now that the H-bomb is.

27 *The more absolute death seems, the more authentic life becomes.*

28 All I love and know may be burnt to ashes in one small hour: London, New York, Paris, Athens gone in less time than it takes to count ten. I was born in 1926; and because of what can happen now in ten seconds, that year lies not forty-one years but a measureless epoch and innocence away. Yet I do not regret that innocence. I love life more, not less.

29 Death contains me as my skin contains me. Without it, I am not what I am. Death is not a sinister door I walk towards; it is my walking towards.

ʄʄ

The more absolute death seems, the more authentic life becomes.

ʄʄ

30 Because I am a man death is my wife; and now she has stripped, she is beautiful, she wants me to strip, to be her mate. This is necessity, this is love, this is being-for-another, nothing else. I cannot escape this situation, nor do I want to. She wants me to make love, not like some man-eating spider, to consume me, but like a wife in love, so that we can celebrate our total sympathy, be fertile and bear children. It is her effect on me and my effect upon her that make all that is good in my time being. She is not a prostitute or a mistress I am ashamed of or want to forget or about whom I can sometimes pretend that she does not exist. Like my real wife she informs every important situation in my life, she is wholly of my life, not beyond, or against, or opposite to it. I accept her completely, in every sense of the word, and I love and respect her for what she is to me.

PART ONE

CULTURAL

PERSPECTIVES

ON DEATH

·1·

CONCEPTS

OF DEATH

Death, perhaps man's greatest mystery and source of fear, has from earliest recorded times been a chief focus of his superstitions and beliefs about his life and his world (and about other possible lives and places). Man's thoughts about death have influenced his philosophies and his religions. This is not at all surprising inasmuch as religion *is* concerned with the myths and mysteries of resurrection, rebirth, and relationship with God. In essence, man seems to generate, in his various cultures, some kind of view of death, what might be called a "strategy" for handling the idea of death. Although in this century death has become vastly secularized—as evidenced by the exalted scientist, the revered doctor, the venerated devices for diagnosis and treatment, and the glorified hospital—the relationship between religion and death is historically rooted and continues, for many, to play an important role in their attitudes (and in their behaviors) toward death.

Always, and in all cultures, the main questions seem to be: What is death? How shall we think of it? (Fear it? Welcome it?) Is death the absolute end? Or is there some sort of survival after death? The selections in this chapter offer the reader a "long view" of death—death as seen from the perspective of various cultures at various times. The Toynbee selection discusses some of the specific strategies that various cultures have worked out for dealing with the fact of death that are functionally related to, or even functionally dependent on, the culture's religions, philosophies, legal and political institutions, and socioeconomic conditions at a particular period. (As the gods evolve and the pantheons change, so do the concepts of death). Some of these concepts are highly durable from culture to culture and from time to time (e.g., Toynbee's ". . . putting one's treasures in future generations . . ."), while others, such as "physical countermeasures," are less durable, albeit they may be retained today in vestigial form (e.g., peasant funeral rites in China, calling for burning of symbolic paper articles to accompany the dead). The "evolution" of perspectives on death within a major culture can be illustrated by comparing early Christian concepts with those of modern Christianity, as is done in the selection by Gatch.

One of the most soothing strategies for dealing with the concept of death is simply to deny that death means the end of the individual (a concept which, in one form or another, is implied in several of the categories described by Toynbee). This is perhaps one of the most "durable" views of death. Both the Heywood and the Russell selections emphasize that survival after death is, of necessity, based on belief; but Heywood sees "evidence" to support such a belief, while Russell sees logic as refuting the whole concept. Heywood's selection is included because this volume is a sampler of current thought, presenting both the firmly established and the avowedly professed, even where the data seem to be shaky.

Bertrand Russell was probably the most intellectually gifted mind of this century. His thoughts and writings have illuminated mathematics, science, philosophy, and morality. His brief essay "Do We Survive Death?" is written in typical pungent Russellian prose, putting to rest (for any logical mind who dares to follow his reasoning) the vexing notion of survival after death and its beguiling twin, immortality.

The penultimate selection in this book is from Simone de Beauvoir's memoir of her mother's death in which she says: "Religion could do no more for my mother than the hope of posthumous success could do for me. Whether you think of it as heavenly or earthly, if you love life, immortality is no consolation for death." At the other extreme is the tragic hunger for immortality of Miguel de Unamuno, the twentieth-century Spanish philosopher and writer. In his famous work *The Tragic Sense of Life*, first published in 1921, he wrote: "For the sake of a name, man is ready to sacrifice not only life but happiness—life as a matter of course. 'Let me die, but let my fame live! Death is bitter, but fame is eternal.'" Unamuno seemed to be obsessed with immortality. A Catholic, he wrote: "If we all die utterly, wherefore does everything exist?" And "If there is no immortality, of what use is God?" He said further: "It is impossible for us, in effect, to conceive of ourselves as not existing, and no effort is capable of enabling consciousness to realize absolute unconsciousness, its own annihilation." This statement is all the more remarkable in that Unamuno, perhaps as far in his beliefs from a psychoanalytic orientation as any twentieth-century thinker could be, practically repeats one of Freud's most often quoted statements about death and immortality: "Our own death is indeed unimaginable, and whenever we make an attempt to imagine it we can perceive that we really survive as spectators. Hence the psychoanalytic school could venture on the assertion that at bottom no one believes in his own death, or to put the thing in another way, in the unconscious everyone of us is convinced of his own immortality." These two statements present an amazing parallel of thought from two distinguished thinkers approaching the beguiling topic of immortality at about the same time from very different philosophic positions.

From the very beginning we sense the oxymoronic quality of death. Death is destroyer and redeemer; the ultimate cruelty and the essence of release; universally feared but sometimes actively sought; undeniably ubiquitous, yet incomprehensibly unique; of all phenomena, the most obvious and the least reportable; feared yet fascinating.

These oxymoronic qualities of death are caught in these lines by Sir Walter Raleigh: "O eloquent, just and mighty Death. Whom none can advise, thou hast persuaded; what none have dared, thou has done; and whom all the world has flattered, thou only has cast out of the world and despised."

Various Ways in Which Human Beings Have Sought to Reconcile Themselves to the Fact of Death

Arnold Toynbee

Arnold Toynbee, an internationally famous English historian, is best known for *A Study of History*, a ten-volume work written between 1934 and 1954. In this selection taken from his remarkable and scholarly book *Man's Concern with Death*, Professor Toynbee lists and discusses numerous ways in which human beings have denied, accepted, embraced, superordinated, or "handled" death.

From *Man's Concern with Death*. Copyright © 1968 by Arnold Toynbee, A. Keith Mant, Ninian Smart, John Hinton, Cicely Yudkin, Eric Rhode, Rosalind Heywood, H. H. Price. Used with permission of McGraw-Hill Book Company, and Hodder and Stoughton Ltd.

(a) *Hedonism.* The most obvious way of reconciling oneself to death is to make sure of enjoying life before death snatches it from us. The catchwords *"Carpe diem"*[1] and "Let us eat and drink, for tomorrow we shall die"[2] are notorious, and Herodotus[3] has preserved an Egyptian folk-tale in which the Pharaoh Mycerinus, when the gods had sentenced him to die after enjoying only six more years of life, successfully doubled the term arbitrarily allotted to him by turning night into day. This hedonistic solution of the problem of death is, of course, illusory. In reality a human being cannot stay awake, enjoying himself, for 24 hours a day, day in and day out, over a span of six years. Nor can he make sure of enjoying himself even for the briefest spells; and, if luck does favor him that far, his foreknowledge that one day he is going to die will be lurking all the time at the back of his mind. The skeleton was simply being brought out of the cupboard in the Egyptian custom, also recorded by Herodotus,[4] of exhibiting a miniature wooden model of a mummy at a feast in order to remind the revellers of the grim fact of death, which they were trying to put out of

---

[1]Horace, *Odes,* Book I, Ode xi, line 8. Cp. Book I, Ode iv, passim.
[2]Isaiah, xxii, 13. Cp. Eccles., iii, 22.
[3]Herodotus, Book II, chap. 133.
[4]In Book II, chap. 78.

their minds for the moment. Eating, drinking, and being merry is, like war and revolution, an intrinsically transient activity. It is, in fact, another name for "sowing one's wild oats," and it is only in fairy tales that this conventional escapade is followed by "marrying and living happily after." In prosaic real life, it is followed by the anxieties and fatigues and maladies of adult life—congenital evils of our human condition, which, if they are severe and long drawn out, may make a human being actually look forward to death as an eventual relief on which he can count for certain.

(b) *Pessimism.* The most obvious alternative to the illusory solace of hedonism is to conclude that life is so wretched that death is the lesser evil. In the 5th century B.C., when the Greeks were at the height of their achievement in all fields, the Greek poet Sophocles declared[5] that "it is best of all never to have been born, and second-best—second by far—if one has made his appearance in this world, to go back again, as quickly as may be, thither whence he has come." The Greek historian Herodotus attributed the same view to the 6th-century-B.C. Greek sage Solon.[6] According to Herodotus's story of Solon's conversation with King Croesus, the human beings cited by Solon as having been the happiest, save for one, within his knowledge, were, not Croesus, as Croesus had hoped, but two young men—a pair of brothers—who had died in their sleep at the height of their strength, achievement, and fame, when their mother had prayed to the goddess Hera to bestow on them the best lot that a human being can hope for. The comment that Herodotus puts into Solon's mouth is that the brothers "met with the best possible end that human life can have, and that God took this opportunity for making it manifest that, for a human being, it is better to be dead than to be alive."

"Those whom the gods love, die young."[7] In many military-minded societies, there have been young men who have looked forward, with pride and exaltation, to the prospect of dying prematurely in battle; and it is significant that when, in the 7th and 6th centuries B.C., some Greeks began to transfer their treasure from their community to their own individual lives, the elegiac and lyric poets who gave expression to this psychological revolution harped plaintively on the brevity of the springtime of an individual

---

[5]In *Oedipus Coloneus,* lines 1224-6.
[6]Herodotus, Book I, chap. 31.
[7]Byron, *Don Juan,* IV, xii.

human being's life, and on the weariness of the long-drawn-out sequel of old age, with its burden of increasing ill-health and debility.[8]

ʧʧ

*The lot of an agricultural laborer who
is the serf of a pauper in the land of
the living is preferable to being king
of all the dead.*

ʧʧ

However, in this age and in all subsequent ages of ancient Greek history, the Greeks continued to be enthralled by the Homeric epics. These were probably composed, or given their final form, in the 8th century B.C., and the hero of the *Iliad*, Achilles, is not at all reconciled to his foreknowledge that he is doomed to die young, nor does his mother the goddess Thetis take satisfaction, as some Spartan human mothers did in later times, in the prospect of her son's dying young on the field of honor. Young though he still is at the siege of Troy, Achilles has already had time to win matchless glory by his outstanding prowess. But the fame that Achilles has already achieved in a short life does not console him for death's imminence; and his experience after death, in the realm of the shades of the dead, justifies posthumously his reluctance, while alive, to lose his life prematurely. In the eleventh book of the *Odyssey*, his shade is represented as saying to Odysseus that the lot of an agricultural laborer who is the serf of a pauper in the land of the living is preferable to being king of all the dead;[9] and, after making this bitter observation, he strides away, unresigned and indignant, though elated at the same time by the news, given him by Odysseus, of the military prowess of his son.[10]

The repining at the prospect of an early death which is attributed to Achilles in the *Iliad* may have corresponded to the average Greek young man's attitude in real life—even a young man who happened to have been

---

[8]E.g. Mimnermus, *Nanno*, Elegies I and II.
[9]*Odyssey*, Book XI, lines 489–491.
[10]*Ibid.*, lines 538–540.

born a Spartan and to have been conditioned by being brought up under the "Lycurgan" regimen. If his mother took the stand of the legendary Spartan mother, his private reaction may have been a wry one. At Sparta, and, *a fortiori,* in other Greek city-states, there is much evidence that the Greeks, even those who paid lip-service to pessimism, got much enjoyment out of life; were not eager to exchange it for death; and did not let the edge be taken off their enjoyment by brooding on a death for which they were in no hurry. The Greeks enjoyed passing the time of day in each other's company, discussing anything and everything; they enjoyed beauty; and they had a genius for bringing these two sources of enjoyment together in choral singing and dancing, theatrical performances, religious processions, and talkative political assemblies.

Compared with Greek pessimism, Indian pessimism has been radical, and it has also been sincere, as is demonstrated by the single-mindedness and the austerity with which it has been put into action. Hinduism regards man's universe as being an illusion; the Buddha, anticipating some of the schools of modern Western psychologists by about twenty-four centuries, held that the soul is an illusion too. He saw in the human psyche only a fleeting series of discontinuous psychological states, which are held together only by desire, and which can be dissipated if and when desire is extinguished. In the Buddha's view, the extinction of desire is the proper goal of human endeavor, because the achievement of this brings with it the extinction of suffering, and, for the Buddha, life and suffering were synonymous. Not death, but re-birth, is the arch-ordeal for a human being. The Buddha took it for granted that the effect of desire, precipitated in the form of karma (the cumulative spiritual effects of action taken in a succession of lives up to the present), is to keep a series of rebirths going *ad infinitum,* unless and until, in one of the lives in this chain, the sufferer, by successfully performing the strenuous spiritual exercises that the Buddha has prescribed, manages to bring the series to an end by attaining the state of extinguishedness (nirvana) in which all passion is spent and rebirth ceases because it is no longer brought on by the momentum of karma, now that karma has been worked off. In this spiritual struggle to attain nirvana, death (i.e. the death of the current life in the series) is an unimportant incident. Nirvana may be attained at death, but it may also be attained while the former sufferer is still living what will now have been the last of his successive lives.

One index of pessimism is suicide. In a society in which life is rated at so low a value that death is held to be the lesser evil, suicide will be held to be one of the basic human rights, and the practice of it will be considered respectable and in some cases meritorious or even morally obligatory.

In the Graeco-Roman world, no stigma was attached to suicide, though the practice of it was not so common as it has been in South and East Asian countries in which the prevailing religions and philosophies have been of Indian or Chinese origin. There were cases of Greek statesmen who committed suicide in a political impasse. Demosthenes and King Cleomenes III of Sparta are examples. Under the Principate, Roman nobles were in some cases allowed to commit suicide as an alternative to execution. The Greek philosopher Democritus is said by Lucretius to have exposed himself to death voluntarily (perhaps by starvation) when he found that his mental powers were failing.[11] But the Greek spectators were surprised and impressed when Peregrinus Proteus burned himself to death ostentatiously at Olympia.[12] (A modern Western psychologist might have convicted him, as Lucian does, of exhibitionism.) It is possible that Peregrinus may have been influenced by an Indian precedent that could have been within his knowledge. According to the geographer Artemidorus of Ephesus, an Indian who had accompanied an Indian embassy to the Emperor Augustus had burnt himself to death at Athens. Strabo[13] cites Artemidorus as saying that "some Indians do this because they are finding life a burden, while others—of whom this one is an example—do it because they are finding life so good. The idea is that, when everything has gone as one likes, it is time to be off, for fear that, if one lingers, one may be overtaken by something that one does not like."

According to Artemidorus, this particular Indian "leaped on to the pyre, laughing, with nothing on but a loin-cloth and with his body well-oiled; and his tomb bears the inscription: 'Zarmanochegas, an Indian from Bargosa [Broach], who made himself immortal by following traditional Indian custom'."

In Hindu society the commonest form of suicide has been *sati*. It used to be deemed a meritorious act for a widow to burn herself to death when her husband died; and, though *sati* was nominally voluntary, it seems often to have been committed under pressure. A widower was under no reciprocal obligation; but male devotees used to throw themselves under the wheels

---

[11]Lucretius, *De Rerum Natura*, Book III, lines 139–141.
[12]Lucian, *De Morte Peregrini.*
[13]*Geographica*, Book XV, chap. 1, § 73 (C.720).

of Juggernaut's car to be crushed to death. In present-day Vietnam, Buddhist monks and nuns have committed suicide by burning themselves to death as a political protest. In China·under the imperial regime, a censor who had felt it to be his official duty to present a memorial to the Emperor, criticising the Emperor's conduct, might follow up this act by committing suicide—a reconciliation of sincerity with loyalty that would increase the pressure on the Emperor while releasing the censor himself from embarrassment. In Japan, it has been a point of honor to commit suicide, not only as a political protest, but as a sign of respect for a defunct emperor or as atonement for some failure in duty, or for some breach of etiquette, which, in a Westerner's eye, would be a quite inadequate ground for making such drastic and such irrevocable amends, even if the Western observer had no objection to suicide in principle.

There have been cases in which Jews, Phoenicians, and Lycians have committed suicide *en masse* rather than allow themselves to be taken prisoner by a victorious enemy. On the other hand, Christians, whose religion is of Jewish origin, have always felt an inhibition against committing suicide, and have branded a suicide as a *felo de se*, who has debarred himself, by his crime, from being given burial in consecrated ground. The Christian's view of this world as being "a vale of tears" is much the same as the Buddhist's view; but the Christian, unlike the Buddhist, does not consider that he has the right to decide for himself to put an end to his life. For the Christian, this is not man's prerogative; it is God's; and it is impious wilfully to anticipate God's action. If this is a Christian superstition—and it is a superstition in Greek, Roman, Hindu, Buddhist, Confucian Chinese, and Japanese eyes—it is a Christian tradition that dies hard. At the present day, many ex-Christians, who have abandoned almost all the rest of the Christian tradition, still retain the Christian feeling that suicide is shocking.

In a community of Australian natives who live by food-gathering and migrate, in search of food, in an annual orbit, the aged will voluntarily drop out and stay behind to die, in order to relieve the community of the burden of continuing to maintain them. In the present-day Western world the average expectation of life has been increased, without any accompanying increase in zest or relief from pressure, while the loosening of family ties has left many old people out in the cold, socially and spiritually. If they had been Australian natives, they would have allowed themselves to die; if they had been Chinese peasants, there would have been a place for them in the home, with their children and grandchildren, as long as they remained alive. Being Christians or ex-Christians, and therefore feeling the traditional

Christian inhibition against committing suicide, many old people in the Western world today linger on, lonely and unhappy, until medical ingenuity ceases to be able to keep them physically alive.

The Christian inhibition against suicide applies, *a fortiori*, to giving to incurably and painfully ailing human beings the merciful release that humane Christians give, as a matter of course, to animals when these are in the same plight. Hitler was not prevented by the conscience of the German Christian public from murdering millions of Jews; yet the German Christian conscience that did not prove effective for deterring Hitler from committing the crime of genocide did make it impossible for Hitler to carry out his plan of killing off aged, infirm, and feeble-minded Germans in order to relieve physically and mentally fit Germans of the burden of continuing to look after the unfit when German energies were being mobilized by Hitler for the waging of the Second World War.

ⱶⱶⱶ

*Ancient tombs have been preserved
in far greater numbers than ancient
dwellings once inhabited by the living.*

ⱶⱶ

(c) *Attempts to circumvent death by physical countermeasures.* One of the commonest primitive assumptions regarding death is that a dead person's life can be prolonged after death by providing the corpse with the food, drink, paraphernalia, and services that were formerly at the disposal of the person whose living body this corpse once was. The burial with the dead of objects that are useful to the living has been a world-wide practice. Archaeologists have been able to reconstruct a culture from the contents of graves in sites in which there has been little or no trace left of the apparatus used by the living. Ancient tombs have been preserved in far greater numbers than ancient dwellings once inhabited by the living. Besides yielding up tools, weapons, ornaments, and clothes, some tombs have been found to contain the remains of slaughtered domestic animals and of human servitors, whose services the dead owner of the tomb was expected still to be able to command.

This naïve strategy for circumventing death was carried to extremes in Ancient Egypt. If the tomb representing a dead pharoah's house was magnified to the dimensions of a gigantic pyramid, if the furniture deposited in his tomb was as lavish in both quantity and quality as the gear that was buried with Tut-ankh-amen; and if the tomb was endowed with lands whose revenues would pay, in perpetuity, for the provision of victuals and for the performance of ritual by priests, it was felt that death could be counteracted and overcome by this massive application of physical countermeasures—in fact, by sheer physical force. Still more naïve was the assumption that preserving a dead body by arresting its natural decay was tantamount to keeping the life in it. Mummification was practiced not only in Egypt but in Peru. The dryness of the climate in both coastal Peru and Upper Egypt was an assistance to the embalmer's work, yet this fine art was manifestly just as incapable of keeping life in a corpse as the Zoroastrian practice of exposing corpses to putrefy until they have been consumed by scavenging birds and beasts.

Another strategy for the circumvention of death by physical counter-measures has been to seek for the tree of life or for the elixir of immortality. But the fruitlessness of this quest has been recognised in mythology. When Adam and Eve had eaten of the fruit of the Tree of Knowledge, they were expelled from the Garden of Eden by the angel with the flaming sword before they had had time to baffle Yahweh by eating the fruit of the Tree of Life as well. Translated into present-day prosaic terms, this myth signifies that man's acquisition of science and technology has not enabled him to acquire immortality as well. The outcome of the Sumerian hero Gilgamesh's quest for immortality was likewise ironical. After performing a series of Herculean labors, Gilgamesh was on the last stage of his journey home with a branch of the Tree of Life in his hand when he accidentally dropped this into the water, where it was immediately snapped up by a snake. So Gilgamesh arrived home still mortal. His labors had, after all, been in vain.

The futility of trying to circumvent death by taking physical counter-measures was demonstrated dramatically in Ancient Egypt at the fall of the Old Kingdom. The fall of this regime was accompanied by a social revolution in the course of which the tombs of the pharaohs and of their courtiers were rifled and the funerary wealth accumulated in the course of three-quarters of a millennium was impudently plundered. The irony of this ignominious end of such careful and elaborate physical provision for the circumvention of death is one of the themes of surviving Egyptian works of literature written in the age of the Middle Kingdom. Yet this recognition of the futility of the practice did not deter succeeding generations from persisting with it, and the principal beneficiaries of the costly furnishing of

Egyptian pharaohs and nobles came to be, not the dead themselves, but living tomb robbers. Tomb robbing became as fine an art as mummification. The robbers penetrated the most massive and most cunningly contrived defences and eluded the watchful eye of the public authorities. They battened on the Egyptian people's invincible naïveté. Yet it is conceivable that the robbers themselves were not altogether immune from the prevailing superstition. We can imagine them going about their professional business with mixed feelings of cynicism and guilt.

(d) *Attempts to circumvent death by winning fame.* Though a dead body cannot be kept alive by physical measures, the memory of the dead, as they were when they were truly alive, can be transmitted to succeeding generations. In an illiterate society the main media of commemoration are the memorization of genealogies and the composition and recital of oral poetry. When a society has become literate, poetry can be reduced to writing and can by supplemented by inscriptions engraved on stone or impressed on clay tablets or written on papyrus or parchment or paper or palm-leaves or slivers of bamboo, to record the foundation of temples and the annals of reigns. These official records, in turn, can be raised to the level of biographies and historical works of literature which can take their place side by side with poetry.

This attempt to circumvent death by commemoration is more sophisticated than the attempt to circumvent it by physical measures; but the outcome of this attempt is ironical too in ways of its own. For instance, the recorder eventually wins greater fame than the men of action whose fame has been preserved by the recorder's pen. Most of what we know about the Athenian statesman Pericles and the Spartan soldier Brasidas today is due to the fact that a minor naval commander, Thucydides, was given the leisure for becoming a major historian thanks to his having been cashiered and exiled, perhaps unfairly, for having failed to prevent Brasidas from capturing Amphipolis. When Horace wrote "non omnis moriar,"[14] he underestimated the length of the time after his death during which his poetry would preserve the memory of the poet himself. He reckoned that his poetry would continue to be read as long as the ritual of Rome's official religion continued to be performed. This ritual was suppressed by the intolerant Christian Roman Emperor Theodosius I in the last decade of the 4th century of the Christian Era, only four centuries after the date of Horace's death. Yet

---

[14]Horace, *Odes,* Book III, Ode xxx, line 6.

Horace's poetry is still being read in the 20th century by readers whose mother tongue is not Latin, and, in the earlier decades of the 19th century, it was still being quoted in speeches made in English by members of the parliament at Westminster.

Horace himself, however, has pointed out the precariousness of this circumvention of death by commemoration—sophisticated and ethereal though this method is by comparison with the naïve circumvention of death by physical measures.

> Vixere fortes ante Agamemnona
> multi; sed omnes illacrimabiles
> urgentur ignotique longâ
> nocte, carent quia vate sacro.[15]

The relics of Agamemnon's predecessors who are not commemorated in the Homeric epic have now been disinterred by modern archaeologists. These have proved to have been mightier monarchs than Agamemnon himself, and, whether or not they employed court poets whose works have not yet come to light, we have now retrieved some of their records—not romantic minstrels' lays but prosaic official inventories, corresponding to what present-day governments call "forms." These pre-Agamemnonian Mycenaean official documents are at least four or five centuries older than the *Iliad* and the *Odyssey*, and we have specimens of rudiments of the Sumerian cuneiform script that date from before the close of the fourth millennium B.C., but mankind's first five millennia of literacy are dwarfed by the dark night of the preceding million years during which our ancestors were already human yet have not left any surviving memorial except their tools and their cave paintings—and even those Late Palaeolithic paintings are estimated to be not more than about thirty thousand years old. Our thousand past millennia of oblivion are a long span of time, compared to our subsequent 30,000 years of pictorial commemoration and 5000 years of literacy. But mankind's first million years, as well as his latest 5000 years, are dwarfed by the span of 2000 million years which is reckoned to be the expectation of life on the surface of this planet. It is difficult to imagine that any existing works of man, either monumental or literary, will have survived until the day when this planet becomes no longer habitable. Will any of the

---

[15]Horace, *Odes,* Book IV, Ode ix, lines 25-28. "There were mighty men before Agamemnon—there were any number of them; yet, one and all, these are buried in a long, long night, unknown and unmournable—and this just because they had no inspired bard [to commemorate them, as Agamemnon has been commemorated by Homer]."

now current languages then still be intelligible? Will any works written in these still survive? Will not the pyramids, and the still more durable tumuli and railway embankments, have been worn down flatter than the most archaic of the rocks that now crop out on the earth's surface?

(e) *Self-liberation from self-centredness by putting one's treasure in future generations of one's fellow human beings.* Another way in which human beings have sought to reconcile themselves to the fact of death has been so ubiquitous and so constant that one might almost venture to infer that it is innate in human nature. Down to this day, since the earliest date to which our surviving records reach back, most human beings have reconciled themselves, to some extent, to their mortality as individuals by putting their treasure in their descendants, while some human beings have expanded their concern to embrace all the other representatives of future generations who, though not their physical descendants, will be their successors and will perhaps be their spiritual heirs.

In the genealogy in the 11th chapter of the Book of Genesis, the high point in the life of Shem and each of his successive descendants is his age when his first child is born. The remainder of his life, from that red-letter day onwards till his death, is represented implicitly as being an anticlimax.

In Yahweh's successive promises to Abraham, the god never promises his human client personal immortality. What he promises him is progeny. "I will make of thee a great nation";[16] "I will make thy seed as the dust of the earth, so that, if a man can number the dust of the earth, then shall thy seed also be numbered";[17] "look now toward heaven and tell the stars, if thou be able to number them: and he said unto him, so shall thy seed be";[18] "thou shalt be a father of many nations";[19] "Abraham shall surely become a great and mighty nation";[20] "in multiplying I will multiply thy seed as the stars of the heaven, and as the sand which is upon the sea shore."[21] Whether or not this prospect of becoming the ancestor of the Hebrew peoples reconciled Abraham to the prospect of his own death, it is evident that the promises that were held to have been made to Abraham by Yahweh were felt, by the authors and editors of the Book of Genesis, to be more valuable and more satisfying than any promise of personal immortality would have been. If the Israelite writers of these passages believed

---

[16]Gen., xii, 2.   [18]Gen., xv, 5.   [20]Gen., xviii, 18.
[17]Gen., xiii, 16   [19]Gen., xvii, 4.   [21]Gen., xxii, 17.

that, after death, the shades of the dead retained a shadowy existence in Sheol, they will have shared the feelings of the author of the 11th book of the *Odyssey*, who, as has been remarked earlier, describes the shade of Achilles as exulting, in Hades, at the news of his son's prowess on earth, unreconciled though Achilles himself was to his own state after death.[22]

It is significant that the belief in the resurrection of the dead did not gain a foothold in the Jewish community until the 2nd century B.C. This belief seems to have been introduced to the Jews through their becoming acquainted with a foreign religion, Zoroastrianism. One of the considerations that led some Jews to believe, from the 2nd century B.C. onwards, in the eventual resurrection of some individuals is thought to have been their confidence in Yahweh's sense of justice. They will have felt that this was bound to move Yahweh to reward those Jews who had suffered martyrdom in resisting the Seleucid Emperor Antiochus IV's attempt to coerce the Palestinian Jewish community into adopting the Greek way of life; and these martyrs would not be adequately rewarded if they were not eventually raised from the dead to become living participants in the messianic kingdom when this was eventually established. The belief that, not only the Jewish martyrs, but all the dead, were destined to rise again seems, in the development of Judaism, to have come later.

It is also significant that this addition of a new article to the traditional corpus of Jewish beliefs was not accepted immediately by the Jewish people as a whole. It was adopted, at first, by the Pharisees only. It was rejected by the Sadducees on the ground that there was no warrant for it in the written Mosaic Law, and that the written Law alone was valid. The Pharisees were originally dissenters; the Sadducees represented the "establishment." The Sadducees were in control of the Temple at Jerusalem, and held at least the key posts in the officiating priesthood. The Sadducees maintained their dominant position in the Palestinian Jewish community, and persisted in their rejection of the belief in the the resurrection of the dead, until the destruction of the Temple in A.D. 70. It was only after this that the Pharisees' hitherto controversial belief became part of the orthodox faith of the Jewish people as a whole; and, among the Jews, this general adoption of the belief in the resurrection of the dead has not weakened the desire for the continuous survival of the Jewish people as a community that perpetuates itself from generation to generation of the mortal men and women who are its successive ephemeral representatives.

---

[22]*Odyssey,* Book XI, lines 538–540.

The pre-Pharisaic Israelites and Jews were not peculiar in reconciling themselves to the prospect of death by taking comfort in the prospect that their race would be perpetuated in their descendants. A prospect that has caused greater anxiety and distress than the prospect of death has been the prospect of dying without being survived by any descendants. According to the Book of Genesis,[23] Abraham felt that Yahweh's announcement that he was going to be Abraham's "exceeding great reward" was meaningless so long as Yahweh suffered Abraham to go childless; and this passionate desire to have descendants, that is attributed to Abraham in this passage, has been widespread. It has been particularly strong in societies, such as the Hindu and the Chinese, in which it has been held to be important for a human being that, after his death, he should be commemorated and be venerated in a cult performed by a surviving son and by this son's descendants in their turn.

Where the cult of ancestors is practised, this is evidence of a concern about what is going to happen after one's own death, but this concern may not be solely a concern for the perpetuation of the race; it may be partly self-centred. The ancestor who has demanded the cult has presumably sought commemoration for himself in the belief that this will have some posthumous value for him; the descendant who performs the cult may be moved to undertake this burden not only by love of a parent or by a feeling of piety towards a more remote ancestor, but also by a belief that dead ancestors have it in their power to benefit or injure their descendants, and that it is therefore advisable for their descendants to give them satisfaction by carrying on the cult. Abraham's longing to have a child is not un-self-regarding either. He points out to Yahweh that, if he dies childless, the heir who will inherit his estate will be, not one of his own kinfolk, but "one born in my house," i.e. a child of one of Abraham's slaves.[24]

This self-regarding aspect of the desire to be survived by a legitimate successor is likely to be prominent in cases in which the estate that the present holder of it will leave behind him at death does not consist just of private property, such as Abraham's flocks and herds, but is the succession to the throne of a kingdom. In this case, no doubt, the self-regarding desire to be succeeded by a descendant may be accompanied by a concern for the public welfare. The reigning sovereign may forebode that, if no near kinsman of his survives to succeed him, his own death may be followed by

[23]Gen., xv, 2–3.
[24]*Ibid.*

a dispute over the succession that might give rise to disorder. If the reigning sovereign has imposed on his subjects reforms that are radical and controversial, and if he is conscious that his own ability and willpower have been the principal agencies by which his reforms have been instituted and have been maintained, his desire that his lifework shall outlast his own lifetime may be stronger than his desire that his successor shall be one of his descendants.

The classic case is Peter the Great's treatment of his son and heir Alexei. After disinheriting Alexei, Peter had him flogged to death. One of Peter's motives for committing this dreadful and unnatural crime was a personal antipathy that was mutual; but Peter was also moved by concern for the future public welfare of the Russian state and people, and this concern of Peter's was justified by facts. Alexei was not, by nature, a man of action; he hated being involved in public affairs and was incompetent in them, and he was under the influence of people who were opposed to Peter's reforms and who would have pressed Alexei to undo these if Alexei had survived Peter and had succeeded him. Posterity will agree with Peter that, for Russia, this would have been a calamity.

The extreme step taken by Peter to ensure that the reforms which he had carried out in Russia should not be undone after his death brings out the truth that it is difficult to feel concern for the future welfare of posterity without also trying to give practical effect to this concern by taking steps to influence or even determine what shall happen after one's death in so far as this lies in one's power. If one feels concern for posterity, one will have one's own ideas about what is going to be beneficial for or detrimental to posterity, and one will then be moved to try to ensure the welfare of these future generations as one sees it, and to secure them against suffering harm as one sees that too. Heads of states who have a life-long tenure of office are, of course, not the only people whose concern for posterity may incline them to try to make their power last longer than their own lifetime by fixing, while they are still alive, what shall happen after they are dead. This possibility also arises whenever any private person makes his or her will, especially if the testator is making bequests, not only to kinsmen and friends of his, but to religious, educational, or charitable institutions. The exercise, by the dead, of this posthumous power has been found so burdensome for posterity that, in some countries, legislation has been enacted that limits a testator's freedom to dispose of his property altogether as he chooses.

However, neither private testators nor rulers with a life-long tenure have been so successful in governing the life of posterity as the founders of the historic philosophies and higher religions. Hundreds of millions of human beings who are alive at this moment are being swayed, on many issues, great and small, by the commandments and precepts of Marx, Muhammad, Saint Paul, Jesus, the Buddha, Confucius, and the redactors of the Pentateuch. The posthumous power of these spiritual authorities has been, and continues to be, incomparably great. Yet the exercise of this posthumous spiritual power has its ironical aspect.

Some of the authentic commandments and precepts of these religious leaders were drafted and promulgated by them on the spur of the moment for dealing with some urgent but local and temporary situation. Cases in point are Saint Paul's epistles and the chapters of the Qur'an that were issued by the Prophet Muhammad when he was the head of the government of the city-state of Medina. Both Muhammad and Paul would probably have been disconcerted if they could have foreseen how literally and earnestly even the most casual of their pronouncements were going to be taken by millions of devout posthumous adherents of theirs, and this for hundreds of years to come. There are other zealously obeyed commandments and precepts and statements that have been attributed falsely to the religious leader whose name has lent them their authority, and some of these might have shocked their alleged authors. What would Jesus, for instance, have felt if he could have foreseen that, after his death, his followers were going to worship him, in company with Yahweh and with the Holy Spirit, as one of the members of a divine trinity? On the evidence of the Gospels themselves, Jesus was an orthodox Jew. He is reported to have said to an enquirer: "Why callest thou me good? There is none good save one; that is God."[25] This saying is likely not only to be authentic but to have been notoriously authentic at the time when the Gospel according to Saint Mark was composed. If it had not been, it would surely have been expurgated; for it is a contradiction, out of Jesus's own mouth, of his posthumous Christian followers' thesis that he was God himself.

Peter's murder of Alexei also brings out, through being an extreme case, the truth that the future generations in whom a living human being can put his treasure may comprise a far wider circle than his own physical descendants. The choice that confronted Peter was not, in itself, a unique one. The reigning occupant of an hereditary office—whether he is the sovereign of a state or the director-in-chief of a family business—may feel obliged to disinherit his son, or some less close kinsman, because he judges

---

[25]Mar, x, 18.

him to be unfit to take over the duties of the office and because his conscience tells him that the interests of the realm or the business—i.e. the interests of people who are not his relatives but for whose welfare he is
responsible—ought to take precedence over his family obligations to his
"kith and kin." The disinheriting of an heir who is his heir by virtue of
kinship does not normally require that he should put his disinherited
kinsman to death. The Roman emperors Nerva, Trajan, Hadrian, and
Antoninus Pius each in turn handed on the imperial office to a successor
who was his son only by the legal fiction of adoption, and in doing this they
were making the future welfare of the Empire and its inhabitants their
paramount concern; but none of them murdered any disinherited kinsman
of his, as Peter murdered Alexei. On the other hand, Marcus Aurelius did
a bad service to the Empire when he departed from the consistent practice
of his four immediate predecessors by bequeathing the imperial office to
his actual son Commodus. For Commodus was not only incompetent in
public affairs and uninterested in them, as Alexei was. Unlike Alexei,
Commodus was a vicious character.

ⵉⵉⵉ

> *Can the transfer of one's concern from*
> *one's own puny self to so vast a*
> *posterity give meaning, value, and*
> *zest to life and deprive death of*
> *its sting?*

ⵉⵉⵉ

Peter the Great's concern for the welfare of future generations embraced a nation that was already a large one, but that was, at the same time,
only one among a number, with some of which it was at enmity. Marcus
Aurelius's four predecessors' concern embraced the whole population of
an empire that was a world-state in the eyes of its rulers and their subjects,
in the sense that the Roman Empire contained within its frontiers as much
of the contemporary civilised world as was within its inhabitants' ken.

Today, anyone who is concerned with the welfare of future generations has to expand his concern not only from his family to his nation, but from his nation to the whole human race. For, in our day, "the annihilation of distance" by the progress of technology has linked together, for good or for evil, the fortunes of all sections of mankind, while the invention of the atomic weapon has put the human species in danger of extinction once again for the first time since, in the Later Palaeolithic Age, Man definitively got the upper hand over all other living creatures on the face of this planet except bacteria. No doubt, Lord Russell was thinking in these ecumenical terms if he said, as he is reported to have said, that, when one has reached old age, it is important to care immensely about what is going to happen after one is dead.

In the present state of military potency, political tension, and scientific knowledge, this means putting one's treasure in seventy million future generations of mankind which will have come and gone, after the present generation has died off, before the surface of this planet will have ceased to be habitable for living creatures. Can a human being reconcile himself to the fact of death by putting his treasure in future generations of all mankind in these almost unimaginably large numbers? Can the transfer of one's concern from one's own puny self to so vast a posterity give meaning, value, and zest to life and deprive death of its sting?

It may seem audacious to say that posterity on this scale is not something great enough to draw a human being completely out of himself, and so to reconcile him entirely to his foreknowledge that he himself is going to die. Yet to sink one's self-centredness in a concern for all future generations of one's fellow human beings would be wholly satisfying only if one knew that mankind was the be-all and end-all of the universe. We do not know this; we have no means of discovering whether or not it is the truth; and it seems unlikely to be the truth, considering that our own planet, solar system, and galaxy are only minute fragments of a physical universe whose bounds, if it has any bounds, are beyond the reach of our powers of observation. Moreover, there is, within the psyche of any single human being, a psychic universe that is apparently proving to be at least as vast, in its own medium, as the physical universe is. Furthermore, the psychic universe, the physical universe, and the relation between the two are not self-explanatory; they are mysterious; they can hardly be the ultimate reality. Can a human being get into touch with this ultimate reality? And, if he can, can he reconcile himself to death by entering into eternal communion with the ultimate reality or by merging himself in it?

(f) *Self-liberation from self-centredness by merging oneself in ultimate reality.*
To get into touch with Ultimate Reality and to merge oneself in it has been
an Indian quest. In India, this has been the principal quest of philosophers
of all schools for the last 3,000 years at least. Round about the turn of the
6th and 5th centuries B.C., the quest produced a sharp cleavage between two
schools which gave different reports of the findings of introspection and
consequently worked out different prescriptions for reaching spiritual goals
that were perhaps identical.

The adherents of one school reported that, when a human being succeeds
in bringing into the light of consciousness the very center of his psyche, he
finds there a "dweller in the innermost"—a soul—that is identical with
Ultimate Reality itself. This finding has been expressed in the three words
"That art thou"—"that" meaning Ultimate Reality, and "thou" meaning a
human soul. Was the recognition of the identity of "thou" with "that" held
to be tantamount to the merging of "thou" in "that"? Possibly it was; for the
recognition of the identity is not just an intellectual discovery; it is the
consummation of long and hard spiritual travail.

The opposing school was the school founded by the Buddha. The Buddha's findings were quite different from those of his contemporaries, and,
so far from being the final consummation of long and hard spiritual travail,
they were a fresh starting point for this. The Buddha reported that in the
psyche there was no soul; he found there only a series of discontinuous
psychic states, held together and kept moving only by the momentum of
the karma engendered by desire. His prescription for merging the self in
Ultimate Reality was not to penetrate to the self's core and recognise the
identity of Ultimate Reality with this; it was to stop the flow of psychic
states by extinguishing desire—i.e. self-centredness—and thus attaining to
the state of "extinguishedness" (nirvana).

A present-day Western observer is likely to be more conscious of the
common ground of these two opposing Indian schools of thought than of
the differences that loomed so large in the minds of their respective Indian
initiators. Both schools take it for granted that all sentient beings are doomed
to go through a round of rebirths which will continue unless and until, in
one of the successive lives, the sufferer succeeds in bringing the series of
lives to an end. Both schools hold that rebirth is a far greater evil than death,
and that to circumvent rebirth, not to circumvent death, ought therefore to
be the supreme goal of human endeavours. Both schools also hold that the
spiritual exertions required for attaining this goal are long and hard, though
their prescriptions for striving to attain it differ. A human being who adheres

to either of these schools of Indian philosophy will have little difficulty in reconciling himself to the fact of death. The fact (taken by him for granted) that death is going to be followed by another rebirth will be this man's nightmare. I have never forgotten the radiant smile that came over the face of a Japanese scholar, Professor Anesaki, when, at a conference held in Kyoto in 1929, he announced: "I am from Tokyo, but also from Kyoto, because I am coming here after I am dead." My guess is that Professor Anesaki's smile was evoked by two thoughts: the thought of the natural beauty of the city that was to cherish his mortal remains, and the thought of the ineffable beauty of nirvana.

(g) *The belief in the personal immortality of human souls.* Hindus believe in a supra-personal immortality (i.e. in the identity of the essence of a human being's psyche with Ultimate Reality). Buddhists believe in a depersonalised immortality (i.e. in the possibility of extinguishing the self through self-release from self-centredness). I have suggested that these two beliefs of Indian origin prove, on analysis, to be more closely akin to each other than they might appear to be at first sight and than they have been held to be in Indian philosophical controversies. A further feature that they have in common is that both alike are more credible than the belief in personal immortality.

It is credible that a human being, in his psychic dimension, may be part and parcel of Ultimate Reality in its spiritual aspect, and it is demonstrable that, in his physical dimension, the same human being is part and parcel of the universe in the material aspect in which we apprehend the universe with our senses and interpret our sense-data in scientific terms. On the other hand, no living human being has ever been able to demonstrate conclusively that he has been in psychic communication with a disembodied human psyche (i.e. with the psyche of a human being whose body was, at the time not alive, but was either a corpse or had decomposed into the chemical elements of which the corpse had consisted at the moment at which it had ceased to be a living body). *A fortiori*, no one has ever been able to demonstrate that he has been in psychic communion with an unembodied human psyche that has never yet been embodied or that has, at the time, been temporarily unembodied in an interval between two successive incarnations (a conception that requires the undemonstrated assumption that a psyche can be, and is, repeatedly re-embodied in successive living bodies, human or non-human, without losing its identity).

Every living human being whom any other living human being has ever encountered has been a psychosomatic entity; and the life of every one of these human psychosomatic entities, like the life of every other sexual living organism inhabiting this planet, has moved, or is in the course of moving, in the time dimension, on a trajectory which describes a course up from birth through infancy to its prime and from its prime through old age down to death, supposing that the human being in question lives out his or her life to the end of its full natural span, and that this particular life is not cut short prematurely by disease, accident, or violent death inflicted by other human beings in war, by law, or by private enterprise.

Death, whatever its cause and its circumstances may be, is an event in which the former living body becomes a corpse which decays (unless its physical decomposition is artificially arrested), while, at the same moment, the psyche passes out of human ken (i.e. ceases to be in communication with the psyche of any human being who is alive at that moment). It is impossible to conceive of a human body being alive without being associated with a human psyche. It has been found possible to imagine a psyche being alive without being associated with a living body. However, this feat of imagination is so difficult that attempts to work out its implications in detail have run into incongruities, inconsistencies, incompatibilities, and self-contradictions.

When believers in personal immortality have sought to describe the state of disembodied souls, they have found no way of describing this hypothetical state that does not involve the drawing of some analogy with the psychosomatic life on earth of which we have actual experience. The shade that has been consigned to Sheol or to Hades or to the underworld as conceived by the Sumerians and their Akkadian and Babylonian cultural heirs is an enfeebled replica of the now dead person who was once alive in psychosomatic form. In fact, the author of the 11th book of the *Odyssey* takes it for granted that the only condition on which the living visitor, Odysseus, can put himself into communication with the shades of the dead in their shadowy world is by partially and temporarily re-endowing them with a modicum of physical life. In order to enable them to talk to him, Odysseus has first to administer to them a physical stimulant. He gives each of them, in turn, a drink of the blood of non-human psychosomatic animals— sheep—which Odysseus has slaughtered for this purpose.[26] As for the privileged minority of the departed who are imagined to be enjoying a

[26]*Odyssey*, Book XI, lines 23–50, 82, 88–89, 98, 153, 232, 390.

blissful existence in the Kingdom of the West or as a star in heaven (if the departed grandee has been an Egyptian pharaoh), or in Elysium (if he has been a pre-Christian Greek hero), or in Valhalla (if he has been a pre-Christian Scandinavian warrior), these favoured few are credited with a vitality that is of a superhuman or even godlike exuberance.

This inability to conceive of disembodied spirits in non-psychosomatic terms also besets those believers in personal immortality who hold that the destiny of the departed is determined, not by their former rank, but by their former conduct. The torments of the damned in hell are depicted on the walls of Etruscan tombs and of Eastern Orthodox Christian refectories in monasteries on Mount Athos, and are described in Dante's *Divina Commedia*, in crassly physical terms—and some of these imaginary torments are so extreme that no living human being could be subjected to them for more than a few seconds without dying of them, though, incongruously, the disembodied spirits that are believed to be suffering these lethal torments are held to have been made immortal in order that their suffering may be everlasting. There have been a number of different conceptions of the nature of the personal immortality of a disembodied or unembodied soul, but they all have one significant feature in common. In some degree, they all involve some incongruities, inconsistencies, incompatibilities, and self-contradictions.

One conception of the immortality of the soul has been that souls are not only immortal but eternal: i.e. that every soul has been in existence eternally before it ever came to be embodied, and that it will remain in existence eternally after having become disembodied once for all. Of all the divers conceptions of the personal immortality of the soul, this is the one that comes nearest to the Indian conception of a supra-personal or a depersonalised immortality. This belief was held by some pre-Christian Greeks, but never, so far as we can judge, by more than a small sophisticated minority. Another small minority believed that, at death, the soul was annihilated. The majority probably believed, from the beginning to the end of the pre-Christian age of Greek history, that each human soul comes into existence together with the body with which it is associated in life, and that, after death, it continues, as a shade, to lead, in Hades, a shadowy life of the kind depicted in the 11th book of the *Odyssey*.

The most prominent of the Greek believers in the eternity of souls were the Pythagoreans (an esoteric semi-philosophical semi-religious organised fraternity) and the Orphics (an unorganised and unsophisticated sect). Both these Greek sets of believers in the eternity of souls were also believers in the transmigration of souls from one incarnation to another, and this latter belief is so arbitrary and so peculiar that its simultaneous appearance, in the 6th century B.C., in the Greek world and in India can hardly have been fortuitous. One possible common source is the Eurasian nomad society, which, in the 8th and 7th centuries B.C., had descended upon India, South-Western Asia, the steppe country along the north shore of the Black Sea, and the Balkan and Anatolian peninsulas in one of its occasional explosive *völkerwanderungen.*

A belief in the personal immortality of souls which does not involve a belief in their being eternal as well as immortal is bound up with the attempts, noted already, to circumvent death by physical countermeasures. The pre-Christian and pre-Muslim Egyptians, for instance, believed in the conditional immortality of the souls of the dead—or, strictly speaking, in the conditional immortality of one of the several souls that were believed to appertain to a human being. The particular soul known as the "ka" was believed to remain in existence, haunting the dead person's tomb, so long as posterity continued to keep the tomb in proper spiritual condition by performing the requisite ritual there and by providing the requisite supplies of food, drink, clothes, and furniture which were conceived of as being necessities of life after death, as they had been before death. This belief was held simultaneously with the incompatible beliefs that the dead person's soul might have migrated to the Kingdom of the West or might have ascended to heaven to shine there as a star or might have descended into the underworld presided over by the god Osiris.

This Egyptian belief in the conditional immortality of souls after death has also been held, though it has not, in all cases, been worked out so systematically, by all the numerous other peoples that have practised ancestor-worship, e.g. the Chinese.

Three other varieties of a belief in the immortality of souls after death that does not involve a belief in their pre-existence before birth or in their eternity have been mentioned already. There has been a belief in a dismal habitation of the souls of the dead, which retain a shadowy existence there. This is the Hebrew Sheol, the Greek Hades, and the Sumerian counterpart of these. There has been a belief in a blissful abode for the souls of dead persons who had been in privileged positions in their lifetime. This is the Egyptian Kingdom of the West and Kingdom of Heaven, the Greek Elysium, the Scandinavian Valhalla. There has also been a belief in the existence of two alternative destinations for the souls of the dead—destinations that are determined, according to this more ethical belief, not by previous rank, but by previous behaviour. The souls of the wicked are consigned, as a punishment, to hell—an everlasting abode which is not merely dismal, as Sheol or Hades is, but is excruciating. On the other hand the souls of the righteous are admitted, as a reward, to Paradise or heaven—an everlasting abode which is as blissful as Elysium or Valhalla, but which, unlike them, is attained in virtue of previous merits, not of previous rank.

For believers in Hades and Elysium, the consignment of a dead person's soul to the one or the other of these two alternative abodes is automatic. It is decided by the dead person's former social rank in his lifetime. For believers in hell and heaven, the decision depends on the dead person's conduct during his lifetime; his conduct cannot be assessed without being examined and appraised; and this requires the passing of a judgment by some authority. The belief in a judgment of souls after death is a necessary corollary of the belief in heaven and hell.

This belief in a judgment of souls after death made its appearance at two widely different dates at two far apart places (far apart, that is to say, before the very recent "annihilation of distance"). The belief appeared in Egypt perhaps as early as the age of the Old Kingdom in the third millennium B.C., and it also appeared in North-Eastern Iran or in the Oxus-Jaxartes basin round about the turn of the 7th and 6th centuries B.C., i.e. in the lifetime of the Prophet Zarathustra, who was the promulgator of the belief in this region. We have no evidence as to whether the Egyptian and the Iranian belief in a judgment by which the soul, after death, is consigned either to hell or to heaven had a common historical origin. It is noteworthy, however, that the Egyptian and Iranian beliefs have a further feature in common. The judge of the souls of the dead—Osiris in the one case and Ahura Mazdah in the other—is a good god who has triumphed, or who is going to triumph, in a hard struggle with a wicked god or wicked semi-divine being. Osiris, after an initial defeat, has been given an eventual victory over his wicked brother and adversary Seth by the prowess of Osiris's son Horus and by the devotion of his sister and wife Isis. Ahura Mazdah is going to be victorious, eventually, over his wicked adversary Ahriman.

The Egyptian belief in a judgment of souls after death, to determine whether they shall be sent to hell or to heaven, was presumably the source of the same belief in the Greek world in the Hellenic Age. Here it was probably a legacy of Egyptian influence in Crete in the Minoan Age. Osiris, in his capacity of serving as the judge of the souls of the dead, has a Cretan counterpart in Rhadamanthus. In Egypt the pyramid texts, inscribed for the benefit of pharaohs in the age of the Old Kingdom, and the later "Book of the Dead," circulated for popular use, are collections of formulae, spells, and instructions designed to help the dead person's soul to find its way successfully to a blissful terminus without falling into any of the pitfalls, traps, and obstacles that will beset the soul in the course of its difficult and dangerous passage. The contents of the Orphic tablets are similar and are designed to serve the same purpose.

In both cases the purpose is practical guidance, not edification, and, in so far as purification enters into it, this is purification in the ritual, not in the ethical, sense. In the pre-Christian Greek picture of hell, Tityus, Sisyphus, Tantalus, and Ixion are four classical representatives of the damned who are suffering everlasting torments. The wall paintings in Etruscan tombs show that the Greek picture of hell made a strong impression on the Etruscans; and it may not be fanciful to guess that there may have been an Etruscan component (preserved in subsequent Tuscan folklore), as well as a Christian component, in the mediaeval Christian Tuscan poet Dante's lurid description of the torments of the damned in the Christian hell.

↑↑

*When the belief in personal immortality
is associated with a belief in a
judgment after death—a judgment that
will consign the dead to either eternal
bliss or eternal torment—the price of a
human being's belief in the survival of
his personality after his death is
anxiety during his lifetime.*

↑↑

The Christian and Muslim conceptions of the judgment of souls after death and of the heaven and the hell to which the souls are consigned respectively, in accordance with the verdict, are evidently derived, in the main, not from the pre-Christian religion of Egypt, but from Zoroastrianism —presumably via Pharisaic Judaism, which—unlike the Sadducean Judaism

of the post-exilic Jewish "establishment" in Judea—laid itself open to
Zoroastrian influences that played upon Judaism after the incorporation of
Babylonia, Syria, Palestine, and Egypt in the Persian Empire in the 6th
century B.C.

In Christian belief the individual judgment of souls immediately after
death, and their consignment, immediately after judgment, to hell, limbo,
or heaven, coexists with the incompatible belief in the universal judgment
of all souls—both the souls of the resurrected dead and the souls of the
human beings alive at the moment—when the Last Trump sounds to give
the signal for the resurrection of the dead and for "the Last Judgment" of
living and of resurrected dead human beings alike.

When the belief in personal immortality is associated with a belief in a
judgment after death—a judgment that will consign the dead to either eternal
bliss or eternal torment—the price of a human being's belief in the survival
of his personality after his death is anxiety during his lifetime.

"For we know Him that hath said, 'Vengeance belongeth unto me;
I will recompense,' said the Lord. And again, 'The Lord shall judge
his people.'
"It is a fearful thing to fall into the hands of the living God."[27]

(h) *The belief in the resurrection of human bodies.* A disembodied or unembodied soul is more difficult to imagine than a soul that is associated with a
living body in the psychosomatic unity with which we are familiar through
our acquaintance with ourselves and with our fellow living human beings.
This union of soul with body in a life after death is easier to imagine if it is
represented as being a reunion, in which the body with which the soul is
now associated is the body—reconstituted, reanimated, and resurrected—
with which this soul was associated before soul and body were parted by
death and the body consequently became a corpse. On the other hand the
reconstitution, reanimation, and resurrection of a corpse is virtually impossible to imagine, considering that, after death, a human body immediately
begins to decay and eventually decomposes completely, unless the entrails
are removed and the rest of the corpse is preserved artificially by being
mummified.

The audience that Saint Paul had attracted at Athens listened to him
patiently till he made the statement that God had raised a man from the
dead; but this assertion brought the meeting to an end. Some of Paul's

---

[27]Hebrews, x, 30–31.

listeners laughed, while others, more courteously, told him that they would wait to hear more from him till they found another opportunity.[28] If Paul had stated that Jesus had an immortal soul which had pre-existed and would continue to exist eternally, his Greek audience might have been willing to hear him out. Personal immortality of souls was a familiar and not incredible hypothesis for Greeks of Saint Paul's generation, but to be asked to believe in the resurrection of the dead was, for them, tantamount to being given notice by the speaker himself that he was wasting their time by talking nonsense.

Paul might have obtained a better hearing for his declaration of belief in bodily resurrection if he had been preaching in contemporary Egypt; for in Egypt, since at least as far back in time as the third millennium B.C., it had been believed that one corpse had come to life again—and this after it had been cut up into fourteen pieces that had been scattered and had had to be reassembled. In Egypt this story was told of a god—the god Osiris who, since his own bodily resurrection, had become the judge of souls after death. When Paul told the Athenians that Jesus had been raised from the dead, he referred to Jesus as being a man and said that it was God who had raised him; but at the same time Paul cited this act of God's as evidence that God had appointed Jesus to judge all mankind at a future date that was already fixed;[29] and Paul believed that Jesus was in some sense God, though he did not divulge this belief of his on this occasion. It will be recognized that the role of being a god who is put to death and is resurrected in order to become mankind's judge is attributed to both Osiris and Jesus.

The belief that Jesus has risen from the dead, the belief that he is to judge mankind, and the linking of these two beliefs with each other thus have an Egyptian precedent; but there is also another tenet of Christianity in which a belief in resurrection is linked with a belief in judgment, and this tenet appears to be of Zoroastrian, not Egyptian, origin. According to Christian doctrine, Christ's judgment of mankind is not an *ad hoc* judgment of the souls of the dead individually, immediately after the death of each of us; it is a future judgment of all mankind simultaneously, including the people who will be alive at the time, as well as all those who will have lived and died by then; and the dead will be brought to judgment by a resurrection of their bodies, which will be brought back to life for the occasion and will be reunited with their souls. This belief in the bodily resurrection of all dead

---

[28]Acts, xvii, 32.
[29]Acts, xvii, 31.

human beings is common to Christianity and Islam, and, like the belief in judgment, noted earlier, it seems to have been derived by both religions from Zoroastrianism via Pharisaic Judaism. According to Zoroastrian doctrine, the discrimination between the righteous and the wicked at the last and general judgment is to be made by means of a physical ordeal by fire and molten metal; and this indicates that, according to Zoroastrianism, in accordance with Pharisaic Judaism, Christianity, and Islam, the dead are expected to rise again physically.

Zoroastrianism anticipated Christianity in believing in two judgments: a judgment of each soul individually, immediately after death, and a final judgment of all human beings simultaneously, the dead as well as those alive at the time. This belief is so peculiar and involves such incongruities that there surely must be an historical connection between its appearances in these two different religions: i.e. Christianity must have adopted the belief from Zoroastrianism. Zoroastrianism's priority is indicated, not only by the chronological fact that Zoroastrianism is about six centuries older than Christianity, but also by the connection, in Zoroastrianism, between the belief in a future last and general judgment and the belief in a final and conclusive victory of the good god Ahura Mazdah over the evil spirit Ahriman in the current war between these two spiritual powers. Ahura Mazdah's coming victory over Ahriman is to have the general judgment of mankind as its sequel.

This belief that mankind is to be judged twice over, besides being incongruous—it seems superfluous to recall souls from heaven or hell, as the case may be, to earth in order to have the same verdict passed on them for the second time—also raises the question whether heaven and hell are to be thought of as existing in the psychic dimension or in the physical dimension. The locus of disembodied souls is presumably not physical. Yet the agony and the bliss of the souls of the dead before the general resurrection are depicted in physical imagery; and if, for the last and general judgment, the temporarily disembodied souls of the dead will have been reunited with their resurrected bodies, the heaven and the hell to which they will then be consigned must be physical localities, if the human beings who are sent there after this second judgment have been restored to the psychosomatic state in which they lived on earth before their deaths—not to speak of those who are overtaken, still alive, by the sounding of the Last Trump.

In Christianity and Islam, as in Zoroastrianism, the resurrection of human bodies is associated with a last and general judgment, which will consign—or re-consign—the resurrected dead, and will also consign the living, to either heaven or hell. Their common mother-religion, Pharisaic Judaism, however, seems—at any rate, to begin with—to have adopted the Zoroastrian belief in bodily resurrection in a version that was less close to the original than the Christian-Muslim version is. In this original Pharisaic Jewish version the resurrection is apparently to be a privilege, not an ordeal. The Jewish martyrs who have given their lives for the Jewish faith and for the Jewish people are to rise again from the dead, not to attend a divine judgment which will consign them either to heaven or to hell, but to participate in the re-establishment on earth of the Kingdom of Judah by "the Lord's Anointed" (the Messiah): a scion of the House of David who will not only reinstate his ancestral kingdom up to its Davidic frontiers, but will transform it into a world-empire that will be the millennial Jewish successor of the successive world-empires of the Assyrians, the Persians, and the Macedonians.

This mundane Jewish adoption of a transcendental Zoroastrian belief brings out the truth that the resurrection of the body does not necessarily imply that the reconstituted psychosomatic human being is going to be immortal. The Messiah himself seems to have been thought of originally as being a mortal man who would be distinguished from his fellow mortals only in being the legitimate Davidic heir to the Kingdom of Judah and in bearing rule over a world-empire that would be still more extensive and more mighty than the realm of the Messiah's ancestor David himself. In the course of nature the Messiah would die, like David and like every one of David's successors and the Messiah's predecessors who, from the 10th to the 6th century B.C. had, each in turn, reigned over the Kingdom of Judah as "the Lord's Anointed," i.e. as the legitimate living representative of the Davidic dynasty. If the Davidic restorer of the Davidic kingdom was destined to be mortal, like his ancestor, the resurrected martyrs would presumably prove to be mortal too. They would be resurrected only to die again eventually—dying, in their exceptional case, for the second time.

It will be seen that, in this first phase, the adoption by the Pharisaic Jews of the Zoroastrian belief in bodily resurrection was subordinated to the traditional Jewish view—expressed in the legend of Yahweh's successive promises to Abraham—that the supreme blessing for a mortal man was to be assured, not of securing personal immortality for himself, but of leaving behind him descendants who would perpetuate his race. It was taken as a matter of course that the Jewish martyrs would be raised from the dead expressly for the purpose of witnessing the eventual military and political triumph of Judah to which they would have contributed by having sacrificed their lives. It was assumed that they would be well content to "depart in peace," together with the Messiah himself, when their eyes had seen God's salvation which He had prepared before the face of all peoples[30]—a salvation that would be the corporate salvation of the Jewish people, and a glory that would be the political glory of a re-established Jewish state which, this time, would be, not a petty local principality, but a veritable world-empire.

(i) *The hope of heaven and the fear of hell.* A Hindu who, as a result of intense introverted contemplation, has attained, as a personal experience, the intuition that the essence of his soul is identical with Ultimate Reality, has presumably been liberated by this experience from all hopes and fears about either life or death. He has become aware of a truth that assures him of the unimportance of life and of death alike. A Buddhist who has learnt that it is possible to make a definitive exit into nirvana from the sorrowful series of rebirths, and who has also been instructed in the strenuous spiritual exercises by means of which this goal may be attained, will be too absorbingly preoccupied with the pursuit of his practical spiritual endeavours to concern himself with either life or death or to entertain either hopes or fears. On the other hand, lively hopes and fears about a human being's destiny after death will be aroused by a belief in personal immortality, whether the believer in this expects to survive everlastingly as a disembodied soul or expects his soul to be reunited, at the sounding of the Last Trump, with his resurrected body, to live on everlastingly thereafter as a reconstituted psychosomatic unity: i.e. as a human being constituted like his own present living self and like the living selves of his contemporaries who, like him, have not yet suffered death.

What is the effect of the belief in personal immortality after death on the feelings, attitude, and conduct of the believer? To what degree, if any, does it influence his behavior while he is alive in the psychosomatic form of life which is the only form of it that is known to us in our experience?

The believer in a conditional personal immortality—an immortality that is dependent on the perpetual performance of rites by the believer's descendants—is likely to suffer anxiety. He will be anxious to make sure both that he is going to leave descendants behind him and that these will have both the will and the means to perform, punctiliously, all that is requisite in order to maintain the immortality of this ancestor of theirs. The believer

---

[30]Luke ii, 29–32.

in a personal immortality in the shadowy realm of Sheol or Hades will repine at the brevity of a human being's full-blooded zestful psychosomatic life on earth—unless, of course, he undergoes so much suffering before death that he comes to contemplate even the bleak prospect of Sheol or Hades with resignation. The grandee who is confident that his own destination is not Sheol or Hades but is Elysium or Valhalla may be nerved by his aristocratic self-assurance to face the prospect of personal immortality after death with equanimity, or even with the pleasurable anticipation with which a Buddhist—the polar opposite of the pagan barbarian warrior—looks forward to his exit into a nirvana in which his personality will have been extinguished.

In so far as the belief in personal immortality after death does captivate a living person's imagination, the believer's mental picture of hell seems generally to be livelier than his mental picture of heaven.

The believer in a personal immortality which he may be going to spend either in heaven or in hell, according to the verdict that will be passed, after his death, on his conduct while he was alive, ought, if he holds this belief *bona fide,* to be the most anxious of all; and his version of the belief in personal immortality ought to have the greatest effect of all on his present behavior. He is committed to the belief that the credit or debit balance of the account of his good and evil deeds during his brief life on earth is going to decide, once for all, whether his destiny is to be weal or woe in the everlasting future of sentient personal life that awaits him after death.

In practice, there is in some cases a considerable discrepancy between the belief on the one hand—even when the believer believes himself to be sincere—and the believer's state of mind and behavior on the other hand.

I have, for instance, known one believer who was intensely afraid of the prospect of death, though he was conscious of having lived righteously in the main and though he was also utterly confident that he was one hundred percent correct in his theological tenets. Logically, he ought to have felt assured that, after death, he could not only go to heaven but would be received there as a V.I.P. All the same, he was unable to face the prospect of death with equanimity. Conversely, there have been people who have believed that the infallible penalty for the commission of serious sins in this life is condemnation, after death, to everlasting torments in hell, yet who have not been deterred by this belief from committing sins that have been so heinous that, according to the sinner's own belief, his condemnation to suffer everlasting torment in hell will be inescapable.

Such discrepancies between belief and behavior indicate that belief has to be supported by experience if its influence on behavior is to be effective. All beliefs, whatever they may be, that relate to what is going to happen or is not going to happen to a human being after death are, intrinsically beyond the range of experience, and they are perhaps even beyond the range of realistic imagination.

In so far as the belief in personal immortality after death does captivate a living person's imagination, the believer's mental picture of hell seems generally to be livelier than his mental picture of heaven. The torments of the damned in hell have, on the whole, been depicted and described more vividly than the bliss of the salvaged in heaven. Lucretius, in the third book of his *De Rerum Natura*,[31] in which he is arguing that death spells complete and permanent annihilation, presents this as a consoling thought for the living, because the prospect liberates them from the fear that, after death, they may be condemned to suffer the legendary everlasting torments that are believed, by the credulous, to be being inflicted on the mythical arch-sinners Tantalus, Tityus, Sisyphus, and Ixion.[32] As Lucretius drives his point home at the close of this passage, it is in this world only that life ever becomes hell, and this only for people who are such fools as to believe in the reality of a life in hell after death.

This fear of hell, which Lucretius is seeking to dispel, is offset, of course, by the hope of reunion, after death, with beloved fellow human beings from whom one has been parted either by dying before them or by surviving them. Bereavement through death is harder to face and to bear than death

---

[31]Lines 978–1023.

[32]Cp. *Odessey*, Book XI, lines 582–600.

itself; and the pain of bereavement is mitigated if the separation that death brings with it is believed to be not everlasting but only temporary. The coming reunion is usually pictured as a blissful one in heaven; yet even the torments of hell are eased if they are shared. The most moving passage in Dante's *Inferno* is his depiction of Paolo and Francesca[33] locked in each other's arms in everlasting love as they are swept round together in an everlasting wind of anguish.

---

[33]*Inferno*, Canto Quinto, lines 73-142.

The Biblical Tradition

Milton McC. Gatch

Milton McC. Gatch, Professor of English at the University of Missouri, was educated at Haverford College, Episcopal Theological School, and at Yale University. This selection, taken from his book *Death: Meaning and Morality in Christian Thought and Contemporary Culture*, presents a brief overview of the Old and New Testament views on death—views that may prove surprising to those who are not students of the Bible.

On the whole, it can be said of the biblical writings that they have no theology of death or of an afterlife. Both Testaments are radically secular in their overriding concern with history, which is to be understood in both in a very special sense as the self-manifestation of God in human events or as the interpretation and judgment of human events in the light of man's highest aspirations—which the Hebraic tradition viewed as the will of God for men.[1] Concerned with the destiny of a People in history, the writers of Scripture had little to say about the significance of the end of the individual's historical existence and were not motivated to speculate about an extrahistorical survival. Passages which seem to belie this generalization must be read very carefully within the special historical circumstances which gave rise to them. Any effort to understand the biblical view of the nature of death and man's destiny must, in other words, keep constantly in mind the resounding silence of the Bible on the subject in general and be tempered by a very careful interpretation of its few specific statements within their historical contexts.

THE OLD TESTAMENT

The Old Testament records the historical and theological reflections of a People for over a millennium, during which time considerable development and alteration of ideas are observable. Despite their wide divergencies of points of view, nevertheless, the Hebrew writers uniformly approached the question of death in a manner quite different from those of either the Greeks or the moderns.[2]

The prevailing opinion concerning death can be expressed in two ways. One might say either that death was regarded as the termination of human existence or that, because the predominant concern was with the People and its historical destiny, the question of the significance of death for the individual rarely arose and was essentially meaningless. From the point of view of the modern world, which is uniquely concerned with the role and identity of the individual, the former restatement of the biblical approach to death is probably the more congenial; historically, the latter is surely the more accurate.

The concerns of the dying patriarch, Abraham, as related in the Yahwist history, touch upon several of the chief themes in the basic biblical understanding of death:

> Abraham was now old, advanced in years; and Yahweh had blessed Abraham in everything.
>
> Abraham said to the senior servant of his household, who had charge of all his possessions, "Place your hand under my thigh, and I will make you swear by Yahweh, God of heaven and God of the earth, that you will not obtain a wife for my son from the daughters of the Canaanites among whom I dwell, but will go to the land of my birth to get a wife for my son Isaac. . . . On no account are you to take my son back there! Yahweh God of heaven, who took me from the home of my father and the land of my birth, and who solemnly promised me, saying, 'I will give this land to your offspring'—he will send his angel before you that you may bring my son a wife from there. . . ." So the servant placed his hand under the thigh of his master Abraham and swore to him concerning this matter. (Gen. 24:1-9)[3]

This account of the death of Abraham is a passage from the Yahwist epic of the history of the Hebrew peoples. The writer of this great narrative was concerned to set out the historical framework within which the present state of the kingdom of Judah was to be understood. He believed that by telling of the nomadic patriarchs, the tribal confederacy, and the emergence of the Davidic kingship, he could explain how it had come to pass that a tribal people had prospered among the other peoples of the ancient Near East, whose cultures and religions contrasted markedly with those of the worshipers of Yahweh. For the Yahwist historian, in other words, history supplanted myth as the means of explaining the meaning of the experience of the People.[4] The account of the life of Abraham holds a pivotal place among the earlier chapters of this epic of the People's history, and the treatment of the death of the patriarch typifies the essential concerns of earlier Hebraic thought in dealing with the termination of life.

At the end of his full and prosperous life, Abraham remembered that one task remained unfinished. He had not provided for the continuation of his line beyond the next generation. Thus, his dying act[5] was to cover this oversight. One can hardly say that he was motivated to this ultimate intervention in Isaac's affairs, after the manner of the dying patriarch of the modern novel, either by a generous desire to see that his son would be cared for when the father was no longer there to oversee his activities or by a malicious compulsion to continue his parental tyranny even in death. Rather, he wanted to see that the achievements of his lifetime would be continued; and this could only be done through Isaac and his progeny.

Abraham believed that he had come to live among the Canaanites through the intervention of Yahweh and that this settlement was not a matter of a generation or two but a permanent one. The Yahwist historian stresses this conviction again and again, but chiefly by means of the quotation of the promise of the "God of heaven and God of the earth." The promise is stated not in terms of Abraham himself but in terms of his "offspring." In other words, the Patriarch conceives of the meaning of his life not in terms of his own accomplishments but in terms of the fulfillment of the promise he had received. He is not to be regarded as a remarkable man of unusual and significant achievements but as an actor in the continuing processes of purposeful historical development. He will remain important only insofar as what he has begun in his lifetime is continued in the history of his offspring. He will assume a place in the genealogies of his people and will remain a vital link in the chain which is being forged in the history of the People. The unusual oath which Abraham makes the servant swear upon his genitals probably underlines this general point of view.[6] In those who proceed from his thighs, both his life and his death assume significance.

There is no attempt (indeed, it is not possible) to speak in individual terms for Abraham, for the Hebraic mind does not conceive of the situation as we do. There is no way to separate Abraham from the clan he produces. Even his personality is indistinct from that of the tribe. Thus, one can only speak anachronistically of his death as an end since, even dead, Abraham continues to be an important aspect of the corporate personality. Such was also the meaning of the priestly historian who, in his account of the death of the Patriarch (Gen. 25:8), says, "he was gathered to his kin.' Like his predecessors, the man who dies becomes one of the fathers, a name in the genealogical list; and as such he never ceases to be a part of the continuing story of the People.[7]

The Greek notion seems to have been that immortality was earned through one's contribution to the state and that the locus of immortality was in the collective memory of the state.

This frame of mind made quite inconceivable the question of an individual afterlife and probably contributed to the fact that Hebrew thought never developed a notion of a soul or life-force which is separable from the historical man.[8] At the same time, the general Old Testament conceptualization is both different from and more profound than the Greek view of political immortality. The Greek notion seems to have been that immortality was earned through one's contribution to the state and that the locus of immortality was in the collective memory of the state. The Hebrew understanding is at once more primitive and more organic. Personality and identity are terms which attach not to the person but to the People; thus, when one dies, personality and identity are not disrupted, for the People continues. Only the possibility that one's line may not be fruitful gives rise to anxiety in the face of death.

In a general way, the kind of view expressed by the Yahwist historian persevered throughout the period of Old Testament writing. The concept of corporate personality tended to be refined (some might say, refined away), but the tradition refrained from assigning to death more than physiological significance and continued to regard the People as the locus both of continuity and of the ultimate meaning of life.

After the fall of the Israelite kingdoms and the period of the exiles, nevertheless, the historical situation of the Jews gave rise to a quite different formulation of the relationship between Yahweh and his People. No longer a member of a nation chosen from among the peoples of the world to fulfill a special calling, the Jew now found himself "essentially an *individual* adrift in the cosmos."[9] The older literature was canonized and reinterpreted so as to provide guidelines for the Jew in this dilemma, and new forms of religious writing emerged to give similar guidance and encouragement.

Chief among these kinds of writings are those of the Wisdom School. Most of the motifs of this literature are found elsewhere in the traditions of the ancient Near East, and they were not unknown to the Hebraic world before the fall of the kingdoms. But the Wisdom tradition came into its own as a theological and literary approach to the problems raised by the new historical situation of the Jews. Psalm 137 is the classic depiction of that situation: the People are captives in an alien land, longing for the familiar ways of Jerusalem (the ways whose importance had been explained by the Yahwist and other epics of the emergence of the People) and not knowing how to worship their God in the foreign place. The situation necessitated a new formulation of the religion (which we know as Judaism) which would guide the individual by instruction and by example and enable him to maintain his integrity in the face of his aloneness in the cosmos.

Thus it is that the Wisdom literature is characterized both by a prescriptiveness which stresses the manner in which the wise man will react to his situation and by a resignation which counsels him to keep the faith in the face of adversity. In its approach to the phenomenon of death, the Wisdom school generally maintained the realism of the Yahwist historian. But the historical hopes of the Yahwist have been dashed: the People is no longer a nation whose emergence and reason for being need to be explained; the individual finds himself without a nation and seeks to understand the nature of his dependence upon Yahweh. Since he has no new picture of the meaning of death, the Wisdom writer tends to counsel resignation and trust in the face of death and other adversities, as in Job. Only occasionally did the school tend toward bitterness over the prospect of the end of life, as in Ecclesiastes and (more characteristically) Psalm 88.

The same phenomena which gave currency to the Wisdom literature gave rise to the apocalyptic literature in which pseudonymous wise men revealed the secrets of the future inbreaking of the divine realm upon the sphere of human life in order to save men. In the book Daniel,[10] for example, the central figure is portrayed as a wise man living among foreigners but strictly adherent to the Law of his People. The visions of Daniel reveal that the Son of Man will come from the heavenly to the human realm for the purpose of redeeming the latter and counsel the faithful to suffer martyr-dom rather than gainsay the commandments and lose their place among the elect.

One of the characteristic teachings of apocalyptic (based ultimately upon extrapolations from certain of the Exilic and post-Exilic prophetic books) is the doctrine of resurrection. Whereas Ezekiel, in the vision of the valley of the dry bones (chapter 37), had spoken metaphorically of the restoration of the nation from its deathlike desolation, the writer of Daniel speaks of the resurrection of those Jews who have died in the interim between the collapse of the kingdoms and the forthcoming revival through Yahweh's agency. But this is not his only innovation. Influenced by the priestly notion that salvation depends upon one's adherence to the law (a notion which also tends to undermine the concept of corporate personality), the author also foresees a judgment of those who are raised: "And many of those who sleep in the dust of the earth shall awake, some to everlasting life, and some to shame and everlasting contempt. And those who are wise shall shine like the brightness of the firmament; and those who turn many to righteousness, like the stars for ever and ever" (Dan. 12:2-3 RSV).

Daniel does not, it must be noted, base this hope of a post-mortem life upon some notion of the nature of man but upon his faith that, in the divine economy, wisdom and virtue must be rewarded. And he can only conceive of this life as a corporate one within a restored and transformed Israel. His view is radically new, but it is also clearly continuous with the traditions of his heritage. It amounts to saying that one's life is not in vain if it is virtuous because, like the life of Abraham and others before, it has its meaning and continuation in the ongoing history of the People. To be dead or with one's kin is not to have become nothing, for the People will be restored. In this sense, Daniel simply reaffirms the tradition in which the Preacher had seen no grounds for continued confidence. Death gave no more grounds for anxiety to Daniel than to Abraham.[11]

THE NEW TESTAMENT

Much of New Testament teaching[12] concerning death developed from the apocalypticism of the Old Testament and the Apocrypha. Yet, it is a mistake to say that Jesus' teaching follows the spirit of apocalyptic eschatology, which tended to point to the exact time when the divine, restorative inter-vention might be expected.[13] Rather, Jesus maintained a careful tension between present and future: his proclamation of the imminent futurity of the Kingdom of God, combined with his assertions of the power and significance of his own work, is meant to state that "he who will bring in the Kingdom of God in the future has appeared in the present in Jesus himself, and in him the powers of the coming aeon are already at work. . . ."[14] Thus, more than that of the apocalyptic school, Jesus' eschatology is unconcerned with speculation concerning the meaning of death or the future destiny of the person.

There is, indeed, no passage in the Synoptic Gospels in which Jesus discourses explicitly on the subject of death. The questions which we characteristically ask about the subject simply did not occur to him or to those who gathered his sayings. It is possible, however, to deduce certain aspects of his attitude on the matter of death from several discourses whose chief subjects were quite different. In the following passage, for example, the intent of Jesus' interlocutors was to confound him by posing an impossible and hypothetical legal question:

> "Teacher, Moses wrote for us that if a man's brother dies and leaves a wife, but leaves no child, the man must take the wife, and raise up children for his brother. There were seven brothers; the first took a wife, and when he died left no children; and the second took her, and died, leaving no children; and the third likewise; and the seven left no children. Last of all the woman also died. In the resurrection whose wife will she be? For the seven had her as wife."
>
> Jesus said to them, "Is not this why you are wrong, that you know neither the scriptures nor the power of God? For when they rise from the dead, they neither marry nor are given in marriage, but are like angels in heaven. And as for the dead being raised, have you not read in the book of Moses, in the passage about the bush, how God said to him, 'I am the God of Abraham, and the God of Isaac, and the God of Jacob'? He is not God of the dead, but of the living; you are quite wrong." (Mark 12:18–27 RSV)[15]

Despite the fact that this passage is concerned with a question of legal interpretation, rather than an expostulation on the meaning of death, it will suit our present purpose of examining Jesus' attitude toward death. He does not speak on the subject directly or because death as a topic interests him. Rather it arises as an incident of an effort to entrap him in heretical teaching. He and the Sadducees are agreed on one point: that human life is to be conceived as a unitive phenomenon in which the physical and that which animates the physical (the Greeks would have called it spirit or soul) are inseparable. No more than the Abraham of the Yahwist historian can Jesus

51

or his interlocutors imagine that body and soul are separable or that, as Socrates put it in the *Phaedo*, human life is a condition in which the soul is temporarily entrapped in flesh. Man is that being who exists on the historical plane and whose existence has both a beginning and an end.

↑↑↑

*Jesus was unconcerned with
speculations either about death or
about the meaning of resurrection.*

↑↑

But the Sadducees, who did not accept the apocalyptists' doctrine of resurrection, tried to confute that notion by resort to the device of *reductio ad absurdum* with their presentation of the impossible case of the woman married successively to seven brothers; and Jesus parried the question neatly. The doctrine of resurrection in Daniel had been an effort to say that life lived well was not in vain even though it bore no apparent fruit because of the present condition of the People. God would not allow such a life to be "vanity" as the Preacher of Ecclesiastes had thought, but would accept it into the genealogy of the restored Israel. It would be judged acceptable at the coming time of restoration or renewal. "He is not God of the dead, but of the living," and therefore, the literalistic question about life after the resurrection is absurdly beside the point. The God who manifested himself to Moses at the burning bush is concerned with the life of a People, the progeny of Abraham, and not with death.

What exactly Jesus conceived to be the nature of the life of resurrection is unclear, and it is unlikely that he ever considered the problem. His preoccupation was with the urgency of life in the present time: with the signs in his own ministry and in general historical phenomena which proclaimed or would soon proclaim that God is about to do something new, to inaugurate his kingship in a decisive way. This is the motif of the parables,[16] and the Synoptic Apocalypse[17] stresses not resurrection but the signs of the end of the present age. The statement: "And then he will send out the angels, and gather his elect from the four winds, from the ends of the earth to the ends of heaven" (Mark 13:27 RSV) is the only sentence (in only two of the three versions) of the Apocalypse which touches on resurrection; and it is very general. The description of the Last Judgment in Matthew 25:31–46 is cast in parabolic form so as to stress rather the importance of being prepared for the impending coming of God's kingship than the nature of the resurrection and its aftermath.[18]

Jesus, in other words, was unconcerned with speculations either about death or about the meaning of resurrection. Nothing he says seems to enlarge upon the traditional Hebraic stance; indeed, he seems to have used the language of apocalyptic while withdrawing from the apocalyptic picture of resurrection in favor of a reaffirmation of the kind of assertion made before the historical dislocation of the People. At the time of his crucifixion, there is abundant evidence in the Synoptic Gospels that Jesus showed both fear and terror in the face of suffering. Unlike Socrates, who faced death with triumphant composure, he took death as a terrible and serious thing.[19] His ultimate appeal was to the will of God, and that same will was his only and bitter comfort.

Jesus was concerned with life, or with the quality of life expected by God of his people, because he believed that the new age was about to begin. Death is the end of historical existence except insofar as one conceives of the dead as being with the fathers or a part of the living heritage of the People. To say that the dead shall be raised is to say that they will, as a part of the living heritage, participate in the life of the restored People which is about to begin.[20]

Of course, Jesus may have had (and probably did have) a more concrete picture than this in mind when he spoke of resurrection. His failure to be much more specific in his pronouncements is, however, made clear by the problems raised almost immediately for his followers in communicating this crucial, eschatological aspect of his teaching. For one thing, the time of the coming of the new order of things, for which Jesus had urged men to prepare, was not so imminent. Thus (rather as the Wisdom and apocalyptic schools emerged to answer questions raised by the historical failure of the expectations of the Hebraic peoples), it became imperative to develop a rationale for life in the interim before the coming of the kingship of God. Furthermore, it was necessary to accommodate Jesus' teaching, addressed only to the Jews, to the universal audience to whom Paul and others came to believe it was appropriate. And, finally, as a consequence of this, a new language was needed to express uniquely Judaic concepts in a society for which the terminology of the followers of Plato was more readily comprehensible.

It is in the writing of Paul,[21] who was attempting to resolve all three of
these problems, that the problem of eschatology and the problem of death
and the afterlife met and for the first time were made inseparable. Clarification of Jesus' vagueness, the lapse of time and the difficulty of cross-
cultural interpretation all loom large in the following passage, which gathers
a number of themes familiar in Paul's day and fuses them for the first time.

> . . . There is one glory of the sun, and another glory of the moon,
> and another glory of the stars; for star differs from star in glory.
> So it is with the resurrection of the dead. What is sown is
> perishable, what is raised is imperishable. It is sown in dishonor,
> it is raised in glory. It is sown in weakness, it is raised in power. It
> is sown a physical body, it is raised a spiritual body. If there is a
> physical body, there is also a spiritual body. Thus it is written,
> "The first man Adam became a living being"; the last Adam became
> a life-giving spirit. . . . I tell you this, brethren: flesh and blood
> cannot inherit the kingdom of God, nor does the perishable inherit
> the imperishable.
> Lo! I tell you a mystery. We shall not all sleep, but we shall all
> be changed, in a moment, in the twinkling of an eye, at the last
> trumpet. For the trumpet will sound, and the dead will be raised
> imperishable, and we shall be changed. For this perishable nature
> must put on the imperishable, and this mortal nature must put on
> immortality. When the perishable puts on the imperishable, and the
> mortal puts on immortality, then shall come to pass the saying that
> is written:
> "Death is swallowed up in victory."
> "O death, where is thy victory?
> O death, where is thy sting?" (I Cor. 15: 41–55 RSV)

No longer can the question of the nature of the resurrection as a mode
of existence for the revivified dead be evaded. It must become what it was
only potentially in the apocalyptic tradition: a special kind of corporeal
existence which is a reward for the righteous who have died and a punishment for the wicked. To spell out what he means by this, Paul has recourse
not only to fundamentally Greek terms like "spiritual" but also to the
typological comparison of Christ and Adam and to the logical forms of
disputation familiar to the philosophical schools and through them, perhaps,
to the rabbinical schools of the Jewish dispersion. The passage is primarily
a careful, rhetorical, and logical development of the antitheses of "physical"
and "spiritual," constructed so as to show that there can be full life (in the

unitive, Hebraic sense) for those who will be raised but that it must be understood symbolically or spiritually (in the dualistic Greek sense) as radically different from historical existence. Just as Jesus was raised, so all men will be raised—or, if they are still living, changed—when the time comes. Therefore, the length of the time interval makes little difference; salvation remains universally available.[22]

Death in Paul's view is the "last" and greatest enemy of man, yet an enemy whose power derives from man's own acts of sinfulness. The moment of death is, thus, one of obliteration or of self-obliteration but for the intervention of God in Christ Jesus, whose own resurrection and glorification constitutes man's only hope of victory over death (I Cor. 15:12–22). Death is, then, an event or phenomenon of awful seriousness; Jesus' own reactions to his impending death were not cowardly or unphilosophical but absolutely realistic. But Jesus' own triumph is the assurance of man's triumph whenever God chooses to inaugurate his own reign. Those who die in Christ are, euphemistically, "asleep" and awaiting the ultimate triumph or the dread judgment—at the resurrection with the rest of the People of God. Ultimately, the dead will be raised, corporeal and yet spiritual; and therefore, we can face death with a sure hope of ultimate triumph by God's grace.

With the possible exception of the radically Hellenized Wisdom of Solomon of the Apocrypha, the first consistently developed theology of death in the Judeo-Christian intellectual tradition is that of Paul. Although none of Paul's assumptions were novel in the first century, he seems to have gone beyond what Jesus said on the subject, so far as we can tell from the meager record of the Gospels; and he makes certain concessions in its vocabulary, at least, to common Greek conceptualizations. But the expansions and the concessions are minimal and were necessary in the light of the apologetic problems of explaining the lengthening of the interim and of speaking to a non-Judaic audience. The fundamental elements of the tradition—the lack of distinction between body and spirit and the overriding concern not with the destiny of the individual but with that of the People—are carefully maintained to the absolute exclusion of either the dualistic and metaphysical or the political notion of immortality which the Hellenistic Age had inherited from fifth-century Greece.

Statements like that of Geoffrey Gorer, that "orthodox Christianity is dogmatic that the soul continues to exist after death,"[23] are, then, absolutely without biblical foundation. Not only do the biblical writers on the whole have no conception of a soul as a separable element of human existence, but also there is agreement that death is the (often dreadful) termination of existence and that there is no such thing as an individual afterlife. The very urgency of living well in the world arises, in the biblical outlook, from the fact of death and from the high mission of the People of the Covenant, old or new, within which People alone the individual's life has meaning and purpose. At the end of the biblical tradition, the Pauline emphasis upon the general resurrection serves simply to underline these points, that all life is corporeal and that the judgment of mankind is general because the People is indivisible. In this view lay the possibility of a further development in which man could be regarded as entering upon an afterlife in the body of his resurrection after the sleep of the interim.

Against this general understanding of death, the Greek views stand in contrast. Whereas the Judeo-Christians maintained the unity of the human being, the Greek philosophical tradition in general conceived of a soul which might or must continue to exist after its separation from the body. Metaphysically speaking, immortality was a necessary logical deduction for the Greek but an inconceivable construct for the Jews and primitive Christians. And, whereas the Hebraic progenitor was understood as always part of the living heritage of the People, the Greek political hero continued to exist in the memory of his city and thus to be granted immortality.

NOTES

1   On the biblical definition of History, see Lloyd G. Patterson, *God and History in Early Christian Thought* (Studies in Early Christian Thought; New York: Seabury Press, 1967), pp. 1–15.

2   For a survey of Old Testament attitudes toward death (with which I disagree at several points), see Robert Martin-Achard, *From Death to Life: A Study of the Development of the Doctrine of the Resurrection in the Old Testament,* trans. John Penney Smith (Edinburgh: Oliver and Boyd, 1960).

3   Trans. E. A. Speiser ("The Anchor Bible," I; Garden City: Doubleday, 1964), p. 174. Used with permission. I am further indebted to Speiser's Introduction and Notes for helpful suggestions; to the Introduction and Commentary of C. A. Simpson in *The Interpreter's Bible,* I (Nashville: Abingdon Press, 1952); and to the articles of Edmond Jacob on "Death" and "Immortality" in *The Interpreter's Dictionary of the Bible* (Nashville: Abingdon Press, 1962). Lack of space has prevented me from taking account of the kinds of evidence presented by Roland de Vaux (*Ancient Israel: Its Life and Institutions,* trans. John McHugh [New York: McGraw-Hill, 1961], esp. at pp. 56–61); I am, however, convinced that these considerations do not fundamentally challenge my discussion.

4   Harvey H. Guthrie, Jr., *Wisdom and Canon: Meanings of the Law and the Prophets* (Winslow Lectures, 1966; Evanston: Seabury-Western Theological Seminary, 1966), pp. 4–5.

5   According to the Yahwist, who is not responsible for Gen. 25:1–11.

6   Here I go beyond other commentators, who are more cautious. The only other reference to this kind of oath is in Gen. 47:29; and it is, significantly, associated with the death of Israel, who is likewise preoccupied with thoughts of the land of the promise of Yahweh.

7   Because of the unique role of Abraham as the first patriarch, "in Abraham's bosom" became a common euphemism for death.

8   *Nephesh,* the Hebrew word which has often been translated "soul," means, rather, "that which is vital in man in the broadest sense" (Gerhard von Rad, *Old Testament Theology,* trans. D. M. G. Stalker [2 vols.; Edinburgh: Oliver and Boyd, 1962 and 1965], I, p. 153). Although *nephesh* is given to man at his creation and it returns to God at his death, the concept is closer to selfhood or life-force than to soul.

9   Guthrie, *Wisdom and Canon.* My statement of the themes of later Hebrew religious thought is heavily influenced by Guthrie in the work cited and in *God and History in the Old Testament* (New York: Seabury Press, 1960), pp. 117–137. See also von Rad, II, pp. 301–315. Not all scholars would agree to their formulation of the relationship between Wisdom and apocalyptic, but it seems to me proper because of the essential contemporaneity of the traditions to see them as related rather than as antipathetic.

10   See von Rad, II, pp. 308–315.

11   I have not treated Wisdom of Solomon, which does incorporate the Hellenistic doctrine of the immortal soul into the Hebraic historical framework, because of its late date (c. 100 B.C.–c. A.D. 40) and its uniqueness. Obviously, however, it shows the inherent possibilities of accommodation to Hellenism via the Wisdom tradition (and this is doubly significant in the light of its association with Alexandria where Christian philosophical theology was to flower and represents a significant movement in late Judaism, the importance of which has only recently been recognized. One might argue that Wisdom only translates Hebraic notions into the Greek philosophical idiom (and I have been tempted to do so, claiming for the author a high level of sophistication and remarkable poetic powers); but in the light of the Christian history of the problem of immortality, that seems to be pushing things. It is easy to see why the Fathers were moved by this document. For further commentary, see Bruce C. Metzgar, *An Introduction to the Apocrypha* (New York: Oxford University Press, 1957), pp. 65–76.

12   My interpretation is heavily influenced by Oscar Cullmann's Ingersoll Lecture for 1955, "Immortality of the Soul or Resurrection of the Dead," reprinted in Stendahl, ed., *Immortality and Resurrection,* pp. 9–47; I go somewhat further than he, however.

13   See Dan. 12:5–13.

14   Werner Georg Kümmel, *Promise and Fulfillment: The Eschatological Message of Jesus,* trans. D. M. Barton ("Studies in Biblical Theology," 23; London: SCM Press, 1957), p. 153. See also Gunther Bornkamm, *Jesus of Nazareth,* trans. Irene and Fraser McLuskey with James M. Robinson (New York: Harpers, 1960), pp. 90–95.

15   See also Matt. 22:23–33.

16   See Joachim Jeremias, *The Parables of Jesus* (rev. ed.; London: SCM Press, 1963), *passim.*

17   Mark 13:5–37; Matt. 24:4–36; Luke 21:8–36.

18   See Kummel, *Promise and Fulfillment,* pp. 88 ff.

19   See Cullmann in *Immortality and Resurrection,* pp. 12–20.

20   Regretfully, considerations of length prevent us from dealing here with the John Gospel, for it has seemed to many to represent a Hellenized point of view. Despite its radically different vocabulary. I regard it more and more as a document in which Hellenic terms are

used to present Hebraic notions. Its real sources lie in the Wisdom movement; but its exegetical interpretation has been shaped by the Alexandrian philosophical theologians.

21 Paul's writing, of course, antedates that of the Evangelists and in some ways influences them. The present order of discussion is based on the assumption that Mark 12:18 ff. is a comparatively untouched *logion*. The signs of the Synoptic Apocalypse are not free from later influences, and even the reference therein to the resurrection may not be authentic.

22 Paul treats this problem more directly in I Thess. 4:13–18.

23 *Death, Grief, and Mourning* (Garden City, N.Y.: Doubleday, 1965), p. 24.

Death and Psychical Research:
The Present Position Regarding
the Evidence of Survival

Rosalind Heywood

Rosalind Heywood is Member of Council of the Society for Psychical Research in England. This selection, which first appeared in *Man's Concern with Death* edited by Professor Toynbee, is one of a number of articles in that volume on psychical research, a study that is particularly popular in England. It has been included as representative of the kind of data upon which many psychical researchers base their approach to the age-old question of survival after death.

From *Man's Concern with Death.* Copyright © 1968 by Arnold Toynbee, A. Keith Mant, Ninian Smart, John Hinton, Cicely Yudkin, Eric Rhode, Rosalind Heywood, H. H. Price. Used with permission of McGraw-Hill Book Company, and Hodder and Stoughton Ltd.

From the point of view of the investigator, then, the findings of psychical research in relation to death seem to amount to something like this. On the one hand the apparent potentialities of E.S.P. make it hard to conceive what kind of evidence could give coercive proof of survival —evidence that could not at a pinch be ascribed to some combination of telepathy, clairvoyance, precognition or retrocognition in relation to events in this world. As against this, the more we learn about the range of these capacities, about man's apparent power to transcend the limitations of the known senses and of time and space as presented to him by those senses, the less inconceivable it may be that the early researchers were on the right track in surmising that there could be something in him—what Professor C. D. Broad discreetly calls some psi component—which might be able to function independently of a physical body.

In a book concerned with attitudes to death some reference should perhaps be made not only to the attitude of the scientific researcher as regards the possibility of survival, but also to those of people who have themselves had E.S.P.-type experiences connected with death. It may be guessed that most actively religious Christians who have such experiences accept them for what they appear to be, and that a number of the non-Christians who have them join some group, such as the theosophists or spiritualists, into whose beliefs their experiences will fit, for this gives them peace of mind. But how many people are there like the flight lieutenant, who appeared to talk quite normally with his dead fellow pilot and yet had no framework of belief which would hold his experience? Judging from the many cases sent to Dr. Louisa Rhine and to other writers of seriously-intentioned books on psi, there must be an appreciable number, and owing to the present orthodox belief that death is the end, it looks as if some of them dare not mention such experiences for fear of being thought out of their minds. Some even wonder, could that perhaps be true? "Can you possibly explain this?" they write, "I have never dared ask anyone before. Do you think I could be mad?"

The experiences most often reported, incidentally, as with most of the authenticated cases in the annals of psychical research, are far removed from the headless, chain-clanking "ghosties and ghoulies" of fiction and Christmas Numbers. Apart from the apparently aimless haunting type, modern "ghosts" usually seem to want to help, or warn, or merely to appear to a loved friend or relative. And sometimes they are not distinguished from living persons until they vanish.

For those of us, then, who are conditioned by the widespread belief that mind and body die together, and who yet have apparent contacts with the purposeful discarnate, what is our rational attitude towards those contacts, especially as they are admittedly sporadic, fleeting, and not to be repeated to order? Perhaps I may be forgiven a personal summarised illustration of this dilemma, since it is not easy to describe other people's experiences as if from the inside.

In the 1950s the expected death occurred of an inventor friend, with whom, as we both accepted that death was the end, I had shortly before agreed regretfully that he would never be able to bring to fruition the many ideas still seething in his brain. About ten days after his death I was astounded and delighted to "meet," quite naturally, his apparently living personality, and to be assured with emphasis that we had been quite mistaken; he now had scope and opportunity beyond his wildest dreams. In some imageless way I seemed able to participate in his awareness of scope and opportunity and I was rejoicing in this when it flashed across my mind that I ought to ask for evidence of his splended liberation. But the reply he made was, "I can't give you any evidence. You have no concepts for these conditions.[1] I can only give you poetic images." Which he did. But quite soon I realized that I could not hold the state into which, unexpectedly, my consciousness had switched, so I said, "Goodbye, I must drop now." And I "dropped" at once to ordinary awareness of mundane surroundings.

ฯฯ

Should we defy the voice of contemporary science and bet on the reality of our own experiences, however fleeting and unpredictable?

ฯฯ

Although this experience does not appear to be very exceptional, there is not a shred of evidence to support my account of it, and investigators will therefore—and quite rightly—feel it their duty to dismiss it as a mere anecdote. But again, what is the rational attitude for the people who have such experiences, sometimes repeatedly? Should we discard them all as illusions, in obedience to orthodoxy? Should we even suspect our own sanity? (I asked two eminent psychiatrists to check on mine and they both gave me a clean bill of health. But one did say sadly, "I'm *afraid* you're quite sane.") Or should we defy the voice of contemporary science and bet on the reality of our own experiences, however fleeting and unpredictable?

---

[1]In an article in *The New Scientist* for August 30th 1962, Dr. Richard Gregory has suggested that travellers in space might be faced with a similar problem. "Suppose," he says, "we were to meet something really odd—say a new life form—could we see it properly? The perceptual system is a computer, programmed by evolutionary experience and by our own personal experience of the world. A new kind of object requires the perceptual computer to solve a new problem with an old programme, which may be neither adequate nor appropriate."

On one thing, perhaps, the psi-experiencing agnostic can afford to bet— that were the whole of humanity to have experiences similar to his own, of the occasional momentary, purposeful presence of discarnate persons he had known in life, it would not occur to them, however mistaken they might be in fact, to doubt the reality of survival. As things are, however, the only place where his reason can feel at ease and honest is on the fence. And there he will at least be encouraged to find a number of distinguished scholars who have thought it worthwhile to study the evidence for survival for many years. This is how three among them summed up their conclusions in the 1960s. First, the well-known American psychologist Professor Gardner Murphy.

> Where then do I stand? To this the reply is: what happens when an irresistible force strikes an immovable object? To me the evidence cannot be bypassed, nor, on the other hand, can conviction be achieved . . . Trained as a psychologist and now in my sixties, I do not actually anticipate finding myself in existence after physical death. If this is the answer the reader wants, he can have it. But if this means that in a serious philosophical argument I would plead the antisurvival case, the conclusion is erroneous. I linger because I cannot cross the stream. We need far more evidence; we need new perspectives; perhaps we need more courageous minds.[2]

Next, the doyen of British psychologists, Professor Sir Cyril Burt.

> The uncertainty leaves the matter open in *both* directions. On the one hand the theoretical psychologist (and that includes the parapsychologist) should, on this particular issue, preserve a strict agnosticism, pressing physicalistic interpretations as far as they will go, and even if in the end he feels compelled to adopt the hypothesis of a surviving mind, he must remember that it is, like the ether of old, no more than a hypothesis. On the other hand, those who, from reasons of faith, metaphysics, or what they take to be personal revelation, still wish to believe in survival for themselves or those they love, need have no grounds for fearing scientific censure. Thus our verdict on the whole matter must be the same as that pronounced by Plato two thousand years ago—the reply he puts into the mouth of Socrates while waiting to drink the hemlock. "I would not positively assert that I shall join the company of those good men who have already departed from this life; but I cherish a good hope." Hope implies not the virtual

---

[2]*Challenge of Psychical Research*, Harpers, New York, 1961, p. 273.

certainty of success but the possibility of success. And it is, I think, one important result of recent psychological and parapsychological investigations to have demonstrated, in the face of the confident denials of the materialists and the behaviourists, *at least the possibility* of survival in some form or other, though not necessarily in the form depicted by traditional piety or fourth century metaphysics.[3]

And finally, Professor C. D. Broad, sometime Knightbridge Professor of Moral Philosophy at Cambridge. He, incidentally, does not hide the fact that he does not want to survive.

The position as I see it is this. In the known relevant normal and abnormal facts there is nothing to suggest and much to countersuggest, the possibility of any kind of persistence of the psychical aspect of a human being after the death of his body. On the other hand, there are many quite well-attested *paranormal* phenomena which strongly suggest such persistence, and a few which strongly suggest the fullblown survival of a human personality. Most people manage to turn a blind eye to one or the other of these two relevant sets of data, but it is part of the business of a professional philosopher to try to envisage steadily both of them together. The result is naturally a state of hesitation and scepticism (in the correct as opposed to the popular sense of that word). I think I may say that for my part I should be slightly more annoyed than surprised if I should find myself in some sense persisting immediately after the death of my present body. One can only wait and see, or alternatively (which is no less likely) wait and not see."[4]

It looks then as if at the present time to step off the fence on either side as regards survival entails an act of faith. On one side we can believe—but cannot prove—that men of science already know enough about the nature of things to be able to assert with safety that it is impossible; on the other we can believe—but equally cannot prove—that certain phenomena demonstrate that it is a fact.

---

[3]*Article,* "Psychology and Parapsychology" in a symposium *Science & E.S.P.,* edited by J. R. Smythies, International Library of Philosophy and Scientific Method, Routledge and Kegan Paul, p. 140.

[4]*Lectures on Psychical Research,* International Library of Philosophy and Scientific Method, Routledge and Kegan Paul, 1962, p. 430.

Do We Survive Death?*

Bertrand Russell

Bertrand Russell, British philosopher, mathematician, and
essayist, was one of the most intellectually gifted individuals
of our century. His many works, characterized by wit, clarity,
and vivid metaphor, are known throughout the world. In
this selection, taken from his book *Why I Am Not A
Christian*, Russell, in his typical no-nonsense, pungent prose,
attacks the notion of survival after death.

Before we can profitably discuss whether we shall
continue to exist after death, it is well to be clear as to the sense in which a
man is the same person as he was yesterday. Philosophers used to think
that there were definite substances, the soul and the body, that each lasted
on from day to day, that a soul, once created, continued to exist throughout
all future time, whereas a body ceased temporarily from death till the resurrection of the body.

The part of this doctrine which concerns the present life is pretty certainly false. The matter of the body is continually changing by processes of
nutriment and wastage. Even if it were not, atoms in physics are no longer
supposed to have continuous existence; there is no sense in saying: this is
the same atom as the one that existed a few minutes ago. The continuity of
a human body is a matter of appearance and behavior, not of substance.

The same thing applies to the mind. We think and feel and act, but there
is not, in addition to thoughts and feelings and actions, a bare entity, the
mind or the soul, which does or suffers these occurrences. The mental continuity of a person is a continuity of habit and memory: there was yesterday one person whose feelings I can remember, and that person I regard as
myself of yesterday; but, in fact, myself of yesterday was only certain

---

*This piece was first published in 1936 in a book entitled *The Mysteries of Life and Death*. The
article by Bishop Barnes to which Russell refers appeared in the same work.

EDITOR'S NOTE: *This is the only selection in this volume that violates our own canon of
limiting all pieces to those published between 1965 and 1975. The reasons for including
this piece—as a counterfoil to the previous one—were persuasive enough to bend our rule.*

mental occurrences which are now remembered and are regarded as part of the person who now recollects them. All that constitutes a person is a series of experiences connected by memory and by certain similarities of the sort we call habit.

If, therefore, we are to believe that a person survives death, we must believe that the memories and habits which constitute the person will continue to be exhibited in a new set of occurrences.

No one can prove that this will not happen. But it is easy to see that it is very unlikely. Our memories and habits are bound up with the structure of the brain, in much the same way in which a river is connected with the riverbed. The water in the river is always changing, but it keeps to the same course because previous rains have worn a channel. In like manner, previous events have worn a channel in the brain, and our thoughts flow along this channel. This is the cause of memory and mental habits. But the brain, as a structure, is dissolved at death, and memory therefore may be expected to be also dissolved. There is no more reason to think otherwise than to expect a river to persist in its old course after an earthquake has raised a mountain where a valley used to be.

*It is not rational arguments but
emotions that cause belief
in a future life.*

All memory, and therefore (one may say) all minds, depend upon a property which is very noticeable in certain kinds of material structures but exists little if at all in other kinds. This is the property of forming habits as a result of frequent similar occurrences. For example: a bright light makes the pupils of the eyes contract; and if you repeatedly flash a light in a man's eyes and beat a gong at the same time, the gong alone will, in the end, cause his pupils to contract. This is a fact about the brain and nervous system—that is to say, about a certain material structure. It will be found that exactly similar facts explain our response to language and our use of it, our memories and the emotions they arouse, our moral or immoral habits of behavior, and indeed everything that constitutes our mental personality, except the part determined by heredity. The part determined by heredity is handed on to our posterity but cannot, in the individual, survive the disintegration of the body. Thus both the hereditary and the acquired parts of a personality are, so far as our experience goes, bound up with the characteristics of certain bodily structures. We all know that memory may be obliterated by an injury to the brain, that a virtuous person may be rendered vicious by encephalitis lethargica, and that a clever child can be turned into an idiot by lack of iodine. In view of such familiar facts, it seems scarcely probable that the mind survives the total destruction of brain structure which occurs at death.

It is not rational arguments but emotions that cause belief in a future life.

The most important of these emotions is fear of death, which is instinctive and biologically useful. If we genuinely and wholeheartedly believed in the future life, we should cease completely to fear death. The effects would be curious, and probably such as most of us would deplore. But our human and subhuman ancestors have fought and exterminated their enemies throughout many geological ages and have profited by courage; it is therefore an advantage to the victors in the struggle for life to be able, on occasion, to overcome the natural fear of death. Among animals and savages, instinctive pugnacity suffices for this purpose; but at a certain stage of development, as the Mohammedans first proved, belief in Paradise has considerable military value as reinforcing natural pugnacity. We should therefore admit that militarists are wise in encouraging the belief in immortality, always supposing that this belief does not become so profound as to produce indifference to the affairs of the world.

Another emotion which encourages the belief in survival is admiration of the excellence of man. As the Bishop of Birmingham says, "His mind is a far finer instrument than anything that had appeared earlier—he knows right and wrong. He can build Westminster Abbey. He can make an airplane. He can calculate the distance of the sun. . . . Shall, then, man at death perish utterly? Does that incomparable instrument, his mind, vanish when life ceases?"

The Bishop proceeds to argue that "the universe has been shaped and is governed by an intelligent purpose," and that it would have been unintelligent, having made man, to let him perish.

To this argument there are many answers. In the first place, it has been found, in the scientific investigation of nature, that the intrusion of moral or aesthetic values has always been an obstacle to discovery. It used to be thought that the heavenly bodies must move in circles because the circle is the most perfect curve, that species must be immutable because God would only create what was perfect and what therefore stood in no need of improvement, that it was useless to combat epidemics except by repentance because they were sent as a punishment for sin, and so on. It has been found, however, that, so far as we can discover, nature is indifferent to our values and can only be understood by ignoring our notions of good and bad. The Universe may have a purpose, but nothing that we know suggests that, if so, this purpose has any similarity to ours.

Nor is there in this anything surprising. Dr. Barnes tells us that man "knows right and wrong." But, in fact, as anthropology shows, men's views of right and wrong have varied to such an extent that no single item has been permanent. We cannot say, therefore, that man knows right and wrong, but only that some men do. Which men? Nietzsche argued in favor of an ethic profoundly different from Christ's, and some powerful governments have accepted his teaching. If knowledge of right and wrong is to be an argument for immortality, we must first settle whether to believe Christ or Nietzsche, and then argue that Christians are immortal, but Hitler and Mussolini are not, or vice versa. The decision will obviously be made on the battlefield, not in the study. Those who have the best poison gas will have the ethic of the future and will therefore be the immortal ones.

Our feelings and beliefs on the subject of good and evil are, like everything else about us, natural facts, developed in the struggle for existence and not having any divine or supernatural origin. In one of Aesop's fables, a lion is shown pictures of huntsmen catching lions and remarks that, if he had painted them, they would have shown lions catching huntsmen. Man, says Dr. Barnes, is a fine fellow because he can make airplanes. A little while ago there was a popular song about the cleverness of flies in walking upside down on the celing, with the chorus: "Could Lloyd George do it? Could Mr. Baldwin do it? Could Ramsay Mac do it? Why, no." On this basis a very telling argument could be constructed by a theologically minded fly, which no doubt the other flies would find most convincing.

Moreover, it is only when we think abstractly that we have such a high opinion of man. Of men in the concrete, most of us think the vast majority very bad. Civilized states spend more than half their revenue on killing each other's citizens. Consider the long history of the activities inspired by moral fervor: human sacrifices, persecutions of heretics, witch-hunts, pogroms leading up to wholesale extermination by poison gases, which one at least of Dr. Barnes's episcopal colleagues must be supposed to favor, since he holds pacifism to be un-Christian. Are these abominations, and the ethical doctrines by which they are prompted, really evidence of an intelligent Creator? And can we really wish that the men who practiced them should live forever? The world in which we live can be understood as a result of muddle and accident; but if it is the outcome of deliberate purpose, the purpose must have been that of a fiend. For my part, I find accident a less painful and more plausible hypothesis.

·2· DEATH AS A SOCIAL DISEASE

In this world there are certain positive attributes (beauty, brains, elegance, talent, etc.) and conversely there are certain stigmas. These stigmas include deformity, disease, outcast status (see Erving Goffman's book *Stigma: Notes on the Management of Spoiled Identity* [1963]), failure, old age, and death. Very few people are permitted to be proud of their aging or dying. This chapter touches on two separate elements: the stigma of death, seen as ugly, brutal, or commercially exploitable; and a core paradox and oxymoron of our century wherein, on the one hand, there are our efforts to prohibit individual death (by prolonging life through technological means) and, on the other hand, our insane addiction to violent and massive death, what Gil Elliot has called "macro-violence in the man-made environment," by which he refers to the mass slaughter by organized governments. This killing by governments is the most serious disease of our world. It is the only malady that could kill us *all*. With the perception of this threat has come a number of psychological concomitants: what Robert Lifton has called "numbing"; what Nathan Leites has referred to as "affectlessness"; what Kenneth Keniston has called "alienation"; what Henry Murray has labelled "the root mood of an articulate depth-sensitive minority." These psychological states may be related to recent increases in crime, use of drugs, disaffection, and violence.

This chapter represents a tightening of focus on the cultural perspectives of death by concerning itself with death as viewed in contemporary culture. The chapter is divided into two sections, each of which talks about death as a disease. The first "disease" aspect is our contemporary treatment of death as a social disease (much like V.D.) not appropriate to "polite society." This attitude stems from the changing characteristics of death ("controlled mortality" as discussed in the next chapter and institutionalization of death—both of which pull death away from our immediate view and make it somewhat "sinful," just as a "glimpse of stocking was shocking" at another age) and from an oxymoronic approach to death. This double-image view of death is underscored in the Gorer selection, already a sociological classic, where it is pointed out that while *violent* death is an increasing part of the fantasy life of mass audiences, *natural* death becomes unmentionable, more taboo in our time than sex was in Victorian days.

Because death is "socially unacceptable," we attempt to interdict it, as the Ariès article shows. In effect we pretend it isn't there by "tarting up" the cadaver so that it's not dead but just sleeping. Ariès, a European, attributes this behavior almost entirely to the United States. The exploitation by the funeral industry of our fastidious rejection of death is reviewed by Baird, who shows how, with enough money, we can "tastefully" unload the dead and suppress bereavement and thereby buttress our ban on socially unacceptable death.

Our increasing acceptance of violent death leads us to the second "disease" aspect—a disease of the society, resulting from the inexorable ubiquity of death. The last three selections of the chapter are about macroviolence. The twentieth century—like the time of the great Asian and European plagues of the fourteenth century (See Ziegler's *The Black Death*)—can be called a Century of Death: atomic death is in the air, omnipresent, possible in any spot or at any moment; there is no place to hide.

Our society embraces violent death (witness our avid attention to the butchery on television programs and our relative indifference to the slaughter on our highways) in various ways; but it should be noted that the emphasis here is on violent death as practiced by governments. The resulting disease of society is expressed by the psychic numbing and guilt of survivors pointed up in the Lifton and Olson selection and detailed on a more personal level by Baruch.

Another expression of the disease is a pervasive fear—fear that nothing will last in the face of possible total destruction and that therefore nothing matters. The overriding aspect of this disease of society is represented by the "technological alienation" described by Elliot. (How can any society behave healthily with a loaded atomic gun constantly pointed at its head?) As Lifton and Olson say, ". . . [in a] sense we are all survivors of this century's holocausts . . ."; and it might be added that we all suffer the special sickness characteristic of survivors.

Every once in a while one comes across a book that is so shocking in its simple recitation of horrible facts that it seems both noble and obscene. Elliot's *The Twentieth Century Book of the Dead* is such a volume. All he does is detail the 110 million deaths committed by *governments* since 1900—a "nation of the dead," created by man himself. The selection from that work reprinted here is about the agents of death—how the killing is done. Elliot's book is not one for the timid; it is for everyone. Read, shudder, and weep.

The Pornography of Death

Geoffrey Gorer
Geoffrey Gorer is a noted English anthropologist who has
written about Africa, Bali and Angkor, Himalayan villages,
and the American people. His first book was about the
Marquis de Sade. This selection, which is taken from his
book *Death, Grief and Mourning*, has in the past few years
already become a classic of its kind. In it, Gorer proposes,
and brilliantly explicates, the dramatic thesis that death
is treated in our society as obscene and pornographic; that
while sex was the pornography of the Victorians, death is
the pornography of our times.

> *Birth, and copulation, and death.*
> *That's all the facts when you come to brass tacks;*
> *Birth, and copulation, and death.*
> —T. S. Eliot, *Sweeney Agonistes* (1932)

Pornography is, no doubt, the opposite face, the
shadow, of prudery, whereas obscenity is an aspect of seemliness. No society has been recorded which has not its rules of seemliness, of words or
actions which arouse discomfort and embarrassment in some contexts,
though they are essential in others. The people before whom one must
maintain a watchful seemliness vary from society to society: all people of
the opposite sex, or all juniors, or all elders, or one's parents-in-law, or
one's social superiors or inferiors, or one's grandchildren have been selected
in different societies as groups in whose presence the employment of certain words or the performance of certain actions would be considered
offensive; and then these words or actions become charged with affect.
There is a tendency for these words and actions to be related to sex and
excretion, but this is neither necessary nor universal; according to Malinowski, the Trobrianders surround eating with as much shame as excretion;
and in other societies personal names or aspects of ritual come under the
same taboos.

Rules of seemliness are apparently universal; and the non-observance of these rules, or anecdotes which involve the breaking of the rules, provoke that peculiar type of laughter which seems identical the world over; however little one may know about a strange society, however little one may know about the functions of laughter in that society (and these can be very various) one can immediately tell when people are laughing at an obscene joke. The topper of the joke may be "And then he ate the whole meal in front of them!" or "She used her husband's name in the presence of his mother!" but the laughter is the same; the taboos of seemliness have been broken and the result is hilarious. Typically, such laughter is confined to one-sex groups and is more general with the young, just entering into the complexities of adult life.

Obscenity then is a universal, an aspect of man and woman living in society; everywhere and at all times there are words and actions which, when misplaced, can produce shock, social embarrassment, and laughter. Pornography on the other hand, the description of tabooed activities to produce hallucination or delusion, seems to be a very much rarer phenomenon. It probably can only arise in literate societies, and we certainly have no records of it for non-literate ones; for whereas the enjoyment of obscenity is predominantly social, the enjoyment of pornography is predominantly private. The fantasies from which pornography derives could of course be generated in any society; but it seems doubtful whether they would ever be communicated without the intermediary of literacy.

The one possible exception to this generalization is the use of plastic arts without any letterpress. I have never felt quite certain that the three-dimensional *poses plastiques* on so many Hindu temples (notably the "Black Pagoda" at Konarak) have really the highfalutin Worship of the Life Force or Glorification of the Creative Aspect of Sex which their apologists claim for them; many of them seem to me very like "feelthy" pictures, despite the skill with which they are executed. There are too the erotic woodcuts of Japan; but quite a lot of evidence suggests that these are thought of as laughter-provoking (i.e. obscene) by the Japanese themselves. We have no knowledge of the functions of the Peruvian pottery.

As far as my knowledge goes, the only Asian society which had a long-standing tradition of pornographic literature is China; and, it would appear, social life under the Manchus was surrounded by much the same haze of prudery as distinguished the nineteenth century in much of Europe and the Americas, even though the emphasis fell rather differently; women's deformed feet seem to have been the greatest focus of peeking and sniggering, rather than their ankles or the cleft between their breasts; but by and large life in Manchu China seems to have been nearly as full of "unmentionables" as life in Victoria's heyday.

Pornography would appear to be a concomitant of prudery, and usually the periods of the greatest production of pornography have also been the periods of the most rampant prudery. In contrast to obscenity, which is chiefly defined by situation, prudery is defined by subject; some aspect of human experience is treated as inherently shameful or abhorrent, so that it can never be discussed or referred to openly, and experience of it tends to be clandestine and accompanied by feelings of guilt and unworthiness. The unmentionable aspect of experience then tends to become a subject for much private fantasy, more or less realistic, fantasy charged with pleasurable guilt or guilty pleasure; and those whose power of fantasy is weak, or whose demand is insatiable, constitute a market for the printed fantasies of the pornographer.

Traditionally, and in the lexicographic meaning of the term, pornography has been concerned with sexuality. For the greater part of the last two hundred years copulation and (at least in the mid-Victorian decades) birth were the "unmentionables" of the triad of basic human experiences which "are all the facts when you come to brass tacks," around which so much private fantasy and semi-clandestine pornography were erected. During most of this period death was no mystery, except in the sense that death is always a mystery. Children were encouraged to think about death, their own deaths and the edifying or cautionary death-beds of others. It can have been a rare individual who, in the 19th century with its high mortality, had not witnessed at least one actual dying, as well as paying their respect to "beautiful corpses"; funerals were the occasion of the greatest display for working class, middle class, and aristocrat. The cemetery was the center of every old-established village, and they were prominent in most towns. It was fairly late in the 19th century when the execution of criminals ceased to be a public holiday as well as a public warning.

In the 20th century, however, there seems to have been an unremarked shift in prudery; whereas copulation has become more and more "mentionable," particularly in the Anglo-Saxon societies, death has become more and more "unmentionable" *as a natural process.* I cannot recollect a novel or play of the last twenty years or so which has a "death-bed scene" in it, describing in any detail the death "from natural causes" of a major character; this topic was a set piece for most of the eminent Victorian and Edwardian writers, evoking their finest prose and their most elaborate technical effects to produce the greatest amount of pathos or edification.

One of the reasons, I imagine, for this plethora of death-bed scenes—apart from their intrinsic emotional and religious content—was that it was one of the relatively few experiences that an author could be fairly sure would have been shared by the vast majority of his readers. Questioning my old acquaintances, I cannot find one over the age of sixty who did not witness the agony of at least one near relative; I do not think I know a single person under the age of thirty who has had a similar experience. Of course my acquaintance is neither very extensive nor particularly representative; but in this instance I do think it is typical of the change of attitude and "exposure."

↑↑

> *Our great-grandparents were told that babies were found under gooseberry bushes or cabbages; our children are likely to be told that those who have passed on (fie! on the gross Anglo-Saxon monosyllable) are changed into flowers, or lie at rest in lovely gardens.*

↑↑

The natural processes of corruption and decay have become disgusting, as disgusting as the natural processes of birth and copulation were a century ago; preoccupation about such processes is (or was) morbid and unhealthy, to be discouraged in all and punished in the young. Our great-grandparents were told that babies were found under gooseberry bushes or cabbages; our children are likely to be told that those who have passed on (fie! on the gross Anglo-Saxon monosyllable) are changed into flowers, or lie at rest in lovely gardens. The ugly facts are relentlessly hidden; the art of the embalmers is an art of complete denial.

It seems possible to trace a connection between the shift of taboos and the shift in religious beliefs. In the 19th century most of the inhabitants of Protestant countries seem to have subscribed to the Pauline beliefs in the sinfulness of the body and the certainty of the afterlife. "So also is the resurrection of the dead. It is sown in corruption; it is raised in incorruption: it is sown in dishonour; it is raised in glory." It was possible to insist on the corruption of the dead body, and the dishonour of its begetting, while there was a living belief in the incorruption and the glory of the immortal part. But in England, at any rate, belief in the future life as taught in Christian doctrine is very uncommon today even in the minority who make churchgoing or prayer a consistent part of their lives; and without some such belief natural death and physical decomposition have become too horrible to contemplate or to discuss. It seems symptomatic that the contemporary sect of Christian Science should deny the fact of physical death, even to the extent (so it is said) of refusing to allow the word to be printed in the *Christian Science Monitor.*

During the last half-century public health measures and improved preventive medicine have made natural death among the younger members of the population much more uncommon than it had been in earlier periods, so that a death in the family, save in the fullness of time, became a relatively uncommon incident in home life; and, simultaneously, violent death increased in a manner unparalleled in human history. Wars and revolutions, concentration camps, and gang feuds were the most publicized of the causes for these violent deaths; but the diffusion of the automobile, with its constant and unnoticed toll of fatal accidents, may well have been most influential in bringing the possibility of violent death into the expectations of law-abiding people in time of peace. While natural death became more and more smothered in prudery, violent death has played an evergrowing part in the fantasies offered to mass audiences—detective stories, thrillers, Westerns, war stories, spy stories, science fiction, and eventually horror comics.

There seem to be a number of parallels between the fantasies which titillate our curiosity about the mystery of sex, and those which titillate our curiosity about the mystery of death. In both types of fantasy, the emotions which are typically concomitant of the acts—love or grief—are paid little or no attention, while the sensations are enhanced as much as a customary poverty of language permits. If marital intercourse be considered the natural expression of sex for most of humanity most of the time, then "natural sex" plays as little role as "natural death" (the ham-fisted attempts of D. H. Lawrence and Jules Romains to describe "natural sex" realistically but high-mindedly prove the rule). Neither type of fantasy can have any real development, for once the protagonist has done something, he or she must proceed to do something else, with or to somebody else, more refined, more complicated, or more sensational than what had occurred before. This somebody else is not a person; it is either a set of genitals, with or without secondary sexual characteristics, or a body, perhaps capable of suffering pain as well as death. Since most languages are relatively poor in words or constructions to express intense pleasure or intense pain, the written portions of both types of fantasy abound in onomatopoeic conglomerations of letters meant to evoke the sighs, gasps, groans, screams, and rattles concomitant to the described actions. Both types of fantasy rely heavily on adjective and simile. Both types of fantasy are completely unrealistic, since they ignore all physical, social, or legal limitations, and both types have complete hallucination of the reader or viewer as their object.

There seems little question that the instinct of those censorious busybodies preoccupied with other people's morals was correct when they linked the pornography of death with the pornography of sex. This, however, seems to be the only thing which has been correct in their deductions or attempted actions. There is no valid evidence to suggest that either type of pornography is an incitement to action; rather are they substitute gratifications. The belief that such hallucinatory works would incite their readers to copy the actions depicted would seem to be indirect homage to the late Oscar Wilde, who described such a process in *The Portrait of Dorian Gray*; I know of no authenticated parallels in real life, though investigators and magistrates with bees in their bonnets can usually persuade juvenile delinquents to admit to exposure to whatever medium of mass communication they are choosing to make a scapegoat.

Despite some gifted precursors, such as Andréa de Nerciat or Edgar Allan Poe, most works in both pornographies are aesthetically objectionable; but it is questionable whether, from the purely aesthetic point of view, there is much more to be said for the greater part of the more anodyne fare provided by contemporary mass media of communication. Psychological Utopians tend to condemn substitute gratifications as such, at least where copulation is involved; they have so far been chary in dealing with death.

Nevertheless, people have to come to terms with the basic facts of birth, copulation and death, and somehow accept their implications; if social prudery prevents this being done in an open and dignified fashion, then it will be done surreptitiously. If we dislike the modern pornography of death, then we must give back to death—natural death—its parade and publicity, readmit grief and mourning. If we make death unmentionable in polite society—"not before the children"—we almost ensure the continuation of the "horror comic." No censorship has ever been really effective.

Forbidden Death

Philippe Ariès
Philippe Ariès is a French writer who specializes in social
history. In his book *Western Attitudes toward Death*, from
which this selection is taken, Ariès traces the development
of these attitudes from the Middle Ages to the present. He
contends that the modern tendency toward interdicting or
in some way denying the presence of death began around
the turn of this century. With a view reminiscent of that expressed by Evelyn Waugh in *The Loved One*, Ariès attributes
this phenomenon almost entirely to America.

From *Western Attitudes toward Death: From the Middle
Ages to the Present* by Philippe Ariès. Copyright © 1974 by
The Johns Hopkins University Press. Reprinted by permission
of the publisher.

It seems that the modern attitude toward death, that
is to say the interdiction of death in order to preserve happiness, was born
in the United States around the beginning of the twentieth century. However, on its native soil the interdict was not carried to its ultimate extremes.
In American society it encountered a braking influence which it did not
encounter in Europe. Thus the American attitude toward death today
appears as a strange compromise between trends which are pulling it in
two nearly opposite directions.

There is as yet very scanty documentation on this subject, but the little
that is available has inspired the following thoughts, which I hope will
evoke comments, corrections, and criticism from American historians. When
I read for the first time G. Gorer, J. Mitford, H. Feifel, etc.,[1] I thought I was
finding in contemporary America traces of the mentality of the French
Enlightenment.

"Forest Lawn" is not as futuristic as Evelyn Waugh thought,[2] and it
made me think of the descriptions of the cemeteries dreamed of by the
French authors of cemetery plans in the late eighteenth century, plans which

---

[1] J. Mitford, *The American Way of Death* (New York, 1963); H. Feifel *et al*, *The Meaning of Death* (New York, 1959), a pioneering work.

[2] E. Waugh, *The Loved One* (London, 1948).

never materialized owing to the Revolution and which were replaced in the early nineteenth century by the more declamatory and figurative architecture of Romanticism. In the United States, everything was happening as if the Romantic interval had never existed, and as if the mentality of the eighteenth-century Enlightenment had persisted without interruption.

This first impression, this first hypothesis, was false. It did not take sufficient account of American Puritanism, which is incompatible with confidence in man, in his goodness, in his happiness. Excellent American historians pointed this out to me, and I was very willing to agree with them. Yet the similarities between a part of the current American attitude toward death and that of enlightened Europe in the eighteenth century are no less troubling. We must concede that the mental phenomena which we have just observed occur much later than the French Enlightenment. In America, during the eighteenth and the first half of the nineteenth centuries, and even later, burials conformed to tradition, especially in the countryside: the carpenter made the coffin (the coffin, not yet the "casket"); the family and friends saw to its transport and to the procession itself; and the pastor and gravedigger carried out the service. In the early nineteenth century the grave was still sometimes dug on the family property—which is a modern act, copied from the Ancients, and which was unknown in Europe before the mid-eighteenth century and with few exceptions was rapidly abandoned. In villages and small towns the cemetery most frequently lay adjacent to the church. In the cities, once again paralleling Europe, the cemetery had in about 1830 been situated outside the city but was encompassed by urban growth and abandoned toward 1870 for a new site. It soon fell into ruin, and Mark Twain tells us how the skeletons would leave it at night, carrying off with them what remained of their tombs ("A Curious Dream," 1870).

The old cemeteries were church property, as they had been in Europe and still are in England. The new cemeteries belonged to private associations, as the French authors of those eighteenth-century plans had fruitlessly dreamed. In Europe cemeteries became municipal, that is to say public, property and were never left to private initiative.

In the growing cities of the nineteenth century, old carpenters or gravediggers, or owners of carts and horses, became "undertakers," and the manipulation of the dead became a profession. Here history is still completely comparable to that in Europe, at least in that part of Europe which remained faithful to the eighteenth-century canons of simplicity and which remained outside the pale of Romantic bombast.

Things seem to have changed during the period of the Civil War. Today's "morticians," whose letters-patent go back to that period, give as their ancestor a quack doctor expelled from the school of medicine, Dr. Holmes, who had a passion for dissection and cadavers. He would offer his services to the victim's family and embalmed, it is said, 4,000 cadavers unaided in four years. That's not a bad rate for the period! Why such recourse to embalming? Had it been practiced previously? Is there an American tradition going back to the eighteenth century, a period in which throughout Europe there was a craze for embalming? Yet this technique was abandoned in nineteenth-century Europe, and the wars did not resurrect it. It is noteworthy that embalming became a career in the United States before the end of the century, even if it was not yet very widespread. We can cite the case of Elizabeth "Ma" Green, born in 1884, who as a young woman began to help the undertaker in her small town. At the age of twenty she was a "licensed embalmer" and made a career of this trade until her death. In 1900 embalming appeared in California. We know that it has today become a very widespread method of preparing the dead, a practice almost unknown in Europe and characteristic of the American way of death.

One cannot help thinking that this long-accepted and avowed preference for embalming has a meaning, even if it is difficult to interpret.

This meaning could indeed be that of a certain refusal to accept death, either as a familiar end to which one is resigned, or as a dramatic sign in the Romantic manner. And this meaning became even more obvious when death became an object of commerce and of profit. It is not easy to sell something which has no value because it is too familiar and common, or something which is frightening, horrible, or painful. In order to sell death, it had to be made friendly. But we may assume that "funeral directors"— since 1885 a new name for undertakers—would not have met with success if public opinion had not cooperated. They presented themselves not as simple sellers of services, but as "doctors of grief" who have a mission, as do doctors and priests; and this mission, from the beginning of this century, consists in aiding the mourning survivors to return to normalcy. The new funeral director ("new" because he has replaced the simple undertaker) is a "doctor of grief," an "expert at returning abnormal minds to normal in the shortest possible time." They are "members of an exalted, almost sacred calling."[3]

---

[3]From Mitford, *The American Way of Death.*

Thus mourning is no longer a necessary period imposed by society; it has become a *morbid state* which must be treated, shortened, erased by the "doctor of grief."

Through a series of little steps we can see the birth and development of the ideas which would end in the present-day interdict, built upon the ruins of Puritanism, in an urbanized culture which is dominated by rapid economic growth and by the search for happiness linked to the search for profit.

The wake, increasingly avoided in industrial Europe, persists in the United States: it exists as "viewing the remains," the "visitation." "They don't view bodies in England."

This process should normally result in the situation of England today, as it is described, for example, by Gorer: the almost total suppression of everything reminding us of death.

But, and this is what is unique about the American attitude, American mores have not gone to such an extreme; they stopped along the way. Americans are very willing to transform death, to put make-up on it, to sublimate it, but they do not want to make it disappear. Obviously, this would also mark the end of profit, but the money earned by funeral merchants would not be tolerated if they did not meet a profound need. The wake, increasingly avoided in industrial Europe, persists in the United States: it exists as "viewing the remains," the "visitation." "They don't *view* bodies in England."[4]

The visit to the cemetery and a certain veneration in regard to the tomb also persist. That is why public opinion—and funeral directors—finds cremation distasteful, for it gets rid of the remains too quickly and too radically.

---

[4]*Ibid.*

Burials are not shameful and they are not hidden. With that very characteristic mixture of commerce and idealism, they are the object of showy
publicity, like any other consumer's item, be it soap or religion. Seen for
example in the buses of New York City in 1965 was the following ad, purchased by one of the city's leading morticians: "The dignity and integrity
of a Gawler. Funeral costs no more. . . . Easy access, private parking for
over 100 cars." Such publicity would be unthinkable in Europe, first of all
because it would repel the customer rather than attract him.

Thus we must admit that a traditional resistance has kept alive certain
rituals of death which had been abandoned or are being abandoned in
industrialized Europe, especially among the middle classes.

Nevertheless, though these rituals have been continued, they have also
been transformed. The American way of death is the synthesis of two tendencies: one traditional, the other euphoric.

Thus during the wakes or farewell "visitations" which have been preserved, the visitors come without shame or repugnance. This is because in
reality they are not visiting a dead person, as they traditionally have, but
an almost-living one who, thanks to embalming, is still present, as if he
were awaiting you to greet you or to take you off on a walk. The definitive
nature of the rupture has been blurred. Sadness and mourning have been
banished from this calming reunion.

Perhaps because American society has not totally accepted the interdict,
it can more easily challenge it; but this interdict is spreading in the Old
World, where the cult of the dead would seem more deeply rooted.

During the last ten years in American publications an increasing number
of sociologists and psychologists have been studying the conditions of death
in contemporary society and especially in hospitals.[5] This bibliography
makes no mention of the current conditions of funerals and mourning.
They are deemed satisfactory. On the other hand, the authors have been
struck by the manner of dying, by the inhumanity, the cruelty of solitary
death in hospitals and in a society where death has lost the prominent place
which custom had granted it over the millennia, a society where the interdiction of death paralyzes and inhibits the reactions of the medical staff
and family involved. These publications are also preoccupied with the fact
that death has become the object of a voluntary decision by the doctors

---

[5]A bibliography of 340 recent works is to be found in O. G. Brim *et al.*, *The Dying Patient*
(New York: Russell Sage Foundation, 1970). It does not include anything to do with funerals,
cemeteries, mourning, or suicide.

and the family, a decision which today is made shamefacedly, clandestinely. And this paramedical literature, for which, as far as I know, there is no equivalent in Europe, is bringing death back into the dialogue from which it had been excluded. Death is once again becoming something one can talk about. Thus the interdict is threatened, but only in the place where it was born and where it encountered limitations. Elsewhere, in the other industrialized societies, it is maintaining or extending its empire.

The Funeral Industry in Boston

Jonathan Baird
Jonathan Baird, a young writer-composer now living in California, wrote this selection in 1968 for a course on death which he took as an undergraduate student at Harvard University. One of seventeen essays published in a book entitled *Death and the College Student,* this article reveals the relationship between the funeral industry and the contemporary American approach toward death.

From *Death and the College Student* by Edwin S. Shneidman, Ed. Copyright © 1972 by Behavioral Publications, Inc., New York. Reprinted by permission.

Mr. A. E. Long of the Long Funeral Home ("Service Is a Long Word") leaned back from his desk, placed his hands together, looked briefly at the full-color 8 × 10 photograph of his wife and children and said with great sincerity, "Our function is to provide counseling to families in need at a very important time, to relieve them of the burden of worrying about the arrangements for the funeral service."

Mr. Long's grandfather founded the establishment in 1876, then more a workshop than the elaborate building that now houses "the oldest funeral home in Cambridge." Today the Long enterprise has under its roof several viewing chambers (or "slumber rooms"), casket display rooms, a basement area the secrets of which are kept from the nonprofessional, two funeral chapels, and a staff of eight including two secretaries. Mr. Long's picture gazes understandingly from a large poster ad in the Harvard Square subway station while an ad in the yellow pages sings the praises of the Home's air conditioning, pipe organ, and "reception facilities."

The growth of the funeral industry in Boston and the rest of the United States has been enormous. When the first A. E. Long founded his establishment, his functions were very limited; Jessica Mitford says in her *The American Way of Death* (1963, p. 199):

> The undertaker's job was primarily custodial. It included supplying the coffin from a catalogue or from his own establishment, arranging to bring folding chairs . . . , taking charge of the pall-bearers, supervising the removal of the coffin and loading it into the hearse, and in general doing the necessary chores until the body was finally lowered into the grave.

Services and care for the dead were done largely by the family, and funerals were simple, small, unceremonious. Cemeteries were usually churchyard ones; "floral tributes" were, if not discouraged, certainly minimal. The entire service was very personal and the importance of the body very small.

While the funeral industry has grown in pretentiousness and plasticity, the conservatism and addiction to tradition that is the soul of Boston has protected her from the disease that has spread so rapidly in the funeral trade throughout America. The virtues of colonial life traditions are here, along with the vices, and in funeral practices these virtues are clearly shown. The presence of the universities in and around Boston has also slowed down the process of "modernization" in funeral practices. Not as wound up in status symbols and less exposed to the mass media (or large amounts of money), the people related to the universities don't get sucked into the game of the "bier barons." This is not to suggest that the American Way of Death hasn't infected Boston, for it certainly has; but the funeral director has been forced to work with these traditions instead of throwing them out as he would obviously prefer to do.

In the funeral trade, a great deal of profit is made in the casket sale. The trade magazines describe scientific methods for arranging casket displays; the art of quoting prices as "$120 more" or "$60 less" rather than, say $727 has been finely developed. Descriptions of caskets border on the ridiculous, such as the one Jessica Mitford (p. 57), notes of the "Valley Forge" model: ". . . designed to reflect the rugged, strong, soldierlike qualities associated with historic Valley Forge . . . symbolizes the solid, dependable, courageous American ideals so bravely tested at Valley Forge. . . ." Inside the casket are such innovations as the "Beautyrama Adjustable Soft-Foam Bed" and the "600 Aqua Supreme Cheney velvet, magnificently quilted and shirred." The wholesale cost of these caskets is a small fraction of the selling price, and nowhere can the key aspects of the funeral trade be seen clearer than in the fantastically equipped casket. I should add that Mr. Chester H. Eastman of Eastman Funeral Service Inc., when asked about caskets, emphatically affirmed that simple wood caskets were also used.

As one moves outside Boston, one can see what the trade will do if given some rope. As near as Arlington, funeral practices become more extravagant, and in places like Wellesley and Milton the colonial spirit is obscenely burlesqued in Georgian buildings with columns and architraves. The suburbs are clearly the lucrative market in the Boston area, and all the aspects of the modern American funeral industry are present.

The largest Boston House, J. S. Waterman & Sons, handles all religions and ethnic groups. But many establishments deal with particular groups: A. E. Long & Son is the largest Protestant house in Cambridge; Daniel O'Brien, which has the highest trade volume in Cambridge, takes mostly Catholics; Levine Chapels is the most popular Jewish undertaker, followed by Benjamin Solomon; Berlund in Arlington takes on the Swedish residents; and so on. Houses stress their age, an aspect that appeals to tradition-conscious Bostonians. A. E. Long can remember no new mortuary since he has taken over. He cites the enormous capital needed to start a business—over $200,000 with no guarantee of immediate return. People come to a house because friends or relatives were handled there, and a new enterprise can't hope to attract many customers for a very long time. If someone wishes to go into business, he generally buys an existing home and retains the name for at least five years. The houses that don't change hands this way (a majority) are like inheritances: they remain in the family.

The nature of the funeral transaction is partly responsible for the expansion of the death industry. The person who is arranging for a burial generally is perturbed, and many emotions run through his, or more usually her, mind. Guilt may sometimes be present—guilt in the form of the question "Could I have done something?" guilt perhaps at being alive while another is dead. Whether motivated by guilt or simply by an honest desire to show one's love for someone who has died the result is a determination to give the deceased the best funeral possible. This plays right into the funeral director's hands, since the trade is always prepared to offer some new "extra" to further show love for the dead; thus, the familiar refrain of every funeral director, "We're only giving the public what it wants." Mr.

Long reiterated this refrain several times with a touch of weary annoyance at a "frequent misconception." In such a situation the suggestion of a person obviously experienced in "how these things are done" has enormous weight. The director with a practiced sincerity guides the family through a casket display room which shows only the most expensive models. If urged, he will move to a less expensive showroom, all the while reminding his client of the importance of showing his or her devotion. The family has had little contact with funeral arrangements, with the pros and cons of embalming, burial versus cremation, viewing the body, etc. With the aid of a little bit of twisted logic many of the mortician's arguments are compelling. Added to this are the frequent concern for "keeping up with the Joneses" and the desire to obtain a funeral that is "worthy of a person's station in life."

People who have been badly burned by the funeral trade don't want to dwell on their experience. They say that it won't happen to them again and often consider criticism of the funeral to be disrespectful to their dead relative.

All these elements serve to drive up the scale and cost of a funeral. When Jessica Mitford wrote *The American Way of Death* in 1963, the price of a funeral for an average adult was $1,405. There has been little change, although the person who is positive about what he wants and is not about to get carried away can generally now get away with about $300 for the whole thing—less than in the early 1960s. Boston is below the national average, although how much none of the directors will say. No one will give any figures on his trade volume or on the average cost of each transaction, but those asked agreed that, on the average, it costs less to die in this city.

In America especially, we relegate the idea of death to the back of our minds; our society is concerned with youth and life, an attitude that manifests itself in many ways that need not be treated here. But the effect of this attitude is that we sweep the thought of death under the carpet, repressing all its aspects to the point of making it taboo. When I mentioned my interviewing activities to several friends, they winced and said, "I don't want to talk about it . . ." Thus, many people simply don't take a good look at the abuses of the funeral industry. Disposal of the dead for most people is such an unpleasant task that the sooner it is over with, the better. People who have been badly burned by the funeral trade don't want to dwell on their experience. They say that it won't happen to them again and often consider criticism of the funeral to be disrespectful to their dead relative.

As always when a subject is taboo, several myths pop up that no one will force himself to think about long enough to explode. Many of these myths concern embalming. Directors used to claim that modern embalming techniques prevented decomposition; that the dead person would eternally remain as his survivors last saw him. A slogan of the industry was "everlasting security for your Loved One." In the late forties, the case of August Chelini v. Silvio Nieri, a funeral director, in a California court completely exploded this myth. Chelini was one of the few people who wanted all the services of the American funeral for his dead mother, especially the "everlasting security." He was happily obliged by Nieri, who assured him that embalming and a sealed metal casket would provide this. Chelini, after the funeral, began to suspect that the crypt his mother lay in might be invaded by the great amount of insects he saw at the cemetery. After a year or so, the 57-year old mechanic and garage owner became so concerned that he had his mother disinterred, only to find, as the doctor said to him, that "this is a hell of a mess and a hell of a poor job of embalming in my opinion." Chelini then sued for $50,000. In the resulting trial it was learned that the practice of embalming can in no way slow down decomposition of a body, and the metal "seal-type" casket only hastens the natural process of decay. Chelini was awarded $10,900, while the funeral trade squirmed uncomfortably. Embalming is also cited as a public health service, especially in the case of communicable diseases. Jessica Mitford did some extensive research on this subject and found no evidence outside the funeral trade to support this contention.

Both Mr. Long and Mr. Eastman contend that viewing the body in a "slumber room" or open casket is effective grief therapy. In Evelyn Waugh's satiric novel *The Loved One* (1950), a "mortuary hostess" gives Dennis Barlow the rationale for this practice (pp. 50–51):

The leave-taking is a very, very great source of consolation. Often the Waiting Ones [survivors] last saw their Loved Ones on a bed of pain surrounded by all the gruesome concomitants of the sick room or the hospital. Here they see them as they knew them in buoyant life, transfigured with peace and happiness. At the funeral they have time only for a last look as they file past. Here in the Slumber Room they can stand as long as they like, photographing a last beautiful memory on the mind.

To create this "Beautiful Memory Picture" (the trade's term) an enormous amount of energy is expended. The recreation of a corpse is looked on by most in the trade as an art form in itself. Waugh describes such an artist inspired by the cosmetician he is preparing his subject for (p. 99):

> And behold, where before had been a grim line of endurance, there was now a smile! It was masterly. It needed no other touch. Mr. Joyboy stood back from his work, removed his gloves and said: "For Miss Thanatogenos."

Despite the trade's justification for viewing the body as a form of grief therapy, one finds evidence supporting it to be highly elusive. My own reaction to the painted restoration of my grandmother was that I thought it obscene, and this sentiment is mirrored by all I have spoken to. Jessica Mitford obtained similar reactions and, despite impressive research, found no psychiatric opinion that viewing the corpse contributed in any way to "grief therapy." The North American continent is apparently the only place in the world where such a practice is tolerated. The attitude of the foreigner to the idea is expressed beautifully in a letter to Mitford from an English friend (p. 76):

> It shook me rigid to get there and find the casket open and poor old Oscar lying there in his brown tweed suit, wearing a suntan makeup and just the wrong shade of lipstick. If I had not been extremely fond of the old boy, I have a horrible feeling I might have giggled. Then and there I decided that I could never face another American funeral—even dead.

If heaven exists somewhere, many Boston residents think it may be somewhere in the Mt. Auburn St. Cemetery. Lying just outside Cambridge on Rt. 2, the cemetery, while not the largest in Boston, is certainly the most impressive. Gentle hillsides, valleys, foliage, churches, streams, and ponds, all beautifully laid out, stretch as far as the eye can see, which is not a great distance since the terrain varies so much one gets a strange feeling of privacy being surrounded by this pastoral landscape. Paths and roads crisscross throughout with such names as "Moss Road," "Ivy Lane," and "Primrose Path." The variety of the foliage is incredible, and each carefully pruned tree is labelled with its generic name. In the spring it is especially lovely, as all colors of blossoms are evident. There are millions of flowers, some planted on gravesites, and the air is heavy with their scent. Monuments are tastefully arranged, varying in scale from simple slabs to a huge reproduction of the sphinx. Many of the monuments have very early dates on them; there is an obviously new marker with the date 1640 on it, showing that many people redesign the gravesites of their ancestors. Epitaphs range from the simple noting of last names to such dripping sentimentalities as "We shall meet in heaven to part no more." Some grave lots say "Father-Mother" and list the first names of their children who died later and were laid under smaller stones next to their parents. Others read "Husband-Wife." Family plots have an address written on the stairs, but all the gravesites have numbers such as "2245 Oak Lane." The office building is in red brick, early English Gothic, perhaps copied from the palace at Hampton Court outside London. The huge gates which mark the entrance display the message, "Then shall the dust return to the earth as it was, and the spirit shall return to God who gave it." The place is simply incredible and no one who spends any time in Cambridge should miss it.

Out on the West Coast and in many other areas, the super-cemetery has emerged, the leading one being Forest Lawn in Los Angeles, the model for Evelyn Waugh's "Whispering Glades." All that is at Mt. Auburn is there tenfold, plus many other features such as decorative statuary, several "romantic" spots for the enormous number of people who visit even with no relative buried there, and an entire mortuary establishment, making it a "one stop" enterprise, a supermarket for the dead. In Boston, difficulties in obtaining large amounts of land as well as local tradition have held back similar projects. There are smaller burial grounds here, and the cemeteries have not become quite as plastic. There are even a few simple areas remaining in Boston, but this is a vision that is fast becoming obsolete.

Cemetery land is tax-free, an old tradition in this country formulated in several Supreme Court decisions. At first glance, the business appears to be nonprofit, and its income is tax-free. But the operation is hardly nonprofit since the promoters, sometimes a land-holding company, work out an arrangement whereby the cemetery will get only, say, 50 percent of the income, while the promoters get the other half. The cemetery is still nonprofit, but the men behind it are raking in awesome amounts (also tax-free). Investment in cemeteries is much more profitable than in regular land because it can be intricately subdivided, and charges can be levied for main-

tenance as well as monuments. Across the street from the cemetery office
is a concern that makes gravestones. One doesn't go in and ask outright if
the same people are running both cemetery and monument business (the
company names are different), but it might not be an unreasonable surmise
that the two lead back to the same promoters.

As cemeteries become crowded, a new invention has broken the space
barrier: the community mausoleum. Piling crypts on top of each other and
charging an average of $720 plus "maintenance costs" for each one, the
cemetery promoters have hit on a most lucrative idea, with unlimited opportunities. The "tenement mausoleums" haven't really caught on in Boston,
however, despite their staggering expansion throughout the rest of the
country.

A recent phenomenon in the funeral industry is "pre-need" buying.
Before, the gravesite negotiation was carried on through the funeral director,
who was not about to urge spending great amounts of money on a gravesite
since it might result in less "investment" in his own services. So the cemeteries created a way to get around the director: "pre-need" door-to-door
selling. This has enabled the cemeteries to obtain the capital to build before
anyone is actually buried; the operation is thus self-financing.

The salesman, who is called a "memorial counselor," uses inflation as his
first sales argument. His second is that of protecting the survivor (generally
the wife) from overspending at a time of emotional strain. Customers buy
because of "the aura of genteel respectability conferred by ownership of
cemetery property" and the self-congratulatory feelings for "planning
ahead." But they ignore the publicly owned cemeteries where gravesites are
much cheaper, fail to see that the practice of "pre-need" sales has pushed
up the price of a cemetery plot, and might even prefer to be cremated.

The funeral directors then picked up the practice of pre-need sales. Mr.
Long said there was "a good deal" of pre-need buying not only for the cemeteries but for the services of his own establishment as well. "These are
mostly aging people who have lived alone for some time," he elaborated.
Neither he nor Mr. Eastman volunteered percentages. The latter expressed
his pleasure with the idea and felt that the industry was offering security
and assurance of "adequate care" to those who bought. More elaborate
justifications are noted by Evelyn Waugh, who has the "mortuary hostess"
speak of bringing the fear of death into the open and removing such anxiety
by preparing now. Her spiel involves a strange interweaving of the fear of
dying and the fear of creating economic burdens at death, spiced with general truisms, "scientific data," and quotes from *Hamlet.*

Faced with the growth of the "American way of death," many people are forming "memorial societies." The purpose of these is stated in the pamphlet "Memorial Associations; What They Are—How They Are Organized," put out by the Cooperative League of the U.S.A. (Nora, 1962):

> Memorial Associations and their members seek modesty, simplicity, and dignity in the funeral arrangements over which they have control. This concern for the spiritual over material values has revealed that a "decent burial" or other arrangement need not be elaborate.

A trade magazine, the *National Funeral Service Journal,* as quoted by Jessica Mitford, said (p. 267): "The movement appeals most strongly to the visionary, ivory tower eggheads of the academic fraternity"—a description that fits Boston and Cambridge in particular quite nicely. The societies are especially popular in Boston. The largest is the Memorial Society of Massachusetts at 874 Beacon St., but there are others in the surrounding communities. The members contribute moderate amounts of money and work through a funeral director who agrees to handle all the society's business. Finding such a director is difficult but not impossible; the extra business, even at lower prices, is enormously appealing to a house that is not at the top of the trade. The Long Home is not one of these. Mr. Long shook his head, wearily perplexed, "I don't know . . . they accept all this money, and I don't know what they do with it. They could get the same service here for the same price." When asked if he did any of their work, he replied, "There's no sense in going along with them—no, we don't cooperate."

The funeral trade has been exposed to a great deal of criticism in the last decade and has grown more and more sensitive. All the Boston houses contacted greeted the request for an interview with suspicion; only two accepted it, and with reluctance. The remaining three didn't openly refuse interviews but rather said their business volume was unmanageable that day and to try again tomorrow. This went on for four days at O'Brien's near Central Square, where a Miss Hanlon, who apparently runs that branch, talked briefly over the phone about the poor publicity and lack of chance to respond. Despite frequent assurances that the research was being conducted with an open mind and that this would be the best way for the trade to defend itself, she would not even grant a ten-minute interview. The other houses were not as frank, but equally adept at putting off the request, Waterman's for three days and Levine for two.

Funeral industry trade magazines are most difficult to get hold of. They are found in no library in the Boston area. I asked Mr. Long for one or two, and he sent me to Miss Hanlon at O'Brien's. She told me that Mr. Long had them too, but wouldn't give them up, and she wouldn't either. She compared my request to "going into a chemical factory and asking to see the formulas," and said I would learn nothing more than technical data such as information about new embalming fluids. Even though it was pointed out that her analogy was hardly applicable, she remained obdurate and wouldn't surrender the journals.

The industry has reacted viciously to criticism from more widely read discussions than this one. Two well-known ones were Bill Davidson's "The High Cost of Dying" in *Collier's* in 1951 and Roul Tunley's "Can You Afford to Die?" published in *The Saturday Evening Post* in 1961. The trade was shaken, and its press responded with charges of atheism and communist sympathies. The second article was particularly resented, for it offered concrete suggestions for remedy: the memorial societies previously mentioned. The most famous investigation has, of course, been Jessica Mitford's *The American Way of Death.* Years after the book appeared, the directors are still shaking. A. E. Long, when asked about the book, quickly became upset: "Money . . . that's all she was out for. If people want to pay good money for a thing like that . . . carry it around with them . . . I don't care." He warmed up and became really talkative for the first time in forty-five minutes. "Admittedly there are a few bad establishments—there are in any profession. There are corrupt lawyers . . . you know a few corrupt lawyers, don't you?" I replied I imagined there were, quite embarrassed at being the cause of this outburst. He continued, "Sure there are, but compared to the huge number of good establishments, the corrupt ones are an infinitesimal amount."

REFERENCES

Mitford, Jessica. *The American Way of Death.* New York: Simon and Schuster, 1963.

Nora, Fred. *Memorial Associations.* New York: Cooperative League of the U.S.A., 1962.

Waugh, Evelyn. *The Loved One.* Boston: Little, Brown and Company, 1950.

Combat Death

Joel Baruch

Joel Baruch, a Vietnam War veteran, was a student at the University of California at Los Angeles when he wrote this selection for a course on death. This essay, which first appeared in *Death and the College Student,* describes death in war as seen in the mind of a naive recruit and as felt in the guts of a disillusioned infantryman.

From *Death and the College Student* by Edwin S. Shneidman, Ed. Copyright © 1972 by Behavioral Publications, Inc., New York. Reprinted by permission.

War is not only the professional soldier's occupation; its prevalence over the earth since the start of recorded time is a warm blessing to him. He does not quake at the hint of violent death; indeed, he welcomes and pursues it. He prefers a glorious battlefield death to the ignominy of natural death, for to him death without honor is the ultimate disgrace. Without war, he is like an itinerant beggar suffering from undernourishment. War, and the death and destruction left in its wake, gives him sustenance. No, more; it gives him the drug he craves for he is an addict.

I know this man well, I lived with him for two years—from the dismal training camps in the United States to the desolate tropical forests of South Vietnam. And ever since I made his acquaintance, I still awake suddenly during the night, sweating profusely, haunted by the memory of what I saw and, worse yet, what I did.

Stone dead, he was. Eyes wide open, staring at nothing. A thin veneer of blood curling at the corner of his lips. Two gaping holes in his chest. Right leg half gone. My first combat fatality. A lifeless body where only moments before a heart beat its customary seventy pumps in one orbit of the minute hand. It is one thing to hear about death; to watch it happen is quite another. I went over to the nearest tree and vomited my guts out.

Combat training had never prepared me for anything like this. The death of an enemy was mentioned in aloof terms as if the enemies were stuntmen on a movie set who would get up and walk away after the take. Your own death was never dwelled upon; the training period was set in a world of illusions in which American soldiers seemed invulnerable to combat death.

Because the possibility of my own extinction was so far removed from the illusory world of the training camp, I frequently fantasized myself in heroic combat roles. Careless of personal safety, I would assault an enemy machine-gun bunker and obliterate it with hand grenades, spitting away the grenade pins I had torn out with my teeth a la John Wayne. The next sequence was invariably an awards ceremony where I would receive a high commendation for gallantry in action—never of course, posthumously, since I always came through unscathed.

Fortunately, these ludicrous daydreams came to a halt when I learned of my destination. Our platoon sergeant gathered us together during a bivouac exercise and stated in his tired, fatherly manner, "Men! So you will have no doubts, let it be known that you are all going to Vietnam following completion of this training course. Some of you, maybe many of you, will not be coming back. But remember! I'd rather die in combat than on the highways. Dying for your country is the only way to go."

I was becoming impervious to the death of my fellow soldiers, and, in addition, I was negating the possibility of my own possible demise.

I felt a peculiar shudder—half thrill and half fright. The epitome of my fantasies was before me in the person of this sergeant, and for the very first time I realized that I could die from charging a machine gun. At the same time a more pervasive fear, that of eradicating another human being, occurred to me. What gave me the right to judge whether or not my enemy should die? To this day, I thank that sergeant for contributing to my maturation.

Changes in personality and mood are rooted in the special climate of the combat zone. These mutations evolve in such a wily fashion that the person who undergoes them is not aware of the alterations himself. Usually, a spectacular event triggers recognition of this attitudinal mutation. That is precisely what happened to me when I saw my second combat fatality.

Our infantry company was on a routine search-and-destroy mission when the staccato burst of a sniper's grease gun found its mark. Moments before I hit the ground, a trooper not more than five meters away fell over backwards as if he had been struck in the face by a professional boxer. I glanced over to see if I would help him. I couldn't. His brains were splattered everywhere; a large chunk had landed on the arm of my fatigue shirt. Later, after helping the medics wrap his body and load it into the plastic-canvas bag, I settled beneath a tree to meditate on my strange reaction.

"God, it was only a short time ago that I viewed my first dead body, and the scene had made me retch uncontrollably. Now, I've seen another human being die, and although I'm certainly distressed and moved, it simply doesn't affect me in the same way. His death brings feelings of sorrow, but that sense of misery and depression is absent. Why should I be so callous?

"That was close! So close that I could hear the unmistakable twang of the bullets followed by the dull, empty thud that accompanies a direct hit. It could have been me just as easily. But why wasn't it? Perhaps I am luckier than most. I don't really think it can happen to me. When I finally die, I will be eighty years old, lying in bed with a heroin syringe protruding from my veins."

These recapitulations of my perceptions of death—death of others and death of self—announced a mutation in my personality: I was becoming impervious to the death of my fellow soldiers, and, in addition, I was negating the possibility of my own possible demise.

General Patton once said something to the effect that "no one ever won a war by dying for his country; he makes the other bastard die for his." This statement presupposes that life is an extremely valuable commodity in a combat zone, that Pyrrhic victories are undesirable. It now seems to me, however, as it did during my combat venture, that the American military command do not share this view. We were treated as if we were inanimate objects, as fuel for the war machine, as cannon fodder. Whenever a member of the American general staff was interviewed as to his principal anxiety about the contingencies of war, he would more often than not, state the tremendous cost in human lives. Some military supervisors probably believe this. Yet I am skeptical about high-ranking officers who are promoted so they can perform the unenviable task of sending men to their death and who, all of a sudden, expound negative feelings toward the very act they are trained and promoted for. I once eavesdropped on a conversation between a major and a lieutenant colonel: "I hope the war doesn't end before I have another chance to earn a higher rank," one said to the other.

Promotions through the military chain of command come much more slowly in peace time. Thus, the career officer who ambitiously pursues his profession needs combat action in order to ascend quickly in the military hierarchy. War is an opportunity for him, and he cannot, by necessity, be overly concerned with the expenditure of human lives.

Irreverence for human life, by both those in command and those in the ranks, is profoundly exemplified by countless stories and articles on military combat. As an adolescent, I had learned to accept cruel behavior on the part of foreign enemies or, thanks to the television westerns, the atrocities of warring Indians. But the "good guys" would never scalp and rape Indian squaws or drive wooden splinters under the thumbnails of their prisoners of war. For they were the heroes, and they wore the "white hats" of purity and goodness. Having been quite naive and therefore a likely target for nationalistic propaganda, I genuinely believed that tortures were exclusively a part of enemy "techniques"—whoever the enemy or "bad guys" might be.

On the day of my rude awakening, our weapons platoon was checking that the hamlet of Cu Chi was not a hideout for Viet Cong recruits. As we approached the outskirts of the village, we took cover and observed only the humdrum activity of the farmers in the surrounding rice paddies. No weapon bearers were detected, so we warily moved into the hamlet. The village chieftain greeted us amicably; he could speak English sufficiently well to be understood and, without the aid of an interpreter, our platoon leader asked him where the "Cong" were. The chieftain denied any association with the enemy. The sergeant greeted this inappropriate response by grabbing the chieftain and slapping him repeatedly back and forth across the face. Then he demanded to interrogate any two men that the chieftain could find at work in the fields. The terrified village head did as ordered and returned with two young boys—no more than fifteen or sixteen years old. Using the old man as an interpreter, the sergeant interrogated the boys: "Are you V.C.?" "Where's your next ambush?" "What are you 'gooks' doing in this area?"

It was quite apparent that the two "suspects" were either tongue-tied out of pure fear or did not savvy what was happening. They couldn't answer, and the sergeant leveled his M-16 rifle at their stomachs. As their eyes widened, the burst of gunfire almost tore them in half. The sergeant, quite unperturbed, took his machete and in two clean motions chopped off their heads. Then, in monster-movie fashion, he picked up the two heads still dripping with blood, one in each hand, and set them atop the hamlet's wooden picket fence; he lit two cigarettes and placed them in their mouths. As the villagers gazed incredulously at the scene, the sergeant warned the chieftain that if his village consorted with the Viet Cong, more incidents like this would occur: "I'll chop everybody's head off!" We left with the chieftain nodding furiously.

ʃʃ

> *A substantial proportion of American war deaths and incapacitating injuries are external to combat. . . .*

ʃʃ

On another occasion, I witnessed the gross differences in the burial of Viet Cong "killed-in-actions" and American dead. When an unusually large number of the enemy were slain in a military operation, a huge trench was dug, and the Viet Cong corpses were carelessly tossed into the ditch. It was reminiscent of a photograph I had seen taken in a German concentration camp showing layers of decaying human bodies being cast into a gigantic crater. If some of the gung-ho "rednecks" in the outfit were assigned to burial detail, they would often make a game of it by desecrating the bodies of the enemy. The American soldier who could invent the most imaginative and outrageous desecration would receive the "ears of his choice." In order to win this sought-after prize, contestants would perform such obscene acts as placing their penis into the open mouth of a corpse or, for variety's sake, insert it into the dead man's anus. As a total antithesis, the "burial" of American dead is a somber affair. (It is not a genuine burial, but a facsimile. The dead soldier, or the parts of his body that can be located, are swathed in a bag that is then sent stateside for appropriate burial.) American flags are cloaked around the body as if to reassure the grief-stricken survivors that the deceased was the epitome of manhood because he died defending freedom and democracy. Instead of a desecration contest, a tranquil and dignified atmosphere surrounds the ceremonious duty of "burying" American troops.

Noninitiates in combat might question, as I once would have, the authenticity of massacre reports involving "civilized" American soldiers. It is common knowledge that Americans are incessantly conditioned to believe that snuffing out the life of another human being for any reason other than self-defense is both legally and morally repugnant. It is erroneous to assume, however, that Americans are incapable of violating their putative ethics. Almost every American has heard about the 1968 My Lai massacre. The resultant murder trials of First Lieutenant William Calley and Captain Ernest Medina certainly served to publicize the atrocities committed at My Lai. Disappointingly, these trials failed to focus public attention on what should have been the primary issue: war can change ordinary human beings into ghouls.

For the most part, Americans are wholly ignorant about many nuances pertaining to the Vietnam War. Their support or displeasure for American involvement directly parallels the weekly casualty statistics in their local newspapers. A high figure elicits cries of indignation, and a lower figure evokes either support or apathy. If they were only aware of the duplicity involved in the compilation of those statistics, then, perhaps, American participation in Vietnam would have taken a different course.

In the first place, a substantial proportion of American war deaths and incapacitating injuries are external to combat. Many soldiers do not die as a result of shrapnel wounds from booby traps or land mines. Nor do a large number of soldiers that "make" the weekly casualty lists die from injuries incurred in direct confrontation with the enemy. For example, rather a sizeable proportion of the American deaths in a combat zone are attributable to their own recklessness. I witnessed instances of such noncombat fatalities during my Vietnam experience. One of these, in particular, stands out as particularly grotesque.

On a humid afternoon, two men in my company were playing "catch" with a live hand grenade. As they foolishly hurled the grenade back and forth, the pin somehow came loose thus activating it. From a distance, I heard the tremendous cacophony of explosions. I dropped the sandbag I was filling and rushed to the scene. A quick glance was sufficient to reconstruct what had happened.

One of the two men was an M-79 grenadier. He had been playing catch while wearing two pouches full of ammunition for his weapon. Unaware that the pin had fallen out, he caught the grenade just as it detonated. The blast set off a chain reaction—his M-79 ammo exploded, which, in turn, triggered the volatile Claymore mines protecting the perimeter of the base camp. The cylindrical steel pellets of these lethal weapons peppered a group of soldiers laying columns of barbed wire. A subsequent body count turned up the incredible figure of fifteen dead and thirty-two injured.

Undoubtedly, the survivors of the dead received an official telegram from the federal government stating that their relative "died from injuries inflicted in combat," a lie which perhaps soothed the survivors and certainly saved military face.

Acts of heroism—real heroism, not the heroism of my fantasies—are not without substantiation in any combat encounter. They do occur, though perhaps not as frequently as the paperback war novel would lead one to believe. During my tour of duty in the tropical jungles of Southeast Asia, I observed a few illustrations of outright heroism and many demonstrations of disconcerting cowardice. Moreover, I experienced both situations myself, and from those encounters I received an invaluable lesson both in human foibles and in human dignity. If some of my internal experiences can be generalized to other soldiers trapped in similar situations (and I think they can be), then I believe I have learned something important about men in combat: most are possessed by an overpowering desire for survival and, at the same time, a humane reluctance to kill the enemy. Of course there were dissenters; a substantial minority of them—the rabble-rousers, the hatemongers, those professional soldiers who actually like to kill—actively relished the idea of staking their lives against those of the enemy in a contest to the death. I know this much: they were a different breed of animal.

The Nuclear Age

Robert Jay Lifton and Eric Olson

Robert Jay Lifton is Professor of Psychiatry at Yale University
and is perhaps most widely known for his book *Death in
Life: Survivors of Hiroshima,* which won a National Book
Award in 1969. This selection, taken from his more recent
work *Living and Dying* (written with Eric Olson), discusses
the effects of the Hiroshima explosion not only on those
who survived that blast and experienced what the authors
call "psychic numbing," but on the rest of humanity as well.

*The 17th century was the century of mathematics, the
18th that of the physical sciences, and the 19th that of
biology. Our 20th century is the century of fear.*

> —Albert Camus, from
> *Neither Victims Nor Executioners*

The sun can't hold a candle to it.

Now we're all sons of bitches.

> —Two reactions of nuclear
> scientists to the first atomic bomb test

Early in the morning of August 6, 1945, the United
States dropped on the Japanese city of Hiroshima the first atomic bomb
ever used on a human population. The destruction and chaos wrought by
that bomb were so immense that it has never been possible to make a precise count of the number of people killed. Most estimates are in the range
of 100,000 to 200,000 people. Even for the hundreds of thousands who
experienced the bombing but remained alive, the vision and taint of nuclear
holocaust left lifelong scars.

The bomb was unexpected; it came as people went about their morning chores of making and eating breakfast and preparing to go to work. Suddenly a blinding flash cut across the sky. There were a few seconds of dead silence and then a huge explosion. Enormous clouds formed and then rose upward in a gigantic dark column. The clouds leveled off and the whole formation resembled an enormous black mushroom.

Those who have seen atomic explosions speak of their awesome and frightening beauty. On that Japanese summer morning, the beauty was immediately eclipsed by the experience of an overwhelming encounter with death. Normal existence had suddenly been massively invaded by an eerie and unknown force. An area of total destruction was created extending for two miles in all directions, and 60,000 buildings within the city limits were demolished.

The reaction of the survivors was at first a sense of being totally immersed by death. Houses and buildings leveled, the sight of dead bodies, the cries and moans of the severely injured, and the smell of burning flesh all combined to leave a permanent death imprint of staggering power.

Among the survivors there quickly developed a profound kind of guilt. This guilt was related both to having remained alive while others (including loved ones and neighbors) died, and to the inability to offer help to those who needed it. All of this became focused in a question that remained at the center of a lifelong struggle for the survivors: "Why did I remain alive when he, she, they died?" And this question itself sometimes became transformed into the haunting suspicion that one's own life had been purchased at the cost of the others who died: "Some had to die; because they died I could live." This suspicion led to a feeling among survivors that they did not deserve to be alive and that one could justly remain alive only by coming in some way to resemble the dead.

The Japanese survivors became psychologically numb, their sensitivities blunted by guilt and by an inability to resume meaningful activity amid the chaos. The boundary separating life from death no longer seemed distinct. By becoming numb, the survivors blocked their awareness of the pain and suffering and effected a kind of compromise between life and death.

The survivors' lives were made even more difficult by a susceptibility to various forms of disease and weakness to which their exposure to atomic radiation made them vulnerable. Many of those exposed have had to struggle to live with maimed bodies; all have had to live with the incredible end-of-the-world image of nuclear holocaust.

For us, now, the image of Hiroshima symbolizes the possibility that what has happened once can happen again. By today's standards, that first atomic bomb was a very small one. The difficulty of imagining the human suffering that followed in the wake of its use is multiplied many times over in trying to contemplate what a world war with atomic weapons would be like now.

The atomic bomb was the product of an extraordinary research program carried out during World War II. In the beginning there had been little confidence that an atomic bomb could actually be made. But the suspicion that German scientists were attempting to put such a weapon into the hands of Hitler led the United States to undertake an all-out effort.

In 1939, a letter to President Roosevelt was drafted by Albert Einstein encouraging full support for a scientific program that would lead to the development of the atomic bomb. Research installations were established at a number of places throughout the country, and work went ahead with unprecedented commitment. By July, 1945, the first atomic bomb was ready for testing in the New Mexico desert. So intense was the effort to create the bomb and so anxious were the scientists about whether it would work that few physicists at Los Alamos were inclined to raise moral questions about the weapon they made.

The bomb worked. Suddenly, it became possible for one plane to deliver a single bomb, the explosive power of which previously would have required two thousand bombs. All who watched were awestruck by what they saw; the experience had a religious quality. Men had released through the bomb a source of power literally beyond imagining. It seemed that the use of this powerful device could bring the war to a rapid conclusion and could in peacetime yield untold energy, and would thus transform the nature of both war and peace.

All these things were possible. But what was immediate and overwhelming was the sheer majesty and power of the bomb itself. Robert Oppenheimer, director of the research project that produced the bomb, later remembered his thoughts at the time of the explosion:

> At that moment . . . there flashed into my mind a passage from the Bhagavad-Gita, the sacred book of the Hindus: "I am become Death, the Shatterer of Worlds!"

Another observer at the time used such phrases as "mighty thunder" and "great silence" to describe his response, and went on to speak in clearly religious language:

On that moment hung eternity. Time stood still. Space contracted to a pinpoint. It was as though the earth had opened and the skies had split. One felt as though he had been privileged to witness the Birth of the World.

Others had more cynical responses: "Now we're all sons of bitches," and, more simply, "What a thing we've made." Still others spoke of "the dreadful," "the terrible," "the dire," and "the awful."

ƒƒƒ

Nuclearism is a peculiar, twentieth-century disease of power.

ƒƒƒ

"This is the greatest thing in history!" was President Truman's response upon hearing of the bomb's successful use in Hiroshima, which seemed to portend a rapid end to the war. And a newspaper report at the time described the force as "weird, incredible, and somehow disturbing."

If we understand the experience of religious conversion as involving a changed image of the cosmos and man's place within it, then certainly the responses of those early witnesses to atomic power would qualify as religious. There was a sense of a "new beginning," of making contact with the infinite and the feeling that life would never be the same again. The bomb took on qualities of a deity, a god whose strange and superhuman power would change the course of human history.

After it became clear that this atomic god was real, the scientists who had unleashed it began to diverge in their responses to the new power. As in any situation, most went on with their professional "business as usual." Some assumed a sense of mission in committing themselves to controlling the use of this threatening force. Others identified themselves with the force, became converts to the religion of nuclearism, and dedicated themselves to propagating the new faith.

Nuclearism is a peculiar, twentieth-century disease of power. We would do well to specify it, trace its roots, and see its connection with other forms of religious and immortalizing expression. Nuclearism is a form of totalism. It yields a grandiose vision of man's power at a historical time when man's precarious sense of his own immortality makes him particularly vulnerable to such aberrations.

Man has always attached deep emotion to his tools. As extensions of his own body and capacities, they have provided him with an image of himself. The centrality of technology to twentieth-century culture has increased this tendency to define life in terms of the tools and techniques that have so deeply transformed the world. In this sense, nuclearism is a manifestation of two underlying contemporary inclinations: to deify tools, and to seize whatever symbols are available in the desperate search for a sense of significance.

The career and personal struggles of Robert Oppenheimer reveal the tensions that have existed in relation to nuclear weapons. Oppenheimer directed the vast and complex research effort at Los Alamos. He and those with whom he worked were convinced that if the bomb could be developed quickly, its availability would hasten the end of the war and could even rid the world of war permanently. Certain nuclear scientists in Chicago who had completed their contribution to the bomb research project tried to raise moral questions about the bomb's use. Oppenheimer, however, remained committed and resisted such reflection. He did not agree that the bomb should merely be "demonstrated" to frighten the enemy into submission rather than be actually used on a human population.

It was not until 1949, when the vastly more powerful hydrogen bomb was nearly completed, that Oppenheimer began to reexamine his convictions. He continued to work on weapons research, and even came to favor the development of small "tactical" hydrogen bombs. But he became concerned that the idea of a "super" H-bomb seemed "to have caught the imagination, both of the Congressional and military people, as the answer to the problem posed by the Russians' advance." With his characteristic brilliance, Oppenheimer then began to expose the dangers involved in letting the bomb dominate all thinking on international relations.

Oppenheimer had been a national hero during and just after the war, when he was widely credited with the success of the atomic bomb research project. But when he began to raise questions about nuclearism and underwent what we might call "nuclear backsliding," he was forced to submit to extreme public humiliation in the form of a long government investigation of his "Americanism" and was eventually denied a security clearance. His earlier strong advocacy of the bomb and his national standing made his subsequent doubts all the more dangerous to those who remained proponents of nuclearism.

Edward Teller, another physicist important in early bomb research who later became known as "the father of the hydrogen bomb," is representative of the opposite sequence. In 1945, Teller opposed the use of the atomic bomb without warning. After the war, he vehemently objected to the moral reservations expressed by other scientists toward the idea of making nuclear weapons. Teller advocated maintaining an "adventurous spirit" in fully exploring the possibilities of atomic weapons—which now meant "his" H-bomb—and he believed that "we would be unfaithful to the tradition of Western civilization if we shied away from exploring what man can accomplish." This combination of ethical blindness and extreme technicism, not just in Teller but in many others as well, inspired the subtitle of the film *Dr. Strangelove, or How I Stopped Worrying and Learned to Love the Bomb*.

No one could argue that the power of the atomic bomb is not impressive, or that it does not readily engender a sense of awe both for nature's power and man's capacity for technological mastery. But the danger of the nuclearist position is that the bomb's power and its limitations are never clearly examined. The terms that were used by the scientists in referring to the bomb—terms such as "the gadget," "the thing," "the device," or simply "It"—served to blunt a continuing awareness of the bomb's deadly purpose. The bomb became enmeshed in utopian hopes for total salvation that seemed otherwise unattainable. Man's own place in the scheme of things was devalued and made subordinate to the demands of the weapon.

The early discussion of bomb shelters and diplomacy in the postwar period are examples of the perversions of logic to which the bomb led. It became clear that the United States could not fully defend itself from nuclear attack in case of another major war. An anxious debate ensued in which the chief issue was whether there would be any survivors of a major nuclear conflagration—shelters or no shelters. Also involved was the question of whether, considering the world into which they would emerge, the survivors would envy the dead. Teller argued that there *would* be survivors and that democratic ideals would survive with them. He insisted that "realistic thinking" demanded facing up to the possible consequences of the use of atomic weapons.

Given the experience of those who actually did survive the atomic bomb in Hiroshima, the question about survivors in this debate was never properly posed. The important question is not "Would there be survivors?" or "Would the survivors envy the dead?" but rather "Would the survivors themselves feel *as if* dead?"

Nuclearist thinking pervaded the field of diplomacy. There was a feeling that "the big atomic stick" (as Edward Teller called it) could solve the political problems of the world. There is no doubt that the presence of nuclear weapons did exercise a deterrent effect in international relations immediately following World War II. But a weapon too awesome and frightening to be used could not be a permanently effective deterrent. Statesmen began to realize that an arsenal consisting only of nuclear weapons would make the punishment for international violations more destructive than the crime. As one writer put it, a policeman armed only with an atomic bomb could not even prevent a housebreaking unless he were willing to sacrifice the entire city in doing so. It is even possible that the restraint on all-out war created by nuclear weapons made smaller, more prolonged conflicts like Vietnam more likely.

Nuclearism involves a failure of the imagination—a failure to conceive in human terms the meaning of the weapons—and the embrace as a means of man's salvation of that which most threatens it. Nuclearism provides an apocalyptic alternative to the already impaired modes of symbolic immortality while itself further undermining the viability of these modes. Nuclearism propels us toward use of the weapons and, equally dangerous, undermines man's capacity to confront the problems they raise.

Each of the modes of symbolic immortality has been affected by the dislocations of the nuclear era. Even without the actual deployment of these weapons, their very existence poses a profound threat to our perceptions of living and dying. The possibility that the human species can annihilate itself with its own tools fundamentally alters the relationship of human imagination to each mode of symbolic continuity.

The biological (and biosocial) mode is perhaps most obviously affected. The assumption of "living on" in one's descendents is made precarious. The aspiration of living on in one's nation is also undermined, for no longer do national boundaries offer the protection and security they once did. National security becomes identical with international security, which is dependent upon the partial relinquishment by each nation of its own exclusive claim on the allegiance of its citizens.

Because ultimate issues of life and death have become more urgent and more problematic, the theological mode has also become problematic. A rational-scientific age had already made commitments of religious faith and the meaning of God difficult issues for many people. Theological imagery of transcending death becomes a dubious promise if the assurance of some form of earthly survival is not also given. If there are none (or few) left among the biologically living, then the image of spiritual survival loses much of its symbolic and comforting power. It is precisely these threats to the belief in salvation that may account for the burgeoning of fundamentalist groups and the insistence of these groups upon the most narrow and literal—one might say desperate—forms of Biblical faith.

In Japan after the explosion of the atomic bomb, neither Eastern nor Western religious imagery seemed capable of providing an acceptable explanation or formulation of the meaning of the disaster. The bomb experience seems to have wounded that deep layer of human confidence and trust to which religious symbolism appeals. No conventional religious expression was adequate to reestablish a sense of trust and continuity.

Partly as a response to this impasse, religious language has come to emphasize the sacred quality of man's earthly commitments and the religious importance of responsible political action. At the same time, there has been a revival of fundamentalist and occult religion—a manifestation of the increased plausibility of apocalyptic visions. Who can now say that an image of the end of the world is merely religious pipe dream meant to frighten people into submission?

Theological imagery has developed in two contrasting directions. There has been a movement toward naturalism, in which religious imagery is more humanistic and closer to observable process. But there has also been a rise of visionary and doom-prophesying religious forms, in which salvation is made conditional upon total repentance. In either case, man's new demonic technological capacity (if not demonic human psychological potential) always threatens to overwhelm and render futile the attempt to immortalize man's spiritual attainments.

Immortality through the creative mode depends upon the conviction that one's works will endure. But what lasts anymore? The existence of nuclear weapons, together with the breakdown of the many forms of collective symbolization and ritual we have discussed, raise doubts about the permanence of any contributions to human culture. The fear is that nothing will last and that, therefore, nothing matters.

This concern about the viability of particular social forms and even about historical continuity itself creates an undercurrent of anxiety and mistrust that is generally not directly felt. But this concern is expressed in the increased need of young people to have a sense of the immediate human impact of their work and has resulted in heightened interest in careers involving teaching, legal practice, social work, and medicine. With regard to scientific work, as more questions are raised about the ethics of various scientific projects, the individual scientist is less able to undertake research without consideration of the lethal or life-enhancing potentials of the new knowledge he may unearth.

These questions and threats lead to a greater reliance upon the fourth mode—that of nature—for an image of permanence. But we now know that nature is all too susceptible to both our weapons and our pollution. Joan Baez's mournful tones in the song "What Have They Done to the Rain?" and Bob Dylan's desperate anger in "A Hard Rain's A-gonna Fall" both suggest a vision, shared by all of us in some degree, of ultimate nuclear violation of our planet.

In the face of this vision, explorations of outer space take on a special symbolic urgency. In these explorations we seek to extend our natural environment almost to infinity. But it would be the most wishful kind of illusion to see in these explorations, or in speculation about life on other planets, a solution to the problems of human continuity on our own endangered planet.

The impairment of these four modes of symbolic immortality has led to a greater reliance on the mode of experiential transcendence. This mode is closely related to immediate sensation. It is therefore less vulnerable to being impoverished by misgivings about historical durability, on which the other modes are more dependent. The resort to pleasure-seeking or mystical experience is common in historically dislocated times. In our own time, we have witnessed great preoccupation with intensified forms of experience through drugs, sex, music, meditation, dance, nature, and even politics.

ↈↈ

The ultimate threat posed by nuclear weapons is not only death but meaninglessness: an unknown death by an unimaginable weapon.

ↈↈ

Beyond enabling one to live more fully in the present, the experiential mode lends itself to something more—to engaging death anxiety directly by experimenting with risk. Almost as artists become a community's conscience by exploring the extremities of the community's unfaced danger, the active pursuit of experiential transcendence plays with fears of death by inviting them, even encouraging them.

In this respect, there may be a strange parallel between nuclearism and the intense forms of experience that many people are now seeking. The most perverse response to the existence of a doomsday machine would be to love the bomb itself joyously: the nightmare of oblivion experienced as ecstasy. This is the malignant phenomenon that the film *Dr. Strangelove* carries even further and portrays in a powerfully bizarre image: a cowboy euphorically riding an atomic bomb as it soars from the plane toward glorious explosion.

Fanciful as this image appears, it has an eerie psychological plausibility. Expressed boldly, there may be a need to destroy one's world for purposes of imagined rebirth, a need which lends itself either to suicidal obliteration or to transformation and regeneration. This need takes advantage not only of every variety of individual and social aggression, but fits as well with the psychological principle of touching death, either imaginatively or literally, as a precondition of new life. Thus, nuclear weapons can achieve vivid symbolic representation in our minds precisely because of their promise of devastation.

The ultimate threat posed by nuclear weapons is not only death but meaninglessness: an unknown death by an unimaginable weapon. War with such weapons is no longer heroic; death from such weapons is without valor. Meaninglessness has become almost a stereotyped characterization of twentieth-century life, a central theme in modern art, theater, and politics. The roots of this meaninglessness are many. But crucial, we believe, is the anxiety deriving from the sense that all forms of human associations are perhaps pointless because subject to sudden irrational ends. Cultural life thus becomes still more formless. No one form, no single meaning or style appears to have any ultimate claim. The psychological implications of this formlessness are not fully clear; while there seem to be more life choices available, fewer are inwardly compelling.

Such broad historical themes as these can influence even the most fundamental of human relationships—the nurturing bond between mother and child. No mother can fully escape the general threat to the continuity and significance of life, nor the resulting death anxiety. Nor can she avoid transmitting these doubts to her offspring. Erik Erikson has emphasized the importance for the child of gaining a sense of "basic trust" early in life. Lack of such a firm sense of basic trust can undermine one's self-confidence for life and can prevent an individual from fulfilling his creative potential. Such childhood deficiencies may result from a lack of parental trust, from misgivings in the parents about the meaning and significance of their own lives.

Fundamental attitudes like these are communicated to children in subtle ways from their earliest days on. The importance of symbolic impairments in parents, such as a lost sense of immortality, in producing individual-psychological difficulties in children has not been much examined. But it is in such ways as this that the psychohistorical themes that characterize an era—like unfaced death anxiety in our time—become enmeshed in the psychological lives of individuals from one generation to another.

We began this discussion by describing some of the psychological struggles of those who survived the atomic bomb in Hiroshima. Those struggles involved guilt, numbing, and a continuing effort to give form and meaning to radically disrupted lives. Perhaps we can achieve little more than a glimmer of the excruciating tensions such extraordinarily painful lives have involved. But in another sense we are all survivors of this century's holocausts.

In cultivating and making clear to ourselves our own status as survivors, we become more fully part of the century in which we live. In doing so we open ourselves to the experience of pain and to the imagery and anxiety of death. We glimpse at such moments the necessity for personal and social transformation in the interest of continued survival and new meaning. The urgency of the tasks of reconstruction are then pressed upon us—though the forms our efforts must take are never fully clear.

Agents of Death

Gil Elliot

Gil Elliot was born in Scotland in 1931 and studied at Glasgow and Sussex universities. In his remarkable work *The Twentieth Century Book of the Dead,* from which this selection is taken, Elliot details the 110 million murders committed by governments in this century.

DEATH MACHINES

In considering violent or untimely death, it is the manner and means of death—not the general phenomenon of death itself—that are of primary philosophical interest.

Can the manner and means of violent death be reduced to a knowable mechanism—a "death machine"?

Of the ways in which we can think of knowing or understanding such a death machine, one is to "know all the facts," another is to ask the question, "how does it relate to me?"

To know the facts is desirable. To know *all* the facts about such a phenomenon as the death machine would clearly be an absurd pretension. Yet, "waiting for science to establish all the facts" is the everyday limbo of the game of factual knowledge. Whilst playing this waiting game we are supposed to suspend the judgment of values, and even to neglect that most sensitive tool of inquiry, sharpened by experience, alert to survive, vivid in its brief life: intuition. Intuition, or the practice of relating oneself to the object in the immediacy of experience, is, like life itself, "unreliable." It seems that the certainties of science are worth waiting for. But when these so-called certainties appear they are as pluralistic, as conflicting, as subject to opinion as anything else. In short, the procedures of "objective" inquiry are just as much modified by self and by fantasy as those of subjective inquiry. The difference is that in the first case the part played by the self is concealed from the observer, and often from the would-be scientist himself.

Shelley said that the poet is the "unacknowledged legislator" of the world. In our grim times the chief unacknowledged legislator has been the subjective fantasy of political leaders, academic theorists, social groups masquerading as "objective reality," "historical necessity," "political realism," "value-free judgment," "scientific objectivity," and so forth.

The death machine, then, is partly a factual object—an ever-incomplete accretion of facts; and partly a philosophical object—uncertain of definition yet conceived as a whole to which I relate myself, so intuitively that the "I" itself will become, if necessary, subject to analysis as part of the death machine!

We might manage a preliminary definition, or at least tease out some of the relevant parts, of the death machine if we look at those versions of it which [can be] loosely identified with different areas of macroviolence. The *war machine*, the *total-war machine,* and the *total-state machine* are pretty well factual objects, identifiable in terms of organization, weapons, production, deployment of plans and personnel.

I took the war machine of the First World War as the type of the twentieth-century war machine. What characterizes it most is a change in the nature of the *alienating process.* War was traditionally a conflict between two alienated sides, "enemies." During the First World War even the men in the trenches ceased to believe that the enemy was the men in the other trenches. The alienating process of the modern war machine divides men into two subjective environments: the physical environment of the victim (the death environment) and the technological environment of the systems and machines which produce death. Some have perceived this in terms of class alienation. According to this view, the killing systems and machines are within the conscious control of the leaders and generals, and it is their class alienation from the poor that prevents them from using restraint in the use of these systems against the chief victims, the ordinary soldiers who without their uniforms are, of course, the poor. I am sure that this process— which I shall call *natural alienation* when I discuss it below in the context of the nature machine—is relevant to a discussion of how the modern war machine came into being, or evolved. The other view is that the machines and systems inhabit a faceless environment of their own, and dominate their users. However it evolved in the first place, it is this, which we can fairly call *technological alienation,* that remains and persists as the most characteristic feature of the twentieth-century war machine.

It is also characteristic of the war machine that the same man, the soldier, operates the killing systems as well as being their victim. The *total-war* machine extends the alienation principle, for here death environments are also created for people who are not themselves involved in operating the killing systems, that is civilians shot, starved, or bombed, soldiers and civilians enclosed in camps. Here the alienation between the environment of the killing system—military or administrative—and the environment of the victim is total. The same is true of the total-state machine, with one additional refinement. The alienated identity of the victim is not merely created by the technological sweep of the machine, as it is in the total-war machine. In this case, before the victim is included in the killing technology (the labor camp, the mass execution, the deportation) a paranthropoid identity, such as class enemy or enemy of the people, is created for him out of the ideology of the total-state machine. That is to say, *ideological alienation* precedes the technological alienation.

↑↑

We should remember, first, that the machines of modern warfare are not merely horrid excrescences, nightmarish extrusions of the human mind. . . . Purely as machines they are truly representative of us and the times we live in.

↑↑

The essential difference between the war machine and the total-war machine is one of *consciousness.* Traditionally war was a ritual in which certain qualities such as bravery, generalship, morale, cunning contributed to the symbolic outcome known as "victory." Where ritual and symbol broke down you had chaotic, meaningless conflicts such as the Thirty Years' War. The First World War was *not* this chaotic, meaningless thing, not merely the war of attrition and exhaustion. It was a case—*the* case—of ritual and symbol being outstripped and replaced by a new logic of war. But it was not yet a conscious logic. Total war as it developed thereafter was a *conscious* departure from the natural order provided by ritual and symbol. But how conscious? and how true has the logic of the new order been to the human consciousness?

As we know, the raw material of total war, and hence the chief premises of its logic are, one, vast numbers of people and, two, machines.

The vast numbers were first represented by the figure of the citizen-soldier, who reached his apotheosis in the First World War. By the Second World War he was already outstripped, in numbers participating, by the plain *citizen*. The next total war will involve very few soldiers as against citizens. Thus the logic of numbers reaches its conclusion, that total war is war between citizens not soldiers. But this logic cannot sustain a theory of war. "Soldiers" means a selective, limited number of people who can be used for purposive action. "Citizens" has no such finite, purposive meaning. It can only mean either "all citizens" or "citizens at random to an infinite number." It is an inchoate principle which cannot sustain a theory of conflict.

The responsibility for providing a rationale of total war thus devolves heavily upon the machines, and the logic of the machines is utterly fascinating. We should remember, first, that the machines of modern warfare are not merely horrid excrescences, nightmarish extrusions of the human mind. That is what they become in action, but purely as machines they are truly representative of us and the times we live in. The force of unprecedented numbers; impersonal answers to the demands of conflicting egos; the development of solutions under pressure; economical concentration of human ingenuity—all of these are represented and symbolized in our machines of warfare. They are our champions on the field of conflict.

It is part of the genius of living things that violence, when not directed to survival (food, protection), is economical in its effects. The biological response to conflict between equals is an instinctive ritual which (a) recognizes and respects the reality of the conflict or disagreement, and (b) reduces the struggle to symbolic dimensions. Animals fighting their own kind have a system of signals symbolizing defeat, victory, submission which allow the conflict to be resolved far short of irreparable physical harm. Human society is far too complex for such patterns to remain in a pure form, but they still survive at the roots of individual behavior. So far as group conflict is concerned, the most economical fighting ritual is that where two champions symbolize two numerous groups of people and fight on their behalf.

When it comes to the *machine as champion*, not only does the machine lack these reductive qualities: its response to the conflict situation is purely quantitative. Where there are two machines confronting one another, there will be soon four, and so on. The symbol or champion becomes greater in importance than what it represents. As the number and power of the machines increase, so does the number of people involved. But . . . the logic of numbers in the context of total war cannot sustain a rationale of

113

conflict. Once again we reach a logical *impasse.* There is only one logical path left, and that is that the machines should fight one another *without the involvement of people.*

There are I think two possible reasons why we do not proceed with this logic and have a War of the Machines. One is the difficulty of arranging it; but I cannot believe this would be an insuperable obstacle. The other reason, and I believe the valid one, is that it would be absurd. For two opposing sides to contemplate arranging a War of the Machines would expose the absurdity of the logic of conflict by destructive machinery, and hence must lead to the dismantling of the machinery. But this is something that we could not bear to contemplate. So great is our spiritual and material investment in the machines, so much do they truly champion our values, so little do we have the wit or resourcefulness to devise other symbols to represent us in our conflicts, that we cannot face up to the logic of what we are doing. So the people and the machines continue to grow in numbers, the function of the people being to lend verisimilitude to the War of the Machines. Thus we achieve the poor man's version of sanity, which is the physical acceptance of whatever happens to exist, supported by whatever rationalization can be concocted at the moment.

. . . How true [has] the logic of total war been to the human consciousness? Well, it is a straightforward denial of consciousness, of course. If the machines are looked upon as the objective results of thought, and in their development as the repositories of an objective logic, then the objective conclusion they display is, as demonstrated above, the need for their own destruction or dismantling. Consciousness demands that we draw this conclusion and act upon it. Indeed, if looked upon in this way the machines of war might provide the basis for a complete rationale of the place of conflict in human society, and of the destruction of human life in particular. In this case they would perform a useful rationalizing function, and would actually take human practice a progressive step beyond the simple logic of survival which governs the instinctive rituals of fighting. But, in the denial of this consciousness, we leave ourselves in that limbo known as the world of objective reality: a world of external objects in which the human being has no greater value than any other object displacing the same physical volume of space, a mental environment as hostile to the survival of life as a concentration camp.

What is the difference between the "nature machine" and these man-made death machines? Well, the *nature machine* is the mechanics of what used to

be called, rather smugly, the balance of nature. It was a kind of long-term
death machine for the poor in their environment, in the form of disease,
epidemic, and shortage of food; tendencies that were exacerbated from time
to time by natural disasters such as flood and crop failure, and by degener-
ate relationships between alienated classes. But the balance of nature was
kept in the sense that life triumphed conspicuously over death.

On the basis of this definition we can draw some comparisons between
death in the natural environment and in the man-made environment.
By "natural environment" I mean the context of living when the world
society as a whole was pre-industrial. Many of the same conditions apply to
present-day "underdeveloped" countries. But remember that however
pre- or non-industrial a society may be today, it almost certainly pos-
sesses two basic ingredients of the man-made environment: modern medicine, which may drastically reduce the death-rate and increase the
population; and, at the least, rapid access to sophisticated military technology in the world community. The essential elements of the new man
made life and death.

If we think of untimely deaths in the natural environment as being the
"violence of nature" then by far the greatest proportion came from *micro-
violence*, by which I mean the regular, widely distributed incidence of disease, infant mortality, malnutrition. Because of the gradual, pervasive nature
of micro-violence we tend to lack direct ways of apprehending its magnitude. For the same reason its impact is taken and absorbed by those directly
affected by it: it does not *apparently* affect the structures of society as a
whole. The macro-violence of nature—floods, famine, pestilence—had more
apparent, dramatic impact, but in fact the quantitative effects were much
smaller; and macro-violence was not institutionalized and given a continuous existence as it is in the man-made environment. The same was true of
the macro-violent forms of fighting, which retained an inherent *reductive
capacity*; whilst in the man-made environment, where the propensity to
fight is invested in machines, the problem of reduction is divorced from
instinct, ritual, and commonsense and is a problem of men and machines,
and which controls which.

The chief reasons the effects of micro-violence are unapparent is because it is an essential *part* of the social structure. The "balance of nature"
depends upon it. So does the large-family structure and hence the specialized roles of men and women. Natural micro-violence has a macro-violent
impact only when the possibility of stopping it is perceived—then it promotes change or revolution; and when it *has* been stopped—then it promotes

115

(in default of birth control) a population explosion with future implications of macro-violence.

The alienation process in the natural environment has the same roots as in the man-made environment, but develops in a radically different way. *Natural alienation* begins as a good and necessary separation of vigorous social elements from their bondage to the earth. As this separation flowers into the skills and arts of social management the classes formed from it, whether aristocratic or middle-class, become physically alienated not only from the earthier aspects of themselves but from the people associated with the earth; hence the despised class of *peasants.* In spite of this actual circumstance, of people living as it were in separate worlds, the Christian ethos claims to unite them. The people are spiritually united in God, and even physically united in a romanticized version of nature. When this unified consciousness is challenged or threatened we have *religious alienation,* the victims being in the post-Reformation period *minority Christian* denominations, in the turbulent and insecure seventeenth century *witches,* and persistently throughout the Christian centuries the *Jews.*

ⲅⲅ

Of the 110 million man-made deaths calculated in this century, sixty-two million died in conditions of privation, forty-six million from guns and bombs, or hardware, and two million from chemicals.

ⲅⲅ

Physical and spiritual alienation is thus, in the natural environment, natural and religious, and in the man-made environment, technological and ideological. The victims are similar and the relevant psychological patterns seem to be very much the same. Peasants and Jews are major victims of both types of environment; they are the link as it were between the paranthropoid identities of one kind of society and the other. The great difference is in the kind of violence they bring about. The natural environment contained a continual micro-violence which took a regular toll of human life and from time to time escalated sufficiently through plague, famine, and the chaos of war to give society a nasty jolt, but it preserved the balance of nature and never at any time threatened the existence of the human species. The man-made environment has brought micro-violence impressively under control, but it threatens to disturb the balance of nature through industrial activity affecting the atmosphere, through the destruction of living species, and through uncontrolled increases in human population; it has brought macro-violence to a level which disastrously upsets the stability of societies, destroys morals, and threatens the continued existence of the human species.

Another link between the two environments is the *death-breeding machine* which at its most chaotic combines the violence of nature with that of technology. If technology is nature moulded by consciousness then we might expect this machine to contain a progression from a less-conscious to a more-conscious process. Certainly human consciousness is embedded in technology, yet apologists of modern war tend to present the technology as a massive simulation of nature about which little can be done; and it does seem more like a progression from blind nature to blind technology. If we extend the meaning of the *death-breeding process* to signify the active principle of all macro-violent systems, we shall see however that some are more conscious than others. Also we should remember that technology proceeds from a knowable first cause: man or, more specifically, scientific man. The death-breeding process leads to the final peak of the *total-death machine,* that which threatens the apocalyptic end and absolutely final appearance of . . . us.

What about . . . us? the celluloid lovers continually ask each other as we catch our breaths in the dark of the cinema, and that is also the question of the total-death machine. I suppose total death is some kind of absolute value and the philosophical core of the man-made death machine. Looking at the death machine as a philosophical entity, we might see the *nature machine* as the basic source of all; the *death-breeding process* as the active principle with its question about consciousness; and *total death* as the final question.

In the natural environment nature is supposed to unite society in happy worship of God. In the man-made environment technology is supposed to unite society in happy worship of Science. But if we look at the technologies of macro-violence we shall soon see that the reality is very different.

117

TECHNOLOGIES OF MACRO-VIOLENCE

Of the 110 million man-made deaths calculated in this century, sixty-two million died in conditions of *privation*, forty-six million from guns and bombs, or *hardware*, and two million from *chemicals*. In separating our *chemicals* as a category on its own I am thinking of the future as well as reflecting the century's progress from the heavy metal industries to the advances in the chemical industries which are such a significant part of our present-day scene. The familiar association of large-scale killing with factory production is not merely a colorful metaphor. Given the scale of modern killing technologies, their parallel development with that of industrial research and methods is inevitable. Hence the latest developments in killing methods are those associated with the fashionable science of the moment, biology.

Privation Technologies

The basic kinds of privation technologies are I think best expressed as operating in *enclosed*, *semi-enclosed* and *diffuse* areas.

Deaths from privation technologies 62 million		
ENCLOSED	SEMI-ENCLOSED	DIFFUSE
Camp privation	City privation	Rural or mixed privation
20 million	16 million	26 million

Enclosed Privation Areas   Camp privation is a highly conscious process, involving collection and movement of people, and selective identity of the victim. The systems of the killing technology are various: camp administration, collection or concentration system, and the wider governmental system directing all. Where the secret police system is a power in the land these functions are vertically integrated. But the people who perform the different functions, even if belonging to the same organization, differ from one another, partly in class and outlook, certainly in their spatial relationship with the victim. Where there is no curb on the power of the state (the first condition for camp privation), the state's victims are passed on *notionally* by those who make the rules, *administratively* by those who run the identification and collection system, and *physically* by the camp administration and guards. They are delivered from one set of people to the next. Arbitrary brutality occurs in those who are brutal by nature. But when the conditions notionally or administratively laid down are inhuman, and are supervised by the kind of people who survive by obeying orders, then the system is brutal and that is a more powerful force than arbitrary brutality. The most powerful force of all is physical neglect.

ENCLOSED PRIVATION AREAS

Camp privation

Enclosed ghetto, 1 m. deaths

Concentration camp, 2.5 m. deaths

Prisoners-of-war camp, 4.5 m. deaths

Labour camp, 12 m. deaths

The *enclosed ghettoes* of Poland—Warsaw, Lodz, Lublin—were used as camps. They were sealed-off city areas into which people from outside were concentrated. They were virtually total-death environments. They are unique as enclosed privation areas in which the identity of the victim was not selective as to age and sex (although it is true that less severe privations have been suffered by entire families in transit camps for deported populations and in displaced person camps for refugees).

The German *prisoner-of-war camps* for Russians were the only enclosed privation areas with entirely male populations. Some of these camps were certainly places of total death. They are the most extreme example of sheer physical neglect, more powerful in its effects (cannibalism, for instance) than enforced human pressures.

Although the degeneration of conditions in the German *concentration camps* was possibly due to the secret police arm in particular, the German camps as a whole reflected the policy of the government over a period and hence to a very large extent the society as a whole. Racist attitudes were responsible for the ghettoes, and for the treatment of Slav prisoners of war in a way different from people of other races. The German camp system in its developed form was possible only as the result of military conquest, and with military co-operation. Nine-tenths of the victims were foreigners. Any individual actions leading to their presence in the camps were committed in response to military aggression. In the chain of people who pass

119

on victims from one to the other, the military acted as delivery men to the secret police, not only in the case of some of the concentration camp victims, but also in the case of the Russian prisoners of war.

Whilst the German camp system lasted little more than the duration of the war, the Russian *labor camps* have the distinction of being a permanent assertion of a national system of injustice, traditional in its present form for over fifty years. This is the only camp system where privation has been imposed on people for more than about five years. Hence the environments created by the system—virtually a conscious re-creation of the micro-violence of nature—are unique. Within the system, all on a large scale, are a survival environment, a random-death environment, and a total-death environment. There are certain special camps where people are deprived of liberty but otherwise not harassed. There are the camps of the survival environment, which Solzhenitsyn's novel describes as *The First Circle.* Beyond this there is the second circle, of the labor camp proper and the random-death environment. Beyond that there is the third circle, the camps of the far North and East and the total-death environment: Komi, Karaganda, Vorkuta.

Semi-enclosed Privation Areas   Privation technologies in semi-enclosed areas emphasize the vulnerability of cities. A city cannot adapt itself to military strategies. It cannot pretend it is not a city, disguise itself as a forest, grow its own food on the sly, and so on. Its citizens depend upon organizational structures and if these are interfered with so is the life of the citizen. Once disruption gets beyond a certain stage there is nothing much that can be done about it. Total war and total revolution bring the random-death environment to the city.

The *unenclosed ghettoes* of Eastern Poland and the Baltic States were subject to harassment and pressures from the occupying forces, for racialist reasons,

SEMI-ENCLOSED PRIVATION AREAS

City privation

Unenclosed ghetto, 1 m. deaths

Siege, 1 m. deaths

Occupation, 6 m. deaths

Civil dislocation, 8 m. deaths

which turned them into total-death environments. The purely military pressures of *siege* almost did the same for Leningrad. On a larger and somewhat more diffuse scale, the cities of Russia became areas of random death from privation during the *dislocation* of the Civil War period and again under the pressures of military *occupation* during the Second World War.

The victims of city privation are of course families in their normal habitats; in time of war their identities are selective to the extent that the younger men are being killed elsewhere.

Diffuse Privation Areas   It's amazing in how many different ways the life can be squeezed out of people. It had never occurred to me that a sizeable number of people might have died in *transit*—in the sheer bungling inefficiency of forced movement. Think of the way human beings have been driven and herded back and forth across Europe and Russia in our century. Deportation of peasants to Siberia. Trains to the labor camps. Deportation of Russian and Ukrainian slave laborers to Germany. Trains from every corner of Europe to the ghettoes and death camps. Rail journeys and forced marches of prisoners of war.

DIFFUSE PRIVATION AREAS

Rural or mixed privation

Combat, 1 m. deaths

Transit, 1.5 m. deaths

Economic blockade, 2 m. deaths

Man-made famine, 5 m. deaths

Scorched earth, 5 m. deaths

War dislocation, 12 m. deaths

Privation deaths among soliders in *combat* conditions include the typhus and wound infections of the First World War, the freezing hardship and disease of the Second World War in Russia, the starvation and typhus of the China War and amongst other ill-equipped armies throughout the century, the malarias and jaundices of Western soldiers in the East.

You would imagine that *diffuse* privation would have a larger element of the accidental about it, if only because of the sheer difficulty of getting at people in far-flung rural areas. But not so. *Economic blockade*, as practised against the Germans in the First World War, against the Biafrans in the Nigerian Civil War; *man-made famine*, as engineered against the Russian peasants during the collectivization; *scorched-earth* tactics, as used by the Germans in Russia and the Japanese in China. They are all highly conscious and deliberate methods of destroying people; killing technologies.

Most of these highly conscious technologies tend to produce an immediate random-death environment. In the case of the general *war dislocation* in China and other places where a slow privation was diffused over a vast population, you might say that the privation deaths were an intrusion into a survival environment, that is to say, a social climate in which death is not random but people still have some room to survive by their own efforts.

Listing these technologies, as objective parts of the death machine, is not difficult. But how can I, as an individual, relate myself to these? Perhaps we all tend to feel we ought to attempt to re-live the sufferings of the dead. Apart from the self-delusion involved in such an attempt, it is difficult to see what object is served by it. It certainly doesn't bring back the dead or heal their agony or expiate the crimes of which they are the victims. In fact, if you read some of the basic factual accounts of the intensest death environments such as concentration or death camps—as you must do, if you hope to reach any understanding of the human story—you will probably have an *involuntary* "reliving" of suffering in any case. The experience of most people I have talked to on this subject agrees with my own—that the simple factual detail of such accounts is so horrifying that it is only bearable for a few pages at a time. Herein I think lies the salutary and sole purpose of "re-living" such sufferings: the perception of the unbearable. If it is bearable something phoney is going on, either on the part of the writer or of the reader.

I cannot then truly relate myself to these technologies of macro-violence through the simulated emotions, feelings, and sufferings of the flesh known as "re-living." But I *can* suffer these structures of reality—these terms descriptive of real event—to enter the mind undistorted by specific color, myth, or image.

Indeed it would be difficult enough to describe the *ghetto*, the *blockade*, the *scorched earth*, the *famine*, in terms of image or metaphor—for these are the basic realities which provide image and metaphor for the rest of ordinary existence. They are the bare bones of reality. Nor is there much need, in order to convey their reality, to explain in great detail how the *siege* or *occupation* comes into being and works its effects, for the bones of death are easily enough achieved. There is nothing extraordinary about any of these—they could be organized by a wise child if there were a wise child willing to organize millions of deaths. If we were describing some complex social fabric where a million conflicting interests were maintained in a living pattern then there would be some call for depth of study . . . but when it comes to the *prison camp*, the *concentration camp*, the *labor camp*, all of these share that cretinous unity of human purpose whereby success and failure achieve the same end of destruction and death. These are the bones, these technologies of the past and those death systems latent in our present, that form the skeleton structure of the death machine.

If it is true that in the twentieth century man has finally come face to face with his own skeleton, it is a structure such as this that he is looking at. I would have the *intellect*, not simulated feelings but the perceiving *mind*, to suffer that skeleton.

Hardware Technologies

Military experts tend to assert that in twentieth-century conflicts many more deaths have been caused by the big guns than by small arms. In this generalization there is an important truth and an important untruth. Quantitatively, the statement is not true. According to my calculations deaths from hardware technologies divide roughly as follows:

Deaths from hardware technologies 46 million			
BIG GUNS	AERIAL BOMBS	SMALL ARMS	DEMOGRAPHIC (mixed)
18 million	1 million	24 million	3 million

But the *significant* untruth lies in the implication that as deaths from the big guns increase, deaths from small arms might, or do, or by some logic should, decline in numbers. Not only is this a demonstrably false proposition, but it is the very opposite that is true. As deaths from big guns increase, they also help to bring about an *increase* in deaths from small arms. This is the important truth about the death-potential of the big guns. It is not a question of a particular type of weapon being chosen for military reasons, or of one type making another type obsolete. It is a question of big guns *creating an environment* of death on the scale of macro-violence. In this

123

environment small arms and other death technologies not only flourish but also tend to increase to the same scale of macro-violence.

Big Guns   Basing itself on the general nature of the First World War and on some evidence suggesting the preponderance of wounds to be from the effects of exploding shells, expert opinion concludes that "ninety percent" or "three-quarters" of the deaths came from the big guns. We may modify that proportion if we assume that experts tend to think exclusively in terms of combat deaths, chiefly in terms of the major theatres of war and mainly of the most characteristic set-piece battles. On the basis of a ten-million total, at least two million deaths (from the economic blockade and from soldier-disease) were outside of combat. If we think of the early part of the war when the machine gun was used intensively, of the massed cavalry charges of the Russian front and the heavy losses on the Italo-Austrian front, as well as continuous small engagements and sniping throughout the war, it becomes at least possible that as many as three million may have died from small-arms fire.

Even if the proportion of deaths from the big guns was as low as five million out of ten, the experts are certainly correct in emphasizing the over-whelming significance of these weapons. The big guns created a physical and mental environment, a list of whose effects on the human race would break the spirit of any computer. The mechnical scale of the big guns deter-mined strategy and the general context in which twentieth-century conflict would take place. The big guns decided that the characteristic form of kill-ing in the twentieth century would be repetitive massacre, with a minimum of felt conflict. Thus the nature of the *small-arms* killings in the First World War was predetermined by the big guns. In the first place, whether they amounted to one or three million, the number was greater than the number killed by small arms in any previous war. Secondly, probably the majority

BIG GUNS

China, 1 m. deaths

Other conflicts, 2 m. deaths

Rest of the Second World War, 5 m. deaths

Second World War, Russians, 5 m. deaths

First World War, 5 m. deaths

took the form of repetitive massacre in situations created by the logic of the big guns.

In the First World War the big guns were heavier and the distinction between them and small arms was cruder than in the Second World War. Rifles and machine guns—dominated, like the minds of generals, by the big guns—did the work of the big guns. That is to say, they were frequently used for massacre in situations where big guns might as well have been used. In the Second World War big guns were generally lighter and the range of weapons wider. Some were even portable. Weapons had been rationalized to meet the techniques of massacre.

The big guns and, later, the mechanized battlefield created a technological environment which men accepted as a simulation of nature, a force which could not ultimately be controlled by men but only guided in certain directions. We can see this development also in the smaller conflicts of the century. The forces which govern the incidence of conflict and the scale of death are still localized, traditional ones: genuine if senseless conflicts, death occurring on a scale with at least some reference to the objects of struggle. But in the post-Second World War period, as the world situation casts its shadow more and more on local conflicts, so the general technological environment of large-scale death is imported into them and the localized effects diminish in importance.

In China, the physical environment created by the big guns has not existed to a very large extent at all. In China, of course, the natural environment was sufficiently deteriorated not to require the massive technological creation of a death environment.

Small Arms   The use of small arms is much wider than the limits of formal wars or conflicts. Big guns are used within the context of a formal war, and indeed often dominate the context and create their own environment. This is probably not true of small arms. There is always, I believe, a controlling system or factor stronger than the weapons themselves. This is clearly evident in the case of *formal executions*, where the legal or pseudo-legal process decides death for every individual; death is certified in advance. Execution can be by a number of means—strangling, guillotine, hanging—as well as by shooting. But it seems unlikely that the executions of this century would have reached such numbers without the rifle and pistol. Pulling a trigger is so easy. The uniquely twentieth-century characteristic of these killings is the scale on which they have occurred. The sinister auspices of state interrogations, trials, summary executions are not new, they are as old as human records. The scale is quite new, and it is of course the scale of military operations and of massacre.

SMALL ARMS

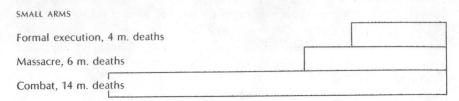

Formal execution, 4 m. deaths

Massacre, 6 m. deaths

Combat, 14 m. deaths

If the massacre by big gun and the massacre by formal execution are rationalized by their apparent connections with traditional human activities—"fighting" and "war," "punishment" and the "legal process"— at least in the massacre by massacre there are no such hypocrisies to obscure the simple truth. Administrative or military orders, men with guns, selected victims, killing: that's the simple recipe. In listing five major areas of massacre with small arms, I shall indicate associated areas where massacres on a smaller scale have occurred, and the approximate figures relate to all the areas mentioned.

The last and largest category of small-arms deaths is those that occurred in military *combat*. My impression is that, on the basis of about fourteen million deaths, half of these would be in the two world wars, and the other half in other wars including those of China. Of the small-arms deaths in the First World War it is is likely the preponderance were in situations where the massed firepower of small arms was used as a means of massacre auxiliary to that of the big guns. This would also be true of Russian combat deaths in the Second World War, and somewhat less true of deaths on other fronts. In the spectrum of smaller wars over the century the pattern would be more erratic. It is probably safe to say that at least half of all the deaths from small arms in the major and minor wars had the characteristics of massacre in environments dominated by big guns.

It becomes necessary to make a distinction between formal combat and what we understand by conflict. Presumably, in conflict in the individual sense, there is some kind of equation such as equal opportunity for both parties or at least a feeling of such, or that the outcome should be dependent on some kind of skill. Conflict in this sense does not exist where people die from privation, or from the big guns, or from the various massacres of small arms. Only in about half the deaths from small arms in combat situations is there the remotest possibility of a conflict situation having existed. If we

Administrative or military orders	Men with guns	Selected victims	Number killed
Suppression of minority and other *ad hoc* orders	Turkish Army and others in "small" wars	Armenians and others	1m.
Enforced collectivization and other administrative tasks	Russian Secret Police	Peasants, camp prisoners, etc.	1m.
Reprisal orders and other law-and-order measures	German Army	People, random selected	2m.
Orders to suppress and destroy Jewry and other groups	German Secret Police	Jews, Gypsies, old and sick people	1m.
Other *ad hoc* orders	Japanese army and other armies in the Second World War	Peasants and others	1m.
		Approximate total	6m.

add to this the category of demographic violence where there is clearly a large element of conflict, we have a figure of about ten million deaths where a situation of conflict *might* have existed; that is to say, in less than ten percent of all the man-made deaths of the century.

Demographic Violence   Each of the three cases I have noted, the Russian Bread War, the Chinese anti-bourgeois campaigns, and the Indian Partition riots—accumulating to a minimum of three million deaths—might be looked upon as escalated forms of micro-violence. That is to say, to some extent they have the character of ordinary civil violence. Yet in each case there is a macro-element in the organizational structure of the event as well as in its incidence, in the form of an instruction or recommendation from the center. In each case an official pronouncement, coming at a time of transition between two systems of government, leads to a violence which reflects the clash between the two forms of government. This reminds us that even in an age of macro-violence the violence of "the people" remains micro-violent, that is taking the form of frequent individual and occasional mob violence which *never* approaches the dimensions of macro-violence *except when organized by the state*. Feelings of violence in the people are only united into a mass in the fantasy of scholar and politician. Thus we have the grotesque paradox that many respectable statesmen, in their fear of "the people" or "the masses" or "disorder," recommend that the best way to keep them off the streets is put them in uniform—the very action that unites vast numbers of people in the potential of macro-violence!

The very exceptional nature of demographic violence in the spectrum of macro-violence—the fact that it involves hand-to-hand fighting reflecting direct conflict, aggression, fear, and struggle in the individual—leads to a necessary question. Do the technologies of macro-violence, with a few exceptions, lead to situations, and ultimately to a general situation, in which violence may explode or proliferate without reference to conflict, aggression, fear, or struggle? Can macro-violence become completely divorced from human psychology and motivation? If it can, then it calls for a completely new dimension of inquiry, for most studies of violence assume a link with aggression, conflict, frustration, boredom, and other human conditions.

ʄʄ

By the time we reach the atom bomb, Hiroshima and Nagasaki, the ease of access to target and the instant nature of macro-impact mean that both the choice of city and the identity of the victim have become completely randomized. . . .

ʄʄ

Aerial Bombing   The number of deaths [from aerial bombing] may be a good deal in excess of the one million I have calculated, but it is most unlikely to be more than two million. The peak level of deaths for an individual city is about 200,000 and the main victims were Dresden, Hiroshima, and Nagasaki, chief targets of Allied terror-bombing in the Second World War. The deliberate bombing of civilians was the chief source of deaths in volume, and other cities attacked in this way during the Second World War (including the Sino-Japanese war) were: Coventry and other English cities; Rotterdam and other Dutch cities; Warsaw and other Polish cities; Stalin-

grad and other Russian cities; Shanghai and other Chinese cities; Frankfurt
and other German cities; Tokyo and other Japanese cities.

In the bombing of cities the technologies of violence are destroying the
technologies of peace. In the early days, bombing was similar to the shelling
of a city, that is the city happened to crop up in the strategic plans. By the
time we reach the atom bomb, Hiroshima and Nagasaki, the ease of access
to target and the instant nature of macro-impact mean that both the choice
of city and the identity of the victim have become completely randomized,
and human technology has reached a final platform of self-destructiveness.
The great cities of the dead, in numbers, remain Verdun, Leningrad, and
Auschwitz. But at Hiroshima and Nagasaki the "city of the dead" is finally
transformed from a metaphor into a literal reality. The city of the dead of
the future is our city and the victims are—not French and German soldiers,
nor Russian citizens, nor Jews—but all of us without reference to specific
identity.

Chemicals and Other Advanced Technologies

About the asphyxiation of between one and two million people by poi-
sonous fumes in specially prepared chambers and vans, there is little to be
said that has not already been said. It should be studied in direct physical
detail as recorded in several books and the reader will then find if he has
not already done so that there is no need to compare it with anything else
in order to get it "into perspective." Since then science and technology have
proliferated the technologies of macro-violence to the extent that every
new technological development has a death-application as well as a life-
use. If you explore the ocean bed and contemplate its human uses you also
devise a means of devastating the ocean bed. If you discover how to isolate
germs and viruses for protective purposes you also proceed to concentrate
them into a technology for killing a million people. If you can deaden the
nerves to lessen surgical pain you can also paralyse the nerves for hostile
purposes, and modify your technology to produce various degrees of agony
and types of death. Whilst scientific discoveries and technologies often
remain hypothetical and open-ended for a considerable time while their
life-uses are being explored, the death-application has the advantage of
unquestionable effectiveness. The technology can thus instantly become a
closed system and acquire that aura of magic and power which has been
sought through the ages by villains, charlatans, psychopaths, and fools.
Thus, for instance, the attempt to connect the subtle detail and variety of

human behavior with physiological processes is delicate—difficult—hypothetical—frustrating—open-ended. But if you approach it from the angle of the *death-application,* you can most certainly by drugs and surgery ensure the deadening of great areas of human behavior, and thus become a magician freed from irritating difficulties.

Such is the romanticization of technology, like the old romanticizing of nature, that the technologies of macro-violence are actually glamourized in modern fiction, with the glossy inanity with which overfed, stupid aristocrats used to dress up as swains and shepherdesses. These corruptions are beginning to eat back at technology so that, in addition to the city of the dead as a future arena of self-destructiveness, we have the possibility of human technology destroying itself at the source. . . .

VALUES: NEGATIVE AND POSITIVE

Seeking an *answer to death* is perhaps the greatest wild-goose chase of human existence. Yet from time to time a new attitude if not solution arises out of our experience. Such an attitude is latent in the connection between *violence* and *death* which, although apparently an obvious one, has not yet been fully expressed in terms of recent experience. Violence in the twentieth century has produced the new phenomenon of *total death.* As an *idea,* total death has existed—in mental pictures of *the day of judgment, doomsday, the end of the world*—at least since the formulation of the great religions. As a *reality* attainable by human means, the science of which is a permanent unalterable part of knowledge, it originates in the notorious half-century from which we are just emerging. *Can* we emerge from the nightmare of reality and vision created in that period? We cannot create a retrospective order for the chaos of the actual events. Can we escape from the chaos of the idea that is left to us? *Total death* could mean the obliteration of particular cities or countries or regions; it could mean the collapse of world civilization or the death of the species; or it could mean the total death of the mind within a variety of physical parameters. *Total death* might be brought about by a wide range of means; by the carefully considered destruction of selected millions; by the direct and secondary effects of pollution or overcrowding; by a death-breeding mixture of every kind of human motivation acting on machineries and systems which are beyond the control of living creatures. *Total death* has a time-span overwhelming the convenient human notion of time. It can "happen" in an instant, in a few days; it can have the monthly, yearly rhythms of traditional warfare or it could create a chronic long-term disruption of the seasons of nature and the years of human life. Its possibility is tomorrow, or in the next two hundred years, or at any "time" in the future. *Total death* is a hard, scientific and immediate reality at the same time as being a speculative idea in search of a philosophy. No existing mental structures, of science, philosophy, or religion, are adequate to contain it.

Death after all is a powerful reality. It is one of two or three fundamental ideas that condition the human attitude to existence. I think we should find, if we examined them in the cool comparative way that is now becoming possible, that some of the great religions have gravely distorted truth in order to accommodate the idea of death—to explain it away, to dodge its straightforward implications. A common result is the identification of *death* with *evil*, or with an unknowable darkness or *chaos.* Hence the rejection in the mind of death as a reality. Hence the reluctance of those who write with such vigor the history of the machines and systems of violence to mention the facts of death and to include these in their historical interpretations. Hence *our need to reject the assumption that reality is chaos,* to insist on *the possibility of knowing the truth about the deaths that result from our behavior, to structure our knowledge of death and deaths and total death* and bring the facts into the light of day. *Bringing into the light of day* is what happens to the soul after death, according to the *Egyptian Book of the Dead.* I made a distinction, between ancient books of the dead and the present one, of *necromancy* and *necrology,* as an indication of the different structures of knowledge of different ages. As a deeper level of truth the distinction is, I admit, a mere quibble. *Our* bringing into the light of day is different in structure but reaches the same end.

Our structure of knowledge is founded in fact. Yet the exposition of total death in terms of fact explodes the ethos of factual knowledge that is so characteristic of our age!

Total death explodes the simple *myths* of belligerent nationalism. It reduces the death-formulas of *religion* to absurdity. As an idea, it cannot be relegated to those rarefied spheres of *philosophy* where all ideas are made silly and ineffectual by the cleverness of philosophers. There is too much grim reality in it for that. As a practical reality, aspects of total death can be governed on a factual basis by a discipline such as *ecology.* But the full reality cannot, for it is too much beyond the predictable, its timespan is too unwieldy, to be contained within the factual parameters of a scientific discipline.

It is not surprising that the idea of total death should crash through established structures of thought. It is the intellectual legacy of a violence that

131

crashed through the physical structures of human societies for half a century. Those who used to live by the *Tibetan Book of the Dead* would not be surprised: yet some of our most "modern," "scientific," "brilliant" minds seem to imagine that we can go on living just as before, with the degradation and nothingness of the public experience expressed in terms of the historical myths and clichés that preceded it! But total death is not simply a myth-destroying reality. It disrupts more than those *intellectual* forms of mediation between man and his surroundings—religion, philosophy, scientific disciplines—already mentioned. It tears apart in the mind some of the forms of *physical* mediation that are most dearly cherished by the advanced societies. Principal among these is the arms pile.

The notion that national "defence" rests in the accumulation of suicidal weaponry is the final surrealism of the factual ethos, for total death is itself the mocking product of this delusion.

And this great scientific proof—that there is no ultimate physical "protection" against one's surroundings—calls in question the whole area of "factual" mediation between man and his surroundings as expressed in technology.

Fact is not superior to myth. Technology is not more efficient than religion. However much factual and technical knowledge we acquire, we shall always have to live with the unpredictable. These are the immediate implications of total death. That is why, although this exploratory study is grounded in fact and systems, the intellectual tools I am most familiar with as a child of my age, it also indicates the possibility of *knowing* this area of reality through myth and through speculative philosophy, and future students may develop the subject in these directions, taking the factual grounding for granted.

It is easy to italicize a few phrases, more difficult to predict how they are to be absorbed into the fabric of existence. The student of total death will not expect immediate technical spin-off from his researches, for he knows the timespan of total death is not that of a generation nor of a lifetime, but of a civilization. A great deal of fuss is made about the pace at which "modern ideas" succeed one another. But these are ideas used as technology, as closed systems of thought. The open-ended idea takes longer to absorb, it continues to breed and stimulate further thought. It was in the nineteenth century that the idea of men as gods came to us, and we still do not know what it means. The turbulence of our own century has produced advances in the idea of consciousness which we have hardly begun to absorb. And in the aftermath of that turbulence we have perforce to change our idea of death.

The discoveries of science and the rapid production of ideas-as-technology are very important and powerful and capable of bringing about the most significant historical events, such as the end of the world and endless other adjustments to life. No one can deny the impressiveness of that claim.

But with the above three ideas alone—god, consciousness, death—and the new interpretations of them afforded by recent experience, it would be possible to build a high civilization, and that is something different.

In our own period we are in the midst of a movement to recover inner values. Among these the values of death must be recycled into our vision of totality so that we may live truly in the world of life and death.

PART TWO

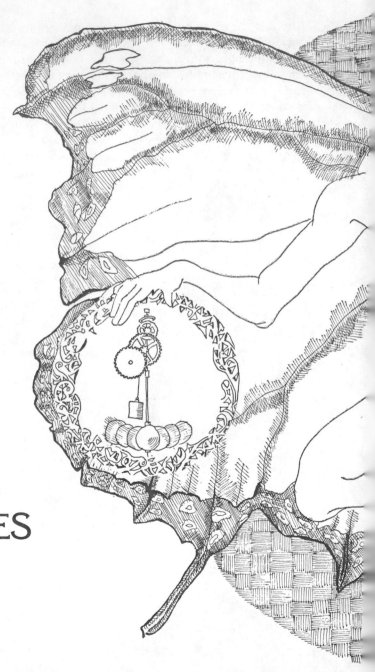

SOCIETAL

PERSPECTIVES

ON DEATH

THE

DEMOGRAPHY

OF DEATH

The four selections that comprise this chapter represent a further tightening of our focus on death—death in our society and in our own time. The chapter also introduces a second oxymoronic aspect of death: the efforts and resources invested by our society in creating a "total death" capability (as discussed in Chapter 2) and at the same time the scientific and medical efforts directed toward saving individual lives and extending the average life expectancy. Both components of this oxymoron express, as Lerner put it, man's extension of his control over nature (the "war machine" replacing the "nature machine" and controlled mortality replacing uncontrolled mortality).

The first selection is current and encyclopaedic, citing up-to-date mortality statistics and providing factual answers to the questions of the when, why, and where of death. Historically, the demographic (or actuarial) approach has been identified largely with the names of an Englishman, John Graunt, who in 1662 published an enormously important book on the London bills of mortality—what later evolved into the current death certificate—and of a Prussian clergyman, Johann Süssmilch, who in 1741 made a systematic attempt to correlate figures on mortality—what used to be called "political arithmetic" and what we now call "vital statistics." Lerner's selection reminds us of our indebtedness to Graunt and Süssmilch and reminds us also how science and knowledge develop over the centuries. Lerner discusses how changes of mortality levels effect changes in social structure, one such change being the increasing institutionalization of death resulting from the effects of controlled mortality, as discussed in the first Goldscheider selection. Other implications of a controlled mortality for today's society include changes in religious views about death over the past few generations. As Goldscheider points out, the changing character and distribution of mortality have had major implications on the functioning of our social systems and on the nature of our social institutions (the desacralization or secularization of death being one of many examples). In two short centuries the primary locus of deaths has changed dramatically from church to hospital.

But the benefits of an increased life expectancy do not accrue to all strata of society, as pointed out in the Sudnow selection and the second Goldscheider selection. In our society today, as in other societies in other times, death is egalitarian only in the ultimate sense; otherwise it is the most undemocratic aspect of life. Sudnow's selection, while not strictly "demographic" in its exposition, can be seen as a companion piece to the second Goldscheider selection because it is, among other grisly things, an extraordinary exploration of the social forces that go into the designation "Dead On Arrival (DOA)." It has been included to give some emotional texture to the "social inequality of death."

The fourth selection, also by Goldscheider, deals with the fascinating (and frightening) social inequalities of death. "Mortality differences," he writes, "may be observed between men and women, young and old, farmers and urbanites, college educated and high school dropouts, professionals and laborers, rich and poor . . ." In this selection, he speaks of the significant social inequities of death specifically related to race and to socioeconomic status. The Surgeon General might well warn us that being black and/or poor is much more dangerous to your life than smoking.

The introductory remarks to Chapter 1 alluded to the secularization of death in this century. There are implications of this secularization even beyond the shift of death's focus from religion to science, the disciplines where the main "priests" of death are to be found today. (Nowadays, when people pray for a dying loved one, they may pray to God to help the *doctor* save the person's life; the realistic appeals are made to medical science.) While we have seen the creation of a megadeath capability in our lifetime, we have also seen, in the crazy oxymoronic century (vis-à-vis death) in which we live, considerable socioeconomic, political, and, especially, technological (medical) advances directed toward the prolongation of human life. Only with the secularization of death has it been possible to effect this increased life expectancy, but "at the price" of rather substantial social changes in various aspects of our attitudes toward death, as we shall see in subsequent chapters which will touch upon the changing character of death in our times. Other *change* themes to follow will include: medical/scientific advances in prolonging life, with implications for defining death (treated in the first part of Chapter 4) and for issues related to euthanasia (treated in Chapter 8); increased involvement in the antecedents of death (second part of Chapter 4) which leads into a changing view about the uniqueness of each death which, in turn, results in an increasingly "humanistic" approach toward the dying (Chapter 5) and toward those immediately affected by death (Chapter 6).

When, Why, and Where People Die

Monroe Lerner
Monroe Lerner is a professor at The Johns Hopkins University where he is a member of the Department of Medical Care and Hospital and of the Department of Behavioral Sciences. This selection, which first appeared in *The Dying Patient* edited by Orville Brim, Jr. and others, is both current and encyclopaedic in its discussion of the many facets of mortality statistics.

Chapter 1, "When, Why, and Where People Die," by Monroe Lerner from *The Dying Patient,* Edited by Orville G. Brim, Jr., Howard E. Freeman, Sol Levine, and Norman A. Scotch (with the Editorial Consultation of Greer Williams), © 1970 by Russell Sage Foundation. Reprinted by permission.

Perhaps one of man's greatest achievements in his endless quest to extend the limits of his control over nature has been his success in increasing the average duration of his lifetime. This success has been particularly substantial in the modern era, beginning with the mid-

seventeenth century, and during the second third of the twentieth century
it extended even to the far corners of the globe. During this period, and
possibly for the first time in human history, the lifetimes of a substantial
proportion of the world's population have been extended well beyond even
the economically productive years, so that most people can now reasonably
expect to survive at least into their retirement period.

The ability to do this has always been highly valued, at least as an ideal,
and perhaps especially in those societies able at best to struggle along only
at the subsistence margin and with almost no economic surplus to support
life during the barren years. But even in other circumstances, more than
one conception of the "good society" has had a component notion that
survival beyond the productive years could be within the realm of possibility for all. Nevertheless, only in the technologically advanced Western
nations of today does the *average* duration of life reach, and even in some
instances exceed, the famous Biblical standard of threescore and ten. If
the average duration of life—life expectancy, to use the technical term of
statisticians and actuaries—is conceived of as an important indicator of
man's control over nature and at the same time also as a crucial element in
the moral evaluation of society, then surely man's difficult journey down
the long paths of history may be described as social progress rather than
merely as evolution.

In any case, whether progress or evolution, man certainly has extended
his average lifetime. This [selection] first traces that process, as much as it
is possible to do so from the inadequate historical data, and only in the
most general terms, from prehistory down to the present situation in the
United States. Life expectancy, however, is in one sense simply a refined
measure of mortality, and for some purposes it is more useful to deal with
mortality rates rather than with life expectancy. Mortality, then, becomes
the focus of the remainder of the present discussion.

Later, mortality trends in the United States are traced from 1900 to the
present, for the total population and separately by age and sex. Young
people—infants, children, and young adults—and females at all ages have
clearly been the chief beneficiaries of this process, although other segments
of the population have also gained substantially. The major communicable
diseases—tuberculosis, influenza and pneumonia, gastritis and duodenitis,
the communicable diseases of childhood, and so on—have declined as leading causes of death, to be replaced by the "degenerative" diseases, that is,
diseases associated with the aging process—heart disease, cancer, and
stroke—and by accidental injury.

Populations may be perceived not only as consisting of sex and age groups, but also as individuals and families ranged along a multi-dimensional, socioeconomic continuum. The problem then becomes: How do people at various points or in various sections of this continuum fare with regard to mortality risk or, in a more literal meaning of the term than was intended by the German sociologist Max Weber who coined it, what are their life-chances?

↑↑

A definite upward progression in life expectancy has been evident in the Western world throughout its history, and this progression is, furthermore, one in which the pace has clearly accelerated with the passage of time.

↑↑

Perhaps the most meaningful way of dealing with this question, if the objective is to identify large groups or strata in the population who actually do experience gross or at least identifiable differences in mortality risk, is to assume the existence of three major socioeconomic strata in this country, each characterized by a distinctive and unique life style—the white-collar middle class, the blue-collar working class, and the poverty population. Various structural factors in the life styles of these populations are conducive to different outcomes in mortality risk. In general, the poverty population experiences relatively high mortality rates at the younger ages and from the communicable diseases, while the white-collar middle class, especially its male members, experiences relatively high mortality rates at mid-life and in the older ages, from the "degenerative" diseases. The blue-collar working class, to the extent that it avoids both types of disabilities, appears for the moment at least to be experiencing the lowest mortality rates among the three strata.

Finally, the place where death occurs—that is, in an institution, at home, or elsewhere—has long been a neglected area of mortality statistics. From national data presented later in this [selection], it seems clear that the proportion of all deaths in this country occurring in institutions has been rising steadily, at least for the last two decades and probably for much longer than that. It may now be as high as, or higher than, two-thirds of all deaths. Almost 50 percent of all deaths occurring outside an institution in 1958 were due to heart disease, and especially to the major component of this cause-of-death category, arteriosclerotic heart disease, including coronary disease, which accounted for 37 percent of the total. Cancer, stroke, and accidents comprised the remaining major components of the total, accounting for another 30 percent of the out-of-institution deaths.

HISTORY AND THE DURATION OF HUMAN LIFE

Scholars can only estimate, in the absence of direct data, what the average duration of life must have been during prehistory. Such estimates have been made, however, and they appear to be roughly consistent with the fragmentary data available from the few surviving contemporary primitive groups, in Africa and elsewhere, whose conditions of life resemble those of our remote ancestors at least in some of their major relevant aspects. Prehistoric man lived, according to these estimates, on the average about 18 years (Dublin, 1951:386–405); life during prehistory was, in the Hobbesian sense, indeed nasty, short, and brutish. Violence was the usual cause of death, at least judging from the many skulls found with marks of blows, and man's major preoccupation was clearly with satisfying his elemental need for survival in the face of a hostile environment including wild beasts and other men perhaps just as wild. Survivorship in those days was very seldom beyond the age of 40. Persons who reached their mid-20s and more rarely their early 30s were *ipso facto* considered to have demonstrated their wisdom and were, as a result, often treated as sages.

With the rise of the early civilizations and the consequent improvements in living conditions, longevity must surely have risen, reaching perhaps 20 years in ancient Greece and perhaps 22 in ancient Rome. Life expectancy is estimated to have been about 33 years in England during the Middle Ages, about 35 in the Massachusetts Bay Colony of North America, about 41 in England and Wales during the nineteenth century, and 47.3 in the death-registration states of the United States in 1900.[1] Thus a definite up-ward progression in life expectancy has been evident in the Western world throughout its history, and this progression is, furthermore, one in which the pace has clearly accelerated with the passage of time.

The upward progression has continued during the twentieth century and, at least in the United States, its rate of increase has accelerated even further. Thus, life expectancy continued to rise in this country after 1900, even if somewhat erratically; by 1915 it had reached a temporary peak at 54.5 years. The 1918 influenza epidemic caused a sharp drop in life expec-tancy, to just below 40 years, a level probably typical of "normal" condi-tions in the United States during the first half of the nineteenth century (Lerner and Anderson, 1963:317–326). But thereafter the upward trend in life expectancy resumed and, between 1937 and 1945 and following the development of the sulfa drugs and the introduction of penicillin during War II, its increase was extraordinarily rapid. From 1946 to 1954, however, although life expectancy in this country continued upward, the *rate* of in-crease tapered off. And from 1954, when life expectancy was 69.6 years, to 1967[2] when it had reached only to 70.2, the gain was at a snail's pace com-pared to what it had been during the earlier period.

In broader perspective, that is, during the first two-thirds of the twentieth century that we have now experienced, life expectancy rose by almost twenty-three years, an average annual gain of about one-third of a year. This is a breathtaking pace compared to any period of human history prior to this century, and it clearly could not be sustained over a long period of time without enormous social disruption. In line with this, however, life expectancy in the country may now have reached a plateau at, or just above, 70 years.

---

[1] All life expectancy and mortality figures presented in this section pertaining to the U.S. in 1900 or subsequent years, unless otherwise specified, are based on various published re-ports of the National Vital Statistics Division of the National Center for Health Statistics (formerly the National Office of Vital Statistics), U.S. Public Health Service. The reports themselves are not specifically cited here, but the source for each figure is available upon request. Rates for years prior to 1933 are based on the "death-registration states" only. In 1900 this group consisted of ten states, primarily in the northeastern part of the country, and the District of Columbia. However, the number of states included in this registration area gradually increased over the years, and by 1933 all states in the continental U.S. were part of it. For comparison purposes, figures for the death-registration states are customarily con-sidered as satisfactorily representing the experience of the entire country, and this practice is followed in the present discussion.

[2] All 1966 and 1967 figures shown in this selection are provisional. Based on past experience, however, the provisional rates are likely to be identical, or nearly so, to the final rates.

Where does the United States stand in life expectancy compared with other nations, and what can we anticipate as the reasonable upper limit, or goal, that this country *should* be able to attain in the present state of the arts? Although international comparisons of this type appear to be a hazardous undertaking, in large part because of the substantial obstacles to comparability, a number of other nations clearly have higher life expectancies than we do, and at least in some instances the differences are fairly substantial. Even cursory observation of a recent international compendium of demographic statistics (United Nations, 1967:562–583) reveals, for example, that in Australia, Denmark, The Netherlands, New Zealand, Norway, and Sweden life expectancy may be as much as two to three years higher than the comparable figure in the United States. Countries such as Belgium, France, East Germany, the Federal Republic of Germany, Switzerland, England and Wales, and many others, also exceed us in life expectancy, but not by so wide a margin. Surely this country should at least be able to reach the level of those listed above, if not to exceed them. It is possible that these countries may be nearing an upper limit, however, one that may persist unless some major medical breakthrough occurs. Returning to our own country, future projections of life expectancy and mortality made prior to 1954 now appear to have been much too conservative (Dorn, 1952); on the other hand, those made subsequent to 1954 were clearly too optimistic. Tarver (1959), for example, projected a life expectancy of about 73.5 years in 1970, but it now appears that we may be a long time in reaching this goal.

Life expectancy by definition is equivalent to the average duration of life. But how are the numbers obtained for this measure? Starting with a hypothetical cohort of one hundred thousand persons at birth, the mortality rates by age and by sex of a given population in a given year are applied to this cohort as it ages and moves through its life cycle, reducing it in number until no survivors of the original cohort remain (Spiegelman, 1968:293). The number of years lived by the *average* person in this cohort is termed the given population's life expectancy. Clearly then, the life-expectancy figure thus obtained is simply the inverse of mortality experience; it depends entirely upon age-and-sex-specific mortality rates. Employment of the measure "life expectancy" as an indicator of the mortality experience of a population is useful for comparison purposes both currently and across time. This is especially true because this measure eliminates the disturbing influence on the mortality rate of variation in the age-and-sex composition of populations. It is precisely because of this characteristic that life expectancy was used in the preceding discussion to make comparisons across the long span of history. For discussion of the immediate past and current situations, however, it is perhaps best to shift the locus of the discussion from life expectancy to mortality.

MORTALITY IN THE UNITED STATES, 1900 TO 1967: TRENDS AND DIFFERENTIALS, OVERALL AND BY AGE AND SEX

Paralleling inversely the increase in life expectancy from 1900 to the present, the mortality rate (deaths per 1,000 population) of the United States population has declined sharply during this century. Thus in 1900 the mortality rate was 17.2 per 1,000 population, but by 1954 had dropped to 9.2 per 1,000, the lowest ever recorded in the United States. Since that time it has fluctuated between 9.3 and 9.6, and in 1967 the rate was 9.4, representing a decline of about 45 percent since 1900. These figures understate the extent of the "true" decline, however, primarily because the age composition of the United States population has changed drastically since 1900. This change has generally been in the direction of increasing the high-mortality-risk age segments of the population as a proportion of the total and at the expense of the low. With age composition held constant, that is, using the 1940 age composition of the United States population as a standard, the hypothetical "age-adjusted" death rate in this country declined between 1900 and 1967 from 17.8 to 7.2 per 1,000, a drop of about 60 percent.

Age and Sex   The pattern of mortality rates by age in this country during 1900 was generally similar to that prevailing today (see Table 1). Thus in 1900 the mortality rate was high during infancy, 162.4 per 1,000, in comparison to the rates at other ages; it dropped to the lowest point for the entire life cycle, 3.9, at ages 5–14; but thereafter it rose steadily with increasing age until at ages 85 and over the mortality rate was 260.9 per 1,000 population. In 1966 the comparable rate was only 23.1 per 1,000 during infancy; the low point was 0.4 at ages 5–14; and again the rates rose steadily with increasing age, to 202 per 1,000 at ages 85 and over. Between 1900 and 1966 the largest *relative* declines in the mortality rates took place at the younger ages, especially during infancy and childhood. Although the declines at the older ages are less impressive percentages, they are, nevertheless, very substantial in absolute numbers. For example, at ages 85 and over the mortality rate dropped by about 59 deaths per 1,000 population, that is, from 261 to 202 per 1,000.

TABLE 1

MORTALITY RATES PER 1,000 POPULATION BY AGE AND SEX,
UNITED STATES, 1900 AND 1966

Age (in years)	1900			1966		
	Both sexes	Males	Females	Both sexes	Males	Females
All ages	17.2	17.9	16.5	9.5	11.0	8.1
Under 1	162.4	179.1	145.4	23.1	25.7	20.4
1-4	19.8	20.5	19.1	1.0	1.0	0.9
5-14	3.9	3.8	3.9	0.4	0.5	0.4
15-24	5.9	5.9	5.8	1.2	1.7	0.6
25-34	8.2	8.2	8.2	1.5	2.0	1.0
35-44	10.2	10.7	9.8	3.1	3.9	2.3
45-54	15.0	15.7	14.2	7.3	9.7	5.1
55-64	27.2	28.7	25.8	17.2	23.6	11.2
65-74	56.4	59.3	53.6	38.8	52.0	28.1
75-84	123.3	128.3	118.8	81.6	98.5	69.5
85 and over	260.9	268.8	255.2	202.0	213.6	194.9

Although the mortality rates for both males and females in the United States population declined substantially since 1900, the *rate* of decline was much sharper for females. Thus the mortality rate for females dropped from 16.5 in 1900 to 8.1 in 1966, a decline of 51 percent. For males the corresponding drop was from 17.9 to 11.0, or by 39 percent. The male death rate has been significantly higher than the female death rate in this country throughout the twentieth century, but the relative excess of male over female rates has increased over the years, from 8.5 percent in 1900 to 36 percent in 1966. When these rates are age-adjusted to a standard population, the excess of male over female rates in 1966 is considerably larger, about 70 percent.

In 1900, the relative excess of male over female mortality rates by age was largest during infancy, at 23 percent. At ages 5–14, the mortality rates for males were actually slightly lower than the comparable rates for females; at ages 15–34, rates were about the same for each sex; and in each of the age groups at 35 and over, the mortality rates for males exceeded the comparable rates for females only by a relatively slight amount, that is, by from

5 to 11 percent. By 1966, however, although the mortality rates at each age were lower for each sex than the comparable rates in 1900, the decline in almost all cases was larger for females. As a result, the percentage excess of male mortality rates over female rates was larger in most age groups during 1966 than it had been during 1900. It was largest (an excess of almost 200 percent in 1966), at ages 15–24.

MORTALITY IN THE UNITED STATES, 1900 TO 1967:
TRENDS AND DIFFERENTIALS BY CAUSE OF DEATH

One of the most significant changes in the mortality experience of this country since 1900 has been the decline in the major communicable diseases as leading causes of death[3] and the consequent increase in *relative importance* of the so-called chronic degenerative diseases, that is, diseases occurring mainly later in life and generally thought to be associated in some way with the aging process. Accidents, especially motor vehicle accidents, have also risen in relative importance as causes of death during this period, but mortality during infancy and maternal mortality, that is, mortality associated with childbearing, have declined sharply.

The Communicable Diseases   The leading cause of death[4] in 1900 was the category: "influenza and pneumonia, except pneumonia of the newborn." This major communicable disease category was listed as the cause of 202.2

---

[3]Cause of death in U.S. mortality statistics is currently determined in accordance with World Heath Organization Regulations, which specify that member nations classify causes of death according to the International Statistical Classification of Diseases, Injuries and Causes of Death, 1955. Besides specifying the classification, World Health Organization Regulations outline the form of medical certification and the coding procedures to be used. In general, when more than one cause of death is reported, the cause designated by the certifying physician as the underlying cause of death is the cause tabulated (cf. World Health Organization, 1957).

[4]The method of ranking causes of death used here follows the procedure recommended by *Public Health Conference on Records and Statistics* at its 1951 meeting. Only those causes specified in the "List of 60 Selected Causes of Death" were included in the ranking, and the following categories specified in that list were omitted: the two group titles, "major cardiovascular-renal diseases" and "diseases of the cardiovascular system"; the single title, "symptoms, senility, and ill-defined conditions"; the residual titles, "other infective and parasitic diseases," "other bronchopulmonic diseases," "other diseases of the circulatory system," and "all other diseases"; and all subtitles represented within a broader title. Causes of death are ranked on the basis of rates unadjusted for age or to a specific Revision of the International List of Diseases and Causes of Death, and the above discussion is based on these "crude" rates. But the *titles* used, and the 1966 rates, are those of the Seventh Revision.

TABLE 2

THE TEN LEADING CAUSES OF DEATH, BY RANK,
UNITED STATES, 1900 AND 1966

1900

Rank	Cause of death	Deaths per 100,000 population	Percent of all deaths
	All causes	1,719.1	100.0
1	Influenza and pneumonia	202.2	11.8
2	Tuberculosis (all forms)	194.4	11.3
3	Gastritis, duodenitis, enteritis, etc.	142.7	8.3
4	Diseases of the heart	137.4	8.0
5	Vascular lesions affecting the central nervous system	106.9	6.2
6	Chronic nephritis	81.0	4.7
7	All accidents	72.3	4.2
8	Malignant neoplasms (cancer)	64.0	3.7
9	Certain diseases of early infancy	62.6	3.6
10	Diphtheria	40.3	2.3

1966

Rank	Cause of death	Deaths per 100,000 population	Percent of all deaths
	All causes	954.2	100.0
1	Diseases of the heart	375.1	39.3
2	Malignant neoplasms (cancer)	154.8	16.2
3	Vascular lesions affecting the central nervous system	104.6	11.0
4	All accidents	57.3	6.0
5	Influenza and pneumonia	32.8	3.4
6	Certain diseases of early infancy	26.1	2.7
7	General arteriosclerosis	19.5	2.0
8	Diabetes mellitus	18.1	1.9
9	Cirrhosis of the liver	13.5	1.4
10	Suicide	10.3	1.1

deaths per 100,000 population in 1900 (see Table 2), and it accounted for 11.8 percent of all deaths in that year. By 1966, however, the mortality rate for this category was down to 32.8, it ranked fifth among the leading causes of death, and it now accounted for only 3.4 percent of all deaths during the year.

Tuberculosis (all forms) and the gastritis grouping[5] second and third leading causes of death, respectively, in 1900, were both reduced so significantly and to such low rates during the course of this century that neither category was listed among the ten leading causes of death in 1966. Tuberculosis had caused 194.4 deaths per 100,000 in 1900, or 11.3 percent of all deaths, while the gastritis grouping, with 142.7 deaths per 100,000, had accounted for 8.3 percent of the total. By 1966 the comparable rates for these two categories were 3.9 and 3.3, respectively, with each accounting for substantially less than one-half of 1 percent of all deaths in that year. The percentage declines for each from 1900 to 1966 were by 98 percent.

Diphtheria had been listed as tenth leading cause of death in 1900, with 40.3 deaths per 100,000 population. In 1966 this condition accounted for only forty deaths all told in this country, that is, considering the entire United States population as at risk, so that the death rate was about one death per five million persons. Other major communicable diseases with impressive declines in mortality were some of the other communicable diseases of childhood, such as whooping cough, measles, scarlet fever, and streptococcal sore throat, and syphilis, typhoid and paratyphoid fevers, rheumatic fever, and typhus.

Hillery *et al.* (1968), comparing recent mortality data from forty-one countries, have shown that the communicable diseases ("infectious diseases" in their terminology) as causes of death decline significantly as a proportion of all deaths in each country as these countries move "up" in the demographic transition, that is, as their birth and death rates decline, and as they concomitantly become at least presumably more "advanced" technologically and socially. Thus, in the "transitional" countries (low death rates but high birth rates), communicable diseases account for about one-third of all deaths on the average, while in the demographically "mature" countries (both death rates and birth rates low), the comparable proportion is about one in twelve of all deaths. This finding is generally in conformity with past experience in this country and elsewhere.

The Degenerative Diseases   "Diseases of the heart" ranked fourth among the leading causes of death in this country during 1900; this category caused 137.4 deaths per 100,000 and accounted for 8.0 percent of all deaths. By

---

[5]The full title of this cause-of-death grouping, in the nomenclature of the Seventh Revision of the International List of Diseases and Causes of Death, is: gastritis, duodenitis, enteritis, and colitis, except diarrhea of the newborn.

1966, however, it had risen so far in importance that it had become the leading cause of death, far outranking all others. Its mortality rate had risen to 375.1 deaths per 100,000 population, and it accounted for nearly 40 percent of all deaths in that year. Between 1900 and 1966 the unadjusted death rate from this disease rose by 173 percent; the rise was much less if the age-adjusted rates for these two years are compared, but even this rise was very substantial.

The pattern of increase for malignant neoplasms (cancer) as a cause of death was generally quite similar. This disease ranked eighth among the leading causes of death in 1900. It accounted for 64 deaths per 100,000 population and less than 4 percent of all deaths. By 1966, however, its rank among the leading causes had risen to second, its rate per 100,000 to 154.8, and its proportion of the total of all deaths exceeded 16 percent. Vascular lesions of the central nervous system, although remaining relatively stable in number of deaths per 100,000 (106.9 in 1900 and 104.6 in 1966), nevertheless rose in rank (fifth to third) and as a proportion of all deaths (6 to 11 percent).

How can we account for the increases, in both absolute and relative terms, in these "degenerative" diseases as causes of death? As the classification implies, these are diseases occurring later in life and closely associated with the aging process. Whereas formerly people died on the average much earlier in life, victims primarily of the communicable diseases, they survive today to a much later age, only to succumb in due time to the degenerative conditions. Hillery and his associates (1968) in their interesting study have generalized this trend also. Thus in their demographically transitional countries (low death rates but high birth rates) the degenerative diseases account for less than one-third of all deaths, whereas in their demographically mature countries (both death rates and birth rates low) these diseases account for just under two-thirds of the total. The net overall gain has clearly been an extension of life by many years.

MORTALITY AND SOCIOECONOMIC STATUS

There appears to be a good deal of confusion in this country today, and perhaps especially among social scientists, demographers, and health statisticians, as to the precise nature of the relationship between mortality and socioeconomic status. This confusion has existed, and perhaps will continue to exist for some time, despite the fact that quite a few studies in the past, and a number of ongoing studies, have attempted to clarify the relationship. Part of this confusion may be occasioned by what is perhaps the changing nature of that relationship, a change which in turn may have been brought about by the tremendous improvements in medical technology and therapies during the past century and by the increasing general affluence of the American population. But part of it results also from the lack of a generally accepted method for the construction of an overall index of socioeconomic status (Lerner, 1968).

In turn, the failure of social scientists to develop a generally accepted method for the construction of an overall index reflects their lack of general agreement on the number or composition of social classes or social strata in the United States, especially when this entire culturally diverse country is considered as the unit of analysis. Different numbers of classes or strata have been identified, depending on definitions and operational purposes, but none of these is a real entity. Various measures of socioeconomic status have been related to mortality, and the results of one very large study along these lines are now beginning to appear (Kitagawa, 1968). Nevertheless, the overall pattern continues to remain quite unclear at this writing.

For present purposes—to relate socioeconomic status to mortality—it appears that the most meaningful division of the United States population from a conceptual, rather than an operational, standpoint is into three socioeconomic strata. These strata are set apart from one another, in the most general terms, by a distinctive and unique life style, even though the boundaries between these strata are not sharp, and there may be a considerable movement of individuals and families among them. The life styles of these strata, in turn, are dependent upon or associated with income, wealth, occupation and occupational prestige, dwelling, ethnic origin, educational attainment, and many other factors, all of which, in some as yet unspecified way, add up to the total. The life styles, in turn, are directly relevant to the health level, and more specifically the mortality experience of each stratum. The structural factors in each of the three major life styles through which the relationship to mortality operates include at least these four: the level of living (food, housing, transportation, or other factors); degree of access to medical care within the private medical care system; occupation of the family head (sedentary or involving physical activity); and the nature of the social milieu for that stratum (that is, its degree of economic or social security).

The highest stratum consists of those who are usually designated as the middle-and upper-class white-collar business executives at all levels and professionals, and all those who are above this category. It even includes the highest echelons of skilled blue-collar workers (tool-and-die makers), foremen, supervisors, or the like. Although the range of variation *within* this stratum is great, the group as a whole shares the essential elements of a "middle-class" way of life, that is, residence in "better" neighborhoods and suburbs, general affluence, and so on.

The second stratum consists of this country's blue-collar workingclass—mainly the semiskilled and unskilled workers in the mass-production and service industries, but also small farmers and possibly even farm laborers, and lower level white-collar workers. These people are also relatively affluent, but not to the same extent as the middle class. Again, although the range of variation *within* this stratum is great, they also share a unique style of life distinctively different from that of the higher stratum. This group will subsequently be designated in the present discussion as the working class.

The lowest of the three strata includes those who are generally designated as the poverty population. By definition, these people generally do not share in the affluence characteristic of this country. It consists of the poor in large-city ghettos and the rural poor (residents of Appalachia or the Deep South, as well as others); the Negro, Puerto Rican, Mexican, and French-Canadian populations, and the other relatively poor ethnic minorities in this country; Indians on reservations; the aged; migratory laborers; and the dependent poor.

Although, as stated above, this mode of classification of socioeconomic status appears to be the most meaningful from a conceptual standpoint in terms of relating it to mortality, it clearly lacks merit from the operational point of view. This is because there would appear to be no ready way of segregating these groups from one another in the available national statistical data, relating either to population data or health statistics, and especially to study their respective mortality experiences. Nevertheless, here and there some attempts have been made, and some studies, mostly local and regional in character and particularly of the poverty population, have been carried out (cf. Chicago Board of Health, 1965; and Lerner, 1968). What follows, therefore, is to be understood as more of an overall gross impression and prediction, rather than anything else, and one based on a general familiarity with the literature of what would be found if the data were available in the form required by the present framework.

The poverty populations generally are likely to have the highest death rates of the three strata on an overall basis, but especially from the communicable diseases. This has been true historically between rich and poor nations in the modern era and still represents the situation in the world today at various levels of wealth and technological advancement (Pond, 1961; Anderson and Rosen, 1960). Within this country, a considerable amount of evidence exists to show that mortality rates among the poverty population are likely to be highest during infancy, childhood, and the younger adult ages. The communicable diseases of childhood, gastrointestinal diseases, and influenza and pneumonia are still a relatively serious health problem among this population, even where public health facilities and services are relatively adequate, as, for example, in the slums of large cities in this country today. What this population lacks most, perhaps, is adequate access to personal health services within the private medical care system. Although these services are to some degree available under other auspices (Strauss, 1967), they may be relatively ineffective and not oriented to the life style of their recipients, while the cultural impediments to their use appear to be substantial.

The blue-collar working class appears to have the best overall mortality record . . . At mid-life . . . they appear to suffer from relatively few of the disabilities associated with middle-class affluence.

In contrast, the white-collar middle class does enjoy relatively adequate access to personal health services under the private medical care system, and their mortality rates during infancy, childhood, and even young adulthood are substantially lower than that of the poverty populations. This is especially true for mortality from the communicable diseases, but appears to extend almost to the entire spectrum of causes of death. The higher levels of living enjoyed by this stratum in general buttress its advantage during the younger years. During mid-life and especially during the later years, however, its mortality rates appear to become substantially higher than those of the rest of the population, primarily for the "degenerative" diseases, especially heart disease, cancer, and stroke.

One possible hypothesis that has been offered in explanation of this phenomenon merits comment here. It may be that, because of improved survival by members of this stratum at the younger ages, many persons are carried into mid-life with a lower "general resistance" factor than that which characterizes persons in the poverty stratum, and that these individuals are perhaps therefore more vulnerable to the diseases and hazards most prevalent at mid-life and beyond. At the moment, at least, there seems to be no possible way of testing this hypothesis.

Another hypothesis is that this excess mortality at mid-life is a concomitant of the general affluence characterizing the life styles of the middle class and of their sedentary occupations (executive and white-collar). Both of these, in turn, may result in obesity, excessive strains and tensions, excessive cigarette smoking, and perhaps ultimately premature death. Men aged 45–64 (mid-life), especially white men, appear to be particularly vulnerable to coronary artery disease and respiratory cancer. Middle-class women, on the other hand, appear to be less affected by these affluence-related forms of ill health than middle-class men, perhaps because of innate resistance, social pressures to avoid obesity, cigarette smoking without inhalation, and generally less stressful lives, or perhaps some combination of these factors. In any case, women in this stratum appear to have the best of all possible worlds, that is, they have none of the health disabilities associated with the sedentary occupations characteristic of their spouses while at the same time enjoying adequate medical care.

The blue-collar working class appears to have the best overall mortality record. This group appears to have relatively low mortality during the younger ages and from the communicable diseases, especially because they do have access to good medical care in the private medical care system. At mid-life, moreover, they appear to suffer from relatively few of the disabilities associated with middle-class affluence.

WHERE DEATH OCCURS

Where people die—in a hospital or other institution, at home, or in a public place—has been a relatively neglected aspect of mortality statistics in this country during the past few years. Although this information is contained on each death certificate and relatively little additional effort or expense would be required to code and tabulate it, this has not been done, perhaps because it has not been at all clear that the returns would be commensurate to the additional expense. As a result, the last national tabulation of these data based on the regular vital statistics data-collection system relates to

1958, and these data were far from complete; many of the cross-tabulations that could have been made were not, in fact, carried out. Some of the states and cities here and there have published tabulations since that time, however.

Recently, some new interest has been expressed in this question among public health circles, possibly stimulated by the coming into being of Regional Medical Programs throughout the country. These in turn were set up under the Heart Disease, Cancer, and Stroke Amendments of 1965 (P.L. 89–239), which provided for the establishment of regional cooperative arrangements for improvement of the quality of medical care through research and training, including continuing education, among medical schools, research institutions, and hospitals, and in related demonstrations of patient care. The new legislation was aimed generally at improving the health, manpower, and facilities available, but one specific purpose was to make new medical knowledge available, as rapidly as possible, for the treatment of patients (Yordy and Fullarton, 1965). The assumption in public health circles was that the place of occurrence of some deaths, and the circumstances, may have been related to an inability to obtain proper medical care either at the moment of death or immediately preceding it, as in cases of sudden death, or at some point during the illness or condition leading to death in other cases. The extent to which this assumption is true is, of course, difficult to test given the present paucity of relevant data.

In 1958, according to the most recent *national* data available (see Table 3), 60.9 percent of all deaths in this country occurred in institutions, that is, in hospitals, convalescent and nursing homes, and in hospital departments of institutions or in other domiciliary institutions. This figure represented a considerable rise over the comparable 49.5 percent recorded in 1949, the most recent preceding year for which a national tabulation was made. On the basis of these data it appeared that the proportion was rising by an average of better than 1 percent annually.

National data to test whether the trend continued beyond that year are unavailable, but state and local data appear to indicate that this, in fact, may have been the case. In New York City, for example, the proportion of deaths occurring in institutions rose steadily, with only one very slight fluctuation, from 65.9 percent in 1955 to 73.1 percent in 1967 (see Table 4). These same data indicate that the proportion of deaths occurring at home dropped commensurately during these years, from 31.4 percent to 24.2 percent. The proportion of deaths occurring elsewhere, primarily in public

TABLE 3

NUMBER AND PERCENT OF DEATHS OCCURRING IN INSTITUTIONS BY TYPE OF
SERVICE OF INSTITUTION, UNITED STATES, 1949 AND 1958

	1958		1949	
	Number	Percent	Number	Percent
Total deaths	1,647,886	100.0	1,443,607	100.0
Not in institution	644,548	39.1	728,797	50.5
In institution	1,003,338	60.9	714,810	49.5
Type of service of institution				
General hospital	784,360	47.6	569,867	39.5
Maternity hospital	1,862	0.1	2,249	0.2
Tuberculosis hospital	9,097	0.6	13,627	0.9
Chronic disease, convalescent and other special hospitals	24,180	1.5	12,402	0.9
Nervous and mental hospitals	57,675	3.5	45,637	3.2
Convalescent and nursing homes, homes for the aged, etc.	98,444	6.0	22,783	1.6
Hospital department of institutions, and other domiciliary institutions	3,646	0.2	41,841	2.9
Type of service not specified	24,074	1.5	6,404	0.4

places, remained relatively constant. Data from the Maryland State Department of Health also indicate a substantial upward progression in the proportion of all deaths occurring in institutions, from 64.4 percent in 1957 to 71.8 percent in 1966 (Maryland State Department of Health, 1967).

Most of the deaths occurring in "institutions," as the data of Table 3 indicate, occurred in hospitals, the vast majority of which were general hospitals. Nervous and mental hospitals during each of the two years to which the table relates, however, accounted for somewhat more than 3 percent of all deaths. The proportion occurring in convalescent and nursing homes, homes for the aged, and similar establishments increased substantially between 1949 and 1958, from 1.6 percent to 6.0 percent.[6]

---

[6]However, there is some lack of comparability between these two figures, and this increase, although undoubtedly substantial, may not be quite as large as these figures indicate.

TABLE 4

NUMBER AND PERCENT OF DEATHS BY PLACE OF DEATH, NEW YORK CITY, 1955-1967

	Number of deaths				Percentage			
	Total	In Insti-tution	At Home	Other	Total	In Insti-tution	At Home	Other
1955	81,612	53,746	25,598	2,268	100.0	65.9	31.4	2.8
1956	81,118	54,716	24,193	2,209	100.0	67.5	29.8	2.7
1957	84,141	57,141	24,609	2,391	100.0	67.9	29.2	2.8
1958	84,586	57,946	24,230	2,410	100.0	68.5	28.6	2.8
1959	85,352	58,859	24,127	2,366	100.0	69.0	28.3	2.8
1960	86,252	59,413	24,341	2,498	100.0	68.9	28.2	2.9
1961	86,855	60,061	24,524	2,270	100.0	69.2	28.2	2.6
1962	87,089	60,409	24,315	2,365	100.0	69.4	27.9	2.7
1963	88,621	61,588	24,677	2,356	100.0	69.5	27.8	2.7
1964	88,026	62,391	23,602	2,033	100.0	70.9	26.8	2.3
1965	87,395	62,308	22,879	2,208	100.0	71.3	26.2	2.5
1966	88,418	63,599	22,576	2,243	100.0	71.9	25.5	2.5
1967	87,610	64,083	21,222	2,305	100.0	73.1	24.2	2.6

Source of basic data: Personal communication from Mr. Louis Weiner, New York City Department of Health.

Table 5 shows the percent of deaths, by color, that occurred in institutions in 1949 and 1958, for the entire country and for each geographic division. In both years the proportion of deaths occurring in institutions was substantially lower for the nonwhite population than for the white when the country as a whole is considered as the unit. However, for the New England, Middle Atlantic, and East North Central states in both years and the West North Central states in 1949 the reverse pattern was true, that is, the proportion of deaths occurring in institutions was higher for the nonwhite population than for the white. In general, the proportions in both years for the East South Central, West South Central, and South Atlantic states, and especially for their nonwhite populations, were very low in comparison to the rest of the country. In Mississippi, even as late as 1958, only 31.0 percent of the nonwhite deaths occurred in institutions. (These data are not shown in Table 5.)

By cause of death, as Table 6 indicates, the most important categories in which the proportion of deaths occurring in institutions was relatively

TABLE 5

PERCENT OF DEATHS OCCURRING IN INSTITUTIONS BY COLOR AND
GEOGRAPHIC DIVISION, UNITED STATES, 1949 AND 1958

Geographic division	1958			1949		
	Total	White	Nonwhite	Total	White	Nonwhite
United States	60.9	61.9	53.2	49.5	50.4	43.2
New England	64.2	64.0	72.4	52.2	52.0	67.1
Middle Atlantic	62.8	62.3	68.9	53.2	52.2	69.0
East North Central	63.6	63.2	67.9	51.5	50.9	59.7
West North Central	63.8	63.9	61.5	50.7	50.6	54.4
South Atlantic	55.8	58.6	48.4	42.5	45.3	36.3
East South Central	47.6	51.8	37.3	34.6	37.8	27.6
West South Central	54.9	57.7	44.2	42.8	45.3	34.3
Mountain	63.5	63.4	64.1	55.2	54.9	61.0
Pacific	66.5	66.3	68.8	58.5	58.1	65.5

TABLE 6

TOTAL DEATHS AND PERCENT OCCURRING IN INSTITUTIONS BY CAUSE,
FOR SELECTED CAUSES OF DEATH, UNITED STATES, 1958

Cause of death	Total deaths, number	Percent in institutions
Tuberculosis, all forms	12,361	80.0
Syphilis and its sequelae	3,469	71.7
Dysentery, all forms	407	62.4
Scarlet fever and streptococcal sore throat	139	57.6
Whooping cough	177	60.5
Meningococcal infections	746	87.9
Acute poliomyelitis	255	91.8
Measles	552	63.8
Malignant neoplasms, including neoplasms of lymphatic and hematopoietic tissues	254,426	67.7
Benign neoplasms	4,961	82.5
Asthma	5,035	55.4
Diabetes mellitus	27,501	68.6
Anemias	3,195	72.4
Meningitis, except meningococcal and tuberculous	2,247	91.8
Vascular lesions affecting central nervous system	190,758	65.8
Diseases of heart	637,246	50.4
Arteriosclerotic heart disease, including coronary disease	461,373	48.5

TABLE 6 (*continued*)

Cause of death	Total deaths, number	Percent in institutions
Other hypertensive disease	13,798	68.5
General arteriosclerosis	34,483	61.8
Other diseases of circulatory system	17,204	79.5
Chronic and unspecified nephritis, etc.	13,827	67.6
Influenza and pneumonia	57,439	68.6
Influenza	4,442	43.1
Pneumonia, except pneumonia of newborn	52,997	70.7
Bronchitis	3,973	61.7
Ulcer of stomach and duodenum	10,801	88.2
Appendicitis	1,845	94.5
Hernia and intestinal obstruction	8,853	90.5
Gastritis, duodenitis, enteritis, etc.	7,838	78.7
Cirrhosis of liver	18,638	79.3
Cholelithiasis, cholecystitis, and cholangitis	4,720	90.0
Acute nephritis, and nephritis with edema, etc.	2,203	76.0
Infections of kidney	6,889	85.5
Hyperplasia of prostate	4,627	81.1
Deliveries and complications of pregnancy, childbirth, and the puerperium	1,581	85.5
Congenital malformations	21,411	86.5
Certain diseases of early infancy	68,960	94.5
Symptoms, senility, and ill-defined conditions	19,729	25.2
Accidents	90,604	47.6
Motor-vehicle accidents	36,981	44.0
Other accidents	53,623	50.0
Suicide	18,519	18.5
Homicide	7,815	34.1

small were the external causes of death (accidents, suicide, and homicide), diseases of the heart, influenza, and the catchall category "symptoms, senility, and ill-defined conditions." Less than one-half of all deaths following accidents occurred in the hospital, and the comparable figure was only 44 percent for motor vehicle deaths. Only about one-half of all deaths from diseases of the heart occurred in an institution, and somewhat less than that figure for arteriosclerotic heart disease, including coronary disease. In the case of each of these conditions, as well as for suicide and homicide, it seems likely that the short time-interval between onset of the condition and death is probably a major reason for the relatively small proportions occurring in hospitals. Finally, only about one-fourth of all deaths for which a cause could not clearly be delineated (deaths attributed to symptoms, senility, and ill-defined conditions) occurred in hospitals.

ⅎⅎⅎ

It would appear . . . that the implicit goal of the health establishment in this country . . . has been far from realized.

ⅎⅎ

Considering the almost 645,000 deaths that occurred outside an institution in 1958, almost one-half (49 percent) were accounted for by diseases of the heart (see Table 7). (Within this category, arteriosclerotic heart disease, including coronary disease, accounted for about 37 percent of the total.) The next three most important causes of death in accounting for all deaths outside of institutions were malignant neoplasms, 13.1 percent; vascular lesions, 10.1 percent; and accidents, 7.4 percent. These first four categories combined accounted for about 80 percent of all deaths occurring outside institutions, but other causes of death—for example, influenza and pneumonia, suicide, general arteriosclerosis, and so on—were also important in the total.

CONCLUSIONS AND IMPLICATIONS

It would appear, at least from the point of view and focus of the preceding discussion, that the implicit goal of the health establishment in this country to "assure for everyone the highest degree of health attainable in the present state of the arts" has been far from realized. For example, with regard to mortality and its derivative, life expectancy, other nations have clearly outdistanced us, and by a substantial margin. It is true that most of these countries are smaller and more homogeneous, and the environmental hazards plaguing them may not be operative in the same manner and to the same degree as they are among us. Nevertheless, we do appear to have fallen short of what has been achieved elsewhere, and it is therefore appropriate to raise questions about the reasons for this apparent failure.

TABLE 7

DEATHS OCCURRING OUTSIDE INSTITUTIONS BY CAUSE, FOR
SELECTED CAUSES OF DEATH, UNITED STATES, 1958

Cause of death	Number	Percent
All Causes	644,548	100.0
1. Diseases of the heart	316,074	49.0
Arteriosclerotic heart disease, including coronary disease	237,607	36.9
2. Malignant neoplasms, including neoplasms of the lymphatic and hematopoietic tissues	84,724	13.1
3. Vascular lesions affecting the central nervous system	65,239	10.1
4. Accidents, all forms	47,476	7.4
Motor-vehicle accidents	20,709	3.2
Other	26,767	4.2
5. Influenza and pneumonia	18,036	2.8
Pneumonia	15,528	2.4
Influenza	2,508	0.4
6. Suicide	15,093	2.3
7. General arteriosclerosis	13,173	2.0
8. Diabetes mellitus	8,635	1.3
9. Homicide	5,150	0.7

Three broad lines of inquiry have been suggested as possible approaches in this [discussion], and a fourth influencing and possibly underlying the others will be mentioned. When one considers the entire spectrum of causes of death and their "places of occurrence," it is not unreasonable to assume *as a working hypothesis* that many deaths are occurring from causes—disease conditions—that are amenable, at least under optimum conditions in the present state of the arts, to medical management and control. Of course, the sex and age of the patient, the general state of health and degree of "resistance" of the organism, and many other factors should be considered in the evaluation of each case before any death is characterized as needless or preventable. Furthermore, it may be very difficult to refrain from setting up, as working standards, ideal conditions that are unattainable anywhere, given the realities and the imperatives of social organization, the relatively low priority of health in the hierarchy of human values and "needs," the "mass" nature of society, and the vagaries and irrational elements in what is colloquially described as "human nature." Nevertheless, the social and economic differentials in mortality discussed in this [selection] would appear to argue that there is much room for improvement, that the low mortality rates now attained by some could be attained, theoretically at least, by all.

If this is true, and if our goal is indeed to assure the highest degree of health attainable *for everyone,* then we must ask ourselves whether the social organization for the provision of health services to the population in some degree shares responsibility for the discrepancy between goal and reality. If responsible inquiry is directed toward this problem, the unknowns in this vital area of public policy may be reduced, and we may begin to re-examine the place of health in our presently implicit hierarchy of values as opposed, for example, to education, other forms of welfare, space exploration, urban crowding, rural poverty, national security, and the myriad national concerns to which we allocate community resources. We may even be able to move toward calm and rational discussion of some alternative forms of social organization of the health care system, including their economic and perhaps social costs, hopefully with the result that we ultimately arrive at intelligent decisions.

REFERENCES

Anderson, Odin W., and George Rosen.
  1960   An examination of the concept of preventive medicine. *Health Information Foundation, Research Series No. 12.* New York: Health Information Foundation.

Chicago Board of Health; Planning Staff of the Health Planning Project.
  1965   *A Report on Health and Medical Care in Poverty Areas of Chicago and Proposals for Improvement.*

Dorn, Harold F.
  1952   Prospects of further decline in mortality rates. *Human Biology* 24, 4(December): 235–261.

Dublin, Louis I., in collaboration with Mortimer Spiegelman.
  1951   *The Facts of Life—From Birth to Death.* New York: Macmillan.

Hillery, George A., Jr., *et al.*
  1963   Causes of death in the demographic transition. Paper presented at the Annual Meeting of the Population Association of America, Boston, Mass.

Kitagawa, Evelyn M.
  1968   Race differentials in mortality in the United States, 1960 (corrected and uncorrected). Paper presented at the Annual Meeting of the Population Association of America, Boston, Mass., April.

Lerner, Monroe.
    1968   The level of physical health of the poverty population: a conceptual reappraisal of structural factors. Paper presented at Conference on New Dimensions in Health Measurements, sponsored by Washington Statistical Society and American Marketing Association, Washington, D.C., January 25.

Lerner, Monroe, and Odin W. Anderson.
    1963   *Health Progress in the United States: 1900–1960.* Chicago: University of Chicago Press.

Maryland State Department of Health, Division of Biostatistics.
    1967   *Annual Vital Statistics Report: Maryland, 1966.* Also, same annual reports for earlier years to 1957. Baltimore.

Pond, M. Allen.
    1961   Interrelationship of poverty and disease. *Public Health Reports* 76 (November): 967–974.

Spiegelman, Mortimer.
    1968   Life tables. Pp. 292–299 in *International Encyclopedia of the Social Sciences.* New York: Free Press.

Strauss, Anselm L.
    1967   Medical ghettos: medical care must be reorganized to accept the life-styles of the poor. *Trans-action* 4(May):7–15 and 62.

Tarver, James D.
    1959   Projections of mortality in the United States to 1970. *The Milbank Memorial Fund Quarterly* 37, 2(April): 132–143.

United Nations.
    1967   *Demographic Yearbook, 1966.* New York.

World Health Organization.
    1957   *Manual of the International Statistical Classification of Diseases, Injuries, and Causes of Death: Based on the Recommendations of the Seventh Revision Conference, 1955.* Vol. I. Geneva, Switzerland.

Yordy, K. D., and J. E. Fullarton.
    1965   The heart disease, cancer, and stroke amendments of 1965 (P.L. 89–239). Reprint from *Health, Education and Welfare Indicators,* November.

The Mortality Revolution

Calvin Goldscheider
Calvin Goldscheider is a Professor of Sociology at the
Hebrew University in Jerusalem. In this selection, which is
taken from his book on sociological demography entitled
Population, Modernization, and Social Structure, he invites
our attention to the "mortality revolution" that has taken
place from the period just preceding the Industrial
Revolution to the present and discusses the effects that this
mortality revolution has had on the structure of our society.

From Calvin Goldscheider, *Population, Modernization, and
Social Structure,* pp. 102-117, 124-132. Copyright © 1971 by
Little, Brown and Company (Inc.). Reprinted by permission.

Historically, mortality levels have been reduced so
radically that high life expectancy, low infant mortality, and the control of
the lethal consequences of infectious diseases and epidemics are conspicuous demographic features of modern societies. Comparatively, not all
countries have participated equally or at the same pace in the "mortality
revolution," and international variations in the extent of mortality control
persist. Examining historical and competitive mortality patterns allows for
the isolation and identification of the causative mechanisms involved in
the transformation from high and uncontrolled mortality to low and controlled mortality; it also permits linking the mortality revolution to other
long-run social processes. Moreover, a revolution in the extent and character
of a vital and intimate event such as death must have major repercussions
not only for those institutions of human society that have developed to cope
specifically and directly with mortality, but also for those features of social
organization that are shaped by, and depend indirectly on, the length of
human life.

The two major issues in analyzing historical and comparative changes in
mortality are (1) the relationship between modernization and mortality,
and (2) the consequences of the mortality revolution for the nature of human
society. These two issues in turn focus on several general questions. First,
what is the substantive nature of the mortality revolution, and what are the
causal connections between mortality reductions and social revolutions

associated with agriculture, industry, urbanization, and technology? More specifically, to what extent are low death rates restricted to "modern" societies; that is, how new or recent is this societal characteristic? If mortality was high in premodern societies, what social forces may be linked systematically and empirically to its reduction? Is low mortality a function of "modernity" or "contemporarity"; that is, does low mortality characterize only modern, industrialized nations of the contemporary world or is it a feature of most or all societies in the post–World War II era? Have imported, low-cost, mass medical and public health projects in underdeveloped countries reduced or eliminated mortality discrepancies between the developed and developing areas of the world? To what degree are mortality changes integral to the modernization of Western societies over time and to levels of socioeconomic development in the contemporary world? We must go beyond any mechanical correlation to specify those elements that connect modernization and mortality.

Second, we must determine the impact and implications of the mortality revolution. Whether or not the reduction of mortality levels is a function of modernization in sociohistorical and socioeconomic contexts, the question remains, What relevance do differing levels of mortality have for the nature of human society? Irrespective of the relative newness or pervasiveness of low death rates, "controlled" mortality is a unique feature of modern society. What are the implications of this uniqueness for economic, political, cultural, and social institutions? How do sociocultural responses to death vary under conditions of high and low mortality? In what ways are ideologies and explanations of death sensitive to the changing quantity and distribution of deaths within society? If mortality reduction is integral to modernization processes, how do declines in mortality facilitate social and economic development and under what conditions is controlled mortality an impediment to modernization?

MODERNIZATION AND MORTALITY REDUCTION

To specify the features of modernization that are linked systematically to mortality changes, some general empirical evidence on historical patterns of mortality processes and comparative contemporary levels of mortality is needed. Thus, the first task in analyzing the relationship between modernization and mortality reduction is to raise and solve the basic *empirical* issues. First, what were the patterns of mortality before the onset of the Industrial

Revolution?[1] If we are to relate changes in mortality to industrialization specifically, or to modernization generally, some overall indication of mortality levels and patterns in preindustrial and premodern societies is necessary. Although this question seems straightforward, it specifies neither how far back into the vast expanse of the preindustrial era we need to venture nor in what areas of the world we should look.

As a corollary, the logical follow-up question is: How did mortality change during industrialization and modernization? Again, this question is not as specific as it might seem. Industrialization is not a uniform process, confined to one time period with discrete starting and ending points. Thus, we should not be surprised if the pace of mortality changes varied between and within countries and related differently to various stages of industrial development. Indeed, we should be skeptical if the evidence showed uniform changes.

These first two general questions focus primarily on the sociohistorical context of "Western" industrialized nations—Europe and North America. A third empirical question considers the relationship between socioeconomic development and mortality levels in the contemporary post-World War II era. Are there general uniformities in mortality levels among contemporary nations, irrespective of their pattern of socioeconomic development or their pace of industrialization? Obviously, to test the hypothesis of mortality "convergence" among contemporary nations or examine the diffusion of mortality control, we need to specify the different types of comparative populations: we may compare nineteenth-century and post-World War II mortality patterns and uncover certain convergences, although different results may be obtained by comparing pre- and post-World War II mortality rates.

Preindustrial Mortality

Mortality conditions before the Industrial Revolution were terrible. But were they high uniformly throughout this long period of human history, in all areas and for all populations? Indeed, how "high" were mortality levels and how accurate are the records from which the evidence is derived? If we were to require a rigorous, scientific, quantitative answer to these questions,

---

[1]In this context, the Industrial Revolution is a shorthand expression for the whole process of industrial, agricultural, and urbanization changes. Although distinct analytically, modernization and industrialization will be used synonymously in this [discussion].

we should have to abandon the search and indicate simply that such an objective is impossible, because the *systematic* collection of detailed information—about mortality as well as other social data—is as unique to modern society as is low mortality. Thus, any attempt to document the pattern of mortality in the preindustrial world must rely on fragmentary evidence for local areas, of sometimes unknown completeness, of uneven quality and detail, using methodologies of estimation that are more in line with the canons of the historian-detective than the scientist-demographer. The scientist will surely err (although to an unknown degree) if in reconstructing mortality patterns in the preindustrial world, the data of historians and anthropologists are presented uncritically. It seems equally unwise to apply modern sophisticated measurement techniques to such information. Evidence on preindustrial mortality presented in tabular form often conveys the impression of exactitude and definitiveness, which may be unjustifiable methodologically.

If data on mortality patterns in fifteenth- or sixteenth-century Europe are scarce and if available data are of uneven, and often unknown, quality, *a fortiori* mortality records of the ancient and early medieval world are limited. Nor does it appear necessary for us to travel back into ancient history. Except for the sheer joy of such intellectual exercises, such an undertaking has little scientific or analytic merit. Fifteenth- through eighteenth-century evidence may in large part be generalized to the more distant past. Attempts at the demographic reconstruction of primitive populations, of prehistoric man, and of the Egyptian, Greek, and Roman populations, may be important for historians or anthropologists or archaeologists but are of little direct value to social scientists interested in analytic demography. For our purposes, the evidence on preindustrial populations will be selected from materials of more recent historical periods, but there is no reason to suspect that these findings cannot be extended to cover the longer history of man before the modern era.

Thus, in our inquiry into mortality conditions of the preindustrial world, we essentially require a "feeling" for the situation, a general portrait pieced together from various sources to form a coherent pattern. The available evidence, particularly of the painstaking research on family reconstruction carried out by historian-demographers in France and England in the 1960s, points to the following general arguments, which, without too much error, may be taken as the overall preindustrial mortality pattern. Preindustrial mortality—that is, mortality throughout the world before about the eighteenth century—was in large part *uncontrolled directly.* By this we mean that *mortality levels were high but not uniformly high; the extent of mortality fluctuation over time within the preindustrial world depended on social, economic, political, and environmental conditions in local areas that affected the response of populations to climatic conditions, food shortages, famines, diseases, epidemics, and sociopolitical disturbances: these same societal forces resulted as well in mortality variation between different areas, and for different subpopulations within areas, at any point in time.* Premodern patterns of mortality were therefore by-products of the general social, economic, political, and cultural conditions in preindustrial societies. Although mortality was "uncontrolled," these general social and cultural conditions were not; hence, mortality patterns were not haphazard. After reviewing evidence on historical fluctuations in preindustrial mortality, Wrigley concludes:

> Some of the most important influences on mortality were altogether outside the control of preindustrial societies. . . . [But] the inability of preindustrial societies to protect themselves against disease by medicine and public health measures does not mean that mortality levels were not greatly influenced by social and economic conditions. On the contrary the level of real income enjoyed by a population played a great part in determining its death rate. Abundant food, good clothing and warm dwellings can cause a vast improvement in mortality even when medical knowledge is slight, while conversely those who face the rigours of winter in rags, those who live with their families in damp and chilly hovels or have no shelter at all are much more likely to fall victim to disease and, having done so, to succumb.[2]

Indeed, social, political, economic, and environmental situations may have played a more decisive role in determining patterns of mortality under conditions of "non-control" than under modern conditions of the medical revolution and its mass public health application. We will return to this argument in a subsequent section.

Preindustrial mortality thus involved three important ingredients: mortality was high, fluctuated over short periods, and varied widely at any point in time between areas and subpopulations. To convey a "feeling" for

---

[2]E. A. Wrigley, *Population and History* (London: Weidenfeld and Nicolson, World University Library, 1969), pp. 127, 129.

these three features of preindustrial mortality, we use selected illustrations that are neither exhaustive of the available, and increasing, evidence nor "random samples" of the existing data. Rather, in large part they represent major mortality features under preindustrial conditions so that comparisons can be made with subsequent changes in mortality patterns during industrialization. These illustrations focus first on presenting a general picture of the fluctuating high levels of mortality in "normal" preindustrial periods; subsequently, mortality variations as a result of famines and epidemics will be illustrated. The period covers the thirteenth through the eighteenth centuries, but concentrates on the sixteenth to the eighteenth centuries, and mostly refers to Europe.

Overall levels of preindustrial mortality may be obtained by examining estimates of life expectancy at birth for European populations. Although it is rare to have accurate information of this sort, because it requires knowledge of the distribution of population and deaths by age, enough material exists to show that mortality levels in preindustrial Europe were high and varied substantially. Based on a review of several studies, the United Nations estimated that between the thirteenth and seventeenth centuries, life expectancy at birth in Europe ranged from twenty to forty years; during the eighteenth century the range was between thirty-three and forty years for Europe and the United States.[3] In seventeenth-century England, life expectancy at birth averaged thirty years,[4] but some local areas enjoyed much more favorable conditions. For example, life expectancy at birth in one small urban parish in England from the sixteenth through the eighteenth centuries is estimated to have been as high as forty-six years and only as low as thirty-five years.[5] Similarly, mortality tables for France in the late eighteenth century show a life expectancy at birth of less than thirty years, whereas in the cities of France and other European countries it was seldom over twenty years.[6] Whereas estimates of life expectancy at birth in Spain and Italy in the eighteenth and nineteenth centuries are below thirty years,[7]

---

[3]United Nations, *The Determinants and Consequences of Population Trends* (New York, 1953), pp. 50–51; Louis Dublin et al., *Length of Life* (New York: Ronald, 1949), p. 41.

[4]Peter Laslett, *The World We Have Lost: England Before the Industrial Age* (New York: Scribner's, 1965), p. 93.

[5]E. A. Wrigley, "Mortality in Pre-Industrial England," *Daedalus,* 97 (Spring 1968), p. 574, table 17.

[6]Wrigley, *Population and History,* p. 131; Dublin et al., *Length of Life,* pp. 35–36.

[7]Massimo Livi-Bacci, "Fertility and Population Growth in Spain in the Eighteenth and Nineteenth Centuries," *Daedalus,* 97 (Spring 1968), pp. 527–529.

in the early days of settlement in Plymouth Colony in New England life expectancy at birth was probably as high as fifty years in some localities.[8]

In the fourteenth century plague is estimated to have killed 25 million persons, one-fourth to one-third of the population of Europe.

Another measure of mortality, considered by many to be the most sensitive indicator of social, economic, and environmental conditions, is the infant mortality rate—the proportion of babies born who die in their first year. Infant mortality among the British aristocracy, which in all likelihood had more favorable mortality patterns than the general population, fluctuated around 20 percent of all births during the sixteenth and seventeenth centuries, dropping to 16 percent during the first half of the eighteenth century.[9] Similarly, fully one-fourth of the babies born in one wealthy urban parish in England in the late sixteenth century and in rural villages of seventeenth- and eighteenth-century France died before their first birthday.[10] Other areas may have had lower or higher rates of infant deaths: Colyton, a small urban English parish, is estimated to have had an infant mortality rate of only 120 to 140 per 1,000 live births during the sixteenth and seventeenth centuries.[11] In some areas of France where the registration of infant births and death appears to have been unusually complete, infant mortality ranged at high levels of 24 to 29 percent during the eighteenth century. In other areas of France at the same time the range was from 15 to 20 percent. In Brittany, France, half the children did not survive to the tenth year, and there was no noticeable improvement during the eighteenth century. In

[8]Wrigley, *Population and History,* p. 131.

[9]Wrigley, "Mortality in Pre-Industrial England," pp. 570–571, table 16; cf. T. H. Hollingsworth, *The Demography of the British Peerage,* Supplement to *Population Studies,* 18 (1964), p. 67, table 52.

[10]Wrigley, "Mortality in Pre-Industrial England," pp. 571–572; Laslett, *The World We Have Lost,* p. 124.

[11]Wrigley, "Mortality in Pre-Industrial England," pp. 557–560; see his revised estimates, p. 570.

Southwest France conditions were better: two out of three children survived to age ten. Indeed, within France, infant mortality through the eighteenth century varied more between regions than between time periods.[12]

If variation and fluctuation around high levels of mortality were the rule for "normal" times in preindustrial societies, periods of crisis—food shortages, famines, disease, epidemics, wars, etc.—accentuated these patterns of diversity. Thus, although the small English parish of Colyton seems to have had favorable mortality levels relative to other areas of England from the sixteenth through the eighteenth centuries (life expectancy at birth of thirty-five to forty-five years and infant mortality between 12 and 14 percent), it too had severe setbacks. For example, in the twelve months beginning November 1645, the plague outbreak reduced the population of Colyton by about a fifth.[13]

In crisis years, local populations throughout Europe experienced crude death rates as high as 200, 300, and even 400 per 1,000 population. National populations and often all of Europe were subject to mortality levels in given years that are hard to imagine. In the fourteenth century plague is estimated to have killed 25 million persons, one-fourth to one-third of the population of Europe.[14] The population of Denmark fell by more than 20 percent in the decade starting in 1650, and in the year 1696–1697, Finland may have lost over one-fourth of its population.[15] In the 1690s, a succession of poor harvests created a "crisis of subsistence" throughout Europe; some regions of Sweden experienced death rates around 160 per 1,000 population.[16] In Norway, the number of deaths in 1741 was three times as high as in the prior four-year period.[17] Moreover, many periods of high mortality were local in their incidence, caused by a local harvest failure, or by an outbreak of an epidemic disease in a circumscribed geographic area, which most likely was never documented fully.

---

[12]Pierre Goubert, "Legitimate Fecundity and Infant Mortality in France During the Eighteenth Century: A Comparison," *Daedalus,* 97 (Spring 1968), pp. 598–601.

[13]Wrigley, *Population and History,* p. 82.

[14]Ibid., pp. 62–63; United Nations, *The Determinants and Consequences of Population Trends,* p. 52.

[15]Wrigley, *Population and History,* p. 63.

[16]Cited in William Petersen, *Population* (New York: Macmillan, 1969), p. 387.

[17]United Nations, *The Determinants and Consequences of Population Trends,* p. 51; cf. H. Gille, "The Demographic History of Northern European Countries in the Eighteenth Century," *Population Studies,* 3 (June 1949), pp. 3–70.

Although local and regional variation in mortality, as a result of harvest failures or epidemics, is difficult to document empirically, a reconstruction of the pattern of the plague epidemic in France, 1720–1722, may be instructive.[18] The evidence on the last important epidemic of the plague in Western Europe suggests that localities were not affected at random; rather, patterns followed communication routes. Moreover, the concentration of population appears to have been decisive in spreading the lethal plague; the larger the population, the more it was affected. All French cities over 10,000 population were affected, although a large number of small areas escaped any mortality consequences. In Marseilles, for example, 44 percent of the population (estimated at 90,000 before the plague) died, 30 percent of Aubagne (population 27,000) died, but small isolated French areas had few deaths. Similarly, whereas the epidemic of 1665 killed about 15 percent of London's population, whole quarters of the city remained untouched.[19] In part, village or areal isolation may have been a safeguard during periods of epidemics but may have resulted in disaster in times of food shortages.

These illustrations of preindustrial mortality picture fluctuating overall national death rates revolving around fairly high levels. Mortality in local areas may have fluctuated even more. If these patterns were plotted on a chart, for almost any time period and for nations as well as local populations, we would end up with the zig-zags of mortality variation over which people had virtually no direct control. Folk medicine does not appear to have been effective and prayers for health and agricultural prosperity must have often been answered in the negative. Because preindustrial mortality patterns were not controlled directly but rather were responsive to social, economic, political, and environmental conditions, it follows that when these conditions were altered, mortality patterns would change as well. Therefore, the impact of the agricultural, industrial, technological, and urban revolutions on mortality must be considered.

Industrialization and Mortality

These preindustrial mortality patterns, so long characteristic of human society, began to change in some areas of Europe as early as the mid-eighteenth century, and followed in most of Europe throughout the nineteenth

---

[18]Jean-Noel Biraben, "Certain Demographic Characteristics of the Plague Epidemic in France, 1720–1722," *Daedalus*, 97 (Spring 1968), pp. 536–545.

[19]Ibid., p. 545, fn. 6. On epidemics in France, see also J. Meuvret, "Demographic Crises in France from the Sixteenth to the Eighteenth Century," in *Population in History*, ed. D. V. Glass and D. Eversley (Chicago: Aldine, 1965), chap. 21.

century. By 1840, the population in the most advanced European countries had a life expectancy of over forty years slowly increasing to forty-five years by 1880, to fifty-one years by the turn of the twentieth century, to over sixty years by 1930, and to over seventy years by the 1950s.[20] The changes in life expectancy and infant mortality for Great Britain from the mid-nineteenth century to the contemporary period are representative.[21] In mid-nineteenth century England and Wales, life expectancy at birth was around forty years for males and forty-two years for females. By 1910, life expectancy at birth had increased eight years for males and ten years for females; continued medical and socioeconomic improvements raised life expectancies for males and females to fifty-nine and sixty-three years, respectively, by the 1930s. In the mid-1960s, life expectation for a newborn was, on the average, sixty-eight years for males and seventy-four years for females. Thus, in a little over a century, life expectancy at birth had improved by 70 percent for males and by 76 percent for females. Similarly, from the mid-nineteenth century to the beginning of the twentieth century, infant mortality in Great Britain fluctuated around 150 per 1,000 live births. After 1900, a period of continuous and steady reduction in infant mortality occurred through the 1960s. In the late 1930s the rate had fallen to around 55 per 1,000 live births; immediately after World War II only 3.2 percent of all babies born died in their first year; by the mid-1960s, the proportion had been reduced below 2 percent. The quality of information in Great Britain allows for a subdivision of infant mortality into neonatal (death during the first month of life) and postneonatal (death during the first to the eleventh month) during the twentieth century. The evidence shows that the neonatal mortality had been reduced in the 1960s by 60 percent of its early twentieth century level, whereas the postneonatal deaths, reflecting genuine social and economic improvements, were reduced by over 90 percent during the same period.

Several important features of this sketch of mortality distinguish it from death patterns in the preindustrial period. First, and foremost, is the level of mortality. During the Industrial Revolution, particularly beginning in the nineteenth century, mortality reached low levels that were unknown, as far as evidence is available, in prior human history. Although some local areas or short time periods may have had preindustrial mortality levels as low or

---

[20]United Nations, *The Situation and Recent Trends of Mortality in the World*, Population Bulletin no. 6 (1963), table IV.1.

[21]Data from R. K. Kelsall, *Population* (London: Longmans, Green, 1967), pp. 24–26.

lower than in the early stages of the Industrial Revolution, never was there such a *continuous* period of lowered mortality levels inching its way downward. In Norway, for example, the crude death rate was steady at about 20 per 1,000 from 1815 to 1850 before falling below 20. In several earlier periods between 1740 and 1815 in Norway, crude death rates were not far above 20 per 1,000 but the pattern was erratic. In 1745, the crude death rate in Norway was 20 per 1,000, but it had fallen from a high of over 50 per 1,000 in 1742–1743 and rose to almost 35 per 1,000 in 1747. So went most of the period before 1815 in Norway. However, after maintaining the steady level of mortality from 1815 to 1850, crude death rates in Norway declined from 20 to 12 per 1,000 by the 1920s.[22] Similarly, infant mortality in Sweden fluctuated around 200 per 1,000 live births from 1750 to 1810, occasionally dipping below 200 only to increase again. But after 1810, the level of infant mortality fell below 200 per 1,000, never to go that high again. Not until the late nineteenth century, however, were fluctuations converted into a steady and precipitous decline.[23]

Thus, along with the decline in the mortality level, a second related feature of the modern period is the virtual elimination of the enormous mortality fluctuations that characterized the preindustrial world. This was the result of the almost complete absence of crises associated with harvest failures and epidemic disease. With the outstanding exception of Ireland, where famines began in 1845, such European countries as France starting in the mid-eighteenth century, and most other industrializing nations beginning in the early nineteenth century, did not experience the mortality devastations that famines and epidemics brought. This virtual disappearance followed the improvements in communications and transportation that facilitated transferring harvest surpluses to deficient areas. In addition, the beginning of the agricultural revolution broadened the variety of crops available. People began to overcome systematically the natural forces of harvest failures and were better able to ward off severe sickness.[24]

Although the modern period effectively reduced the large mortality fluctuations that resulted from food shortages and epidemics, wars continued to have major demographic consequences in general, and mortality consequences in particular. Mortality patterns in the Russian Empire and

---

[22]Data from Wrigley, *Population and History*, fig. 5–2, pp. 162–163.
[23]Data from Donald Bogue, *Principles of Demography* (New York: Wiley, 1969), fig. 16–4, p. 562.
[24]Wrigley, *Population and History*, pp. 165–169.

the Soviet Union from 1861 to 1965 are extreme but instructive.[25] Crude death rates fluctuated around 35 per 1,000, beginning a slow descent in the last decade of the nineteenth century. By 1917, crude death rates were around 25 per 1,000. But the downward trend was interrupted by both world wars; in 1919 and 1941 the crude death rate was estimated at over 50 per 1,000. After World War II, crude death rates again resumed their downward trend, at an accelerated pace, remaining at below 10 per 1,000 from 1950 to 1965.

But aside from wars and local sociopolitical disturbances, nineteenth-century Europe experienced reductions in mortality levels and controlled significantly the fluctuations of the preindustrial era. Most mortality changes in Europe during the initial period did not result from medical break-throughs or public health applications, which were not causal to any degree in reducing mortality until the end of the nineteenth century, when mortality had already begun to decline. As a result, the third feature of mortality reduction in Europe was its greater initial impact on children above age one and on adults, rather than on infants below age one or on the older population. Infant mortality, as noted earlier, did not visibly decline in England and Wales until the late nineteenth century, whereas overall mortality began to fall earlier. The same pattern is true of France.[26] Knowledge of the causes of infant deaths and effective countermeasures came later than the improvement in standards of living and food supplies. Thus, the initial decline in mortality appears to have been the result of better food, housing, and "rising living standards," whereas public health measures and the control of infant mortality were clearly slower and later developments.[27]

Changes in mortality in Europe, because they initially reflected improved living standards, were neither swift nor spectacular. Rather they mirrored

---

[25]For data and discussion, see Jean-Noel Biraben, "Essai sur l'evolution demographique de l'U.R.S.S.," *Population,* 2A (June 1958), pp. 41–44; David Heer, "The Demographic Transition in the Russian Empire and the Soviet Union," *Journal of Social History,* 1 (Spring 1968), pp. 193–240; D. Peter Mazur, "Expectancy of Life at Birth in 36 Nationalities of the Soviet Union," *Population Studies,* 23 (July 1969), pp. 225–246.

[26]E. A. Wrigley, *Industrial Growth and Population Change* (Cambridge, Eng.: Cambridge University Press, 1961), p. 101, table 24.

[27]Wrigley, *Population and History,* pp. 169–172; Thomas McKeown and R. G. Brown, "Medical Evidence Related to English Population Changes in the Eighteenth Century," in *Population in History,* ed. Glass and Eversley, pp. 285–307; T. McKeown and R. G. Record, "Reasons for the Decline of Mortality in England and Wales During the Nineteenth Century," *Population Studies,* 16 (November 1962), pp. 94–122; cf. P. E. Razzell, "Population Change in Eighteenth Century England," *The Economic History Review,* 28 (August 1965), pp. 312–332.

the steady but slow spread of many improvements in private and public hygiene and in the variety and quality of obtainable foods.[28]

Preindustrial mortality patterns varied among areas as a result of local responses to food shortages, famines, diseases, epidemics, and the like. During the early periods of industrialization, mortality variations were accentuated, but for different reasons. Obviously, all European nations and all areas and subpopulations within nations did not have equally improved living standards. For example, in the last years of the nineteenth century, infant mortality in the poorest areas of England affected one out of four babies born, two and one-half times the level of infant deaths among the wealthy. Life expectancy at birth was as low as twenty-four years in some areas of nineteenth-century England and as high as fifty-one years in other areas, although it was forty-one years nationally.[29] Hence, most initial "depths of misery" commonly associated with the early stages of Western industrialization are more appropriately viewed as the result of early urbanization and differential gains in living standards. Late nineteenth-century popular, reformist, and scholarly literature portrays vividly the poor mortality conditions of the slums. Yet, overall mortality declined and, in time, medical advances, public health programs, and improved sanitation along with the continuing rise in living standards reduced urban mortality levels considerably. Thus, the poorer mortality conditions in urban areas of Europe and the United States during their early industrialization should not obscure the overall relationship between industrialization and mortality reduction. As Wrigley notes:

> The literature of all the industrializing countries of Western Europe is full of novels examining the depths of misery into which people sank in the worst of the new slums and the immense toll of life exacted at all ages. Yet it would be as dangerous to base an assessment of the effect of the industrial revolution upon mortality on these facts and impressions as it would be to assume that the conditions which occurred in preindustrial Europe during the periodic demographic crises were typical of preindustrial times generally, for what was then concentrated into certain short periods of time was later concentrated into certain restricted areas.[30]

---

[28]Wrigley, *Population and History*, p. 170.
[29]Ibid., p. 173.
[30]Ibid., pp. 173–174.

Although, in the short run, urbanization brought a concentrated number of people into closer contact, which helped spread communicable diseases, and although urban areas were unprepared in housing, sanitation, and minimum health and environmental levels for the influx of rural migrants, urbanization within the industrializing nations of the late nineteenth and early twentieth centuries was part of social and economic modernization. Hence, over time, improved living conditions and increased health and wealth in cities conspired to bring mortality under control.

ᵠᵠ

The slowness and regularity of mortality declines characteristic of nineteenth-century Europe reflected the slowness and regularity of economic and social development.

ᵠᵠ

The transformation of European mortality patterns from conditions of noncontrol to societal control, from high fluctuating rates to low steady rates, must be understood therefore in the context of the social, economic, and political revolutions that transformed European society. In the initial stages of the agricultural and industrial revolutions, mortality improved as living standards improved. The causitive mechanisms were largely the same in nineteenth-century Europe as in preindustrial periods. The difference in mortality levels between the periods reflected economic and social developmental differences: as economic and social conditions became better, mortality levels were reduced. But beginning in the late nineteenth century another intermediate force began to obscure the clear-cut relationship between socioeconomic modernization and mortality reduction. The developing science and technology of medicine began to revolutionize mortality patterns even further. Once the causes of death were uncovered and preventive public health measures were applied, a diffusion of direct mortality control occurred not only within Europe but throughout the world. Thus, the slowness and regularity of mortality declines characteristic of nineteenth-century Europe reflected the slowness and regularity of economic and social development. But the applications of medical discoveries and the development of medical and public health technologies, which were themselves by-products of the Industrial Revolution, affected the pace and sharpness of mortality reduction directly, *independent of developmental levels.*

The Spread and Pace of Mortality Control

The fall in mortality within the industrializing world after the turn of the twentieth century, particularly infant mortality, was swifter than previous periods. Moreover, countries outside of the industrialized nations, without undergoing any dramatic alterations or even slight improvements in their social and economic development, around 1930 began to import medical and public health technologies that had developed slowly in Europe. The technological diffusion model of mortality decline, in contrast to the socio-economic developmental model, may be observed in the mortality pattern of almost every underdeveloped, nonindustrialized country. For example, life tables for Latin American countries show an expectation of life at birth below thirty years before the twentieth century, which reflected poor social and economic circumstances. These conditions in nineteenth-century Latin America were worse than in eighteenth-century Europe; hence the higher mortality rates in Latin America. Between 1900 and 1930 some Latin American countries experienced social and economic improvements; standards of living increased and mortality levels were reduced slowly as a result. But after 1930, mortality levels not only decreased much more sharply in Latin America than they had previously and faster than in nineteenth-century Europe, but did so irrespective of social and economic changes. Between 1930 and 1950, expectation of life at birth increased to thirty-seven years, on the average, for Latin America and jumped another fourteen years in the next decade. Between 1930 and 1960, for selected Latin American countries, about three-fourths of a year were added *annually* to life expectancy at birth, a pace three times as rapid as that between 1910 and 1930 and five times as rapid as that between 1860 and 1910.[31]

Although only a small island in the Indian Ocean, mortality changes in Mauritius may also illustrate the swiftness of mortality reduction without major economic or social development. Mauritius had a fairly constant

---

[31]For historical trends in mortality in Latin America, see Eduardo Arriaga and Kingsley Davis, "The Pattern of Mortality Change in Latin America," *Demography* (August 1969), pp. 223–242. The pattern of declining mortality and socioeconomic development in nineteenth-century South Asian populations is discussed in Gunnar Myrdal, *Asian Drama: An Inquiry into the Poverty of Nations,* vol. 3 (New York: Pantheon, 1968), pp. 1557–1559.

crude death rate in the first four decades of the twentieth century—over 35 per 1,000. Between 1941 and 1947, the crude death rate declined from 36 per 1,000 to 20 per 1,000; by 1961 the rate had fallen to 10 per 1,000. Infant mortality declined from 155 per 1,000 live births, 1944–1948, to 62 per 1,000 live births in 1961; life expectancy at birth was around thirty-two years, 1942–1946, and reached close to sixty years by the 1960s. These mortality changes in Mauritius can in no way reflect major social or economic revolutions.[32] Not only was the pace in mortality reduction dramatic but, relative to the experience of European nations, unprecedented. Within the eight-year period following World War II, Mauritius raised its average life expectancy from thirty-three to fifty-one years, a gain that took Sweden a century and a quarter to achieve.[33]

This impressive accelerated pace of mortality decline in developing countries during the twentieth century, when compared to the experience of the industrializing nations of the world during the 1800s, is further illustrated in comparing mortality changes in Sweden with several other developing nations. Infant mortality began to fall regularly in Sweden around the turn of the nineteenth century; it took about a hundred years before the rate fell by 50 percent to below 100 per 1,000 live births. But Chile took less than three decades to achieve this decline starting with the mid-1930s.[34] Similarly, the increase in life expectation at birth in Ceylon between 1946 and 1954 required half a century in Sweden; for the decade beginning in 1946, Barbados experienced increases in life expectancies that took Sweden four times as long beginning in 1890. In 1921, Jamaica had the same life expectancy at birth that Sweden had in 1780; by 1951, Jamaica had the same life expectancy at birth that Sweden had in 1910, i.e., what it took Sweden one hundred and thirty years to accomplish was completed in three decades in Jamaica.[35]

---

[32]Population Reference Bureau, "The Story of Mauritius: From the Dodo to the Stork," *Population Bulletin*, 18 (August 1962), pp. 93–115; cf. R. M. Titmuss and B. Abel-Smith, *Social Policies and Population Growth in Mauritius* (London: Methuen, 1960).

[33]Kingsley Davis, "Population," *Scientific American*, 209 (September 1963), p. 69.

[34]Basic data derived from materials presented by Bogue, *Principles of Demography*, fig. 16–4, p. 562; table 16–9, p. 586.

[35]United Nations, *The Situation and Recent Trends of Mortality in the World*, p. 50. For other comparisons see Arriaga and Davis, "The Pattern of Mortality Change in Latin America"; George Stolnitz, "Comparison Between Some Recent Mortality Trends in Underdeveloped Areas and Historical Trends in the West," in *Trends and Differentials in Mortality* (New York: Milbank Memorial Fund, 1956), pp. 26–34.

These examples could be multiplied by substituting other developed and underdeveloped areas. Mortality declines, particularly since the 1930s, have accelerated and have been compressed. This acceleration has taken place independent of economic and social development and may be understood only as a result of the diffusion of direct mortality control techniques from the developed to the underdeveloped world. Even within the industrialized world, the clear-cut one-to-one relationship between socioeconomic improvements and mortality reductions is no longer observable during the twentieth century, particularly since the 1930s.

The swift mortality decline after the 1930s may be observed as well with measures of infant mortality. For the 1936–1938 period, infant mortality rates for over forty countries have been compiled by the United Nations.[36] Of course, some countries with the highest rates were omitted, e.g., India, China, and almost all of Africa, due to an absence of reliable information; but a sufficient range of countries and rates is represented to illustrate pre-World War II patterns. Of forty-three countries, 1936–1938, twenty-three had infant mortality rates over 10 percent of all births (a bare minimum because Asian and African countries not listed because of poor data had rates at least that high). Of the twenty countries with rates below 10 percent only three (Netherlands, Australia, and New Zealand) had rates below 4 percent. Comparison of these same countries in the mid-1960s shows that only one country out of the forty-three had a rate over 10 percent (Chile), despite the fact that Chile's infant mortality rate had declined 55 percent in the thirty-year period. Fully twenty-two countries had rates below 3 percent. The pace of the decline during these three decades varied. Most countries cut their infant mortality rates by over 60 percent; only one country (New Zealand) reduced its rate by less than 40 percent—but it had the lowest recorded rate in the 1930s. The most impressive declines in infant deaths for this period occurred in the Soviet Union (from 184 to 31 per 1,000), Singapore (from 162 to 28 per 1,000), Japan (from 113 to 23 per 1,000), Taiwan (from 145 to 26 per 1,000) and Czechoslovakia (from 115 to 22 per 1,000).

Changes in specific causes of death also illustrate these new unprecedented patterns of mortality reduction through the use of swift, inexpensive, and mass public health applications. This is particularly the case for malaria

---

[36]United Nations, *The Situation and Recent Trends of Mortality in the World,* table IV.8, reproduced with additions from the U.N. *Demographic Yearbook* in Bogue, *Principles of Demography,* p. 586, table 16–9.

control and declines in tuberculosis. Ceylon is a favorite demographic example, although it is clearly an extreme case. The overall death rate in Ceylon fell from 20 to 14 per 1,000 in 1946-1947 following DDT spraying, which virtually wiped out the malarial mosquito, a major cause of death. Such a fall in death rates took seventy years in England and Wales.[37] In Guatemala, the deaths due to malaria dropped from 6,238 to 124 in 1958-1959; India's annual incidence of malaria ranged upward to over 100 million before World War II, but dropped in 1966 to fewer than 50,000; in the United States malaria caused 200,000 to 400,000 deaths annually before 1946 and has since been eliminated entirely.[38] In 1945, malaria caused 3,534 deaths in Mauritius, 25 percent of all deaths; by 1955 only three people died of it.[39] Among the Maori population, the decline in the crude death rate due to reduction in tuberculosis was about 50 percent for males and 43 percent for females (1945-1956).[40] . . .

ʃʃʃ

. . . it is . . . significant, and often overlooked, that mortality control facilitates *in important ways social and economic development.*

ʃʃʃ

MORTALITY AND SOCIETY

The historic and comparative pattern of mortality reduction, the general outline of causative factors involved, and the persistence of mortality differentials among contemporary nations of the world are for the most part known in broad outline among students of population. The context or framework within which the mortality revolution is analyzed may differ somewhat between the demographer and the sociologist; the former might

---

[37]Political and Economic Planning (PEP), *World Population and Resources* (London: George Allen and Unwin, 1955), p. 12.

[38]Cited in Petersen, *Population,* pp. 562-563.

[39]Population Reference Bureau, "The Story of Mauritius," p. 101.

[40]D. I. Pool, "Post-War Trends in Maori Population Growth," *Population Studies,* 21 (September 1967), pp. 87-98.

stress the role of mortality in the demographic revolution, whereas the latter may emphasize the broader context of social and economic modernization. In analyzing the general patterns of mortality reduction and its determinants, these contexts overlap substantially, and differences between the demographic and sociological contexts largely reflect differences of emphasis. However, when connections between mortality reduction and social change are examined, i.e., when the focus is on the consequences of death control for the nature of human society, the population analyst often reverts to demographic parochialism. In most discussions of the "consequences" of the mortality revolution, analyses are restricted to the impact of mortality changes and variations on population growth, age structure, fertility, and to a lesser extent, on migration. If the "social" consequences of mortality changes are discussed at all, it is usually in the context of by-product results that flow *indirectly* from the impact of mortality on population dynamics. Notwithstanding the very important relationships between mortality and other population processes, and the significance of mortality reduction as a generator of social problems through its association with population growth under some conditions, mortality levels and changes have *direct* social structural implications.

Because the role of mortality as a dependent variable has been so often emphasized, it is useful to explore the complementary side of the relationship—the impact of mortality changes on modernization. It is reasonably clear that mortality reduction is *integral* to the complex changes associated with modernization, that is, modernization is unthinkable without major alterations in the level and pattern of death. Obviously, social, economic, and technological changes that are manifestations of modernization operate as powerful agents for the control of mortality, but it is also equally significant, and often overlooked, that mortality control *facilitates* in important ways social and economic development. The use of the word *facilitates* rather than *causes* is important for two reasons: First, in analyzing the consequences of mortality reduction for social and economic development it is often impossible, theoretically or empirically, to isolate the causal chain, although we know that the two processes are correlated. This is due to the constant interaction of these processes, the complexity of modernization, and the likelihood that intervening factors connect mortality reduction to modernization. Second, even where the connections are less obscure, mortality changes set up *potentialities* for elements of modernization, in the sense that low mortality is a *necessary* but surely not a *sufficient* condition for social and economic development.

One illustration of the consequences of mortality reduction for social and economic modernization examines the impact of changing patterns and levels of death on key social institutions: family and kinship, socioeconomic, and religiocultural systems. For analysis it is helpful first to construct ideal-typical models of the mortality structure under the extremes of "non-control" and "control." We may extract four key interrelated features of mortality under extreme noncontrolled conditions. First, mortality levels are high—crude death rates are around 50 per 1,000; life expectancy at birth is less than thirty years, and infant mortality rates are at least 35 percent of all births. These levels of mortality mean an *ever-presence of death* within society. Second, mortality levels fluctuate widely over short periods of time. When harvests are poor or when epidemics are rampant, not infrequent occurrences, mortality takes a heavy toll of the total society. Combined with the generally high mortality levels, such fluctuations imply *great uncertainties about length of life* over time. A third feature of mortality under noncontrolled conditions is the *mystery of death*. Mortality patterns in these circumstances are by definition uncontrolled; when death occurs it cannot be explained in terms of scientific or "rational" causal sequences, because these are in large part unknown, but rather must be "explained away" by nonrational, sometimes mystical, reasoning. Fourth, mortality under noncontrolled conditions is not randomly distributed throughout all ages but takes extraordinary large numbers of the very young. The timing of death is thus *accentuated in the early few years of life*. In short, life under extreme conditions of the noncontrol of mortality is precariously short, death is ever-present, shrouded in mystery and uncertainty, and is concentrated among the very young.

At the opposite extreme is the ideal-typical condition of death where mortality is controlled. The level of mortality is low—crude death rates are below 10 per 1,000; life expectancy is over seventy years, and only about 1 percent of all babies born die in their first year. Death rarely interrupts the daily activities of societies, and when it occurs it is largely to older persons dying in institutions from degenerative diseases. The quantity of life is discussed not in terms of uncertainties but as "probabilities," and death is explained largely in rational, scientific vocabularies. These two ideal-typical models have been abstracted from reality and presented in extreme form for analytic purposes, but they are not far removed from the real world. Non-controlled mortality conditions, as discussed earlier, are in large part characteristic of the preindustrial world of Europe and North America before the seventeenth or eighteenth centuries, and of Latin America before the 1930s. With qualification, preindustrial, noncontrolled mortality continues to characterize parts of Asia and significant sectors of Africa in the 1960s. In contrast, controlled mortality, in its more accentuated but not in its "final" form, is typical only of the most socially and economically developed areas of the contemporary world, i.e., Europe, North America, Japan, and some selected smaller populations.

Mortality and Socioeconomic Development

If uncontrolled mortality is characteristic of traditional societies and controlled mortality is a feature of modern societies, we can begin to link other key features of traditional and modern societies to mortality. In traditional societies, kinship units are the primary sources of identification and power; they dominate the allocation of status to individuals, the distribution of goods, and the exercise of power. The emphasis on kinship "fits" well with facts of uncontrolled mortality. Emphasis on individual merit or the nuclear family in isolation would be difficult to sustain given the precariousness and shortness of life. Societal organization and social identification must be formed around some unit that is more permanent and less likely to be eradicated in brief periods. It is therefore not surprising that the wider kin group or even larger clan or tribe unit is invested with such power. In contrast, one feature of modern societies is the breakdown of kin dominance through structural differentiation and the assignment of social identification through the nuclear family. Combined with the emphasis on "individualism," the small nuclear family is *possible* only by extending life and reducing infant deaths. Although individualism and nuclear family structure vary somewhat between modern societies and are determined by many complex features of modernization processes, the *potential* emergence of the nuclear family as *the* social unit and the emphasis on individual worth are limited to conditions where the length of human life is relatively long.

Another characteristic of traditional societies is large family size. The number of babies born to a family in traditional societies was high. One conditioning factor for high fertility is high mortality, particularly of infants. For societies to survive under high mortality conditions, that is, to have two or three children survive to adulthood to have children of their own, a much larger number of babies has to be conceived. The institutionalized emphasis on high fertility in high mortality societies results, in part, from the fact that replacement of the family unit is circumscribed by the extent of mortality. Only after mortality is reduced can families have a smaller number of children in confidence that two or three will survive to adulthood. But we should take care in viewing the causal relationship only as one way, that is, that reduced mortality leads to reduced fertility. It is equally valid to argue, and some scattered evidence supports this, that reduced family size may have resulted in lower mortality. Nevertheless, it is inconceivable that an average family size of two or three children could for very long characterize a society with uncontrolled mortality without resulting in demographic suicide. Controlled mortality thus is one of the many complex factors that sets up the potential for the emergence of the small family system. Although approximating a "necessary" condition for lower fertility, reduced mortality is by no means a "sufficient" condition.

Several other features of family structure, family formation, and family life are related to changing mortality levels,[41] four of which have special interest in historical and comparative contexts. First, a common pattern in many traditional and preindustrial societies is for marriages to be arranged either by the parents of the prospective bride and groom, or through some relative, or through a formal intermediary. In modern societies, "romantic love" replaces arranged marriages, and individuals usually select their own marriage partners. It is likely that one basis shaping this transformation is increased length of life. Choosing a marriage partner requires at least time for exploration, particularly when that decision involves emotional and romantic components. Entering into the game of marriage selection, seeking and searching for a partner, is less likely to occur under precarious mortality conditions than when time is not a major consideration. Similarly, the higher mortality among the young in traditional societies reduces the probability of strong emotional involvements and investments between parent and child. Where child mortality is low, greater emotional attachments between parent and children are more likely to be institutionalized. A third family feature that has changed over time is the increased potential for longer marriages and, as well, for several changes in marriage partners within the life span. Whether individual marriages remain intact longer depends on many complex factors; but both the possibility of longer marriages and the option for "serial monogamy," or divorces and remarriages, are shaped by the average length of human life. Finally, due to the high mortality of traditional societies a large proportion of the population consists of orphans or widowed persons.[42] Moreover, the widowed are more likely to be younger in traditional communities. Such is not the case, in large part, for modern

---

[41]See the brief discussion in David M. Heer, *Society and Population* (Englewood Cliffs, N.J.: Prentice-Hall, 1968); pp. 43–45.

[42]See Laslett, *The World We Have Lost*, pp. 95–96.

societies. The conspicuousness of bereavement as reflected in the proportion of widowed and orphaned has declined sharply as mortality patterns become concentrated among the elderly.

Along with major alterations in family-kinship systems in modernization, major changes in socioeconomic institutions occurred. In general, the revolutionary changes in mortality set up the conditions under which socioeconomic modernization takes shape. Under conditions of constant sickness and early death, men in traditional societies had neither time nor energy to improve very much upon subsistence conditions or acquire the knowledge necessary to plan for its improvement. A description of morbidity and mortality conditions in contemporary Africa is revealing.

In the African social drama sickness has a strong claim to being the arch-villain. It is bad enough that a man should be ignorant, for this cuts him off from the commerce of other men's minds. It is perhaps worse that a man should be poor, for this condemns him to a life of stint and scheming. . . . But what surely is worst is that a man should be unwell, for this prevents his doing anything much about either his poverty or his ignorance.[43]

The "nonpresence" of death in modern societies physically and socially removes the death of man from the life of society.

In more general terms, modernization implies the need for occupational specialization, fluid labor markets, career preparation, social mobility, and others, which require training and skill circumscribed by time factors. Moreover, modern economies require social and personal planning and rational calculations. Such planning requires time. People under preindustrial mortality conditions lived in a "moving present" and "short-term prospects

---

[43]George Kimble, *Tropical Africa*, vol. 2 (Garden City, N.Y.: Doubleday, Anchor Books, 1962), p. 156; cf. William McCord, *The Springtime of Freedom: Evolution of Developing Societies* (New York: Oxford University Press, 1965).

185

occupied most of their attention. Even the seven fat and seven lean years of scripture cover a longer span than would have entered the calculations of most men."[44]

An interrelated feature of kinship and stratification systems in premodern communities is the emphasis on ascription, and the relative absence of major intergenerational or intragenerational social mobility. In contrast, achievement is emphasized in modern societies and, in turn, social mobility is fostered. Again, these changing patterns fit the mortality picture of these ideal-typical societies. It is unthinkable that men should acquire the knowledge and skills based on long-term training when mortality is high and life is precarious. Spending a dozen or more years in formal education and training is absurd, when life is short and uncertain.[45] Similarly, the processes of socioeconomic mobility depend not only on time per se, but on a *Weltanschauung* that includes planning ahead, saving, and deferred gratification, all of which are difficult conceptions of self when people live in the moving present.

Mortality and Religiocultural Systems

Most of the indirect impact of mortality levels on social institutions and social processes depends on time factors that are shaped by mortality. If the transformation from high to low death rates has facilitated social and economic changes tied indirectly to the length of human life, it should be expected that those social institutions that are concerned directly with mortality will be responsive to its structure and frequency. In particular, we should expect that the dominance of death in premodern societies would influence both the social relevance and content of institutions organized around death.[46]

In every society—traditional and modern—man must explain and understand the meaning of life and death and has to cope with his own mortality and that of his family and friends. The press for explanation must be greater under conditions where death is open, frequent, and conspicuous on a

---

[44]Wrigley, *Population and History,* pp. 77–78.

[45]See Holger R. Stub, "Education, the Professions, and Long Life," *British Journal of Sociology,* 20 (June 1969), pp. 177–189.

[46]Cf. Robert Blauner, "Death and Social Structure," *Psychiatry,* 29 (1966), pp. 378–394, reprinted in Rose Coser (ed.), *Life Cycle and Achievement in America* (New York: Harper Torchbook, 1969), pp. 223–260.

regular basis. In the preindustrial world the society was "inured to bereavement and the shortness of life. It clearly had to be."[47] In a description of village life in India, McCord notes:

> How long one can live is the primary preoccupation of every villager. For in Khampur (Uttar Pradesh, India), where half of the children die before they are ten and rats carry the bubonic plague and every adult has at times experienced malarial fever, death cannot be hidden.[48]

In sharp contrast, the low level of death in modern society and its segregation from the ongoing social system reduce regular confrontations with the mortality of man. When death is confined largely to the elderly—those retired from work, finished with direct parental responsibilities—and handled within specialized bureaucracies, mortality becomes removed from the daily business of social life. The constant presence of death in traditional societies means that society has to incorporate its regularity within the ongoing system of life. The "nonpresence" of death in modern societies physically and socially removes the death of man from the life of society.

An important feature of traditional societies is the emphasis on, and dominance of, religious institutions. The decline of religion and the emergence of secularism is, in part, tied to the changing needs that religion can satisfy. When life is precarious, when death is frequent and mysterious, social institutions are needed to explain death. With the decline in mortality, its removal from daily concern, and its concentration among the elderly, the pressing need for social reinforcement in times of bereavement is considerably reduced. Moreover, the decline of "fate" or "God's will" as explanatory concepts and fatalism as a dominant religious theme are, in part, related to the extension of the length of life and the concomitant changes in the timing of death.[49]

Therefore, religious institutions must redefine the content of their message, or at least place different emphasis within that content, if they are to remain vital in the modern world. Indeed, it is not surprising that, along with the decline in mortality, shifts occur from an emphasis on "otherworld" orientations to "this-world" matters, in both general values and

---

[47]Laslett, *The World We Have Lost*, p. 96.

[48]McCord, *The Springtime of Freedom*, p. 22.

[49]Ibid., p. 22; Stub, "Education, the Professions and Long Life," p. 183. On India, see Kingsley Davis, *The Population of India and Pakistan* (Princeton: Princeton University Press, 1950), p. 64.

in context of religious institutions. Rewards for religious adherence are no longer placed in other worlds or other lives but in the quality of life in this world.[50] In premodern societies, people live in the present but, paradoxically, are other-world oriented. In modern societies, people plan for the future and are this-world oriented. Both patterns fit the facts of mortality and its meaning in these different types of society. The current emphasis among religious institutions and their philosophers on social theologies of the quality of life could hardly attract the attention of persons surrounded by the quantitative shortness of life. Conversely, emphasizing cities of God seems too far removed from the long span of time people have to live in the cities of man.

Some have gone so far as to suggest that the stress on religion in general and on ghosts and communities of the dead in particular may be attributed to the nearness and frequency of deaths in premodern societies. Hence, the absence of stress on ghosts and extrahuman forces in modern society is not simply the routing of superstition by science and rational thought but "reflects the disengaged social situation of the majority of the deceased."[51] The removal of death from everyday life in modern society and the bureaucratized control of death further disengage the ongoing society from concern and interest in death. Mortality in modern society rarely interrupts the business of life.[52] If the revolution in mortality has not influenced directly the shift from religiousness to secularism, it surely has played an integral, supporting role.

In sum, the decline in mortality and its changing character and distribution has had major implications, direct and indirect, on the functioning of social systems and the nature of social institutions. Modern society in all its social, economic, and cultural dimensions is inconceivable under conditions of high mortality. The integral role of the mortality revolution in the transformation from traditional to modern is beyond dispute, because mortality processes are responsive directly to modernization and also because mortality reduction shapes the potential for socioeconomic development. The former reason has almost always been stressed; the latter argument is by no means less important. As Heer suggests: "It is possible that

[50]On this point, see Heer, *Society and Population,* p. 44.
[51]Blauner, "Death and Social Structure," in *Life Cycle and Achievement in America,* pp. 232–235.
[52]Ibid., p. 228; cf. David Sudnow, *Passing On: The Social Organization of Dying* (Englewood Cliffs, N.J.: Prentice-Hall, 1967); Barney Glazer and Anselm Strauss, *Awareness of Dying* (Chicago: Aldine, 1965).

the dramatic decline in mortality since the end of the nineteenth century has evoked more changes in social structure than any other single development of the period."[53] In this sense, social scientists concerned with modernization cannot neglect mortality.

Death, Uses of a Corpse, and Social Worth

David Sudnow
David Sudnow is Associate Professor in the Sociology Department at Brooklyn College. This selection is taken from his book *Passing On* and describes the rather startling treatment accorded both the living and the dead as they pass through a hospital's emergency room.

From David Sudnow, *Passing On*, © 1967, pp. 95–107. Reprinted by permission of Prentice-Hall, Inc., Englewood Cliffs, New Jersey.

In County's Emergency Ward, the most frequent variety of death is what is known as the "DOA" [dead on arrival] type. Approximately forty such cases are processed through this division of the hospital each month. The designation "DOA" is somewhat ambiguous insofar as many persons are not physiologically dead upon arrival, but are nonetheless classified as having been such. A person who is initially classified as "DOA" by the ambulance driver might retain such a classification even though he might die some hours after his arrival at the hospital.

When an ambulance driver suspects that the person he is carrying is dead, he signals the Emergency Ward with a special siren alarm as he approaches the entrance driveway. As he wheels his stretcher past the clerk's desk, he restates his suspicion with the remark "possible," a shorthand reference for "Possible DOA." The use of the term *possible* is required by law which insists, primarily for insurance purposes, that any diagnosis unless made by a certified physician be so qualified. The clerk records the arrival in a log book and pages a physician, informing him, in code, of the arrival. Often a page is not needed as physicians on duty hear the siren alarm and expecting the arrival wait at the entranceway. The "person" is rapidly wheeled to the far end of the ward corridor and into the nearest available foyer or room, supposedly out of sight of other patients and possible onlookers from the waiting room. The physician arrives, makes his examination and pronounces the patient dead or alive. A nurse then places a phone call to the coroner's office, which is legally responsible for the removal and investigation of all DOA cases.

Neither the hospital nor the physician has medical responsibility in such cases. In many instances of clear death, ambulance drivers use the hospital as a depository for disposing of a body, which has the advantages of being both closer and less bureaucratically complicated a place than the downtown coroner's office. The hospital stands as a temporary holding station, rendering the community service of legitimate and free pronouncements of death for any comers. In circumstances of near-death, it functions more traditionally as a medical institution, mobilizing lifesaving procedures for those for whom they are still of potential value, at least as judged by the ER's [emergency room] staff of residents and interns. The boundaries between near-death and sure-death are not, however, altogether clearly defined.

In nearly all DOA cases, the pronouncing physician, commonly that physician who is the first to answer the clerk's page or spot the incoming ambulance, shows, in his general demeanor and approach to the task, little more than passing interest in the event's possible occurrence and the patient's biographical and medical circumstance. He responds to the clerk's call, conducts his examination, and leaves the room once he has made the necessary official gesture to an attending nurse (the term "kaput," murmured in differing degrees of audibility depending upon the hour and his state of awakeness, is a frequently employed announcement). It happened on numerous occasions, especially during the midnight-to-eight shift, that a physician was interrupted during a coffee break to pronounce a DOA and returned to his colleagues in the canteen with, as an account of his absence, some version of "Oh, it was nothing but a DOA."

It is interesting to note that while the special siren alarm is intended to mobilize quick response on the part of the ER staff, it occasionally operates in the opposite fashion. Some ER staff came to regard the fact of a DOA as decided in advance, and exhibited a degree of nonchalance in answering the siren or page, taking it that the "possible DOA" most likely is "D," and in so doing gave authorization to the ambulance driver to make such assessments. Given that time lapse which sometimes occurs between that point at which the doctor knows of the arrival and the time he gets to the patient's side, it is not inconceivable that in several instances patients who might have been revived died during this interim. This is particularly likely as apparently a matter of moments may differentiate the reviveable state from the irreversible one.

ꞁꞁ

Currently, at County [Hospital], there seems to be a rather strong relationship between the age, social backgrounds, and perceived moral character of patients and the amount of effort which is made to attempt revival when "clinical death signs" are detected. . . .

ꞁꞁ

Two persons in "similar" physical condition may be differentially designated as dead or not. For example, a young child was brought into the ER with no registering heartbeat, respirations, or pulse and was, through a rather dramatic stimulation procedure involving the coordinated work of a large team of doctors and nurses, revived for a period of eleven hours. On the same evening, shortly after the child's arrival, an elderly person who presented the same physical signs, with what a doctor later stated, in conversation, to be no discernible differences from the child in skin color, warmth, etc., "arrived" in the ER and was almost immediately pronounced dead, with no attempts at stimulation instituted. A nurse remarked later in the evening: "They (the doctors) would never have done that to the old lady (attempt heart stimulation) even though I've seen it work on them too." During the period when emergency resuscitation equipment was being readied for the child, an intern instituted mouth-to-mouth resuscitation. This same intern was shortly relieved by oxygen machinery and when the woman "arrived," he was the one who pronounced her dead. He reported shortly afterwards that he could never bring himself to put his mouth to "an old lady's like that."

It is therefore important to note that the category "DOA" is not totally homogeneous with respect to actual physiological condition. The same is generally true of all deaths, death involving, as it does, some decisional considerations, at least in its earlier stages.

There is currently a movement in progress in some medical and lay circles to undercut the traditional distinction between "biological" and "clinical" death, and procedures are being developed and their use encouraged for treating any "clinically dead" person as potentially reviveable.[1] This movement, unlike late nineteenth-century arguments for life after death, is legitimated by modern medical thinking and technology. Should such a movement gain widespread momentum, it would foreseeably have considerable consequence for certain aspects of hospital social structure, requiring, perhaps, that much more continuous and intensive care be given

---

[1]There is a large popular and scientific literature developing on efforts to "treat the dead," the import of which is to undercut traditional notions of the nonreversibility of death. Some of this discussion goes so far as to propose the preservation of corpses in a state of nondeterioration until such time as medical science will be able to do complete renovative work. See particularly R. Ettinger, *The Prospect of Immortality* (Garden City: Doubleday & Company, Inc., 1964). The Soviet literature on resuscitation is most extensive. Soviet physicians have given far more attention to this problem than any others in the world. For an extensive review of the technical literature, as well as a discussion of biomedical principles, with particular emphasis on cardiac arrest, see V. A. Negovskii, *Resuscitation and Artificial Hypothermia* (New York: Consultants Bureau Enterprises Inc., 1962). See also, L. Fridland, *The Achievement of Soviet Medicine* (New York: Twayne Publishers, Inc., 1961), especially Chapter Two, "Death Deceived," pp. 56–57. For an account of the famous saving of the Soviet physicist Landau's life, see A. Dorozynski, *The Man They Wouldn't Let Die* (New York: The Macmillan Company, 1956).

For recent popular articles on "bringing back the dead" and treating death as a reversible process, see "The Reversal of Death," *The Saturday Review,* August 4, 1962; "A New Fight Against Sudden Death," *Look,* December 1, 1964.

Soviet efforts and conceptions of death as reversible might be seen to have their ideological basis in principles of dialectics:

For everyday purposes we know and can say, e.g., whether an animal is alive or not. But, upon closer inquiry, we find that this is, in many cases a very complex question, as the jurists know very well. They have cudgelled their brains in vain to discover a rational limit beyond which the killing of the child in its mother's womb is murder. It is just as impossible to determine absolutely the moment of death, for physiology provides that death is not an instantaneous, momentary phenomenon, but a very protracted process.

In like manner, every organized being is every moment the same and not the same . . .

From F. Engels, *Socialism: Utopian and Scientific* (New York: International Publishers Co., 1935), p. 47.

For a discussion of primitive conceptions of death with particular attention to the passage between life and death, see I. A. Lopatin, *The Cult of the Dead Among the Natives of the Amur Basin* (The Hague: Mouton and Company, 1960), pp. 26–27 and 39–41.

"dying" and "dead" patients than is presently accorded them, at least at County. At Cohen Hospital, where the care of the "tentatively dead" is always very intensive, such developments would more likely be encouraged than at County.

Currently, at County, there seems to be a rather strong relationship between the age, social backgrounds, and perceived moral character of patients and the amount of effort which is made to attempt revival when "clinical death signs" are detected, as well as the amount of effort given to forestalling their appearance in the first place. As one compares practices at different hospitals, the general relationship seems to hold, although at the private, wealthier institutions, like Cohen, the overall amount of attention given to "initially dead" patients is greater. At County, efforts at revival are admittedly superficial, with the exception of the very young and occasionally wealthier patient, who by some accident, ends up at County's ER. No instances have been witnessed, at County, where external heart massage was given a patient whose heart was stethoscopically inaudible, if that patient was over forty years of age. On the other hand, at Cohen Hospital heart massage is a normal routine at that point, and more drastic measures, such as injection of adrenalin directly into the heart, are not uncommon. While these practices are undertaken for many patients at Cohen if "tentative death" is discovered early, as it generally is because of the attention "dying" patients are given, at County they are reserved for a very special class of cases.

Generally, the older the patient the more likely is his tentative death taken to constitute pronounceable death. Before a twenty-year-old who arrives in the ER with a presumption of death, attached in the form of the ambulance driver's assessment, will be pronounced dead by a physician, very long listening to his heartbeat will occur, occasionally efforts at stimulation will be made, oxygen administered, and oftentimes stimulative medication given. Less time will elapse between initial detection of an inaudible heartbeat and nonpalpable pulse and the pronouncement of death if the person is forty years old, and still less if he is seventy. As well as can be detected, there appeared to be no obvious difference between men and women in this regard, nor between white and Negro "patients." Very old patients who are considered to be dead, on the basis of the ambulance driver's assessment, were seen to be put in an empty room to "wait" several moments before a physician arrived. When a young person is brought in as a "possible," the ambulance driver tries to convey some more alarming sense to the arrival by turning the siren up very loud and continuing it after

The Demography of Death

he has already stopped, so that by the time he has actually entered the wing, personnel, expecting "something special," act quickly and accordingly. When it is a younger person that the driver is delivering, his general manner is more frantic. The speed with which he wheels his stretcher in, and the degree of excitement in his voice as he describes his charge to the desk clerk, are generally more heightened than with the elderly "DOA." One can observe a direct relationship between the loudness and length of the siren alarm and the considered "social value" of the person being transported.

The older the person, the less thorough is the examination he is given; frequently, elderly people are pronounced dead on the basis of only a stethoscopic examination of the heart. The younger the person, the more likely will an examination preceding an announcement of death entail an inspection of the eyes, attempt to find a pulse and touching of the body for coldness. When a younger person is brought to the hospital and while announced by the driver as a "possible" is nonetheless observed to be breathing slightly, or have an audible heart beat, there is a fast mobilization of effort to stimulate increased breathing and a more rapid heart beat. If an older person is brought in in a similar condition there will be a rapid mobilization of similar efforts; however, the time which will elapse between that point at which breathing noticeably ceases and the heart audibly stops beating, and when the pronouncement of death is made, will differ according to his age.

One's location in the age structure of the society is not the only factor which will influence the degree of care he gets when his death is considered to have possibly occurred. At County Hospital a notable additional set of considerations can be generally termed as the patient's presumed "moral character." The detection of alcohol on the breath of a "DOA" is nearly always noticed by the examining physician, who announces to his fellow workers that the person is a drunk, and seems to constitute a feature he regards as warranting less than strenuous effort to attempt revival. The alcoholic patient is treated by hospital physicians, not only when the status of his body as alive or dead is at stake, but throughout the whole course of medical treatment, as one for whom the concern to treat can properly operate somewhat weakly. There is a high proportion of alcoholic patients at County, and their treatment very often involves an earlier admission of "terminality" and a consequently more marked suspension of curative treatment than is observed in the treatment of nonalcoholic patients. In one case, the decision whether or not to administer additional needed blood to an alcoholic man who was bleeding severely from a stomach ulcer was decided negatively, and that decision was announced as based on the fact of his alco-holism. The intern in charge of treating the patient was asked by a nurse, "Should we order more blood for this afternoon?" The doctor answered, "I can't see any sense in pumping it into him because even if we can stop the bleeding, he'll turn around and start drinking again and next week he'll be back needing more blood." In the DOA circumstance, alcoholic patients have been known to be pronounced dead on the basis of a stethoscopic examination of the heart alone, even though that person was of such an age that were he not an alcoholic he would have likely received much more intensive consideration before being so designated. Among other categories of persons whose deaths will be more quickly adjudged, and whose "dying" more readily noticed and used as a rationale for palliative care, are the sui-cide, the dope addict, the known prostitute, the assailant in a crime of vio-lence, the vagrant, the known wifebeater, and other persons whose moral characters are considered reproachable.

✓✓

DOA cases are very interestingly "used" in many American hospitals. . . . A set of procedures can be performed upon those bodies for the sake of teaching and research.

✓✓

Within a limited temporal perspective at least, but one which is not necessarily to be regarded as trivial, the likelihood of "dying" and even of being "dead" can thus be said to be partially a function of one's place in the social structure, and not simply in the sense that the wealthier get better care, or at least not in the usual sense of that fact.[2] If one anticipates having

---

[2]The "DOA" deaths of famous persons are reportedly attended with considerably pro-longed and intensive resuscitation efforts. In Kennedy's death, for example, it was reported:

> Medically, it was apparent the President was not alive when he was brought in. There was no spontaneous respiration. He had dilated, fixed pupils. It was obviously a lethal head wound.

> Technically, however, by using vigorous resuscitation, intravenous tubes and all the usual supportive measures, we were able to raise the semblance of a heart beat.

The New York Times, November 23, 1963, p. 2.

a critical heart attack, he best keep himself well-dressed and his breath clean if there is a likelihood he will be brought into the County Emergency Unit as a "possible."

There are a series of practical consequences of publicly announcing that a patient is dead in the hospital setting. His body may be properly stripped of clothing and jewelry, wrapped up for discharge, the family notified of the death, and the coroner informed in the case of DOA deaths. In the Emergency Unit there are a special set of procedures which are partially definitive of death. DOA cases are very interestingly "used" in many American hospitals. The inflow of dead bodies, or what can properly be taken to be dead bodies, is regarded as a collection of "guinea pigs," in the sense that a set of procedures can be performed upon those bodies for the sake of teaching and research.

In any "teaching hospital" (in the case of County, I use this term in a weak sense, a hospital which employs interns and residents; in other settings a "teaching hospital" may mean systematic, institutionalized instruction), the environment of medical events is regarded not merely as a collection of treatable cases, but as a collection of experience-relevant information. It is a continually enforced way of looking at the cases one treats under the auspices of a concern for experience with "such cases." This concern can legitimately warrant the institution of a variety of procedures, tests, and inquiries which lie outside and may even, on occasion, conflict with the strict interests of treatment; they fall within the interests of learning "medicine," gaining experience with such cases and acquiring technical skills. A principle for organizing medical care activities in the teaching hospital, and perhaps more so in a county hospital where patients' social value is often not highly regarded, is the relevance of any particular activity to the acquisition of skills of general import. Physicians feel that among the greatest values of such institutions is the ease with which they can selectively organize medical attention so as to maximize the benefits to knowledge and technical proficiency which working with a given case expectably afford. The notion of the "interesting case" is, at County, not simply a casual notion, but an enforced principle for the allocation of attention. The private physician is in a more committed relation to each and every one of his patients, and while he may regard this or that case as more or less interesting, he ideally cannot legitimate the interestingness of his patients' conditions as bases for devoting varying amounts of attention to them. His reward for treating the uninteresting case is, of course, the fee, and physicians are known to give more attention to the patients who will be paying more.

At County Hospital, a case's degree of interest is a crucial fact, and one which is invoked to legitimate the way a physician does and should allocate his attention. In surgery I found many examples. If on a given morning in one operating room a "rare" procedure was scheduled, and in another a "usual" procedure planned, there would be no special difficulty in getting personnel to witness and partake in the "rare" procedure, whereas work in the "usual" case was considered as merely work, regardless of such considerations as the relative fatality rate of each procedure or the patient's physical condition. It is not uncommon to find interns at County interchange among themselves in scrubbing for an appendectomy, each taking turns going next door to watch the skin graft or chest surgery. At Cohen*, such house staff interchanging was not permissible. Interns and residents were assigned to a particular surgical suite and required to stay throughout the course of the procedure. On the medical wards, on the basis of general observation, it seems that one could obtain a high order correlation between the amount of time doctors spent discussing and examining patients and the degree of unusualness of their medical problems.

I introduce this general feature to point to the predominant orientation, at County, to such matters as "getting practice," and the general organizational principle which provides for the propriety of using cases as the basis for this practice. Not only are live patients objects of practice, so are dead ones.

There is a rule, in the Emergency Unit, that with every DOA a doctor should attempt to insert an "endotracheal" tube. This should be done only after the patient is pronounced dead. The reason for this practice (and it is a rule on which new interns are instructed as part of their training in doing emergency medicine) is that such a tube is extremely difficult to insert, requiring great yet careful force and, insofar as it causes great pain, cannot be "practiced" on live patients. The body must be positioned with the neck held at an angle that this large tube will go down the proper channel. In some circumstances when it is necessary to establish a rapid "airway" (an open breathing canal), the endotracheal tube can apparently be an effective substitute for the tracheotomy incision. The DOA's body, in its transit from the scene of the death to the morgue constitutes an ideal experimental

---

*A private hospital in the same city.—ED.

opportunity. The procedure is not done on all deceased patients, the reason apparently being that it is part of the training one receives on the Emergency Unit, and to be learned there. Nor is it done on all DOA cases, for some doctors, it seems, are uncomfortable in handling a dead body whose charge as a live one they never had, and handling it in the way such a procedure requires. It is important to note that when it is done, it is done most frequently and most intensively with those persons lowly situated in the social structure. No instances were observed where a young child was used as an object for such practice, nor where a well-dressed, middle-aged, middle-class adult was similarly used.

On one occasion a woman, who had seemingly ingested a fatal amount of Clorox, was brought to the Emergency Unit and after her death several physicians took turns trying to insert an endotracheal tube, after which one of them suggested that the stomach be pumped to examine its contents to try to see what effects the Clorox had on the gastric secretions. A lavage was set up and the stomach contents removed. A chief resident left the room and gathered together a group of interns with the explanation that they should look at this woman because of the apparent results of such ingestion. In effect, the doctors conducted their own autopsy investigation without making any incisions.

On several similar occasions, physicians explained that with these cases they didn't really feel like they were prying in handling the body, but that they often did in the case of an ordinary or "natural death" of a morally proper person. Suicidal victims are frequently the object of curiosity, and while among the nursing staff there is a high degree of distaste in working with such patients and their bodies, doctors do not express such a high degree of distaste. There was a woman who came into the Emergency Unit with a self-inflicted gunshot wound, which ran from her sternum downward and backward, passing out through a kidney. She had apparently bent over the rifle and pulled the trigger. Upon her "arrival" in the Emergency Unit she was quite alive and talkative, and while in great pain and very fearful, was able to conduct something of a conversation. She was told that she would need immediate surgery, and was taken off to the O.R. She was followed by a group of physicians, all of whom were interested in seeing what damage the path of the bullet had done. One doctor said aloud, quite near her stretcher, "I can't get my heart into saving her, so we might as well have some fun out of it." During the operation, the doctors regarded her body much as they would during an autopsy. After the critical damage was repaired and they had reason to feel the woman would survive, they en-

gaged in numerous surgical side ventures, exploring muscular tissue in areas
of the back through which the bullet had passed but where no damage
requiring special repair had to be done, with the exception of tying off
bleeders and suturing. One of the operating surgeons performed a side
operation, incising an area of skin surrounding the entry wound on the
chest, to examine, he announced to colleagues, the structure of the tissue
through which the bullet passed. He explicitly announced his project to be
motivated by curiosity. One of the physicians spoke of the procedure as an
"autopsy on a live patient," about which there was a little laughter.

In another case, a man was wounded in the forehead by a bullet, and
after the damage was repaired in the wound, which resembled a natural
frontal lobotomy, an exploration was made of an area adjacent to the path of
the bullet, on the forehead proper below the hairline. During this exploration the operating surgeon asked a nurse to ask Dr. X to come in. When
Dr. X arrived, the two of them, under the gaze of a large group of interns
and nurses, made a further incision, which an intern described to me as unnecessary in the treatment of the man, and which left a noticeable scar down
the side of the temple. The purpose of this venture was to explore the structure of that part of the face. This area of the skull, that below the hairline,
cannot be examined during an autopsy because of a contract between local
morticians and the Department of Pathology, designed to leave those areas
of the body which will be viewed, free of surgical incisions. The doctors
justified the additional incision by pointing out that since he would have a
"nice scar as it was, a little bit more wouldn't be so serious."

During autopsies themselves, bodies are routinely used to gain experience in surgical techniques, and many incisions and explorations are conducted that are not essential to the key task of uncovering the cause of the
death. On frequent occasions, specialists-in-training came to autopsies
having no interest in the patient's death. They would await the completion
of the legal part of the procedure, at which point the body is turned over to
them for practice. Mock surgical procedures are staged on the body, oftentimes with two coworkers simulating actual conditions, tying off blood
vessels which obviously need not be tied or suturing internally.

When a patient died in the Emergency Unit, whether or not he had been
brought in under the designation "DOA," there occasionally occurred
various mock surgical procedures on his body. In one case a woman was
treated for a chicken bone lodged in her throat. Rapidly after her arrival via
ambulance a tracheotomy incision was made in the attempt to establish an
unobstructed source of air, but the procedure was not successful and she

died as the incision was being made. Several interns were called upon to practice their stitching by closing the wound as they would on a live patient. There was a low peak in the activity of the ward, and a chief surgical resident used the occasion to supervisorily teach them various techniques for closing such an incision. In another case the body of a man who died after being crushed by an automobile was employed for instruction and practice in the use of various fracture-setting techniques. In still another instance several interns and residents attempted to suture a dead man's dangling finger in place on his mangled hand.

The Social Inequality of Death

Calvin Goldscheider

Calvin Goldscheider's work explicates, in a fascinating and frightening manner, the social inequalities of death. In this selection. Professor Goldscheider focuses on these inequalities as they relate specifically to race and socioeconomic status.

From Calvin Goldscheider, *Population, Modernization, and Social Structure*, pp. 259–265. Copyright © 1971 by Little, Brown and Company (Inc.). Reprinted by permission.

SOCIOECONOMIC STATUS AND MORTALITY

On April 14, 1912, the maiden voyage of the *Titanic* met with disaster. However, not all the passengers died at sea. The official casualty lists revealed that only 4 first-class female passengers (3 voluntarily chose to stay on the sinking ship) of 143 were lost; among second-class passengers, 15 of 93 females drowned; among third-class female passengers, 51 out of 179 died.[1] The social class selectivity among females on the *Titanic*—from 3 percent to 45 percent who died—dramatically illustrates the general inequality in death associated with social class levels.

---

[1] Cited in Aaron Antonovsky, "Social Class, Life Expectancy and Overall Mortality," *Milbank Memorial Fund Quarterly*, 45 (April 1967), pt. I, p. 31.

The unequal distribution of death for various social classes has been observed regularly since the turn of the twentieth century. Sir Arthur Newsholme wrote in 1910 about England that "no fact is better established than that the death rate, and especially the death rate among children, is high in inverse proportion to the social status of the population." In a review of infant mortality conditions in the United States during the first quarter of this century, Woodbury notes that low socioeconomic status, particularly low-income earnings, is the "primary cause" of excess mortality.[2]

Let us review briefly the relationship between social class and mortality for several European countries, where data have been more accurate and more readily available for a longer period of time, and for the United States. The countries to be considered include Scotland, England and Wales, the Netherlands, Denmark, the United States, and one underdeveloped country, Chile.

ffffffffffffffffffffffffffffffffffffffffffffffffffffffffffffffffffff

Rates of infant deaths among the lowest class lag thirty years behind infant death rates among the highest class.

ffffffffffffffffffffffffffffffffffffffffffffffffffffffffffffffffffffff

In Scotland, infant and fetal mortality rates for all social classes (defined by father's occupation) have declined over the last three decades, but the mortality differential between the lowest and highest social class has widened. In 1939, the fetal death rate of the lowest occupation class was one and one-quarter times as high as that of the highest occupational class grouping; in 1963, it was two and one-third times as high. Similarly, in 1939, the highest social class had a neonatal mortality rate of 30 per 1,000 live births, whereas the lowest social class had a neonatal mortality rate of 40 per 1,000 live births; in 1963, the gap widened with the highest social class having a neonatal mortality rate of 9.5, and the lowest social class a rate of

---

[2]Both Newsholme and Woodbury are cited in Edward G. Stockwell, "Infant Mortality and Socio-Economic Status: A Changing Relationship," *Milbank Memorial Fund Quarterly*, 40 (January 1962), pp. 102–103.

22.3. Moreover, the gap between these two class extremes was most evident in the postneonatal period, where socioeconomic environmental conditions clearly outweigh biological factors. In 1939, postneonatal deaths in the lowest occupational class were six times that of the highest occupational class, whereas in 1963, the differential more than doubled, and postneonatal death rates were more than thirteen times as great among the lowest than among the highest social classes.[3]

Since 1911, British statistics have repeatedly shown this same inverse relationship between parental social class (father's occupation) and infant mortality. Although significant declines in infant mortality *within* each social class during the first half of the twentieth century have been reported, the relative differences *between* classes have not decreased.[4] The gap is indeed large: mortality among infants born into families of unskilled laborers is two and one-half times that of infants born into families of professionals and rates of infant deaths among the lowest class lag thirty years behind infant death rates among the highest class.[5] This has occurred in Britain and Scotland even when medical care is readily available to the entire population and where maternity hospital accommodations are ample. Moreover, some evidence shows that the steep mortality gradient from the highest to the lowest occupational class has widened in England and Wales, as in Scotland, precisely during the same period when the gap between the incomes of these class extremes has decreased.

The Danish evidence reveals the same pattern of considerable mortality differences from one occupation group to another. In a 1967 report, data derived in 1954–1955 show that two and one-half times as many children of "domestic workers" (lowest occupational rank) died in their first year of

---

[3]The data for Scotland are based on a report by Dr. Charlotte Douglas reviewed in U.S. Department of Health, Education and Welfare, *Report of the International Conference on the Perinatal and Infant Mortality Problem of the U.S.*, National Center for Health Statistics, ser. 4, no. 3 (June 1966), p. 3. (Similar findings are cited for France and Hungary.) Although Dr. Douglas notes the difficulty in understanding the widening class differential in infant mortality in Scotland, she suggests that nutrition, housing, economic conditions, and general life styles conspire to produce the class gap.

[4]See the summary by Dr. Katherine M. Hirst, in ibid., pp. 4–5; Cf. K. Hirst et al., *Infant and Perinatal Mortality in England and Wales*, National Center for Health Statistics, ser. 4, no. 12 (November 1968), pp. 31–32; Helen Chase, *International Comparison of Perinatal and Infant Mortality*, National Center for Health Statistics, ser. 3, no. 6 (March 1967), p. 67.

[5]See R. K. Kelsall, *Population* (London: Longmans, Green, 1967), pp. 47–50; for earlier reports, see R. M. Titmuss, *Birth, Poverty and Wealth* (London: H. Hamilton Medical Books, 1943); J. N. Morris and J. A. Heady, "Social and Biological Factors in Infant Mortality," *Lancet*, 268 (March 1955), pp. 554–560; and several studies cited in Kelsall, *Population*, p. 98.

life when compared to the children of self-employed persons in professional services.[6] The widening of class inequalities in life chances, particularly between the highest and lowest social classes, has also been observed for Denmark.

The Netherlands data provide an interesting confirmation of the persistence of inequality in death rates between social classes. Infant mortality in the Netherlands (15 per 1,000 live births in 1964) is one of the lowest recorded in the world (second only to Sweden) and probably one of the lowest recorded in world history. After World War II, the Netherlands became one of the Western European welfare states characterized by social security for the great masses, moderate wages increasing with the living standard, relatively little unemployment, and no real poverty. Yet, despite the fact that infant loss has reached low levels, the classic rule still prevails: unfavorable social conditions increase perinatal and postnatal mortality. Mortality is lowest in the highest social class and increases more or less progressively with decreases in social class. Data for 1961–1962 show a wide mortality range by social class in the Netherlands. Neonatal and postneonatal mortality among children with parents in the highest occupational class was about 20 percent below the averages for the country as a whole, whereas in the lowest occupational class, the mortality rates were 10 percent above the national average. The influence of father's occupation on infant mortality is unmistakable. Infant mortality in the lowest social class shows a lag of about seven years in reaching the level attained by the highest social class. The lag would be even greater if the highest income group included in the highest occupational class were compared with the lowest income group in the lowest occupational class. The decline in infant mortality has been fairly uniform for all occupational groups and, at least over the last decade, no appreciable increase in the gap between the highest and lowest class has been observed.[7]

Most European data available on social class differences in general mortality are based on the occupation of father. For overall mortality, it is difficult to separate deaths associated with the "risks" or hazards of various

[6]P. C. Matthiessen et al., *Infant and Perinatal Mortality in Denmark*, National Center for Health Statistics, ser. 3, no. 9 (November 1967), pp. 15–16, and tables 5 and 12, p. 55. The same pattern was observed in earlier years.

[7]Data on the Netherlands were derived from J. H. de Haas-Posthuma and J. H. de Haas, *Infant Loss in the Netherlands*, National Center for Health Statistics, ser. 3, no. 11, pp. 16–24 and table 11. Social class differences in mortality remain practically the same when adjustment is made for parity and age of mother. See ibid., p. 32.

occupations from deaths due to the social and economic implications of life styles associated with occupational class. But the data on infant mortality classified by the occupation of father unmistakably reflect life style and social class factors. In addition, information in England on social class differentials in mortality of women classified by the occupation of their husbands show the same mortality gradient by social class. In these cases, the relationship found could only be a function of differential social and economic life styles indicated by occupational groupings.[8]

Comparable data on socioeconomic class differences in mortality are unavailable for the United States. The several community, ecological studies (ranking census tracts by some measure of socioeconomic status and correlating census tract mortality measures), direct studies for New York State and California, and preliminary national estimates based on death record-census matching of 1960 have all noted the inverse relationship of social class indicators and mortality. These findings, based on various methodologies, gain in reliability not only because of the consistency of results but because of the overall similarity with the European evidence, which is based on more accurate data for a longer period of time. Several United States studies illustrate similar findings using the three methodologies cited.

First, one of the most carefully executed ecological-correlation studies, of Providence, Rhode Island, found infant mortality to be less a sensitive indicator of socioeconomic status as it was in the past. However, when neonatal mortality was separated from postneonatal mortality, i.e., where the major causes of death are farther removed from the physiological processes of gestation and birth, the findings point clearly to an inverse relationship between postneonatal mortality and socioeconomic status.[9]

In a 1961–1963 special study of health problems associated with poverty in New York City, sixteen poverty areas were identified by low income and high frequency of social problems. In 1961–1963, infant mortality in New York City was 26 per 1,000 live births, but in the sixteen poverty areas the rate was 35 per 1,000. The maternal mortality rate for the sixteen poverty areas was almost 2½ times that of the rest of New York City. When health districts were grouped by housing quality in New York City, districts with poor housing had an infant mortality rate over twice that of

---

[8]Cf. Harold Dorn, "Mortality" in *The Study of Population*, ed. Philip Hauser and Otis D. Duncan (Chicago: University of Chicago Press, 1959).
[9]Stockwell, "Infant Mortality and Socio-Economic Status," pp. 101–111

districts with good housing and a maternal mortality rate almost four times as high.[10]

*The
Demography
of Death*

Studies of upstate New York, for the 1950-1952 period, reaffirm the inverse relationship between level of father's occupation and infant deaths. Neonatal mortality ranged from 14 per 1,000 births among the children of professionals to 20 per 1,000 among the children of laborers; postneonatal mortality (28 days to 11 months per 1,000 survivors to 28 days among births) ranged from 3.5 to 3.7 among professionals and managers to 9.6 among nonfarm laborers.[11]

Finally, carefully matched death and census records (350,000) in the United States resulted in the following estimates of mortality (twenty-five years of age and older) by years of school completed and family income.[12]

1 Among white males with no schooling, mortality was about 10 percent higher than among the college educated; among females mortality was about 50 percent higher among those with no schooling than among those with some college education. The inverse gradient characterizes both sexes and most age groups.

2 Among white males with family incomes below $2,000 a year, mortality was over 50 percent higher than among males with incomes $10,000 a year or more; among females mortality was slightly less than 50 percent greater among those with the lowest family incomes than among those with the highest family incomes.

3 A strong inverse relationship between mortality and level of educational attainment was found for the 1960 nonwhite population. Among nonwhite males, from 25 to 64 years of age, mortality was 31 percent higher for those with less than five years of schooling when compared to males with some high school or college education. Poorly educated nonwhite females from 25 to 64 years of age had mortality rates 70 percent higher than better educated nonwhite females.

---

[10]Eleanor Hunt and Earl Huyck, "Mortality of White and Non-White Infants in Major U.S. Cities," *Health, Education and Welfare Indicators* (January 1966), pp. 1-18.

[11]Chase, *International Comparison of Perinatal and Infant Mortality,* pp. 67-68.

[12]Evelyn Kitagawa and Philip Hauser, "Education Differentials in Mortality by Cause of Death, United States, 1960," *Demography,* 5:1 (1968), pp. 318-353; Evelyn Kitagawa, "Social and Economic Differentials in Mortality in the United States, 1960" (paper presented to the General Assembly, International Union for the Scientific Study of Population, London, 1969).

205

Health can be measured not only by length of life but also by positive elements of good health. Information from the United States National Health Survey clearly confirms the generally accepted positive relationship between poor health and low income.[13] People in families with a total income of less then $2,000 a year (in 1961) had twenty-nine restricted days of activities per year, per person; for those with family incomes of $2,000 to $4,000 a year, disability days dropped to eighteen, and in families with incomes of $4,000 a year and over the number was thirteen. To some extent income may be low because of greater illness just as illness may be low because of higher incomes—but it is clear that the two misfortunes exist together.

↑↑

Evidence . . . points consistently to the social inequality of death for members of different social strata.

↑↑

The National Health Survey in the United States further reveals that lower income persons, despite their increased level of illness and greater need for health care, receive fewer health services than people with higher incomes. Information gathered between 1963 and 1964 shows that 59 percent with family incomes below $2,000 a year consulted a physician at least once during the preceding year, compared with 66 percent of those with annual incomes between $4,000 and $7,000 a year and 73 percent of those with annual incomes of $10,000 a year. Finally, twice as many of those with higher incomes ($7,000 a year or more) avail themselves of medical specialists when compared to those with the lowest income status (below $2,000 a year).

In sum, the evidence from several European countries and the United States points consistently to the social inequality of death for members of different social strata. Some evidence, by no means universal or documented fully, also indicates an increased mortality discrepancy between

---

[13]Data from the National Health Survey have been presented in Forrest E. Linder, "The Health of the American People," *Scientific American*, 214 (June 1966), pp. 21-29.

the highest and lowest classes since World War II, paralleling the findings for racial mortality differentials in the United States and South Africa. Sufficient materials are not yet available to account for these increased mortality discrepancies, if they do in fact exist. Two points of conjecture are worthy of intense and rigorous testing. First, social class mobility may result in the movement out of the lower classes of persons who are healthier and more motivated to achieve a positive state of health. In the process, the lower classes, over time, may become composed of social and physical "rejects," whose mortality patterns may be consequently higher. This selective upward mobility may have increased after World War II, and, in part, may account for increased discrepancies between the lowest and higher classes. A second possibility relates to processes of urbanization and changing environmental densities since the end of World War II. The increasing urbanization of the lower classes, especially Negroes, as a result of rural-to-urban and interurban mobility, and the increasing concentration of urban residents among the poor in substandard housing and deprived social environments, may have increased mortality rates between classes and races. Although static areal measures show lower mortality rates in overall urban areas, more refined measures that subdivide urban areas into homogeneous socioeconomic sections are needed. A contributing and interrelated factor beyond the changing social-environment situation of millions of poor persons relates to the differential availability of health and medical facilities and services and, more significantly perhaps, differential motivation to utilize services when they are available. Whether these motivational elements have changed in the last decades requires careful research. These suggestions for research may illuminate the specific problem of the social inequality of death, its persistence and increase, and in the process may suggest alternative solutions for diminishing such inequalities.

• 4 •

THE

DETERMINATION

OF DEATH

Among the many current changes in the "thanatological wind," one can determine a number of
threads of change relating to death-in-our-time.
In the previous chapter we have noted changes in
the increase in general longevity and in the secularization of death. In this chapter, several additional
current death-threads can be mentioned: (a) an
appreciation of the increasing complexity of what
constitutes "death" and a concomitant concern with
a refinement of the technical definition of death, as
reflected in the selection by Mant; (b) the advent
of organ transplantation and the obvious implications for defining legally and ethically when a
"viable" organ can be taken from a "dead" body,
a topic touched upon in the selection by Veatch;
(c) as part of the general secularization of death, the
"institutionalization" of death in hospitals, which has
led to the development of certain institutional
methodologies for the handling of death, such as
"death trajectories" and planning of "hospital
careers," described in the Glaser and Strauss selection; and (d) a new concern with reconceptualizing
the psychological dimensions of death in light of
changes in our understanding of man, especially our

increasing awareness of the role of man's conscious and unconscious intentions in his movement through life, including his possible movements toward his own death—as touched upon in the selections by Shneidman and by Shaffer.

From the standpoint of knowledge about the dying process (especially in the hospital), no discipline has contributed more in the past ten years than has sociology. Contemporary sociologists like Sudnow or Glaser and Strauss have actually gone into hospitals and emerged to "tell it like it is." They have revealed the impersonal methodologies used in regimenting the activity of dying. They have documented the cruel isolation of the dying person and have described the tactics that hospital personnel use to avoid dealing with dying and death. What is clear is that death has become a legitimate topic for serious sociological study; what is surprising is that it took so long.

Within the contemporary sociological study of death, one can discern at least two kinds of approaches: the rather traditional approach (following Emile Durkheim, the great nineteenth-century French sociologist) which employs statistical measures and emphasizes large-scale trends, and the "new look"—called ethnomethodology (and identified with the teachings of Harold Garfinkel, currently a professor at UCLA)—in which sociologists attempt to give an accurate accounting of the events of everyday life, recording and commenting on what people actually do in various situations, e.g., a verbatim report of two young physicians talking across the body of a dying person about his autopsy as though he were already dead.

Long before death became as secular as it has in this century, death and dying were associated primarily with the physician, and not unreasonably so. The doctor treated life-threatening illnesses and served as the goalie between the quick puck of death and the awful irretrievable score. Today, more than ever, the physician has become the arbiter of death, although not everyone (including many physicians) believes that this is best. Nevertheless, the physician deals with such questions as *what* is death, *who* is dead, *when* is one dead, and *how long* should a human being in pain and in obvious indignity be kept alive. These questions obviously burden the physician—and all of us—with some of the deepest moral and ethical issues.

The "determination of death" in the first three selections of this chapter relates to plotting the path to, and defining the point of, death. In the last two selections the approach to death and the meaning of the expression "determining death" undergo a mutation. "Determining" now relates to the state of mind of the person as he approaches death, and we shift from the relatively cold institutional approach to reintroduce man into his own death.

209

The Shneidman selection objects to the traditional approach to the certification of death that "leaves man out" of his own death, and the Shaffer selection focuses on the role of "intention" in a person approaching death. This interest in the role of intention points to a growing social awareness of the complexity of death (reflecting a different facet of the chapter's opening discussion) and foreshadows discussion in later chapters in which man is treated as "more than a biological machine to which things happen."

Initial Definitions of Dying Trajectory

Barney G. Glaser and Anselm L. Strauss
Barney G. Glaser and Anselm L. Strauss are both Professors of Sociology at the University of California School of Nursing in San Francisco. This selection, taken from their book *Time for Dying*, discusses how hospitals seek to project the path that a terminal patient takes on his way to death.

When the dying patient's hospital career begins—when he is admitted to the hospital and a specific service—the staff in solo and in concert make initial definitions of the patient's trajectory. They expect him to linger, to die quickly, or to approach death at some pace between these extremes. They establish some degree of certainty about his impending death—for example, they may judge that there is "nothing more to do" for the patient. They forecast that he will never leave the hospital again, or that he will leave and perhaps be readmitted several times before his death. They may anticipate that he will have periods of relative health as well as severe physical hardship during the course of his illness. They predict the potential modes of his dying and how he will fare during the last days and hours of his life.

They anticipate how much relative control the patient, the family, and they, the staff, will have over different stages of his dying trajectory, thus anticipating who will shape the dying patient's existence, and in what way, as the trajectory runs its course. For example, during what stages, if any, in the trajectory will the family feel it necessary to search for a cure—a "reprieve"—from any quarter of the medical community? And the staff, even at the outset, may begin considering which would be the best place for the patient's life to end—in the hospital or at home?—and, if in the hospital, how to manage the death watch, the constant care before death, and the family.

At this early stage of rehearsing these aspects and critical junctures of the dying patient's trajectory, the staff may perceive a temporally determinant trajectory—its total length with clearcut stages—or an indeterminant trajectory—its stages or length or both are unclear. Although they assign as complete a trajectory as possible to the dying patient, the clarities and vagaries of the several aspects of any trajectory generate differentials in definitions among the various staff members. The legitimate definitions . . . come from the doctor. Since the definition of trajectory influences behavior, these differing definitions may create inconsistencies in the staff's care of and interaction with the patient, with consequent problems for the staff itself, family, and patient.

No matter how full and clear they may appear at the patient's admission, the initial definitions of the dying trajectory seldom remain unchanged. The staff is continually redefining the trajectory as the patient's hospital career proceeds and his condition changes. Defining the dying trajectory is, then, an open-ended process, which continually explains to the staff what they must do now, next, and in the future in caring for the dying patient. Changes in definition cause them to revise their ideas of hospital organization to help in this care, and reformulate their feelings about the patient as he proceeds toward death. Defining and redefining the dying trajectory is, in effect, a process by which the staff maps the care of the hospitalized dying patient over long and short periods of time.

The defining process allows the staff to *temporalize* every aspect of the hospital career of the dying patient. They can temporally organize their work, its associated activities and interactions, and their sentiments. Without this temporalization afforded and guided by the dying trajectory, they could neither follow nor keep up with the constant shifting and changing condition of the patient as he dies. Without this temporalization, the hospital organization, the organization of the service, and the sentimental order of the ward would be under constant threat of breaking down, and often in a state of disarray. By defining trajectories, the staff establish for themselves a *broad-range "explanation"* of what will happen to the patient, and thereby provide an *organizing perspective* on what they will do about handling the impending flow of events.

ꞁꞁꞁ

In the case of dying patients, the family . . . tend[s] to see the hospital as a custodial institution that is taking over the management of the patient's dying.

ꞁꞁꞁ

They also engage in what we shall call a *structural process.* As the dying trajectory proceeds, it generates the need for various structural aspects of hospital organization to be brought into play (the patient is, say, sent to the Intensive Care Unit or is put through dismissal procedures). Each such action moves the trajectory along, and changing conditions force other structural aspects of the hospital to be brought into play—some of them routine, as procedures for disposing of the body or for readmitting the patient, and others created to handle infrequent events, such as the announcement of a surprise death to an unsuspecting family. As the trajectory runs its course, its process is linked with the hospital organization as a structure in process. At different stages of the trajectory, different aspects of hospital procedures and facilities become relevant for the care and handling of the dying patient. These "structural relevancies" in turn become conditions and processes tied to the staff's work and mood in caring for the patient. The open-ended redefinition of the trajectory, and its linkage with the structural processes of hospital care, come to an end in any given case when the body is removed and the family sent home. However, it must be kept in mind that the hospital is usually dealing with a number of dying trajectories at once, each with various staff definitions. Hence there is a constant tendency toward disorder in the work and sentiments of staff.

GOING TO THE HOSPITAL

There is an old adage that people in general no longer believe, but that is
well understood by hospital staffs: "Never go to the hospital, because
hospitals are a place where people die." It is clear to most of us that large
numbers of people go to hospitals to recover; it is clear to staff members
that more people than ever before are going to hospitals to die. In either
case, hospitalization delegates considerable responsibility to the hospital
and the medical staff. Determination of what is going to happen to the
patient and the style in which it will happen become an institutional-
professional, rather than a personal, issue. The degree of delegation of
responsibility and control over the patient is in the beginning never quite
appreciated by the patient or his family, for they are typically rather ignorant
of hospital structure, hospital staff, and hospital careers.

In the case of dying patients, the family is perhaps even less willing to
recognize the extent of the delegation, for they tend to see the hospital as a
custodial institution that is taking over the management of the patient's
dying. In their eyes the hospital will protect them from the ordeal of having
the patient at home and will structure and limit the ordeal of his dying for
all concerned. The dying patient may be delegating more control over his
style of living while dying than he wishes. When they realize this, some
patients leave the hospital without their doctor's advice. But most stay (unless sent home), supporting the loss of control over their living as best they
can, while trying to learn how to be acceptable dying patients. Of course,
at some point in their dying trajectory, their physical condition may require
the staff to manage their existence completely, no matter what they may
wish.

In the case of patients who are expected to recover, the patient's and
family's delegation of responsibility and control to the hospital is made "in
the service of recovery." They see the hospital as a rehabilitating institution—a concentration of equipment and know-how designed to produce a
cure. To reject going to the hospital is, perhaps, to risk dying. If such a
patient dies, the bewildered family is likely to accuse the hospital and staff
of negligence, questioning their curative ability and pretensions. This point
is made clear by the following extreme example: A family in Greece sent a
relative to the hospital to get well; however, he died—a complete surprise to
everyone involved. The family gathered and stoned the hospital, breaking
several windows. (In the United States, the family considers a malpractice or
negligence suit.)

213

In sum, even when seen as a place for recovery, the hospital sometimes serves as the locus of dying. Its resources are better organized to handle the problems of dying, however, when the patient comes to it to die. Yet even under this condition, as we shall show, staff and organization preparations for the social-psychological problems of dying are not as adequate as those for recovery.

ENTERING THE HOSPITAL

Entering a hospital juxtaposes a hospital career and a dying trajectory. The doctor, patient, or family who chooses the hospital must anticipate some kind of career in the hospital suitable to the patient's dying trajectory. Hospitals vary in their ability to mobilize the resources necessary to cope with all stages of a trajectory. For example, when a hospital does not have a particular piece of equipment, such as a kidney machine, it can mean potential death to the patient who suddenly requires one. In one such case, it was discovered that a well-known private hospital did not have such a machine (which everyone assumed it ought to have). When a dying patient suffered a renal failure, he had to be rushed to a nearby medical center. A hospital's resources—its adequacies and limitations—must be considered when linking a dying trajectory to a hospital career.

Hospital resources significantly influence the staff's initial definition of the patient's dying trajectory, and they plan accordingly for his hospital career. They have a good idea of what hospital care they can provide, and this knowledge sets limits on how they define his dying trajectory. The doctor, the patient, and the family may or may not consider this hospital career and trajectory acceptable. If not acceptable, they will seek another hospital that can, by virtue of its resources, provide a more favorable career and dying trajectory. This process of fitting resources, careers, and trajectories together accounts in large measure for the drift of patients toward the large, research-oriented, medical centers whose resources permit more optimistic dying trajectories—either longer or less certain to end in death.

Some patients who would wish it cannot be moved to a medical center because their dying is too rapid or because their physical condition or their dependence on a machine does not allow them to be moved. They are locked in a particular hospital career until the end of their trajectories. Other patients prefer a career in a hospital where excessive heroics are not possible. They prefer not to be subjected to unique machines, equipment, or drugs thay may prolong their trajectories painfully. These patients and their families do not consider moving but focus on living and preparing themselves for a trajectory shaped only by the resources of their current hospital. With still other patients, the dying trajectory does not permit a move to any hospital, and they must remain at home to die. In some such cases, a hospital may send equipment into the home to ease or prevent the dying for a time, and a nurse may attend the patient. These patients experience, out of context, some aspects of a hospital career.

Moving between hospitals is also contingent on the type of dying trajectory. If a patient is dead on arrival, his hospital career starts with the end of trajectory—usually a very short one, occasioned, for example, by a heart attack or accident. Trajectories that last a few days or weeks typically do not allow time for more than one hospital career, unless a nearby hospital can provide an emergency measure deemed advisable. The patient either dies in the first hospital or is sent home to die. With their typical pattern of entry and re-entry, trajectories and occasional reprieves may last over several months or years. This long duration allows much time for "hospital hopping," especially in the search of new cures or more reprieves. Thus the lingering dying patient may have several different hospital careers before he dies. On the other hand, the lingering patient in a large urban center may keep returning to the same hospital, and even the same ward, throughout the course of his dying trajectory.

*There is an acceptable dying trajectory
for each ward in a hospital.*

In sum, different hospitals may provide different hospital careers and different initial definitions of dying trajectories. When the patient or his family chooses the hospital, they are exercising a measure of control over the patient's trajectory—how he will fare as a human being and as a patient. The more their decision is based on experience with hospitals, the more control they exercise over the differentials associated with dying in them. To be sure, frequently the patient simply goes to the hospital with which his doctor is affiliated, and no control is exercised. Sometimes control may be sought by changing to a doctor with access to the hospital preferred by the patient or family. Some doctors can take a patient to several hospitals and so allow their patients a choice; by briefly reviewing the conditions at the various hospitals, they give a patient a basis of control over his impending hospital career. In the case of short trajectories, the only choice may be the nearest hospital, chosen with the hope that its facilities can handle the emergency.

ADMITTANCE TO A WARD

There is an acceptable dying trajectory for each ward in a hospital. Upon entering, the dying patient is assigned to the appropriate ward on the basis of initial definitions of his trajectory; and the ward staff accept him or not on the basis of *their* initial definitions of his trajectory. When the initial definitions of ward staff and admitting personnel or private doctor differ significantly, the patient may be refused admittance to the ward. In this section we shall examine admission processes to several different kinds of wards—emergency, intensive care, cancer, medical, and premature baby— particularly the relationship of the ward staff's initial definitions of the dying trajectory to the admission requirements and procedures.

Generally, we are concerned here exclusively with admission to United States hospitals that separate illnesses by ward or departments within wards. In most large American hospitals, patients are placed on the basis of some notion of an "ideal" trajectory for each ward. This approach helps the hospital and ward staff codify their initial and subsequent definitions of the patient's dying trajectory. In contrast, European and Asian hospitals in the main have large, open wards that admit *all* patients, no matter what their trajectories may be. It is harder for the staff in these hospitals to maintain clear definitions of the diverse multiple dying trajectories; open wards create many problems in handling the dying situation. American hospitals, however, introduce an initial orderliness by screening patients on the basis of initial definitions of trajectory.

There are, to be sure, exceptions. Some county hospitals in rural areas in the United States have large open wards. On the other hand, the university hospital in one Italian city has separate wards for each department specializing in particular classes of illness. Each doctor-professor in this hospital has his own ward. Some are so jealous of their realms that they pass no records on to another ward when a patient is moved. Thus, upon being admitted to the new ward the patient's trajectory must be defined anew, repeating the whole process of examinations and history-taking. The trajectory of a patient who must pass from ward to ward is repeatedly being "initially" defined, in contrast to the redefinition process in American hospitals, where some records are usually passed along with the patient who must travel between wards.

Not all wards have the space or personnel to accept appropriate dying patients; this can have drastic consequences for the unaccepted patient. He may be sent to a ward not accustomed to his particular trajectory, which cannot offer the suitable hospital career. For example, if a patient needing constant care is placed in a ward where he can receive only periodic care, he may die between routine checks, unattended. We found precisely this situation in a county hospital whose emergency ward has a rule prohibiting accepting patients once all beds are full, regardless of consequences. Some patients are sent home to await a bed and, while waiting, become sicker or even die. Other patients, nearer death, are sent to appropriate wards. For example, a patient in danger of dying from a drug was sent for the night to the "psych" ward, where being "drugged" qualified him for admittance as suicidal. Patients on the "psych" ward, once asleep, are not checked until morning. The staff member reporting this observed: "If he did have a bad reaction there, he was as good as dead. Do you realize that just that sort of thing happened a hundred and some-odd times last year?" On the wrong ward, even a recoverable patient can become a dying patient. Another patterned hospital condition that might put the patient on the wrong ward appears when the inexperienced aide, under doctor's orders, takes a patient who needs oxygen periodically down to x-ray, where there is no oxygen supply. Conditions such as these, which mate a dying trajectory with an inappropriate hospital career, can increase both the likelihood and the speed of dying. . . .

Where and how a patient is placed on the ward upon admission or soon after can also be for him a very telling indicator of his chances for recovery, especially if he has had some experience in hospitals either as patient or visitor. For example, being placed in a room alone with the door left ajar, being screened off immediately after being placed in a multipatient room, or being placed as close to the nursing station as possible can lead to realizations that perhaps he is dying. These realizations are based both on comparisons with other patients, indicating that the common ward career does not entail isolation, and on the recognition that isolation prevents one's dying from disturbing other patients. In short, the patient's trajectory is not quite acceptable, and he is being provided a slightly different career. Explaining to themselves the unusual placements may easily lead both patient and family to formulate definitions of a dying trajectory.

217

The definitions of a dying trajectory that may occur to a patient as he passes through the conditions and procedures of entering a hospital and ward are just beginning and concern mostly the certainty (or uncertainty) of dying. Definitions of time, mode and shape of trajectory come later. Whether or not correct, the initial definitions will be imbued with doubt, and are, therefore, liable to much redefinition as the patient's trajectory and hospital career proceed with their attendant changing conditions.

The Medical Definition
of Death

A. Keith Mant

A Keith Mant is an English physician associated with Guy's Hospital in London. This selection is taken from a chapter entitled "Definition of Death" which first appeared in *Man's Concern with Death* edited by Arnold Toynbee. Mant's discussion offers some straightforward medical definitions that effectively set the stage for any further discussion of "what death is."

A true medical definition of death and an accompanying morbid fear of premature burial or dissection has exercised the mind of man from the earliest times. Modern techniques and practices have, under certain circumstances, tended to increase the difficulties of a precise definition rather than lessen them.

DIAGNOSIS OF DEATH

The importance attached to the certification of death by a duly qualified medical practitioner is known to all persons who are familiar with the procedure of coroners' inquests and have heard the police officers who were called to the scene of the death state, "Dr. X arrived at Y hours and pronounced life extinct." Some may feel that it is superfluous to call a medical practitioner to certify a death which had clearly occurred some days before the body was discovered, but in many countries a doctor must by law certify the fact of death. In Great Britain no cadaver can be legally disposed of without the production of a death certificate, and a death certificate can only be issued by a registered medical practitioner or a coroner. When a death is reported to a coroner the fact of death must be certified by a doctor after he has examined the body. On the other hand, provided a doctor has been in attendance during the last illness he may issue a death certificate without ever having seen the body after death—although this information must be recorded in the death certificate. This occasionally leads to certificates being issued prematurely or for the wrong person.

In a case brought to my notice a few years ago a child was sent round to a doctor's surgery with a message that grandpa had died and a request for the doctor to issue a certificate. Grandpa's front door was open, so the doctor could enter the house if he wished. The practitioner went round to the house and saw the old man apparently dead in bed, and as he had been treating him for a heart condition he wrote out the death certificate and left it by the bedside. On returning to his surgery he remembered that he had not seen his patient alive during the last fortnight, so he informed the coroner of the facts. The coroner's officer went round to the house, and whilst reading the death certificate was surprised by the "deceased" sitting up in bed and asking what he was doing. He explained his presence by stating that he was a police officer and that as the front door was open he had come in to investigate. The old man was still walking around six months later! Here we have an example of death being certified because the doctor accepted information he was given and did not bother to establish whether death had in fact occurred. Errors in pronouncement of death by doctors who do not examine the body or or merely give a cursory examination are rare but not unknown.

Taylor's *Medical Jurisprudence*[1] records recent cases of wrong certification. An old lady who had been found lying on some common ground was brought to hospital by ambulance. A doctor summoned from the Casualty Department felt that she was cold, and he was unable to feel a pulse or heart beat when he placed his hand on her chest. It was only after she had

---

[1]Taylor's *Principles and Practice of Medical Jurisprudence*, 12th edition, Ed. Simpson, K., Churchill, London, 1965, p. 104.

been undressed and placed on the mortuary table that it was noticed that she was still breathing.

Professor Simpson[2] mentions a 78 year old woman who was found apparently dead, having written suicide notes and with an empty sleeping tablet container by her side. She was removed to the public mortuary where six hours later a police officer dealing with her identification found her to be breathing.

In both these cases errors arose because the doctors relied too much on the circumstances surrounding the discovery of the bodies and did not carry out a detailed examination. In the first case, severe natural disease of the kind which in itself will weaken the heartbeat, together with cooling of the body following collapse in the open, produced signs of apparent death. In the second case the woman was under deep narcosis. In this condition the breathing is shallow and there is slowing and weakening of the pulse and a loss of body temperature. This state of drug-induced suspended animation is referred to in *Romeo and Juliet* (iv. i. 98) when Friar Laurence gives Juliet a potion which will put her into a deep sleep and says, "No warmth or breath shall testify thou liv'st."

On November 3rd 1967 several newspapers carried the story of an American soldier who was severely injured by an explosion in Vietnam. The soldier was taken to hospital apparently dead, and efforts to resuscitate him were abandoned after 45 minutes. He was sent to the mortuary where, however, the embalmer noticed he was still alive, and he was eventually flown back to the United States, where he subsequently recovered.

When lay persons attempt to certify death the chances of error are increased. After an air raid in Europe during the last war, I was asked by a civilian if I would examine someone who appeared to be alive in a pile of corpses. I not only confirmed that this body was alive but also removed two other "live corpses" from the heap. The deaths of all persons in the heap of corpses had been certified by the local air raid wardens, who had certified death rather by a visual examination of the injuries than as a result of any clinical examination. It must be admitted that the three live persons I removed were all suffering from severe injuries. One survived a long ambulance journey to die in hospital and, as she had been certified dead some two to three hours before I was sent for, it may well be that an earlier arrival at hospital would have saved her life.

---

[2]Simpson, K. *Abbotempo*, 1967, 3, 22.

Some of the earlier textbooks on forensic medicine have omitted any definition of death or have been intentionally ambiguous. For instance, if we look up the criteria of death in Smith's *Principles of Forensic Medicine* written in 1821,[3] we read, "If we are aware of what indicates life, which everyone may be supposed to know, though perhaps no one can say that he truly and clearly understands what constitutes it, we at once arrive at the discrimination of death. It is the cessation of the phenomena with which we are so especially familiar—the phenomena of life." Other early writings, although listing signs of death, give far more space to errors which may arise by placing reliance in these signs. Many quote examples of apparent suspended animation, premature burials and premature caesarean sections and autopsies.

The continental medico-legists of the 18th and 19th centuries wrote much on the uncertainty of signs of death and gave many examples of errors in certification. One finds, however, that cases which were reliably authenticated are quoted by many different authors, and this suggests that errors, although admittedly occurring from time to time, were certainly not as common as was made out by the more sensationalist writers.

John Bruhier,[4] a Paris physician of the 18th century, collected histories of persons alleged to have been buried alive. He gave 52 alleged examples of premature burial and 72 mistaken certifications of death, and recommended that burial should not take place until early putrefaction had occurred. A century later Fontenelle[5] recorded 46 cases of either premature burial or errors of certification; while Carré[6] asserted that there had been 46 cases of persons who had been certified dead and had recovered whilst awaiting inhumation. In the late half of the 16th century a Norman gentleman, M. Francois Civille, was alleged to have been three times dead, three times buried and three times disinterred and resuscitated.[7] In England the case of Colonel Townsend[8] was extensively quoted in textbooks of medical jurisprudence. Colonel Townsend voluntarily went into a state of suspended animation in the presence of Dr. Cheyne, another doctor and an

---

[3]Smith, J. G. *Principles of Forensic Medicine.* Underwood, London, 1821, p. 16.

[4]Bruhier-d'Ablaincourt, J. J., *Dissertation sur l'incertitude des signes de la mort et de l'abus des enterrements et des embauments précipités,* Paris, 1742.

[5]de Fontenelle, J., *Récherches médico-légales sur l'incertitude des signes de la mort, etc.,* Paris, 1834.

[6]Carré, *De la mort apparente,* Thèse de Paris, 1845.

[7]Sedillot, *Manuel complet de médecine légale,* Paris, 1835.
  Orfila, M. *Médecine légale,* Paris, 1823, p. 460.

[8]Cheyne, G. *The English Malady,* Risk, Ewing & Smith, London, 1733.

apothecary. His respirations and heart apparently ceased and after half an hour, as they were leaving him for dead, he slowly recovered.

The famous Professor Louis,[9] doyen of French medical jurisprudence, described a curious case of conception whilst apparently dead. A young monk stopped at a house where a young girl was laid out for burial and offered to spend the night in the room where the coffin was placed. He stripped the body during the night and had intercourse with it. The following morning, after he had left, the girl was resuscitated as she was about to be interred, and nine months later she gave birth to a child!

A leading article in the *Lancet* of 1866[10] reported a speech made by the Cardinal Archbishop Donnet of Bordeaux to the French Senate. In his speech the Cardinal described how as a young priest he had collapsed in the pulpit of a crowded church on a hot and sultry day. He was pronounced dead by a doctor and preparations were made for his funeral. Although he could see nothing he could hear what was being said. The Cardinal said that it was hearing a voice which he had known from infancy that produced the effort to get himself out of the trance. The next day he stood in the same pulpit. The Cardinal went on to say that he had himself saved several persons who had been considered dead and prepared for interment. One case he described was of a young girl who was about to be finally covered before burial. He did not feel certain that the girl was dead so he called out to her. The girl recovered and grew up to become the mother of a family.

There are several records of surgeons performing caesarean sections on women mistakenly considered to have died during labour. Before the days of anaesthesia, antisepsis and modern surgery, such an operation performed during life was invariably fatal, but the law of Numa Popilius demanded a caesarean section on women who died undelivered. A number of premature operations are recorded and the eminent Parisian obstetrician and gynaecologist Peu,[11] having carried out a caesarean section on a woman believed to be dead, vowed never to undertake such an operation again.

Mistakes in the pronouncement of death were not confined to the inexperienced doctors. Vesalius,[12] the founder of modern anatomy and physician to both Charles V and Philip II of Spain, carried out an autopsy on a man who was supposed to be dead and whose heart was seen to be beating,

---

[9]Louis, A., *Lettre sur le certitude des signes de la mort*, Paris, 1752.

[10]*Lancet* (1866), 1.295.

[11]Peu, P., *Prax. Obstetr.* 11 c 11. 2.

[12]Paris, J. A. and Fonblanque, J. S. M., *Medical Jurisprudence*, Phillips, London, 1823, vol. 2, p. 6.

together with other signs of life, when the thorax was opened. Vesalius was charged with homicide and impiety and taken before the Tribunal of the Inquisition, and his life was spared only by the intercession of the King of Spain.

There is no doubt that during the plagues and epidemics which swept Europe during the 17th and 18th centuries, several persons were prematurely buried owing to the natural desire to dispose of infected bodies as soon as possible.

Hadwen[13] cites numerous cases culled from the English, American and continental literature of dramatic recovery shortly before proposed interment, and horrifying examples leaving no doubt that persons were buried alive.

Of those who recovered before interment, all persons would appear to have gone into a trance-like state similar to that of Colonel Townsend. They were all fully aware of what was going on but were quite unable to make any movement. Some of these states lasted for several days, and the absence of any sign of putrefaction resulted in continued resuscitative measures. The resuscitative measures applied, for instance keeping the body warm and applying mustard poultices, would, if the person had been dead, have accelerated the onset of putrefaction. These trance-like states, like the fashionable "vapors" of the 19th century, appear to have disappeared in the 20th century. However, should a person in such a trance-like state be certified dead today, his chances of resurrection would be diminished because bodies are not usually kept at home but transferred to refrigerators in public mortuaries or undertakers' chapels, where any trance-like state would rapidly become permanent!

Of those buried alive, and Hadwen cites several examples, it would appear that some might have been saved were it not for superstition, disbelief and formality. One reads of persons hearing sounds from a fresh grave, disbelief and then many hours' delay before the formalities are completed for the exhumation. When the coffin is eventually opened we are told of the twisted shrouds, the doubled-up body, often with fresh injuries which have been bleeding, and all the signs of suffocation. Are these authentic cases? Dr. T. K. Marshall,[14] in a paper to the Medico-Legal Society, considers most of the accounts far from convincing and describes how some, though not all, of the criteria upon which evidence of premature burial was

---

[13]Hadwen, W. R., *Premature Burial*, Swan Sonnenschein, London, 1905.
[14]Marshall, T. K., (1967) *Med-leg F.* 35; 14.

based could have a natural explanation, for example the action of rodents, putrefaction and the plundering of vaults.

Hadwen[15] records that during the 1849 epidemic of cholera, when 119 persons died in Gloucester alone, the man and woman in charge of the ward informed a solicitor, for whom they later worked, that as soon as the patients were dead they put them in shells and screwed them down so as to get them out out of the way as soon as possible. Sometimes they revived afterwards and were heard kicking in their coffins. They were never released as it was considered by the man and wife in charge that they had got to die anyway. A number of writers in the 19th century considered that there was a danger of premature burial during epidemics.

ʃʃ

The morbid fear of premature burial prompted some persons even [to] demand that they be decapitated before burial.

ʃʃ

MEDICAL SIGNS OF DEATH

The signs of death listed by the earlier medico-legists differ little from those found today in medico-legal textbooks. They are briefly: cessation of respiration and heart beat, changes in the eye, insensibility to electrical stimuli, rigor mortis, pallor, hypostasis and relaxation of the sphincters. The difficulties which existed in the early days in pronouncing death still exist, although they are often made easier today by increased knowledge and improved techniques. The fallibility of holding a feather before the nostrils was recorded by Shakespeare when in *Henry IV, Part II*, the Prince of Wales removed his father's crown believing him to be dead, with the words:

". . . By his gates of breath
There lies a downy feather which stirs not:
Did he suspire, that light and weightless down
Perforce must move." (*Henry IV, Part II*, iv. v. 30)

---

[15]Hadwen, W. R. (*ibid.*), p. 118.

Shakespeare refers also in *King Lear* to another fallible method of determining life, that of holding a mirror to the nostrils, as proof that Cordelia was dead:

"Lend me a looking-glass;
If that her breath will mist or stain the stone,
Why, then she lives." (*King Lear,* v. iii, 263)

From the earliest medical writings on death such methods were recognised as unreliable and dangerous. The morbid fear of premature burial prompted some persons to order in their wills that before burial death must be proved surgically by incision or by the application of boiling liquids or a red hot iron to the skin. Some even demanded that they be decapitated before burial.

Some of the earlier medico-legists placed weight on one particular sign of death. Professor Louis[16] placed emphasis on eye changes: the drying of the cornea, followed within a few hours by flaccidity of the eyeballs. Nysten[17] considered death present when muscles failed to contract with the application of a galvanic current, as response to electrical stimuli may be elicited normally up to some two hours after death has occurred. Professor Louis and others also placed reliance on the development of rigor mortis and wrote at considerable length on the differentiation of rigor mortis from other conditions such as tetanus.

Foderé[18] recommended the opening of an intercostal space in the left side of the chest and the insertion of a finger to palpate the heart to see if it were beating.

All these earlier medico-legists were agreed that the only incontrovertible sign of death was the onset of putrefaction.

SOMATIC AND CELLULAR DEATH

In 1836 Ryan[19] made a profound statement which is pertinent today: "Individuals who are apparently destroyed in a sudden manner, by certain wounds, diseases or even decapitation, are not really dead, but are only in

---

[16]Louis, A., *op.cit.*

[17]Nysten, *Recherches de physiologie et de chimie pathologiques, pour faire suite à celles de Bichat, sur la vie et la mort,* Paris, 1811.

[18]Foderé, F. E., *Traité de médecine légale,* Paris, 1813, 2nd edition, vol. 2, p. 366.

[19]Ryan, M., *Manual of Medical Jurisprudence and State Medicine,* Sherwood, Gilbert & Piper, London, 1836, 2nd edition, p. 499.

conditions incompatible with the persistence of life." Here Ryan recognises the differences between somatic death, the extinction of personality, and molecular death, the actual death of the cells which make up the body.

This is the problem that faces doctors today when considering the question of organ transplantation: when is the person from whom the organ is to be removed in a state which is incompatible with the persistence of life?

Somatic death is the cessation of all vital functions such as the heart beat and respiration. Molecular or cellular death follows. Many cells in the body will continue to live for some time after somatic death. Muscles will respond, for instance, to electrical stimuli for up to two hours. The well-known death-stiffening of the body, rigor mortis, is due to cellular metabolism continuing after somatic death. Groups of cells may be removed from a body after death and kept alive, sometimes indefinitely, in tissue culture. The rate at which cellular death occurs varies in different organs. The more specialised the organ, the more rapidly its cellular death follows somatic death. The advent of organ transplantation surgery has greatly increased the importance of cellular death.

Owing to the fallibility of the diagnosis of death many writers advocated a delay between death and burial. Bruhier[20] advocated four days or until putrefaction had commenced. In France burial could not officially take place until 24 hours after the death certificate had been issued, and in certain parts of the continent regulations insisted that bodies should be left in a mortuary which was under the direction of a cemetery inspector with medical knowledge until unequivocal signs of post-mortem decomposition had appeared. A special room was attached for the resuscitation of those who were only apparently dead. In France in particular the fear of premature burial was widespread during the 19th century. Research into the signs of death was carried out in the various academies and prizes were offered for papers on the subject. Dr. E. Bouchet[21] was awarded the Manni prize of 1,500 francs in 1846 for the discovery of a certain sign of death. Bouchet relied on auscultation. He showed conclusively that in apparent death even when there appeared to be a complete cessation of vital functions, including cooling of the body, the heart beat was not at any time suspended but merely reduced in force and frequency.

---

[20]Bruhier-d'Ablaincourt, J. J., *Mémoire sur la nécessité d'un réglement général au sujet des enterrements et des embauments, et projet de réglement*, Paris, 1746.

[21]Bouchet, E., *Traité des signes de la mort et des moyens de prévenir les enterrements précipités*, Paris, 1849.

The Prix Dusgate, a quinquennial prize of 2,500 francs, was awarded in 1890 to Dr. Maze who considered, as others had done before, that putrefaction was the only sure sign of death, and advocated the provision of mortuaries in cemeteries where bodies could be placed until putrefaction commenced. Two later prizes were awarded to Dr. Icard, who recommended the injection of a dye into the circulation. If life were present the entire body would be colored in a few minutes. Numerous other novel tests were recommended such as the plunging of a needle into the heart to observe movement, the application of steam or heat to the skin and the passage of a galvanic current.

The profound interest in methods of determining real from apparent death in the 18th and 19th centuries is emphasised by Gannal's[22] textbook on the subject which was published in 1890. His bibliography contains no fewer than 418 references.

MODERN CRITERIA OF DEATH

So much for the history of the search for a reliable sign of death. What about the present day? With all our acquired knowledge can one succinctly give the medical criterion of death?

During the last few years this matter has been discussed at various international and other scientific meetings and has been the subject of several papers. There is still no unanimity, as death is not an instantaneous process and sometimes its initial phases may be reversible. For instance, a person collapses from a heart attack. He is apparently dead. There are no respiratory movements and no heart beat. If this attack should have taken place in a hospital, where all the modern methods for resuscitation are available and immediately at hand, it is possible that his heart beat may be restored and the man literally brought back to life. Without these procedures, unknown a few years ago, death would have been permanent. Can one be alive and dead at the same time?

The United Nations Vital Statistics define death as the permanent disappearance of every sign of life. Dr. Voigt[23] considers that this definition is not sufficiently comprehensive and should read: "Death has occurred when every spontaneous vital function has ceased permanently." But what if we

---

[22]Gannal, F., *Mort apparente et mort réelle*, Muzard et fils, Paris, 1890.
[23]Voigt, J., (1967), *World Med. J.*, 14; 144.

apply this definition to a man who has been beheaded or hanged? Spontaneous vital functions may continue for several minutes after decapitation or judicial hanging.

Today the medical criteria of death have a significance undreamed of by the earlier physicians, whose chief concern was the prevention of premature burial. If inhumation were delayed, as by law in some European countries, for a specified period after the issue of a death certificate, premature burial would appear impossible, and it would be quite impossible if burial were delayed until the onset of putrefactive processes.

ORGAN TRANSPLANTATION AND ARTIFICIAL PROLONGATION OF LIFE

Today, with the transplantation of cadaver organs to living persons, the exact moment of death is of great importance, as the sooner the organs are removed from the cadaver after somatic death, the better the chance of the grafted organ surviving. The potential donors of their organs are usually young persons who are dying as the result of some serious accident. Their lives are often being artificially maintained by apparatus which is carrying out the functions of their heart and lungs. When the apparatus is switched off they will have no spontaneous heart or respiratory movements. These mechanical substitutes for the vital functions would normally only be employed in the first place if it were considered that they might tide the patient over a period, until the vital centers could again function spontaneously. The doctor has to decide when the limit of usefulness of these artificial aids is reached—that is, when centers in the brain controlling the vital functions of the body are irreversibly damaged. Is it right that the doctor in charge of the case should maintain artificial somatic life in order that an organ may be removed for grafting purposes whilst it is still being circulated with oxygenated blood?

Professor Simpson[24] points out an important medico-legal issue arising from the artificial maintenance of life. Supposing a person, anxious that his estate should escape death duties, should make a deed of gift, and a few days before the specified period is up should have an accident in which his vital centers are irreversibly damaged to such an extent that they can never again function spontaneously. Should the doctor try to maintain somatic life artificially until the specified period is reached, or risk being sued by the beneficiaries if he does not? One can see such a case leading to a definition of death in the legal sense.

---

[24]Simpson, K., (1967), *Guy's Hosp. Gaz.*, 81; 605.

The persistence of normal life is dependent upon the integrity of that part of the central nervous system which controls the vital functions and upon the integrity of the vital organs themselves. If one fails, they all fail. Until relatively recently the certification of the fact of death was based upon the cessation of the heart beat—or "heart death." Today with our increase in knowledge and the introduction of the electroencephalogram (E.E.G.) we now also have "brain death." Under normal circumstances "heart death" precedes "brain death," but with modern techniques of resuscitation "brain death" may precede "heart death."

It has been known for a long time that if certain brain cells, the more recently specialised, are deprived completely of oxygen for more than a few seconds they die and can never recover their function, as there is no regeneration of brain tissue. The more primitive parts of the brain, those that control the vital functions, can put up with far greater insults, and therefore, under certain circumstances, the individual may lose personality, that part of the brain which deals with thought and voluntary movement, and yet survive as a vegetable because the vital centers are intact. Thus one might conclude that if there is a flat E.E.G. reading, that is to say a complete absence of brain function, for five minutes, that life is extinct. In fact some biologists[25] accept one minute as incontrovertible proof of death. In a normal case this is acceptable, but as with other signs of somatic death there are exceptions. Professor Hamburger[26] reported complete recovery after a flat E.E.G. reading was recorded for several hours in two patients suffering from severe barbiturate poisoning. At the low temperatures which are reached by the hypodermic techniques employed in modern heart surgery the oxygen requirements of the brain are greatly reduced, and the circulation of oxygenated blood may be maintained with a heart-lung machine, although the circulation and respiration have ceased to function spontaneously owing to the low body temperature which is below that compatible with life. By the older definitions the patient is dead, but he is in fact in a state of artificially induced hibernation or suspended animation. Both the E.C.G. and E.E.G. recordings show that neither the brain nor the heart is functioning, but when the body is re-warmed at the end of the operation the vital functions start to operate spontaneously and normal function is restored.

---

[25]*Ethics in Medical Progress*, Ciba Foundation Symposium, Churchill, London, 1966, p. 68.
[26]*Ibid.*, p. 69.

Likewise a person who suffers a cessation of heart beat due to some acute lesion, such as a coronary thrombosis, is dead by old criteria—he has had a cardiac death. The moment of cerebral death, however, has not arrived and, if the heart beat is restarted by artificial means before the onset of cerebral death, the patient may make a complete recovery.

Under certain circumstances, the use of artificial aids to maintain a vital function for long or indefinite periods appears reasonable. For example, the patient who has complete paralysis of the nerves controlling respiration following poliomyelitis may live for many years in a respirator. The patient with certain types of heart disease may live much longer if an artificial pacemaker is introduced to take over the control of the heart beat. Machines are available to take over the work of the kidneys, and life, which was otherwise impossible, may be prolonged. In all these examples, once the artificial aid is taken away the patient will die. These cases differ from those described earlier in that the patients still have their personality. The higher centers of the brain are intact although disease has interfered with the brain's control of certain vital functions or with the functioning of certain vital organs. Provided these functions are maintained artificially the person is alive in every other sense.

Dr. Voigt[27] considers that in a particular case, if brain function is abolished and spontaneous circulation and respiration have ceased, then the definition of death in the United Nations Vital Statistics is fulfilled. No one can dispute this statement. Differences of opinion arise only in diagnosis.

Recently Dr. Henry Beecher[28] of Harvard stated in a lecture that the cessation of the heart beat was no longer synonymous with the onset of death but there were now three competing definitions.

1 The moment at which irreversible destruction of brain matter, with no possibility of regaining consciousness, was conclusively determined.
2 The moment at which spontaneous heart beat could not be restored.
3 "Brain Death" as established by the E.E.G.

Dr. Beecher went on to say that any up-to-date determination of death would be a legal impossibility at this time, however theologically and scientifically sound it might be.

---

[27]Voigt, J., (1967), *World Med. F.*, 14; 145.
[28]Beecher, H., *The Times*, December 12th 1967.

CONCLUSIONS

The medical criteria of death have not radically changed since the earliest days except for the concept of cerebral or brain death. Modern apparatus such as the electroencephalogram and the electrocardiogram when available enable the clinician to apply more efficient and searching tests. Under normal circumstances a person is as dead today as he was a thousand years ago if his heart does not beat for five minutes. It is when a patient is subjected to an abnormal environment or is in an abnormal state as the result of drugs, disease or treatment that exceptions to a single or several of the accepted criteria of death may arise. The certifying doctor should always exercise extreme vigilance and exclude the remote possibility of any extraneous factor inducing a state of suspended animation. In 1884 the *Lancet*[29] in an annotation on burying cholera cases alive said, "It is not so much the undue haste as inexcusable carelessness that must be blamed for the premature burying of persons who are not really dead." The few mistakes in certification that are made today, as in the past, are due to carelessness and ignorance.

---

[29]*Lancet* (1884), 2; 329.

Brain Death

Robert M. Veatch
Robert M. Veatch is the Associate for Medical Ethics and
Director of the research group on Death and Dying at the
Hastings (New York) Institute of Society, Ethics and the Life
Sciences. Dr. Veatch's article reports a fascinating and
poignant case (involving a heart transplant) that touches
on morality, religion, law, science, praxis, and prejudice.

Robert M. Veatch, "Brain Death: Welcome Definition . . .
or Dangerous Judgment?" *Hastings Center Report*, Vol. 2,
No. 5 (November 1972). Reprinted by permission.

CASE NO. 23 *The following case, decided by a Virginia jury,
may be a crucial one for medical ethics. It may be used as precedent in deciding* when
a patient is dead *and for establishing* where the proper authority lies *for
changing public policy regarding such fundamental decisions as those of human life
and death. It appears that there were serious mistakes, both in interpretation and in
judgment, by all involved. A more thorough exploration is certainly called for.*

On May 25, 1968, at the beginning of the era of transplantation, Bruce
Tucker was brought to the operating room of the hospital of the Medical
College of Virginia. Tucker, a 56-year-old black laborer, had suffered a
massive brain injury the day before in a fall. He sustained a lateral basilar
skull fracture on the right side, subdural hematoma on the left, and brain
stem contusion.

The following timetable is taken from the summary of the case by Judge
A. Christian Compton:

6:05 p.m.	Admitted to the hospital.
11:00 p.m.	Emergency right temporoparietal craniotomy and right parietal burr hole.
2:05 a.m.	Operation complete; patient fed intravenously and received "medication" each hour.
11:30 a.m.	Placed on respirator, which kept him "mechanically alive."
11:45 a.m.	Treating physician noted "prognosis for recovery is nil and death imminent."
1:00 p.m.	Neurologist called to obtain an EEG with the results showing "flat lines with occasional artifact. He found no clinical evidence of viability and no evidence of cortical activity."

2:45 p.m.	Mr. Tucker taken to the operating room. From this time until 4:30 p.m. "he maintained vital signs of life, that is, he maintained, for the most part, normal body temperature, normal pulse, normal blood pressure and normal rate of respiration."
3:30 p.m.	Respirator cut off.
3:33 p.m.	Incision made in Joseph Klett, heart recipient.
3:35 p.m.	Patient pronounced dead.
4:25 p.m.	Incision made to remove Tucker's heart.
4:32 p.m.	Heart taken out.
4:33 p.m.	Incision made to remove decedent's kidneys.

Tucker's heart and kidneys were removed by the surgical team. The heart was transplanted to Joseph G. Klett, who died about one week later.

William E. Tucker, brother of the dead man, sued for $100,000 damages, charging the transplant team was engaged in a "systematic and nefarious scheme to use Bruce Tucker's heart and hastened his death by shutting off the mechanical means of support." According to the judge's summary, "a close friend of the deceased was searching for him and made an inquiry at three of the hospital information desks, all without success." Tucker's brother, William, was "at his place of business, located within 15 city blocks of the hospital, all day on May 25th until he left his business to go find his brother in the afternoon when he heard he had been injured. Among the personal effects turned over to the brother later was a business card which the decedent had in his wallet which showed the plaintiff's (brother's) name, business address and telephone number thereon." The suit charged that the removal of organs was carried out with only minimal attempts to notify the victim's family and obtain permission for use of his organs.

ꜛꜛ

There is a great deal at stake at the
policy level in the definition of death.

ꜛꜛꜛ

This case is one of the most complicated and significant in the current debate about the brain locus for death. Whether or not it should, in fact, be treated as a "brain death" case we shall consider later, but certainly that is the way the principals in the case and the press have handled it. The Internal Medicine News Service headed their report, " 'Brain Death' Held

Proof of Demise in Va. Jury Decision." The *New York Times'* headline said, "Virginia Jury Rules That Death Occurs When Brain Dies." *Internal Medicine News,* in one of the best stories covering the case, claimed—quite accurately—that "the landmark decision is not binding elsewhere but it is certain to be cited as precedent in related cases." In fact, not one news story with which we are familiar saw this as other than a brain death case.

The surgeons who removed Tucker's heart evidently also interpreted it as a case of deciding when a patient is dead. Dr. Hume is quoted as saying that the court's decision in favor of the physicians "brings the law up to date with what medicine has known all along—that the only death is brain death."

Asked to decide whether the physicians were guilty of causing the death of the heart donor, the jury in the Tucker case were in effect being asked to make a public policy judgment about whether the irreversible loss of brain function is to be equated for moral, legal, and public policy purposes with the death of an individual.

The task of defining death is not a trivial exercise in coining the meaning of a term. Rather, it is an attempt to reach an understanding of the philosophical nature of man and that which is essentially significant to man which is lost at the time of death. When we say that a man has died, there are appropriate behavioral changes; we go into mourning, perhaps cease certain kinds of medical treatment, initiate a funeral ritual, read a will, or, if the individual happens to be president of an organization, elevate the vice president to his presidency role. According to many, including those who focus on the definition of death as crucial for the transplant debate, it is appropriate to remove vital, unimpaired organs after, but not before, death. So there is a great deal at stake at the policy level in the definition of death.

CANDIDATES FOR "DEATH"

There are several plausible candidates for the concept of death. All are attempts to determine that which is so significant to man that its loss constitutes the change in the moral and legal status of the individual. The traditional religious and philosophical view in Western culture was that a man died at the time when his soul left the body. This separation of body and soul is difficult to verify experimentally and scientifically and is best left to the religious traditions, which in some cases still focus upon the soul-departure concept of death.

Traditional secular man has focused on the cessation of the flow of the vital body fluids, blood and breath; when the circulatory and respiratory functions cease, the individual is dead. This is a view of the nature of man which identifies his essence with the flowing of fluids in the animal species.

There are also two new candidates. One of these is the complete loss of the body's integrating capacities, as signified by the activity of the central nervous system. This is the now-popular concept frequently though inaccurately given the name "brain death." Most recently in the literature there are those who are beginning to question the adequacy of this notion of brain death, claiming that it already has become old fashioned. They ask why is it that one must identify the entire brain with death; is it not possible that we are really interested only in man's consciousness: in his ability to think, reason, feel, experience, interact with others, and control his body functions consciously? This is crucial in rare cases where the lower brain function might be intact while the cortex, which controls consciousness, is utterly destroyed.

↑↑↑

The claim that death occurs when the brain dies is opinion to be sure, but it is not, and by the very nature of the case cannot be, medical opinion.

↑↑↑

MORAL, NOT TECHNICAL

The public policy debate about the meaning of death involves a choice among these several candidates for death. The Harvard Ad Hoc Committee to Examine the Definition of Brain Death established operational criteria for what it called irreversible coma, based on very sound scientific evidence. These four criteria are: 1. unreceptivity and unresponsivity; 2. no movements or breathing; 3. no reflexes; 4. flat electroencephalogram ("of great confirmatory value").

What the Committee did not do, however, and what it was not capable of doing, was establishing that a patient in irreversible coma is "dead," i.e., that we should treat him as if he were no longer a living human being who is the possessor of the same human moral rights and obligations as other human beings. While it may be the case that a patient in irreversible coma, according to Harvard criteria, has shifted into that status where he is no longer to be considered living, the decision that he is "dead" cannot be derived from any amount of scientific investigation and demonstration. The choice among the many candidates for what is essential to the nature of man and, therefore, the loss of which is to be called "death," is essentially a philosophical or moral question, not a medical or scientific one.

This being the case, it is troubling, indeed, to hear physicians say as Dr. Hume did, that the Virginia legal decision "brings the law up to date with what medicine has known all along—that the only death is brain death." If some physicians have believed this (and certainly there is no consensus among medical professionals), they know it from their general belief system about what is valuable in life and not from their training as medical scientists. It is therefore distressing that "expert" witnesses, including Dr. William Sweet of Harvard Medical School, were called by the defense to testify before the jury. Dr. Sweet said, "Death is a state in which the brain is dead. The rest of the body exists in order to support the brain. The brain is the individual." This may or may not be a sound moral philosophical argument. It is certainly not a medical argument. And to ask a chief of neurosurgery at Massachusetts General Hospital to make the moral argument is certainly a kind of special pleading on the part of legal counsel for the defense. This led to the *New York Times'* story which began, "A medical opinion that death occurs when the brain dies, even if the heart and other organs continue to function, has been reinforced by a jury here in a landmark heart transplant suit." The claim that death occurs when the brain dies is opinion to be sure, but it is not, and by the very nature of the case cannot be, medical opinion. To leave such decision-making in the hands of scientifically trained professionals is a dangerous move.

Especially in such a fundamental matter as life and death itself, it is very difficult to see how the rest of society can shirk its responsibility in deciding what concept of death is to be used. To be sure, the scientific community can and should be asked to establish the criteria for measuring such things as irreversible coma, once the public, acting through its policy-making agencies in the legislature, has determined that irreversible coma is to be equated with death.

But let us return to the Tucker trial to see how this confusion between social and medical responsibilities developed. In the state of Virginia, according to the judge, there was a definition of death operative and that

definition was specifically "the cessation of life; the ceasing to exist; a total
stoppage of the circulation of the blood, and a cessation of the animal and
vital functions consequent thereto such as respiration and pulsation." On
a motion for summary judgment for the defendants, the judge ruled that
the law-book definition of death must take precedence over medical opinion. In this opinion, Judge Compton directed that the court was bound by
the legal definition of death in Virginia until it was changed by the state
legislature. Three days later, however, after considerable debate, Judge
Compton may have backtracked on his commitment to the publicly established concept of death. He instructed the jury:

> In determining the time of death, as aforesaid . . . you may consider
> the following elements none of which should necessarily be
> considered controlling, although you may feel under the evidence that
> one or more of these conditions are controlling: the time of the total
> stoppage of circulation of the blood; the time of the total cessation
> of the other vital functions consequent thereto, such as respiration
> and pulsation; the time of complete and irreversible loss of all
> functions of the brain; and whether or not the aforesaid func-
> tions were spontaneous or were being maintained artificially or
> mechanically.

This instruction is ambiguous, to say the least. It could be that Judge
Compton meant no innovation here. It could be that the "complete and
irreversible loss of all function of the brain" might have been merely the
"cause" of death traditionally defined, i.e. "a cessation of the animal and
vital functions." Presumably if the head injury to Tucker led to the cessation
of all brain function and thereby to the cessation of all other vital functions,
death could have occurred in the traditional sense without or prior to the
intervention of the surgeons. This almost certainly would have been the
case if Mr. Tucker had received no medical attention. Then (traditional)
death would have occurred and the "complete and irreversible loss of all
function of the brain" would have been simply a relevant factor.

But it also is possible to interpret the judge's instructions as authorization for the jury to use a new concept of death—one based directly on brain
function—in determining the time of the patient's death. If this is the case
it is a complete reversal of the judge's earlier statement and a major change
in public policy. It would appear that this contradicts Judge Compton's
earlier conclusion that "if such a radical change is to be made in the law of
Virginia, the application should be made therefore not to the courts but to

the legislature wherein the basic concept of our society relating to the preservation and extension of life could be examined and, if necessary, reevaluated." Let us hope that the judge's later instruction to the jury should not be taken as backing down from this important principle.

WHO SHOULD HAVE MADE THE DECISION?

The other candidates for decision-making in this case obviously are the relatives of the patient. While it is the state's obligation to establish fundamental policy in this area, it would seem reasonable and in the interest of the state that they would judge that no organs may be removed from an individual after death unless there is some authorization by the individual patient, such as is now called for in the Uniform Anatomical Gift Act, or by the patient's relatives, also as provided by that Act. If it is true, in this case, that the relatives of the patient were not consulted and sufficient time was not taken to establish that relatives were available, this would seem to have been a most serious infringement upon the rights of the patient and the patient's family.

The removal of organs in the rare situations where relatives cannot be found raises a serious, if rather unusual, problem for transplant surgeons. It would appear to be far wiser to avoid the risk of abuse in these cases, which will frequently involve indigent and lonely patients, by simply forbidding the use of organs. Certainly four hours (from the time Mr. Tucker was placed on a respirator until the respirator was turned off) was not sufficient time to seek permission from the next of kin.

WAS THIS REALLY A DEFINITION OF DEATH CASE?

Up to this point, we have assumed that the defense, the prosecution, and the press were correct in interpreting this case as one focusing upon the meaning and concept of death. Yet the case record, as presented to the court, leaves open some very serious questions. The medical team was operating with a definition of death which focused on the brain. Medical witnesses for the defense claimed that Mr. Tucker was "neurologically dead" several hours before the transplant operation. Yet according to the records presented of the case, at 11:45 a.m. Mr. Tucker's physician says prognosis is nil and death imminent. At 1:00 p.m. the neurologist took an EEG reading and found it "showing flat lines with occasional artifact" and he "reports no evidence of viability and no signs of cortical activity." Presumably, according to a brain-oriented concept of death, Mr. Tucker was thought to be dead at that time by the surgeons. Yet we are told by the surgeons that at

3:30 p.m. they turned the respiratory off. One must ask what possible moral
principle would justify turning off a respirator on a dead patient. Presumably if one is dealing with a corpse, the moral imperative would be to
preserve the organs for the benefit of the living in the best possible condition—by continuing the respiration process until the heart could be removed. We would find no moral problems with such behavior; in fact,
one would say that it would be morally irresponsible to run the risk of
damaging the tissue. Yet the respirator was turned off—from which one can
only surmise that it must have been done in order to permit the heart and
lungs to stop functioning. The only plausible reason for this would be that
there was some lingering doubt about whether or not Mr. Tucker was dead.
Of course, to introduce this dimension is to place doubt on the claim that
the patient was dead at 1:00 p.m. when the EEG showed a flat tracing "with
occasional artifact."

If, however, the purpose was to turn the respirator off in order to allow
the patient to die all the way, the case is not one of a new definition of death
at all; it is instead the common one of morally, and possibly legally, deciding
to continue treatment no longer on an irreversibly terminal patient. The
morality of ceasing treatment on such a terminal patient has been accepted
widely in medical ethics. Such procedures are practiced and accepted by
Catholic, Protestant, and Jewish moral traditions alike. It could be, then,
that this is really a case of deciding when it is morally acceptable to stop
treatment on a dying patient, rather than a case of deciding when a patient
was dead. This seems to be the most plausible and morally acceptable reason
for turning off the respirator under law then existing in Virginia. It is very
important to note that the jury never announced that the brain-oriented
concept of death is now appropriate or that they themselves used such a
concept. They were not asked or permitted to do this. They merely concluded that they found the defendants not guilty of wrongful death of the
decedent. It may well be that at least some of them reasoned that the physicians did indeed hasten the dying process by turning off the respirator, but
given the patient's condition this was an acceptable way to behave; i.e., they
may have considered that the physician could have justifiably decided to
withdraw the mechanical means of support as "extraordinary for a patient in
Tucker's irreversibly dying condition." We do not know this of course, but
we also do not know that the jury accepted a brain-oriented concept of
death.

At 3:35 p.m., five minutes after the respirator was turned off, the patient
was pronounced dead. One would think this was because there had been a

cessation of heart beat and respiratory function and the death was pronounced according to the traditional heart/lung criteria. If this were the case, the physicians would be operating under the traditional moral and legal requirements, and the removal of organs for transplantation, presumably with the permission of the next of kin, would be an acceptable procedure. They would not be using the brain-oriented concept of death at all.

WAS HE NEUROLOGICALLY DEAD?

There is one final problem which must be resolved. The summary of the proceedings raises some doubt as to whether the patient was dead even according to the concept of brain death which focuses upon the brain. The Harvard criteria call for the use of irreversible coma. But the Harvard report appeared in the *Journal of the American Medical Association* dated August 5, 1968, and the surgeons at the Medical College of Virginia had to make their decision two months earlier, on May 25, 1968. Obviously they could not be expected to have followed the Harvard criteria precisely. Nevertheless, Mr. Tucker definitely could not have been declared dead according to the criteria since established by the Harvard Committee and widely used as being the minimal tests for establishing irreversible coma. At the very least, the tests were not repeated twenty-four hours later. The patient was pronounced dead less than two hours and thirty-five minutes after the electroencephalogram reading.

In order to accept the jury's decision in this case and accept it as demonstrating that the physicians were justified in the use of brain evidence of death, one would have to accept four highly questionable premises. The first is that the jury did indeed base its decision on a brain-oriented concept of death. Second, that a man is really dead when he no longer has any capacity for brain activity. The third is that it was reasonable under 1968 conditions to conclude that the patient had irreversibly lost the capacity for any brain activity based on one EEG reading without repetition. Such a conclusion is premature even for the scientific evidence which exists today, some four years later. Finally, one would have to accept that individual medical professionals should be vested with the authority to change public policy on an area as fundamental as life and death. This no one should be willing to tolerate.

The Death Certificate

Edwin S. Shneidman
Edwin S. Shneidman is Professor of Thanatology and
Director of the Laboratory for the Study of Life-Threatening
Behavior at the University of California at Los Angeles. In
this selection, which is taken from his book *Deaths of Man,*
Dr. Shneidman discusses the development, the uses, and the
main deficiencies of the death certificate. He notes that
the contemporary death certificate fails to reflect the
psychological role of the decedent in his own demise.

As this book is about death, so this selection is about a unique document that memorializes death. We have seen that death is an epistemologically curious event that cannot be experienced and never has been directly reported. The document of which we speak is one that must, without exception, be completed (in due time) for each reader, and which, under no possible circumstances in this world, can any reader ever see completed for himself. The document is, of course, the death certificate.

That interesting document is much more than just a document. It is better understood as that special form which gives operational meaning to death and which, in fact, defines its current dimensions. It reflects the ways in which man—administrative and forensic man, at any rate—thinks about death and the ways in which he believes it occurs.

The impact of the death certificate is considerable. It holds a mirror to our mores; it reflects some of our deepest taboos; it can directly affect the fate and fortune of a family, touching both its affluence and its mental health; it can enhance or degrade the reputation of the decedent and set its stamp on his postself career. But if the impact of the death certificate is great, its limitations are of equal magnitude. In its present form the death certificate is a badly flawed document.

Today most states follow the format of the U.S. Standard Certificate of Death. Most relevant to our present interests is the item which reads: "Accident, suicide or homicide (specify)." When none of these is checked, a natural mode of death is, of course, implied. Only two states, Delaware and Virginia, have made all four of these modes of death explicit on the death certificate (and have included "undetermined" and "pending" categories as well). Curiously enough, Indiana included these modes of death on the death certificate form from 1955 to 1968, but then revised the form in 1968 and now provides no item for mode of death; nor, surprisingly, does the current Massachusetts death certificate contain an accident-suicide-homicide item.

In addition to the U.S. Standard Certificate, the International Classification of Diseases and Causes of Death plays a major role in determining the way a specific death may be counted—and thus in the apparent change in statistical causes of death from decade to decade. For example, the definitions of suicides and accidents were changed in the Seventh Revision (1955) and Eighth Revision (1966) of the International Classification, and the numbers of suicides and accidents changed along with the definitions. When the Seventh Revision was put into effect for the data year 1958, the death rate for suicides increased markedly over 1957. In part, one can find the explanation in this paragraph (U.S. Department of Health, Education and Welfare 1965):

> About 3.3 percent of the total suicide rate for 1958 as compared with that for 1957 resulted from the *transfer of a number of deaths from accidents to suicide.* In 1958 a change was made in the interpretation of injuries where there was some doubt as to whether they were accidentally inflicted or inflicted with suicidal intent. Beginning with the Seventh Revision for data year 1958, "self-inflicted" injuries with no specification as to whether or not they were inflicted with suicidal intent and deaths from injuries, whether or not self-inflicted, with an indication that it is not known whether they were inflicted accidentally or with suicidal intent, are classified as suicides. The change was made on the assumption that the majority of such deaths are properly classified as suicide *because of the reluctance of the certifier to designate a death as suicide unless evidence indicates suicidal intent beyond the shadow of a doubt.* The magnitude of the comparability ratios for suicide varied considerably with means of injury, from 1.02 for suicide by firearms and explosives to 1.55 for suicide by jumping from high places. [Emphasis added.]

It would seem that this redefinition led to an apparent 55 percent increase from one year to the next in suicides by jumping from high places. Even more interesting is the official observation that the death certifier would be reluctant to indicate suicide "unless evidence indicates suicidal intent beyond the shadow of a doubt." Clearly the certifier plays an important role in the process of generating mortality data. It is he who makes the subjective judgment of what constitutes conclusive evidence of the decedent's intent. The Eighth Revision (1966), which made the category "Undetermined" available, introduced still further problems, apparently shifting many suicidal deaths to the Undetermined category. What is urgently needed is an explanation and description of the current practices of certifying deaths, especially deaths by suicide. We need a uniform system that would eliminate such inconsistencies (or confirm the differential unequivocally) as for example, 10.9 deaths by suicide per 100,000 population for Idaho versus 20.2 for Wyoming. What is required is a "correctional quotient" for each reporting unit—county, state, and nation. Until such information is obtained, available suicidal statistics are highly suspect.

That is what the situation is now. At the turn of the century, an early reference book of the medical science (Abbot 1901) urged reliable death registration bookkeeping:

> The objects secured by a well devised system of death certification are manifold and may be enumerated as follows:
>
> 1 Questions relating to property *rights* are often settled by a single reference to a record of a death.
> 2 The official certificate of a death is usually required in each case of claim for *life insurance.*
> 3 Death certificates settle many disputed questions in regard to *pensions.*
> 4 They are of great value in searching for records of *genealogy.*
> 5 A death certificate frequently furnishes valuable aid in the *detection of crime.*
> 6 Each individual certificate is a contribution *causa scientiae.* Taken collectively they are of great importance to physicians, and especially to health officers, in the study of disease, since they furnish valuable information in regard to its causes, its prevalence, and its geographical distribution.

All that is well and good. But that was three-quarters of a century ago. It is time to take full account of the enormous scientific and intellectual developments of the twentieth century, especially the psychiatric revolution that began with Freud and has grown steadily during the past three generations. At least four more functions for the death certificate might be added to the half-dozen listed in 1901:

7 The death certificate should reflect the dual nature of death; that is, its private nature (as it is almost experienced by the decedent) and its public nature (as it is experienced and accounted for by others).

8 It should reflect the type of death that is certified—[for example,] brain death (a flat electroencephalographic record) [or] somatic death (no respiration, heartbeat, reflexes).

9 It should include space for the specification of death by legal execution, death in war or military incursions, death by police action, and others of the sort.

10 Perhaps most important, it should abandon the anachronistic Cartesian view of man as a passive biological vessel on which the fates work their will, and instead reflect the contemporary view of man as a psycho-socio-biological organism that can, and in many cases does, play a significant role in hastening its own demise. This means that the death certificate should contain at least one item on the decedent's *intention* vis-à-vis his own death. It is not enough to state that a death was natural, accidental, suicidal, or homicidal; we should know too whether it was intentioned, subintentioned, or unintentioned.

Let us look at the typical death certificate reproduced here. What is there seems fairly straightforward. The items speak for themselves. But not everything is so obvious. For example, it is possible to think of the items on the death certificate as being divided into three groups: The top third of the certificate has to do with identification of the decedent. It establishes exactly who that person was: name, date of birth, place of birth, spouse's name, mother's maiden name, Social Security number, etc.—items calculated to distinguish one John Allen Smith from any other.

ffffffffffffffffffffffffffffffffffffffffffffffffffffffffffffffffffffffff

In the Western world death is given its administrative dimensions by the death certificate.

ffffffffffffffffffffffffffffffffffffffffffffffffffffffffffffffffffffffff

The middle section of the certificate relates to cause or causes of the death. There is some worldwide agreement as to what causes are to be listed. Indeed, . . . there is an international classification of diseases and causes

INDIANA STATE BOARD OF HEALTH
DIVISION OF VITAL RECORDS
MEDICAL CERTIFICATE OF DEATH

Local No._____

State No._____

1. PLACE OF DEATH a. COUNTY		2. USUAL RESIDENCE (Where deceased lived. If institution: Residence before admission) a. STATE	b. COUNTY
b. CITY, TOWN, OR LOCATION	c. Length of Stay in 1b	c. CITY, TOWN, OR LOCATION	
d. NAME OF HOSPITAL OR INSTITUTION (If not in hospital, give street address)		d. STREET ADDRESS	
e. IS PLACE OF DEATH INSIDE CITY LIMITS? YES☐ NO☐		e. IS RESIDENCE INSIDE CITY LIMITS? YES☐ NO☐	f. IS RESIDENCE ON A FARM? YES☐ NO☐

3. NAME OF DECEASED (Type or print)	First	Middle	Last	4. DATE OF DEATH	Month	Day	Year

5. SEX	6. COLOR OR RACE	7. MARRIED ☐ NEVER MARRIED ☐ WIDOWED ☐ DIVORCED ☐	8. DATE OF BIRTH	9. AGE (In years last birthday)	IF UNDER 1 YEAR Months / Days	IF UNDER 24 HRS. Hours / Min.

10a. USUAL OCCUPATION (Give kind of work done during most of working life, even if retired)	10b. KIND OF BUSINESS OR INDUSTRY	11. BIRTHPLACE (State or foreign country)	12. CITIZEN OF WHAT COUNTRY?

13. FATHER'S NAME	14. MOTHER'S MAIDEN NAME

15. WAS DECEASED EVER IN U. S. ARMED FORCES? (Yes, no, or unknown) (If yes, give war or dates of service)	16. SOCIAL SECURITY NO.	17a. INFORMANT'S NAME

17b. INFORMANT'S ADDRESS	17c. RELATIONSHIP TO DECEASED

18. CAUSE OF DEATH [Enter only one cause per line for (a), (b), and (c).] PART I. DEATH WAS CAUSED BY: IMMEDIATE CAUSE (a)_____	INTERVAL BETWEEN ONSET AND DEATH
Conditions, if any, which gave rise to above cause (a) stating the underlying cause last. DUE TO (b)_____ DUE TO (c)_____	
PART II. OTHER SIGNIFICANT CONDITIONS CONTRIBUTING TO DEATH BUT NOT RELATED TO THE TERMINAL DISEASE CONDITION GIVEN IN PART I (a).	19. WAS AUTOPSY PERFORMED? YES☐ NO☐

20a. ACCIDENT ☐ SUICIDE ☐ HOMICIDE ☐	20b. DESCRIBE HOW INJURY OCCURRED. (Enter nature of injury in Part I or Part II of item 18.)
20c. TIME OF INJURY Hour Month Day Year a. m. p. m.	
20d. INJURY OCCURRED WHILE AT ☐ NOT WHILE ☐ WORK AT WORK	20e. PLACE OF INJURY (e. g., in or about home, farm, factory, street, office bldg., etc.) 20f. CITY, TOWN, OR LOCATION COUNTY STATE

21. ATTENDING PHYSICIAN: I certify that I attended the deceased from_____, to_____and last saw her/him alive on_____Death occurred at_____M (C.S.T.) on the date stated above; and to the best of my knowledge, from the causes stated.

22. HEALTH OFFICER: I certify that I investigated cause of death of deceased and find that death occurred at_____M (C.S.T.) from causes stated and on above date.

23a. Signature of Attending Physician or Health Officer.	23b. ADDRESS	23c. DATE SIGNED

24a. BURIAL, CREMATION, REMOVAL (Specify)	24b. DATE	24c. NAME OF CEMETERY OR CREMATORY	24d. LOCATION

DATE REC'D BY LOCAL HEALTH OFFICER	SIGNATURE OF HEALTH OFFICER	25. FUNERAL DIRECTOR	ADDRESS

S.B.H.—6-24-3—Revised 1955   U. S. Department Health, Education and Welfare.   Form Approved Budget Bureau No. 68-R375

EMBALMER'S NAME_____

LICENSE No._____

MEDICAL CERTIFICATION

FUNERAL DIRECTOR'S LICENSE No._____

of death: an Abbreviated List of 50 Causes and an Intermediate List of 150 Causes. The International Conference for the Eighth Revision of the International Classification of Diseases, held in Geneva in 1965 (U.S. Department of Health, Education and Welfare 1966), considered compilation of a longer list of 250 to 300 causes.

The bottom third of the death certificate contains a number of items usually related to injury and to such miscellaneous items as place of burial or cremation, name of funeral director or embalmer, and so on—none of which interests us especially. But there is one item of very special interest in this section, usually relative to "violent death," which typically contains only three words: accident, suicide, homicide. The important point is this: If none of these three is checked, it is implied that the death was natural. These four terms, then, represent the four traditionally implied modes of death: natural, accidental, suicidal, and homicidal—what, acronymically, I have called the NASH classification (Shneidman 1963). (The use of modifications and combinations of these terms to yield other labels, such as "probable suicide," "probable accident," "suicide-accident undetermined," and so on, does not change the fact that there are only four main modes of death stated or implied on the present certificate.)

It should be immediately apparent that the cause of death stated on the certificate does not automatically carry with it information as to the specific mode of death. One example should suffice: Asphyxiation due to drowning in a swimming pool does not clearly communicate whether the decedent struggled and drowned (accident), entered the pool with the intention of drowning himself (suicide), or was held under the water until he was drowned (homicide).

In the Western world death is given its administrative dimensions by the death certificate. It is the format and content of this document that determines and reflects the categories in terms of which death is conceptualized and death statistics reported. The ways in which deaths were described and categorized in John Graunt's day* and earlier set deep precedents for ways

---

*John Graunt, a London tradesman, published in 1662 a small book of observations on the "bills of mortality" that were published in London at the end of each year. Graunt separated the various bits of information contained in these bills into categories and organized them into tables. He focused on individual causes of death and on the subject of population estimation, and constructed a mortality table which was the first attempt to organize data in this manner. Of greatest significance was his success in demonstrating the regularities that can be found in medical and social phenomena when one is dealing with large numbers. John Graunt's book was to have great social and medical significance. —ED.

of thinking about death, and they govern our thoughts and gut reactions to death to this day. . . . Deaths were then assumed to fall into one of two categories: there were those that were truly adventitious—accidents, visitations of fate or fortune (called natural and accidental)—and there were those that were caused by a culprit who needed to be sought out and punished (called suicidal and homicidal deaths). In the case of suicide, the victim and the assailant were combined in the same person and the offense was designated as a crime against oneself, a *felo de se*. England did not cease to classify suicide as a crime until 1961, and in this country it remains a crime in nine states to this day (Litman 1970).

The importance of the certification of the mode of death—of the coroner's function—can now be seen: it not only set a stamp of innocence or stigma upon the death, but also determined whether the decedent's estate could be claimed by his legal heirs (natural or accidental deaths) or by the crown or local lord (a suicide or a murderer). That was certainly one important practical effect of the death certificate. This bias (in relation to suicide, at any rate) is reflected today in the ways insurance policies are written. I would assert that the NASH categories of death were implied as early as the sixteenth century in English certification, and that this submanifest administrative taxonomy of death has beguiled most men into thinking that that is the way death phenomena really are, which, of course, is not necessarily so at all.

Although it may be platitudinous to say that in each life the inevitability of death is an inexorable fact, there is nothing at all inexorable about our ways of dimensionalizing death. Conceptualizations of death are man-made and mutable; what man can make he can also clarify and change. Indeed, changes in the conceptualizations of death are constantly occurring, notwithstanding the NASH notions of death that have held on for centuries after they became anachronistic. Each generation becomes accustomed to its own notions and thinks that these are universal and ubiquitous.

From the time of John Graunt and his mortuary tables in the seventeenth century through the work of Cullen in the eighteenth century and William Farr in the nineteenth century, the adoption of the Bertillon International List of Causes of Death in 1893, and the International Conference for the Eighth Revision of the International Classification of Diseases as recently as 1965, the classification of causes of death has constantly been broadening in scope, the changes characterized primarily by attempts to reflect additions to knowledge, particularly those contributed by the new professions as they have developed—anesthesiology, pathology, bacteriology, immunology, advances in obstetrics and surgery, and most recently, the behavioral sciences.

The traditional natural-accident-suicide-homicide classification of modes of death is demonstrably insufficient: certain deaths cannot be classified as other than equivocal. This can be true, of course, even when *cause* of death is clearly established. Indeed, in the modern medical examiner-coroner's office, it is a very rare case—given the available skills of pathologist, microscopist, and toxicologist—in which the cause of death cannot be determined. But it does not follow at all that mode of death can be so clearly stated; . . . an estimated 10 to 15 percent of all coroners' cases are equivocal as to mode of death, the alternatives usually being accident and suicide.

ͼͼͼ

> *A total autopsy ought to include the services of the behavioral scientist—psychologist, psychiatrist, sociologist, social worker.*

ͼͼͼ

The most serious fault in the certification of equivocal death is the lack of any attempt to establish the *intention* of the decedent in regard to his own demise. The decedent's intention—not his stomach or lung contents or his brain pathology—is what operationally distinguishes suicide from the other three modes. And the decedent's intention cannot be found in the test tube or under the microscope. Often, however, it can be discovered by conscientious interviewing of people who knew various aspects of his life style and specific behavior immediately prior to his death. A total autopsy ought to include the services of the behavioral scientist—psychologist, psychiatrist, sociologist, social worker. We call this procedure the "psychological autopsy. . . ."

Much of what I have had to say about the NASH classification of death has impugned its heuristic and scientific usefulness. What, in fact, is its major shortcoming? By far its greatest inadequacy lies in the fact that it emphasizes relatively trivial elements in the death of a human being while omitting altogether the psychological role he may have played in his own demise. The NASH classification, Cartesian and apsychological in spirit, implies that the human being is a biological machine to which things happen, rather than a vital, introspective, unique individual who often unconsciously plays a decisive role in his own fate. In other words, it leaves man out.

I propose that we put him in. We could begin by adding the item I have already suggested—an indication of the decedent's intention regarding his own death. This item might be labeled "Imputed Lethality," since this judgment can only be inferential, and I suggest that it consist of four designations: "High," "Medium," "Low," "Absent."

High imputed lethality would indicate that the decedent definitely wanted to die, and played a direct and conscious role in his own death. The death was due primarily to the decedent's conscious wish to be dead, and to his actions in carrying out that wish either by some recognized means of suicide (jumping from a high place, shooting himself in the head) or by deliberately goading someone to kill him, refusing life-saving procedures, stopping a prescribed medical regimen, or some other act of commission or omission that he knew would result in his death.

Medium imputed lethality would indicate that the decedent played an important role in effecting his own death. His behavior in some degree hastened the event—carelessness, foolhardiness, neglect of self, rash judgment, gambling with death, laxness in following a prescribed life-saving medical regimen, active resignation to death, drug abuse, habitual drunkenness, "tempting fate," "asking for trouble."

Low imputed lethality would indicate that the decedent played some small but insignificant role in effecting or hastening his own demise. The difference between medium and low imputed lethality is one of degree, not of kind.

When imputed lethality is absent, the decedent has played no role in effecting his own death. The death was due entirely to assault from outside the body (in no way invited by the decedent) or to failure within the body (in a decedent who unambivalently wished to continue to live).

This is a classification that seems to me to be meaningful; it is more fair than the NASH categories alone. At present, individuals of higher social status who commit suicide are more likely to be assigned the mode of accident or natural death than are individuals of low social status whose suicidal intent appeared no less ambiguous. If the term is to have any meaning at all, it should be used fairly across the board, measured by the individual's intention.

Perhaps more important from the larger view, the lethality-intention item would provide an unexampled source of information by means of which biostatisticians, public health officials, and social scientists could assess the mental health of any community. It is obvious that the number of deaths that are caused, hoped for, or hastened by the decedents themselves is a measure of the prevalence of psychological disorder and social stress. At present we do not have this measure, and we need it.

It might be protested, inasmuch as the assessments of these intention states involve the appraisal of unconscious factors, that some workers (especially lay coroners) cannot legitimately be expected to make the kinds of psychological judgments required for this type of classification. But medical examiners and coroners throughout the country are making judgments of precisely this nature every day of the week. When a coroner must evaluate a possible suicide, he acts, perhaps without realizing it, as psychiatrist and psychologist, as both judge and jury: any certification of death as suicide implies some judgment or reconstruction of the victim's motivation or intention. But it would be far better if these psychological dimensions of death were made explicit through use of a lethality-intention scale than to allow them to remain implicit and be used in an influential manner. The dilemma is between the present usable, oversimplified classification on the one hand, and a somewhat more complex but more precise classification on the other.

In Marin County, California, the coroner's office* is currently assessing each death processed by that office in terms of both the traditional NASH classification of mode of death and the lethality intention of the decedent. For a two-year period, 1971–1972 (978 cases), the breakdown was as follows:

(1) Natural deaths (630): high lethality intent, none; medium lethality, 33 (5%); low, 37 (6%); absent, 560 (89%).

(2) Accidental deaths (176): high lethality intent, 2 (1%); medium; 77 (44%); low, 40, (22%); absent, 57 (33%).

(3) Suicidal deaths (131): high lethality intent, 131 (100%).

(4) Homicidal deaths (37): high lethality intent, none; medium, 20 (54%); low, 9 (24%); absent, 8 (22%). Four deaths were of unknown origin.

The first thing we notice is that *some* natural, accidental, and homicidal deaths were classified as having *some* degree of lethal intention. If the medium- and low-intention categories are combined, then over one-fourth

---

*I am especially grateful to Keith C. Craig, coroner's deputy, Marin County, for his interest and help in supplying these data.

(26 percent) of all natural, accidental, and homicidal deaths (216 of 847) were deemed to be subintentioned. If one adds the suicidal deaths (in which the decedent obviously has played a role), then only 64 percent—or 625 of 978—of all deaths were deemed to have been totally adventitious; or, conversely, 36 percent were deemed to have some psychological components.

Also of special interest in these Marin County data is the finding that coroners can, with no more apparent difficulty than they experience in assigning deaths to the NASH categories, simultaneously (and by essentially the same processes of inference and induction) assign deaths to psychological (intentional) categories as well. It is an important pioneer effort that deserves widespread emulation.

REFERENCES

Abbott, Samuel W. Death Certification. In Albert H. Buck (Ed.), *Reference Handbook of the Medical Sciences.* New York: William Wood, 1901.

Litman, Robert E. Medical-Legal Aspects of Suicide. In Edwin S. Shneidman, Norman L. Farberow, and Robert E. Litman, *The Psychology of Suicide.* New York: Science House, 1970.

Shneidman, Edwin S. Orientations toward Death: A Vital Aspect of the Study of Lives. In Robert W. White (Ed.), *The Study of Lives.* New York: Atherton, 1963.

Shneidman, Edwin S. *Deaths of Man.* New York: Penguin Books, 1974.

U.S. Department of Health, Education and Welfare. *Mortality Trends in the United States, 1954–1963.* Washington, D.C.: U.S. Government Printing Office, 1965.

U.S. Department of Health, Education and Welfare. *Report of the United States Delegation to the International Conference for the Eighth Revision of the International Classification of Diseases, Geneva, Switzerland, July 6–12, 1965.* Washington, D.C.: U.S. Government Printing Office, 1966.

World Health Organization. *Manual of the International Statistical Classification of Diseases, Injuries, and Causes of Death: Based upon the Recommendations of the Seventh Revision Conference, 1955.* Geneva: World Health Organization, 1957.

Psychological Autopsies
in Judicial Opinions

Thomas L. Shaffer*

Thomas L. Shaffer is Professor of Law at Notre Dame
University. In this selection, Professor Shaffer discusses with
both psychological and juridical sophistication, the role
of intention in death and then, in detail, presents a "psychological autopsy" of an eighty-year-old man from a legal
viewpoint.

From *Death, Property, and Lawyers: A Behavioral Approach*
by Thomas L. Shaffer. Copyright © 1970 by the Dunellen
Publishing Company, Inc. Reprinted by permission.

The court's inquiry . . . is into the mind of the
decedent, into that "heap or collection of different perceptions."
Transfers prompted by the thought of death, even if they are also
prompted by other motives, are includable in the gross estate. The
tax law does not require us here to determine "motive". . . but it
seeks an equally elusive shadow from the recesses of the mind of
the deceased; did the thought of death prompt him to act? The
conclusion may not be wholly intellectual. Decision may result also
from intuition, emotional reaction, and visceral response to the
composite picture that results from the images imposed on each other
in court by advocates with opposite motives, one bent on proving
that the deceased, whatever his age or health, was convinced of his
own immortality and impervious to thoughts of death, and the other
seeking to show that the donor was weak of body and sick of mind,
preoccupied by the converging approach of the grim reaper and the
tax collector.[1]

It is surprising how many cases have been litigated under Section 2035 of
the Internal Revenue Code, which imposes an estate tax on inter-vivos

*Dr. Robert S. Redmount and Dr. Herman Feifel contributed comments to this discussion. I
am grateful to them for their contribution and for their suggestions on other material in
this selection.

gifts in contemplation of death.* It is also surprising that those hundreds of
judicial opinions embody rigid perceptions of human life and of attitudes
toward death, perceptions which range from incisive to callous. They disclose a judicial system of death psychology which is detailed, systematic,
and sometimes, probably, accurate. This is an inquiry into those opinions
(and decisions) as psychological autopsies. The inquiry has several practical possibilities:

1 It may indicate something about the legislative wisdom in retaining a tax
   provision which turns on a post-mortem assessment of the attitude a dead
   man had toward his death.[2]
2 It may indicate something about the judicial wisdom in construing a
   statutory word ("contemplation") literally.[3] Compare this, say, with the
   judicial wisdom in construing a similar word ("intended"), in a similar
   section of the same Code, to refer only to the mechanical operation of a
   property-transfer device.[4]
3 It may indicate something about trial tactics within a legislative and
   judicial system which continues to impose death taxes on transfers which
   are made in contemplation of death. (It is an open secret that the process
   as it now exists is chaotic and probably presents the only common factual
   issue in the federal estate tax on which taxpayers can usually expect
   victory.)
4 It may indicate something about the way men are as they approach death.
   That assumes, of course, that judges are able to detect human facts and
   to report them accurately. At least one can hope that the Section 2035
   opinions will tell him how judges think men are as they approach death.

I make the inquiry against a model suggested by the eminent "suicidologist,"
Dr. Edwin Shneidman, who has recently worked at the National Institute of
Mental Health, and as a Fellow of the Center for Advanced Study in the
Behavioral Sciences. Dr. Shneidman proposed several years ago a "psycho-
logical post-mortem."[5] He designed his system primarily for death certifica-
tion, and he demonstrated that it is a model upon which attitudes toward

---

*"The value of the gross estate shall include the value of all property to the extent of any
interest therein of which the decedent has at any time made a transfer . . . in contemplation
of his death. If the decedent within a period of three years ending with the date of his death
. . . transferred an interest in property . . . such transfer shall, unless shown to the contrary, be deemed to have been made in contemplation of death within the meaning of this
section. . . ."

death can be reconstructed after the man being studied is dead. And that is exactly what judges do in Section 2035 cases.

Dr. Shneidman's objective was "a psychologically oriented classification of death phenomena, an ordering based in large part on the role of the individual in his own death." His analysis had an affirmative premise that a man's death is a personal event and a negative premise that our culture, specifically those public officials concerned with death certification, accept "natural" death as an ideal. Both premises apply to the Section 2035 literature, where, because of *United States* v. *Wells*, the inquiry is a personal inquiry; and where judges make their decisions in reference to an ideal decedent who has lived his life to the end, with courage, and who has predicated what he did in his last days on his life rather than on his death. (One might call that ideal the "natural" attitude toward death.) This ideal death (or attitude) is what Shneidman calls "the idyll that living and dying are separate." It should be some consolation to lawyers and judges that Shneidman aims this "idyll" primarily at physicians and coroners.

This view of death, in Shneidman's world and in the chambers of judges deciding "contemplation of death" cases, assumes that death is something that happens to a man, rather than something a man does:

> What has been confusing in this traditional approach is that the individual has been viewed as a kind of biological *object* (rather than psychological, social, biological organism), and as a consequence, the role of the individual in his own demise has been omitted.

This leads Shneidman, as it led Freud, to forsake an analysis of death and focus instead on an analysis of *dying*. He avoids even the word "death" and substitutes instead four other words for dying: (1) *cessation* ("the last line of the last scene of the last act of the last drama of that actor"); (2) *termination* (a biological end which one might plan to survive, as Tom Sawyer did); (3) *interruption* (cessation, temporarily, without termination, as in sleep or a coma); and (4) *continuation* (the opposite of interruption: continuation relates to death because people may want to be delivered from continuation but not from life itself). These concepts are useful in a consideration of property disposition at, or "in contemplation of," death. Testamentary transfer is evidently a matter of termination without cessation; the testator expects to live on in his property. He may therefore view his death as an interruption, and he may view as continuation the aspects of property ownership which impose responsibilities on him.

Shneidman suggests that the decedent might have approached his cessation in any one of four general frames of mind: intentioned, subintentioned, unintentioned, and contraintentioned. Each category is further subdivided:[6]

Intentioned:
>   cessation-seekers
>   cessation-initiators (who would rather quit than be fired)
>   cessation-ignorers (who contemplate cessation without termination)
>   cessation-darers (who, for instance, "fly" airplanes without knowing how)

Subintentioned:
>   cessation-chancers
>   cessation-hasteners (alcoholics; people who refuse to use medicine)
>   cessation-capitulators
>   cessation-experimenters (who seek an altered continuation)

Unintentioned:
>   cessation-welcomers (the ideal old person who is thought to welcome the end)
>   cessation-acceptors (heroic acceptance)
>   cessation-postponers
>   cessation-disdainers (the supercilious death attitudes of some young people)
>   cessation-fearers (for example, hypochondriacs)

Contraintentioned:
>   cessation-feigners
>   cessation-threateners (for example, people who "attempt" suicide as a way to manipulate others)

The decedent in every factually detailed, reported Section 2035 case could probably be located within this scheme. I see an illustrative parallel in two cases Shneidman puts on the confusion involved in the psychopathology of suicide: The first case involved a woman who shot herself, with drastic physical damage short of death. The second case involved a woman

> who had cut herself with a razor blade. She had, she said, absolutely no lethal intention, but had definitely wished to jolt her husband into attending to what she wanted to say to him about his drinking habits.

Classifying both cases, as medicine has been likely to do, as "attempted suicide," would have "run the risk of masking precisely the differences we might wish to explore." The two classifications suggested in Shneidman's "contraintentioned" category preserve the distinction. An analogue is possible to (1) the person who makes testamentary transfers for vindictive reasons and to (2) the person who talks about or threatens testamentary changes (whether or not he makes them) for manipulative reasons. . . .

↑↑↑

There is a difference between giving one's property away because one is going to die and making written plans for what is to be done with one's property when one is dead.

↑↑↑

Fitting Section 2035 cases into Shneidman's scheme will sometimes be the result of looking at the evidence objectively.[7] It will sometimes be the result of the subjective needs and views of death in the judge or judges deciding the case. The prototypes which arise from decided Section 2035 cases should in either event give way to a psychologically sophisticated view of death attitudes in the donors under judicial examination, and that will be analogous to the sophistication Shneidman suggests for the medical and paramedical professions in suicide treatment.

The prototype judicial view of a gift in contemplation of death case implies that the dead man expressly, overtly, considered death as the fact which would bring a series of plans into operation. Giving in contemplation of death is seen as goal-striving behavior which death will facilitate. I suspect and even hypothesize that this view is unsound because it equates "gift in contemplation of death" with "testamentary disposition." That equation is unquestionably at work in most of the cases. It is a judicial rule of thumb. But it is probably psychologically inaccurate. There is a difference between giving one's property away because one is going to die and making written plans for what is to be done with one's property when one is dead. I suggest, very tentatively, that the first is analogous to cessation-feigning and the second analogous to cessation-postponing.

In a second paper, Shneidman applied his system to Herman Melville. There is one aspect of his venture which is particularly interesting in the psychology of testation. Shneidman believes that Melville's preoccupation with death, combined with his almost obsessional resentment of literary critics, led him to a choice between protest and withdrawal. Melville chose withdrawal "disdainful, ignoring . . . critics as though they did not exist, as though they were dead, reducing them to the unimportant position of impotence by robbing them of their power to influence and especially of their power to hurt." Shneidman believes that Melville's withdrawal was a sort of death:

> This maneuver, by its very nature, tragically can be executed only at the price of one's own total or partial self-ostracism and thus at the expense of the death of part of one's social and hence psychological self.

Melville was, in this view, focusing on a "post-self," on a future in which his real self (the self which he expressed in his work) would be vindicated:

> The self or ego relates to the core of one's active functioning, his cognitive and emotional masterings and maneuvers in the present life; the post-self, on the other hand, refers to the ways in which one might live on, survive, or have some measure of impact or influence after the event of his own physical death—for example, through one's children, or through one's published works. . . .

This is cessation *without* termination; and it is far better as a matter of human anticipation than cessation *with* termination: "To cease as though one had never been . . . to abandon any hope . . . of impact or memory . . . beyond one's death, to be obliterated . . . to be naughted . . . that is a fate literally far worse than death."

I mention this in introduction because the post-self concept has application in considering contemplation of death. A man survives his death (cessation) in those he loves and in the things he owns. He lives on (when the context is gratuitous transfer) in an expression that involves both those he loves and his property. He lives on in the act of giving property. And this is the same sort of living-on that Shneidman discovered in Melville; it is a part of things one contemplates when he contemplates death. . . .

I have been generously assisted and encouraged in this and other aspects of the study of the psychology of testation by Dr. Shneidman and by two other distinguished clinical psychologists, Dr. Robert S. Redmount, who is also a lawyer, and Dr. Herman Feifel, who should probably be considered the founder of modern death psychology.

COMMISSIONER v. ESTATE OF VARNER (TAX COURT)

William Varner died at the age of 80 years, four months. At issue are three transfers he made during his life.[8] The first, made two years, ten months before his death, was of a summer cottage in Michigan; this transfer was made to his son, William Varner, Jr., "for the use of the grantor's granddaughter, Linda Snopes Cole." Linda Snopes Cole was the decedent's daughter's daughter; the decedent's daughter and her husband died in an airplane accident ten years before the transfer of the summer cottage.

The second transfer was of shares of stock in the Frenchman's Bend Realty Company, a corporation which owned and managed farm property in areas near the decedent's home. This transfer, made 18 months before the decedent's death, was of all the decedent's interest in the corporation; it was made, outright, to William Varner, Jr., the decedent's son.

The third transfer, made six months before the decedent's death, was of several parcels of real estate: two farms, ten acres of undeveloped land, and the house on which the decedent's home stood. This transfer was to William Varner, Jr., in trust for Linda Snopes Cole. It was accompanied by an extensive and complex trust instrument which restrains on its alienation, elaborate restrictions on the alienation of equitable interests (spendthrift provisions), and directions for the distribution of corpus and income to Linda Snopes Cole and to her children, if she had any.

William Varner, Jr., as executor of his father's estate, timely filed a federal estate-tax return, reporting these three transfers as not taxable, and a gross estate exclusive of these transfers of $15,000. Since the gross estate reported was well below the exemption allowed, the estate reported no taxable estate and paid no estate taxes. The values at death of the property transferred during life are stipulated in this Court and are:

the summer cottage, $65,000;

stock in Frenchman's Bend Realty Company, $150,000;

real estate in trust, $210,000.

The evidence is that these transfers had approximately the same values on the dates they were transferred inter vivos and that after the transfers were completed the decedent's owned property did not exceed $20,000 in value.

The Commissioner of Internal Revenue objected to the estate's position on the three inter-vivos transfers and issued notices of deficiency. He claimed estate taxes of $96,200, which assessments the estate protested. The case is here on the following issue: Were the three inter-vivos transfers includable in the gross estate under Section 2035 of the Internal Revenue Code of 1954, which provides:

> The value of the gross estate shall include the value of all property to the extent of any interest therein of which the decedent has at any time made a transfer . . . by trust, or otherwise, in contemplation of his death.[9]

This Court must decide whether the dominant motive of the decedent in making each of these transfers was prompted by the thought of death. The leading authority on the tests which are to be applied is the decision of the Supreme Court of the United States in *United States* v. *Wells,* which said that the question is whether "the decedent's purpose in making the gift was to attain some object desirable to him during his life, as distinguished from the distribution of his estate as at death." The Court there stated that the Congressional purpose in Section 2035 was "to reach substitutes for testamentary dispositions and thus to prevent the evasion of the estate tax." We have determined that the transfers were *not* in contemplation of death.

The Cottage   The decedent was 77 years old when he transferred the cottage. The testimony is that he made the transfer in order to provide a restful, pleasant atmosphere for his granddaughter, so that she could spend her summer vacations there. The reason he transferred to his son, Mrs. Cole's uncle, rather than to Mrs. Cole, was that Mrs. Cole was somewhat unstable mentally. She had twice been hospitalized for "nervous breakdowns"; her husband had divorced her about a year before this transfer; she lived in the decedent's home when she was not on vacation; the decedent cared for her during periods of emotional tension in her life. The evidence is that Mrs. Cole found the summer heat in Frenchman's Bend oppressive and that she enjoyed staying at the Michigan cottage and had stayed there off and on during summers since she was a child. The decedent spoke many

259

times before the transfer of making the cottage available to Mrs. Cole, so that she would not need to ask his permission to stay there.

Five years before he died and shortly after the death of his wife, the decedent stopped going to the cottage himself. Aside from a two-month visit there by Mrs. Cole, the cottage was in caretaker status for a year and a half after the death of the decedent's wife. About three and one-half years before his death, however, Mr. Varner visited the cottage on what he later referred to as an "inspection tour." When he arrived at the cottage he found that the caretaker had neglected it. In fact, Mr. Varner found the caretaker intoxicated and unconscious in one of the bedrooms of the cottage. (This caretaker was replaced by William Varner, Jr., after the transfer which is at issue here.) Witnesses testified that this discovery disturbed Mr. Varner and that he decided to "get rid of the cottage." There is in evidence a letter he wrote William Varner, Jr., enclosing a copy of the executed, recorded deed; that letter said, in part:

> Your mother always preferred Michigan, but I have never liked it. Besides that, the worry of it has become too much for me; you have just got to go ahead and run it. I have had enough, and, besides, I need to reduce my tax bite. It has served its purpose so far as I am concerned. I have my home in Frenchman's Bend.

(As a matter of fact, Mr. Varner still had, at that time, extensive ownership of real estate other than his home, as well as 25 percent of the common stock of a real estate holding company there.) The letter said nothing of Mrs. Cole's use of the cottage, but the oral testimony was that William Varner, Jr., understood that the cottage "was really for Linda," that the deed made that clear to him, and that he managed the cottage for her and intends to continue doing so.

The decedent's health, prior to seventeen months before his death, was excellent for a man of his age. The first evidence of his terminal illness arose after the transfer of the cottage *and* of the corporate securities, when he visited his physician with the complaint that he was not able to hold on to things. The physician diagnosed his ailment as amyosthenic lateral sclerosis of the spinal cord, a chronic degenerative disease of the central nervous system which leads to the wasting away of the body from want of nourishment. The disease is usually fatal in from two to six years after diagnosis. The physician did not inform Mr. Varner of this condition; he told Mr. Varner that he had a nervous condition, that he (the doctor) would prescribe medication for it, and that Mr. Varner should return for "checking up" at intervals of one month. At the time of this diagnosis, Mr. Varner was active, cheerful, and optimistic. The physician never told him about his fatal condition, but he did tell Williar Varner, Jr., about seven months before Mr. Varner's death, and the testimony is that William Varner, Jr., told his father about the condition shortly thereafter.

We think that Mr. Varner, who made this transfer before he had any information on his illness—even partial, undisturbing information—was not significantly affected by an altered attitude toward life, that is, by thoughts of death. The evidence is that he was cheerful, pleasant, active, interested in many facets of life, sociable, and fond of many forms of entertainment, including circuses, card games, and, when he was in Memphis, burlesque shows. Few men many years his junior could match his zest for living, both physically and mentally. We find as a fact that the transfer of the cottage was not in contemplation of death.

The Corporate Securities   This transfer was made 18 months before death and one month before the decedent visited his physician for what turned out to be a diagnosis of fatal illness. The transfer was of all the decedent's interest in a corporate venture he had founded in 1928, and of which he had been variously president, secretary, and treasurer; he resigned from office in the corporation three years before his death, and turned the day-to-day management of the business over to his associate, Colonel V. K. Ratliff. He remained as a director and saw that his son, William Varner, Jr., (who was then a nominal shareholder) was employed as secretary and business manager for the corporation. Eighteen months before his death, Mr. Varner resigned as a director and transferred all of his shares (about one-third of those outstanding) to William, Jr.

Mr. Varner's health at this time remained good, although he had begun to suffer some muscular instability. His physician testified that there was nothing in his physical condition, at the time of the transfer of corporate securities, "which would lead any physician to anticipate his death at any time in the near future." Cross-examined about the spinal condition which was diagnosed a month later, the physician said he was not sure that a diagnosis would have disclosed this condition at the time of the transfer, and that in any event the prognosis at that time would have been survival for at least two years.

Mr. Varner's transfer of the securities was, of course, a part of his general retirement from business. Counsel for the Government contends that he was "letting go, preparing to cash in his chips." That charming metaphor

261

is not as apt as it may appear. Mr. Varner remained active in the management of rural real estate for another year; he climbed atop houses to inspect roofs, walked in fields which he owned to estimate crop yields, and even attempted minor repairs on his buildings. He began at about that time to make extensive plans for travel, and even to carry out some of them. He told his son and Mrs. Cole that he would make a sea trip around the world within a few months of retirement. He took an airplane trip to the World's Fair in New York City shortly after the transfer of securities, and he went on extensive automobile trips around his home region—some of them by himself. These travels were strenuous, and included hiking in the hills of his native state. Mr. Varner's only complaint about his trips was that he was unable to deduct their cost on his income-tax return. He took his physician on two of these trips into the hills; the physician testified that he (the physician) tired more readily in hiking than Mr. Varner did. William Varner, Jr., hired a servant to assist his father around the house, but his father resisted the servant and resented his presence. He never complained about his health or talked of death.

This evidence is similar to that on the cottage transfer. In the first situation Mr. Varner's manifest motive was to provide a pleasant summer retreat for his disturbed, unhappy granddaughter; in the case of the securities, the transfer was to provide a secure business future for his son, to reduce income taxes, and to enjoy, while he lived, his son's growth and success in a challenging business. Here, as in the transfer of the cottage, the dominant motives were living motives. Neither transfer was made in contemplation of death.

The Real Estate   Six months before he died, Mr. Varner transferred all of his remaining real estate to William Varner, Jr., as trustee for Mrs. Cole. The estate argues that this transfer, like the transfer of the cottage, was motivated by a desire to see Mrs. Cole provided for. The Government points to an additional circumstance, a steady, continuing deterioration in Mr. Varner's health. Beginning about eight months before his death (two months before this transfer), Mr. Varner had been forced to curtail his activity. He cancelled his world-wide trip. One month before this trust transfer, he was hardly able to walk; he had to use a wheelchair when he visited his physician. He ceased to complain about his servant and, in fact, became friendly with him. At the time of the trust transfer, he could no longer use either hands or legs. The physician continued to tell Mr. Varner that he had a nervous condition from which, he implied, Mr. Varner would recover. One month before the third transfer, however, the physician finally told William Varner, Jr., about the gravity of his father's condition. William, Jr., testified that he relayed this information to his father within two or three days. This was apparently before the second transfer. He said his father took the information calmly, and that his father's disposition remained cheerful. Not even then was Mr. Varner given to morbid thoughts; he did not refer to his condition again, not even in the final moments of his life. When he executed the trust instrument at issue, he told William, Jr., that his reason for the transfer was to see to it that Mrs. Cole was provided for. The estate argues that this fact, taken with Mr. Varner's continuing optimism about life, is evidence of a life motive, and we agree with that assessment. The size of the transfer, although significant, did not leave Mr. Varner without funds and is therefore not determinative, particularly in view of the fact that William Varner, Jr., as trustee, did not disturb his father's possession and use of the family home.

Mr. Varner is not shown to have entertained thoughts of death, even when he was dying.[10] He was not reticent about his physical condition, but he was not dominated by it either—that is especially apparent when one considers the transfers for Mrs. Cole, who was herself in poor health.[11] The gifts for her benefit were to establish her financial independence and to protect her from the eventualities of a life which had been cruel to her.[12] A person who retains a healthy mental condition normally does not make gifts in contemplation of death.[13] Mr. Varner's were not thoughts of death, nor were they thoughts which combined death and the desire to avoid estate taxes.[14] "Standing alone, the desire to avoid death taxes cannot be deemed conclusive of a mental state such as is contemplated by the statutory phrase."[15] His was a more cheerful, more "life-ful" frame of mind.[16] He was interested in the happiness of his children and in helping them financially.[17] He was determined to carry out "promises and plans that were unconnected with the thought of impending death."[18]

Conclusions of Law   The principal question in a gift-in-contemplation of death case is factual, but a consideration of precedent supports and confirms our factual conclusions.[19] The decedent's health, which was progressively worse at each of these transfers, is of course an important consideration.[20] But this Court has repeatedly held that health is not determinative of purpose in making life-time transfers. In *Coffin*[21] and *Beurman*[22] we held that the existence at transfer of serious, even fatal, conditions was not controlling in the face of evidence of living motives. This attitude is mirrored in opinions and jury charges from the federal district courts, in which it is emphasized that cheerful demeanor and a disdain for morbid preoccupation indicate that a decedent has living motives even as he, quite literally, wastes into death.[23] The controlling test, as the court said in *Peck*, is whether the decedent "was motivated, moved, propelled, by the same considerations that cause one to make testamentary dispositions of property, and whether the gift made was a substitute for such testamentary dispositions, without awaiting death."[24] We find here that Mr. Varner's transfers were for the care of his granddaughter and the business success of his son and therefore not substitutes for testamentary dispositions.

An additional factor as to the first two transfers is that Mr. Varner did not know he was dying. Early decisions in the Eighth Judicial Circuit turn in part on the fact that the decedents had no knowledge of their fatal conditions.[25] In *Neal*, as here, doctors did not tell the decedent about his condition but did tell his family. The trial judge in *Delaware Trust Co.* v. *Handy* reached a similar decision where it was shown that the decedent suffered from arteriosclerosis but did not know about it.[26] Other cases in the federal courts are in accord, as are *Mills*, *MacDonald*, and *Bloise* in this Court.[27] The decedent in *Mills* was told he was ill but not how long he had to live. *MacDonald* turned on medical evidence that "the decedent may have been suffering from the disease for several years without any awareness of being ill."[28] There, as here, the fatal disease was serious but the life expectancy was at worst uncertain.[29] There, as here, the decedent did not talk about the condition even after he learned of it. *Bloise* held for the Commissioner, but is distinguishable because the condition there—terminal cancer—was diagnosed shortly before the transfers at issue (not, as here, after two of the three transfers) and because it was much more likely to bring speedy death.[30] Other decisions in this Court buttress our reliance on the rule that serious illness is only minimally relevant when it is not shown that the decedent knew he was ill.[31]

We detect in Mr. Varner's later life three features which emphasize that his thoughts were not thoughts of death. The first of these is the relinquishment of his business life in favor of a pleasant retirement, devoted to the care of his troubled granddaughter. The second is what we regard as an effort to draw closer to the two loved ones who remained to him. The third is his manifest desire to spend his last years in vigorous activity and travel. These factors combine, in our view, in a "life style" which seemed almost to turn away from thoughts of death; it was that life style which dictated the transfers here at issue.

This life style can co-exist with illness and even with concern about health, as we held in *Coffin,* in *Suchs,* and in *Johnson.*[32] Transfers made in these circumstances tend to contemplate pleasant retirement from the burdens of life rather than from life itself. This is obvious, as we held in *Tetzlaff,* when one considers that careful and burdenless living *prolongs* life.[33] Mr. Varner's acquisitive years were over, but that is not necessarily a circumstance in which he would begin to contemplate death. On the contrary, he seemed to contemplate closer relations with his loved ones, a factor which tends to prove living motives for property transfer.[34] This factor is often present when the transfer is one to restore family harmony.[35] It can equally be present, however, where the family has been decimated by tragedy.[36] We think Mr. Varner was concerned more with what was thought of him while he lived than with happy memories after he was dead.[37] It is interesting to reflect how different the case might have been had he had no loved ones to draw near him in his last years.[38]

Dying people often foresee their deaths at a virtually conscious level, and even more often sense death unconsciously and begin an almost instinctive preparation for it.

He was also determined to enjoy the life which was left to him. There are scores of cases in which physical activity, vigor, and, especially, travel and plans for travel, are held to be indicative of living motives. In *Delaware Trust Co.* v. *Handy* the federal district court was influenced by the fact that the decedent, at the time of transfer, contemplated a two-year trip around the world.[39] In *Heiner* v. *Donnan,* which was reversed on other grounds in the Supreme Court, the Circuit Court of Appeals took account of the fact that the decedent was an inveterate traveller, that he had, as Mr. Varner had, taken extensive automobile trips, and that he regularly went to Europe and travelled in the United States.[40] In *Commissioner* v. *Gidwitz's Estate*, the court noted that the decedent, despite a serious heart condition, "did not believe at that time that he was in danger of imminent death but . . . expected to live for a number of years."[41] Evidence of this inter alia, was the decedent's habitual travel in the United States and abroad, his fishing and automobile trips, and the fact that he did his own driving. In that case the executor listed the decedent's last illness as lasting for 15 years; the transfer involved was one that did not in fact benefit beneficiaries until after the decedent's death. Despite these factors the court found that Gidwitz's cheerful attitude toward life, his energetic interest in travel and activity, was determinative evidence of living motives for the transfer involved. Finally, in the *Old Colony Trust* case, the federal district court in Massachusetts, deciding a case in which the decedent took his own life, held that an active business life and domestic and foreign travel within this year before death indicated living motives in a trust transfer for children.[42] The case resembled Mr. Varner's in several respects and differs notably only in the fact that Mr. Varner held onto his life until the last. A number of decisions for the taxpayer in the federal courts of appeal have relied on the fact that the decedent's general pattern of travel and activity indicated that he had no thought of death at the time of transfer.[43] Decisions from federal district courts and from this Court are essentially similar on this point.[44] In many of these cases the decedent had been actively traveling at the time of the transfer in question.[45] In others he was making plans for future travel.[46]

We are aware of the limitations of our process in cases such as this. We are not so much determining here what William Varner was like as we are determining what the evidence shows he was like. "We cannot be certain that our portrait . . . is a lifelike replica . . . but we are confident that it accurately reflects the portrait . . . drawn by the evidence in the record."[47] We find that none of the transfers at issue was made in contemplation of death.

COMMENTARY

The tax Court's opinion in *Varner* . . . *suggest[s] that the judiciary is finding in precedent and then applying six "group norms" about death and property. They are something like this:*

1 *Contemplation Is Surrender* The court is at some pains to point out that the transfer of the cottage was a relatively insignificant transfer in terms

of Mr. Varner's total assets, even though this point should, logically, embarrass the court when it talks about the cumulative effect of all three transfers. The court also labors the fact that Mr. Varner had enough to support a gracious retirement after transferring the corporate securities, and even enough to keep body and soul together (given his son's permissiveness in letting him live in the house) after all three transfers. Finally, the court finds that, since Mr. Varner could and did live in the house until he died, its transfer was not death-motivated. In other words, a death-motivated transfer is one that lacks present-day operation; this last point could as well be made in reverse in other words, since Mr. Varner wanted the house to be used for his granddaughter and at the same time to live in it until he died (a clearly "testamentary" frame of mind), the transfer was within the statute. It is interesting to compare the judicial assumption, that dying people give up, with clinical information discovered by Zinker and Fink:

> Individuals on the brink of death or individuals who knew they
> were to die in the near future experienced the greatest insights, the
> greatest joys, and important re-evaluation of their past lives . . .
> greater religious strength, greater love . . . integration and closure
> of their past lives and sometimes "grew."
>
> We have found . . . that many patients often are . . . concerned
> with being respected as human beings, with being loved, and with
> understanding the nature of their illness. We have come in contact
> with several critically ill patients who showed signs of psychological
> growth. These individuals seemed to accept the fact of their coming
> death and, having freed themselves from the burden of fighting for
> physical survival, felt free to feel close to their fellow patients, to be
> creative, and to experience greater religious strength. . . .
>
> Despite the fact that some dying individuals get "stuck" on
> certain basic needs and often deteriorate psychologically, other
> individuals begin to think in a more fluid way and are stimulated to
> examine their past lives, to examine their beliefs, and to examine
> afresh the nature of things around them. For the first time, they are
> able to cope with questions that continually have plagued them.

2 *Death Is a Medical Matter* Civilized Western man is the only animal to whom this norm is applied; it is assumed that other animals, such as elephants and birds, Eskimos and Indians, know enough to prepare for death without being told to do it.[48] The medical-death norm had two applications in the *Varner* opinion, both well justified by the precedents. The first ap-

plication assumed that Mr. Varner, even though he was almost 80 years old and declining physically, would not be biologically or psychologically aware that his condition portended death. The second and corollary application of the medical-death norm is the court's treatment of the fact that a physician (at the time the securities were transferred) did not know Mr. Varner was dying, and therefore Mr. Varner cannot have known. The insight supporting both applications is that dying is not a matter of human experience, or of instinct; it is a matter of medical information. Behavioral research is to the contrary; there is now good clinical evidence, and some more systematic evidence, that dying people often foresee their deaths at a virtually conscious level, and even more often sense death unconsciously and begin an almost instinctive preparation for it.[49]

3 *Travelers Forget Death*   This norm relates to the first two norms and is applied whether or not the traveler is dying or, if dying, knows that he is dying. The *Varner* court is candid about its assumption, both in terms of negative evidence (Mr. Varner's surrender of the cottage was actuated by compassion for his granddaughter, who arguably gained nothing by it) and in terms of affirmative evidence (Mr. Varner continued to climb atop houses, go hunting, and take trips, even when he was dying). The genesis and growth of this travel-and-activity norm is probably related on the death-is-surrender norm (or to a general attitude that death is something that happens to a man, rather than something he does). There is a substantial amount of literary indication that it is not true (which is relevant because judges often adhere to literary insight even though they usually spurn psychological insight). Tolstoy's story *Three Deaths*, in which a dying consumptive woman believes she will survive if she can make her way out of Russia, is an example. (And, incidentally, her family and doctor think she doesn't know she is dying.) O'Connor's recent memoir on the last days of the Irish poet and editor George Russell relate the fact that Russell suddenly left his home in Dublin, gave away his possessions, and moved to London. Yeats remarked that this was a matter of his "giving up the world to go on a world cruise." But O'Connor thought not:

> Of all the men I have known, Russell was most a creature of habit, and for him to give up everything—his house, his books, his pictures, his friends—was already a sort of death.

And there is solid behavioral evidence to support the poetic insight.[50] Even practicing lawyers know that travel and death are psychologically related;

those I have interviewed said that the prospect of a trip is the usual reason clients come in to have wills prepared.

4 *Dying People Are Sad*   This norm has a tacit assumption—that people who are dying may make gifts in contemplation of death—but the court did not state it because it would have tended to undermine the court's conclusions on the house transfer. In explaining the cottage transfer the court was almost intemperately anxious to mention Mr. Varner's contemporaneous optimism, even though the evidence also indicated sadness at the relatively recent death of his wife and disgust at the fickleness of caretakers. In explaining the house transfer, the most difficult part of the opinion, the court relied almost exclusively on Mr. Varner's optimism in the face of a death which was obvious by this time even to Mr. Varner himself. Mr. Varner's disapproval of the servant his son provided for him was taken by the court to indicate that the servant symbolized death; life-centered man's reaction to symbols of death is resentment. The court did not express that assumption, possibly because Mr. Varner later grew closer to the servant, and even then, according to the court, did not contemplate death.

5 *Support Is Only for Life*   Following what is perhaps the most commonplace of all platitudes in these cases, the court gave it as the law that a person who is concerned about the support of loved ones is not concerned about his death.[51] The norm has a couple of subnorms. One is that no one worries about how his loved ones will be taken care of after he is dead (the life-insurance industry to the contrary notwithstanding). The other is that satisfactions derived from providing support are seen in terms of one's lifetime. This is a judicial denial of the insight represented by Shneidman's "post-self" concept.

6 *Dying People Withdraw*   This norm seems superficially to resemble Shneidman's analysis of Melville's "social death," but the resemblance is only superficial. The factual basis for it in this case is the conclusion that Mr. Varner's retirement—retirement, ultimately, even from the ownership of the roof over his head—was carried out so that he could devote more time and attention to those he loved and so that he could, by giving them property, entice them into unfamiliar intimacy with him. The court takes this aspiration for togetherness to be the opposite of withdrawal. Melville, by contrast, withdrew *toward* his work (and would, Shneidman says, have withdrawn toward his family too, if he could have). Melville and Mr. Varner did

similar things, but Shneidman's conclusion from this fact is that Melville was dying; the court's conclusion is that Mr. Varner was not dying, at least not in the tax sense.

NOTES

1 Fatter v. Usry, 20 A.F.T.R.2d, para. 147,154 (E.D. La. 1967) (Rubin, J.).

2 See generally Lowndes and Kramer; Lowndes and Stephens; Riecker; Kimbrell; Hochman and Lindsay.

3 United States v. Wells, 283 U.S. 102 (1931).

4 Shukert v. Allen, 273 U.S. 545 (1927); see Lowndes and Kramer, note 2 supra at 81–82; Wishard v. United States, 143 F.2d 704 (7th Cir. 1944); Estate of Hofford, 4 T.C. 542, 790 (1945).

5 Shneidman, *Orientations Toward Death: A Vital Aspect of the Study of Lives* in Robert W. White (Ed.), *The Study of Lives.* New York: Atherton, 1963); Shneidman, *Orientation Toward Cessation: A Reexamination of Current Modes of Death.*

6 Shneidman used the word "psyde" as a prefix to these classifications, but he explains that he uses the Greek word as a synonym for "cessation"; he now uses the word "death."

7 See Mills, *Medicolegal Ramifications of Current Practices and Suggested Changes in Certifying Modes of Death,* which suggests a parallel between familiar elaborate systems of arriving at intention in negligence and criminal litigation (contributory negligence, assumption of risk, subtleties in workmen's compensation, etc.) and the prediction of levels of "self determinism" in attitudes toward death. This is similar to what judges do in Section 2035 cases, although judicial classifications have not yet been subjected to anything resembling Shneidman's elaborate rational taxonomy.

8 This is a composite of the following cases: Fatter v. Usry, 20 A.F.T.R.2d para. 147,154 (E.D. La. 1967); Kniskern V. United States, 232 F. Supp. 7 (S.D. Fla. 1964); American Trust Co. v. United States, 175 F. Supp. 185 (N.D. Cal. 1959); Estate of Want, 29 T.C. 1223 (1958); Estate of Hinds, 11 T.C. 314 (1948) *aff'd* 180 F. 2d 930 (5th Cir. 1950); Estate of Atwater, T.C.M. 44,375. The notes which follow the text are, through the end of the *Varner* opinion, the court's.

9 The same section in S2035(b), creates a statutory, rebuttable presumption that transfers within three years of death are in contemplation of death, and an irrebuttable presumption that transfers more than three years before death are not in contemplation of death. In addition to these specific presumptions, determinations of the Internal Revenue Service are presumptively correct. See Neal v. Commissioner 53 F.2d 806 (C.C.A. 8, 1931).

10 See Moylan v. United States, 18 A.F.T.R.2d 6240 (N.D.N.Y. 1966) (jury charge).

11 Tetzlaff, T.C.M. 43,034, *aff'd* 141 F.2d 8 (8th Cir. 1944); see Estate of Neilson, T.C.M. 67,219.

12 Neilson, Ibid., involved a trust for a retarded child, which is similar to the trust for Mrs. Cole in this case.

13 See Peck v. United States, 16 A.F.T.R.2d 6125 (M.D. Ga. 1965) (jury charge).

14 See Stiles v. United States, 2 A.F.T.R.2d 6391 (S.D. Fla. 1958) (jury charge).

15   Rhoads v. United States, 12 A.F.T.R.2d 6195 (E.D. Pa. 1963) (jury charge); see Farmers Loan and Trust Co. v. Bowers, 68 F.2d 916 (C.C.A. 2, 1934), *cert. den.* 296 U.S. 649 (1935); Denniston v. Commissioner, 106 F.2d 925 (C.C.A. 3 1939); Estate of Higgins, T.C.M. 50,132.

16   The decedent of Altendorf v. United States, 14 A.F.T.R.2d 6134 (D. N. Dak. 1964) (jury verdict for taxpayer), was a cheerful 85; in Estate of Johnson, 10 T.C. 680 (1948), he was more than 90; and in Metzger v. United States, 181 F.Supp. 830 (N.D. Oh. 1960), he was an optimistic alcoholic. See Carlson v. United States, 7 A.F.T.R.2d 1825 (D. Minn. 1960) (jury verdict for taxpayer).

17   Estate of Bond. T.C.M. 66,021; Estate of Flynn, T.C.M. 44,387.

18   Metzger v. United States, 181 F. Supp. 830, 834 (N.D. Oh. 1960).

19   Kentucky Trust Co. v. Glenn, 217 F.2d 462 (6th Cir. 1954).

20   Estate of Johnson, 10 T.C. 680 (1948).

21   T.C.M. 54,338.

22   T.C.M. 65,114.

23   For example, Gordon v. United States, 163 F. Supp. 542 (W.D. Mo. 1958); Peck v. United States, 16 A.F.T.R.2d 6125 (M.D. Ga. 1965) (jury charge); Stiles v. United States, 2 A.F.T.R.2d 6391 (S.D. Fla. 1958) (jury charge).

24   Ibid. at 6129.

25   Neal v. Commissioner, 53 F.2d 806 (C.C.A. 8, 1931); Willcuts v. Stoltze, 73 F.2d 868 (C.C.C. 8, 1934).

26   53 F.2d 1042 (D. Dela. 1931).

27   Commissioner v. Gidwitz's Estate, 196 F.2d 813 (7th Cir. 1952), citing and quoting Allen v. Trust Co., 326 U.S. 630 (1946); United States Trust Co. v. United States, 23 F. Supp. 476 (Ct. Cl. 1938); *cert. den.* 307 U.S. 633 (1938): First National Bank of Birmingham v. United States, 25 F. Supp. 816 (N.D. Ala. 1934) (knowledge in family, but not in decedent); Estate of Wolfe v. United States, 10 A.F.T.R.2d 6292 (E.D. Tex. 1962) (jury charge); Seattle-First National Bank v. United States, 11 A.F.T.R.2d 1824 (W.D. Wash. 1963): "The decedent did not at any time have any serious thought of death or the imminence thereof. . . ." T.C.M. 46,216; T.C.M. 51,326; T.C.M. 66,044.

28   See Estate of Larsh, T.C.M. 49,221; Estate of VanDever, T.C.M. 52,352.

29   See Estate of Martin, T.C.M. 43,498; Estate of Burr, T.C.M. 45,364.

30   See Estate of Awrey, 5 T.C. 222 (1945).

31   Estate of Delaney, 1 T.C. 781 (1943); see Estate of Vardell, 35 T.C. 50 (1960); Estate of Macaulay, 3 T.C. 350 (1944); Estate of Fry, 9 T.C. 503 (1947); Estate of Fleishmann, T.C.M. 54,111.

32   T.C.M. 54,338; see Estate of Hite, 49 T.C. 580 (1968); T.C.M. 55,239: "A man who is not in good health may, nevertheless, make a transfer which is . . . for purposes connected with life"; 10 T.C. 680 (1948).

33   T.C.M. 43,034, at p. 43–107: "[H]is interest in and care for his health indicates that he was devoting his attention and thought to the extension of his life as long as possible."

34   See Peck v. United States, 16 A.F.T.R.2d 6125 (M.D. Ga., 1965) (jury charge).

35   For example, Estate of Jacobson, T.C.M. 50,301.

36 See Estate of Neilson, T.C.M. 67,219.

37 Estate of MacDonald, T.C.M. 51,326: "We cannot overlook the fact that the decedent appears as interested in what his family thought, during his lifetime, but indifferent to their views after his death."

38 See Estate of Maxwell, T.C.M. 44,366, and compare it with Metzger v. United States, 181 F. Supp. 830 (N.D. Oh. 1960).

39 53 F.2d 1042 (D. Dela. 1931). See also Dunn v. United States, 1968 Prentice-Hall para. 147,235 (S.D. Ill. 1968) (jury charge); Estate of Mills, T.C.M. 46,216; Rea v. Heiner, 6 F.2d 389, 391 (W.D. Pa. 1925); "The week before she died, she drove to Pittsburgh three times, was preparing to go to Canada for the summer, making arrangements for building a boathouse and seawall there, and for changing the barn and building a dairy on the farm at home"; Beeler v. Motter, 33 F.2d 788 (D. Kan. 1928).

40 61 F.2d 113 (C.C.A. 3, 1932); 285 U.S. 312 (1932).

41 196 F.2d 813, 815 (7th Cir. 1952).

42 15 F. Supp. 417 (D. Mass. 1936).

43 Bradley v. Smith, 114 F.2d 161 (C.C.A. 7, 1940); Tait v. Safe Deposit and Trust Co., 74 F.2d 851 (C.C.A. 4, 1935); Brown v. Commissioner, 74 f.2d 281 (C.C.A. 10, 1934). This factor was held not determinative, though, in United States v. Tonkin, 150 F.2d 531 (C.C.A. 3, 1945); Buckminster's Estate v. Commissioner, 147 F.2d 331 (C.C.A. 2, 1944); Northern Trust Co. v. Commissioner, 116 F.2d 96 (C.C.A. 7, 1940); Updike v. Commissioner, 88 F.2d 807 (C.C.A. 8, 1937); *cert. den.* 301 U.S. 708 (1936); and Stubblefield v. United States, 6 F. Supp. 440 (Ct. Cl. 1934). See United States v. Wells, 283 U.S. 102 (1931).

44 In re Kroger's Estate, 145 F.2d 901 (6th Cir. 1944); Flannery v. Willcuts, 25 F.2d 951 (C.C.A. 8, 1928); Poor v. White, 8 F. Supp. 995 (D. Mass. 1934); Welsh v. Hassett, 15 F. Supp. 692 (D. Mass. 1936), *rev'd on other grounds* 90 F.2d 833 (C.C.A. 1, 1937), *aff'd* 303 U.S. 303 (1938); Estate of Ridgely v. United States, 20 A.F.T.R.2d 5946 (Ct. Cl. 1967). Estate of Fleischmann, T.C.M. 54,111; Estate of Hinde, T.C.M. 52,016; Estate of O'Neal, T.C.M. 47,167; Estate of Cook, 9 T.C. 563 (1947); Estate of Burr, T.C.M. 45,364; Estate of Koussevitsky, 5 T.C. 656 (1945).

45 Estate of Vardell, 35 T.C. 50 (1960); Estate of Ackel, T.C.M. 58,027; Estate of Weir, 17 T.C. 409 (1951); Estate of Macaulay, 3 T.C. 354 (1944).

46 Estate of Green, T.C.M. 45,086; Estate of Bickerstaff, T.C.M. 42,358.

47 Estate of Johnson, 10 T.C. 680 (1948).

48 Lorenz discusses and compares the Freudian "death wish" theory with his ethological findings and relates both to Margolin's study of Ute Indians. Goody discusses property transfers *propter mortem* in primitive societies in Africa.

49 See Hutschnecker; Glaser and Strauss; Eissler; Joseph; Weisman and Hackett. Some federal judges demonstrate similar insight. See Gregg v. United States, 13 F. Supp. 147 (Ct. Cl. 1936); Kengel v. United States, 57 F.2d 929 (Ct. Cl. 1932). The facts in Estate of Kent, T.C.M. 47,233, are the kind of facts these psychological researchers talk about.
    Ridden v. Thrall, 125 N.Y. 572, 26 N.E. 627 (1891), is an interesting, largely implied judicial recognition of the fact that men somehow foresee in their tissues not only the time of death but maybe even the occasion of death. The decedent there had given property *causa mortis* as he was about to undergo a relatively minor operation. He died from a heart ailment, shortly after surgery. The question was whether he contemplated the cause of death and the court

held that he did, even though his physician did not. See also CALIFORNIA CIVIL CODE §§ 1150–53 (codifying property rules on gifts "in view of death").

50 Feifel, *Attitudes of Mentally Ill Patients Toward Death;* Jung, *The Soul and Death;* Stern, Williams, and Prados, *Grief Reactions in Later Life.* Rogers reports a course of psychotherapy which took a sudden, sharp turn for the worse when the patient ("client") was about to leave for a vacation trip. The reported interview and diary material surrounding this event is filled with allusions to death. See the psychological sources in note 69 supra, and Fox.

51 The collection of suicide notes in Shneidman and Farberow, *Clues to Suicide,* is evidence to the contrary.

PART THREE

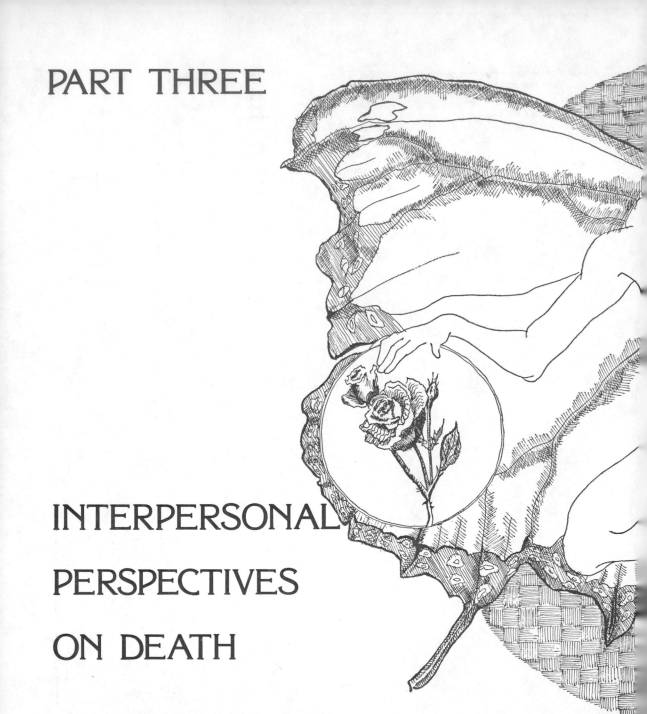

INTERPERSONAL
PERSPECTIVES
ON DEATH

·5·

THE

PARTICIPANTS

OF DEATH

Rarely is the drama of dying played by a single actor. Usually some supporting cast is involved and, as a result, the drama partakes of the complications (and shortcomings) of all human interaction, including such reactions and emotions as withdrawal, fear, disgust, shame, guilt, and ambivalence. Interactions between a dying person and his survivors-to-be—loved ones, doctors, nurses and others—are rather complicated because parties on both sides are participating in an unusual and extraordinarily stressful situation. One of the most important developments in the current thanatological scene is a growing awareness and understanding of how the terminal person views his condition and how he seeks to cope with the prospect and process of dying; and further, how these awarenesses and understandings are reflected in the new approaches being used (by the medical profession in general and by thanatologists in particular) to treat and help terminal patients. We now are beginning to recognize, for example, that dying persons are human beings who dislike being abandoned as much as anyone else and that wanting human contact while facing death is biologically and psychologically sound and normal.

In this chapter too there is a shift of focus, this time centering on those immediately concerned with death. A concomitant of the institutionalization of death is the creation of a set of relationships between the institution (as represented by the hospital staff) and the dying. This, in turn, gives rise to a set of interpersonal interactions. How these interactions are structured is discussed in the first selection of this chapter (Glaser and Strauss), in which the "implicit understandings" that patients and staff often have with each other in relation to the patient's death are explicated. This selection describes a sort of courtly dance of death, a grisly ballet in which unspoken "contracts" are carried out, sometimes by mutual consent, but oftentimes unilaterally without the patient's knowledge and perhaps at the cost of the patient's life, days or weeks or months sooner that he otherwise might have lost it.

Another set of interpersonal reactions—those between the terminal patient and his family—is investigated next by Kübler-Ross. Through her writings, films, and appearances, she has had a great deal of influence on our thinking about the care of the dying person. Her selection not only contains much practical wisdom on how to handle a terminal illness within a family but also points up the current changes toward a more humanistic approach which, in effect, help to offset some of the problems created by the trend toward institutionalizing death.

The new humanistic approach theme is continued by the Hinton selection, which addresses the importance of communication tailored to the specific needs of the dying or death-contemplating individual. The final selection expands on this theme stressing the need for communication among terminal patients, their families, and the hospital staff. The essential "gift" that can be given the terminal patient is the knowledge that someone is ready and willing to share his concerns—a gift that may in the end be "the silence that goes beyond words," to use Kübler-Ross's words.

It is interesting to speculate how the increasing humanistic approach by and toward the "participants of death" is related to the general humanistic trend in other sectors of society (for example, as in humanistic psychology developed by Henry Murray, Abraham Maslow, Carl Rogers, Gordon Allport, and others) and to wonder whether this approach may return to death and dying a portion of the human dimension that has been lost as death has become increasingly institutionalized and desacralized.

In order to appreciate the nature of working with a dying person, it is important to understand some of the significant characteristics of such an interaction, specifically the difference between a *conversation* (or "ordinary talk") and a *professional exchange,* and to recognize that therapeutic efforts should be of the latter sort. A person who systematically attempts to help the dying individual is either a therapist or is acting in the role of a therapist. He cannot escape this role. This is not to say that many others—relatives, dear friends, church members, neighbors—cannot also play extremely important roles. The distinction between *conversation* and *professional exchange* is exceptionally elementary, but, because understanding it is at the very heart of effective therapeutic work, some rudimentary ideas need to be made explicit. The differences between the two can be charted in the form of some contrasts between ordinary talk (e.g., "I'm so sorry to hear about the death," "Please accept my most sincere condolences," "Time will heal the wounds") and a professional exchange.

	In a *Conversation* the focus is on:	In a *Professional Exchange* the focus is on:
Content	1 Substantive content, i.e., the talk is primarily about things, events, dates—the surface of the world.	1 Affective (emotional) content, i.e., the exchange focuses (not constantly but occasionally) on the feelings and the emotional tone of the patient, sometimes minimizing the "facts."
Level	2 Manifest level, i.e., conversation focuses on what is said, the actual words which are uttered, the facts which are stated.	2 Latent level, i.e., the professional person listens for what is "between the lines," below the surface, for what is implied, not expressed, for what may be unconsciously present.
Meanings	3 Conscious meanings, i.e., dealing with the other person as though what was said was meant and as though the person	3 Unconscious meanings, i.e., listening for unconscious meanings and latent intentions (e.g. double-entendres, puns,

were "a rational man"
and that he "knows his
own mind."

hidden meanings, latent
implications, etc.).

Abstraction	4	Phenotypic, i.e., concern with the ordinary interesting details of life, where	4	Genotypic, i.e., search for congruencies, similarities, commonalities, *generalizations* about the patient's psychological life.
Role	5	Social role, i.e., an exchange between two people who are essentially equals (like neighbors or friends, etc.) or who depend on the prestige of age, rank, status, etc., but who have an equal right to display themselves, to ask each other banal or intimate questions, neither being the "doctor" and neither being the "patient." A conversation is the most democratic of all human exchanges.	5	Transference, i.e., the exchange is between nonequals; between one person who wishes help (and tactitly agrees to play the patient's role) and another person who agrees to proffer help (and thus is cast in the role of physician, priest, father, magician, witch doctor, helper). Much of what is effective in the exchange is the patient's "transference" onto the therapist.

What the student should learn from the above chart is that the thanatologist's professional work with dying persons is not "just talk," as is generally the case in exchanges between the dying and friends and loved ones. This is not to suggest that there is not an enormously important place for the mere presence of friends and loved ones, for their sitting in communicative silence, and for their just talking about either the most trivial or, literally, the most vital of issues.

The Ritual Drama of Mutual Pretense

Barney G. Glaser and Anselm L. Strauss

This selection, taken from the book *Awareness of Dying* by
Barney C. Glaser and Anselm L. Strauss, reflects some of
the current thinking of the "new sociology" concerning
death and discusses an "implicit mutual understanding"
about death between terminal patients and hospital staffs.

Reprinted from Barney G. Glaser and Anselm L. Strauss
Awareness of Dying (Chicago: Aldine Publishing Company,
1965); copyright © 1965 by Barney G. Glaser and Anselm
L. Strauss. Reprinted by permission of the authors and Aldine
Publishing Company.

When patient and staff both know that the patient
is dying but pretend otherwise—when both agree to act as if he were going
to live—then a context of mutual pretense exists. Either party can initiate his
share of the context; it ends when one side cannot, or will not, sustain the
pretense any longer.

*One nurse remarked: I may know they
are going to die, and the patient knows
it, but (usually) he's just not going to
let you know that he knows."*

The mutual-pretense awareness context is perhaps less visible, even to
its participants, . . . because the interaction involved tends to be more
subtle. On some hospital services, however, it is the predominant context.
One nurse who worked on an intensive care unit remarked about an unusual patient who had announced he was going to die: "I haven't had to
cope with this very often. I may know they are going to die, and the patient
knows it, but (usually) he's just not going to let you know that he knows."

280

Once we visited a small Catholic hospital where medical and nursing care for the many dying patients was efficiently organized. The staff members were supported in their difficult work by a powerful philosophy—that they were doing everything possible for the patient's comfort—but generally did not talk with patients about death. This setting brought about frequent mutual pretense. This awareness context is also predominant in such settings as county hospitals, where elderly patients of low socioeconomic status are sent to die; patient and staff are well aware of imminent death but each tends to go silently about his own business.[1] Yet, as we shall see, sometimes the mutual pretense context is neither silent nor unnegotiated.

The same kind of ritual pretense is enacted in many situations apart from illness. A charming example occurs when a child announces that he is now a storekeeper, and that his mother should buy something at his store. To carry out his fiction, delicately cooperative action is required. The mother must play seriously, and when the episode has run its natural course, the child will often close it himself with a rounding-off gesture, or it may be concluded by an intruding outside event or by the mother. Quick analysis of this little game of pretense suggests that either player can begin; that the other must then play properly; that realistic (nonfictional) action will destroy the illusion and end the game; that the specific action of the game must develop during interaction; and that eventually the make-believe ends or is ended. Little familial games or dramas of this kind tend to be continual, though each episode may be brief.

For contrast, here is another example that pertains to both children and adults. At the circus, when a clown appears, all but the youngest children know that the clown is not real. But both he and his audience must participate, if only symbolically, in the pretense that he is a clown. The onlookers need do no more than appreciate the clown's act, but if they remove themselves too far, by examining the clown's technique too closely, let us say,

---

[1]Robert Kastenbaum has reported that at Cushing Hospital, "a Public Medical Institution for the care and custody of the elderly" in Framingham, Massachusetts, "patient and staff members frequently have an implicit mutual understanding with regard to death . . . institutional dynamics tend to operate against making death 'visible' and a subject of open communication. . . . Elderly patients often behave as though they appreciated the unspoken feelings of the staff members and were attempting to make their demise as acceptable and unthreatening as possible." This observation is noted in Robert Kastenbaum, "The Interpersonal Context of Death in a Geriatric Institution," abstract of paper presented at the Seventeenth Annual Scientific Meeting, Gerontological Society (Minneapolis: October 29–31, 1964).

then the illusion will be shattered. The clown must also do his best to sustain the illusion by clever acting, by not playing too far "out of character." Ordinarily nobody addresses him as if he were other than the character he is pretending to be. That is, everybody takes him seriously, at face value. And unless particular members return to see the circus again, the clown's performance occurs only once, beginning and ending according to a pre-arranged schedule.

Our two simple examples of pretense suggest some important features of the particular awareness context to which we shall devote this [discussion]. The make-believe in which patient and hospital staff engage resembles the child's game much more than the clown's act. It has no institutionalized beginning and ending comparable to the entry and departure of the clown; either the patient or the staff must signal the beginning of their joint pretense. Both parties must act properly if the pretense is to be maintained, because, as in the child's game, the illusion created is fragile, and easily shattered by incongruous "realistic" acts. But if either party slips slightly, the other may pretend to ignore the slip.[2] Each episode between the patient and a staff member tends to be brief, but the mutual pretense is done with terrible seriousness, for the stakes are very high.[3]

INITIATING THE PRETENSE

This particular awareness context cannot exist, of course, unless both the patient and staff are aware that he is dying. Therefore all the structural conditions which contribute to the existence of open awareness (and which are absent in closed and suspicion awareness) contribute also to the existence of mutual pretense. In addition, at least one interactant must indicate a desire to pretend that the patient is not dying and the other must agree to the pretense, acting accordingly.

A prime structural condition in the existence and maintenance of mutual pretense is that unless the patient initiates conversation about his impending

---

[2]I. Bensman and I. Garver, "Crime and Punishment in the Factory," in A. Gouldner and H. Gouldner (eds.), *Modern Society* (New York: Harcourt, Brace and World, 1963), pp. 593–96.

[3]A German communist, Alexander Weissberg, accused of spying during the great period of Soviet spy trials, has written a fascinating account of how he and many other accused persons collaborated with the Soviet government in an elaborate pretense, carried on for the benefit of the outside world. The stakes were high for the accused (their lives) as well as for the Soviet. Weissberg's narrative also illustrated how uninitiated interactants must be coached into their roles and how they must be cued into the existence of the pretense context where they do not recognize it. See Alexander Weissberg, *The Accused* (New York: Simon and Schuster, 1951).

death, no staff member is required to talk about it wi
Americans, they are unlikely to initiate such a convers
fessionals they have no rules commanding them to talk ab
patient, unless he desires it. In turn, he may wish to initia
tion, but surely neither hospital rules nor common conven
him. Consequently, unless either the aware patient or the
breaks the silence by words or gestures, a mutual pretense r
open awareness context will exist; as, for example, when th
does not care to talk about death, and the patient does not press
though he clearly does recognize his terminality.

ↂↂ

*It is remarkable how a patient can
flash cues to the staff about his own
dread knowledge, inviting the staff to
talk about his destiny, while the nurses
and physicians decide that it is better
not to talk too openly with him about
his condition lest he "go to pieces."*

ↂↂ

The patient, of course, is more likely than the staff members to refer
openly to his death, thereby inviting them, explicitly or implicitly, to respond in kind. If they seem unwilling, he may decide they do not wish to
confront openly the fact of his death, and then he may, out of tact or genuine
empathy for their embarrassment or distress, keep his silence. He may
misinterpret their responses, of course, but . . . he probably has correctly
read their reluctance to refer openly to his impending death.

Staff members, in turn, may give him opportunities to speak of his death,
if they deem it wise, without their directly or obviously referring to the topic.
But if he does not care to act or talk as if he were dying, then they will
support his pretense. In doing so, they have, in effect, accepted a complementary assignment of status—they will act with pretense toward his

...se. (If they have misinterpreted his reluctance to act openly, then they ...ve assigned, rather than accepted, a complementary status.)

Two related professional rationales permit them to engage in the pretense. One is that if the patient wishes to pretend, it may well be best for his health, and if and when the pretense finally fails him, all concerned can act more realistically. A secondary rationale is that perhaps they can give him better medical and nursing care if they do not have to face him so openly. In addition, as noted earlier, they can rely on common tact to justify their part in the pretense. Ordinarily, Americans believe that any individual may live—and die—as he chooses, so long as he does not interfere with others' activities, or, in this case, so long as proper care can be given him.

To illustrate the way these silent bargains are initiated and maintained, we quote from an interview with a special nurse. She had been assigned to a patient before he became terminal, and she was more apt than most personnel to encourage his talking openly, because as a graduate student in a nursing class that emphasized psychological care, she had more time to spend with her patient than a regular floor nurse. Here is the exchange between interviewer and nurse:

INTERVIEWER: Did he talk about his cancer or his dying?
NURSE: Well, no, he never talked about it. I never heard him use the word cancer. . . .
INTERVIEWER: Did he indicate that he knew he was dying?
NURSE: Well, I got that impression, yes. . . . It wasn't really openly, but I think the day that his roommate said he should get up and start walking, I felt that he was a little bit antagonistic. He said what his condition was, that he felt very, very ill that moment.
INTERVIEWER: He never talked about leaving the hospital?
NURSE: Never.
INTERVIEWER: Did he talk about his future at all?
NURSE: Not a thing. I never heard a word. . . .
INTERVIEWER: You said yesterday that he was more or less isolated, because the nurses felt that he was hostile. But they have dealt with patients like this many many times. You said they stayed away from him?
NURSE: Well, I think at the very end. You see, this is what I meant by isolation . . . we don't communicate with them. I didn't, except when I did things for him. I think you expect somebody to respond to, and if they're very ill we don't . . . I talked it over with my instructor, mentioning things that I could probably have done; for instance, this isolation, I should have communicated with him . . .

INTERVIEWER: You think that since you knew he was going to die, and you half suspected that he knew it too, or more than half; do you think that this understanding grew between you in any way?

NURSE: I believe so . . . I think it's kind of hard to say but when I came in the room, even when he was very ill, he'd rather look at me and try to give me a smile, and gave me the impression that he accepted . . . I think this is one reason why I feel I should have communicated with him . . . and this is why I feel he was rather isolated. . . .

From the nurse's account, it is difficult to tell whether the patient wished to talk openly about his death, but was rebuffed; or whether he initiated the pretense and the nurse accepted his decision. But it is remarkable how a patient can flash cues to the staff about his own dread knowledge, inviting the staff to talk about his destiny, while the nurses and physicians decide that it is better not to talk too openly with him about his condition lest he "go to pieces." The patient, as remarked earlier, picks up these signals of unwillingness, and the mutual pretense context has been initiated. A specific and obvious instance is this: an elderly patient, who had lived a full and satisfying life, wished to round it off by talking about his impending death. The nurses retreated before this prospect, as did his wife, reproving him, saying he should not think or talk about such morbid matters. A hospital chaplain finally intervened, first by listening to the patient himself, then by inducing the nurses and the wife to do likewise, or at least to acknowledge more openly that the man was dying. He was not successful with all the nurses.

The staff members are more likely to sanction a patient's pretense than his family's. The implicit rule is that though the patient need not be forced to speak of his dying, or to act as if he were dying, his kin should face facts. After all, they will have to live with the facts after his death. Besides, staff members usually find it less difficult to talk about dying with the family. Family members are not inevitably drawn into open discussion, but the likelihood is high, particularly since they themselves are likely to initiate discussion or at least to make gestures of awareness.

Sometimes, however, pretense protects the family member temporarily against too much grief, and the staff members against too immediate a scene. This may occur when a relative has just learned about the impending death and the nurse controls the ensuing scene by initiating temporary pretense. The reverse situation also occurs: a newly arrived nurse discovers the patient's terminality, and the relative smooths over the nurse's distress by temporary pretense.

285

THE PRETENSE INTERACTION

An intern whom we observed during our field work suspected that the patient he was examining had cancer, but he could not discover where it was located. The patient previously had been told that she probably had cancer, and she was now at this teaching hospital for that reason. The intern's examination went on for some time. Yet neither he nor she spoke about what he was searching for, nor in any way suggested that she might be dying. We mention this episode to contrast it with the more extended interactions with which this [selection] is concerned. These have an episodic quality—personnel enter and leave the patient's room, or he occasionally emerges and encounters them—but their extended duration means that special effort is required to prevent their breaking down, and that the interactants must work hard to construct and maintain their mutual pretense. By contrast, in a formally staged play, although the actors have to construct and maintain a performance, making it credible to their audience, they are not required to write the script themselves. The situation that involves a terminal patient is much more like a masquerade party, where one masked actor plays carefully *to* another as long as they are together, and the total drama actually emerges from their joint creative effort.

A masquerade, however, has more extensive resources to sustain it than those the hospital situation provides. Masqueraders wear masks, hiding their facial expressions; even if they "break up" with silent laughter (as a staff member may "break down" with sympathy), this fact is concealed. Also, according to the rules ordinarily governing masquerades, each actor chooses his own status, his "character," and this makes his role in the constructed drama somewhat easier to play. He may even have played similar parts before. But terminal patients usually have had no previous experience with their pretended status, and not all personnel have had much experience. In a masquerade, when the drama fails it can be broken off, each actor moving along to another partner; but in the hospital the pretenders (especially the patient) have few comparable opportunities.

Both situations share one feature—the extensive use of props for sustaining the crucial illusion. In the masquerade, the props include not only masks but clothes and other costuming, as well as the setting where the masquerade takes place. In the hospital interaction, props also abound. Patients dress for the part of not-dying patient, including careful attention to grooming, and to hair and makeup by female patients. The terminal patient may also fix up his room so that it looks and feels "just like home," an activity that supports his enactment of normalcy. Nurses may respond to these props with explicit appreciation—"how lovely your hair looks this morning"—or even help to establish them, as by doing the patient's hair. We remember one elaborate pretense ritual involving a husband and wife who had won the nurses' sympathy. The husband simply would not recognize that his already comatose wife was approaching death, so each morning the nurses carefully prepared her for his visit, dressing her for the occasion and making certain that she looked as beautiful as possible.

The staff, of course, has its own props to support its ritual prediction that the patient is going to get well: thermometers, baths, fresh sheets, and meals on time! Each party utilizes these props as he sees fit, thereby helping to create the pretense anew. But when a patient wishes to demonstrate that he is finished with life, he may drive the nurses wild by refusing to cooperate in the daily routines of hospital life—that is, he refuses to allow the nurses to use their props. Conversely, when the personnel wish to indicate how things are with him, they may begin to omit some of those routines.

During the pretense episodes, both sides play according to the rules implicit in the interaction. Although neither the staff nor patient may recognize these rules as such, certain tactics are fashioned around them, and the action is partly constrained by them. One rule is that dangerous topics should generally be avoided. The most obviously dangerous topic is the patient's death; another is events that will happen afterwards. Of course, both parties to the pretense are supposed to follow the avoidance rule.

There is, however, a qualifying rule: Talk about dangerous topics is permissible as long as neither party breaks down. Thus, a patient refers to the distant future, as if it were his to talk about. He talks about his plans for his family, as if he would be there to share their consummation. He and the nurses discuss today's events—such as his treatments—as if they had implications for a real future, when he will have recovered from his illness. And some of his brave or foolhardy activities may signify a brave show of pretense, as when he bathes himself or insists on tottering to the toilet by himself. The staff in turn permits his activity. (Two days before he returned to the hospital to die, one patient insisted that his wife allow him to travel downtown to keep a speaking engagement, and to the last he kept up a lively conversation with a close friend about a book they were planning to write together.)

A third rule, complementing the first two, is that each actor should focus determinedly on appropriately safe topics. It is customary to talk about the daily routines—eating (the food was especially good or bad), and sleeping (whether one slept well or poorly last night). Complaints and their management help pass the time. So do minor personal confidences, and chatter about events on the ward. Talk about physical symptoms is safe enough if confined to the symptoms themselves, with no implied references to death. A terminal patient and a staff member may safely talk, and at length, about his disease so long as they skirt its fatal significance. And there are many genuinely safe topics having to do with movies and movie stars, politics, fashions—with everything, in short, that signifies that life is going on "as usual."

A fourth interactional rule is that when something happens, or is said, that tends to expose the fiction that both parties are attempting to sustain, then each must pretend that nothing has gone awry. Just as each has carefully avoided calling attention to the true situation, each now must avert his gaze from the unfortunate intrusion. Thus, a nurse may take special pains to announce herself before entering a patient's room so as not to surprise him at his crying. If she finds him crying, she may ignore it or convert it into an innocuous event with a skillful comment or gesture—much like the tactful gentleman who, having stumbled upon a woman in his bathtub, is said to have casually closed the bathroom door, murmuring "Pardon me, *sir.*" The mutuality of the pretense is illustrated by the way a patient who cannot control a sudden expression of great pain will verbally discount its significance, while the nurse in turn goes along with his pretense. Or she may brush aside or totally ignore a major error in his portrayal, as when he refers spontaneously to his death. If he is tempted to admit impulsively his terminality, she may, again, ignore his impulsive remarks or obviously misinterpret them. Thus, pretense is piled upon pretense to conceal or minimize interactional slips.

Clearly then, each party to the ritual pretense shares responsibility for maintaining it. The major responsibility may be transferred back and forth, but each party must support the other's temporary dominance in his own action. This is true even when conversation is absolutely minimal, as in some hospitals where patients take no particular pains to signal awareness of their terminality, and the staff makes no special gestures to convey its own awareness. The pretense interaction in this case is greatly simplified, but it is still discernible. Whenever a staff member is so indelicate, or so straightforward, as to act openly as if a terminal patient were dying, or if the patient does so himself, then the pretense vanishes. If neither wishes to destroy the fiction, however, then each must strive to keep the situation "normal."[4]

THE TRANSITION TO OPEN AWARENESS

A mutual pretense context that is not sustained can only change to an open awareness context. (Either party, however, may again initiate the pretense context and sometimes get cooperation from the other.) The change can be sudden, when either patient or staff distinctly conveys that he has permanently abandoned the pretense. Or the change to the open context can be gradual: nurses, and relatives, too, are familiar with patients who admit to terminality more openly on some days than they do on other days, when pretense is dominant, until finally pretense vanishes altogether. Sometimes the physician skillfully paces his interaction with a patient, leading the patient finally to refer openly to his terminality and to leave behind the earlier phase of pretense.

Pretense generally collapses when certain conditions make its maintenance increasingly difficult. These conditions have been foreshadowed in our previous discussion. Thus, when the patient cannot keep from expressing his increasing pain, or his suffering grows to the point that he is kept under heavy sedation then the enactment of pretense becomes more difficult, especially for him.

Again, neither patient nor staff may be able to avoid bringing impending death into the open if radical physical deterioration sets in, the staff because it has a tough job to do, and the patient for other reasons, including fright and panic. Sometimes a patient breaks his pretense for psychological reasons, as when he discovers that he cannot face death alone, or when a chaplain convinces him that it is better to bring things out into the open than to remain silent. (Sometimes, however, a patient may find such a sympathetic listener in the chaplain that he can continue his pretense with other personnel.) Sometimes he breaks the pretense when it no longer makes sense in light of obvious physical deterioration.

Here is a poignant episode during which a patient dying with great pain and obvious bodily deterioration finally abandoned her pretense with a nurse:

---

[4] A close reading of John Gunther's poignant account of his young son's last months shows that the boy maintained a sustained and delicately balanced mutual pretense with his parents, physicians and nurses. John Gunther, *Death Be Not Proud* (New York: Harper and Bros., 1949). Also see Bensman and Garver, *op. cit.*

There was a long silence. Then the patient asked, "After I get home from the nursing home will you visit me?" I asked if she wanted me to. "Yes, Mary, you know we could go on long drives together. . . ." She had a faraway look in her eyes as if daydreaming about all the places she would visit and all the things we could do together. This continued for some time. Then I asked, "Do you think you will be able to drive your car again?" She looked at me, "Mary, I know I am daydreaming; I know I am going to die." Then she cried, and said, "This is terrible, I never thought I would be this way."

In short, when a patient finds it increasingly difficult to hang onto a semblance of his former healthy self and begins to become a person who is visibly dying, both he and the staff are increasingly prone to say so openly, whether by word or gesture. Sometimes, however, a race occurs between a patient's persistent pretense and his becoming comatose or his actual death—a few more days of sentience or life, and either he or the staff would have dropped the pretense.

𝟙𝟙

A chief organizational consequence of the mutual pretense context is that it eliminates any possibility that staff members might "work with" patients psychologically, on a self-conscious professional basis.

𝟙𝟙

Yet, a contest may also ensue when only one side wishes to keep up the pretense. When a patient openly displays his awareness but shows it unacceptably, as by apathetically "giving up," the staff or family may try to reinstate the pretense. Usually the patient then insists on open recognition of his own impending death, but sometimes he is persuaded to return to the pretense. For instance, one patient finally wished to talk openly about death, but her husband argued against its probability, although he knew better; so after several attempts to talk openly, the patient obligingly gave up the contest. The reverse situation may also occur: the nurses begin to give the patient every opportunity to die with a maximum of comfort—as by cutting down on normal routines—thus signaling that he should no longer pretend, but the patient insists on putting up a brave show and so the nurses capitulate.

We would complicate our analysis unduly if we did more than suggest that, under such conditions, the pretense ritual sometimes resembles Ptolemy's cumbersomely patched astronomical system, with interactants pretending to pretend to pretend! We shall only add that when nurses attempt to change the pretense context into an open context, they generally do this "on their own" and not because of any calculated ward standards or specific orders from an attending physician. And the tactics they use to get the patient to refer openly to his terminality are less tried and true than the more customary tactics for forcing him to pretend.

CONSEQUENCES OF MUTUAL PRETENSE

For the patient, the pretense context can yield a measure of dignity and considerable privacy, though it may deny him the closer relationships with staff members and family members that sometimes occur when he allows them to participate in his open acceptance of death. And if they initiate and he accepts the pretense, he may have nobody with whom to talk although he might profit greatly from talk. (One terminal patient told a close friend, who told us, that when her family and husband insisted on pretending that she would recover, she suffered from the isolation, feeling as if she were trapped in cotton batting.) For the family—especially more distant kin—the pretense context can minimize embarrassment and other interactional strains; but for closer kin, franker concourse may have many advantages. . . . Oscillation between contexts of open awareness and mutual pretense can also cause interactional strains. We once observed a man persuading his mother to abandon her apathy—she had permanently closed her eyes, to the staff's great distress—and "try hard to live." She agreed finally to resume the pretense, but later relapsed into apathy. The series of episodes caused some anguish to both family and patient, as well as to the nurses. When the patient initiates the mutual pretense, staff members are likely to feel relieved. Yet the consequent stress of either maintaining the pretense or changing it to open awareness sometimes may be considerable. Again, both the relief and the stress affect nurses more than medical personnel, principally because the latter spend less time with patients.

But whether staff or patient initiates the ritual of pretense, maintaining it creates a characteristic ward mood of cautious serenity. A nurse once told us of a cancer hospital where each patient understood that everyone there had cancer, including himself, but the rules of tact, buttressed by staff silence, were so strong that few patients talked openly about anyone's condition. The consequent atmosphere was probably less serene than when only a few patients are engaged in mutual pretense, but even one such patient can affect the organizational mood, especially if the personnel become "involved" with him.

A persistent context of mutual pretense profoundly affects the more permanent aspects of hospital organization as well. (This often occurs at county and city hospitals.) Imagine what a hospital service would be like if all terminal patients were unacquainted with their terminality, or if all were perfectly open about their awareness—whether they accepted or rebelled against their fate.[5] When closed awareness generally prevails the personnel must guard against disclosure, but they need not organize themselves as a team to handle continued pretense and its sometimes stressful breakdown. Also, a chief organizational consequence of the mutual pretense context is that it eliminates any possibility that staff members might "work with" patients psychologically, on a self-conscious professional basis. This consequence was strikingly evident at the small Catholic hospital referred to a few pages ago. It is also entirely possible that a ward mood of tension can be set when (as a former patient once told us) a number of elderly dying patients continually communicate to each other their willingness to die, but the staff members persistently insist on the pretense that the patients are going to recover. On the other hand, the prevailing ward mood accompanying mutual pretense tends to be more serene—or at least less obviously tense—than when open suspicion awareness is dominant.

---

[5]For a description of a research hospital where open awareness prevails, with far-reaching effects on hospital social structure, see Renée Fox, *Experiment Perilous* (New York: Free Press of Glencoe, 1959).

Coping with the Reality
of Terminal Illness in the Family

Elisabeth Kübler-Ross

Elisabeth Kübler-Ross is a Swiss physician now practicing in Chicago where she began a seminar on death and dying that was initially greeted with considerable resistance by physicians but was welcomed by terminal patients. In this selection taken from her book *On Death and Dying*, Dr. Kübler-Ross introduces the family as a participant in the dying drama.

Family members undergo different stages of adjustment similar to [those of the] patients. At first many of them cannot believe that it is true. They may deny the fact that there is such an illness in the family or "shop around" from doctor to doctor in the vain hope of hearing that this was the wrong diagnosis. They may seek help and reassurance (that it is all not true) from fortune-tellers and faith healers. They may arrange for expensive trips to famous clinics and physicians and only gradually face up to the reality which may change their life so drastically. Greatly dependent on the patient's attitude, awareness, and ability to communicate, the family then undergoes certain changes. If they are able to share their common concerns, they can take care of important matters early and under less pressure of time and emotions. If each one tries to keep a secret from the other, they will keep an artificial barrier between them which will make it difficult for any preparatory grief for the patient or his family. The end result will be much more dramatic than for those who can talk and cry together at times.

Just as the patient goes through a stage of anger, the immediate family will experience the same emotional reaction. They will be angry alternately with the doctor who examined the patient first and did not come forth with the diagnosis and the doctor who confronted them with the sad reality. They may project their rage to the hospital personnel who never care enough, no matter how efficient the care is in reality. There is a great deal of envy in this reaction, as family members often feel cheated at not being able or allowed to be with the patient and to care for him. There is also

293

much guilt and a wish to make up for missed past opportunities. The more we can help the relative to express these emotions before the death of a loved one, the more comfortable the family member will be.

ⰧⰧⰧ

> *Genuine emotions on the part of a member of the family are much easier to take than a make-believe mask which the patient can see through anyway.*

ⰧⰧⰧ

When anger, resentment, and guilt can be worked through, the family will then go through a phase of preparatory grief, just as the dying person does. The more this grief can be expressed before death, the less unbearable it becomes afterward. We often hear relatives say proudly of themselves that they always tried to keep a smiling face when confronted with the patient, until one day they just could not keep that facade any longer. Little do they realize that genuine emotions on the part of a member of the family are much easier to take than a make-believe mask which the patient can see through anyway and which means to him a disguise rather than a sharing of a sad situation.

If members of a family can share these emotions together, they will gradually face the reality of impending separation and come to an acceptance of it together. The most heart-breaking time, perhaps, for the family is the final phase, when the patient is slowly detaching himself from his world including his family. They do not understand that a dying man who has found peace and acceptance in his death will have to separate himself, step by step, from his environment, including his most loved ones. How could he ever be ready to die if he continued to hold onto the meaningful relationships of which a man has so many? When the patient asks to be visited only by a few more friends, then by his children, and finally only by his wife, it should be understood that that is the way of separating himself gradually. It is often misinterpreted by the immediate family as a rejection, and we have met several husbands and wives who have reacted dramatically to this normal and healthy detachment. I think we can be of greatest service to them if we help them understand that only patients who have worked through their dying are able to detach themselves slowly and peacefully in this manner. It should be a source of comfort and solace to them and not one of grief and resentment. It is during this time that the family needs the most support, the patient perhaps the least. I do not mean to imply by this that the patient should then be left alone. We should always be available, but a patient who has reached this stage of acceptance and decathexis usually requires little in terms of interpersonal relationship. If the meaning of this detachment is not explained to the family, problems can arise. . . .

The most tragic death is perhaps—aside from the very young—the death of the very old when we look at it from [the] point of view of the family. Whether the generations have lived together or separately, each generation has a need and a right to live their own lives, to have their own privacy, their own needs fulfilled appropriate to their generation. The old folks have outlived their usefulness in terms of our economic system and have earned, on the other hand, a right to live out their lives in dignity and peace. As long as they are healthy in body and mind and self-supporting, this may all be quite possible. We have seen many old men and women, however, who have become disabled physically or emotionally and who require a tremendous sum of money for a dignified maintenance at a level their family desires for them. The family is then often confronted with a difficult decision, namely, to mobilize all available money, including loans and savings for their own retirement, in order to afford such final care. The tragedy of these old people is perhaps that the amount of money and often financial sacrifice does not involve any improvement of the condition but is a mere maintenance at a minimal level of existence. If medical complications occur, the expenses are manifold, and the family often wishes for a quick and painless death, but rarely expresses that wish openly. That such wishes bring about feelings of guilt is obvious.

I am reminded of an old woman who had been hospitalized for several weeks and required extensive and expensive nursing care in a private hospital. Everybody expected her to die soon, but day after day she remained in an unchanged condition. Her daughter was torn between sending her to a nursing home or keeping her in the hospital, where she apparently wanted to stay. Her son-in-law was angry at her for having used up their life savings and had innumerable arguments with his wife, who felt too guilty to take her out of the hospital. When I visited the old woman she looked frightened and weary. I asked her simply what she was so afraid of. She looked at me and finally expressed what she had been unable to communicate before, because she herself realized how unrealistic her fears were. She was afraid of "being eaten up alive by the worms." While I was catching my breath and tried to understand the real meaning of this statement, her daughter blurted out, "If that's what's keeping you from dying, we can burn you," by which she naturally meant that a cremation would prevent her from having any contact with earthworms. All her suppressed anger was in this statement. I sat with the old woman alone for a while. We talked calmly about her lifelong phobias and her fear of death which was presented in this fear of worms, as if she would be aware of them after her death. She felt greatly relieved for having expressed it and had nothing but understanding for her daughter's anger. I encouraged her to share some of these feelings with her daughter, so that the latter might not have to feel so bad about her outburst.

When I met the daughter outside the room I told her of her mother's understanding, and they finally got together to talk about their concerns, ending up by making arrangements for the funeral, a cremation. Instead of sitting silently in anger, they communicated and consoled each other. The mother died the next day. If I had not seen the peaceful look on her face during her last day, I might have worried that this outburst of anger might have killed her.

Another aspect that is often not taken into account is what kind of a fatal illness the patient has. There are certain expectations of cancer, just as there are certain pictures associated with heart disease. The former is often viewed as a lingering, pain-producing illness, while the latter can strike suddenly, painless but final. I think there is a great deal of difference if a loved one dies slowly with much time available for preparatory grief on both sides, compared to the feared phone call, "It happened, it's all over." It is easier to talk with a cancer patient about death and dying than it is with a cardiac patient, who arouses concerns in us that we might frighten him and thus provoke a coronary, i.e., his death. The relatives of a cancer patient are therefore more amenable to discussing the expected end than the family of someone with heart disease, when the end can come any moment and a discussion may provoke it, at least in the opinion of many members of families whom we have spoken with.

I remember a mother of a young man in Colorado who did not allow her son to take any exercise, not even the most minimal kind, in spite of the contrary advice on part of his doctors. In conversations this mother would often make statements like "if he does too much he will drop dead on me," as if she expected a hostile act on the part of her son to be committed against her. She was totally unaware of her own hostility even after sharing with us some of her resentment for having "such a weak son," whom she very often associated with her ineffective and unsuccessful husband. It took months of careful, patient listening to this mother before she was able to express some of her own destructive wishes toward her child. She rationalized these by the fact that he was the cause of her limited social and professional life, thus rendering her as ineffective as she regarded her husband to be. These are complicated family situations, in which a sick member of the family is rendered more incapable of functioning because of the relative's conflicts. If we can learn to respond to such family members with compassion and understanding rather than judgment and criticism, we also help the patient bear his handicap with more ease and dignity.

The following example of Mr. P. demonstrates the difficulties that can occur for the patient when he is ready to separate himself, but the family is unable to accept the reality, thus contributing to the patient's conflicts. Our goal should always be to help the patient and his family face the crisis together in order to achieve acceptance of this final reality simultaneously.

Mr. P. was a man in his mid-fifties who looked about fifteen years older than his age. The doctors felt that he had only a poor chance to respond to treatment, partially because of his advanced cancer and marasmus, but mainly because of his lack of "fighting spirit." Mr. P. had his stomach removed because of cancer five years prior to this hospitalization. At first he accepted his illness quite well and was full of hope. As he grew weaker and thinner, he became increasingly depressed until the time of his readmission, when a chest X-ray revealed metastatic tumors in his lungs. The patient had not been informed of the biopsy result when I saw him. The question was raised as to the advisability of possible radiation or surgery for a man in his weak condition. Our interview proceeded in two sessions. The first visit served the purpose of introducing myself and of telling him that I was available should he wish to talk about the seriousness of his illness and the problems that this might cause. A telephone interrupted us and I left the room, asking him to think about it. I also informed him about the time of my next visit.

When I saw him the next day, Mr. P. put his arm out in welcome and signaled to the chair as an invitation to sit down. In spite of many interruptions by a change of infusion bottles, distribution of medication, and routine pulse and blood pressure measurements, we sat for over an hour.

297

Mr. P. had sensed that he would be allowed to "open his shades" as he called it. There was no defensiveness, no evasiveness in his accounts. He was a man whose hours seemed to count, who had no precious time to lose, and who seemed to be eager to share his concerns and regrets with someone who could listen.

The day before, he made the statement, "I want to sleep, sleep, sleep and not wake up." Today he repeated the same thing, but added the word "but." I looked at him questioningly and he proceeded to tell me with a weak soft voice that his wife had come to visit him. She was convinced that he would make it. She expected him home to take care of the garden and flowers. She also reminded him of his promise to retire soon, to move to Arizona perhaps, to have a few more good years. . . .

He talked with much warmth and affection about his daughter, twenty-one years old, who came to visit him on a leave from college, and who was shocked to see him in this condition. He mentioned all these things, as if he was to be blamed for disappointing his family, for not living up to their expectations.

I mentioned that to him and he nodded. He talked about all the regrets he had. He spent the first years of his marriage accumulating material goods for his family, trying to "make them a good home," and by doing so spent most of his time away from home and family. After the occurrence of cancer he spared every moment to be with them, but by then, it seemed to be too late. His daughter was away at school and had her own friends. When she was small and needed and wanted him, he was too busy making money.

Talking about his present condition he said, "Sleep is the only relief. Every moment of awakening is anguish, pure anguish. There is no relief. I am thinking in envy of two men I saw executed. I sat right in front of the first man. I felt nothing. Now, I think he was a lucky guy. He deserved to die. He had no anguish, it was fast and painless. Here I lie in bed, every hour, every day is agony."

Mr. P. was not so much concerned about pain and physical discomfort as he was tortured by regrets for not being able to fulfill his family's expectations, for being "a failure." He was tortured by his tremendous need to "let go and sleep, sleep, sleep" and the continuous flow of expectations from his environment. "The nurses come in and say I have to eat or I get too weak; the doctors come in and tell me about the new treatment they started, and expect me to be happy about it; my wife comes and tells me about the work I am supposed to do when I get out of here; and my daughter just looks at me and says, 'You have to get well'—how can a man die in peace this way?"

For a brief moment he smiled and said, "I will take this treatment and go home once more. I will return to work the next day and make a bit more money. My insurance will pay for my daughter's education anyway, but she still needs a father for a while. But you know and I know, I just cannot do it. Maybe they have to learn to face it. It would make dying so much easier!"

Mr. P. showed . . . how difficult it is for patients to face impending and anticipated death when the family is not ready to "let go" and implicitly or explicitly prevents them from separating themselves from the involvements here on earth. [One patient's] husband just stood at her bedside, reminding her of their happy marriage which should not end and pleading with all the doctors to do everything humanly possible to prevent her from dying. Mr. P.'s wife reminded him of unfulfilled promises and undone tasks, thus communicating the same needs to him, namely, to have him around for many more years to come. I cannot say that both these partners used denial.* Both of them knew the reality of the condition of their spouses. Yet both, because of their own needs, looked away from this reality. They faced it when talking with other people but denied it in front of the patients. And it was the patients who needed to hear that they too were aware of the seriousness of their condition and were able to accept this reality. Without this knowledge "every moment of awakening is pure anguish," in Mr. P.'s words. Our interview ended with the expression of hope that the important people in his environment would learn to face the reality of his dying rather than expressing hope for a prolonging of his life.

Once the patient dies, I find it cruel and inappropriate to speak of the love of God.

This man was ready to separate himself from this world. He was ready to enter the final stage when the end is more promising or there is not enough strength left to live. One might argue whether an all-out medical effort is appropriate in such circumstances. With enough infusions and transfusions, vitamins, energizers, and antidepressant medication, with psychotherapy and symptomatic treatment, many such patients may be given an additional "lease on life." I have heard more curses than words

---

*For a discussion of the mechanisms of denial, see Weisman's selection on this topic. —ED.

of appreciation for the gained time, and I repeat my conviction that a patient has a right to die in peace and dignity. He should not be used to fulfill our own needs when his own wishes are in opposition to ours. I am referring to patients who have a physical illness but who are sane and capable enough to make decisions for themselves. Their wishes and opinions should be respected, they should be listened to and consulted. If the patient's wishes are contrary to our beliefs or convictions, we should express this conflict openly and leave the decisions up to the patient in respect to further interventions or treatments. In the many terminally ill patients I have so far interviewed, I have not seen any irrational behavior or unacceptable requests, and this includes . . . two psychotic women . . . who followed through with their treatment, one of them in spite of her otherwise almost complete denial of her illness.

THE FAMILY AFTER DEATH HAS OCCURRED

Once the patient dies, I find it cruel and inappropriate to speak of the love of God. When we lose someone, especially when we have had little if any time to prepare ourselves, we are enraged, angry, in despair; we should be allowed to express these feelings. The family members are often left alone as soon as they give their consent for autopsy. Bitter, angry, or just numb, they walk through the corridors of the hospital, unable often to face the brutal reality. The first few days may be filled with busy-work, with arrangements and visiting relatives. The void and emptiness is felt after the departure of the relatives. It is at this time that family members feel most grateful to have someone to talk to, especially if it is someone who had recent contact with the deceased and who can share anecdotes of some good moments towards the end of the deceased's life. This helps the relative over the shock and the initial grief and prepares him for a gradual acceptance.

Many relatives are preoccupied by memories and ruminate in fantasies, often even talk to the deceased as if he were still alive. They not only isolate themselves from the living but make it harder for themselves to face the reality of the person's death. For some, however, this is the only way they can cope with the loss, and it would be cruel indeed to ridicule them or to confront them daily with the unacceptable reality. It would be more helpful to understand this need and to help them separate themselves by taking them out of their isolation gradually. I have seen this behavior mainly in young widows who had lost their husbands at an early age and were rather unprepared. It may be more frequently encountered in the days of war where death of a young person occurs elsewhere, though I believe a war always makes relatives more aware of the possibility of no return. They are therefore more prepared for that death than, for example, for the unexpected death of a young man through a rapidly progressing illness.

A last word should be mentioned about the children. They are often the forgotten ones. Not so much that nobody cares; the opposite is often true. But few people feel comfortable talking to a child about death. Young children have different concepts of death, and they have to be taken into consideration in order to talk to them and to understand their communications. Up to the age of three a child is concerned only about separation, later followed by the fear of mutilation. It is at this age that the small child begins to mobilize, to take his first trips out "into the world," the sidewalk trips by tricycle. It is in this environment that he may see the first beloved pet run over by a car or a beautiful bird torn apart by a cat. This is what mutilation means to him, since it is the age when he is concerned about the integrity of his body and is threatened by anything that can destroy it.

Also, death . . . is not a permanent fact for the three-to-five-year-old. It is as temporary as burying a flower bulb into the soil in the fall to have it come up again the following spring.

After the age of five death is often regarded as a man, a bogey-man who comes to take people away; it is still attributed to an outward intervention.

Around the ages of nine to ten the realistic conception begins to show, namely, death as a permanent biological process.

Children will react differently to the death of a parent, from a silent withdrawal and isolation to a wild loud mourning which attracts attention and thus a replacement of a loved and needed object. Since children cannot yet differentiate between the wish and the deed . . . , they may feel a great deal of remorse and guilt. They will feel responsible for having killed the parents and thus fear a gruesome punishment in retribution. They may, on the other hand, take the separation relatively calmly and utter such statements as "She will come back for the spring vacation" or secretly put an apple out for her—in order to assure that she has enough to eat for the temporary trip. If adults, who are upset already during this period, do not understand such children and reprimand or correct them, the children may hold inside their own way of grieving—which is often a root for later emotional disturbance.

With an adolescent, however, things are not much different than with an adult. Naturally adolescence is in itself a difficult time, and added loss of a parent is often too much for such a youngster to endure. They should be listened to and allowed to ventilate their feelings, whether they be guilt, anger, or plain sadness.

RESOLUTION OF GRIEF AND ANGER

What I am saying again here is, let the relative talk, cry, or scream if necessary. Let them share and ventilate, but be available. The relative has a long time of mourning ahead of him, when the problems for the dead are solved. He needs help and assistance from the confirmation of a so-called bad diagnosis until months after the death of a member of the family.

↑↑↑

The most meaningful help that we can give any relative, is to share his feelings before the event of death and to allow him to work through his feelings, whether they are rational or irrational.

↑↑↑

By help I naturally do not assume that this has to be professional counseling of any form; most people neither need nor can afford this. But they need a human being, a friend, doctor, nurse, or chaplain—it matters little. The social worker may be the most meaningful one, if she has helped with arrangements for a nursing home and if the family wishes to talk more about their mother in that particular set-up, which may have been a source of guilt feelings for not having kept her at home. Such families have at times visited other old folks in the same nursing home and continued their task of caring for someone, perhaps as a partial denial, perhaps just to do good for all the missed opportunities with Grandma. No matter what the underlying reason, we should try to understand their needs and to help relatives direct these needs constructively to diminish guilt, shame, or fear of retribution. The most meaningful help that we can give any relative, child or adult, is to share his feelings before the event of death and to allow him to work through his feelings, whether they are rational or irrational.

If we tolerate their anger, whether it is directed at us, at the deceased, or at God, we are helping them take a great step towards acceptance without guilt. If we blame them for daring to ventilate such socially poorly tolerated thoughts, we are blameworthy for prolonging their grief, shame, and guilt which often results in physical and emotional ill health.

Speaking of Death with the Dying

John Hinton

John Hinton is an English physician and Professor of Psychiatry at Middlesex Medical School. In this selection, taken from his indispensable, book *Dying*, Dr. Hinton discusses the issues involved in speaking with a terminal patient and notes that *how* one speaks with the dying is far more important than *what* one says.

The frequently debated question "Should the doctor tell?" tends to carry a false implication that the doctor knows all about the patient's approaching death and the patient knows nothing. The resultant discussion and controversy [are] therefore often irrelevant or, at least, tangential to the real problem. Doctors are far from omniscient. Even if they have no doubt that their patients' condition will be fatal, they can rarely foretell the time of death with any accuracy unless it is close at hand. Furthermore . . . patients are not necessarily unaware of what is happening; many have a very clear idea that they are dying.

Rather than putting a choice between telling or not telling, it would be more useful to ask other questions. Should we encourage or divert a patient who begins to speak of matters that will lead to talk of dying? How freely should we speak to him about it? Should we lie to him if we suspect he only wants to be told that all will be well? If he sincerely wishes to know if his illness will be fatal, should his suppositions be confirmed? If he never asks outright, have we a duty to tell him? Is it right to deny knowledge of dying

303

to those who ask, or wrong to tell those who show no wish to know? Should we allow the awareness of dying to grow gradually, or should patients who are mortally ill know this early on, so that they may attain greater acceptance of dying? If they are to be told more openly, how should such knowledge be given? How do people react to being told? These questions—all part of that oversimplified "Should the doctor tell?"—can have no universally accepted answer. Individuals differ, and ethical beliefs or current opinions will influence judgment.

TO SPEAK FREELY?

There are some good reasons for speaking freely about the possibility of dying to those with fatal conditions. An ill person who strongly suspects that he is dying, but is denied the least opportunity to question or discuss this, can feel cruelly isolated if he does not want this conspiracy of silence. He may be surrounded by people whose every manifest word or action is designed to deny or avoid the fact that he is dying, and he is aware of the artificiality of their deception. How can he gain the ease of wholly sincere talk with others if all maintain the pretence that his imminent departure from life, his leaving them for ever, is just not taking place? It would be thought preposterous and cruel if throughout a mother's first pregnancy and delivery all around conspired to treat it as indigestion and never gave her an opportunity to voice her doubts.

The view that we have a duty to inform the dying man has some support on material and spiritual grounds. If a doctor conceals from a patient that he is mortally ill, the person may fail to order his family affairs or may embark on business ventures which he would not contemplate if he knew his likely fate. The doctor's legal responsibility to warn the dying person appears to be a matter of debate. Most doctors however will bear in mind how far a person needs to set his affairs in order, when considering what they should tell a dying patient. Imparting advice to a man that it might be a wise precaution to tidy up business arrangements serves more than that single function. (Kline & Sobin, 1951). Conveyed with tact, it is a hint that an ill man can discuss further with his doctor if he is of a mind to know more, or it is advice he can just accept at its face value.

The spiritual need for a man to know that he is dying may well take precedence over material matters in the terminal phase. Frequently the dying person spontaneously turns or returns to his religious beliefs. He may already have prayed for help in his serious illness, perhaps with rather unfamiliar voice. If it appears that recovery is unlikely, most ministers hold strongly that the patient should know this, so that he can prepare for eternal life.

At times there is an increasing need to be frank with a patient over his prognosis, because he has short periods of feverish hopes followed by long periods of despairing misery. He may waste effort and money on unjustified and quite hopeless treatments, only to have bitter disappointment as proclaimed panaceas fail. If a patient is seriously ill and appears to be getting worse, while his physician appears content with ineffective remedies, he may feel that opportunities of cure are being lost. This may lead to a feeling of frustration or a desperate tour of other doctors. Of course, a second opinion from a respected source may be a great help to all concerned. This may bring assurance that no important possibility is being neglected. When a troubled patient who has been seeking fruitlessly for cure comes to a better understanding with his doctor on the nature of his disease and how much hope is justifiable, he may regain confidence and find greater peace.

In spite of these arguments which favor frankness with the dying, many doctors are reluctant to speak with them of death. They feel that most patients do not wish to raise the subject except to get reassurance, and that the truth is likely to be hurtful. This common medical attitude is uncomfortably combined with a considerable hesitation over practising deliberate evasion and deceit on patients who have put their trust in the doctor, even if the "white lies" are intended to avoid distress. Some forthright physicians, however, make plain their belief that it does patients no good to be told that they are dying (Asher, 1955). It is a viewpoint easy to attack on theoretical grounds; but when truth can give rise to considerable distress, when kindly half-truths do not materially alter the course to death, and when dying people would like to hear that they will recover, it takes a very convinced man to condemn evasion or even the occasional untruth. Many scrupulous people who care for the dying find themselves concealing the truth in a manner they always wished to avoid.

In practice relatively few doctors tell patients that there is no hope of recovery. In one study of medical opinion, for example, a group of over two hundred doctors, working in hospital and private practice, were asked if they favored informing those patients found to have a cancer very likely to prove fatal (Oken, 1961). Patients so defined would include, of course, some whose symptoms were investigated early while they were in reasonable general health, with death some way off. Such patients might have little reason at this stage to suspect their illness to be mortal, and if a doctor did tell them, it would give some unanticipated bad news. Eighty-eight percent of these doctors would not tell the patient, although some of them would make exceptions. The doctors felt that usually the patient's questions were pleas for reassurance. The other 12 percent usually told the patients that they had cancer, especially if the latter were intelligent and emotionally stable. Most of the doctors felt that they should inform a relative and were glad to share the burden of their knowledge. Incidentally no less than 60 percent of these same doctors said that they would like to be told if they themselves had an equally sinister form of cancer. This inconsistency of opinion between imparting and receiving such information was explained by the doctors on the basis of their own greater fortitude or responsibilities. It might be so, but it is more likely to be the emotionally determined attitude found among lay and medical people alike. This was indicated by the fact that these physicians were not any more frank with doctors whom they treated for cancer than any other patients with cancer. Equally, lay people are more in favor of themselves being told they have developed a cancer than of recommending that others in a similar condition should be told (Kelly & Friesen, 1950).

Although the majority of practising doctors may believe that it is better for them to be reticent with the dying, this opinion must be reconsidered in the light of the fact that an equally large proportion of lay people say that they would like to be told. On the surface, it seems quite perverse that 80 or 90 percent of physicians say that they rarely, if ever, tell patients that their illness is mortal (Oken, 1961), whereas about 80 percent of patients say they would like to be told (Gilbertsen & Wangensteen, 1961). If a doctor sees the question in rather unreal black-and-white terms of either pressing unpleasant news of impending death upon a patient or keeping him in happy ignorance of his fate, this will sway him towards expressing an opinion against telling. This travesties the usual situation, however, where the dying person, with gathering doubts and clues, becomes increasingly suspicious that his condition is mortal.

It is often suggested that the very high percentage of people who give the theoretical answer that they would like to know if they had cancer, do so because they feel secure in their present state of good health. They might be less confident if there was an immediate possibility of having a fatal illness. Albeit, almost as high a proportion of patients actually being treated for cancer in Manchester were just as much in favor of being told of their diagnosis (Aitken-Swan & Easson, 1959). They had been told they had a treatable cancer and later on were asked if they approved or disapproved of being informed. Two thirds were glad to have been told, only 7 percent disapproved, and 19 percent denied having been told—the familiar phenomenon of failing to hear or remember what one does not wish to learn. This particular group of patients, however, had curable cancers. Is it the same for those with incurable cancers?

The answer appears to be that they equally wish to know. In the University Hospitals at Minnesota it is the practice of doctors to tell their patients the diagnosis (Gilbertsen & Wangensteen, 1961). A group of patients with advanced cancer were asked if they knew their diagnosis and 86 percent did know. Most had been told by their doctor, although some found out in other ways. Many of the remaining 14 percent, who did not know, had asked at one time and been given evasive answers. As many as four-fifths of these very ill patients thought that cancer patients should be told. They said it had helped them understand their own illness and given them peace of mind. It also allowed them to plan for further medical care, religious matters, and for other aspects of their families' and their own lives.

HOW TO SPEAK OF DYING?

There are, therefore, several good reasons justifying considerable candor with people who are fatally ill. If this were to be more widely accepted in principle, how and when should such sincere conversation take place? Clearly an abrupt statement to every patient with incurable disease that he is going to die is likely to do more harm than good.

Some wish to know only a little of their illness. As with non-fatal disease a person may be helped by simple explanations of the illness, together with a general plan of investigating or treating the condition. An intelligent young woman, who was admitted to hospital with an obviously growing lump on one rib, was very troubled while investigations were done and treatment started without anyone telling her what it was. There was not much reassuring information to give her, as it was the sign of a widespread cancer. She wanted to know something, however. She was told that it was a tumor and that the X-rays had shown up one or two smaller ones. They would be treated by radiotherapy and, it was correctly said, her condition would improve considerably. This was as much as she wanted to know at that time. She had been very anxious, but after this talk she was less so. She was quite sad for a day or two, and then her spirits recovered. This sort of response of sorrow on learning of having serious disease, followed by greater equanimity as acceptance grows, is the usual understandable reaction.

307

Some dying patients want to know even less than this sort of edited version of the truth. They may not want to hear a word about the nature of their condition. They may well have a hidden suspicion and gladly enter a tacit conspiracy to avoid the whole subject. They wish others to take over all responsibilities, anxieties, and decisions. This total surrender of all decision to the doctor may be somewhat less common now, especially as doctors tend to lose a little of their former authoritative manner, and more patients refuse to put up with it. But when seriously ill, it can be easier for a patient to relinquish all control, all knowledge, to his doctor. If the dying person indicates openly that he does not want to know, if he shows by his manner or by his talk that he does not wish to regard his illness as fatal, it would be uncharitable to force the truth upon him. The aim is to make dying a little easier, not to apply a dogma of always divulging truth (Alvarez, 1952).

It is not an easy problem when a patient asks about his incurable illness in a way that indicates his need for reassurance or, at least, hope. He is probably more likely to ask such questions as "It's not cancer, is it, doctor?" if his doctor has shown no sign of giving any spontaneous comment about his condition. If a patient does blurt out this loaded question, or suddenly asks, "Will I get better?" of someone ill-prepared to answer, the situation is potentially distressing to both. The result is often a hasty untruthful reassurance. If this is given in an atmosphere of doubt and anxiety, present in both their minds, little good will be done to the ill person's morale. If the question has been met with a hasty denial or a misleadingly optimistic view, this may be accepted with gratitude. Sometimes it is taken as a more definite answer than was intended. The ill person may even, by a series of further questions based on the first slanted answer, wring out a more emphatic denial of fatal disease than one would wish to give. This is disturbing, but is not necessarily a catastrophe, even if the patient later comes to realize that his first misgivings were well-founded. Nevertheless, an emotional balance achieved on a basis of assurances bound to be proved false, is no stable adjustment. When the original loaded question is put, it is often better not to answer the dying person's anxious inquiry straight away. Returning the question, asking him to describe more fully what anxieties he has in mind, and listening sympathetically to his doubts and fears will meet some of his needs. Then the fuller description may show the basis of his anxiety. It may be a totally unwarranted fear which can be allayed, such as an anticipation of prolonged agony. It may be a well-founded apprehension, but one that can be borne with help. In the long run, especially if there is someone at hand to help with any subsequent doubts, allowing a person to discuss his fears may prove more valuable than a hasty, consoling, but untrue, answer.

In practice, probably the best and easiest way to broach the matter of dying with a mortally ill person is just to allow him to speak of his suspicions or knowledge of the outcome. If necessary, he can be asked how he feels and shown that more than the polite stereotyped answer is wanted. If the patient mentions that he feels upset he can be encouraged to talk about it. Then frequently the doctor will find that there is little for him to "tell," all that is required is for him to listen with sympathy. In these circumstances the dying person does not usually ask for reassurance or praise for his courage. He may glance up for confirmation of mutual understanding. He may want to know a little more to clarify some aspect of the situation. It is quite possible for the doctor to be uncertain of the exact course of an illness and yet, when asked, to give an honest qualified answer without lying or undue prevarication. To many people this brings firmer comfort than the flimsy props of obviously false promises or the chaos of apparently bewildered ignorance. In treating any disease it is common enough to be thinking in terms of probabilities and possibilities rather than certainties. As compensation for our having to endure uncertainty, it is uncommon to be in a position where there is no comforting straw of hope for survival.

While doctors are trying to judge their patients' capacity to stand unpleasant news, many patients are equally making their intuitive judgments of whether their doctor can bear sincere but difficult questions.

If it is unclear if an ill person desires to know the whole truth, it is possible to start by giving gentle hints. A simple explanation of the disease, mentioning the favorable aspects of treatment and touching upon the other serious possibilities, will enable the ill person to take up the aspects he wishes and ignore others (Aldrich, 1963). The beginnings of awareness may be started early. A surgeon before operating upon a suspected cancer will often tell the patient that if the condition is serious he will need to perform an extensive operation. The patient who has such an operation can then pursue the matter with the doctor as much as he wishes. He can apprehend the threat of the illness, or concentrate on the curative value of the treatment.

Many doctors prefer to use an oblique approach for letting the patient know that he may be dying. Without any deception or lies, they aim to allow an awareness of the outcome to grow. If need be, a germ of realization is planted, but hope is never utterly excluded. Discussion can be reasonably frank, but the emphasis is on the favourable aspects (Gavey, 1955). If, indeed, the awareness of dying is going to grow, those who care for the patient must be prepared to keep pace with this increasing realization. They should be ready to listen and let the patient know that some of his surmises are true and some of his fears are unjustified. In this way the dying person should not feel too lonely, too uncertain, nor plunged into acute emotional distress.

Although it is not an infallible guide to how much the dying patient should be told, his apparent wishes and questions do point the way. This means that the manner in which he puts his views should be closely attended to—the intonations and the exact wording may be very revealing. It also means that he must be given ample opportunity to express his ideas and ask his questions. If the questions are sincere, however, then why not give quiet straight answers to the patient's questions about his illness and the outcome? It makes for beneficial trust (Leak, 1948).

It is to be remembered that while doctors are trying to judge their patients' capacity to stand unpleasant news, many patients are equally making their intuitive judgements of whether their doctor can bear sincere but difficult questions. They often have a very accurate idea of which doctor is quite unaccustomed or unsuited to being frank about fatal illness to the person most concerned. I have often been told by understanding people, towards the end of their life, that they knew that the doctor looking after them could not easily talk about this. "He feels he's got to get people well, and I couldn't very well talk to him about not getting better," said a woman who knew she would soon die. If a patient is firmly insistent and his doctor is honest, frank conversations do take place. "I asked him what they'd found and then I asked him if it was cancer. And now I know it's cancer, and they haven't been able to take it all away. There's only one in a thousand chance of recovery." The physician who had been questioned by this man said that he felt that he had probably been more perturbed by the conversation than the patient had.

Occasionally those concerned with a patient's care hold conflicting views over his need to be told. Such unpleasant disagreements, when they do occur, are not resolved as often as they should be by discovering what the patient already knows. Nor do those with his interest at heart meet as often as they should to see what common ground they have between their seemingly opposed and entrenched beliefs.

It is perhaps strange that there is so much more agreement over talking frankly to members of the family about their relative's fatal illness rather than to the patient himself, even if he shows a wish to know. It reverses the usual convention of the doctor keeping confidential the information concerning an adult and telling other people only if the patient agrees. A few doctors, if they tell the patient the serious nature of the illness, do discuss with them who else should be informed. Usually the next of kin is told, but often it is clear that some other responsible member of the family is better able to receive the information and pass on the appropriate knowledge to the rest. As with the patient, the families receiving these tidings often need more than just a bulletin of bad news.

REACTIONS TO SPEAKING OF DEATH

Many patients have said what a relief they have felt when at last they have had a chance to talk openly about the probability that they are dying. As so many gain comfort from this, it is clearly unkind to deny them the opportunity. They do not get the chance because people are fearful of embarking on such conversations. In the book *Awareness of Dying* by Glaser and Strauss (1965), the authors refer to the fact that some people who care for patients are recognized by their colleagues to have an aptitude for speaking easily and honestly to the dying and bring them comfort. I am sure that many more people could do this if the climate of opinion changed towards greater frankness, and more people realized how much they could help in this way. Most nurses, medical students, and young doctors do not receive as much help as they should, during their training, over the problems raised in caring for the dying.

If more people become prepared to speak freely with the dying there will be a need for caution, because although many would benefit, some would react adversely. A proportion of people, nearing the end of life, are very distressed by implicit or explicit references to death's coming. A little exploratory conversation may indicate a patient's likely reaction. He may

311

say quite clearly what he wants. A man who was pretty sure that he had abdominal cancer said, "I want them to tell me if they *are* going to operate. If they aren't, I want them to give me the wire. Then I'll know what to make of it." It was clear that he was not one who only wanted to know as long as the news was good.

There can be some intuitive judgment of how much particular individuals should be told. Their habitual manner of dealing with life can be a useful guide, their style of facing former difficulties or attaining their social position (Ogilvie, 1957). This was illustrated by one equable man who had risen to a responsible position supervising a group of shops. He had always coped well with problems in life, once he knew what was needed to be done. The previous year he had had a kidney removed and had been told that all should be well after the operation. His wife, however, had been told that he had a cancer and also warned, according to his doctor's usual policy, not to tell the patient. When the patient entered hospital again with a spread of his cancer, he insisted on being told the true state of affairs. He took it very well, but regretted that he had not been told before, so that he and his wife could have openly acknowledged that he might have little time to live. Naturally, a patient's expressed wishes and clues from his past life as to his manner of facing difficulties give no perfect prediction. The man who has succeeded in life, developing strong friendships and warm family ties may, in spite of his apparent stability, be unable to cope with the threat of so much loss. The less happy person may be better prepared to give up his life (Aldrich, 1963). Nevertheless, the view that a stable person will probably retain this characteristic when facing death usually proves correct.

In general, learning that an illness is likely to be fatal produces a period of disquiet, even dismay, although this may be effectively concealed. However well the knowledge has been conveyed, it is almost bound to cause some emotional reaction. If frank discussions were often to result in patients becoming severely or persistently distressed, even suicidal, few doctors would wish to speak to them of dying. There does tend to be an exaggerated fear that dying patients will kill themselves if they are told that their illness may be fatal. The chances are that the suicidal acts which occur in those with mortal disease are due to the suffering and the spiritual isolation when the sick are lonely, rather than any despair following a sympathetic discussion of their outlook. Although suicide remains a threatening possibility, inhibiting some from frank discussion with the dying, it is hard to find a case where a humane conversation on these lines precipitated any suicidal act. It is much more likely to have prevented it. "I knew what I'd got," said a young woman who had attempted suicide, "I'd seen it in my notes. I'd looked it up in the medical books and I knew I couldn't recover. I wanted to talk about it with the doctor, but he always seemed too busy, or just called it inflammation."

Clumsy telling of a fatal illness can cause great distress, but this extreme is generally avoidable. There is an account of one Veterans' Administration Hospital in North America where it was the practice to tell the patient the nature of his illness, including fatal illness (Glaser & Strauss, 1965). Many of the patients in this hospital were from a low social class or destitute, and, it seems, not necessarily treated with much dignity. Some of the doctors made a practice of short, blunt announcements to the patients and walking away. Some softened it a little and assured the patient that pain would be controlled. Although they could justify telling the truth because the patients become "philosophical" about it after a few days, this technique seems hard. The sociologists describing the situation wrote that the abrupt disclosure tended to result in a more immediate profound depression. As a result the patients were more apt to try and cope with such potential distress by denying the reality of their situation, rather than being helped to accept it.

In order to evaluate more reliably the effect of telling patients that they have a mortal illness, a careful and courageous investigation was carried out by some of the medical staff at Lund University (Gerle et al., 1960) Some patients with an incurable illness were told and others were not. Personal contact was maintained throughout the further course and treatment of their illness, taking care to note if the greater frankness or reticence was more helpful to them. A psychiatrist made a preliminary assessment of the patients to see if there were any indications of emotional instability in the past or present to contraindicate telling. In the overwhelming majority of those he thought it suitable to tell, the patients maintained their emotional balance and did not regret being told. In some patients it was suspected that they would be upset initially, but later regain composure; and this was largely borne out. Among both those who were told and those who were not, there were equally small groups who never achieved serenity in this last illness. None of the patients in this group, told with care, reacted in a dramatic or excessive way on learning that they had incurable cancer. On the contrary, the social worker, who continued visiting the patient and family throughout the illness, was impressed by the improved family relationships among those who had been told. There appeared to be less tension and desperation at the progressive deterioration in health.

313

This maintenance of contact and care by people who have imparted tidings of fatal illness is most helpful. People cannot take in all such information of emotional importance immediately. They must be given the opportunity to ask again. Indeed the patient with a serious disease may ask the same questions about his condition again and again, while gradually coming to terms with it. Others deny that they have ever been told (Aitken-Swan & Easson, 1959). There would seem little kindness in insisting that they realize it if they do not want to hold it in their consciousness. At a later time they may wish to know more. It is a chilling, cruel experience to be told of having an incurable disease and then to be apparently dismissed with no mention of further care, just discarded. Those who confirm a patient's suspicion that he now has little time to live should surely see that he can return to them or some other suitable person who knows of the situation, if he wishes to talk more of the matter. Then he will gain comfort from this honesty.

REFERENCES

Aitken-Swan, J., and Easson, E. C. Reactions of Cancer Patients on Being Told Their Diagnosis. *British Medical Journal,* 1959, *1,* 779.

Aldrich, C. K. The Dying Patient's Grief. *Journal of the American Medical Association,* 1963, *184,* 329.

Alvarez, W. C. Care of the Dying. *Journal of the American Medical Association,* 1952, *150,* 86.

Asher, R. Management of Advanced Cancer. *Proceedings of the Royal Society of Medicine,* 1955, *48,* 373.

Gavey, C. J. Discussion on Palliation in Cancer. *Proceedings of the Royal Society of Medicine,* 1955, *48,* 703.

Gerle, B., Lunden, G., and P. Sandblom. The Patient with Inoperable Cancer from the Psychiatric and Social Standpoints. *Cancer,* 1960, *13,* 1206.

Gilbertsen, V. A., and Wangensteen, O. H. Should the Doctor Tell the Patient that the Disease is Cancer? In *The Physician and the Total Care of the Cancer Patient.* New York: American Cancer Society, 1961.

Glaser, B. G., and Strauss, A. L. *Awareness of Dying.* Chicago: Aldine, 1965.

Kelly, W. D., and Friesen, S. R. Do Cancer Patients Want to Be Told? *Surgery,* 1950, *27,* 822.

Kline, N. S., and Sobin, J. The Psychological Management of Cancer Cases. *Journal of the American Medical Association,* 1951, *146,* 1547.

Leak, W. N. The Care of the Dying. *Practitioner,* 1948, *161,* 80.

Ogilvie, H. Journey's End. *Practitioner,* 1957, *179,* 584.

Oken, D. What to Tell Cancer Patients. *Journal of the American Medical Association,* 1961, *175,* 1120.

Therapy with the Terminally Ill

Elisabeth Kübler-Ross

In this selection from her book *On Death and Dying*, Dr. Elisabeth Kübler-Ross discusses, with characteristic gentleness and concern, therapy for the terminally ill and concludes with a memorable phrase about the care that can be given in "the silence that goes beyond words."

Death belongs to life as birth does.
  The walk is in the raising of the foot as in the laying of it down.

  —Tagore, from *Stray Birds*, CCXVII

The terminally ill patient has very special needs which can be fulfilled if we take the time to sit and listen and find out what they are. The most important communication, perhaps, is the fact that we let him know that we are ready and willing to share some of his concerns. To work with the dying patient requires a certain maturity which only comes from experience. We have to take a good hard look at our own attitude toward death and dying before we can sit quietly and without anxiety next to a terminally ill patient.

The door-opening interview is a meeting of two people who can communicate without fear and anxiety. The therapist—doctor, chaplain, or whoever undertakes this role—will attempt to let the patient know in his own words or actions that he is not going to run away if the word cancer or dying is mentioned. The patient will then pick up this cue and open up, or he may let the interviewer know that he appreciates the message though the time is not right. The patient will let such a person know when he is ready to share his concerns, and the therapist will reassure him of his return at an opportune time. Many of our patients have not had more than just such a door-opening interview. They were, at times, hanging onto life because of some unfinished business; they cared for a retarded sister and had found no one to take over in case of their death, or they had not been able to make arrangements for the care of some children and needed to share

315

this worry with someone. Others were guilt-ridden about some real or imagined "sins" and were greatly relieved when we offered them an opportunity to share them, especially in the presence of a chaplain. These patients all felt better after "confessions" or arrangements for the care of others and usually died soon after the unfinished business was taken care of.

//

We have to take a good hard look at our own attitude toward death and dying before we can sit quietly and without anxiety next to a terminally ill patient.

//

Rarely an unrealistic fear prevents a patient from dying, as earlier exemplified in the woman who was "too afraid to die" because she could not conceive of "being eaten up alive by the worms." She had a phobic fear of worms and at the same time was quite aware of the absurdity of it. Because it was so silly, as she herself called it, she was unable to share this with her family who had spent all their savings on her hospitalizations. After one interview this old lady was able to share her fears with us and her daughter helped her with arrangements for a cremation. This patient too died soon after she was allowed to ventilate her fears.

We are always amazed how one session can relieve a patient of a tremendous burden and wonder why it is so difficult for staff and family to elicit their needs, since it often requires nothing more but an open question.

Though Mr. E. was not terminally ill, we shall use his case as a typical example of a door-opening interview. It is relevant because Mr. E. presented himself as a dying man as a consequence of unresolved conflicts precipitated by the death of an ambivalent figure.

Mr. E., an eighty-three-year-old Jewish man, was admitted to the medical service of a private hospital because of severe weight loss, anorexia, and constipation. He complained of unbearable abdominal pains and looked haggard and tired. His general mood was depressed and he wept easily. A thorough medical work-up was negative, and the resident finally asked for a psychiatric opinion.

He was interviewed in a diagnostic-therapeutic interview with several students present in the same room. He did not mind the company and felt relieved to talk about his personal problems. He related how he had been well until four months before admission when he suddenly became "an old, sick, and lonely man." Further questioning revealed that a few weeks before the onset of all his physical complaints he lost a daughter-in-law and two weeks before the onset of his pains his estranged wife died suddenly while he was on a vacation out of town.

He was angry at his relatives for not coming to see him when he expected them. He complained about the nursing service and was generally displeased with the care he received from anybody. He was sure that his relatives would come immediately if he could promise them "a couple of thousand dollars when I die," and he elaborated at length about the housing project in which he lived with other old people and the vacation trip they all were invited to attend. It soon became evident that his anger was related to his being poor and that being poor meant that he had to take the trip when it was planned for his place of residence, i.e., he had no choice in the matter. On further questioning it became clear that he blamed himself for having been absent when his wife was hospitalized and tried to displace his guilt on the people who organized the vacation.

When we asked him if he did not feel deserted by his wife and was just unable to admit his anger at her, an avalanche of bitter feelings poured out in which he shared with us his inability to understand why she deserted him in favor of a brother (he called him a Nazi), how she raised their only son as a non-Jew, and finally how she left him alone now when he needed her the most! Since he felt extremely guilty and ashamed about his negative feeling towards the deceased, he displaced his feelings on the relatives and nursing staff. He was convinced that he had to be punished for all those bad thoughts and that he had to endure much pain and suffering to alleviate his guilt.

We simply told him that we could share his mixed feelings, that they were very human and everybody had them. We also told him bluntly that we wondered if he could not acknowledge some anger at his former wife and express it in further brief visits with us. He answered to this, "If this pain does not go away I will have to jump out of the window." Our answer was, "Your pain may be all those swallowed feelings of anger and frustration. Get them out of your system without being ashamed and your pains will probably go away." He left with obviously mixed feelings but did ask to be visited again.

The resident who accompanied him back to his room was impressed with his slumped posture and took notice of it. He reinforced what we had said in the interview and reassured him that his reactions were very normal, after which he straightened up and returned in a more erect posture to his room.

A visit the next day revealed that he had hardly been in his room. He had spent much of the day socializing, visiting the cafeteria, and enjoying his food. His constipation and his pain [were] gone. After two massive bowel movements the evening of the interview, he felt "better than ever" and made plans for his discharge and resumption of some of his former activities.

On the day of discharge, he smiled and related some of the good days he had spent with his wife. He also told of the change in attitude towards the staff "whom I have given a hard time" and his relatives, especially his son whom he called to get acquainted a bit better, "since both of us may feel lonely for a while."

We reassured him of our availability should he have more problems, physical or emotional, and he smilingly replied that he had learned a good lesson and might face his own dying with more equanimity.

The example of Mr. E. shows how such interviews may be beneficial to people who are not actually ill themselves, but—due to old age or simply due to their own inability to cope with the death of an ambivalent figure— suffer a great deal and regard their physical or emotional discomforts as a means of alleviating guilt feelings for suppressed hostile wishes toward dead persons. This old man was not so much afraid to die as he was worried about dying before he had paid for his destructive wishes toward a person who had died without having given him a chance "to make up for it." He suffered agonizing pains as a means of reducing his fears of retribution and displaced much of his hostility and anger onto the nursing staff and relatives without being aware of the reasons for his resentment. It is surprising how a simple interview can reveal much of this data and a few statements of explanation, as well as reassurance that these feelings of love and hate are human and understandable and do not require a gruesome price, can alleviate much of these somatic symptoms.

For those patients who do not have a simple and single problem to solve, short-term therapy is helpful, which again does not necessarily require the help of a psychiatrist, but an understanding person, who has the time to sit and listen. I am thinking of patients like Sister I., who was visited on many occasions and who received her therapy as much from her fellow patients as she did from us. They are the patients who are fortunate enough to have time to work through some of their conflicts while they are sick and who can come to a deeper understanding and perhaps appreciation of the things they still have to enjoy. These therapy sessions, like the brief psychotherapy sessions with more terminally ill patients, are irregular in time and occurrence. They are individually arranged depending on the patient's physical condition and his ability and willingness to talk at a given time; they often include visits of just a few minutes to assure them of our presence even at times when they do not wish to talk. They continue even more frequently when the patient is in less comfort and more pain, and then take the form of silent companionship rather than a verbal communication.

We have often wondered if group therapy with a selected group of terminally ill patients is indicated, since they often share the same loneliness and isolation. Those who work on wards with terminally ill patients are quite aware of the interactions that go on between the patients and the many helpful statements that are made from one very sick patient to another. We are always amazed how much of our experiences in the seminar are communicated from one dying patient to another; we even get "referrals" of one patient from another. We have noticed patients sitting together in the lobby of the hospital who have been interviewed in the seminar, and they have continued their informal sessions like members of a fraternity. So far we have left it up to the patients how much they choose to share with others, but we are presently looking into their motivation for a more formal meeting, since this seems to be desired by at least a small group of our patients. They include those patients who have chronic illnesses and who require many rehospitalizations. They have known each other for quite a while and not only share the same illness but they also have the same memories of past hospitalizations. We have been very impressed by their almost joyful reaction when one of their "buddies" dies, which is only a confirmation of their unconscious conviction that "it shall happen to thee but not to me." This may also be a contributing factor why so many patients and their family members . . . get some pleasure in visiting other perhaps more seriously ill patients. Sister I. used these visits as an expression of hostility, namely, to elicit patients' needs and to prove to the nursing staff that they were not efficient. . . . By helping them as a nurse, she could not only temporarily deny her own inability to function, but she could also express her anger at those who were well and unable to serve the sick more effectively. Having such patients in a group therapy set-up would help them understand their behavior and at the same time help the nursing staff by making them more accepting of their needs.

Mrs. F. was another woman to be remembered as she started informal group therapy between herself and some very sick young patients, all of whom were hospitalized with leukemia or Hodgkin's disease, from which she had suffered for over twenty years. During the past few years she had an average of six hospitalizations a year, which finally resulted in her complete acceptance of her illness. One day a nineteen-year-old girl, Ann, was admitted, frightened of her illness and its outcome and unable to share this fear with anyone. Her parents had refused to talk about it, and Mrs. F. then

319

became the unofficial counselor for her. She told her of her sons, her hus-band, and the house she had taken care of for so many years in spite of the many hospitalizations, and finally enabled Ann to ventilate her concerns and ask questions relevant to her. When Ann was discharged, she sent another young patient to Mrs. F., and so a chain reaction of referrals began to take place, quite comparable to group therapy in which one patient re-places another. The group rarely consisted of more than two or three people and remained together as long as the individual members were in the hospital.

ʄʄ

Watching a peaceful death of a human being reminds us of a falling star; one of the million lights in a vast sky that flares up for a brief moment only to disappear into the endless night forever.

ʄʄ

THE SILENCE THAT GOES BEYOND WORDS

There is a time in a patient's life when the pain ceases to be, when the mind slips off into a dreamless state, when the need for food becomes minimal, and the awareness of the environment all but disappears into darkness. This is the time when the relatives walk up and down the hospital hallways, tormented by the waiting, not knowing if they should leave to attend the living or stay to be around for the moment of death. This is the time when it is too late for words, and yet the time when the relatives cry the loudest for help—with or without words. It is too late for medical interventions (and too cruel, though well meant, when they do occur), but it is also too early for a final separation from the dying. It is the hardest time for the next of kin as he either wishes to take off, to get it over with; or he des-perately clings to something that he is in the process of losing forever. It is the time for the therapy of silence with the patient and availability for the relatives.

The doctor, nurse, social worker, or chaplain can be of great help during these final moments if they can understand the family's conflicts at this time and help select the one person who feels most comfortable staying with the dying patient. This person then becomes in effect the patient's therapist. Those who feel too uncomfortable can be assisted by alleviating their guilt and by the reassurance that someone will stay with the dying until his death has occurred. They can then return home knowing that the patient did not die alone, yet not feeling ashamed or guilty for having avoided this moment which for many people is so difficult to face.

Those who have the strength and the love to sit with a dying patient in the *silence that goes beyond words* will know that this moment is neither frightening nor painful, but a peaceful cessation of the functioning of the body. Watching a peaceful death of a human being reminds us of a falling star; one of the million lights in a vast sky that flares up for a brief moment only to disappear into the endless night forever. To be a therapist to a dying patient makes us aware of the uniqueness of each individual in this vast sea of humanity. It makes us aware of our finiteness, our limited lifespan. Few of us live beyond our three score and ten years and yet in that brief time most of us create and live a unique biography and weave ourselves into the fabric of human history.

> *The water in a vessel is sparkling; the water in the sea is dark.*
> *The small truth has words that are clear; the great truth has great silence.*
>
> —Tagore, from *Stray Birds*, CLXXVI

•6•

THE SURVIVORS

OF DEATH

To be a survivor, to have suffered a grievous loss
of someone close, is a terrible plight. If grief is not
an illness, often its effects are so severe that it might
as well be one. Grief and mourning are powerful and
stressful emotional states which can touch off
unconscious psychological reactions that actually
jeopardize the individual's life. A recent study shows
that loss of a loved one is absolutely at the top of
the list of stressful, abrasive, and disruptive events
that can happen to one. (A reader interested in the
general topic of stress can refer to the substantial
works of Hans Selye.) For a while—at least a year or
so—the grieving person is an individual "at risk,"
more apt not to take adequate care of self, more
apt to be sick and hospitalized, and even more apt
to die or be killed.

Currently there is a much-needed and overdue
concern with widows and widowers, bereaved
parents, orphaned children, who have, by and large,
been a rather neglected group. This chapter concerns
itself with the psychological needs of the mourners
and grievers who are left behind.

Toynbee's selection sets the tone for this chapter
in his emphasis on death as an essentially dyadic

event—an event in which there are always "two parties to the suffering that death inflicts; and, in the apportionment of this suffering, the survivor takes the brunt." This, for Toynbee is the heart of the relation between the living and the dying, between life and death. As a corollary of his notion about the greater burden on the survivor, Toynbee suggests that if one truly loves one's spouse one would wish for one's spouse to die first so that the spouse can be spared the anguish of bereavement.

Perhaps the most impressive systematic studies in the field of bereavement have been done by Parkes. His selection can be said to offer factual grounds for Toynbee's fears by documenting some of the practical perils of being a survivor. Parkes and his associates studied a number of London widows, under the age of sixty-five, for thirteen months following the deaths of their husbands. His interesting findings indicate that the widows have a "search" for their dead spouses, an inner push toward aggressive behavior, and, compared to nonwidows, a greater number of unexplained illnesses and deaths. He calls his piece "The Broken Heart."

This "peril of survivorship" leads Shneidman in the next selection to talk about "survivor-victims" and "postvention." A growing appreciation of the survivor as a victim has led to the development of special postventive therapies for the survivors. The goal of postvention is to reduce the possible harmful physical and psychological aftereffects resulting from the death of a loved one.

A practical example of postvention, in the form of a self-help program for widows, is described in the selection by Silverman. The article is of further interest in that it stems from the pioneer theoretical work by Erich Lindemann in the 1940s, relating to the (Boston) Coconut Grove fire, from which tragic event he developed many of the concepts of short-term crisis intervention.

The Relation Between Life and Death, Living and Dying

Arnold Toynbee

In the moving Epilogue to his book *Man's Concern with Death* from which the following essay is excerpted, Professor Toynbee introduces us to the concept that the suffering of death is a dyadic event, involving two parties. These passages serve excellently to introduce the other selections in this chapter.

From *Man's Concern with Death.* Copyright © 1968 by Arnold Toynbee, A. Keith Mant, Ninian Smart, John Hinton, Cicely Yudkin, Eric Rhode, Rosalind Heywood, H. H. Price. Used with permission of McGraw-Hill Book Company, and Hodder and Stoughton Ltd.

Premature death may be incurred in various ways. It may be inflicted by human hands deliberately either by public enterprise (war and the execution of judicial death sentences) or by private enterprise (murder). It may be inflicted by non-human living creatures (bacteria, sharks, man-eating tigers). It may be caused by hunger, thirst, or exposure to the elements—defeats of man by non-human nature that have been becoming less frequent in the economically "developed" minority of mankind, though the reduction of the rate of premature deaths from these causes among this minority is being offset by an increase in the rate of premature deaths caused by accidents—particularly in the form of miscarriages of our increasingly high-powered machinery which, in its application to our means of locomotion, has enabled us to "annihilate distance" at the price of a high toll of deaths in road-vehicles and in aeroplanes. (The toll taken by the now obsolescent railway train was comparatively light.)

Since death is irretrievable, the deliberate infliction of premature death by one human being on another is surely a heinous offence—and this not only in murder and in war, but also in the execution of judicial death sentences. Murder has been almost universally condemned—though there have been, and still are, some exceptional societies in which a youth does not qualify for being accepted as a man until he has taken another man's life. Killing in war has, till now, been almost universally regarded as being respectable—though a misgiving about its respectability is betrayed in the euphemistic use of the word "defence" to signify war and preparation for war, however aggressive the intention. For instance, the Spartan official formula for a mobilisation order with the object of invading a foreign country was "to declare a state of defence" *(phouran phainein);* and the costs of genocidal atomic weapons are entered under the rubric "defence" in the budgets of present-day states. The infliction of premature death by process of law has been approved of still more widely and confidently than the infliction of it by act of war. When the abolition of the death penalty has been mooted, this has usually aroused violent controversy; yet the abolition of it is now an accomplished fact in some states in the present-day world. The reason for this obstinately resisted abandonment of an age-old practice is that "while there is life there is hope." A change of heart may be experienced by even the most apparently hardened criminal.

We ought not to be reconciled to premature death when this is caused by human design or callousness or incompetence or carelessness. Yet there are cases in which even premature death is acceptable—the cases in which it has been risked and suffered voluntarily for the benefit of some fellow human being or of mankind in general. Voluntary premature death in war is the form of heroic self-sacrifice that has been both the most frequently performed and the most enthusiastically applauded; yet this is also the form of heroism that is the most ambivalent, since a man who is killed in war dies prematurely in the act of trying to inflict premature death on some of his fellow human beings. There is nothing questionable about the heroism of the premature death of someone who sacrifices his or her life in trying to save a fellow human being from meeting death by, say, drowning or burning; and we can also accept, while we lament, the premature death of pioneers and inventors who have deliberately risked their lives in the cause of making life better for mankind as a whole.

Many men have sacrificed their lives prematurely in winning for mankind, by daring and dangerous experimentation, the art of domesticating wild animals, the art of navigation, the art of aviation. (Scaling the Matterhorn, reaching the Poles, and breaking out of the earth's air-envelope into outer space do not seem to me to be objectives for which lives ought to have been risked and lost.) Many physicians have sacrificed their lives prematurely by tending the victims of deadly contagious diseases, or by experimenting perilously on themselves. My grandfather, who was a doctor, killed himself, unintentionally, when he was at the height of his powers, by experimenting on himself, in the early days of the use of anaesthetics, in order to discover what the right degree of dosage was. So there are circumstances in which premature death is not unacceptable, however grievous it may be.

What are we to say about the premature death of the spirit in a human body that still remains physically alive? I am familiar with this form of premature death too—the death-in-life of insanity and senility. I have been at very close quarters with a human being who lived on physically to a higher age than I have reached now for more than thirty years—about three-eighths of his total span of physical life—after he had suffered the death of the spirit. I have also known intimately three persons—two of them dominating personalities and the third a robust one—who have succumbed to senility in old age. This premature death of a human spirit in advance of the death of its body is more appalling than any premature death in which spirit and body die simultaneously. It is an outrage committed by nature on human dignity. "Slay us," nature or God, if you choose or if you must, but slay us "in the light."[1] Allow the light of reason—the faculty that makes a human being—to survive in us till the end of the life of the body. The spectacle of insanity and senility has always appalled me more than the witnessing or the hearing of a physical death. But there are two sides to this situation; there is the victim's side, as well as the spectator's; and what is harrowing for the spectator may be alleviating for the victim.

It will not, of course be alleviation for him if the failure of his mental faculties overtakes him only gradually and then only to a degree that leaves him aware of what is happening to him. I can think of no worse fate than this, and I have seen it befall my oldest and closest friend—a man three months younger than myself. Our friendship had begun at school when we were thirteen years old and had continued for more than sixty years before he died. One could hardly suffer a greater loss than I suffered in losing him. Yet I could not and cannot regret his death, grievously though I miss him; for his death was, for him, a merciful release from a distress that was irremediable and that was becoming excruciating for him. As for those other three friends of mine, they did not suffer as my poor school fellow suffered; for their mental eclipse was, not partial, but total—as complete as if they had been dead physically as well as mentally—and, for two of the three, this

---

[1] *Iliad*, Book XVII, line 647.

mental death, so far from being a torment, was a release from acute un-happiness. One of these two had previously been in a constant state of painful anxiety, fretfulness, and tension; and, for her, senility brought with it a serenity that she had not enjoyed since her early years. The other, who was love incarnate, had been inconsolable for the loss of her husband till she was released from her unbearable grief by oblivion—a mental death which was a merciful anticipation of the physical death that was tardy in coming to her rescue.

The two-sidedness of death is a fundamental feature of death—not only of the premature death of the spirit, but of death at any age and in any form. There are always two parties to a death; the person who dies and the survivors who are bereaved.

This two-sidedness of death is a fundamental feature of death—not only of the premature death of the spirit, but of death at any age and in any form. There are always two parties to a death; the person who dies and the sur-vivors who are bereaved.

Death releases its prey instantly from all further suffering in this world—and from any further suffering at all, if one does not believe in personal im-mortality or in metempsychosis, but believes either that death spells annihilation or that it spells reabsorption into the Ultimate Spiritual Reality from which the life of a human personality is a temporary aberration.

Lucretius believed that death spells annihilation, and that it therefore confers on the dead a total and everlasting immunity from suffering, either

327

mental or physical. He preaches this nihilist gospel of salvation with a passionate conviction and a fervent concern for the relief of his fellow mortals that make this passage of his poem[2] particularly memorable.

> Death, then is null for us—null and irrelevant—in virtue of the conclusion that the spirit of man is mortal. We felt no ill in that past age in which the Phoenicians were flocking to battle from all quarters— an age in which the whole earth was rocked by the fearful turmoil of war, rocked till it quaked horrifyingly under the lofty ceiling of the air; an age in which the fate of all mankind was trembling in the balance. One of the two contending powers was going to win worldwide dominion on both land and sea, and none could foresee which of the two would be the winner. Well, we felt no ill in that age, and we shall feel no ill, either, when we have ceased to exist—when once soul and body, whose union constitutes our being, have parted company with each other. We shall have ceased to exist; that is the point; and this means that, thenceforward, nothing whatsoever can happen to us, that nothing can awaken any feeling in us—no, not even if land were to fuse with sea, and sea with sky . . .[3]
>
> We can feel assured that, in death, there is nothing to be afraid of. If one is non-existent, one is immune from misery. When once immortal death has relieved us of mortal life, it is as good as if we had never been born . . .[4]
>
> So, when you see someone indulging indignantly in self-pity [at the thought of his body's destiny after death], you may be sure that, though he himself may deny that he believes that, in death, he will retain any capacity for feeling, his profession of faith does not ring true. It is belied by a latent emotion that is subconscious. As I see it, he is not really conceding his premise and its basis. He is not removing and ejecting himself from life radically. Unconsciously he is making some vestige of himself survive . . . He is not dissociating himself fully from his cast-away corpse; he is identifying himself with it and is infusing into it his own capacity for feeling, under the illusion that he is standing there beside it. This is the cause of his indignant self-pity at having been created mortal. He fails to see that, in real death, he will have no second self that will be still alive and capable of lamenting to itself over its own death, or of grieving,

---

[2]Lucretius, *De Rerum Natura,* Book III, lines 830–930, minus lines 912–918, which have been misplaced in the surviving manuscripts.

[3]Lines 830–842.

[4]Lines 866–9.

as he stands, in imagination, over his prostrate self, that he is being mangled by beasts of prey or is being cremated.[5]

Lucretius goes on to put his finger on the difference between the fate of the dead and the fate of the survivors. He pictures a dead man's wife and children saying, as they stand by his funeral pyre:

"Poor wretch, what a wretched fate. One cruel day has deprived you of all the blessings of life." But, in this pass, they do not go on to say: "However, death has simultaneously released you from any desire for these blessings." If they realised this truth clearly and matched it in what they said, they would be able to release their souls from a heavy burden of anguish and fear. "You," they would say, "are now oblivious in death, and in that state you will remain until the end of time, exempt from all pain and grief. It is we who are the sufferers; it is we who, standing by you, reduced to ashes on the appalling pyre, have mourned you to the limit of human capacity for grief, and find ourselves still inconsolable. Our sorrow is everlasting. The day will never come that will relieve our hearts of it."[6]

From this Lucretius draws the following conclusion in the lines that immediately follow.

So this man [who feels an indignant self-pity in contemplating his future after death] has to be confronted with the question: What is there that is particularly bitter in this future, if it is just a return to sleep and quiet? What is there in this prospect that should make anyone pine away in everlasting grief?[7]

This lapse of a sensitive spirit into such obtuse complacency pulls up Lucretius's reader with a jerk. Is a man who is feeling distress at the prospect of his own death going to be totally relieved by the realization that his death will automatically bring with it an immunity from suffering for himself? Is he going to feel no concern for the grief of his bereaved wife and children? Is his certainty of "everlasting" peace and quiet for himself in death going to console him for the "everlasting" sorrow of the survivors?

It may be answered that, though the poet has used—and perhaps deliberately used—the same word "everlasting" to describe the respective states of the survivors and of the dead, the application of the word to the

[5]Lines 870–887.
[6]Lines 898–908.
[7]Lines 909–911

survivors is an exaggeration, considering that they, in their turn, are going to attain, sooner or later, "the return to sleep and quiet" that death brings to every mortal in the end. Meanwhile, they are going, on Lucretius's own showing, to experience the extreme of suffering; and Lucretius has denied himself the license to play this suffering down on the ground that it will be only temporary; for in a later passage,[8] he argues, eloquently and convincingly, that the fancied everlasting torments of the damned in hell after death are fabulous projections of genuine torments--mostly self-inflicted—which we experience in this life. "It is here, in this world," he sums up the argument of this passage in its last line, "that people make life hell through their own stupidity." Yet he has admitted that bereavement makes life hell, here in this world, for the bereaved. Is he prepared to write off their torment, too, as the self-inflicted penalty for a stupidity that is avoidable and reprehensible?

The truth is that Lucretius has been preoccupied by his characteristically impetuous effort to deprive death of its sting and the grave of its victory for the person who is dreading the prospect of death for himself. He has overlooked the crucial fact that, in a death, there are two parties to the event. "For none of us liveth to himself and no man dieth to himself."[9] Man is a social creature; and a fact of capital importance about death's sting is that it is two-pronged. Lucretius may have succeeded in excising the sting for the person who dies, but he has failed to excise it for the dead's survivors. It looks, indeed, as if he has been blind to the significance of the pain of bereavement that he has described incidentally in such moving words. Euripides had been more perceptive. After asking if the experience that we call dying is not really living, and if living is not really dying,[10] he immediately goes on to observe that the spectators of a death are not saved from suffering by their awareness that the dead are exempt from all suffering and from all ills.

When, therefore, I ask myself whether I am reconciled to death, I have to distinguish, in each variant of the situation, between being reconciled to death on my own account and being reconciled to it on the account of the other party. Supposing that I am really reconciled to the prospect of my own death at a ripe old age, am I also reconciled to the prospect of the sorrow and the loneliness that death is going to bring upon my wife if she survives me?

---

[8]Lines 973–1023.

[9]Romans, xiv, 7.

[10]Fragment from Euripides' lost play *Phrixus*, quoted on p. 182.

Supposing that I feel that people who have risked and suffered premature death deliberately for the sake of fellow human beings have found a satisfactory fulfilment of the possibilities of life for themselves, am I reconciled to the loss that their premature deaths have inflicted on mankind, including me? (This question is the theme of George Meredith's novel *Beauchamp's Career*.) Supposing that I feel that the oblivion conferred by senility or insanity has been a boon for someone who was suffering spiritual agony so long as he was in full possession of his mental and spiritual faculties, am I reconciled to my loss of this friend through his lapse into a death-in-life? And, apart from my personal loss, am I reconciled to the brutal affront to human dignity that nature has committed in choosing this humiliating way of releasing a human being from spiritual suffering?

Finally, am I reconciled to the prospect that I may survive my wife, even supposing that she lives to a ripe old age in full possession of her faculties and without suffering more than the minimum of physical pain that is the normal accompaniment of death even in its easiest forms, with the exception of instantaneous deaths and deaths in sleep? The hard fact is that the ways of dying that impose the lightest ordeal on the person who dies are, by their very nature, the ways that inevitably make the shock for the survivors the severest. I have mentioned an old friend of mine whose unbearable grief for the death of her husband was eventually obliterated by the oblivion of senility. The shock that she had suffered had been extreme. She had found her husband lying dead in his bed one morning. He had appeared to be in normal health the day before; but for some years his heart had been weak, and he had died from heart failure in his sleep—peacefully and almost certainly painlessly; I myself recently had the experience of receiving a severe shock from learning of the sudden death of someone with whom my life had once been intimately bound up, though, in this case too, the death had not been a lingering one or been physically very painful, and had come at an age—six months younger than mine—at which death is to be expected.

If one truly loves a fellow human being, one ought to wish that as little as possible of the pain of his or her death shall be suffered by him or by her, and that as much of it as possible shall be borne by oneself. One ought to wish this, and one can, perhaps, succeed in willing it with one's mind. But can one genuinely desire it in one's heart? Can one genuinely long to be the survivor at the coming time when death will terminate a companionship that is more precious to one than one's own life is—a companionship without which one's own life would be a burden, not a boon? Is it possible for love to raise human nature to this height of unselfishness? I cannot answer this question for anyone except myself, and, in my own case, before the time comes, I can only guess what my reaction is likely to be. I have already avowed a boastful guess that I shall be able to meet my own death with equanimity. I have now to avow another guess that puts me to shame. I guess that if, one day, I am told by my doctor that I am going to die before my wife, I shall receive the news not only with equanimity but with relief. This relief, if I do feel it, will be involuntary. I shall be ashamed of myself for feeling it, and my relief will, no doubt, be tempered by concern and sorrow for my wife's future after I have been taken from her. All the same, I do guess that, if I am informed that I am going to die before her, a shameful sense of relief will be one element in my reaction.

My own conclusion is evident. My answer to Saint Paul's question "O death, where is thy sting?" is Saint Paul's own answer: "The sting of death is sin." The sin that I mean is the sin of selfishly failing to wish to survive the death of someone with whose life my own life is bound up. This is selfish because the sting of death is less sharp for the person who dies than it is for the bereaved survivor.

This is, as I see it, the capital fact about the relation between living and dying. There are two parties to the suffering that death inflicts; and, in the apportionment of this suffering, the survivor takes the brunt.

The Broken Heart

Colin Murray Parkes

Colin Murray Parkes is a psychiatrist at Tavistock Institute of Human Relations in London and is on the staff of St. Christopher's Hospice. Dr. Parkes and his associates have conducted perhaps the most impressive systematic study in the field of bereavement with an investigation of twenty-two London widows for a period of thirteen months following the deaths of their husbands. In this selection, Dr. Parkes relates some of his more significant findings concerning the impact of death on survivors.

From *Bereavement* by C. M. Parkes, published by Tavistock Publications Ltd. Copyright © 1973 by International Universities Press. Reprinted by permission.

He only without framing word, or closing his eyes, but earnestly viewing the dead body of his son, stood still upright, till the vehemence of his sad sorrow, having suppressed and choaked his vitall spirits, fell'd him starke dead to the ground.

> —Montaigne's description of the death of John, King of Hungaria

Is grief a cause of death? You will not find grief on a death certificate, not today. But the notion that one may die of grief is a popular theme among novelists and it is not long ago that it was a recognized cause of death.

Thus, in Dr Heberden's Bill classifying the causes of death in London during the year 1657 we find:

Flox and Small Pox	835
Found dead in the streets, etc.	9
French Pox	25
Gout	8
Griefe	10
Griping and Plague in the Guts	446
Hang'd and made away 'emselves	24

Such figures would today be dismissed as examples of medical mythology, but is there in fact any evidence that grief is sometimes a cause of death?

There is, of course, no doubt that psychological factors play a part in many illnesses, but it is only in rare cases of "vagal inhibition" and in so-called voodoo deaths that they appear to be the sole cause. Vagal inhibition is a pseudo-scientific term sometimes used by doctors for the cause of death following a sudden emotional shock. A classic example is provided in the story of some students who held a mock trial and sentenced a man to death. He was led to the place of execution, blindfolded, and hit on the back of the neck with a towel—whereupon he died. Not dissimilar are the numerous well-authenticated cases of death from witchcraft. Although the witchcraft can take many different forms, such deaths seem to follow a general pattern. The "victim" is told that the appropriate ritual curse has been carried out; if he has faith he at once becomes deeply depressed, stops eating, and within a few days is dead. In neither the vagal inhibition type of death nor death from witchcraft is there any post-mortem finding that explains the phenomenon.

Three-quarters of the increased death rate during the first six months of bereavement was attributable to heart disease, in particular to coronary thrombosis and arteriosclerotic heart disease.

Such occurrences are fortunately very rare, but there is other evidence of the effect of psychological factors on mortality among the unhealthy and aging. Aldrich and Mendkoff, for instance, discovered a major increase in mortality among chronically sick patients when a Chicago Home for In-curables was closed for administrative reasons. Of 182 patients who were relocated in other homes, thirty were dead within three months—a mortality rate five times greater than expectation. Mortality was highest among those patients whose grasp on reality was most tenuous, particularly among the thirty-eight whom Aldrich rated as "psychotic" before relocation, of whom twenty-four died within a year (Aldrich & Mendkoff, 1963).

Apart from a few isolated cases of doubtful authenticity, I have come across no evidence that phenomena such as these are responsible for death following bereavement. The examples have been quoted simply to remind the reader that psychological factors can have profound effects even on healthy people.

For many years it has been known that widows and widowers have a higher mortality rate than married men and women of the same age. But then so have bachelors and spinsters, and it is not unreasonable to suspect that some of the fitter widows and widowers remarry, thereby ensuring that those who remain will have a relatively high mortality rate.

This explanation might certainly account for an increased mortality rate among the widowed population as a whole but it would not explain the peak of mortality in widowers during the first year of bereavement as discovered by Michael Young and his colleagues (Young, Benjamin & Wallis, 1963). They found an increase in the death rate among 4,486 widowers over the age of 54 of almost 40 percent during the first six months of bereavement. This dropped off rapidly thereafter to around the mortality rate for married men of the same age.

Independent confirmation of this observation has more recently come from a study of a semi-rural community in Wales (Rees & Lutkins, 1967). A survey of 903 close relatives of 371 residents who died during 1960–65 showed that 4.8 percent of them died within one year of bereavement compared with only 0.7 percent of a comparable group of non-bereaved people of the same age, living in the same area. The mortality rate was particularly high for widows and widowers, 12 percent of whom died during the same period.

These two studies established a statistical relationship between bereavement and an increase in the death rate, but they did not explain this association, and it is still not known why bereaved people tend to die more readily than the non-bereaved.

Several diseases seem to contribute to the higher mortality but recent work has indicated that the most frequent cause of death is heart disease. The paper by Young *et al.* (1963) on the death rate among widowers was used as the basis of a further study (carried out by Parkes, Benjamin & Fitzgerald, 1969) of the causes of death among these same widowers as revealed on their death certificates. It was soon apparent that three-quarters of the increased death rate during the first six months of bereavement was attributable to heart disease, in particular to coronary thrombosis and arteriosclerotic heart disease.

The origin of the term "broken heart" goes back to biblical times. "Bind up the broken hearted," says Isaiah, and the idea seems to have persisted ever since that severe grief can somehow damage the heart. Benjamin Rush, the American physician and signatory of the Declaration of Independence, wrote in his *Medical Inquiries and Observations upon the Diseases of the Mind* (1835): "Dissection of persons who have died of grief, show congestion in, and inflammation of the heart, with rupture of its auricles and ventricles." Rupture of the heart is, of course, a rare condition, but when it does occur it is usually caused by a coronary thrombosis. All of which leads us to suspect that the old physicians may not have been as foolish as we suppose. (In case any bereaved reader is now clutching his chest and preparing to call an ambulance may I hasten to point out that palpitations and a feeling of fullness in the chest are normal concomitants of anxiety and that bereaved people often experience them without developing heart disease.)

The fact that bereavement may be followed by death from heart disease does not prove that grief is itself a cause of death. We do not even know whether bereavement causes the illness or simply aggravates a condition that would have occurred anyway. Perhaps bereaved people tend to smoke more or to alter their diet in a way that increases their liability to coronary thrombosis. Even if emotional factors are directly implicated we still have to explain how they affect the heart. Stress is known to produce changes in the blood pressure and heart rate, in the flow of blood through the coronary arteries and in the chemical constituents of the blood. Any of these changes could play a part in precipitating clotting within a diseased coronary artery and thereby produce a coronary thrombosis, but without further research we can only speculate.

It may be that measures aimed at reducing the stress of bereavement will help to prevent such consequences. If so, then giving help to the bereaved is a practical contribution to public health.

What other effects does bereavement have upon health? Many physical and mental illnesses have been attributed to loss. Usually the attribution is based on the observation that the illness in question came on shortly after a loss. But since losses of one sort or another occur in the lives of all of us, a chance association between illness and loss is always possible. Furthermore, the distinction between physical and psychological symptoms soon breaks down. In this selection I discuss, first, the types of condition that are commonly brought to the attention of a physician or general practitioner, and I then go on to look at the symptoms of bereaved psychiatric patients. But it will soon be obvious that there is a considerable overlap.

Some of the better studies of the psychosomatic effects of loss have come from the Strong Memorial Hospital in Rochester, USA, where a group of psychiatrists have developed the theory that it is the feelings of helplessness and hopelessness that may accompany loss that are responsible for physical illness. In one remarkable study, women suspected of having cancer of the womb were "diagnosed" by a psychiatrist with striking accuracy (Schmale and Iker, 1966). These women had been admitted for investigation after a routine vaginal smear had revealed the presence of ugly-looking cells which might or might not indicate cancer. At this stage nobody knew whether a cancer was present or not, and a minor operation was necessary to prove or disprove such a diagnosis. The psychiatrist, who was as ignorant as anyone of the true situation, interviewed each woman and asked her about her feelings about any recent losses in her life. When he found evidence of both loss and feelings of helplessness or hopelessness, he predicted that this woman would, in fact, be found to have cancer. In 71 percent of cases his diagnosis proved to be correct.

The sceptic will point out that perhaps unbeknown to the doctor, these women did have an inkling of their true diagnosis and it was this knowledge that influenced their feelings or their tendency to recall recent losses in their lives. Similar bias could conceivably explain the high rates of loss which have been reported in cases of leukemia, ulcerative colitis, and asthma. But these results cannot be ignored and it is to be hoped that the necessary work will soon be done to establish the chain of causation. It will indeed be remarkable if psychiatrists have discovered a cause of cancer.

In studies of this type the investigator starts with a person who is sick, or suspected of being sick, and attempts to find out whether he has suffered a loss prior to the onset of his illness. Such studies always carry a risk of retrospective bias. Another way of proceeding is to start with a person who is known to have suffered a loss and to find out what illnesses he contracts thereafter. This approach has been adopted in several studies of bereaved people. For example, seventy-two East London widows were interviewed by Peter Marris on average two years after they had been bereaved; thirty-one (43 percent) thought that their general health was now worse than it had been before bereavement (Marris, 1958). In another study by Hobson (1964), a similar proportion of widows (seventeen out of forty) from a Midland market town made the same assertion. According to both these studies the number of complaints attributed to bereavement was very large. Headaches, digestive upsets, rheumatism, and asthma were particularly frequent.

But such symptoms were common enough in any group of women and might have occurred by chance alone. Moreover, "general health" is a woolly concept of doubtful validity. In a study of twenty-two London widows (referred to henceforth as the London Study) I attempted to obtain a number of different estimates of general health. I asked the widows to rate their own health as "good," "indifferent," or "bad" at each of five interviews carried out at intervals during their first year of bereavement. I also counted the number of consultations each widow had with her GP in the course of the year, and in addition checked off on a standard list the symptoms she claimed to have suffered each time I visited her. Naturally I anticipated that the widows who said that their general health was bad would be the ones who had consulted their GP most frequently and suffered the largest number of symptoms. It came as a surprise to find that this was not the case. The only thing that was found to distinguish the widows who said that their health was bad was a quite separate series of assessments of irritability and anger. Anger and irritability, it seemed, were accompanied by a subjective feeling of ill health which was not reflected in any particular symptom or in a tendency to consult the doctor (Parkes, 1971).

There is evidence, nevertheless, that newly bereaved people do consult their doctors more often than they did before bereavement. In one study of the case records of eight London general practitioners I was able to identify forty-four widows who had been registered[1] with their GP for two years before and one and a half years after bereavement.

Three-quarters of these widows consulted their GP within six months of bereavement and this was a 63 percent increase over the number who had consulted him in a similar period prior to bereavement. The largest increase was in consultations for anxiety, depression, insomnia, and other psychological symptoms, which were clearly attributable to grief. But it was surprising to find that the rise in consultations for such symptoms was confined to widows under 65 years of age. Older people did not, apparently, consult their doctor about these matters.

Consultations for physical symptoms, however, had increased in all age groups, most notably for arthritis and rheumatic conditions. Psycholog-

---

[1]Under the National Health Service each member of the British population is registered with a general practitioner who keeps a medical record on an envelope-card designed for the purpose. Most wives are registered with the same GP as their husband.

ical factors are known to play a part in rheumatism but many of these widows had osteoarthritis, a condition that takes years to develop. It seems therefore that, as with coronary thrombosis, the bereavement probably did not originate the condition but aggravated one that was already present. It is possible, too, that the widows were using their arthritis as an excuse to visit their doctor and that the higher consultation rate reflected a need for help which had little to do with their physical state (Parkes, 1964b).

A useful series of studies which does not rely on the widow consulting her doctor has been carried out by Professor Maddison from the University of Sydney, Australia (Maddison and Viola, 1968). Maddison has devised a postal questionnaire which asks respondents fifty-seven questions about their health over the preceding year. This has now been completed by 132 American and 221 Australian widows thirteen months after bereavement, and by control groups of married women. All were under the age of 60. Of the total sample of widows, 28 percent obtained scores indicating "marked" deterioration in health, compared with only 4.5 percent of the married women.

Symptoms that were commoner in the bereaved than in the married groups included: nervousness, depression, fears of nervous breakdown, feelings of panic, persistent fears, "peculiar thoughts," nightmares, insomnia, trembling, loss of appetite (or, in a few, excessive appetite), loss of weight, reduced working capacity, and fatigue. All these symptoms are features of "normal" grief and it is not surprising to find them complained of by a group of newly bereaved widows. But Maddison found also, in the widows, excessive incidence of symptoms that were less obviously features of grieving. These included headaches, dizziness, fainting spells, blurred vision, skin rashes, excessive sweating, indigestion, difficulty in swallowing, vomiting, heavy menstrual periods, palpitations, chest pains, shortness of breath, frequent infections, and general aching.

Many of Maddison's findings have subsequently been confirmed in a study of sixty-eight Boston widows and widowers under the age of 45, which I have been carrying out with Ira Glick, Robert Weiss, Gerald Caplan, and others at Harvard Medical School (Glick, Weiss, and Parkes, 1974). (This study is henceforth referred to as the Harvard Study.) These unselected widows and widowers were interviewed fourteen months after bereavement and compared with a control group of sixty-eight married men and women of the same age, sex, occupational class, and family size. The bereaved group showed evidence of depression and of general emotional disturbance as reflected in restlessness and insomnia, and in having difficulty in making decisions and remembering things. Also, they consumed more tranquillizers, alcohol, and tobacco than they had done prior to bereavement. They were distinguished from the non-bereaved group by the frequency of their complaints of physical symptoms indicative of anxiety and tension; however, they did not show, as older bereaved subjects have shown in other studies, a large increase in physical ailments. The incidence of headaches, for instance, and of muscular and joint affections was no greater in the bereaved than in the control group.

There are certain potentially fatal conditions which seem in some cases to be precipitated or aggravated by major losses.

Four times as many bereaved as non-bereaved had spent part of the preceding year in hospital, and the bereaved group sought advice for emotional problems from ministers, psychiatrists, and (occasionally) social workers more often than did the non-bereaved. But it came as a surprise to find that there was no difference between the two groups as regards the number of outpatient or private consultations they had had with a doctor. Clearly, the physician is not the person to whom the young Boston widow or widower turns for help. As far as the widows are concerned, financial considerations may play a part here. Like her British counterpart, the American widow tends to suffer a sharp drop in income; unlike the British widow, however, she has to pay her own medical bills. Although three-quarters of the American widows had health insurance, this does not usually cover the cost of private consultation with a physician which, in Britain, would be obtainable without charge. Inpatient services, on the other hand, are covered by health insurance and it did not appear that American widows and widowers were deterred from entering hospital for treatment (see Parkes and Brown, 1972).

In presenting evidence gleaned from several different studies concerning the effects of bereavement on physical health, I may be producing confusion

when my aim is to dispel it. It would be so much simpler if one could state
dogmatically that bereavement is a cause of headaches, osteoarthritis, and
coronary thrombosis, and leave it at that; or, better still, go on to explain
how it causes such conditions. But the evidence (which is reviewed fully in
Parkes, 1970) does not yet justify dogmatism. So what conclusions are
possible?

I think we can justly claim that many widows and widowers seek help
during the months that follow the death of their spouse, and that the professional persons they most often go to are medical practitioners and ministers of religion. I accept the evidence that bereavement can affect physical
health, and that complaints of somatic anxiety symptoms, headaches, digestive upsets, and rheumatism, are likely, particularly in widows and widowers
in middle age. Finally, there are certain potentially fatal conditions, such as
coronary thrombosis, blood cancers, and cancer of the neck of the womb,
which seem in some cases to be precipitated or aggravated by major losses.

Beyond this we cannot go. I have no doubt that further research in these
areas will soon be undertaken and that many of the questions raised by
these findings will be answered.

Is there also evidence that bereavement can produce frank mental illness? Here it is possible to speak with more confidence since grief has been
a subject of detailed study in recent years. Nevertheless we shall soon enter
the realms of speculation when we try to explain why one person recovers
more easily than another from the psychological effects of bereavement. The
only safe course is to review the evidence as concisely as possible so that the
reader can make up his own mind what conclusions are justified.

From the case summaries of 3,245 adult patients admitted to two psychiatric units during 1949–51, I was able to identify ninety-four (2.9 percent)
whose illness had come on within six months of the death of a parent,
spouse, sibling, or child. No doubt there were others among these patients
who had been bereaved, but this fact was not mentioned in the case summary; and I am sure that there would be others again in whom the onset of
mental illness had been delayed for more than six months after the bereavement that caused it. However, it was necessary to confine attention to
those patients whose illness could reasonably be supposed to have something to do with bereavement.

Since bereavement is not an uncommon event, it was necessary to discover first whether the association between bereavement and mental illness
could be due to chance alone. That is to say, would the patient have become
ill at this time whether he had been bereaved or not? I compared the number

of spouse bereavements which had actually occurred in the psychiatric population with the number that could have been expected to occur by chance association. The expected number of spouse bereavements was calculated from the Registrar General's mortality tables for England and Wales covering the same years as the study. It transpired that thirty of the ninety-four patients had been admitted for illnesses which had come on within six months of the death of a spouse, whereas only five spouse-bereaved patients would have been expected by chance alone (see Parkes, 1964a).

Similar conclusions were reached by Stein & Susser (1969) in two carefully conducted studies of psychiatric care in Salford, England. These studies showed an abnormally large proportion of widows and widowers among people coming into psychiatric care for the first time in their lives and an abnormally large proportion of recently bereaved among these widowed patients.

To return to the ninety-four bereaved psychiatric patients identified from their case notes: the diagnoses made by the psychiatrists in these cases were ascertained and compared with the diagnoses made on the 3,151 patients who had not, according to their case records, been bereaved. Two main findings were: first, that the bereaved patients had been diagnosed as suffering from many different types of psychiatric illness; and, second, that the most common single diagnosis in this group was reactive or neurotic depression. This was the diagnosis for 28 percent of the bereaved patients and for only 15 percent of those who had not been bereaved.

From the case records of the bereaved patients it became apparent that, at the time of their admission to hospital, which was usually about a year after bereavement, many of them were still suffering from grief. Grief, which one normally expects to occur shortly after bereavement and to fade gradually in intensity as time passes, was not only still being experienced by these patients but was an integral part of the illness that had brought them into psychiatric care.

In other cases, however, the mental illness did not seem to involve grieving. For instance, several patients who had always been heavy drinkers had developed alcoholic psychoses after the death of a close family member. Here the symptoms were the symptoms of alcoholism, and if there was any persisting tendency to grieve this was not an obvious part of the clinical picture. Bereavement, in these cases, had been the "last straw," resulting in the breakdown of individuals whose previous adjustment had been precarious.

This study (henceforth referred to as the Case-note Study) revealed quite clearly the important part that bereavement can play in producing mental illness. It also indicated that the mental illnesses that follow bereavement often seem to comprise pathological forms of grieving. But case notes are not the most reliable source of research data and, while many of the case histories contained a full and convincing account of the patient's reaction to bereavement, there were others in which the reaction was not described in any detail. Obviously, a more systematic investigation of bereaved psychiatric patients was required. Research was needed, too, to determine what is a "normal" or "typical" reaction to bereavement.

Two studies were undertaken with these aims in view, the Bethlem Study and the London Study. . . . The London Study, to which reference has been made above, was carried out after the Bethlem Study but it will simplify matters if it is discussed first.

It is sometimes said that psychiatrists get a distorted view of life because they see only people who have failed to master the stresses they encounter. The London Study was an attempt to find out how an unselected group of twenty-two London widows under the age of 65 would cope with the stress of bereavement. It was undertaken with the intention of establishing a picture of "normal grief" among young and middle-aged widows. Older widows were excluded because . . . there is reason to regard grief in old age as a rather different phenomenon from the grief of younger people. Whatever the cause of this, it would have confused the overall picture too much to include older people in this survey.

Widows who agreed to help were brought to my attention by their general practitioners. These GPs had been asked to refer every woman in their practice who lost her husband and not to pick out those with special psychological difficulties. However, there were some widows who were not referred, either because they refused to take part or because the GP did not want to upset them. On subsequent inquiry, GPs did not think that these widows differed to any marked extent from those who were referred and it appears that those who were interviewed were a fairly representative sample of London widows.

They were seen by me at the end of the first month of bereavement, and again at the third, sixth, ninth, and thirteenth months, a minimum of five interviews in all. Essentially I was studying the first year of bereavement. However, in order to include but not be over-influenced by the anniversary reaction, I carried out the "end-of-year" interview one month late. This enabled me to obtain an account of the anniversary reaction and also to get an idea of how the widow was adjusting now that this crisis was past.

At the outset I had some misgivings about the entire project. It was not my wish to intrude upon private grief and I was quite prepared to abandon the study if it seemed that my questions were going to cause unnecessary pain. In fact, discussion of the events leading up to the husband's death and of the widow's reaction to them did cause pain, and it was quite usual for widows to break down and cry at some time during our first interview; but with only one exception they did not regard this as a harmful experience. On the contrary, the majority seemed grateful for the opportunity to talk freely about the disturbing problems and feelings that preoccupied them. The first interview usually lasted from two to three hours, not because I had planned it that way but because the widow needed that amount of time if she was to "talk through" the highly charged experiences that were on her mind. Once she found that I was not going to be embarrassed or upset by her grief she seemed to find the interview therapeutic and, although I took pains to explain that this was a research project, I had no sense of intrusion after the first few minutes of the initial contact. (Statistical findings are given in Parkes, 1970a.)

The aim of the Bethlem Study was to investigate atypical reactions to bereavement. Interviews were obtained between 1958 and 1960 with twenty-one bereaved patients at the Bethlem Royal and Maudsley Hospitals. Of the twenty-one patients, four were male and seventeen female. Most of them were seen soon after entering psychiatric treatment, at which time they had been bereaved for an average of seventy-two weeks (the range was from four to 367 weeks). (For further details see Parkes, 1965.)

In both the London Study and the Bethlem Study bereaved people were asked to tell me, in their own words, about their bereavement and how they reacted to it. Questions were kept to a minimum and simply ensured that comparable information about critical events was obtained in each case. Some notes, particularly records of significant verbatim statements, were taken at the time and some assessments were made immediately after the interview. These were recorded on a survey form which was also used as an *aide-mémoire* during the interview.

Following these two studies, which revealed, respectively, typical and atypical forms that the reaction to bereavement can take, the Harvard Study was carried out. This investigation had a rather different object in view. It had been established from earlier work that grief normally follows a certain pattern but that pathological variants sometimes occur, and a group of us now wanted to discover why most people come through the stress of bereavement unscathed whereas others break down with some physical or mental illness. We also wanted to see if it was possible to identify, at the time of a bereavement, those who would be likely to get into difficulties later. Since previous research had shown that the health risk was greatest in young widows, we focused our attention on people under the age of 45 who had lost a spouse. And because widowers had rarely featured in earlier investigations we included a group of them in this one. We contacted forty-nine widows and nineteen widowers by letter and telephone, and visited them in their homes three weeks and six weeks after bereavement, and again fourteen months after they had been bereaved when an assessment was made of their health. Our aim was to discover whether we could predict, from the evidence of the earlier interviews, how our subjects would be feeling and behaving a year later.

The Harvard Study confirmed my expectation that American widows would be found to react to bereavement in a similar manner to the British widows who had been the subjects of my earlier studies. These studies were not carried out to prove or disprove any particular theory, but inevitably I felt constrained to group certain features together and to attempt an explanation of the process of grieving which would make sense of the data.

When, in 1959, I first reviewed the scientific literature on loss and grief I was struck by the absence of any reference in it to the common observation that animals, in their reaction to loss, show many of the features that are evident in human beings. One of the few people who have made this point is Charles Darwin who, in *The Expression of the Emotions in Man and Animals* (1872), described the way in which sorrow is expressed by animals, young children, and adult human beings. His work caused me to formulate a "biological theory of grief" which has been developed over the last decade but has not required major modification.

My preliminary formulation, which formed part of a dissertation for the Diploma in Psychological Medicine, had no sooner been submitted to the examiners when I was lent a duplicated copy of a paper which showed that many of the conclusions I had reached had been reached quite independently by John Bowlby (1951, 1961, 1963, 1969). Bowlby's review of the effects of maternal deprivation in childhood had appeared as a World Health Organization monograph in 1951 and has been followed by a series of papers aimed at clarifying the theoretical questions to which it gave rise. By 1959 Bowlby was well set in working out a comprehensive theory, the first part of which was already in print. I sent him a copy of my own dissertation at that time and subsequently (in 1962) joined his research staff at the Tavistock Institute of Human Relations. Since that time our collaboration has been close and I have made use of many of his ideas. These biographical details are mentioned because I am no longer sure which of us deserves the credit (or blame) for originating many of the ideas that make up the overall theory on these pages. All that I can say, with confidence, is that my debt to John Bowlby is great.

REFERENCES

Aldrich, C. K. and Mendkoff, E. (1963). Relocation of the Aged and Disabled: a Mortality Study, *J. Amer. Geriat. soc.* II:185.

Bowlby, J. (1951). *Maternal Care and Mental Health.* WHO Monograph 2.

————— (1960). Grief and Mourning in Infancy and Early Childhood, *Psychoanal. Study Child* 15:9.

————— (1961a). Processes of Mourning. *Int. J. Psycho-Anal.* 44:317.

————— (1961b). Childhood Mourning and Its Implications for Psychiatry: the Adolf Meyer Lecture. *Amer. J. Psychiat.* 118:481.

————— (1963). Pathological Mourning and Childhood Mourning. *J. Amer. Psychoanal. Ass.* 11:500.

————— (1969). *Attachment and Loss.* Vol. I, *Attachment.* London: Hogarth; New York: Basic Books.

Darwin, C. (1872). *The Expression of the Emotions in Man and Animals.* London: Murray.

Glick, Ira O., Weiss, Robert S., and C. Murray Parkes. (1974). *The First Year of Bereavement.* New York: John Wiley & Sons.

Hobson, C. J. Widows of Blackton. *New Society,* September 14, 1964.

Maddison, D. and Viola, A. (1968). The Health of Widows in the Year Following Bereavement. *J. Psychosom. Res.* 12:297.

Marris, P. (1958). *Widows and their Families.* London: Routledge.

Parkes, C. M. (1959). Morbid Grief Reactions: a Review of the Literature. Dissertation for DPM, University of London.

————— (1964a). Recent Bereavement as a Cause of Mental Illness. *Brit. J. Psychiat.* 110:198.

————— (1964b). The Effects of Bereavement on Physical and Mental Health: A Case Study of the Case Records of Widows. *Brit. Med. J.* (2):274.

————— (1965). Bereavement and Mental Illness. Pt. I, A Clinical Study of the Grief of Bereaved Psychiatric Patients. Pt. 2, A Classification of Bereavement Reactions. *Brit. J. Med. Psychol.* 38:I.

————— (1970). The Psychosomatic Effects of Bereavement. In Oscar W. Hill (ed.), *Modern Trends in Psychosomatic Medicine.* London: Butterworth.

————— (1970a). The First Year of Bereavement: a Longitudinal Study of the Reaction of London Widows to the Death of their Husbands. *Psychiatry* 33:444.

Parkes, C. M., Benjamin, B. and Fitzgerald, R. G. (1969). Broken Heart: a Statistical Study of Increased Mortality among Widowers. *Brit. Med. J.* (I):740.

Parkes, C. M. and Brown, R. J. (1972). Health after Bereavement: A Controlled Study of Young Boston Widows and Widowers. *Psychosomatic Medicine,* 34:449–461.

Rees, W. D. and Lutkins, S. G. (1967). Mortality of Bereavement. *Brit. Med. J.* (4):13.

Rush, B. (1835). *Medical Inquiries and Observations upon the Diseases of the Mind.* Philadelphia: Grigg & Elliott.

Schmale, A. H. J. and Iker, H. P. (1966). The Affect of Hopelessness and the Development of Cancer. I, Identification of Uterine Cervical Cancer in Women with Atypical Cytology. *Psychosomat. Med.* 28:714.

Stein, Z. and Susser, M. W. (1969). Widowhood and Mental Illness. *Brit. J. Prev. & Soc. Med.* 23:106.

Young, M., Benjamin, B. and Wallis, C. (1963). Mortality of Widowers. *Lancet* (2):454.

Postvention and the Survivor-Victim

Edwin S. Shneidman

The following selection is taken from *Deaths of Man.* Here Dr. Shneidman introduces the view of the survivor as a victim and discusses working with survivors for several months after the death of a loved one—a type of therapy he calls "postvention."

A person's death is not only an ending; it is also a beginning—for the survivors. Indeed, in the case of suicide the largest public health problem is neither the prevention of suicide (about 25,000 suicides are reported each year in the United States but the actual number is much higher, probably twice the reported rate) nor the management of suicide attempts (about eight times the number of reported committed suicides), but the alleviation of the effects of stress in the survivor-victims of suicidal deaths, whose lives are forever changed and who, over a period of years, number in the millions.

This is the process I have called "postvention": those appropriate and helpful acts that come *after* the dire event itself (1968, 1971). The reader will recognize prevention, intervention, and postvention as roughly synonymous with the traditional health concepts of primary, secondary, and tertiary prevention, or with concepts like immunization, treatment, and rehabilitation. Lindemann (1944) has referred to "preventive intervention in a four-year-old child whose father committed suicide"; it would be simpler to speak of postvention.

ʯʯ

Recent investigations of widows . . . seem to imply that grief is itself a dire process, almost akin to a disease, and that there are subtle factors at work that can take a heavy toll unless they are treated and controlled.

ʯʯ

Postvention, then, consists of those activities that serve to reduce the aftereffects of a traumatic event in the lives of the survivors. Its purpose is to help survivors live longer, more productively, and less stressfully than they are likely to do otherwise.

It is obvious that some deaths are more stigmatizing or traumatic than others: death by murder, by the negligence of oneself or some other person, or by suicide. Survivor-victims of such deaths are invaded by an unhealthy complex of disturbing emotions: shame, guilt, hatred, perplexity. They are obsessed with thoughts about the death, seeking reasons, casting blame, and often punishing themselves.

The recent investigations of widows by Dr. C. M. Parkes (1970) are most illuminating. The principal finding of his studies is that independent of her age, a woman who has lost a husband recently is more likely to die (from alcoholism, malnutrition, or a variety of disorders related to neglect of self, disregard of a prescribed medical regimen or commonsense precautions, or even a seemingly unconscious boredom with life) or to be physically ill or emotionally disturbed than nonwidowed women. The findings seem to imply that grief is itself a dire process, almost akin to a disease, and that there are subtle factors at work that can take a heavy toll unless they are treated and controlled.

These striking results had been intuitively known long before they were empirically demonstrated. The efforts of Erich Lindemann (1944), Gerald Caplan (1964), and Phyllis R. Silverman (1969) to aid survivors of "heavy deaths" were postventions based on the premise of heightened risk in bereaved persons. Lindemann's work (which led to his formulations of acute grief and crisis intervention) began with his treatment of the survivors of the tragic Coconut Grove night-club fire in Boston in 1942, in which 499 people died. Phyllis Silverman's projects, under the direction of Gerald Caplan, have centered around a widow-to-widow program. These efforts bear obvious similarities with the programs of "befriending" practiced by the Samaritans, an organization founded by the Reverend Chad Varah (1966; 1973) and most active in Great Britain.

On the basis of work with parents of adolescent (fifteen- to nineteen-year-old) suicides in Philadelphia, Herzog (1968) has enumerated three psychological stages of postventive care: (1) resuscitation: working with the initial shock of grief in the first twenty-four hours; (2) rehabilitation: consultations with family members from the first month to about the sixth month; and (3) renewal: the healthy tapering off of the mourning process, from six months on.

A case can be made for viewing the sudden death of a loved one as a disaster and, using the verbal bridge provided by that concept, learning from the professional literature on conventionally recognized disasters—sudden, unexpected events, such as earthquakes and large-scale explosions, that cause a large number of deaths and have widespread effects. Martha Wolfenstein (1957) has described a "disaster syndrome": a "combination of emotional dullness, unresponsiveness to outer stimulation and inhibition of activity. The individual who has just undergone disaster is apt to suffer from at least a transitory sense of worthlessness; his usual capacity for self-love becomes impaired."

A similar psychological contraction is seen in the initial shock reaction to catastrophic news—death, failure, disclosure, disgrace, the keenest personal loss. Studies of a disastrous ship sinking by P. Friedman and L. Lum (1958) and of the effects of a tornado by A. F. Wallace (1956) both describe an initial psychic shock followed by motor retardation, flattening of affect, somnolence, amnesia, and suggestibility. There is marked increase in dependency needs with regressive behavior and traumatic loss of feelings of identity, and, overall, a kind of "affective anesthesia." There is an unhealthy docility, a cowed and subdued reaction. One is reminded of Lifton's (1967) description of "psychic closing off" and "psychic numbing" among the *Hibakusha*, the survivors of the atomic bomb dropped on Hiroshima:

> Very quickly—sometimes within minutes or even seconds—*Hibakusha* began to undergo a process of "psychic closing off"; that is, they simply ceased to feel. They had a clear sense of what was happening around them, but their emotional reactions were unconsciously turned off. Others' immersion in larger responsibilities was accompanied by a greater form of closing off which might be termed "psychic numbing." Psychic closing off could be transient or it could extend itself, over days and even months, into more lasting psychic numbing. In the latter cases it merged with feelings of depression and despair. . . . In response to this general pattern of disintegration, *Hibakusha* did not seem to develop clearcut psychiatric syndromes. To describe the emotional state that did develop they frequently used a term which means a state of despondency, abstraction or emptiness, and may be translated as "state of collapse" or "vacuum state." Also relevant is a related state . . . a listlessness, withdrawn countenance, "expression of wanting nothing more," or what has been called in other contexts "the thousand-mile stare." Conditions like the "vacuum state" or "thousand-mile stare" may be thought of as apathy but are also profound expressions of despair: a form of severe and prolonged psychic numbing in which the survivor's responses to his environment are reduced to a minimum—often to those necessary to keep him alive—and in which he feels divested of the capacity either to wish or will . . . related forms of psychic numbing occur in people undergoing acute grief reactions as survivors of the deaths of family members—here vividly conveyed in a psychiatric commentary by Erich Lindemann (1944):
> "A typical report is this, 'I go through all the motions of living. I look after my children. I do my errands. I go to social functions, but it is like being in a play; it doesn't really concern me. I can't have any warm feelings. If I would have any feelings at all I would be angry with everybody.' . . . The absence of emotional display in this patient's face and actions was quite striking. Her face had a mask-like appearance, her movements were formal, stilted, robot-like, without the fine play of emotional expression."

All this sounds remarkably like Henry Murray's (1967) description of partial death, those "psychic states characterized by a marked diminution or near-cessation of affect involving both hemispheres of concern, the inner and the outer world."

Postventive efforts are not limited to this initial stage of shock, but are more often directed to the longer haul, the day-to-day living with grief over a year or more following the first shock of loss. Postvention is in the honored tradition of holding a wake or sitting *shiva;* but it means more. Typically it extends over months during that critical first year, and it shares many of the characteristics of psychotherapy: talk, abreaction, interpretation, reassurance, direction and even gentle confrontation. It provides an arena for the expression of guarded emotions, especially such negative affective states as anger, shame, and guilt. It puts a measure of stability into the grieving person's life and provides an interpersonal relationship with the therapist which can be genuine, in that honest feelings need not be suppressed or dissembled.

An example may be useful: Late one afternoon a beautiful nineteen-year-old girl was stabbed to death by an apparent would-be rapist in a government building. Within an hour her parents were hit between the eyes with the news (and this is the way these matters are usually handled) by two rather young, well-meaning, but inexperienced policemen. The victim was the couple's only child. Their immediate reactions were shock, disbelief, overwhelming grief, and mounting rage, most of it directed at the agency where the murder had occurred.

A few days later, right after the funeral, they were in the office of a high official who was attempting to tender his condolences when the mother said in an anguished tone: "There is nothing you can do!" To which, with good presence of mind, he answered that while it was true the girl could not be brought back to life, there was something that could be done. Whether he knew the term or not, it was postvention that he had in mind.

I began seeing the parents, usually together, sometimes separately. The principal psychological feature was the mother's anger. I permitted her to voice her grief and to vent her rage (sometimes even at me), while I retained the role of the voice of reason: empathizing with their state, recognizing the legitimacy of their feelings when I could, but not agreeing when in good conscience I could not agree. I felt that I was truly their friend, and I believed they felt so too.

A few months after the brutal murder, the mother developed serious symptoms that required major surgery, from which she made a good recovery. I had insisted that each of them see a physician for a physical examination. Although the mother had had similar difficulty some years before, the situation raises the intriguing (and unanswerable) question in my mind whether or not that organic flurry would have occurred in her body if she had not suffered the shock of her daughter's death. Whatever the answer to that may be, I doubt very much that she would have recovered so well and so rapidly if she had received no postventive therapy.

The parents had an extraordinarily good marriage. Many relatives gave them emotional support. The husband, more laconic and more stoic, was my principal co-therapist—although I did not forget his needs and saw him alone occasionally, when for example, his wife was in the hospital.

Several months after the tragedy the parents seemed to be in rather good shape, physically and emotionally, everything considered. They still had low-level grief, and no doubt always will. But what is most important for this discussion is that each of them has stated that the process of working through their grief was made easier for them and that the outcome was better and more quickly achieved (though not with undue haste) as a result of our postventive sessions, that something of positive value had been done for them, and that they felt that something of this nature ought to be done for more people who found themselves in similar situations.

Quite a few months have passed since the homicide, and the murderer has still not been apprehended. If an arrest is ever made, it will inevitably present renewed conflicts for the girl's parents, and a new question will be raised: Should someone also be concerned with the welfare of the parents of the accused after his arrest?

Most deaths occur in the hospitals, and the dying patient is often isolated and his awareness clouded by drugs. (We nowadays rarely see our loved ones die "naturally" at home—a common event a few generations ago.) The topic of death is an especially unpleasant one for medical personnel. Death is the enemy; death represents failure. It has been noted that physicians constitute one of the few groups (along with policemen and combat soldiers) licensed to take lives in our society; at the same time, however, relatively few physicians deal with dying patients (consider the vast numbers of orthopedists, dermatologists, obstetricians, pediatricians, psychiatrists, and other specialists who deal with conditions that only rarely result in death) and are therefore ill equipped to teach others about death comfortably and meaningfully.

From the point of view of the staff-patient relationship vis-à-vis death, there are essentially three kinds of hospital wards or services. They can be labeled benign, emergent, and dire. A benign ward is one on which deaths are not generally expected and the relationship between staff and patient may be of short or long duration: obstetrical services, orthopedic wards, psychiatric wards. A death on such a service is a sharp tragedy and cause for special self-examination. The reaction is both to loss of a person and to loss of control. The staff, typically, is not so much in mourning as in a state of shock at administrative and professional failure.

Emergency services are quite different. These are the hospital emergency room and the intensive care unit. Here death is not an uncommon experience but the relationship between staff and patient is short-lived; the patient is hardly known as a person, and there is typically no time for meaningful interpersonal relationships to develop: the focus is on physiological functioning. Patients are often unconscious and almost always acutely ill. Death on such a service is not mourned as deep personal loss. It is a "happening," distressing but seldom totally unexpected. The staff—often self-selected—must be inured to the constant psychological toll of working in such a setting. The dangers are callousness, depression, and even acting out, especially in the forms of alcoholism, drug abuse, and heightened sexual activity.

It is the dire service that poses the most stressful problems for physicians and nurses. On such a ward the patients have grim prognoses (and are often doomed when they come to the ward, their illnesses diagnosed as cancer, leukemia, scleroderma, or whatever), and they remain there for an extended period of time, long enough for personal relations to be formed and for them to be known, loved, and then mourned as "real" human beings. Physicians practicing specialties dealing with fatal conditions—certain hematologists, oncologists, radiologists, and so on—know death all too intimately. Often there is not a week that is free of a death. The psychological stresses on such a service may be even greater for nurses, for they face the problem of giving intimate care, risking personal investment, and then dealing with loss.

Consider the following case: A thirty-year-old man was admitted to a hospital ward diagnosed as having leukemia in the terminal stage. He had an unusual combination of physical and personality characteristics that made him an especially "difficult" patient—not difficult in behavior, but difficult to see grow more ill and die: he was handsome, good-natured, alert; he had a keen sense of humor and was flirtatious with nurses, and through intermittent spells of depression and concern with dying he was remarkably brave, reassuring doctors and nurses and telling them not to worry about him or take it so hard. (It would have been much easier for them if he had been difficult in the usual sense—querulous, demanding, complaining; then they could have accommodated more easily to his death, with no great sense of loss.)

As a consultant on the ward, I visited him each day, having been asked to see him because of his depression. He talked openly about the topic of death and his fears of pain, aloneness, and loss, and specifically about his own death and its meaning for his wife and children. These sessions were, by his own account, very meaningful to him. It was the kind of death work that is not unusual in this kind of circumstance. But what was of special professional interest was the behavior, both before and after his death, of a nurse and of his physician.

The nurse, an exceptionally attractive young woman, grew to like the patient very much, with feelings that seemed to strike deeper than routine professional countertransference. I once witnessed a fascinating scene in which the nurse was massaging the patient's back while his wife stood stiffly off to one side; it was an interesting question as to who, at that moment, "owned" the dying patient. (But this nurse was extraordinarily good with the wife, taking her out to dinner, helping her with her young children, making, in a friendly and noncompetitive way, a number of practical arrangements for her.) After the young man's death there were several mourners for whom postvention was necessary, and the nurse was one of them. She grieved for one she had loved and lost, and her grief was sharpened and complicated by its somewhat secret and taboo nature.

The reaction of the physician in the case, a hematologist in his forties, was rather different but no less intense. We had planned to get together after the patient's death to discuss, I thought, interesting features of the case and possible plans for future collaborative efforts. Instead, he came into my office and announced that the young man's death had been the last straw. He was sick and tired of having all the doctors in the country dump their dying patients on him. He wondered how I could bear to see the young man every day while he was dying, and I countered candidly that I had wondered the same thing about him. Mainly he wanted a safe arena in which to vent his feelings about having had enough of death and dying for a while. Within a few weeks he followed his announced intention of making a major change in his professional life: he accepted a faculty position in a medical school in another state and in a specialty other than hematology.

In my own postventive work I have come to at least a few tentative conclusions:

1   Total care of a dying person needs to include contact and rapport with the survivors-to-be.

2   In working with survivor-victims of dire deaths, it is best to begin as soon as possible after the tragedy; within the first seventy-two hours if possible.

3   Remarkably little resistance is met from survivor-victims; most are willing to talk to a professional person, especially one who has no ax to grind and no pitch to make.

4   The role of negative emotions toward the deceased—irritation, anger, envy, guilt—needs to be explored, but not at the very beginning.

5   The professional plays the important role of reality tester. He is not so much the echo of conscience as the quiet voice of reason.

6   Medical evaluation of the survivors is crucial. One should be alert for possible decline in physical health and in overall mental well-being.

Three brief final points: Postvention can be viewed as prevention for the next decade or for the next generation; postvention can be practiced by nurses, lawyers, social workers, physicians, psychologists, and good neighbors and friends—thanatologists all; and a comprehensive mental health program in any enlightened community will include all three elements of care: prevention, intervention and postvention.

REFERENCES

Caplan, Gerald. *Principles of Preventive Psychiatry*. New York: Basic Books, 1964.

Friedman, Paul, and Lum, L. Some Psychiatric Notes on the *Andrea Doria* Disaster. *American Journal of Psychiatry*, 1957, *114*, 426–432.

Herzog, Alfred. A Clinical Study of Parental Response to Adolescent Death by Suicide with Recommendations for Approaching the Survivors. In Norman L. Farberow (Ed.), *Proceedings of the Fourth International Conference for Suicide Prevention*. Los Angeles: Delmar Publishing Co., 1968.

Lifton, Robert Jay. *Death in Life: Survivors of Hiroshima*. New York: Random House, 1967.

Lindemann, Erich. Symptomatology and Management of Acute Grief. *American Journal of Psychiatry*, 1944, *101*, 141–148.

Murray, Henry A. Dead to the World: The Passions of Herman Melville. In Edwin S. Shneidman (Ed.), *Essays in Self-Destruction*. New York: Science House, 1967.

Parkes, Colin Murray. The First Year of Bereavement: A Longitudinal Study of the Reaction of London Widows to the Death of Their Husbands. *Psychiatry*, 1970, *33*, 444–467.

Shneidman, Edwin S. Prevention, Intervention and Postvention of Suicide. *Annals of Internal Medicine,* 75, 1971, 453–458.

Shneidman, Edwin S. *Deaths of Man.* New York: Penguin Books, 1974.

Silverman, Phyllis R. The Widow-to-Widow Program: An Experiment in Preventive Intervention. *Mental Hygiene,* 1969, 53, 333–337.

Varah, Chad. *The Samaritans.* New York: Macmillan, 1966.

Varah, Chad. *The Samaritans in the 70's.* London: Constable, 1973.

Wallace, A. F. *Tornado in Worcester: An Exploratory Study of Individual and Community Behavior in an Extreme Situation.* Washington, D.C.: National Research Council, 1956.

Wolfenstein, Martha. *Disaster: A Psychological Essay.* New York: Macmillan, 1957.

The Widow-to-Widow Program: An Experiment in Preventive Intervention

Phyllis Rolfe Silverman

Phyllis Rolfe Silverman is a psychiatric social worker who works at Harvard Medical School where she directs a program for helping widows during their period of bereavement. Dr. Silverman's innovative clinical efforts, which she terms "an experiment in preventive intervention," stresses self-help and a form of group therapy among widows.

Phyllis R. Silverman "The Widow-to-Widow Program: An Experiment in Preventive Intervention." Reprinted from *Mental Hygiene,* Vol. 53, No. 3, 1969, by permission.

Open discussion of death is usually avoided (Gorer, 1955). In part this is possible because the lowered death rate has made death a less frequent visitor and because most people die in hospitals or other institutions, away from the family. Only hospital personnel and funeral directors daily confront death. The former have the reputation of withdrawing from the dying person (Glaser & Strauss, 1965), and the funeral director's job is to make the deceased look as "natural" as possible and thereby to disguise the fact of his death. We are all aware of our own mortality, but we don't like to be reminded of it.

Many caregivers who work with the dying person and his family have recently been exploring ways of being more responsive to their needs and of helping the family through its period of grief. This is happening in the medical profession, and also among funeral directors. The mental health professional has long been aware of the emotional problems that loss of a loved one and the resulting grief can cause (Freud, 1953). We are, however, no more comfortable in confronting death and its consequences than are other people.

ᚚᚚ

The mental health professional has long been aware of the emotional problems that loss of a loved one and the resulting grief can cause. We are, however, no more comfortable in confronting death and its consequences than are other people.

ᚚᚚ

The work here reported is an attempt to find more effective ways of responding to the problems caused by death—an inescapable fact of life. The Laboratory of Community Psychiatry at Harvard Medical School is studying the normal process of grief, what human and institutional resources are utilized by bereaved people, and what might be an appropriate way to provide additional assistance.

Bereavement and grief represent a crisis and a critical transition for the family of the deceased. The crisis aspects were first studied by Lindemann

357

(1944), when he treated victims of the Coconut Grove fire in 1942. Those he worked with were seriously depressed as a result of the major personal losses they sustained in addition to their physical injury. Lindemann observed several stages in their grieving and discovered that, unless people went through these stages, they did not recover from their physical injury or their depression. He identified the irrational aspects of grief that he saw as transient; the process of recovery was enhanced as the person was allowed to experience these transient irrational emotions.

Grief can be understood as a process that has a beginning, a middle, and an end, at which point the bereaved should be recovering. Some deaths are expected, such as those occurring in old age. These are normal, and most of us make some adjustment to the anticipated end. However, there are accidental crises that occur out of time in the life cycle, such as those that arose from the fire referred to above.

Our work at Harvard is concerned with the untimely death of a spouse in young families. Statistics show that young widows and widowers have a proportionately greater risk of needing treatment for an emotional disorder than would be expected from their numbers in the population. To minimize this risk, we are experimenting with ways of intervening that might ease the distress of the bereaved, carry them through the process of their grief, and lessen the possibility of their developing an emotional disorder.

Most caregivers shy away from the bereaved (Silverman, 1966). Widows I have talked with felt that neither friends, family, physicians, nor clergymen, for that matter, were very helpful. All wanted them to recover as quickly as possible. On the other hand, they found that other widows could be extremely helpful: they were least likely to tell them to "keep a stiff upper lip" at a time when the widows felt their lives were ended and any hope for the future gone. Other widows realized that grief was temporary and had to run its course before it was possible to feel better again.

Most mental health agencies serve people who suffer from a defined psychiatric disorder rather than those going through a life crisis. Further, most people suffering from the "hazard of living" that occurs with the death of a spouse do not typically think of turning to such agencies for aid unless they have had previous contact with them.

If the most helpful person is likely to be another widow, then this is the caregiver who should be available to a woman during her time of grief. However, the distances between people in our society do not make widow-to-widow contact easy to accomplish. People tend to live in homogeneous communities; for example, married couples with children in a certain age range tend to live near each other. In this kind of a society, it is very hard to find other people like oneself if one falls into a special category, such as that of widow.

The widow-to-widow program has grown out of this realization (Silverman, 1967). A target community has been chosen in which all new widows under the age of 60 are offered assistance. Information about the deceased and his widow is gotten from death certificates obtained through the bureau of vital statistics; information on race and religion is provided by funeral directors.

Five widows have been recruited to offer aid and have now been working for more than a year. They represent the dominant religious and racial groups in the community. We have assumed that someone from the widow's own background and faith might be more acceptable to her. (A time when a family is in extreme grief does not seem appropriate for the initiation of integration or ecumenicalism.) In addition, the aides live in or near the community in which they work, which facilitates the easy interchange between themselves and the new widows that can come only if they are neighbors.

The aides are women without any special educational background: two of them did not go past the eighth grade; the others are high school graduates. They were chosen not because of their educational background, but because of their personal skills with people—that is, their ability to empathize and understand what the people they visit are going through. They are all women who have been active in their community in social clubs or in other kinds of volunteer activities before or since they were widowed. Four of them are in their mid-forties; the fifth is in her early sixties.

The aides have been visiting new widows since June 1, 1967. A letter is sent to each widow, on personal note paper, offering condolences, explaining that the aide is also a widow, and proposing a time when she might visit. It is suggested that the widow call if she does not want the aide to visit.

In the first seven months, 110 widows came into the sample. Of these, 19 could not be located: the letters to them were returned, or the aides learned from neighbors that the widow had moved out of town, or they could not locate the address or the apartment. Of the remaining 91, 11 told the aides not to visit; they were abrupt and disinterested. Twelve other widows thought that the program was an excellent idea, but they did not see themselves as requiring any such assistance. (Our concern is that the people who refuse aid may be those who need us the most. However, we must exercise caution; in our zeal to help, we must always respect people's right to refuse to see us.)

The aides have been in touch with 64 widows; half of these they have seen in person, and the other half they have talked with regularly, at great length, on the telephone. A question to be answered in the future is why some women are unwilling to meet the aides in person but are willing to develop, in some instances, very intimate relationships on the telephone.

At this point it is possible to talk about the contacts the aides have had with the widows within one month after the death of their husbands. It seems that the new widow primarily wants to talk. She talks about the circumstances of her husband's death, about her fear of loneliness, about financial problems and how she will manage her future, raising the children alone and perhaps needing to work. When her children are already grown, she talks about the emptiness of the house—the fact that there is no one to take care of, and no one with whom she can share her evenings and weekends. Initially, most of the widows report that they are managing since there is so much to do. They are glad for chores such as straightening out insurance and Veterans and Social Security benefits, since these give them something to keep them busy. Most people are quite able to care for themselves and really need only the special help that comes from having a friendly ear to listen and a shoulder on which they can, in a sense, cry without feeling that they are imposing or being told to "keep a stiff upper lip" and to control themselves.

The aides' responses to the widows' needs vary. They sometimes provide concrete services, such as help in finding a job; they may help the widow sort out her finances and understand how it is possible to live on her new income; they may give needed advice. Most important, they offer friendship. The following vignettes illustrate the kind of work the aides do:

1 Mrs. I. provided the J. family with *moral support* and *showed family members how to be more considerate in their expectations of a new widow; further, she helped Mrs. J. get a job.* When Mrs. I. first visited Mrs. J., the latter was not at home. Mrs. I. then talked to Mrs. J.'s sister, who complained about the new widow's not being able to make up her mind: one minute she wanted to move, the next she was very morose, and spent all her time listening to church music she and her husband had enjoyed together. Mrs. I. explained to the sister something about the bereavement process and suggested that she be patient with her sister, encouraging her little by little to move out.

When the aide saw Mrs. J. in person the next day, she found her painting her apartment, with her teenage children's help. They were listening to church music as they worked. Mrs. J. had decided not to move, and to make her apartment more attractive. She also wanted to go back to work, doing housework so that she could be home when the children returned from school. Mrs. I. made two phone calls that evening and found Mrs. J. work for two days a week.

2 Mrs. N. offered Mrs. Q. *direct advice* about how to cope with her emotional problems. Mrs. Q. called Mrs. N. as soon as she received her letter and wanted her to come immediately. She was in a panic: she couldn't sleep and couldn't stop crying. Mrs. N. went right over.

Mrs. Q. had been accustomed to riding to work every day with her husband on the streetcar. She had gone back to work immediately after the seven days of mourning *(Shiva)* were over, but had become increasingly uncomfortable with each passing day. By the time she arrived at work she was depressed and crying. The trip constantly reminded her of her husband's death. She thought of changing jobs, of working in a different place; but she didn't want to offend her employer, who had been very good to her; in addition, she was frightened of looking elsewhere for a job at her age (50). Mrs. N. told her that changing jobs might be a good idea, but that she should first take a week's vacation, then try going back to her usual job. If she still couldn't face the situation, she should talk to her boss and look for another job.

Mrs. Q. followed this advice. She phoned Mrs. N. frequently, even when she couldn't sleep at night. In the end, she had no trouble finding a new job.

Friendship, to the aide, means visiting back and forth in each other's homes, exploring each other's experience with widowhood, and finding out about each other as people. The aides often invite the new widows to dinner, go out socially with them, and introduce them to other widows.

As we reviewed the services we were providing, it became clear that some people were able to deal with the trauma of the initial impact of the bereavement themselves, or with little assistance from either the aide or their family and friends. This did not ensure recovery, however. To meet the changing needs of the new widow, we organized group meetings to which all the widows were invited. These meetings dealt with questions that widows had raised: what to do with their leisure, what was involved in getting back to work, and how to help children understand their father's death. (We found that widows were most troubled by their children's reactions to their father's death: they had not anticipated that this event would have such an impact on their youngsters.) The meetings brought together the widows who had not seen an aide in person as well as those the aides had come to know quite well.

Our aides have reported that they got through the first few months of their bereavement in one manner or another, but that the loneliness and depression really became most difficult six months or a year after their husbands had died. By then they had in some way settled their lives so that they were carrying on, and only then did a great feeling of loss overwhelm them. Their experience in working with other widows has corroborated this.

ʄʄʄ

I believe that the base for preventive work is not the mental health clinic . . . : prevention should be the work of people and agencies that deal with people as they move through the normal phases of a life cycle.

ʄʄʄ

Our program, therefore, is designed not to have just one or two interviews with people initially, but rather to develop some kind of ongoing relationship to help widows at the different stages of their grief. Our goal is to explore all of the various needs that people have during bereavement and to find ways of helping them expand their resources so they can be more effective in coping with their problems. The end result, hopefully, will be that the mourners will recover and find some future for themselves. The means to this end may be a resource they develop themselves, such as a club for widows and widowers that would, in fact, be a self-help group. If what we do proves to be effective, we hope that it may serve as a pilot program and that, eventually, churches and other agencies and groups in the community will pick up the work and carry it forward.

I believe that the base for preventive work is *not* the mental health clinic, which should reserve its highly skilled services for those who are seriously disturbed and require special care: prevention should be the work of people and agencies that deal with people as they move through the normal phases of a life cycle. I think, for example, of physicians, school teachers, clergymen, neighbors, and funeral directors—all of whom can be forces for positive mental health. Perhaps the most effective preventive program can come from self-help groups, which is basically what our widow-to-widow program is. Here we have a very specialized group of "experts": they have lived through the crisis, they have recovered, and they teach others that it can be done and how to do it. Are we perhaps simply formalizing and making applicable to urban life a procedure that would naturally be followed in rural and more closely knit communities?

REFERENCES

Freud, S.: Mourning and Melancholia. In: Jones, E. (ed.): *Collected Papers of Sigmund Freud, The International Psycho-Analytical Library*, vol. 4, no. 10. London, Hogarth Press, 1953, pp. 152–170.

Glaser, B. G., and Strauss, A. L.: *Awareness of Dying.* Chicago, Aldine, 1965.

Gorer, G.: *Encounter,* 5:49, 1955.

Lindemann, E.: *American Journal of Psychiatry,* 101:141, 1944.

Silverman, P. R.: Services for the Widowed. In: *Social Work Practice, 1966* New York, Columbia University Press, 1966, pp. 170–189.

Silverman, P. R.: *Community Mental Health Journal,* 5:37 (Spring), 1967.

PART FOUR

PERSONAL
PERSPECTIVES
ON DEATH

·7· PSYCHOLOGICAL ASPECTS OF DEATH

As we shall see in each of the remaining chapters, the patient who is dying is very much a *person;* so we have a final shift of focus, this time to a concentrated look at the dying person. A standard textbook of clinical medicine states that "each man dies in a notably personal way." It may not be inaccurate to say that an individual is never more like himself than when he is dying. People come to death with a variety of beliefs, attitudes, superstitions, and fears, and hopes. (But wracking pain and systematic neglect can tear away at their hopes.) And further, there are deep and important unconscious orientations toward death or cessation, different perhaps in each person, some of these moving him toward death and some pulling him away. Today, many behavioral scientists believe that there are definite psychological components in the dying process. In many cases, death can be considered to be a psychosomatic disease. Further, many deaths can be thought of as being *subintentioned,* that is, they are deaths in which the decedent has played an indirect, covert, latent, unconscious role in hastening his own demise. Examples of subintended deaths would be any deaths (excluding clear-cut suicide or absolutely adventitious accident or failure of a vital body part) in which the person has acted with some imprudence, excessive risk taking, disregard of medical regimen, abuse of drugs including alcohol, and so on. One can see immediately that subintentioned deaths include many deaths now labelled as natural, accidental, or homicidal. We all know people who are "prone" to accidents, and we can now add the concept of "victim-precipitated homicide" in which the individual has played some conscious or unconscious part in creating his own fate.

In general, it is possible to say that there are two main approaches to the topic of death: the sociological and the psychological, identified with the names of Emile Durkheim and Sigmund Freud, respectively. In the last several years there have been many psychologists and psychologically oriented physicians who have concerned themselves directly with death. The names of Karl Menninger, Avery Weisman, John Hinton, Herman Feifel, Elisabeth Kübler-Ross, Laurens White, Leon Epstein, Robert Kastenbaum, Richard Kalish, Robert Fulton, and others come to mind. These psychologists and psychiatrists of death (thanatologists) are concerned with the individual's attitudes, development, mental states and orientations, and what are called "psychic mechanisms" of the mind. The six selections in this chapter touch upon different aspects of the new psychology of death.

The Feifel and the Kastenbaum and Aisenberg selections can be thought of as background material for the "Personal Perspectives on Death." Kastenbaum and Aisenberg offer such a background by acquainting the reader with the various stages of the life cycle an individual passes through in acquiring his personal understanding about the meaning of death. It is important to note that there are considerable variations in the manner in which individuals gain an understanding of death—variations that are often reflected in their approaches to dying.

The Feifel selection may be seen as providing a bridge into Part IV since it touches on many topics discussed earlier (e.g., desacralization and institutionalization of death, taboos on death, "total death" by nuclear annihilation, and interactions among the participants of death) relating them to the individual and to the need for a new look at the problems surrounding death and dying. Feifel discusses briefly how the individual copes with the prospect of death.

Feifel's discussion is picked up and shown in finer grain (and from a different premise) by Feder, who offers some new views on various maneuvers ("tactics of the dying") of terminal patients coping with the threat of death. Feder sees a great danger in a progressive isolation and a development of a sense of aloneness among terminal patients. Some of the reasons for this aloneness and isolation stem from, and are the result of a number of "common fallacies about dying patients," which are discussed in the Weisman selection. Once again the humanistic theme is picked up as Weisman urges against stereotyping people and problems and recommends that each patient be treated as a special case. He is certainly one of the most thoughtful writers in the field of thanatology today, and his "common fallacies" about the dying person provide an excellent overview to help the reader dispense with his own possibly erroneous views about death.

In the next selection Shneidman continues and expands the theme of humanistic treatment of the dying by discussing the unique way in which each person prepares himself and others for his death—"death work." This selection points up the need to understand the interplay of certain coping mechanisms such as acceptance and denial. The subject of denial and the importance of understanding this mechanism by which the individual attempts to cope with the prospect and process of dying is elaborated in the last Weisman selection. Weisman spells out various important aspects of denial, showing us that denial is a vital tactic in the person's wrestling with the specter of death.

Death as a Thought

Robert Kastenbaum and Ruth Aisenberg
Robert Kastenbaum is Professor of Psychology at the University of Massachusetts, and Ruth Aisenberg is a Research Psychologist at the Children's Hospital Medical Center in Boston. This selection, taken from their book *The Psychology of Death*, discusses what "death" may mean to a person and delineates the various life stages that a person passes through in acquiring a fully formed concept about death.

Reprinted from Robert Kastenbaum and Ruth Aisenberg *The Psychology of Death*, pp. 4-39. Copyright © 1972 by Springer Publishing Company, 200 Park Ave. S., New York. Used with permission.

D-e-a-t-h. This sequence of five letters is fixed and familiar. It is easy to assume that the *meaning* of this term is also fixed (unvarying) and familiar (truly known to us). Furthermore, one is tempted to assume that d-e-a-t-h refers to a "real something" (or a "real nothing") *out there*.

These assumptions will not be honored in the present discussion. For the moment we are setting aside most of what we know or think we know about "real death." Instead we will try to become aware of those mental operations through which we develop and utilize concepts of death. The elementary logic we are invoking here might be stated as follows:

1 Terms such as "dying," "dead," and "death" generally are *intended* by us to *refer* to phenomena that are outside of or beyond our minds. For example, I *think* of Socrates as dead—but the important point is that Socrates *really is* dead.

2 But we never "really" know what is *out there*. We never even know (beyond the possibility of plausible counter-argument) that there *is* an *out there* out there. We live within and by our own psychological processes. The correspondence between our personal thoughts and feelings and anything else in the universe is a matter for conjecture (as it has been for centuries).

3 We do know that concepts of death have a particular form of existence that is amenable to analysis and understanding. It is even amenable to

controlled empirical investigations. Concepts of death are: *concepts*. We can study the development and structure of death concepts in the individual. We can learn how death concepts get along within the individual's entire community of concepts. We can attempt to discover relationships between concepts of death and such covert states as anxiety or resignation. We can attempt to discover relationships with overt behaviors, such as risk-taking actions or the purchase of "life" insurance. We can examine cultures and subcultures with respect to their concepts of death and their implications for social structure and function.

4 This level of analysis is highly relevant because it is clearly within the realm of psychology. Even if our present knowledge is quite limited, there is some security perhaps in the feeling that we are looking at death from a perspective that is germane to our scientific background.

In short, we are attending to death first as a psychological concept. It is at least a psychological concept, even if it is more. . . .

Too little is known at the present time to assume that there is an obvious developmental goal toward which early conceptions of death advance inch by inch by inevitable inch.

A FEW GENERAL PROPOSITIONS

Perhaps we should expose some of our conclusions ahead of time. In this way the reader may be better prepared to dispute or agree with the materials to come.

1 *The concept of death is always relative.* We will emphasize its relativity to *developmental level*, although a case could be made for other frameworks of relativity. By developmental level we do not necessarily mean the

individual's chronological age. It is obvious that chronological age provides important clues to the person's mode of thinking. But we are concerned with developmental level in a structural sense that will already be familiar to those acquainted with the writings of Heinz Werner (1), Jean Piaget (2), and some others. The point, in any event, is that the concept of death should be interpreted within its organismic context.

2 *The concept of death is exceedingly complex.* In most instances it is not sufficient to express the death concept in one or two propositions. Along with the sheer complexity of the death concept we find it does not invariably hold together as a unified, internally consistent structure. In short, we must be cautious in thinking about somebody having a concept of death in the same way that he has a Social Security number or a big toe.

3 *Concepts of death change.* This proposition is implied by those already mentioned. When we characterize a person's concept of death at a particular point in time we should not suppose that this description will continue to hold true for him indefinitely.

4 *The developmental "goal" of death concepts is obscure, ambiguous,* or *still being evolved.* It is customary to trace growth curves from starting point to apex. To mention one of the clearest examples, we expect the child's height to increase until it attains its "goal": adult height. (One might also persevere to trace the decline of the growth curve after a period of relative stability during the early and middle years of adulthood.)

Conceptions of death cannot be graphed with the same degree of confidence. Technical reasons for this limitation include difficulties in assessing conceptions of death, and in establishing appropriate quantitative units by which progress or lack of progress can be demonstrated. But the more crucial problem has to do with content, not method: we just do not know what constitutes the most mature or ideal conception of death. There are opinions, of course (too often passed off as though established facts). These opinions represent value orientations rather than inexorable conclusions derived from systematic theory or research. Seldom are attitudinal components distinguished from the more purely cognitive aspects of the conception. Is there, in fact, one and only one mature conception of death? And how can we be certain that the individual does not achieve a mature conception of death relatively early in life, but then retreat to a socially sanctioned position that is less adequate from a developmental standpoint? These questions are merely illustrative. We are suggesting that too little is known at the present time to assume that there is an obvious developmental goal toward which early conceptions of death advance inch by inevitable inch.

5 *Death concepts are influenced by the situational context.* How we conceptualize death at a particular moment is likely to be influenced by many situational factors. Is there a dying person in the room with us? A corpse? Does the situation contain a possible threat to our own life? Are we alone or with friends? Is it bright noon, or black midnight? The situation may selectively draw out one type of death cognition among the several we possess. Or, the situation may even stimulate us to develop new or modified death conceptions.

6 *Death concepts are related to behavior.* Most immediately, perhaps, we think of a person engaging in an action that is directly and positively related to his death cognition. He comes to the conclusion, for example, that death is the gateway to eternal bliss. Suicide follows as his relevant behavior. But the relationship is seldom, if ever, that simple. Similar death cognitions can lead to different behaviors, just as similar behaviors can be preceded by different sequences of psychologic. Another person with the "eternal bliss" conception of death stays alive so that he can bring his message of hope and comfort to others. Still another person commits suicide without giving much thought to the prospect of an afterlife; he is totally absorbed in his need to escape from unbearable life stress.

One's concept of death can influence behavior in remote and complex ways. Behavior patterns that do not seem to have anything in particular to do with death may nevertheless be influenced by these cognitions. Insomnia, for example, or panic upon temporary separation from a loved one, sometimes can be traced to death concerns. Clinicians Hattie Rosenthal (3) and Herman Feifel (4) are among the experienced observers who have discovered death thoughts to be closely interwoven with many types of behavior.

KNOWING AND RELATING

It is difficult, in practice, to maintain a clear distinction between concepts and attitudes. In this selection, we concentrate upon the ways in which we explain or interpret death to ourselves [rather than] upon our attitudes or orientations toward death.

Illustration: We ask a child what a shaggle-toothed boondoggler would look like, were there such an animal. He provides us with a vivid drawing or verbal description. He has, in effect, conveyed his understanding of the boondoggler. Now we inquire what he would do if he saw one of them coming down the street. Here he has the opportunity to express his attitude or orientation ("I would run away—fast!" or "I'd say, 'Here snaggle-tooth, here's some nice milk for you. Will you give me a ride on your back'?")

Our total relationship with any object involves both conceptual and attitudinal components. The mere fact that we know, or think we know something about this object, is sufficient to guarantee some kind of relationship. We are related to this object *through our own cognitive activity.* Similarly, the existence of an orientation (e.g., approach or avoidance) presumes some cognitive component. At the least, we have performed the mental operation of classifying the object as something-to-be-avoided.

We shall not insist upon an artificial separation of death concepts from our total organismic relationship to death. But it will be useful to begin with an emphasis upon death as a psychological concept. Taken by itself, the topic is complex enough. And consideration of this specific problem will provide helpful perspective for the variety of other problems that lie ahead.

"YOU ARE DEAD"

At least two forms of the death conception should be clearly distinguished at the outset. The first of these is death-of-the-other. There is reason to believe that the cognition "You are dead" develops more rapidly than the inward-looking "I will die." Later, both types of death conception will be considered in some detail from a developmental viewpoint. At the moment, we are interested only in sketching some of their implications.

"You are dead" is a proposition that is related to the following considerations:

1 You are *absent.* But what does it mean to be absent? We must appreciate the observer's frame of reference. For a young child, the frame of reference is largely perceptual. Absence means *not* here-and-now. The child is not yet equipped to distinguish adequately between spatial and temporal distance. Suppose that you are "away," in another city. From an adult frame of reference, you have a spatial existence at the present time. But the child experiences your absence (5). You are not in *his* perceptual space at this time, therefore you are *not.* (There will be an important amendment to this statement later.)

2 I am *abandoned.* This statement is almost a reciprocal of the preceding proposition. Your disappearance from my perceptual frame of reference

has an effect upon my sense of security. As a parent or other crucial person, you constitute a significant aspect of the universe that is known to the child. As the child, I am not merely aware of *your absence*, but of the *presence of discomfort feelings within myself.*

3 Your absence plus my sense of abandonment contributes to the general sense of *separation.* I have been alienated from one of my most important sources of contact and support. If this separation is sufficiently critical to me, then I may experience a pervasive sense of losing contact with the environment, not just with you. Furthermore, I may also have the impression of being wrenched away from you. This trauma could intensify the already bleak picture of absence and abandonment.

4 The separation has *no limits.* The young child does not grasp the concept of futurity, or of time in general, in the way that most adults have come to develop these concepts. This is a multidimensional problem. It may be sufficient at this point to say that the child's immediate sense of separation is not modulated by future expectations. He cannot tell himself, "Mother has gone away . . . but she will return in five days." He cannot distinguish among short-term, long-term, and final (irreversible) separations. Once the separation experience has been induced, he has no dependable way of planning, estimating, or anticipating its conclusion. What the outsider may regard as a brief separation (based upon consensual clock or calendar time) may be indistinguishable in the child's mind from the prospect of prolonged separation.

5 The child's involvement in *recurring psychobiological rhythms* complicates his relationship to separation and death. He is not fully a knowing participant in the world of "objective" time that moves unit by standard unit from the past, through the present, to the future (6). His time begins each morning when he awakes. His midday nap signals a "time out." External rhythms of night and day and internal rhythms of hunger-satiation, sleep-activation, etc., exert a strong influence over his appreciation of time.

How does this relationship to time affect his conception of death-of-the-other? The four preceding points emphasize, in various ways, the child's vulnerability to separation. He cannot, for example, distinguish well between the prospect of moderate-length and long-term or final separation. Now we must add a factor that might seem contradictory. Bear in mind these two points: a) the child's time experience is conditioned by cyclical rhythms, and b) he is apt to experience sensations of absence, abandonment, and separation in situations where adults would argue that the child has not "really" been abandoned.

We see that the sense of *limitless* separation or the *endlessness* of any experience conflicts with the periodic nature of his experiences. It is a bit difficult to express this relationship. As a child who feels abandoned, I have no way of establishing a future limit upon my present experience. In fact, one of the reasons I am so distressed is that this unpleasant experience shows no signs of being self-limiting. Nevertheless, my psychobiological state is always in transition. I am becoming hungry or sleepy. And the environment in which I am embedded is also in transition. The sun is coming up or it is going down. Various periodic household routines are being started or completed. Concretely, as a cyclical creature in a cyclical environment, I am not likely to maintain a constant frame of reference over a protracted period of (clock or calendar) time. There are breaks and interruptions in even my most steadfast thought and behavior patterns. In other words, despite my inability to posit *limits* to the separation experience, I do not actually have a continuous experience. Periodic changes in my inner state and my external environment distract and rest me. There will be more to say later about the relationship we have been proposing here.

ᛏᛏᛏ

Death essentially is a nonexperience.
The very mental operations I use in
my efforts to fathom death falsify as
they proceed.

ᛏᛏ

What is relevant now is the connection between periodicity and the child's vulnerability to separation experiences. Again, as a child I may "misinterpret" your temporary departure as being a consequential separation. By this same token, however, I may underestimate a consequential separation—even your death. My cyclical patterns of functioning lead me to anticipate that every end has a fresh beginning, just as every beginning has an end. You have been away a long time now (by clock-calendar as well as subjective time). But I do not "know" how long this has been. And I have deeply rooted within me the expectation that the familiar pattern of separation-reunion will be completed. This is another point that we will want to keep in mind when we attempt to trace the entire developmental sequence of death conceptions. The proposition, for now, is that the child is more vulnerable to the death-implications of trivial separations, and more protected from the death-implications of substantial separations than what might appear to be the case from the viewpoint of an observing adult.

"I WILL DIE"

This proposition assumes that one has developed quite a constellation of abstract concepts. The set we offer below is not intended to be exhaustive. The statement "I will die" implies such related concepts as the following:

1 *I* am an individual with a life of my own, a personal existence.
2 I belong to a *class* of beings one of whose attributes is mortality.
3 Using the intellectual process of logical deduction, I arrive at the conclusion that my personal death is a *certainty.*
4 There are *many possible causes* of my death, and these causes might operate in many different combinations. Although I might evade or escape one particular cause, *I cannot evade all causes.*
5 My death will occur in the *future.* By future, I mean a time-to-live that has not yet elapsed.
6 But I do not know *when* in the future my death will occur. The event is certain; the timing is uncertain.
7 Death is a *final* event. My life ceases. This means that I will never again experience, think, or act, at least as a human being on this earth.
8 Accordingly death is the *ultimate separation* of myself from the world (7).

"I will die" thus implies self-awareness, logical thought operations, conceptions of probability, necessity, and causation, of personal and physical time, of finality and separation. It also seems to require the bridging of a tremendous gap: from what I have experienced of life to the formulation of a death concept. It is a good deal easier to develop a concept of a shaggle-toothed boondoggler; I have had contact with many different animals, so it is just a matter of selecting and combining attributes. Death, however, essentially is a nonexperience. I have not been dead (the state). I have not experienced death (the process of life coming to a final halt). The very

mental operations I use in my efforts to fathom death falsify as they proceed. The mind's own modus operandi equips it for interpreting life or
life-like processes better than the alien void. Perhaps now and then I permit
myself to believe that I have actually perceived or formed a concept *of* death.
Closer to the truth, however, is the realization that I have simply observed
my mind as it scurries about in the dark.

Having seen a dead person, animal, or plant is likely to contribute to
my conception of death. Yet these perceptions do not truly bridge the gap.
The deadness is perceived from the outside only. What it feels like not
to feel eludes me. Furthermore, under some circumstances I am liable to
misinterpret my perceptions, seeing the living as dead, or vice versa. Experiences with the dead, however, is another one of those topics we will
keep in mind as we attempt to understand the development of death
conceptions.

DEATH CONCEPTIONS IN INFANCY AND EARLY CHILDHOOD

Most developmental psychologists believe that the very young child (from
birth to about two years) has no understanding of death (8). This opinion
is consistent with the more general contention that young children lack the
ability to grasp *any* abstract conception. Jean Piaget, for an important example, has offered a fine-grained analysis of mental development from early
infancy through adolescence (9). He identifies many stages of development
that seem to have been overlooked by previous observers. Within the
period of infancy alone, Piaget recognizes six different stages of mental
development. But he does not consider that genuine "formal operations"
(abstract conceptualization) enter into the picture until many years have
passed. Even the ten-year-old, with all the intellectual resources he now has
at his disposal, has only just reached the stage of "concrete operations."
He can deal adequately with the "actual," but is just beginning to take
proper account of that which is "potential" or "possible." Finally, in adolescence, one is able to think about thought and, thus, bring to bear the full
intellectual resources that seem to be required for comprehension of death.

Nevertheless, we believe there is much yet to be learned about conceptions of death in early childhood. It may be true enough that highly abstract
and well-verbalized conceptions are beyond the toddler's range. But we
do not share the frequent assumption of developmental psychologists that
very young children do not have any understanding of death (or, for that
matter, that they are incapable of powers of abstraction and generalization).
Between the extremes of "no understanding" and explicit, integrated ab-

stract thought there are many ways by which the young mind can enter into relationship with death. This topic deserves more attention than can be provided here. We cannot, for example, examine all the ways in which conceptions of death are relevant to stages of mental development even in one psychologist's (Piaget's) system. And empirical data on death concepts is sparse in this age range. But we can at least attempt to reopen this area that seems to have been so prematurely sealed off. (Psychoanalytically oriented observers have been more alert than most "straight" developmentalists to early conceptions of death, as we shall see.)

Early Exposure to Death-of-Others

Let us first consider the young child's response to the death of a significant person in his life. This exploration is intended chiefly to provide some clues as to how death registers itself on the minds of the very young. It will not tell us precisely how the infant or small child thinks of death, but it will tell us something about the nature and extent of his response to that event to which we adults give the term "death."

One of the earliest researches into the psychology of death touched upon this question. G. Stanley Hall and Colin Scott (10) of Clark University obtained responses to death questionnaires. The respondents were adults, but part of their task was to recall their earliest experiences with death. Hall later wrote that ". . . the first impression of death often comes from a sensation of coldness in touching the corpse of a relative and the reaction is a nervous start at the contrast with the warmth that the contact of cuddling and hugging was wont to bring. The child's exquisite temperature sense feels a chill where it formerly felt heat. Then comes the immobility of face and body where it used to find prompt movements of response. There is no answering kiss, pat, or smile. In this respect sleep seems strange but its brother, death, only a little more so. Often the half-opened eyes are noticed with awe. The silence and tearfulness of friends are also impressive to the infant, who often weeps reflexly or sympathetically" (11).

He continues: "Children of from two to five are very prone to fixate certain accessories of death, often remembering the corpse but nothing else of a dead member of the family. But funerals and burials are far more often and more vividly remembered. Such scenes are sometimes the earliest recollections of adults" (12).

It is worth adding here that recent investigations of adults' earliest memories also have turned up death experiences such as those to which Hall has alluded (13, 14).

Funeral customs have changed since the childhood of Hall's respondents (most of whom were born in the middle third of the nineteenth century). Perhaps children tend to be more insulated from funerary proceedings today. But it is interesting to read what Hall has to say about children's cognitive reactions to death when they did have the opportunity to be on the scene: "Little children often focus on some minute detail (thanatic fetishism) and ever after remember, for example, the bright pretty handles or the silver nails of the coffin, the plate, the cloth binding, their own or others' articles of apparel, the shroud, flowers, and wreaths on or near the coffin or thrown into the grave, countless stray phrases of the preacher, the fear lest the bottom of the coffin should drop out or the straps with which it is lowered into the ground should slip or break, a stone in the first handful or shovelful of earth thrown upon the coffin, etc. The hearse is almost always prominent in such memories and children often want to ride in one" (15).

And Hall even has an explanation to offer for the latter observation: "This, of course, conforms to the well-known laws of erotic fetishism by which the single item in a constellation of them that alone can find room in the narrow field of consciousness is over-determined and exaggerated in importance because *the affectivity that belongs to items that are repressed and cannot get into consciousness is transferred to those that can do so*" (16). [Italics ours.]

The observations we have been considering so far were made retrospectively. There are formidable difficulties involved in attempting to determine how accurately these adult-looking-backward reports convey what actually took place in early childhood. The same problem holds true for memories reported within the context of psychoanalytic therapy. This does not mean that we are free to neglect these observations, but that additional sources of information should be obtained.

Retrospective studies are a bit less hazardous when we limit our concern to "objective" or "factual" information. One especially relevant fact is the death of a parent. In many (but not all) instances it can be established that a person had lost one of his parents by death at a particular age. Let us turn to one of the most carefully performed studies available on this topic, with special reference to parental bereavement very early in childhood. (We cannot remain strictly within the birth-to-two-years range, because investigators have tended to make larger grouping of years in their data analysis.) Felix Brown, a British psychiatrist, examined the relationship between childhood bereavement and the development of depressive illness in later life (17). He obtained his basic data from the records of 216 unselected depressive patients who were receiving psychiatric services at the time. Brown made use of two control groups: orphanhood tables from the 1921 census, and the records of 267 medical patients who were receiving treatment at the same time as those suffering from depression. His results are closely tied to a series of statistical comparisons which we do not have space to report in detail. We would like to call attention, however, to some of the findings which are most relevant to our present focus.

Brown concludes from his total findings that "bereavement in childhood is one of the most significant factors in the development of depressive illness in later life."

Approximately two out of every five adult depressive patients had lost at least one parent by death before the age of 15. This compares with 1-in-8 and 1-in-5 figures for the control groups. One of the more striking findings (from our viewpoint) was that the death of the father had occurred by the age of four in approximately *twice* the number of cases of boys who later experienced depressive pathology (as compared with both control groups). Paternal bereavement was probably higher than usual among very young children during this period in history because of the high death rate of young men in World War I. This unfortunate fact may account for the relatively large number of paternal bereavements, but it does not account for the differences in adult depression that seem to be related to childhood bereavement.

Brown concludes from his total findings that "bereavement in childhood is one of the most significant factors in the development of depressive illness in later life" (18). However, he does not attempt to oversimplify the etiology of depression, and recognizes the role played by several other factors. This British psychiatrist considers that the effects of bereavement may be long delayed, or at least, their manifestations in clearly psychopathological behavior.

Brown's findings give us some reason to believe that exposure to death in the early years of life can exert an important influence upon the child's subsequent development. Three of his case illustrations involve people whose bereavement had occurred prior to age two.

With all of its limitations, the clinical case method still remains a valuable source of observations and hypotheses. David M. Moriarty, M.D., director of psychiatry at Worcester State Hospital, believes that his psychotherapeutic work has revealed a connection between early bereavement and a girl's later fear of mothering. One of his patients was a woman in her thirties who was more than depressed: she was also in a state of fear that she might kill her own child. "This woman . . . had a brother who died at the age of one year, when she was three years old. The patient's illness coincided in time with the birth of a nephew who was given the same name as the brother who had died" (19).

This case suggests that bereavement as early as the third year of life can have its implications for death-related behavior several decades later. It also attests to the frequent occurrence, as Brown has also noted, of precipitating factors in the current life situation that seem to activate the early trauma. Most of Moriarty's cases seem to have involved bereavement that took place a little later in childhood than the case we selected for mention. Our aim was to indicate the *possibility* that very early exposure to death is registered forcefully upon the child's mind.

Moriarty reports another interesting and relevant case in more detail (20). Here the focus is upon the effect of bereavement, on total development, rather than mothering behavior alone. "Mrs. Q." had undergone severe depressive episodes for over a decade. She attempted to take her life on three occasions, and twice was treated with electroshock therapy (but not successfully). Her personality disturbance was obviously of major proportions.

Mrs. Q's mother had died of appendicitis when the patient was a child of three. She recalled standing beside her uncle at the graveside, her arm around his leg. According to Moriarty, "During her treatment, she used to call me in a panic and would say she felt 'the world is coming in on me.' The thought behind this fear was traced to this graveyard scene when they threw a shovel full of dirt on the lowered coffin" (21). The psychotherapist concluded from his work with this patient that "Mrs. Q. lived most of her life afraid that she would lose other people she loved. . . . She felt her children had *no* mother and that someone ought to take her place and do a better job. She felt dead, non-existent, wanted to die, and feared dying."

. . . The most impressive fact was that she talked and thought about the death of her mother as much as if it had just happened. This tragic event of forty years ago was still uppermost in her mind" (22).

Such observations as these provide circumstantial evidence for the proposition that the very young child can be impressed by his exposure to death. He may not have high level thought operations at his disposal, but death-related *perceptions* can make a strong and enduring impact. Note that both Hall and Moriarty (years apart in their observations and employing different methods of obtaining their data) have called attention to vivid recollections of perceptual details. This is not surprising. The very young child cannot label and classify his experiences the way an older and more verbal person can. How is he able to register and maintain the memory of significant experiences? The camera of his mind seems to be equipped for this purpose. He records the perceived scene. This perceptual recording then serves as an organizing point for the inner feelings and thoughts which could not find verbal expression at the time. *Perceptions* of death thus may be important predecessors of subsequent *concepts.*

Actual observations of children's behavior in death situations (as contrasted with adult memories of the same) have been made. However, these observations are none too plentiful or detailed. Information is particularly scarce concerning the response of very young children. At least two factors are probably responsible for the scarcity of such reports: (a) often it is *assumed* that very young children do not know enough about death to respond in a way that is worth studying; and (b) the limited verbal capacity of the very young child stands as a formidable barrier to exploring his inner response. Systematic research should be possible on this topic if one is prepared to devote sufficient time to the development of appropriate procedures. Exploratory work by psychiatrist Gregory Rochlin, for example, has indicated that a series of fantasy-play sessions can reveal important aspects of the child's interpretation of death (23). Illustrations from his observations will be given a little later.

Consider the "death-exposure" responses of these two very young boys. These responses afford us opportunities to glimpse something of the young child's mind as it tries to come to terms with death, and something of the difficulties adults encounter in attempting to interpret the child's interpretations.

David, at 18 months, was toddling around the back yard. He pointed at something on the ground. Daddy looked. It was a dead bird. The boy labeled what he saw, "buh . . . buh" (his approximation, at the time, for bird). But he appeared uncertain and puzzled. Furthermore, he made no effort to touch the bird. This was unusual caution for a child who characteristically tried to touch or pick up everything he could reach. David then crouched over and moved slightly closer to the bird. His face changed expression. From its initial expression of excited discovery it had moved to puzzlement: now it took on the aspect of a grief mask. To his parent's surprise, the child's face was set in a frozen, ritualized expression resembling nothing so much as the stylized Greek dramatic mask for tragedy. Daddy only said, "Yes, bird . . . dead bird." In typically adult conflict, the parent thought of adding, "Don't touch," but then decided against applying this injunction. In any event, David made no effort to touch.

Every morning for the next few days, David would begin his morning explorations by toddling over to the dead-bird-place. He no longer assumed the ritual-mask expression, but he still restrained spontaneously, from touching. The bird was allowed to remain there until greatly reduced by decomposition. The parents reasoned that he might as well have the opportunity to see the natural processes at work. This had been, to the best of the parents' knowledge, David's first exposure to death. No general change in his behavior was noted (nor had any been expected). The small first chapter had concluded.

But a few weeks later there was a second dead bird to be discovered (this fatality was clearly the work of a local and well-known cat). David had quite a different orientation toward death #2. He picked up the bird and gestured with it. What was on his mind? Something—because he was also "speaking" with insistence. When his parents did not seem to comprehend his wishes, the boy reached up toward a tree, holding the bird above his head. He repeated the gesture several times. Finally (perhaps) comprehending, Daddy tried to explain that being placed back on the tree would not help the bird. David continued to insist, accompanying his command now with gestures that could be interpreted as a bird flying.

All too predictably, the bird did not fly when returned to the tree. David insisted that the effort be repeated several times. Then he lost interest altogether.

But there was a sequel a few weeks later (by now, autumn). David and Daddy were walking in the woods. There were many little discoveries to be made. After a while, however, the boy's attention became thoroughly engaged by a single fallen leaf. He tried to place it back on the tree himself. Failure. He gave the leaf to his father with "instructions" that the leaf be restored to its rightful place. Failure again. When Daddy started to try again,

David shook his head, "no." He looked both sober and convinced. Although leaves repeatedly were seen to fall and dead animals were encountered every now and then, little David made no further efforts to reverse their fortunes.

These observations illustrate some of the reporter's difficulties: (a) He does not know *when* the death-exposure will occur. (b) Although his "reading" of the child's emotional response may be accurate, there is no way to confirm his impressions directly, and he may be either attributing too much or not enough to the child's mind. (c) It is possible that the observer either does not see or fails to recognize other incidents that belong in the sequence. (d) A trained observer who is not related to the child would likely be more "objective," but also would lack sufficient context to interpret specific behavior.

Recognizing these and other limitations attendant upon the parent-child "generation gap," it is still worthwhile to keep in mind some of the implications of what has been observed: (a) The exposure to death did seem to call forth unprecedented and unusual behavior in this child (that is, behavior *he* had not shown before). (b) It is not entirely out of question that there may be a disposition to behave toward death in a certain way that is available even to the very young; we hesitate to speak of an "instinctual" reaction, but there is insufficient evidence to dismiss the possibility altogether. (c) Responses generated from one death-situation may be capable of generalization to related situations even when the child is quite young (as a matter of fact, limited verbal and conceptual development might serve to facilitate *increased* generalization as one is less able to identify similarities and dissimilarities). (d) *Learning* about the properties of death may take place at an early age.

Complexity of the child's relationship to death increases rapidly within the first few years of life. Consider Michael, whose known encounters with death began when he was about two-and-a-quarter years of age. For the following information we are grateful to his father, psychologist Szandor Brent. A more extended account and analysis will be offered elsewhere (24).

Michael had not drunk from a bottle in more than a year. But now, for a period of about six weeks, he had been waking up several times during the night screaming hysterically for a bottle. He could not be satisfied unless the ingredients included both warm water and sugar. Attempts to talk him out of it were useless. He would tearfully insist, "But I *have* to have it!"

One evening his father comforted the boy for a while, and then asked, "What will happen if you don't get your bottle?" Michael replied, "Then I won't (or can't) make contact!" What did that reply mean? Michael explained sobbing: "If I run out of gas, I can't make contact—my engine won't go. You know!" This statement was punctuated by sobs. The elder Brent reports that at this point "the pieces suddenly began to fall together. During the first two weeks in August we had gone to a country cottage for vacation. At the cottage, we *ran out of gas* three times. . . . The second time, in a motorboat, far out in the center of a large lake, at high noon, with a strong off-shore wind, and no one else visible out on the lake. At that time I had become anxious. . ." (25).

Michael was asked, "What are you afraid will happen if you run out of gas?" "My motor won't run and then I'll die," he announced, still tearful.

↑↑

Developmental psychologists and educators tend to emphasize the young child's lack of conceptual ability. He is not yet mentally equipped to understand death. But the corollary too often is neglected: the young child tries to understand.

↑↑

The psychologist then remembered how he and a student had spoken in the boy's presence about how their motor had "died" while they had been puttering with an old car some weeks previously. One of them had also said, "The battery's dead." Dr. Brent asked his boy, "Is that what you are afraid of . . . that your bottle is like gasoline, and like, when the car runs out of gas, the car dies, so if you run out of food, you die?" Michael shook his head, "Yes." But this first attempt at a reassuring explanation did not come across. It was only when he provided the following explanation that Michael understood and relaxed.

"But a car has a key, right? (Michael nods.) And we can turn it on and off anytime we like, right? (I feel him relaxing now.) But where's *your* key? (I lift his shirt playfully and look at his belly button.) Is this your key? (He laughs.) Lemme see. Can I turn your motor on and off? (He laughs again.) See. You are really nothing like a car. Nobody can turn you on and off. Once your motor's on, you don't have to worry about it dying. You can sleep through the whole night, and your motor will keep running without you ever having to fill it up with gas. Do you know what I mean?" (He answers, 'Yes,' and I feel his body relax.)" That night, Michael slept through—without a bottle.

Yet even at this early age, Michael's "death history" was more complex than what has already been reported. Upon further thought his father could piece together a series of incidents that began as far back as his 21st month, when a pet parakeet died. Subsequent incidents included observing his baby sister's umbilical cord fall off during a bath, and his seemingly endless questions about the status of a dead relative whose photograph he had seen.

With this second "case history" before us it would be possible to illustrate a number of additional points. We will concentrate, however, upon three implications that are worth keeping in mind:

1 Exposure to death can contribute, directly or indirectly, to emotional and behavioral disturbances in early childhood. This supplements the material reported previously to the effect that early bereavement experiences may be related to disturbances many years later.

2 Ambiguities in adult language and thought are apt to confuse the young child as he attempts to make sense out of death. At the same time, however, these ambiguities help to introduce him to symbolic usages. Death has more than one meaning; context is important. It is difficult to comprehend how both a battery and a person can be "dead," but in different ways. As he matures, he will be even more versatile in his application of the death concept (e.g., "dead" center, "dying for a cigarette," "aborted" campaign, "deathly silence," etc.). Right from the beginning, then, the infant has the complicated task of learning what is meant by death both in the basic physical sense of the term, and in its varied metaphoric applications.

3 Michael's questioning, so difficult to satisfy, and David's look of puzzlement and uncertainty attest to the fact that death already is providing an intellectual challenge. As we have noted, developmental psychologists

and educators tend to emphasize the young child's lack of conceptual ability. He is not yet mentally equipped to understand death (even to the limited extent that his elders are equipped). But the corollary too often is neglected: the young child *tries* to understand. He is able to recognize that a problem has risen before his eyes. And he may persist in his efforts to solve the problem. We err if we simply compare the child's conceptual structure with our own. Such a comparison does little except to confirm the obvious. Would it not be more instructive if we observed the young child's mental operations for their own sake? Patient, unbiased research might be rewarded in many ways. Most relevantly, perhaps, we might discover that the problem of death is the first vital intellectual challenge to engage the child's mind and, as such, is a prime stimulus to his continued mental development. How can we have ignored this possibility so long?

Intimations of Self-Mortality

Observing a young child's response to death (whether of a bird or a motor) has some advantages. Much remains to guess-work. But at least we can establish that a death stimulus was present; therefore, the child's response has some relationship to the stimulus. However, it is exceptionally difficult to ascertain when and how a very young child is concerned about death in the absence of any stimulus that can be perceived by us. An older child can tell us that he is thinking about death. But we are unlikely to hear this from even an unusually verbal sub-two-year-old.

At one extreme it could be argued that "out of sight, out of mind" applies completely in the case of the very young child. We should not allow ourselves to imagine that he has any thoughts or feelings oriented toward death when no relevant stimuli are present (a large assumption is made in this argument; namely, that adults are capable of judging what is a relevant stimulus for what kind of mental activity in a young child). The advocate of this position is also likely to contend that, even in the presence of obvious death stimuli, the very young child does not begin to approach the adult conception. This is a persuasive argument when we recall our previous analysis of the proposition "I will die." We do not expect the very young to possess *any*, let alone *all*, of the intellectual resources that are implied by the statement of personal mortality.

At the other extreme, however, it has been proposed that the infant is already tuning himself in to the d-e-a-t-h wavelength. Adah Maurer is a spokesman for this challenging view (26). She begins by calling attention to the periodic alternation of experiences in the newborn. This is a phenomenon that was mentioned earlier in this discussion and upon which a number of other observers have commented. No controversy so far.

Next, Maurer suggests that periodic alternations such as the sleep-waking cycle endow the infant with a basic appreciation of the dichotomy between *being* and *non-being.* This leads to the additional proposition that the infant is capable of *experimentation.* In fact, Maurer seems to be proposing that experimentation with the states of being and non-being is involved in some of the infant's very earliest behavior patterns:

> By the time he is three months old, the healthy baby is secure enough in his self feelings to be ready to experiment with these contrasting states. In the game of peek-a-boo, he replays in safe circumstances the alternate terror and delight, confirming his sense of self by risking and regaining complete consciousness. A light cloth spread over his face and body will elicit an immediate and forceful reaction. Short, sharp intakes of breath, vigorous thrashing of arms and legs removes the erstwhile shroud to reveal widely staring eyes that scan the scene with frantic alertness until they lock glances with the smiling mother, whereupon he will wriggle and laugh with joy. . . . To the empathetic observer, it is obvious that he enjoyed the temporary dimming of the light, the blotting out of the reassuring face and the suggestion of a lack of air which his own efforts enabled him to restore, his aliveness additionally confirmed by the glad greeting implicit in the eye-to-eye oneness with another human (27).

Maurer claims that the term, "peek-a-boo" derives from an Old English phrase meaning "alive or dead?" In her view, the infant and toddler's first "games" are not to be dismissed as irrelevant to subsequent development. She believes these activities should be regarded as a crucial part of the long-term process of developing a self identity. Beyond "peak-a-boo," the very young child is likely to engage in a variety of disappearance-and-return games. These are little experiments with non-being or death.

"During the high-chair age, babies persist in tossing away a toy and fretting for someone to return it. If one has patience to replace the toy on the tray a dozen or twenty times, the reward is a child in ecstasy" (28). Gradually, the child learns that some things do not return. "All-gone" becomes one of his earliest and most useful expressions. The child's next line of research may focus upon all-goneness. Three examples are cited by Maurer: "Offer a two-year-old a lighted match and watch his face light up with demonic glee as he blows it out. Notice the willingness with which he helps his mother if the errand is to step on the pedal and bury his banana peel in the covered garbage can. The toilet makes a still better sarcophagus until he must watch in awed dismay while the plumber fishes out the Tinkertoy from the overflowing bowl" (29).

No doubt, these statements by Maurer will be received skeptically (if not increduously) by some readers, and enthusiastically by others. She has left herself open to the criticism of reading much too much into infant behavior. Those who do not object too strenuously to Maurer's approach may nevertheless object to her specific interpretations. How can she be so sure, for example, that the infant experiences "terror" during the blackout phase of his periodic alternations? Sleep is natural and basic. There is no good reason why a healthy baby should experience sleep as an unpleasant state, or become apprehensive as sleep approaches. Is it not more likely that "terror" and other dysphoric affects develop as *learned* associations to darkness or sleep? In our own observations, uneasiness about being in a dark room usually is absent in infancy and early childhood, appearing toward the end of the preschool period. And if Maurer is using terms such as "terror" in a literary rather than a precise sense, then what *is* she actually saying about the infant's mental life vis-a-vis being and non-being? The foregoing is just one example of how one might object to Maurer's views.

Nevertheless, we believe it is important for improved understanding of human development (including, but not limited to conceptions of death) that some investigators take very seriously the possibility that significant processes are in operation very early. We would direct your attention to such factors as the following:

1 It is all too easy for us, even the developmental specialists among us, to become entangled in theoretical fashions of the day. Whether we insist that the infant already is in possession of enormous psychological resources, or that he is simply a noisy tabula rasa, our contentions are likely to be based upon the general social climate as much as upon scientific considerations per se. Historian Philippe Aries, for example, has shown how conceptions of infancy and childhood have changed markedly over the centuries (30). Even closer to home, psychiatrist Martha Wolfenstein has provided an amusing (if disconcerting) analysis of how the all-American baby has altered his basic personality makeup several times during the course of the present century alone (31). Her material is drawn from "official" pronouncements about infant development and care. One

389

has to conclude, of course, that it is the doctrine rather than the infant who changes so radically every few years. The lesson for us should be one of readiness to consider any potentially useful approach to understanding human development, free from the blinders of contemporary (and temporary) "establishment" orientations.

2 "How does a person ever come to understand that he will die, when he has never died before?" Questions such as these appear especially formidable if we ignore early clues because they are subtle and ambiguous. Careful exploration of *possibly* death-related experiences right from the beginnings of postnatal life would provide us with a long series of clues. We would not be forced to shrug our shoulders philosophically or maintain that the adult *suddenly* grasps the essence of personal mortality without any relevant preparation. Whether or not Maurer is correct in her specific observations and interpretations, it seems quite sensible to consider the *possibility* that very early behavior patterns have some relevance to subsequent conceptions of life and death.

3 For us, one of the most persuasive or promising aspects of Maurer's viewpoint is her description of the infant's total involvement in his (assumed) being/non-being games. The three-month-old baby is by no means aloof from his little experiments. He is *organismically* involved ("Short, sharp intakes of breath, vigorous thrashing of arms and legs. . ."). This description appears to be consistent with several of the most astute theoretical models available in the area of human development, notably, those of Kurt Goldstein (32), Kurt Lewin (33), and Heinz Werner (34). From all these models we would expect the infant to respond in a general, undifferentiated mode. In current jargon, we might say he is really "turned on," not holding anything back from his present moment of experiencing. It makes sense that subsequent *concepts* of death gradually would be differentiated out of preconceptual experiences. Although neither Maurer nor the above theoreticians seem to make this point explicitly, it does seem in keeping with their approaches. And this leads us to a further elaboration of our account of death experiences in early childhood.

4 Earlier we proposed that death *perceptions* probably are forerunners of death conceptions. Now we move back a step in the hypothetical series: First, there may be the infant's experiences of the alternations in his own internal states. Then, if Maurer is correct, he actively seeks out experiences of coming-and-going, appearing-and-disappearing. This is a stage

of organismic participation. Later (but still in childhood), he is able to stand a little apart from what he observes. He *perceives* death or death-like attributes in the situation. Still later (beyond early childhood, perhaps) he develops the type of cognitive structures to which the term "conceptions" ordinarily is applied.

5 Those developmentalists whose primary interest is in understanding the emergence of the sense of self-integrity may also find these considerations relevant. Perhaps we should not expect to find evidences of self-mortality awareness until the sense of self has itself been fairly well established. But it is also possible that the sense of self develops with an intimate relationship to the dynamics of being/non-being or presence/absence. If this is the case, then subsequent threatened dissolution of the self (e.g., impending death in old age) can be understood partially in relationship to the coordinated development of self and death concepts years before.

In general, we are taking the position here that much experiencing and behavior relevant to death takes place during infancy and early childhood. Some fairly specific suggestions have been made, all of which require systematic investigation if they are to be confirmed or disconfirmed. Although we have made reference to the work of several other researchers and observers, the reader should not blame them for the way in which we have used their materials in offering our own formulations.

Now we can proceed further along the developmental trail with the amiable prospect before us of having more data available from which tentative interpretations might be advanced.

DEATH CONCEPTIONS IN MIDDLE AND LATE CHILDHOOD

A four-year-old girl is conversing with her 84-year-old great-grandmother: "You are old. That means you will die. I am young, so I won't die, you know." This excerpt from the conversation suggests that the little girl knows what it means to die, even if she has not entirely grasped the relationship between age and death. However, a moment later, she adds: "But it's all right, Gran'mother. Just make sure you wear your *white* dress. Then, after you die, you can marry Nomo (great-grandfather) again, and have babies" (35).

Words such as "dead" and "die" are fairly common in children's conversation. Often enough, as in the above example, they are used with some sense of appropriateness. Yet an additional spontaneous comment ("Then, after you die, you can marry Nomo again, and have babies") or a little questioning by the adult is likely to reveal that the child's understanding of death is quite different from our own. In the following discussion we will be concerned chiefly with the development of the concept of personal mortality, but related topics will also be touched upon.

The most important research contribution in this field was made by psychologist Maria Nagy two decades ago (36). Although her investigation involved Hungarian children, there have been no subsequent indications that her findings require significant modifications when applied to children in the United States. We will consider her study in some detail.

ʃʃʃ

> *The preschool child usually does not recognize that death is* final. *However, he also looks upon death as being continuous with life, that is, deadness is a diminution of aliveness.*

ʃʃʃ

Her respondents ranged in age from three to ten years. They all lived in or around Budapest. Nagy spoke with each of the 378 children to elicit their thoughts and feelings regarding death. The older children (six to ten) also made drawings to represent their ideas of death. In some cases these children were able to write their own explanations of the drawings. Children aged seven and above were asked to "Write down everything that comes to your mind about death." Nagy's sample was almost equally divided between girls and boys, and she made an effort to include children with various social and religious backgrounds, and with a broad spectrum of intellectual functioning.

Nagy found that her results could be categorized into three major developmental phases. Overlapping does occur, she reported, but it remains possible to identify three fairly discrete states of thought which occur in a particular sequence:

Stage One: present until about age five   The preschool child usually does not recognize that death is *final*. This is probably the most significant charac-

teristic of the first stage. However, he also looks upon death as being continuous with life, that is, deadness is a diminution of aliveness. Nagy's
youngest subjects gave two variations on the theme that the dead are still,
in a sense, alive: "(a) death is a departure, a sleep—this denies death entirely;
and (b) the child recognizes the fact of physical death but cannot separate
it from life—he considers death as gradual or temporary" (37).

A close relationship is seen between death and departure. The person
who has gone away is sort of dead. And the dead person has sort of gone
away. "To die . . . means the same as living on but under changed circumstances. If someone dies no change takes place in him, but rather our lives
change since we can no longer see the dead person as he no longer lives
with us" (38). Given this interpretation of death, the child is most likely to
be distressed by its aspect of *separation*.

> Most children, however, are not satisfied when someone dies that he
> should merely disappear, but want to know where and how he
> continues to live. Most of the children connected the facts of absence
> and funerals. In the cemetery one lives on. Movement is to a certain
> degree limited by the coffin, but for all that the dead are still capable
> of growth. They take nourishment, they breathe. They know what is
> happening on earth. They feel it if someone thinks of them and they
> even feel sorry for themselves. Thus the dead live in the grave.
> However, the children realize—with a resulting aversion for death—
> that this life is limited, not so complete as our life. Some of them
> consider this diminished life exclusively restricted to sleep (39).

A number of Nagy's illustrative cases resemble the example we used to
open this section. The child first speaks of death in what seems to be realistic
terms, but subsequent remarks reveal that death is seen as partial or reversible. In particular, Nagy's children typically seem to begin their remarks
with the description of a death *perception*. The perception appears authentic
and accurate enough. It is the mental elaboration upon the perception that
goes astray (according to adult standards). This characteristic of Nagy's
protocols, then, tends to support our suggestion that clear perceptions of
death-related phenomena are possible early in life even if the child does not
yet possess a mature framework within which to interpret and contain them.

Stage Two: between the ages of five and nine   The distinguishing characteristic of this stage is that the child now tends to *personify* death. Although
images of death in the form of a person occurred at all ages Nagy studied,
this was the dominant view for the five-to-nine age range. She found two

general forms of the personification: death is seen as a separate person, or death is himself a dead person.

A number of her respondents spoke about a "death-man" who goes about principally at night. He is difficult to see, although one might get a glimpse of him just before he carries you away. But death may also be a skeleton-man, an angel, or someone who looks like a circus clown, among other variations.

The child now seems to comprehend that death is final. This is obviously an important shift in his thinking. (Unfortunately, Nagy does not report those facets of her data which she interprets as establishing the child's grasp of death as definitive; it might be worthwhile to investigate this point again.) But the second or middle stage view of death retains another protective feature: personal death can be avoided. Run faster than the deathman, lock the door, trick him, somehow elude Mr. Death and you will not die. As Nagy puts it "Death is still outside us and is also not general" (40). . . .

Stage Three: ages nine and ten (and, presumably, thereafter)   The oldest children in Nagy's study tended to have a clear recognition that death is not only final but *inevitable*. It will happen to them, too. The nine- or ten-year-old child knows that everybody in the world will die. Death is universal as well as inevitable. "It is a thing from which our bodies cannot be resurrected. It is like the withering of flowers" (41), one of her ten-year-old girls explained to Nagy.

With Nagy's three stages still in mind as an organizing structure, let us branch out to consider some other observations. First we will touch upon other reports of children's death conceptions, then we will briefly explore some closely related aspects of mental development.

One of the most interesting contributions to this topic was made by psychologist Sylvia Anthony with the guidance of psychoanalyst J. C. Flugel. Her explorations into *The Child's Discovery of Death* (42) were made in Great Britain during 1937–39. A study in mental development, it also "gained deeper topical significance from events occurring as its last words are written. In this and other countries millions of young children have been separated from their parents and taken away to other billets. As the imminence of danger fluctuates, families in each country are separated or re-united. In many countries of Europe now, young children's fathers are under arms, and the shadow of death hangs over the families they come from" (43). Anthony could not have known at the time that the shadow of death hovered not only over the men-at-arms, but also over women and children to an extent that people were not prepared to expect in warfare among "civilized" nations. Today we still do not know precisely what is to be attributed to war and other social conditions, and what is to be considered as "intrinsic" to the child's conception of death. . . .

Because Anthony reported her observations in a somewhat discursive fashion, subsequent authors have tended merely to note that she performed a "classic" or "pioneering" study without summarizing her specific results. We will consider her work in enough detail to convey the gist of her contribution.

Part of her study was concentrated upon a small number of children whose families agreed to maintain Home Records of questions, remarks, or responses on the subject of death. The observations were to be recorded as soon as possible, following their occurrence. Thirteen children from five families were involved in this aspect of the study.

The other part of her study involved an additional 117 children. Most of these were "normals," but she also included 11 from a school for mental defectives, and 26 who were being treated for behavioral or emotional problems at a child guidance clinic. Most (but not all) of the children were given both a story completion test and the 1937 revision of the Stanford-Binet test of intelligence. The particular story completion test selected for this purpose had been devised by M. Thomas at the Institut Jean Jacques Rousseau, in Geneva (44). Previous use of this procedure had indicated that a high proportion of children made reference to death in their responses—even though the story openings themselves did not mention death. Anthony made a few modifications in the Vocabulary section of the Stanford-Binet test, the most relevant of which was the addition of the word "dead" between the fourth and fifth items on the standard list. (We are reminded by Anthony that the Binet includes a number of death-stimulus items, e.g., "In an old graveyard in Spain they have discovered a small skull which they believe to be that of Christopher Columbus when he was about ten years old." This is one of the Verbal Absurdity items. The original Binet test had an even more salient presentation of death stimuli, i.e., a girl cut up into 18 pieces who was supposed to have killed herself in this way. Anthony used the revised form from which this item had been deleted.)

Perhaps the clearest and most pervasive finding throughout the total range of materials was that normal children often think of death. Depending upon the method of scoring employed, Anthony found between 46 and

60 percent of the children making some reference to death in their test responses or in spontaneous remarks made to her. Anthony adds that "Obviously it is impossible that children should think about death *less* than they speak about it. And since these story openings present the children with situations which they can and do immediately envisage in terms of their own daily life, the results certainly suggest that the thought of death comes readily to their minds" (45).

The investigator also points out that the specific nature of the answer varied quite a bit from one child to another (she offers many examples of these responses throughout her book). Furthermore, although some story openings elicited more death themes than did others, the children also varied considerably in terms of which cues stimulated their own particular thoughts of death. "Normal" and "problem" children did not differ from each other in the number of death-oriented responses given.

Can anything be deduced from Anthony's data about the types of themes that are most likely to elicit death ideas from children? She finds two themes to be dominant: ". . . death as sorrowful separation and . . . death as the ultimate result of aggression stand out as the main typical connotations of the idea by whatever method we have studied it. We trace them not so much through the direct word-response of the children, as by the context in which they produce a response that has reference to death" (46). The *sorrow* theme often was associated with the loss of a child by a parent, or the loss of a parent by a child. Death was seen primarily as separation and loneliness. The *fear of agression* theme involved death as the ultimate outcome of violent actions (*e.g.*, a burglar breaking into the house, and then starting to attack its occupants).

The observations that have been mentioned up to this point are not linked to any particular theoretical approach. Let us now sample a few of the psychoanalytic interpretations that Anthony offers from her inspection of the children's fantasy-responses. She notes that, on an *unconscious* level of the child's thought, death by drowning may be identified with prenatal life in the womb. One of her subjects, for example, said that mother was sad because "the child was paddling in the water, and a great big fish came up and ate her." In a later response, the girl's mother was said to have "heard someone crying in the bedroom, and it was a lovely new baby for her, and the same name as the other little girl." Anthony suggests that "here we see clearly the association of death with natal life, and the logical conclusion of that identification in the rebirth of the same person. Occasionally the association of death with drowning, and the suggestions of womb symbolism, occur in another context: For instance, Freddie feared that the burglar who killed him would put his body in a sack and throw it in the river" (47).

Another common fantasy centered around the "bird's-nesting" theme. We will just mention the following typical elements from this complex material: (a) the child fantasies that a boy has "accidentally" broken eggs that he discovered in a nest; (b) later, he feels guilty about this action; (c) fears that he will be punished for this aggression, *e.g.*, by being taken away and destroyed by a giant; and (d) he then turns to his mother for protection, wishing to remain snug and safe in his own "nest."

Interpretation of this type of response is difficult to follow because Anthony (probably with Flugel's collaboration) attempts to explore its ramifications at several different levels at the same time. It seems to us that these interpretations can be sorted into three levels:

Psychosexual Developmental Stage   Anthony proposes that the bird's-nest theme is intimately associated with the oedipal complex. The boy wants mother all for himself (*e.g.*, destroying sibling eggs and taking on the characteristics of a powerful father who can destroy competitors). But this daring act exposes him to the wrath of father-giant. The boy is sent scurrying back to his uncompetitive role as a baby bird under mother's wing.

Moral Law   The child is a firm believer in the "law of the talion." This, of course, is the time-honored "eye-for-an-eye" principle. His own aggressive behavior is bound to result in aggressive actions being carried out upon him. (From both a psychoanalytic and a developmental-organismic viewpoint, we would expect the child to be somewhat vague in his distinction between thought and action. Therefore, even if he has merely played with the idea of doing something violent, he may feel that he has marked himself for retaliation.)

Primitive Organization of Thought   The talion dynamics involve oscillation. One is the aggressor; then one is aggressed-upon. However, Anthony suggests that there is a type of mental oscillation that is more basic, perhaps even more primitive than the law of the talion itself (which is usually considered to be about as "primitive" as any law related to psychic functioning). "The impression is given that the idea of retaliation itself, primitive as it is, develops from a manner of thought still more general and primitive. This manner of thought is an oscillation of attention, by which a whole fantasy or thought-complex is alternately seen in primary and then in reversed aspect, and then again in primary. Thus, a mother loses her child by death, and then the mother herself dies; and then the child (or a substitute) is alive again; and then the mother comes back, too" (48).

Anthony continues this line of reasoning by suggesting that oscillation of attention in *fantasy* has a parallel with oscillation or fluctuation of attention in *perception:*

> In the laboratory we find that if we fix our eyes on a pattern of dots or a figure in ambiguous perspective, after a time the pattern changes before our eyes, independently of our volition, and after going through one or more such changes, returns to the original phase; and this process will continue so long as we maintain our attention on the same object. In the oscillations of fantasy, however, the phenomenon is complicated by the fact that each phase is to some extent affected by the experiences that precede it. Thus, if a mother loses her child by death (primary phase), there is a suggestion of remorse associated with her own death (secondary phase); the birth of another child or of some substitute involves reparation and forgiveness, so that we revert to the primary phase but with richer connotations; and the mother, or her motherhood, can now return to make everything just and right (secondary phase) (49).

Complicated? Yes, but what actually takes place is probably a good bit more complicated than what has been described above, as Anthony herself points out. At least two of the additional factors should be mentioned here. One factor concerns the *origin* of the oscillation tendency. Anthony suggests that this might be traced back to very early infancy, specifically to the feeding situation. First in fantasy, then in overt behavior, the infant may exchange places (oscillate) with his mother with respect to who is feeding and who is being fed. "Infants barely weaned, long before they can walk or talk, may be seen spontaneously to offer their biscuit to their mother to eat. . ." (50).

The second factor concerns more directly the relationship between mental oscillation and the development of the death conception. The tendency for the child's cognitive pendulum to swing back and forth makes it natural for him to replace "He is dead" with "I am dead," and vice versa. In other words, the implication is that the child does not have two completely independent lines of development for personal mortality and death-of-the-other. Whenever the thought of death enters his mind he is likely to put it through both orientations. Furthermore, the continuing shifts between self-and-other do not end where they began. The child's thoughts and feelings on this subject become refined and enriched as he proceeds. Retaliation, for example, tends to give way to fantasies of reparation, which is a more complex and sophisticated concept.

ↆↆↆ

A "magical" quality pervades much of children's thought about death. Of particular interest is the notion that an angry thought or intention directed toward somebody makes the child, in effect, a murderer.

ↆↆↆ

There is much more in Anthony's materials and interpretations than can be presented here. But at least brief mention should be made of several of her other observations:

1 The idea of death in children seems to draw much of its emotional component from its links with birth anxiety, and with aggressive impulses.

2 A "magical" quality pervades much of children's thought about death. By "magic," Anthony means the child tends to believe that events *happen* in a certain way because he *thinks* about them in a certain way. There are many "magical" ways of thinking about death. Of particular interest is the notion that an angry thought or intention directed toward somebody makes the child, in effect, a murderer.

3 The example of magical thinking mentioned above is probably related to the sense of *guilt* that children often seem to experience when a person (or animal) in their lives actually dies. Guilt is a psychological condition that has strong cognitive and affective components. In the child, at least, the cognitive component of guilt ("I am really responsible for his death") can be understood by what has already been described about magical thinking. There is also an important practical implication here: adults may fail to recognize that guilt *is* one of the child's typical reactions to death. The child thus may be given no opportunity to relieve himself of this painful frame of mind. He may even, inadvertently, be made to feel more guilty by what adults say and do.

The studies we have considered so far have used the following general types of methodology: retrospective-questionnaire (Hall-Scott), retrospective-demographic (Brown), retrospective-clinical (Moriarty), contemporaneous-interview/testing (Nagy, Anthony), and short-term longitudinal diaries (Anthony). Two additional types of methodology have been applied directly to the study of death conceptions in childhood.

Many child psychotherapists have had the opportunity to make direct observations of children's death-oriented conversation and behavior while conducting or viewing "play" sessions. One will encounter occasional references to "death play" in many clinical case reports. The work of Gregory Rochlin is of particular interest here, because he has been conducting such sessions with "normal" or "undisturbed" children for the express purpose of understanding their interpretations of death. He has studied children between the ages of three and five. Rochlin and the child would play together on several occasions while a hidden microphone recorded the proceedings. The method appears to be a successful one, although the therapist-investigator has to be patient enough to devote between three and five sessions before sufficient material is obtained. Because this method combines a measure of control and standardization along with a sense of naturalness and the opportunity for direct observation, it obviously has important advantages.

Considering the difference in methodology from what has been reported previously, it is interesting to note that Rochlin's playmates behaved in ways that were quite consistent with the data reported by Nagy and Anthony. A three-and-a-half-year-old boy, for example, knocks a whole family of dolls out of their chairs. First, the victims are to be taken to the hospital. But then they are moved to a sink with running water. The boy indicates the doll-people are scared because they will die: "No more. He'll be all-gone. He died. He goes down the pipe." "Not really." "Yup. Down the sewer. He gets died. The pipe and the sewer is where he goes down." (He eats candy and then says) "They have to have some food." "But they're dead. Food for the dead ones?" "Yes, they're hungry." (He puts another doll down the drain.) "If you're dead, don't you stay dead?" "No, you grow again. You don't stay dead" (51).

The perceptive reader will see that this brief excerpt from one of Rochlin's sessions confirms many of the observations that have been made by less direct means. Perhaps we can be fairly confident that some of the major aspects of the child's view of death have, indeed, been discovered.

Among Rochlin's other observations, we would like to call attention to the following:

1 When somebody in his own life has died, the child is apt to become fearful that others will also leave him by death. Increased fears of separation and questioning about where people have gone may be expected as typical responses to death (even if the deceased person was not very well known to the child).

2 Death play may serve an important denial function for the young child. Rochlin describes, for example, how a four-year-old boy reacted, in his play, to the impact of two actual deaths (grandfather, and a friend of his father's). "His play emphasized dolls who became ill and had nothing further happen to them. Planes would crash with no effect on the passengers. Operations on tonsils, being boiled in a tub or being burned, led to no harm. He did not want to talk about people being killed. It was, he admitted, too sad" (52). Apparently, this young boy was attempting to master or neutralize death through these play maneuvers.

3 In general, Rochlin's observations lead him to the conclusion that "at a very early age well-developed mental faculties are functioning to defend oneself against the realization that life may end. An elaborate system of psychological defenses may be observed" (53).

Unlike those writers whose views are conditioned by academic or psychometric studies of mental development, Rochlin believes that the young child *does* realize that death is inevitable. He contends that the child brings all of his resources to bear upon this threatening realization. He does not claim that the young child entertains adult conceptions of dying or death, but he does argue that the child understands *enough* to organize his thoughts and feelings protectively against these threats.

The controlled *experimental* method has also been employed in this area of inquiry, although sparingly. Irving E. Alexander and Arthur M. Adlerstein demonstrated that laboratory-type procedures could be employed to investigate at least certain parameters of death sensitivity (54). Although their experiment was chiefly concerned with the child's affective (or emotional) response to death, it has implications for understanding his cognitive response as well.

The subjects for this study were 108 boys between the ages of five and sixteen (but only one at each of the age extremes). Most of the children were summer campers from low-income families. None of the children was known to have a psychiatric history.

In contrast to the preceding studies, Alexander and Alderstein concentrated upon objective, quantitative methods. . . . The investigators were at pains to avoid any possible intrusion of subjective or other uncontrolled factors. These precautions seem to exceed those which were exercised in any of the other investigations. It is fairly typical, of course, for early, exploratory studies in a particular area to be qualitative and semi-controlled, giving way eventually to "tighter" research designs.

The boys were given individual testing sessions during which time they were asked to say the first word that came into their minds when a stimulus word was presented (word association task). The time lag between presentation and response was recorded. In addition, a psychophysiological measurement was taken. Changes in skin resistance (galvanic skin responses, GSR) were obtained from the palm and dorsal surface of the boys' right hands. The stimulus words consisted of three sets, each of which was equivalent to the others with respect to frequency of usage in the language, length, and number of syllables. One set was comprised of "neutral" or base-level words. Another set was made up of words that were likely to arouse emotions in children (e.g., mama, papa, child, love, kiss). The critical set consisted of three "death" words: buried, kill, and dead. These words were separated from each other during the presentation sequences.

For all the boys, taken as a group, the death words seemed to make a difference. They were slower in giving a verbal association to the death words, and their skin resistance decreased. The interpretation was that death words led to heightened emotional arousal.

But there also were age differences in response. Although the youngest (five through eight years) and oldest (thirteen through sixteen years) children in this sample showed decreased skin resistance to death words, the middle group had the same skin resistance response to both death and non-death words. How might this pattern be explained? Alexander and Adlerstein suggest that "death has a greater emotional significance for people with less stable ego self-pictures than people with an adequate concept of the self. . . . The interval from the ninth through the twelfth year has been labeled the preadolescent period, a time of latency. . . . No great new demands calling for marked change in response patterns are introduced" (55).

In other words, if ever a child has a "breathing space" in his life to consolidate his gains and develop his skills, it is in this period immediately preceding the adolescent quest for individual identity. . . . Important here from the cognitive standpoint is that the *saliency* of the death concept may be regarded as a function of amount of psychosocial stress upon the individual. More specifically, we are referring to forms of stress which challenge or complicate the individual's sense of selfhood. Perhaps the sense of uncertainty or disorganization in "who-I-am" brings to mind the concern that "I-may-be-not." There is the implication that latency-age and adolescent boys may differ not so much in the *content* of their death conceptions, but rather in how *significant* a role these conceptions play in their total mental life.

SOME CONCEPTS RELATED TO DEATH

Animism

Now let us consider a few of the other concepts whose developmental careers intertwine with the concept of death. One of the most relevant concepts is *animism*, or the tendency to impute life to nonliving entities. This, of course, is not identical with the idea of death per se. It is the distinction between living and nonliving that concerns us at the moment.

Perhaps we should begin by recognizing that the term most typically is meant to imply immature or deviant thinking. If the child declares that the squirrel running across the lawn is alive, we would not ordinarily describe this as an "animistic" concept; it is simply being "accurate." But we would consider him to be animistic if he attributed life to a mechanical squirrel, the lawnmower, a squirrel-tailed cap, etc.

The observations and theoretical formulations of Jean Piaget are important with respect to this as with respect to so many other topics in mental development. Piaget maintains that animism is one of the earliest characteristics of the child's thought (56). It is, in fact, based on a "primitive mental structure." The young child does not differentiate between mental and physical realms as clearly as he will when he becomes an adult. Among other implications, this means that he is likely to see external objects in his own image, that is, as live and conscious beings. There is a converse side to this animism: the child is also likely to treat mental phenomena as though they were physical. (We have already touched upon a related phenomenon: the child's tendency to respond as though his angry thoughts had *caused* somebody to die.)

Piaget views animism as undergoing a developmental transformation that is very much in keeping with the general pattern of mental growth. We move, in other words, from the relatively diffuse and undifferentiated to the specific and differentiated. In broad outline, this is also the position of the other premier mental developmentalist of our day, Heinz Werner (57). The young child is said to interpret most activity as the activity of living creatures. Almost everything is alive, or could be alive under the right conditions (water, when it flows; clouds, when they move, etc.). Gradually, the child learns to restrict this category. He progressively excludes certain phenomena from the ranks of the living. He also reduces the amount of consciousness and purpose he is willing to attribute to the non-alive objects he still regards as living. For example, no longer does he regard a table as being alive in any sense of the word, but the moon may retain a more limited kind of "aliveness" because it floats up in the sky "on its own."

Research stimulated by Piaget's ideas has been conducted on Chinese (58) and Swedish (59) as well as American (60) children. The results confirm at least part of Piaget's thesis, namely, that children, especially young children, do have difficulty in distinguishing living from nonliving objects. However, Piaget, as we have seen, had more than this limited proposition in mind. It would appear that his broader formulations have not been as clearly confirmed, at least not in the opinions of some of the independent investigators. A Swedish researcher, Gote Klingberg (61), has offered an alternative explanation of findings in this area. Instead of assuming that the child fundamentally thinks differently and more "primitively" than the adult, why not simply say that the child begins in ignorance and must learn gradually how to make the distinction between living and nonliving? In other words, we should not exaggerate the difference between the basic mental structure of child and adult. It is more a question of learning and experience.

Klingberg's view does seem consistent with some of the findings obtained both by herself and by other investigators. The data indicate that the younger the child, the more likely he is to make errors of over-inclusion. The data do not show precisely that children *think* that much differently from adults. There are also some indications that children abandon their "animistic" thinking somewhat earlier than Piaget reckoned. (But Piaget himself was more interested in establishing the basic stages through which animistic thought passes than in pinning down a standard timetable by which one traverses the stages.) Another interesting trend is the apparent close similarity between children of different nations (as different as the Swedes and the Chinese) in their designation of particular objects as living or nonliving.

We suggest that theories and research on the topic of "animistic" thinking in children may have the following implications for our understanding of the concept of death:

1 By adult standards, the child begins with "inaccurate" interpretations of both life (or perhaps we should say "livingness") and death. These interpretations become increasingly more "accurate" with age, i.e., they come to resemble the concepts of the parental generations.

2 The directionality of the "error" in both instances may possibly reflect the same underlying bias in the child's mind. It is a bias in favor of life. All that is active pertains to life, or is not distinguishable from "livingness." And all that is alive now will continue to be alive (even though subject to disappearances and interruptions).

3 With both concepts, it remains unclear how much of the discernible change reflects an intrinsic, more-or-less built-in developmental program, and how much is a function of learning experiences within a particular psychosocial milieu. Those who emphasize the intrinsic developmental-stages approach tend to regard the young child as fundamentally more different from his elders than do those who attribute the changes to learning and experience. One's position on this question is likely to affect both the nature and the extent of educational or other efforts to influence the child's conceptions of life and death.

4 Surprisingly, there do not seem to have been any developmental studies directed at examining the relationship between concepts of life and death in the same children. Therefore, we do not know, for example, if those children who lag in their tendency to differentiate between the living and the nonliving also are slower or otherwise idiosyncratic in their attainment of death concepts. We have very little information on the general relationship between these two sets of concepts during the early years of life—only separate studies that cannot really be combined.

5 Theoretically, we should expect the relationship between the two concepts to change with age. The child "should" at first be unable to differentiate between the question: living or nonliving? and the question: what is it for living to become dead? The more specific distinction between nonliving and dead should take even longer to become clear to the child (e.g., the stone is not alive, but is not dead; the bird is dead). The discrimination between nonliving and dead is another problem that seems to lack for research attention. And the general theoretical expectation we have suggested here remains in limbo because of the neglect of research into the relationship between the development of life and death concepts, already mentioned.

405

6 Data regarding both concepts (and general theory on mental development) suggest that the adult versions usually are attained by the pre-adolescent or early adolescent years. It is taken for granted that there are individual differences. It would appear that the "mature" or adult concepts for both life and death occur at about the same time.

7 There is evidence of various kinds to suggest that the concept of death is quite important both in the child's daily life and in his future personality. But we know very little about the significance of the living/nonliving ("animistic") distinction for the child's current adjustment and subsequent maturation.

Object and Self Constancy

We continue our sampling of death-related concepts with one of the most elusive ideas in both philosophy and individual experience. This mystery has been given many names (none of which, however, truly provide a solution). By speaking here of *self constancy* we mean only to make it a little easier to relate this concept to material that is more familiar to specialists in developmental psychology. *Object constancy* or "conservation" is, of course, a household, or laboratory word among developmentalists these days. There is abundant theory and research on this topic (again, much of it derived from Piaget). Much less attention in the form of systematic theory and controlled research has been given to the development of *self* constancy.

Let us first have a word or two about object constancy. For thousands and thousands of words on this topic, the reader will have no difficulty in finding expert treatises (62, 63). The moon is a traditional example here. Sliver, crescent, half, or full, no matter how this object in the sky presents itself to our eyes we recognize it as moon. To update this example a little, we are also capable of identifying the lunarity of the lunar body whether it is viewed in its customary guise as a relatively small object displayed within the larger visual field of the evening sky, or in its new aspect: a television-screen-filling expanse of detailed bleakness. Whether we see the "full" moon as a discrete object within its celestial context or a bit of the moon displayed over our entire visual field, moon it remains.

But it was not always thus. As children, presumably we had to learn to identify those varying shapes in the sky as all being the same. Even earlier in our development, we had to recognize that yesterday's moon and tonight's are the same. A number of observers have pointed out that some children tend to speak of "moons" even at a time when they have already begun to apply the singular/plural distinction correctly in regard to other objects. In any event, a period of development or learning experience is required before we appreciate the constancy of an object through its various transformations. Some objects are trickier than others. Piaget-type experiments often are designed to learn if a child can see his way through the visual manipulations and distractions that are presented to him, and demonstrate his command of the true constancy of the object or object-dimension in question.

Now here is what we wish to say on the topic of object constancy:

1 Disappearance or destruction of the object—"death of the object," if you will permit this phrase—cannot be conceived or appreciated unless the constancy of the object has already been established. We cannot experience the disappearance of an object unless we have already acknowledged its existence as a relatively enduring entity.

2 But constancy of the object itself has little or no meaning if the child has not already come to appreciate the phenomena of change, destruction, disappearance. The basic notion of constancy implies the possibility of nonconstancy.

ⅎⅎ

In infancy and early childhood, the disappearance or destruction of objects probably is experienced as a partial loss of the individual himself. In a sense, he disappears, too, when his mother leaves the room.

ⅎⅎ

3 In other words, we are suggesting that the child must develop the concepts of constancy and change in tandem. Each concept is in a sense "prior" to the other. Right from the start, the concept of enduring qualities is intimately related to the concept of transient or oscillating qualities. This proposition links research and theory on object constancy with . . . the child's early experience of time as periodical and circular. It is also

related to . . . our interrelated thoughts of birth and death, and our tendencies to "kill the thing we love." *We are proposing that "the death-of-the-object" is one of the earliest and most fundamental protoconcepts in the child's long progression toward mature cognitive functioning; it is not really to be separated from development of object constancy.*

4 The distinction between death-of-the-object, and death-of-the-object-that-was-once-alive probably requires developmental and learning pre-conditions. The general theoretical expectations that applied to the concepts of "livingness" and of death should apply here as well. We would expect, for example, that all three concepts are fused together in a very general cognitive orientation, and only gradually differentiated from each other.

5 In infancy and early childhood, the disappearance or destruction of objects probably is experienced as a partial loss of the individual himself. In a sense, he disappears, too, when his mother leaves the room. We do not intend to exaggerate the significance of all object losses. Many of these "losses" are trivial, and are replaced by other objects that are fully as satisfying to the child. In principle, however, the child experiences sense of self-loss whether it is a crucial or trivial object that has disappeared. That facet of the child (or that quanta of "libidinal energy") that he invested in the object has become stranded. This cognitive and affective investment of his *self*—is defunct until reinvested elsewhere. He may even "feel dead" when the object has become dead within his own perceptual and phenomenological field.

6 Suppose that a visual field were to be presented in a perfectly stable or static array. Would it be perceived or experienced as unchanging? The answer probably is in the negative, especially if we are concerned with the human eye and the human mind. Our eyes move to traverse the visual field, therefore we bring change and movement to the static array. Furthermore, what we have in mind by "mind" is mental *activity*, events, processes, currents of perception and thought. To the extent, then, that we do perceive and think, to that extent we introduce a certain level of activity and change into even a hypothetically static external world.

But there is another step to be taken here. We ourselves change over time. The changes are especially rapid and profound during precisely those years of early development that have been our concern in this discussion. Our perceptual, cognitive, and affective orientations are in transition—how, then, can *object* constancy be achieved or maintained? We raise this conundrum only to emphasize the intimate relationship between development of *self* constancy or identity and *object* constancy. A comprehensive account of human development must, we think, give full attention to both aspects, and with appreciation for their mutual influences. Even if we liked to believe that we were interested only in object constancy, we would be unlikely to develop a profound understanding of this topic without also concerning ourselves with what is happening to the self that is achieving or failing to achieve object constancy.

We turn now to a brief consideration of self constancy as this relates to the development of death concepts. (If at this point, the wary reader is expecting another of those apparently obsessive little lists to which he has been exposed so far in this book, his expectation is all too well justified.)

1 It seems unlikely to us that object constancy can run very far ahead of self constancy. There are two related but not identical implications. One implication pertains to the constancy of objects. The other implication is concerned with the constancy of the concepts themselves—but we are going to ignore that problem here.

Whatever interferes with the development of a firm sense of self constancy will make it difficult for the child to comprehend constancy external to himself. More accurately, perhaps, he will be too preoccupied with his unsettled internal state to make adequate distinctions between the enduring and transient qualities in his perceptual field. We might expect such a child to have more than the usual difficulty in achieving clear distinctions between living and nonliving objects, and in moving toward the adult concept of death.

2 The previously cited suggestion of Alexander and Adlerstein (64) also seems relevant here. These researchers reasoned that death becomes a more significant or salient concept when the individual's identity is challenged by psychosocial stress. They noted that, in American culture at least, certain periods of early development are more likely to be stressful than others. Threat to the child's self constancy might well arouse more salient thoughts of death. Yet, as we have proposed, problems in achieving or maintaining self constancy might be expected to make it more difficult for the child to understand death and related matters. There is the possibility of a "vicious circle" here: Formidable losses, challenges, or demands shake up the child's sense of identity. This turbulence tends

to bring thoughts of death and destruction to mind. But the cognitive effects of this shaky self constancy may be such as to increase his difficulties with death and related concepts.

3 It is likely that difficulties could *begin* from the death-loss-separation axis. In the present discussion, we have been regarding death concepts as the function of self constancy, which itself is influenced by role expectations, psychosocial stress, developmental level, and physical condition. But the child who has experienced painful separations from important people may develop a kind of death concern that interferes with the development of both self and object constancy. Some earlier material in this selection is consistent with this proposition. Moriarty's motherless mothers (65), for example, may have difficulty in deciding whether they are themselves, their dead mothers, or their own children.

4 We move deeper into the thicket. Forget the child and his vulnerabilities for the moment. Consider the adolescent or the young adult. The adolescent's *individuality* is likely to be a salient aspect of his total identity. It has taken him a long time to become as individual as he now feels himself to be, and he may be aware that he still has a way to go. But what does it mean to experience oneself as an individual, especially when the experience is of recent vintage? It means to experience oneself as *alone.*

To be individual and to be alone is also to be in a new kind of relationship to death. One is likely to feel more vulnerable to death, or so we believe. And the death to which he is vulnerable is itself more threatening in some respects. . . . The acute perception of individuality-aloneness seems to invite a sharpened sense of personal mortality. Although he has achieved a higher level of integration than he possessed as a child, the adolescent or young adult has not eluded the relationship between self constancy and the prospect of death. The relationship has changed, however, and it will continue to be subject to change throughout his life.

Futurity

What remains of our lives is "in" the future. But death is "there," too. Small wonder, then, that we may, at times, have mixed feelings about futurity.

Thoughts of time and death have a natural affinity for each other. It is difficult to imagine how we could form any conception of death without some conception of time. To keep this section within limits, we will concentrate upon *futurity,* referring to other aspects of time only for background and context. The interested reader will find an extensive literature on the more general topic of the meaning of time in human experience (66, 67, 68). Here, our purpose is simply to explore a few mutual implications of futurity and death concepts in cognitive development.

The young child's relationship to time and death has been touched upon several times in this discussion. We will not repeat what has already been ventured, especially under the rubrics of "You are dead," and "I will die." Let us move ahead to that station in his developmental career which marks the child's attainment of culturally mature time concepts.

As one might expect, there is a lack of agreement among researchers concerning the precise age at which it is customary for a child to achieve a solid grasp on time. In their pioneering investigation of this topic, E. C. Oakden and Mary Sturt (69) concluded that the adult's conception of time is not achieved until about age 13 or 15. This estimate is probably close to the mark. Futurity and other basic time concepts probably are attained by most boys and girls somewhere between late childhood and early adolescence. We are assuming approximately normal intellectual endowment, and a reasonably adequate psychosocial environment. There are some reasons for believing that intellectual level and social milieu are related to concepts of futurity (70, 71).

We are considering now the older child who knows that future time is *qualitatively* different from past and present time. Things that have already happened have happened in one particular way. They will never re-happen or un-happen. What is *yet* to happen? That is a different story. The future is indeterminate, a zone of possibility, of contingency. This is an exciting discovery for the child. The future is really different from what one has already experienced, from what one already *is*. We leave this discovery for a moment, but place an identification tag on it: both "hope" and "dread" begin with the appreciation of futurity as qualitatively distinct from "used" time.

Our sophisticated child also appreciates the existence of world or "objective" time. There is a constant pulse and flow of time apart from his own personal experiences. His thoughts neither initiate nor terminate external time. If this were not true, then he would never be "late," "early," "impulsive," or "dawdling": his own phenomenological world would justify any tempo at which he cared to function. He knows that he cannot truly take "time out." This insight perhaps bestows special meaning on certain organized games in which one legitimately can suspend time. Even in the game situation, however, he comes to realize that the "time out" must be taken in accordance with consensual rules that govern the total situation.

The discovery of objective time may be one of the major psychic events that force magical thinking into the mind's darker and more remote crevices. If external time is impervious to his control, then how is he to influence events in the world simply by doing things inside his head?

From this point on, it becomes difficult (and perhaps arbitrary) to distinguish between what the individual *knows* about futurity and how he *uses* what he knows. Unlike the younger child, he does not seem limited by lack of basic comprehension. The adolescent is quite capable of engaging in high level mental operations, of "thinking about thought" (72). How he orients himself to time is as much a matter of attitudes and personality structure as it is of cognitive development *per se.* Consider, for example, the results of a multi-dimensional study of time perspective in normal adolescents (73). Three findings are of particular relevance:

1 Typically, these young people directed their thoughts to the future—but only to the near future. Almost everything important in life was "just up the road a piece." The second half of their life-span was almost barren. It was uncommon for these people to express any thoughts regarding the fourth or fifth decades of their own lives, let alone the seventh, eighth, or ninth decades.

2 The past was neglected or "blanked out" as well. Not only was scant attention given to one's personal past, but there was the strong impression that these adolescents felt uneasy when asked to turn their thoughts toward where they had been, in contrast to where they were going.

3 There was a prevailing sense of rapid movement from the present to the future. The adolescents felt they were moving somewhere, and in a hurry. However, there was *not* a strong relationship between the sense of forward motion and the extent to which the individual actually was thinking ahead into the future. It will be recalled that for this population in general there was a disinclination to conceptualize the later years of life. One hurtled from "now" to "next" with all possible speed—but what comes after "next"? Few ideas were expressed on this subject.

All of these adolescents could conceive of futurity. But why did they, as a group, limit themselves to the immediate future? Why did they tend to exclude the past? And why were there important individual differences within this group, as well as within other groups that have been studied? Possible explanations are offered both in the study cited above, and in related investigations (74, 75). The most relevant point here is that any explanation must take motivational and socioemotional factors into account. It is not enough that the adolescent can think about the future. He must also develop a personal orientation toward his future.

Mention has already been made of the likelihood that heightened awareness of one's self as an individual also tends to heighten one's concern about death (an hypothesis that is almost begging for empirical investigation). Studies such as the one summarized above suggest that the adolescent's identity is closely linked to who-he-will-be in the near future. Seen from this viewpoint, death becomes much more than an abstract logical concept. The prospect of death is a threat to who-the-adolescent-is-now because it clouds the possibility that he will ever become the self that he values and is moving toward. Threatened loss of futurity (premature death) confronts the adolescent with an implicit denial of his basic identity. He cannot look back upon a full lifetime to bolster his sense of individual identity, nor is he at a relatively stable point in his present existence. He is emerging. But what is the point of emerging if one is never to attain his full development?

From this line of reasoning we should expect that the adolescent and the elderly adult would differ markedly in their conceptions of death even though both appreciate the same basic conceptual dimensions (e.g., death is inevitable, final, personal). They would be expected to differ because, among other circumstances, they stand in different relationships to futurity. We will touch upon the older person's view of death and futurity in a moment. Let us remain a little longer with the adolescent—just how concerned is he with the prospect of a foreshortened life? What has been learned about the relationship between conceptions of futurity and conceptions of death?

Psychologists Louis Dickstein and Sidney Blatt studied the relationship between preoccupation with death and two measures of future-time perspective or anticipation (76). The death questions were quite straightforward, for example: "I think about my own death . . . more than once a week, once a week, once a month, once every few months." One of the futurity measures was a set of four story roots from which the subject is requested to construct a story. A sample story root: "Joe is having a cup of coffee in a restaurant. He is thinking of the time to come when. . ." (77). The subjects, all of them Yale undergraduates, were also given the Picture Arrangement subtest of the Wechsler Adult Intelligence Scale, which is regarded by some psychologists as a measure of the capacity to anticipate future events.

Students who scored very high or very low on the death questionnaire were compared with respect to their futurity scores. It was found that young men with *low* manifest death concern showed significantly *greater* extention into the future. Putting it the other way around, high manifest concern over death was associated with a more limited tendency to project into the future.

This finding is based upon correlational techniques, thus it does not tell us much about the processes involved. Nevertheless, it does allow us to ponder a bit further. Is it possible that apprehension about death is one of the main factors in the (apparently typical) adolescent tendency to rein in his thoughts of futurity? Perhaps one does not care to gaze too far down the road because he just might see something (i.e., *nothing*) there. If death concern does serve to restrain one's view of the future, then it may also impair the ability to plan ahead, to anticipate both hazards and opportunities. One might appear from the outside to be impulsive or short-sighted—even blundering or stupid—when there is in fact no actual cognitive impairment involved. It is just that one has averted his attention from an important source of information (futurity) in consequence of an emotionally aversive reaction to one component of the future (annihilation of the self).

This argument can also be put into reverse. It is possible that the individual's general strategy for organizing his temporal experience is the most relevant factor. The person who organizes his life around one hour or one day at a time may, as a result, be more easily dismayed by the prospect of death. He does not have as much insulation from death as does the person who projects many events, goals, and experiences between his present situation and the remote prospect of his own gravestone.

It is pertinent to remind ourselves that while both of these alternatives seem especially germane to adolescence, the dynamics that are involved can also occur at later points in the life-span. Perhaps the adolescent has more built-in reason for fearing death than does his elder. The young person has the task of conceptualizing a longer future, and must do so, of course, from the base of a shorter past. It is likely that he has not had as much occasion to exercise his ability to schedule and organize events in time—this will come later as he moves into occupational, parental, and other social obligatory realms. At any adult age, however, there is probably an important relationship between ability to conceptualize futurity and one's orientation toward death, and the reverse. Again, more research is needed if we are to evaluate the relative significance of the directions: (a) death concern affecting futurity, and (b) futurity affecting death concern.

For another window on the adolescent's relationship to futurity and death, let us consider an investigation by Neil McLaughlin and Robert

Kastenbaum (78). The subjects in this study were also college students, in this case all were co-eds. Each subject was asked to write six personal essays. The conditions included: a pleasant future event, pleasant past event, unpleasant future event, unpleasant past event, your earliest memory, and the day of your death. The young women were also asked to rate each of their essays on a 5-point scale of engrossment or self-involvement. Those who felt objective and detached, as though they were writing about somebody else, would have a low engrossment score. Those who felt so involved with themselves as depicted in their essay that they were vicariously reliving or pre-living the situation would have a high engrossment score. The remainder of the experimental design need not concern us here.

The most relevant point is that the subjects tended to describe their own deaths in a rather tranquil—and distant—manner. The day of death was seen as being a long way off, into their sixties. Not much emotional conflict was expressed, in fact, not much emotion at all. Graceful, peaceful acceptance and resignation were the general themes. The reported engrossment for the death projections was the lowest of all the essays written.

It would seem that college-age women are not nearly as concerned with death as we might have expected from the preceding discussion. In contrast with a number of other studies that might be mentioned, they did tend to project ahead into the fairly remote future (setting their own deaths in the sixth decade of life). But there was more to this piece of research.

After completing the above procedures, the subjects were then asked to imagine the day of their death in a *different* way. Having obtained and, in a sense removed, the image that came most readily to their minds, the investigators attempted to learn what alternate image, if any, was available to them.

The second projected day of death was markedly different from the first. Death was now viewed as a much more proximate event. Many of the young women described deaths that would occur within the next few years. For the total group, the distance between one's present situation and death *decreased* by more than twenty years.

The specific form taken by death also changed. Accidents and acts of violence became much more frequent. The death situations were described more vividly, in greater detail, with more use of emotion-laden words. The writing style became less restrained and proper—apparently, the subjects were now expressing themselves more spontaneously and idiosyncratically. Emotions and emotional conflicts were much in evidence. Judges who read both set of stories ("blind") had no trouble in determining that the second set conveyed more emotional impact and seemed to represent a greater sense of involvement on the part of the authors.

Yet the subjects themselves reported, through their self-ratings, that they were even *less* engrossed in these essays than they had been in the first set! There was thus a major contradiction between the form and content of the essays as they appeared to outsiders, and as the subjects themselves evaluated them. At the same time that these young women were depicting their deaths as being closer to them in time and in raw affective impact, they were reporting that they felt very little involvement in the situation.

Methodologically, this study underscores the importance of going beyond the subject's first or most accessible response. The subjects' total orientation toward death and futurity would have been badly and incompletely represented had the inquiry been limited to their first responses only.

ιιιιιιιιιιιιιιιιιιιιιιιιιιιιιιιιιιιιιιιιιιιιιιιιιιιιιιιιιιιιιιιιιιιιιιιιιιιιιιιιιιιιιι

In all of the adolescent/young adult populations studied to date, there have been an appreciable number of subjects who expect to live longer than they care to live.

ιιιιιιιιιιιιιιιιιιιιιιιιιιιιιιιιιιιιιιιιιιιιιιιιιιιιιιιιιιιιιιιιιιιιιιιιιιιιιιιιιιιιιιιιιι

What does this study suggest about the relationship between concepts of death and futurity in young adults? Futurity is stretched out when the topic of personal death is first introduced. Time serves as an insulation between the one's present self and eventual death. The reasonable success of this insulation may be judged by the fact that other aspects of the personal death essay were neutral and tranquil. The subject could rely upon readily available stereotyped expressions. But the requirement to deal twice with the same question forced the respondents to find an alternative organization of thought and feeling within themselves. This turned out to be a more personal kind of response. It was especially interesting to see that as the future shrank, the subject simultaneously introduced a greater *psy-*

chological distance between herself and death. The day of death was seen as much closer at hand, but who was dying? A character on a piece of paper, somebody with whom the writer preferred not to identify.

Which conception of futurity and death was the "real" or "basic" one for these subjects? Perhaps it is more appropriate to inquire: how are these two types of conception related within the same individual? Do adolescents and young adults (and the rest of us) understand our own internal complexity? Is there a clear gap between the conceptions of death and futurity that we have developed on a social expectation level, and our more personal, less often communicated thoughts? It would be useful to know more about this topic.

Let us take up one further point regarding death and futurity in adolescence. One's expectation of personal longevity is an aspect of his future perspective. A series of interrelated studies (79) has been looking into both personal expectations of longevity and their correlates. One of the more interesting findings thus far concerns the relationship between expectations and *preferences*. In all of the adolescent/young adult populations studied to date, there have been an appreciable number of subjects who expect to live longer than they care to live. The (projected) value of being alive seems to run out sooner than life itself. There is some further evidence that people who have this pattern of expectation and preference are relatively less likely to come to the aid of other people who are in life-endangering situations (80).

We see once again that conceptions of time and death are difficult to separate from attitudes or preferences, especially after we leave the early years of childhood. (It is not that easy to differentiate cognitions from attitudes in children, but there, at least, we have the developmental progression of thought to use as a guideline.) We also see that the relationship between futurity and death can be complex within the same individual, let alone from one individual to another. For example, the same young person may (a) feel himself moving rapidly into the future, (b) look forward to this future self as being the "real me," yet (c) think very little about the second half of his life-span, and (d) even be convinced that he has more future ahead than he cares to use. Additionally, his #1 expectation that he has a long life-span ahead may alternate with a strong secondary expectation that sudden, violent death will snuff out his life in the near future.

We move now to a brief exploration of futurity and death conceptions in elderly adults. It is true that some aged people are afflicted by chronic brain syndrome or senility. Suffering from organic impairments or deficits, they are not able to think very clearly about the future, or about other matters that require high-level cognitive activity. Some observers may prefer to interpret the deterioration of future-oriented thought as a "natural" accompaniment of the aging process. There is no hard evidence for such an interpretation. It is based upon an inclination to regard the pathology of later life as identical with normal aging.

This is not an idle point. If loss of futurity is part of an inevitable and intrinsic biological process, then it may be as "natural" for the elder to turn away from the future realm as it is for the child to discover this same realm. We prefer to distinguish between (a) a general syndrome of age-related decline in which futurity is but one of the psychological casualties, and (b) the thought and behavior of individuals who are not incapacitated by massive organic changes as they move into their later years of life. In the former situation, the impaired elderly person is likely to show obvious difficulty in recalling the recent past and registering the present. He may not even be able to distinguish reliably among past, present, and future. In the latter situation, the "normal" aging person may perhaps think and speak less of futurity, but he does not exhibit a general pattern of deterioration.

There is the implication that reduction in future orientation in later life, when it does occur, may be related as much to socioemotional as to cognitive factors. One study has found that mentally alert geriatric patients could use futurity successfully as a category for organizing experience—providing it was not their personal experience at stake (81). But this same study revealed that the elders in question could not (or, at least, did not) offer much about futurity within a personal framework.

If an elder can "work with the future" (as shown by his performances on story construction tasks), why, then, does he not show a propensity to "live in the future?" The investigator proposed two alternative explanations:

A particular elderly person happens to be depressed, institutionalized or fearful of death. This quasi-Aristotelian application of the term "accident" is intended to suggest that elderly people do not *necessarily* have to be limited in their future outlook. . . . Specific conditions have occurred in the particular individual's total life situation which have brought about the observed restriction. That such a restriction might be rather common would be no argument for its necessity. By analogy, even when all oak trees in a given area are blighted with the same disease, no one suggests that this affliction is a necessary and intrinsic characteristic of being an oak tree. This view has practical implications: There would be the prospect that "something could be done" to prevent or remedy this "unfortunate accident" of restriction of future outlook.

An alternative explanation is that there is a certain "necessity" involved in the observed restriction of personal futurity. This might be an individual matter, i.e., not every elderly person would "necessarily" possess this "necessity"—but for those who did, its structuring power would be great. What we mean to suggest here is that certain life-styles imply rather definite self-contained limits. Some elderly people consider that they have lived out their life plan, and thus exist on a sort of "surplus time" that is not part of their lifelong system of values (82).

With respect to the latter point, we are reminded of those young adults who believe they are doomed to an undesired longevity. There are some elders who also seem to feel that they are somewhere between a completed life and a delayed death. (But these orientations are subject to change in both young and old as the conditions of present life change—health, finances, and interpersonal relationships, for example.)

The scarcity of objective future time is likely to confront the elderly person with a problem as fundamental, though qualitatively different, as that which he faced as an identity-conscious adolescent. Should he "write off" the future because so little remains of it? Or should he value the future all the more for precisely the same reason? Again, perhaps he should alter his scale of values and meanings so that *small futures* (tomorrow, not ten years from now) become the relevant frame of reference? Should he retreat into the past? Project himself into a vicarious future through the lives of younger relatives or personally significant endeavors? Bury himself in the present moment, denying both past and future? Whatever solution a particular individual may adopt, it must be acknowledged that the whole pattern of his life is operating within the lengthening shadow of death.

REFERENCES

1 Werner, H. *Comparative psychology of mental development.* New York: International University Press, 1957.

2 Piaget, J. *The psychology of intelligence.* New York: Littlefield, 1960.

3 Rosenthal, H. R. The fear of death as an indispensable factor in psychotherapy. *American Journal of Psychotherapy,* 1963, *17,* 619–630.

4 Feifel, H. Symposium comments, Gerontological Society, Oct., 1965. Cited by R. Kastenbaum: Death as a research variable in social gerontology: An overview. *Gerontologist,* 1966, *7,* 67–69.

5 Kastenbaum, R. Engrossment and perspective in later life. In R. Kastenbaum (Ed.), *Contributions to the psychobiology of aging*. New York: Springer, 1965. Pp. 3–18.

6 Schecter, D. E., Symonds, M., & Bernstein, I. Development of the concept of time in children. *Journal of Nervous and Mental Diseases*, 1955, *21*, 301–310.

7 Kastenbaum, R. The child's understanding of death: How does it develop? In E. Grollman (Ed.), *Explaining death to children*. Boston: Beacon Press, 1967. Pp. 89–110.

8 Gesell, Arnold & Ilg, F. L. *The child from five to ten*. New York: Harper & Bros., 1946.

9 Piaget, J. & Inhelder, B. *The growth of logical thinking from childhood to adolescence*. New York: Basic Books, 1958.

10 Hall, G. S. *Senescence*. New York: Appleton, 1922.

11 *Ibid.*, p. 440.

12 *Ibid.*

13 Tobin, S. The earliest memory as data for research in aging. In D. P. Kent, R. Kastenbaum, & S. Sherwood (Eds.), *Research, planning, and action for the elderly*. New York: Behavioral Publications, in press.

14 Kastenbaum, R. & Sherwood, S. Unpublished data. Detroit: Wayne State University; Boston: Hebrew Center for Rehabilitation of the Aged.

15 Hall, *op cit.*, p. 440.

16 Hall, *op. cit.*, p. 441.

17 Brown, F. Depression and childhood bereavement. *Journal of Mental Science.*, 1961, *107*, 754–777.

18 *Ibid.*, p. 775.

19 Moriarty, D. *The loss of loved ones*. Springfield, Ill.: Charles C. Thomas, 1967. P. 63.

20 *Ibid.*, pp. 67–89.

21 *Ibid.*, p. 67.

22 *Ibid.*, p. 88.

23 Rochlin, G. How younger children view death and themselves. In E. A. Grollman (Ed.), *Explaining death to children*. Boston: Beacon Press, 1967. Pp. 51–88.

24 Brent, S. Untitled manuscript, prepared for publication. Detroit: Wayne State University.

25 *Ibid.*

26 Maurer, A. Maturation of concepts of death. *British Journal of Medicine and Psychology*, 1966, *39*, 35–41.

27 *Ibid.*, p. 36.

28 *Ibid.*, p. 37.

29 *Ibid.*

30 Aries, P. *Centuries of childhood*. New York: Knopf, 1962.

31 Wolfenstein, M. The emergence of fun morality. *Journal of Social Issues*, 7, 4, 1951, 15–25.

32 Goldstein, K. *The organism*. New York: American Book, 1939.

33 Lewin, K. *Principles of topological psychology*. New York: McGraw-Hill, 1936.

34 Werner, *op. cit.*

35 Conversation overheard on the ward of a geriatric hospital.

36 Nagy, M. The child's view of death. *Journal of Genetic Psychology,* 1948, *73,* 3–27. Reprinted in H. Feifel (Ed.), *The meaning of death.* New York: McGraw-Hill, 1959. Pp. 79–98 (page citations are to the more accessible reprinted version).

37 *Ibid.,* p. 81.

38 *Ibid.,* p. 83.

39 *Ibid.,* p. 83.

40 *Ibid.,* p. 96.

41 *Ibid.,* p. 96.

42 Anthony, S. *The child's discovery of death.* New York: Harcourt, Brace & World, 1940.

43 *Ibid.,* p. 1.

44 Thomas, M. Cited by Anthony, *Ibid.,* p. 36.

45 Anthony, *op. cit.,* pp. 36–37.

46 *Ibid.,* p. 45.

47 *Ibid.,* p. 46.

48 *Ibid.,* p. 46.

49 *Ibid.,* p. 50.

50 *Ibid.,* p. 51.

51 Rochlin, *op. cit.,* p. 74.

52 *Ibid.,* p. 60.

53 *Ibid.,* p. 61.

54 Alexander, I. & Adlerstein, A. M. Affective responses to the concept of death in a population of children and early adolescents. *Journal of Genetic Psychology,* 1958, *93,* 167–177.

55 *Ibid.,* p. 176.

56 Piaget, J. *The construction of reality in the child.* New York: Basic Books, 1954.

57 Werner, *op. cit.*

58 Huang, I., & Lee, H. W. Experimental analysis of child animism. *Journal of Genetic Psychology,* 1945, *66,* 69–74.

59 Klingberg, G. The distinction between living and not living among 7–10 year-old children with some remarks concerning the so-called animism controversy. *Journal of Genetic Psychology,* 1957, *105,* 227–238.

60 Russell, R. W. Studies in animism: II. The development of animism. *Journal of Genetic Psychology,* 1940, *56,* 353–366.

61 Klingberg, *op. cit.*

62 Piaget, *op. cit.*

63 Smedslun, J. The acquisition of conservation of substance and weight in children. I. Introduction. *Scandinavian Journal of Psychology,* 1960, *1,* 49–54.

421

64 Alexander & Adlerstein, *op. cit.*

65 Moriarty, *op. cit.*

66 Fraisse, P. *The psychology of time.* (Translated by Jennifer Lieth.) New York: Harper & Row, 1963.

67 Poulet, G. *Studies in human time.* (Translated by Elliott Coleman.) New York: Harper Torchbooks, 1959.

68 Campbell, J. (Ed.), *Man and time.* New York: Pantheon, 1957.

69 Sturt, M. *The psychology of time.* New York: Harcourt, Brace, 1925.

70 LeShan, L. Time orientation and social class. *Journal of Abnormal and Social Psychology,* 1952, *47,* 589–592.

71 Schneider, L., & Lysgaard, S. The deferred gratification pattern: A preliminary study. *American Sociological Review,* 1953, *18,* 142–149.

72 Piaget & Inhelder, *op. cit.*

73 Kastenbaum, R. Time and death in adolescence. In H. Feifel (Ed.), *The meaning of death.* New York: McGraw-Hill, 1959. Pp. 99–113.

74 Kastenbaum, R. The dimensions of future time perspective, an experimental analysis. *Journal of Genetic Psychology,* 1961, *65,* 203–218.

75 McLaughlin, N., & Kastenbaum, R. Engrossment in personal past, future and death. Presented at annual meeting, American Psychological Association, New York City, September, 1966.

76 Dickstein, L., & Blatt, S. Death concern, futurity, and anticipation. *Journal of Consulting Psychology,* 1966, *31,* 11–17.

77 Wallace, M. Future time perspective in schizophrenia. *Journal of Abnormal and Social Psychology,* 1956. *52,* 240–245.

78 McLaughlin & Kastenbaum, *op. cit.*

79 Center for Psychological Studies of Dying, Death and Lethal Behavior. Detroit: Wayne State University.

80 Branscomb, A., & Kastenbaum, R. Orientations toward protecting, extending and foreshortening the lifespan: A preliminary study. Center for Psychological Studies of Dying, Death, and Lethal Behavior. Detroit: Wayne State University, 1969, unpublished manuscript.

81 Kastenbaum, R. Cognitive and personal futurity in later life. *Journal of Individual Psychology,* 1963, *19,* 216–222.

82 *Ibid.*

Attitudes toward Death:
A Psychological Perspective

Herman Feifel

Herman Feifel, Chief Clinical Psychologist at the Veterans Administration Mental Hygiene Clinic in Los Angeles, was one of the pioneers of thanatology during the late 1950s and early 1960s. The publication, in 1959, of *The Meanings of Death* which he edited was a landmark not only because it was a significant contribution to the dissemination of thanatological knowledge, but also because it *was* published. In the following selection, Dr. Feifel observes that the changes in a person's attitudes toward death occurring throughout his life cycle reflect psychological as well as biological changes in life.

Herman Feifel, "Attitudes toward Death," *Journal of Consulting and Clinical Psychology* 33, pp. 292-295. Copyright © 1968 by the American Psychological Association. Reprinted by permission.

Two major developments influenced psychology's halting approach in probing attitudes toward death as a relevant variable in human conduct. One was psychology's natal need to raise its flag independently of philosophy and ethics. Scientific respectability meant occupying oneself with measurable stimuli and responses which were repeatable and public. A consequence was restraint in scrutinizing consciousness as a datum and neglect of personality. The other was a waning of faith in the providential and sacred accompanied by a lack of transcending significance for death. This secular turn was further associated with a decline in the kinship group and increasing social fragmentation of the family, a growing impersonality emerging from a technologically dominated society, and deritualization of grief and mourning practices—all fusing to exacerbate our hostility toward and repudiation of death.

The events of World War II, however, and the ensuing press of urgent social problems forced psychology to look beyond its traditional positivism and enter into the bailiwick of moral issues and life choices. The view that a vital psychology must be rooted in man, not in a mathematical physics model, became more insistent. At the same time, a legacy of the same war thrust all of us into a baleful situation in which the world annihilation

fantasies of the schizophrenic patient no longer appeared unrealistic. Physical science has presently made it possible for us all to share a common
epitaph. Not only the individuality of death but posterity and social immortality are now menaced.

In this junction of psychology's waxing interest in the existential richness
of human life, and sharpened awareness of life's temporality and recognition that all truth is germane to the exigencies of survival, research in the
area of death is emerging as an authentic and fertile enterprise.

Consideration of death is undoubtedly one of the foremost sources of
anxiety for man. Indeed, a major task of both religion and philosophy has
been to grapple with its intensity and complexity. Psychology, in coming
to grips with the meaning of death for the individual, asserts its responsibility to reexamine its philosophic and humanistic heritage in the context
of its generic ideal of science.

*Only with consciousness of mortality
does concern with human fulfillment,
salvation, and the notion of the
uniqueness and individuality of each
one of us receive complete meaning.*

Investigation of attitudes toward death and bereavement makes available
a supplementary entryway in understanding adaptational strategies used
in coping with pain, crisis, and stress. It further affords the possibility of
improving treatment of the seriously sick and others facing the prospect
of oncoming death. Additionally, it extends our comprehension of how
death affects the social fabric of society. Overriding these, however, may be
our due recognition of the importance of the future in steering present
behavior. It is man's excelling capacity to conceptualize a future—and inevitable death—which distinguishes him from other species and makes
myopic imitative application of a physical sciences methodology to him.
Anticipation guides a majority of our actions, and expectation serves as a
principal mediator of goal-directed and purposeful behavior. As human

beings, the present contains not only the psychological past but psychological future as well. Death is an absent presence even before its actual arrival. Only with consciousness of mortality does concern with human fulfillment, salvation, and the notion of the uniqueness and individuality of each one of us receive complete meaning.

The piloting force of awareness of death is active at all age levels. Its domain is not confined to the sick, aged, suicidal, or combat soldier. In this regard, it may be pertinent to emphasize that we not shut out children from the realities of death. The efforts of investigators as Anthony (1940), Maurer (1966), Nagy (1948), and Wahl (1958) disclose that we do not protect the child by attempting to shield him from death. Rather, we hinder his emotional growth. In actuality, this proscription displays more of the adult's or parent's own anxieties and strong emotions concerning death than the child's genuine capacity to manage knowledge of the existence of death. Naturally, level of explanation, timing, and individual differences have to be appreciated.

Until recently, the psychoanalytic conceptualization of attitudes toward and fear of death as derivative events was dominant. Sentiments about death were essentially manifestations of a more ultimate reality, that is, separation anxiety or conflicts about castration. Doubtless, such clinical displacement does occur. Death fears can be secondary phenomena. Nevertheless, incoming data increasingly suggest that the reverse may be more to the point. Apprehensiveness over bodily annihilation and concerns about finitude themselves assume dissembling guises. The depressed mood, fears of loss, sundry psychosomatic symptoms, and varying psychological disturbances all have evidenced affinity to anxieties concerning death. Gillespie (1963), the English psychiatrist, for example, goes so far as to declare that fear of death is the most traumatic factor in fashioning senile psychosis. Feifel (1959) and Searles (1961) have both advanced the hypothesis that *one* of the intentions of schizophrenic denial of reality, in certain persons, may function as a magical holding back, if not undoing, of possible death. If living leads inevitably to death, the way not to die is not to live. We need to incorporate thoughts and emotions about death into our personality studies and therapeutic sights. Too frequently do we numb their impetus by engaging ourselves with the symbolic as divorced from the *real* aspects of death.

We are currently more knowing about the multidimensional meanings which death holds for people. Death can be the "gentle night" or "great destroyer." It can reflect surcease from pain and tribulation, reunion with one's family, loss of control, punishment, or loneliness. Developmental changes, cultural conditioning, religious orientation, personality characteristics, and level of threat, among others, contribute their shaping power.

There is also the implication that attitudes toward death can oscillate in the same individual, from strong avoidance through anxious hope and uneasy resignation to calm acceptance. The point in time one centers on can be crucial. In this context, Feifel (1965) has indicated the coexistence of contradictory attitudes toward death, for example, realistic acceptance of death and its simultaneous rejection in a subtle equilibristic balance in many seriously ill and terminally ill patients. He has suggested that this counterpoise seems to serve adaptational needs of the patient, allowing him to maintain communal associations and yet organize his resources to contend with oncoming extinction.

Additionally, we are discovering that treatment of the seriously ill and dying may be too conditioned to considerations and wants of the healthy rather than to the needs of the sick. Research findings underscore the desire of most patients for honest and sharing talk from physicians and family about the seriousness of their illness (Feifel, 1959). This is in strong contrast to the prominent orientation of physician, nurse, and family to avoid such confronting discussion (Feifel, 1965; Glaser & Strauss, 1965). The threat to professional narcissism and existing social scruples about death are obviously contributory. Reappraisal of what and how we instruct our medical, nursing, and seminary students concerning dying, death, grief, and bereavement seems in order.

Truth and what sustains one's sense of reality tend to be more supporting and beneficial to the patient than deception and denial. We must resist disinheriting the patient psychologically and socially at the very time we enhance attention to his physiological requirements. Approaching death is better integrated when the patient feels understood and can voice his feelings and thoughts about dying and death. Clinical experience demonstrates that when this happens, less depression, deviant behavior, and blame of others show themselves in patients. Further opening channels of communication tends to attenuate feelings of inadequacy and guilt not only in the patient but in the professional people involved in treatment and family as well.

Some terminally ill patients, when apprised of their prognosis, manifest an adjustment equal to or better than that seen in similar patients who have not been so informed (Zinker, 1966: Zinker & Fink, 1966). Realization of possible death appears to give permission, even freedom, to some to be themselves rather than extensions or mirrors of other people's values. One can learn, apparently, not only to live with enormous stress but to grow and change under its goad. Indeed, history furnishes us with numerous examples where recognition of impending death has fostered creativity rather than paralysis.

Magnified cognition exists that death represents a fact of social as well as psychological import. The funeral ceremony, although personal in design, is certainly societal in consequence. A person's death affects the emotional life of the bereaved but it also entails changes in the status and social position of the survivors.

What are some deductions from these perceptions? Man is a creature in time and space whose consciousness permits him to nullify their strictures. This brings into his ken the awareness of inexorable death as a compelling stimulus. As a time-ridden being, man is faced with the task of identifying himself with eternity. His most viable response will issue from basic philosophical, religious, or psychological deliberations about death already in his possession. The agony of selfhood is not endurable for most of us in pondering death without resources, be they transcendental, inspirational, or existential. We pay expensively for the taboo we affix to the subject of death. Closer psychological familiarity with death is called for in our developmental upbringing and culture. Our socially repressive outlook encourages neurotic anxieties about death. The evolution of an *ars moriendi* prior to the advent of death is the charge.

Cutting across all the populations the author has studied (Feifel, 1959, 1965) is the view of death as the extreme abomination in man's experience. Despite invocation of denial and a host of other strategems, fear of finitude is never quite hushed. Withstanding all jeremiads and alienation, in the face of death the vast majority in all the author's groups, that is, terminally, seriously, chronically, and mentally ill, as well as normal subjects, assess the world as good and not to be ceded if possible.

Man has a legitimate need to face away from death. In truth, who is to say that under certain conditions this may not be salutary? Unfortunately, excessive camouflage and expulsion of the notion of death prevail in the United States leading to a falsification of the essence of man. If we accept death as a necessity rather than strive to demote it to the level of accident, there may be less need to project fear of death outside ourselves. This might possibly mute some of the violence of our times. Energies now bound up in continuing attempts to shelve and repress the concept of death would be available to us for more constructive aspects of living—perhaps even fortify man's gift for creative splendor against his genius for destruction. Forster (1962, p. 394) has commented penetratingly that "death destroys a man but the *idea* of death saves him."

Finally, what of psychology's more specific assignment in the area of death? Psychotherapeutic functioning and models of personality and psychopathology need amplified representation of the future and death in their horizons. Findings suggest that one's philosophy of life and death lies at the nexus of meaning, value, and personality.

The thrust of empirical attack requires extension. Theoretical expressions must be more rooted in the reasonably precise bases of systematic observation and experimentation. It may be that psychology is particularly favored to be enlightening here since some feel that it is a sector where humanistic and physicist-engineer cultures, too often insulated and at cross-purposes with one another, intersect. Clearly, psychology's own imperative for interdisciplinary perspective should not be minimized.

Methodology will have to capture, in more astute form, the manifold meanings of death not only between individuals but within the same person. We must tighten our grasp of the bonds existing among verbally expressed attitudes toward death, fantasy notions, and below-the-level-of-awareness ideas. As in other areas, we have the bedeviling challenge of making constructs, such as fear of death, operationally definable yet integrating the cogency of such explanatory concepts as purpose, anxiety, redemption.

The pivotal undertaking for psychology has been alluded to by Murphy (1959, p. 320): "Instead of looking at the grim skeleton and crossbones and being told *this* is reality, let us study the observer himself, regard him as the reality and ask why skulls and crossbones are the chief realities for *him.*"

Only by encompassing the concept of death into his life will man fully understand himself—and only the culture which countenances death will truly savor life.

REFERENCES

Anthony, S. *The Child's Discovery of Death.* New York: Harcourt, Brace, 1940.

Feifel, H. *The Meaning of Death.* New York: McGraw-Hill, 1959.

Feifel, H. The function of attitudes toward death. In, *Death and Dying: Attitudes of Patient and Doctor.* Vol. 5, Symposium No. 11, New York: Group for the Advancement of Psychiatry, 1965.

Forster, E. M. Aphorism. In W. H. Auden & L. Kronenberger (Eds.), *The Viking Book of Aphorisms*. New York: Viking Press, 1962.

Gillespie, W. H. Some regressive phenomena in old age. *British Journal of Medical Psychology*, 1963, 36, 203–209.

Glaser, B. G., & Strauss, A. L. *Awareness of Dying*. Chicago: Aldine, 1965.

Maurer, A. Maturation of concepts of death. *British Journal of Medical Psychology*, 1966, 39, 35–41.

Murphy, G. Discussion. In H. Feifel (Ed.), *The Meaning of Death*. New York: McGraw-Hill, 1959.

Nagy, M. H. The child's theories concerning death. *Journal of Genetic Psychology*, 1948, 73, 3–27.

Searles, H. Schizophrenia and the inevitability of death. *Psychiatric Quarterly*, 1961, 35, 631–665.

Wahl, C. W. The fear of death. *Bulletin of the Menninger Clinic*, 1958, 22, 214–223.

Zinker, J. C. *Rosa Lee: Motivation and the Crisis of Dying*. Lake Erie College Studies, Vol. 6. Painesville, Ohio: Lake Erie College Press, 1966.

Zinker, J. C., & Fink, S. L. The possibility for psychological growth in a dying person. *Journal of General Psychology*, 1966, 74, 185–199.

Attitudes of Patients
with Advanced Malignancy

Samuel L. Feder
Samuel L. Feder is Clinical Professor of Psychiatry at Mount
Sinai School of Medicine of the City University of New York.
In his article (taken from a report published by the Group
for the Advancement of Psychiatry), Dr. Feder relates with
compassion his observations on one hundred patients
suffering from advanced malignancies and discusses their
attitudes, their concerns, and their secret and often unconscious wishes for immortality.

From the Group for the Advancement of Psychiatry,
Symposium No. 11, *Death and Dying: Attitudes of Patient
and Doctor* (New York: GAP, 1965), pp. 614–622. Reprinted
by permission.

The observations reported here are based primarily
on a study of approximately 100 patients in varied stages of malignant
diseases seen in the Radiotherapy Department of the Mount Sinai Hospital,
New York City. Additional data come from the intensive treatment of five
patients, whom I saw continually over a period of two or three years as their
disease progressed. Many were approaching death (e.g., of 20 patients with
lung carcinoma, 19 were dead within six months to a year). As a psychiatrist
I have had no experience with people just at the point of death. Others have
considered this particular situation and have undertaken to establish a
guide for the physician (1,2).

NATURE OF THE PROBLEM

My original interest derived from a single experience with a woman dying
of a metastatic malignancy who showed a remarkable ability to face the
prospects of death. Knowing that she had a fatal disease, she was able to
change her goals in life in a most satisfactory and gratifying way. I then
felt there must be some great value in trying to do something about the
current uncertainty as to whether or not a patient should face the fact of his
malignant disease. In this study, then, I started to explore the question of
whether to tell the cancer patient the truth. Many others have explored the
same problem (3,4). I soon decided that this was the wrong question, and

430

perhaps this is the reason we never come up with a generally satisfactory answer.

ꜰꜰ

*In the patients I saw the greatest
threat was not so much death,
whatever dying is, but rather the
danger of progressive isolation and the
development of a sense of "aloneness."*

ꜰꜰꜰ

It has been my experience that practically all patients who have a malignant disease "know" in some way that they have it. The pertinent question, therefore, became one of understanding what was going on in the patient, how he was seeing the threat, what mechanisms he was using to cope with it, and how we could best keep our touch with the individual as he went along this usually progressive and inevitable course.

In the patients I saw the greatest threat was not so much death, whatever dying is, but rather the danger of progressive isolation and the development of a sense of "aloneness." The major task of the physician, then, was to try properly to interpret the patient's various maneuvers, to understand how he was trying to cope with the threat, and so to be able to stay with the patient in order to prevent this particular threat of isolation.

I had the complete cooperation of John Boland, M.D., Director of the Department of Radiotherapy at Mount Sinai Hospital, and worked closely with him. Having come from Christie Hospital in Manchester, England, where they at one time attempted to tell every other cancer patient he had a malignant disease, Dr. Boland was greatly interested in the problem. Nevertheless, I found that the members of his staff were extremely wary of telling anyone he had a malignant disease. At the time I started my study—and, I must admit, also at the time I finished it—most patients were not being told. I was therefore seeing patients in the active stages of some kind of therapy for the malignant disease who had been told their disease was something else and who generally appeared not to know the true nature of their illness.

431

All these patients, when they were asked to see me as a "new doctor," reacted with great anxiety. Of the first 50 patients, the only one who showed no anxiety was a woman in her fifties who was overtly psychotic in every respect and who reacted with no apparent anxiety to anything. All the other patients were terrified at going to see a new doctor. They wondered: "What has gone wrong? . . . This is it. . . . Now I am going to hear *it*." These were the same patients who had convinced the radiotherapy staff that they accepted the diagnosis of "inflammation," "tumor," or "arthritis." In my discussion with the staff, it was clear that most of them believed, or wanted to believe that their patients accepted the diagnosis of some other illness; yet every patient reacted with great anxiety. I had an experience unique in my work as a psychiatrist. All but two of the patients were delighted to discover that I was a psychiatrist. They were glad I was not "one of those other doctors"—"those other doctors" being the bearers of bad tidings. The two who were not particularly happy were an alcoholic man who had had his difficulties with psychiatrists elsewhere and a woman with insanity in the family who was afraid this would have some bearing on her.

When my interest in the subject become known, I was asked to see several patients in private practice. Despite the fact that I had been talking about the need to try to understand what was going on with the patient, the referring physician often begged, urged, or even ordered me not to change his pattern of denying to the patient that something serious was the matter; I was told that the patient would "go crazy" or would "commit suicide," or that "the bottom would fall out." Yet in every case where the referring physician was most forceful about this concern, the first thing the patient talked about, on the occasion of his first visit to me, was referrable to his progressive illness. Usually the first response to my question "Why have you come to see me?" was a direct reference to the fact that "I am dying," or "I just can't take it any more," or "I don't have much time." It is true that as we went along, they dropped the subject, as many patients do. At the time of the initial interview, however, they had an opportunity to openly express this great concern. There was the fact that I, at the same time, was willing to face this fear and discuss it with them as much as they were willing to deal with it. I believe this established a relationship that enabled us to deal appropriately with other concerns as they emerged.

Starting with the fact that, except in cases of total psychotic disassociation, there is never complete denial of this threat of progressive illness and isolation, of wasting and dying, what can we understand about the patient, and how can we meet his problems?

The enormity of the insult to the ego and the body ego in progressive illness has been well established (5). . . . The threat to the coping mechanism that results from this situation . . . is one of the most important patterns, and is one of the major ingredients in the depressed moods seen in these patients. I think these depressions are difficult to explain according to ordinary theories. The melancholia is not one that fits into the theories of object loss, introjection of the good and the bad objects, and so forth. What occurs here is a threat to the usual adaptive mechanisms, in which the individual feels that he is going to become helpless (6), or will have to give up his usual defense or become an invalid. He is afraid he will become unloved, and that, unlovable, he will become progressively isolated.

WHAT MOST CONCERNS THE CANCER PATIENT

For the cancer patient there are special threats. There is, of course, the image of the progressive destruction of the body ego. This is much more marked in people who have hidden disease than in those who have overt disease. People with skin cancer or cancer that presents a visible mass handle the threat far better than those who have an internal malignancy that cannot be kept under their observation and that they cannot follow very carefully (7). In other words, they have less mastery over the situation, at least in their thoughts, and react more intensely.

"If it is malignant, will you please tell me; you have the doctor to talk to, and you have my children to talk to, but whom will I talk to if I am not informed?"

The role of the specific body part has been documented very well, one of the most specific and explicit situations being cancer of the breast in women (8). One woman with Hodgkin's disease showed this clearly. She was very upset, for instance, by the fact that there were indelible marks on the body (to guide the radiotherapist). She told me, "Until the day comes that I can clean off this ink, this imaginary marker, I am going to feel exposed to the world." Her "insides were on the outside," and this was the situation that she could not tolerate. Particularly in these days with replacement and suppressive therapy, one cannot minimize the problem of women who are given corticosterone or testosterone and who develop hair on the face, although the problem is usually minimized by their attending physician.

In the many talks I have had with these patients I have found that their concern is not so much with death itself. I believe this is different from the experience reported by Dr. Feifel.* We don't really know what death is. We are usually frightened of things about which we have some memory. We all know the terrors of loneliness, rejection, and pain. But I don't think we are able really to conceptualize the terrors of death in a way that has any real meaning. There is no experience for death. Therefore, the thing that most concerns patients is the fear that they are going to be hurt or deserted. They want to share some of the experiences, and they are not sure they are going to find somebody with whom to do this. Eissler (1) says that a portion of the therapist's ego dies with the patient. Although I do agree with this, he is also saying that an essential ingredient of the therapeutic process is the patient's ability to share experiences with the therapist. For example, one woman told me, when she was to be operated on for a breast tumor, that she said to her sister, "If it is malignant, will you please tell me; you have the doctor to talk to, and you have my children to talk to, but whom will I talk to if I am not informed?" Another patient with intense and progressive pain from metastatic malignancy came into my office one day, practically collapsed into the chair, and started out by saying that she was in terrible pain. When I spontaneously started to respond to this, she stopped me and said, "Don't say anything. There is nothing for you to say. I just want you to know." If a patient can share some of the pain, if the doctor does not try to dissuade her from having the pain, or from being frightened and distressed, he has done a great deal to prevent this sense of isolation.

I feel that these patients are oriented toward reality. It may be their way, as Dr. Dovenmuehle has pointed out, of partially denying what is going on. But they are certainly oriented toward the problems of living. A fundamental principle in working with these patients is to be prepared to face with them, on a very respectful and realistic level, many of these problems of living. This is true even at those times when both of you know or suspect what the

*See preceding selection.—ED.

patient is talking about is the problem of dying. A patient who will come in and say "It is a very gloomy day today," when it is actually a gloomy day, may in effect be saying, "I feel a little closer to death," or "I am in more pain." Nevertheless, I believe that once you have established a firm base of understanding by letting the patient know that you recognize the seriousness of his situation, you are then in a position to deal either with the weather or with some of the other problems.

When I first started the study and was trying to find out whether to tell the patients they had cancer in so many words, I always offered them an opportunity to ask questions at the end of my rather extensive interviews. One of the first men said, "I am so glad I had a chance to speak to you. It has made me see a great many things, but there is one thing I want to ask you." I must admit that while I had great theoretical ideas about its being much better to come out and talk realistically about the cancer, at this particular moment I reacted with some anxiety. I said to myself, "Here it comes; what shall I do?" This was a man of 65 whose wife had died the previous year, who had a lung cancer, and who himself was to be dead within six months. His question was: "Shall I get married?" I don't think there is much reason to doubt that he was asking me how long he was going to live. Had I said, "Why, of course, get married," I would have given him one kind of obvious answer; and if I had said, "Of course not, don't get married," I would have given him another kind of obvious answer. I adopted the course that I think is best. I said, "This is an important subject, and I think we ought to talk about it." We then were able to go on and talk about how he was feeling.

Another woman in her middle forties who knew she had a metastatic malignancy said one day, "I am getting some crows' feet about my eyes. Should I have plastic surgery?" She too was thinking about the progress of her disease. To tell her casually to go ahead or to pass it off lightly as unimportant would impart a sense of hopelessness. This must never be done.* Here, too, a response that respected her concern about herself enabled her to drop this subject and to speak of her deeper feelings. Another patient was concerned about a child's school phobia; still another was concerned that he would not be able to clear up his desk work.

*Unpublished data from a questionnaire submitted to a group of 75 patients attending a cured-cancer congress showed repeatedly how important a sense of hopefulness was even after the five-year period.

IMPORTANCE OF COMMUNICATION

It seems clear that patients approaching death want the opportunity to talk about daily things, not only as a way of avoiding the subject of death but because these are the only realities they have. In this way the crucial element of hope is maintained in a believable manner. Even those who at one point in the illness openly face the direct consequences will change as the disease progresses. One very aggressive active woman whose character structure was such that *she* prescribed antidepressant medication for her husband, insisted upon knowing what was going on. She had lung cancer and was so informed. She said, "I know I have cancer of the lung, and I understand you are interested in people who have malignancy. I am willing to cooperate with you." At the end of the interview this woman could ask for further help only by saying to me, "If you would like to see me again, I will be glad to cooperate further"; of course I felt that her need for help was very important, and I did ask to see her again. A month later she was readmitted to the hospital with severe pain in the back; she then said to me as honestly as anybody could say anything, "I don't understand why the doctors can't decide what is wrong with me."

I have seen other people who will hear only what they want to hear. No matter how frankly they are told that they have a malignant disease, they will appear later never to have heard what was said. In a study at Christie Hospital, where every other cancer patient was told he had a malignant disease (9), it was discovered in follow-ups that those people who, by documentation, had been told, sometimes acted as though they never heard anything about it. No study was made of how complete this denial was. However, I don't think such denials obviate the advantages of being honest at the beginning. I feel very strongly that once you have said to the patient—however you say it—that you recognize that this is a serious and potentially fatal illness, you have established a relationship upon which you can base future communications at various levels.

QUEST FOR IMMORTALITY

Brodsky (10) has described the Liebestod fantasy, and Eissler (1) speaks of the importance of giving the dying patient a gift. I have observed what I call the "Liebesleben Fantasy," in which the person who is dying really wants to give something to the living. In this way the illusion of immortality is created by leaving something behind, rather than by the expectation of a reunion in the hereafter.

My first experience with this occurred some sixteen years ago while I was a medical resident and cared for a patient who was dying of widespread metastatic breast disease. Not really knowing what else to do I spent a lot of time at her bedside, discussing our mutual interest in Heine's poetry. She left the hospital and died within two weeks. Shortly after her death I received a thick packet of Heine's poems, handwritten in German. An accompanying note from the patient's daughter described how she had spent the last two weeks of her life doing very little but copying out the poetry to send to me. This can be interpreted on a number of levels, but I think it was her way of leaving a bit of herself behind, of perpetuating her life after she died.

Another patient, the same woman I saw so intensively for three years, spent her last days (she knew she was going to die) making bequests of small personal belongings. A week after her death her husband brought me a very small piece of jewelry that she had inherited from a grandmother. The stipulation was that this piece of jewelry be worn. It was a woman's piece of jewelry and obviously I could not wear it, but the idea was that this would be a way of perpetuating herself.

I believe these situations illustrate what can be done to help the patient to meet the threat of isolation. Permitting a situation in which the dying person can leave something behind is very often a great source of comfort. People don't tolerate being cut off in time any more than they like isolation in person. This is illustrated further, I believe, in the interest in ancestry and the desire for offspring.

In an article entitled "Reactions of a Man to Natural Death," Leon Saul wrote: "Is it possible that the wish to live, like other strong wishes that cause symptoms, can be dealt with therapeutically so that its frustration is less painful during the months of decline?" (11) The implication is that the acceptance of death eases the conflict. I can't agree. I don't have any idea how we help a person to die, but I am sure we can do much to help a person to *live* until the time of death.

REFERENCES

1 Eissler, K.: *The Psychiatrist and the Dying Patient,* International Universities Press, Inc., New York, 1953.

2 Rynearson, E.: "You are Standing at the Bedside of a Patient Dying," *CA,* May–June, Vol. 9, No. 3, 1959, p. 85.

3 Meyer, B. C.: 'Should the Patient Know the Truth?," *Journal of The Mount Sinai Hospital,* Vol. 20, No. 6, March-April, 1954, p. 344.

4 "Symposium: What Shall We Tell the Cancer Patient?" *Proceedings of the Staff Meetings of the Mayo Clinic,* Vol. 35, No. 10, May 11, 1960, p. 239.

5 Chodoff, P.: "A Psychiatric Approach to the Dying Patient," *CA,* Vol. 10, No. 1, January-February, 1960, p. 29.

6 Bibring, E.: "The Mechanism of Depression," in Phyllis Greenacre, ed., *Affective Disorders,* International Universities Press, Inc., New York, 1953, pp. 13–48.

7 Aitken-Swan, J., and Paterson, R.: "The Cancer Patient: Delay in Seeking Treatment," *British Medical Journal,* March 12, 1955, p. 623.

8 Shands, H., et al.: "Psychological Mechanisms in Patients with Cancer," *Cancer,* Vol. 6, 1953, p. 474.

9 Boland, J.: Personal communication.

10 Brodsky, B.: "Liebestod Fantasies in a Patient Faced with a Fatal Illness," *International Journal of Psychoanalysis,* Vol. 40, No. 1, 1959, p. 13.

11 Saul, L. J.: "Reactions of a Man to Natural Death," *Psychoanalytic Quarterly,* Vol. 28, 1959, p. 383.

Common Fallacies about Dying Patients

Avery D. Weisman

Avery D. Weisman is a psychoanalyst, physician, and
Professor of Psychiatry at the Harvard Medical School and
at the Massachusetts General Hospital where he heads
Project Omega—the study of dying persons. He is one of
the most thoughtful writers in the field of thanatology
today. In this selection from his book *On Dying and
Denying,* he attacks some of the myths and fallacies
concerning the attitudes and actions of the dying.

The plight of the dying awakens every man's sense of
dread and annihilation. Yet, as Swift said, "It is impossible that anything so
natural, so necessary, and so universal as death, should ever have been
designed by providence as an evil to mankind." Nevertheless, our common
belief, augmented by cultural bias, is that death is a deplorable, evil, unnecessary and premature event. Death is encased by custom. Our rituals,

formal and spontaneous, reflect an enormous concern about being in the presence of the dying and the soon-to-be dead.

In this section I use the physician as the prototype for anyone who is forced to consider the interface between life and death. As a professional, however, the physician influences the way that other people approach death. Because dying people are simply living people who have reached an ultimate stage, the doctor's misconceptions may distort their image of death.

Medicine is only partially scientific. Much of what a practitioner does depends upon empirical procedures, ethical precepts, sanctioned mythology, and much, much magic. Were any doctor to depend wholly upon scientific knowledge, he would be as constrained and disabled as anyone who could act only upon proven principles: He would be lost and ineffectual.

To be a responsive and responsible physician is almost an impossible profession, in the presence of incurable disease and dying. Just at the time when a doctor needs his skill and knowledge, they fail him, out of the nature of things. He is forced to improvise, and at times, his art becomes artifice.

Fortunately, patients tend to endow physicians with the aura of the priest and medicine man, both of whom can perform magic. The advantage of magic over science is that it does not need to be true. Magic and sorcery have nothing to do with truth and proof. They are strategies for dealing with special beliefs about reality. Medical practice draws upon folk-wisdom, and it is as indebted to folk-fallacies as to folk-truths. In the realm of death and dying, magical formulas and incantations frequently pass as principles. Consequently, physicians can readily, even inadvertently, call upon their prejudices and act upon preconceptions. As a result, fallacies about dying patients may be perpetuated from one generation to the next, insulated by a tradition that exempts these beliefs from investigation.

Here are a few typical, widespread fallacies about the dying:

1 Only suicidal and psychotic people are willing to die. Even when death is inevitable, no one wants to die.

2 Fear of death is the most natural and basic fear of man. The closer he comes to death, the more intense the fear becomes.

3 Reconciliation with death and preparation for death are impossible. Therefore, say as little as possible to dying people, turn their questions aside, and use any means to deny, dissimulate, and avoid open confrontation.

4 Dying people do not really want to know what the future holds. Otherwise, they would ask more questions. To force a discussion or to insist

439

upon unwelcome information is risky. The patient might lose all hope. He might commit suicide, become very depressed, or even die more quickly.

5 After speaking with family members, the doctor should treat the patient as long as possible. Then, when further benefit seems unlikely, the patient should be left alone, except for relieving pain. He will then withdraw, die in peace, without further disturbance and anguish.

6 It is reckless, if not downright cruel, to inflict unnecessary suffering upon the patient or his family. The patient is doomed; nothing can really make any difference. Survivors should accept the futility, but realize that they will get over the loss.

7 Physicians can deal with all phases of the dying process because of their scientific training and clinical experience. The emotional and psychological sides of dying are vastly overemphasized. Consultation with psychiatrists and social workers is unnecessary. The clergy might be called upon, but only because death is near. The doctor has no further obligation after the patient's death.

Fallacies lead physicians into inconsistencies, and to judgments that confuse the clinical with the moralistic. Precepts help to rationalize assumptions and to shelter the doctor from undue anxiety. Assumptions, particularly false assumptions, decide conclusions in advance. For example, these seven fallacies are, in effect, tacit justifications for not getting involved with death. Were the physician openly to confess his reluctance, he might paraphrase the fallacies like this: "Anyone who is willing to die must be out of his mind. Death is a dreadful business, because I am afraid of dying. I have done everything for this patient that I know. I wish I could do more. I don't want to be blamed, but I can't stand being around anyone who is going to die, especially if I know him. Even though we all know what is going to happen, let's pretend that all is well or soon will be. Maybe he doesn't know, after all. He hasn't ever asked me about his sickness, and certainly never mentioned dying. If he suspects, and he may, I suppose he would rather not know. Leave well enough alone. If we did force him to talk about the future, maybe he'd be more discouraged, or even take matters into his own hands. The family is pretty helpless, too, but I'll make sure that his pain is under control. Why did that family think I was going to upset him when we first found out what was wrong? We've never mentioned it, so far as I can tell. Now, the best thing to do is keep him comfortable, let him die in peace. We don't want to make anyone suffer unnecessarily. The facts are there, but it will do no good to dwell on death. The family seems to be taking it pretty well, but they'll get over it, they always do. Nature will take its course, if things can just be kept quiet. I don't need a psychiatrist to tell me what I know already. When the time comes, I'll ask the family minister to get in on this and offer some consolation. He'll be taking over soon, anyway!"

ⁱⁱⁱ

*Only someone who is extremely
apprehensive himself would fail to
see that many dying patients accept
death with equanimity and without
mental disturbance.*

ⁱⁱ

Dying patients who are attended by physicians who feel this way are probably fortunate. The scene is sympathetic, compared with the bleak prospect of dying alone and unattended. My point, however, is not to argue the merits of one kind of doctor as opposed to the management of another. Compassion and concern are in this mythical doctor's words, but the management he advocates is primarily intended to comfort and console himself.

Only someone who is extremely apprehensive himself would fail to see that many dying patients accept death with equanimity and without mental disturbance. To regard acceptance of death as a sign of being suicidal or psychotic amounts to believing that anyone who attempts suicide is insane and, therefore, beyond help, just as psychotics are beyond help—egregious fallacies, all.

To be more specific about these seven fallacies: the first three rationalize withdrawal and establish more distance between doctor and patient. The fourth fallacy infers that the patient is also disinclined to talk about death. Unwise confrontation is, by definition, apt to cause mental disturbance. We cannot assume, as this doctor does, that someone who asks no questions has no questions to ask. He may have no opportunity to ask, or he may be afraid to ask, lest he repel people on whom he depends. Families cannot decide judiciously about what to tell. They rely upon the expert for advice and can be swayed according to the doctor's beliefs. The fifth and sixth

441

fallacies presuppose that when the patient is not regarded as responsible, with eyes to see and ears to hear, his silence is assumed to mean that he is both ignorant and complacent. Withdrawal does not necessarily mean serenity, nor is open accessibility equivalent to inflicting "unnecessary suffering." It is commonly heard that physicians do not talk about death with very sick patients in order to keep up their hope. But they usually add that the patients are probably already aware of their condition, and so do not need to be told! If there are rationalizations ready for any contingency, how can anyone be wrong?

Let us continue: survivors do not always get over a serious loss and return to "normal," without first suffering a great deal. Sometimes, bereavement leads to serious somatic and psychological symptoms during the next year or two.* Mourners may become patients. Yet, some doctors continue to believe that anticipatory bereavement is peripheral to more genuine medical concerns.

What is "unnecessary suffering," that is so often cited as a reason for nonintervention? Who is to judge what varieties of suffering are necesssary or not? Whose suffering are we concerned about? During the terminal phase, not many patients ask for miracles, only for evidence of care and concern.

The most damaging and lethal fallacy in this, as in most other situations, is that of stereotyping people and problems. When we categorize anyone, doctor or patient, we reduce them to a least common denominator, and they become less than what they are or could be. The alternative, then, is to look for the exceptions, and meanwhile, to treat everyone as a special case.

---

*Colin M. Parkes, "The Psychosomatic Effects of Bereavement," in *Modern Trends in Psychosomatic Medicine,* ed. Oscar W. Hill (London: Butterworth, 1970). See also "The Broken Heart," this volume.

Death Work and Stages of Dying

Edwin S. Shneidman

In this selection from *Deaths of Man*, Dr. Shneidman
discusses what, if any, are the discernible "stages" of dying.
He notes that there are certain psychological features of the
dying process, characteristic of almost every dying person,
that must be understood if one is to comprehend the mind
and behavior of those approaching death.

. . . Death [is] the most mysterious, the most
threatening, and the most tantalizing of all human phenomena. Death is
destroyer and redeemer; it is the ultimate cruelty and the essence of release.
Death is universally feared but, paradoxically, sometimes is actively sought.
Although undeniably ubiquitous, death is incomprehensibly unique. Of all
phenomena it is the most obvious and the least reportable; it encompasses
the profoundest of man's perplexities and ambivalences. Over the ages
death has been the source of fear, the focus of taboo, the occasion for poetry,
the stimulus for philosophy—and remains the ultimate mystery in the life of
each man.

"Death is the one thing you don't have to do. It will be done for you." So
said philosopher Abraham Kaplan to me. But there is more to that statement
than first meets the mind. Admittedly it implies that everyone dies, that no
one can circumvent his own death. But it makes no attempt to explicate certain lesser truths: that persons die at various rates (from sudden to protracted), at various ages, and with various degrees of participation in their
own death. In those special cases—nowadays rather frequent—in which a
sensitive adult has been told (or knows) that he will die of a fatal disease
within a relatively short time, he has the opportunity (and the chore thrust
upon him) of preparing for his own death, that is, doing his own "death
work."

In the phrase "knows that he will die" the word "knows" has a special
connotation that is critical in any discussion of death. To "know" that one is
doomed to die soon is epistemologically different from "knowing" almost
anything else about oneself or about the world. It is a kind of "knowing"
infused not only with uncertainty but also with several layers of conscious

443

and unconscious mental functioning. Of course, everyone "knows" he is going to die ("Life is a fatal disease"; "No one gets out of life alive"), but when one is seriously ill and has been informed that he is moribund, then his "knowing" about his imminent death is typically mixed with magic, hope, disbelief, and denial. After all, death has never happened to him before.

ʔʔ

*People often do seem to "know" at
some deep unconscious or primitive
level when they are about to die.*

ʔʔ

No one can ever really "know" that he is about to die. There is always the intermittent presence of denial. The recurrent denial of death during the dying process seems to be the manifestation of the therapeutic gyroscope of the psyche. (We must not forget that one of the principal functions of the personality is to protect itself against itself—against its own ravages, assaults, and threats.) And yet seemingly contradictorily—but not really contradictorily, because we are dealing with different levels of the human mind—people often do seem to "know" at some deep unconscious or primitive level when they are about to die and then, in a very special and identifiable way, they withdraw, perhaps to husband their last energies, to put themselves together and prepare for their end.

One implication of this view of "knowing" relates to the question "To tell or not to tell?" In the situation of a person with a fatal disease—as in many aspects of psychotherapy—there is almost anything that can be done badly and almost anything that can be done well. The issue of telling is thus not so much a question of whether or not, but of how, how much, how often, how euphemistically, how hopefully, and how far beyond what the patient (and various members of his family) already "knows" at that moment. Hinton (1967) and Weisman (1972) present excellent discussions of this complicated issue.

Death work imposes a two-fold burden: intrapsychic (preparing oneself for death) and interpersonal (preparing oneself in relation to loved ones and, simultaneously, preparing the loved ones to be survivors). The task is further compounded by pervasive emotional states: grief and anguish over the death to come; anger at one's impotence, at fate, and often, by unconscious extension, at key persons in one's life who are not dying, especially the young; and beneath these, a low-grade anxiety related to fear of pain, to loss of competence, to loneliness and abandonment, to fear of the unknown. But always, intermittently coming and going, is the fervent denial that death will really occur to him.

Dr. Elisabeth Kübler-Ross has delineated five psychological stages in the process of dying, based on her work with terminally ill patients in a Chicago hospital. Her deep concern with their welfare is evident; her book *On Death and Dying* (1969) is a clear manifesto of care for those who are benighted by the shadow of death. At the least, it stands as an antidote to some of the callous conventional hospital procedures surrounding the dying patient, described so well by Sudnow in *Passing On* (1967) and by Glaser and Strauss in *Awareness of Dying* (1965) and *Time for Dying* (1968).

Her book grew out of an interdisciplinary seminar at the University of Chicago, in the course of which dying patients were interviewed, or more accurately, were invited to speak of their fears and hopes, dreams and nightmares. The results of this unexampled open discussion were strikingly salutary for both the stressed dying person and the stressed hospital personnel. The interviews often have an evocative and haunting quality, resonating deep within one and stirring buried aspirations and fears. One cannot help being moved by the great human spirit in the voices of these dying fellow beings.

Kübler-Ross explicates five psychological stages of dying, or sets of reactions to one's awareness of imminent death. Categorized primarily "in terms of coping mechanisms at the time of a terminal illness," these stages are defined as: (1) denial and isolation ("No, not me; it can't be true!"); (2) anger—rage, envy, resentment ("Why me?"); (3) bargaining ("If you'll . . . then I'll . . ."); (4) depression ("What's the use?"); and (5) acceptance (the final rest before the long journey). According to her analysis, "the one thing that persists through all these stages [is] hope" ("I will not die"). One is reminded of Maurice Farber's *Theory of Suicide* (1968), in which self-destruction is seen as "a disease of hope," and of Kobler and Stotland's *The End of Hope* (1964), a case study of the death of a hospital.

Dr. Kübler-Ross does not tell us what percentages of the dying patients lived through each of these five stages or what the consequences were if any were cut off before they achieved the last stage. One key question is how one makes the transition from the negative affective states (which characterize the first four stages) to a state of acceptance. One might wish that she had extended her explorations of the nature of acceptance, as Henry Murray did so superbly in "Dead to the World: The Passions of Herman Melville" (1967). The last of Murray's five "psychic stages" in Melville's psychological development vis-à-vis death is "I accept my annihilation." But Murray then ponders the possible meanings of this acceptance, demonstrating that "acceptance" obviously has many dimensions:

> Did this last station of Melville's pilgrimage constitute a victory of the spirit, as some think? an ultimate reconciliation with God at the end of a lifelong quarrel? or was it a graceful acquiescence to the established morality and conventions of his world with Christian forgiveness toward those who had crushed him in their name? or a forthright willing of the obligatory? or was it an acknowledgment of defeat? a last-ditch surrender of his long quest for a new gospel of joy in this life? or was it a welcoming of death?

My own limited work has not led me to conclusions identical with those of Kübler-Ross. Indeed, while I have seen in dying persons isolation, envy, bargaining, depression, and acceptance, I do not believe that these are necessarily "stages" of the dying process, and I am not at all convinced that they are lived through in that order, or, for that matter, in any universal order. What I do see is a complicated clustering of intellectual and affective states, some fleeting, lasting for a moment or a day or a week, set, not unexpectedly, against the backdrop of that person's total personality, his "philosophy of life" (whether an essential optimism and gratitude to life or a pervasive pessimism and dour or suspicious orientation to life).

Philosophers—all but the twentieth-century analytic so-called philosophers—have traditionally taken life and death as their core topics. In relation to death and philosophy, the interested reader can turn to Choron's *Death and Western Thought* (1963) for a résumé of what major philosophers have thought about death. As the tie between philosophic reflection and easing the burden of one's own death, I know of nothing more illuminating than Pepper's crisp and insightful essay, "Can a Philosophy Make One Philosophical?" (1967).

What of that nexus of emotions manifested by the dying person? Rather than the five definite stages discussed above, my experience leads me to posit a hive of affect, in which there is a constant coming and going. The emotional stages seem to include a constant interplay between disbelief and hope and, against these as background, a waxing and waning of anguish, terror, acquiescence and surrender, rage and envy, disinterest and ennui, pretense, taunting and daring and even yearning for death—all these in the context of bewilderment and pain.

One does not find a unidirectional movement through progressive stages so much as an alternation between acceptance and denial. Denial is a most interesting psychodynamic phenomenon. For a few consecutive days a dying person is capable of shocking a listener with the breathtaking candor of his profound acceptance of imminent death and the next day shock that listener with unrealistic talk of leaving the hospital and going on a trip. This interplay between acceptance and denial, between understanding what is happening and magically disbelieving its reality, may reflect a deeper dialogue of the total mind, involving different layers of conscious awareness of "knowing" and of needing not to know. Weisman's recent book, *On Dying and Denying* (1972), focuses on these complicated psychodynamics of dying, expecially on the role of denial.

The optimal working techniques for the clinical thanatologist (the professional or lay person, staff or volunteer) who deals directly with the death-laden aspects of the dying person have yet to be evolved. Admittedly, working with a dying person is a very special kind of intervention and would seem to require some special approaches and skills. As a beginning, one might say that the primary goals of such thanatological efforts are to help the dying person achieve a better death ("an appropriate death") and to help the survivors deal better with their loss, specifically to forestall morbidity or mortality. The interactions with the dying person are, understandably, different from almost any other therapeutic exchange, though they contain typical elements of rapport building, interview, conversation, psychotherapy (including interpretation), history taking, just plain talk, and communicative silences.

There are many ways in which a clinical thanatologist can find an appropriate occasion to speak with a dying person of feelings about death. Even dreams can be used to this end. (On a closely related topic, Litman, in 1964, wrote of the almost prophetic role of dreams in suicide). An example: A singularly beautiful and serene young woman, rapidly dying of metastacized cancer, had not talked about the possibility of her own death. One day, immediately after I came into her hospital room, she stated that she had had a dream the night before that she wanted to tell me. In her dream, she wandered down a street that she almost recognized but had never travelled, in a city that was vaguely familiar but one that she had never visited, and went to a house that seemed like home but clearly was not hers. In response to her ringing the bell, her mother answered the door, but that person was definitely no longer her mother. She then woke up.

"What does it all mean?" she asked me. In turn, I asked her what her mood had been during her dream. She said that it was one of pervasive sadness and nostalgia. She volunteered that perhaps the dream reflected her wish to be more independent of her mother, to lead her own life, living by her own standards. I asked her under what circumstances her mother might not be her mother. To this, she answered if her mother were dead, but she certainly did not wish for that; or, if it turned out that her mother were really not her biological parent, that she had been adopted, but that did not seem to make any sense. I went one step further: I asked if there might be any other circumstance. No, she said, she could not think of any. Her face then clouded and with some surprise she whispered, "If *I* were dead!" After she said this, her expression seemed to brighten. "Of course!" she said, and then asked, "Is that what I've been trying to keep from myself?" In the following few days she spoke of many details of her life, but intermittently, at a pace which she herself set, she talked about the realistic possibility of her death, her fear of dying, her concern for her loved ones, her deep regret at having to die, and the many joys she had had in her brief life. She said that she was glad that she and I could talk "honestly." Five days after her dream of death she died.

The thanatologist, if he examines his own mind, may very well discover that he is almost constantly aware of the expected "death trajectory" of his patient, and he governs the intensity of the sessions, their movement, the climaxes, the protective plateaus, and so on, over that projected time span— just as a skilled psychotherapist tries to control the intensity of the flow of material within any psychotherapeutic hour, trying not to leave the patient disturbed at the end of the session. The benign interventionist always needs to keep his hand on the rheostat governing the intensity of affect. The best results are achieved by turning affective intensity up gradually during the session and shading it down somewhat toward the end. So it is in the thanatological treatment of a dying person over the last months, weeks, days, hours, of his life.

In my belief, the transference and countertransference aspects of death work are unique, different in subtle ways from any other human exchange;

both Hinton and Kübler-Ross mention this point.* For one thing, the situation itself, because of its obvious poignant quality and its time-limited feature, permits a depth of investment which in any other circumstances might border on the unseemly, yet in this setting is not only appropriate but perhaps even optimal. We can love a dying person, and permit a dying person to love us, in a meaningful way that is not possible in any other psychotherapeutic encounter.

It is difficult (and admittedly complicating) to speak meaningfully about Thanatos and its theoretical opposite, Eros. (Nor, parenthetically, do I view these concepts as anything other than figurative metaphoric polarities. I do not at all believe in a death instinct.) But considering the special nature of the transference and countertransference with dying persons, one might ask: Is it possible to fight death with love, or with loving care as a kind of substitute for love? Is it appropriate? Can it work? In some cases of dying persons I have worked with there was little question in my mind that Eros had helped to sustain them in their terminal periods and to lighten their dying days, that is, if by Eros we mean sympathy, support, and concern, all the opposite of neglect.* One cannot always give the necessary transfusions of hope, but one should not fail to transmit one's honest feelings of interest, affection, and respect for the other's dignity—presaging one's own real sense of grief at the loss to come.

Working with dying persons seems to have some curious attractions and mystiques, some akin, I believe, to those associated with the very beginnings of life, the primal scene. In a sense the mysteries connected with sexuality are not as great as those lifelong uncertainties about the components of ideal love. In somewhat the same way, one can be continually intrigued, mystified, and even voyeuristic about working with individuals who are in the process of dying. As I see a dying person moving from day to day toward that ultimate moment, I hope that perhaps I can learn something

---

*Hinton: "Often we came to know each other well—friendships grew fast in these circumstances and sometimes, it seemed difficult to believe we met only a few times"; and "The physician who had been questioned by this man [with cancer] said that he felt that he had probably been more perturbed by the conversation than the patient had" (1967, pp. 96, 134). Kübler-Ross: "We find the same to be true among many patients who developed strong positive feelings towards us and were still able to pass through a stage of rage and anger often displaced onto others in the environment who reminded them of their own failing strength, vitality and functioning," (1972, p. 57).

*Arnold Toynbee, at eighty, says, "Love cannot save life from death, but it can fulfill life's purpose."

about how dying is done, something about the arcane mysteries of the magic moment of transition from life to nonlife, something about the components of an ideal death, and even, if the gods are gracious, some guidelines that will teach me how to die well when my own turn comes.

ⵢⵢ

The physician would do well to interact intensively with a few, perhaps only one dying person at a time, treating that person as a paradigm of all his dying patients. Further, a physician needs to take vacations from death.

ⵢⵢ

Some practical words may be in order especially for the physician who sees a great number of dying persons in his practice—the oncologist and the hematologist primarily, but many others as well. A busy professional simply cannot take the time to deal intensively with each of his dying patients, and even if he had the time, he would not have the psychic reserves to do so. The physician would do well though to interact intensively with a few, perhaps only one dying person at a time, treating that person as a paradigm of all his dying patients. Further, a physician needs to take vacations from death. A gynecological oncologist, for example, should intersperse his practice with obstetrical cases, delivering babies as a balance for others of his patients who are dying of cancer of the uterus. And, as a further principle, a physician in oncological practice should not fail to seek out psychological or psychiatric consultation for his patients if they are significantly depressed or disturbed about dying and *for himself* if he senses that his own equanimity has been touched. This type of psychotherapeutic consultation might well be made a routine part of a physician's dealing with dying patients, lest he fall prey to the predictable consequences of the unusual psychological stress that comes from working constantly around and against death.

REFERENCES

Choron, Jacques. *Death and Western Thought*. New York: Collier Books, 1963.

Farber, Maurice. *Theory of Suicide*. New York: Funk & Wagnall, 1968.

Glaser, B. G., and Strauss, A. *Awareness of Dying*. Chicago: Aldine, 1965.

Glaser, B. G., and Strauss, A. *Time for Dying*. Chicago: Aldine, 1968.

Hinton, John. *Dying*. Baltimore: Penguin Books, 1967.

Kobler, Arthur, and Stotland, Ezra. *The End of Hope*. New York: Free Press, 1964.

Kübler-Ross, Elisabeth. *On Death and Dying*. New York: Macmillan, 1969.

Kübler-Ross, Elisabeth. Review of Hinton's *Dying*. *Life-Threatening Behavior*, 1972, *2*, 56–58.

Litman, Robert E. Immobilization Response to Suicidal Behavior. *Archives of General Psychiatry*, 1964, *11*, 282–285.

Murray, Henry A. Dead to the World: The Passions of Herman Melville. In Edwin S. Shneidman (Ed.), *Essays in Self-Destruction*. New York: Science House, 1967.

Pepper, Stephen C. Can a Philosophy Make One Philosophical? In Edwin S. Shneidman (Ed.), *Essays in Self-Destruction*. New York: Science House, 1967.

Sudnow, David. *Passing On*. Englewood Cliffs, N.J.: Prentice-Hall, 1967.

Toynbee, Arnold *et al. Man's Concern with Death*. New York: McGraw-Hill, 1969.

Weisman, Avery D. *On Dying and Denying*. New York: Behavior Publications, 1972.

Denial and Middle Knowledge

Avery D. Weisman

In this selection, which is taken from Dr. Weisman's book *On Dying and Denying,* the author describes and discusses the important role that denial plays in the dying process.

From *On Dying and Denying: A Psychiatric Study of Terminality* by Avery D. Weisman Copyright © 1972 by Behavioral Publications, Inc., New York. Reprinted by permission.

SURVIVAL AND FATAL ILLNESS

For most people, sickness is uncomfortable, inconvenient, temporary, but rarely a menace. Then, if sickness persists, enduring beyond the healing effects of treatment and time, the personal dimensions of being sick gradually become more conspicuous. Prolonged illness means not only primary derangements in bodily functions and organs, but secondary incapacity of otherwise intact organs and functions. Like the sick person himself, physical functions and organs may be affected by having nothing to do. Healthy activity requires that we have tasks to perform. If this is not possible, everyday performance becomes more and more difficult until we deteriorate into someone who is concerned merely about the meager necessities of survival alone.

Health means far more than simply not being sick. Similarly, recovery from an illness means more than merely being able to survive. There is a dimension of health that assures us of gratification in being able to do for ourselves. We are not only able to survive, but can act on our own behalf according to the values and standards of the ego ideal.

The patient who is afflicted with a potentially fatal illness is forced to contend with both a threatening disease and impairment of his personal significance. The healing effect of treatment and time are not his. Therefore, as his illness progresses, he is forced to settle for less and less, to compromise his expectations, and to become less than what he had been or might be. Finally, survival becomes an end in itself. He is cut off from most of the satisfactions and significance that he had enjoyed and in which he had found most of his personal meaning.

The process of dying takes place in many ways and on different levels of experience. We die to many things before we die of a disease. Small, partial deaths gradually become confluent, so that we may cease to be as an autonomous person long before literal terminus takes place.

The full sense of viability is determined by three factors: (a) biological survival, (b) competent behavior, and (c) responsible conduct.

Biological survival in the course of serious illness means physical continuity, pain relief, reduction of suffering, and adaptation to diminished strength and capacity. *Competent behavior* means that, to some extent, a sick person can choose the way in which he solves daily problems and carries out his customary tasks. *Responsible conduct* is determined by how closely a patient's competence permits him to fulfill the directives and avoid the prohibitions dictated by his ego ideal.

These three factors contribute to the complete meaning of viability, which is *significant survival*, not merely biological existence. Organic disease can precipitate sickness, but not all sickness is due to disease. Many nonorganic factors and processes enter into survival and recovery, and can aggravate, precipitate, and redirect the course of illness. Moreover, sickness and its resolution may require a strategy of adaptation to the various psychosocial issues generated by organic incapacity. To a significant degree, assessment of denial is based upon the extent and style in which a patient accepts and repudiates the personal impact of sickness.

THE MECHANISM CALLED DENIAL

Few books in the literature of psychiatry have been as influential as Anna Freud's *The Ego and the Mechanisms of Defence* (1948). Stripped to essentials, its major contribution is a theory that defense mechanisms are based upon a primitive response to danger called *denial*. Although A. Freud confined her examples to children, describing denial by word, act, and fantasy, her viewpoint could readily be expanded to include more differentiated and sophisticated defenses, as found in adults. Indeed, a wholly appropriate title might have been, "The Ego and the Mechanisms of Denial."

Since her book, many psychiatrists have described more elaborate forms of defenses and have extended the concept of denial. As a result, "denial" now covers almost any situation, act, or verbal expression in which anyone seeks to "avoid reality," or to escape confrontation with something unpleasant and alarming, at least in the opinion of the observer.

Lewin (1950) asserted that denial is necessary for mood-enhancing and manic states. He compared the manic patient to an infant who has been stimulated and satisfied in a feeding relationship with mother. Eating, sucking, sleeping, and dreamless death are not only closely allied in Lewin's opinion, but can be induced by extensive denial.

Fenichel's encyclopedic treatise on psychoneurosis (1945) depends upon the idea that denial permeates practically the entire range of psychopathology. Schizophrenic reactions, fetishism, memory defects, anxiety attacks, sleep disturbances, and even seizures are attributed to the excessive operation of the mechanism called denial. His hypothesis seems to be that denial is always available whenever a person is threatened, from whatever source. Its usual effect is to negate a painful perception or neutralize a distressing conflict. By frequent reiteration, the reader gains the impression that denial is a mechanism that can be set in motion by any crisis or conflict, and that most defenses, if not all symptoms, depend upon denial.

In general, denial has been used as a fictitious *mechanism*, an *as if* entity that can be triggered promptly by a threatening event or perception, as well as a hypothetical *explanation* for different kinds of psychopathology. Anna Freud regarded denial as a *unifying* concept for different defenses, but she did not suggest that denial is a *unitary* mechanism which serves only to repudiate reality. In fact, she pointed out that denial is expressed in words, acts, and fantasies, but these are what people *do* in order to counter, neutralize, and reorient themselves in the presence of danger. In other words, denial is but one aspect of what defenses do. Denial helps us to do away with a threatening portion of reality, but only because we may then participate more fully in contending with problems.

Terminology simplifies communication, but it can often defeat itself. Terms such as "denial" and "defense mechanisms" are outstanding examples of "misplaced concreteness." Not only are these terms frequently assumed to represent well-established entities, but they are used as explanatory concepts. When this happens, further inquiry and investigation are tacitly discouraged, because custom decides that the words are synonymous with the facts. For example, were we to assume that "memory" is synonymous with "remembering," and that it was a basic, irreducible mental fact, then we would not be able to analyze remembering further. We would be oblivious to the complexities of how information is acquired, registered, stored, scanned, and retrieved.

Psychiatrists often speak about defense mechanisms as if they were independent mental operations which are almost dissociated from the ebb and flow of interpersonal events. They imply that defenses are characteristic of each individual, and that external "dangers" simply elicit a familiar response with comparatively little selectivity. Defenses are very real events, but the hypothesis designating the reality of defense mechanisms is very dubious. Defenses are ways in which the individual selectively participates in ongoing events, but defense "mechanisms" are only general terms which characterize broad similarities between them. There is nothing fundamentally wrong about generalizing acts and statements that separate us from a threatening situation, and calling the effect "denial," unless we believe that denial is the exclusive function of an inner mechanism whose sole purpose is to mitigate the meaning of an external danger.

We must distinguish between the *process of denying* and the *fact of denial*. Denial is a total process of responding within a specific psychosocial context. Negation is only one of the consequences of this process; denial is a final fact, not the process itself. To confuse a total process with one of its defensive aims is like saying that the purpose of driving an automobile is to avoid accidents.

THE PROCESS CALLED DENYING

The mechanistic interpretation of denial has wholly a negative aim—to avoid a painful perception, or, more generally, to keep a distance between a perception and the person who is frightened by it. However, any purposeful act may have its defensive side which serves the aim of avoidance and aversion. The familiar expression "using denial" suggests that denial is a primary defense, having no other function but that of aversion and negation. In contrast with this mechanistic interpretation, the dynamic interpretation of denial does not accept negation and aversion as static products of a process, but rather as incomplete interpretations of a variety of related acts.

The process called denying is both an act and a fact—the act of denying and the fact of denial. Both depend upon personal interaction to define what, how, and when denying takes place.

The act of denying precedes the fact of denial by four successive steps. These steps are:

1 Acceptance of a primary and public field of perception.
2 Repudiation of a portion of the shared meaning of that field.
3 Replacement of the repudiated meaning with a more congenial version.
4 Reorientation of the individual within the scope of the total meaning, in order to accommodate the revised reality.

The fifth step brings about the fact of denial.

Acceptance of a primary and public field of perception means that no one can deny by himself, in utter solitude. He may repudiate events or flee from an impending danger, but he cannot deny unless a portion of that field is shared with someone else.

Repudiation of a portion of the shared meaning may take place by simple negation, but a person may also behave inappropriately for the existing situation, as if the painful portion of the field were not perceived or shared with anyone else. Directly or indirectly, *replacement* of the repudiated meaning occurs. *Reorientation* means that not only is the threat contained, or, possibly, excluded from the field, but earlier relationships and prior conditions are restored.

From the inside, people do not recognize that they have denied a reality, whether it is a perception or a meaning. They only know that every action, aggressive and aversive, is affirmative, fight, flight, or immobilization. The only criterion for understanding its meaning is whether the act is effective and accurate. Only in retrospect do people sometimes see that they have avoided, denied, or negated an obvious reality. The *fact* of denial needs another person who judges that denial of their shared reality has occurred. But the fact of denial means more than simply the presence of an outside judge. Shared and public realities are as much created as contended with. We test reality, but part of the process called "reality testing" is that we are tested by reality, as well. In the interpersonal field, we test out our perceptions and performances, but we are also tested by others seeking confirmation of their realities. Consequently, whenever anyone alters the meaning of a commonly accepted reality, declaring that his version is correct, he can expect to be challenged, simply because everyone within a specific field needs to protect and reaffirm what seems self-evident to him.

The mechanistic interpretation of denial is static, because it does not allow for the modulating participation of the other person to whom the denial is expressed. It assumes that denial is a constant, and that someone who denies does so out of his inner workings, not in order to redefine a relationship with another person in a specific context. As a rule, clinicians tend to ignore the significance of the external observer or participant in making the diagnosis of denial. They assume that denial is merely a matter of more-or-less deviation from an accepted norm, which usually means their own. Depending upon whether a patient is thought to deny a great deal or hardly at all, some doctors recognize major, partial, and minor denial. Patients who minimize are thought to show minor denial, while those who substitute delusions for reality are major deniers.

As a rule, denial is found most frequently when the doctor looks for it, least often when he takes his patient's statements at face value. Naturally, any judge presumes his own accuracy. But sometimes, inappropriate answers to questions may be the correct response, providing that the judge can correct for his special viewpoint and bias. Expectations often determine responses, and this is equally true when judging the extent of denial.

ʃʃ

The purpose of denial is not simply to avoid a danger, but to prevent loss of a significant relationship. This explains why patients tend to deny more to certain people than to others.

ʃʃ

THE PURPOSE OF DENIAL

It is not enough merely to decide that someone has denied a self-evident reality. What form does the denial take? To whom is the denial communicated? What are the circumstances in which denial is expressed? What is threatened?

Although a potential danger is apt to evoke denial (as I shall call the combined act and fact), a common threatened danger is a *jeopardized relationship with a significant key person.* Hence, the purpose of denial is not simply to avoid a danger, but to prevent loss of a significant relationship (Weisman & Hackett, 1967). This explains why patients tend to deny more to certain people than to others. Patients who deny a great deal seem to do so in order to preserve a high level of self-esteem. For this reason, they need to preserve contact and stabilize their relationship with someone essential to self-esteem. Even when there seems to be no one in particular who threatens or could be threatened by a patient's illness, deterioration, or death, the patient himself may deny because he wants to maintain the *status quo* of already existing relationships.

CASE 2* A 48-year-old married woman with advanced, but not terminal, cancer of the cervix was admitted to the hospital for further evaluation

---

Case 1 is included in a previous section of Dr. Weisman's work and is not reproduced here—ED.

and treatment. She seemed calm, even optimistic, and behaved as if hospitalization would be only perfunctory. A social worker, who had known her for a long time, found it strange that this intelligent woman asked no questions about her own condition. She seemed much more preoccupied with her husband's duodenal ulcer than with her cancer. Despite many previous discussions, the patient seemed to ignore the uncertainty of the treatment, with the ultimate uncertainty about life itself.

The extent of denial was so baffling that a psychiatric consultant was called upon. Almost as soon as the interview began, the patient suddenly asked, "Tell me, Doctor, is Grade 3 carcinoma of the cervix more malignant than Grade 1?" She then went on to talk about her serious condition, with no evidence of further denial. Her concern about the husband's ulcer stemmed from worry about how he would get along after her death. She had phrased her worry in terms of his proper diet, but the significant concern was whether he could keep the family together. There had been many arguments between her husband and their children. Without her intercession, she feared that the children would leave home, and, as a result, her husband's ulcer might get worse.

What prompted this patient to talk about her death with the consultant? She had already discussed these concerns with her social worker, but in the hospital, she denied worry, except to the psychiatrist, someone she had not seen before and, probably, would not see again. We should also note that she used an ostensibly medical question as a means of introducing more important problems.

This apparent paradox is very common: patients with serious illnesses will ask about their diagnosis and prognosis, but only to someone not in authority, such as a ward aide, a medical student, a consultant. These are, in effect, not significant people, so the patient can venture to speak with them about deeper concerns, not risking a rupture of significant relationships.

Denial helps to maintain a simplified, yet constant relationship with significant others, especially at a moment of crisis. Case 2 feared that she might lose her family as a result of her illness, part of which was symbolized by hospital admission. If she could manage to reduce the threat through denial, claiming that hospitalization was brief and trivial, that her husband's ulcer was more important, then already existing relationships could be preserved.

MIDDLE KNOWLEDGE

Somewhere between open acknowledgment of death and its utter repudiation is an area of uncertain certainty called *middle knowledge*. Case 1, for example, accepted death as an abstract plausibility. However, at moments of stress, such as after the pathological fracture, or shortly before his death, he voiced plans for a healthy future, or at least spoke about doing things that terminal illness precluded.

As a rule, middle knowledge tends to occur at serious transition points, such as when a patient begins the descent to death, undergoes a setback, or finds obvious equivocation among the people on whom he depends. Fluctuation between denial and acceptance takes place throughout the course of illness, except that denial is more readily diagnosed when there is less reason to hope.

CASE 3   A 35-year-old widow entered the hospital for diagnostic evaluation. She had had a mastectomy several years earlier, but until recently, no further symptoms developed. Shortly after the tests were completed, it became apparent that despite slight clinical symptoms, she had extensive metastases. The problem of planning further treatment for what seemed to be a hopeless situation led to equivocation among her doctors, protracted bedside discussions, and unexplained delay in discharge. Although the doctors had been quite candid before, now they talked in riddles, each one contradicting the other. She asked to go home, but then, for no good reason, she was asked to stay a while longer.

In a conversation with the psychiatric consultant, the patient seemed to recognize the full import of her diagnosis, but then talked as if she had many years left and could even go back to work. She could not grasp the current treatment difficulties and was puzzled by her symptoms. Her operation had been so long ago, she complained, why was she so very weak now? A few days later, she lapsed into stupor, and died.

Middle knowledge is marked by unpredictable shifts in the margin between what is observed and what is inferred. Patients seem to know and want to know, yet they often talk as if they did not know and did not want to be reminded of what they have been told. Many patients rebuke their doctors for not having warned them about complications in treatment or the course of illness, even though the doctors may have been scrupulous about keeping them informed. These instances of seeming denial are usually examples of middle knowledge that herald a relapse. When a patient with a fatal illness suddenly becomes unable to draw plausible inferences about himself, slipping back into an exacerbation of denial, it is often a sign that the terminal phase is about to begin.

DEGREES OF DENIAL

Any statement can be contradicted, and our mental apparatus can nullify any reality, including its own. The roots of denial are planted in the biolog-

459

ical, social, and emotional soil of life, not in the rules of logic. The various interactions that give rise to denial are so fluid and diversified that it is quite impossible to catalogue all the forms in which denial expresses itself. Even when we restrict the manifestations of denying and denial to the topic of threatened and incipient death, the scope of denial is never exhausted. People may deny facts about illness, symptoms, diagnosis, causes of illness, treatment, outlook, disability, family history, relationships, social resources, and, of course, impending death.

The familiar triad established by A. Freud does not mean that denial by word, act, or fantasy adequately classifies all forms of denying and denial. Words, acts, and fantasies are general ways in which we get to know another person. What he says, does, or thinks about are clues to his personality, whether he denies or not. Denying is a process, not a static event, so degrees of denial are never constant. Someone who is a major denier at one moment and under certain circumstances may be a minor denier in another situation.

Because this study was primarily concerned with denial as it related to terminality and the threat of death, our classification was based upon three degrees or orders of denial pertaining to death. *First-order denial* is based upon how a patient perceives the primary facts of illness. *Second-order denial* refers to the inferences that a patient draws, or fails to draw, about the extensions and implications of his illness. *Third-order denial* is concerned with the image of death itself: denial of extinction.

Denial of Facts

First-order denial is usually unequivocal from the observer's viewpoint Because the discrepancy between a patient's report and perceptions and what the observer sees is so great, he has little difficulty in deciding that denial is present. For example, one aged woman refused to accept the fact of her son's death from cancer. Despite efforts of her family, she insisted that he was merely out of town on business, and that the body in the coffin was another man's.

It is not unusual for patients to deny and disavow the primary facts of illness and disease, even when previous experience might have alerted them to recurrences. One man who had coronary heart disease awakened one morning with chest pain. He then went out and bought pork sausages for breakfast. When the pain continued, he was forced to seek medical help, but he complained that his pain was due to his gall bladder, which was usually affected by eating pork sausages! He did not deny the fact of pain, but only the cause of the chest pain. Nevertheless, this was an instance of first-order denial.

Denial of clinical facts, such as chest pain, is not the same as denial of the diagnosis, but when a patient could be expected to recognize tell-tale symptoms of recurrence, it amounts to the same thing. Patients will often use words as instruments of denial, even when the word used is correct. For example, the term "cancer" has secondary meanings that are not shared with the more euphemistic word "tumor." Cancer, unfortunately, evokes images of decay, wasting away, corruption, and so forth. Tumor implies that the lesion is circumscribed, removable, and not apt to be very serious. Similarly, patients do not like the diagnosis of "heart attack." Instead, they may prefer to say that "something was wrong with my ticker," "the blood vessels in my heart were too narrow," or "the doctor told me that I almost had a heart attack."

Euphemisms and circumlocutions are so commonly used in medicine that it would be unfair to label anything less than calling a spade a dirty shovel an example of first- or second-order denial. Nevertheless, when clincial facts are explained by diluted diagnoses and trivial terms, it is not that a patient prefers euphemisms, but that these terms help him to avoid and nullify a recurrent threat. Gravely ill patients, for example, may explain their presence in the hospital by saying, "My doctor wants to be sure I don't have anything serious" or "I've been working too hard and need a rest."

Obviously, first-order denial precludes second- and third-order denial. When facts are negated, it is unnecessary to consider their implications.

CASE 4   Although she had a large abdominal tumor that interfered with daily life, a 48-year-old housewife had minimal complaints. She complied with the treatment program, asked very few questions and showed no apparent interest in the cause of the gross swelling. Her husband had a colostomy for bowel cancer about 20 years before. He criticized his wife's doctors for being alarmists, fools, or charlatans. The first physician she consulted attempted to be candid, but her husband became irritated and claimed that the doctor was mistaken about the diagnosis. She avoided any doctor for a long time, but then, as her tumor grew and incapacity became more pronounced, she finally found a physician who was almost unrealistically reassuring.

When hospitalization became necessary, her attitude was so inconsistent with clinical facts that a psychiatric assessment seemed obligatory. But her physician refused, fearing that the patient would become too upset. Finally, he permitted a social worker to interview the patient. To the surprise

461

of the staff, the patient dramatically responded by pouring out her feelings about having an incurable illness. She was relieved and consoled by the interview, rather than upset. Further conversations disclosed that she had managed to keep her concern within bounds because her husband and doctor had expected denial from her, corresponding to their own reluctance to face the facts.

CASE 5   After recovering from an acute myocardial infarction, a 55-year-old factory worker returned to the medical clinic regularly, but always for complaints unrelated to his heart. Then, one day, while working, severe chest pain recurred. Although it spread to his jaw, shoulder, and left arm, he did not report to a doctor for 3 days. When finally brought to the hospital, he denied suspecting that the symptoms might be another heart attack. He explained that during the first attack, the pain had extended to his fingertips. This time, however, the pain stopped at his wrist. Therefore, it could not be the same trouble he had before!

CASE 6   A 52-year-old widow was being treated for two small epitheliomas. One morning she felt a lump in her breast. Instead of calling it to her doctor's attention, she waited until he was about to discharge her after treatment for the skin cancer ended. She then casually inquired if she would now be all right, not mentioning the tumor of the breast. He promptly reassured her, and the treatment was concluded. Thereafter, she avoided any contact with her affected breast, even doubling up the bath towel so she would not feel the mass. Months later, she was admitted to the hospital with extensive ulceration of her breast.

First-order denial is usually short-lived, although people may persistently minimize their symptoms throughout most of the prediagnostic period. Prediagnostic delay may be due to denial, especially when a patient has someone to help foster and encourage denial. Sometimes, it is the doctor who encourages the patient to false security. Hence the doctor transmits first-order denial to his patient. In fairness, however, many patients hear only what they want to hear, and then protest that they had not been warned about possible qualifications and complications.

CASE 7   A 65-year-old widower developed severe chest pain, but instead of calling his own physician, turned to a doctor who had erroneously minimized symptoms of cerebral thrombosis in his late wife. The doctor said that she suffered "only nerves" at the time when she was about to become paralyzed and then die. The patient later admitted that his call to the wife's physician was the first contact they had had in about seven years, so it was obvious that he preferred a doctor who would minimize his chest pain, even at the risk that another serious illness might be overlooked.

Second-order denial refers to patients who accept the primary facts of illness, even the diagnosis, but cannot visualize the implications and possible extensions of the lesion. It is reasonable, of course, to feel encouraged after a successful operation or period of convalescence, especially when a patient recovers and his doctor is reassuring. However, it is less reasonable when a patient retrospectively minimizes his illness and turns the future into a supportive set of rationalizations. For example, one man after a heart attack claimed that his heart was stronger than ever, because his doctor had compared recovery from coronary thrombosis with scar formation after a wound. "Everyone knows how tough a scar is, so my heart will be tough, too!"

Denial of implications often takes place when a patient fractionates his illness and persistent symptoms into many minor complaints, each of which can then be handled separately. As a result, the total illness cannot amount to much. Generally, patients who refuse to comment about their future and deny the possible implications of illness are seldom very optimistic. They tend to postpone specific plans on one pretext or another. Often they interpose another period of recovery between the original illness and a highly positive future. In this way, the second period is seen in more optimistic terms than if it were simply an extension of the primary disease. "Just as soon as this bleeding stops (or the wound heals, or this infection clears up), I'll be on my way!"

> CASE 8   A 34-year-old mother of two children had extensive treatment for breast cancer. Although she was not terminal, she could not care for herself or the children, and was tended by her widowed mother.
>
> There was a large ulcer at the site of the mastectomy. The patient referred to this as "a tendency to infection." She avoided situations that might expose her to further infections, fearing that she might catch cold. In the hospital she insisted that her bed not be near anyone with pneumonia. Half-heartedly, she complained that "No one ever tells me anything," even though she had been told about the diagnosis and purpose of treatment. "Doctors don't tell me what is going on. I wish they would because then I'd know when I'll be well!"

Throughout her extended illness, she wove a pattern of plausible fictions around every exacerbation and complication. Many of these rationalizations concerned fear that her divorced husband would take the children away. Part of the denial was sustained by her mother, an energetic woman who had also nursed her husband and sister during their terminal illnesses. She was proud that her sister had lived for a time after doctors had given up all hope, and therefore was adamantly optimistic about her daughter. That both her husband and sister had finally died did not sway her conviction that good nursing care would prevail.

CASE 9 A 37-year-old housewife, mother of three teen-aged sons, consulted a gynecologist because of uterine bleeding. In the course of the examination, a breast nodule was discovered. She was operated upon the following day, and after a biopsy showed malignancy, a mastectomy was immediately performed. Because the mutilating operation had not been anticipated, her doctor feared that the lack of preparation might cause the patient to become extremely alarmed, and possibly, suicidal. A psychiatric consultant was asked to intervene, almost as soon as the patient returned to her room.

She surprised everyone by her euphoria, and enthusiastic acceptance of the mastectomy. For several years, she had not attended church because of claustrophobia. As a devout Catholic, she feared eventual punishment. When the psychiatrist told her how fortunate she was, that the tumor was small and had been so promptly detected, she interpreted this "good fortune" as a sign of divine intercession and forgiveness.

While the staff appreciated, with relief, this highly positive response, the patient refused to return for later treatment. She insisted that God had not only forgiven her but had performed a miracle, as well! Why would God in his goodness stop at an early diagnosis? Would he not also cure her? Therefore, she was cured. Her denial extended to other phases of life, which she idealized beyond all fact and reality. The psychiatrist knew about her serious domestic problems from her husband, but after the operation, she claimed that they had never had trouble. Follow-up psychiatric treatment was also refused. The patient would accept appointments, but then cancel, saying that she was too well to see any doctor.

Denial of Extinction

Patients may, after a time, fully accept their diagnosis, with its complications and hazards, but still resist the conclusion that incurable illness results in death. Denial of extinction resembles inability to imagine personal death, which is a sign of the primary paradox.

Third-order denial does not refer to healthy people who espouse a strong creed of immortality. It is found only among patients who have already acknowledged the facts of illness and their extensions, and face imminent confrontation with death. Aside from any philosophical and religious belief, they will behave and talk as if their present state would be indefinitely prolonged.

CASE 10 A 42-year-old unmarried, practical nurse was admitted to a hospital for terminal care, about one month after she was found to have extensive abdominal metastases from carcinoma of the caecum. She had been self-supporting throughout most of her life. With the exception of a sister in a convent, she had no relatives. Her surgeon asked a social worker to arrange the transition from private life to permanent hospitalization for the patient. She accepted the diagnosis and knew the significance of the transfer, speaking frankly and without self-pity. Pain was not a prominent symptom, but she talked about not living much longer.

Several months later, the social worker received an urgent call, asking her to visit that evening. When she arrived, the patient was openly distressed, in contrast to her customary composure. The social worker and the patient had become very friendly during her hospitalization, and had spoken about death, family ties, and illness on many occasions. Now, it seemed apparent that the terminal period was about to begin. To her surprise, however, the patient said that the reason for the telephone call was to help engage a nurse to look after her when she went home. Never had the patient seemed less likely to go home or more likely to die.

It was learned that earlier that day the patient's doctor had returned from a 3-week vacation. He had little to say, and the perceptive patient realized that he was disappointed in her condition. In keeping with her policy of gentle candor, the social worker ventured to suggest that the patient was reexperiencing some of her earlier fears about dying. The patient agreed at once, recognizing the incongruity between her grave condition and plans about going home. Her distress abated promptly, and she merely commented that everyone in her situation must go through similar periods of disappointment and self-deception. Then she dropped off to sleep, but awakened to apologize for ignoring her visitor. She commented serenely that she hoped she wouldn't live much longer. After pausing a very long moment, the social worker took the patient's hand, and softly said she agreed. The woman smiled and said, "Thank you, my dear." Death occurred within 24 hours.

Denial of extinction is difficult to diagnose because it is usually assumed to be a sign of courage, hope, faith, or some other helpful attribute. However, while the patient in Case 10 showed middle knowledge briefly, the main focus of denial was death itself, not the implications of illness. Even though it occurs only at the far end of life, third-order denial is still denial because it appears only in selective situations and is communicated only to certain people with whom a patient wants to maintain a relationship. This patient wanted to spare her doctor further disappointment, and it was natural to to ask her other friend, the social worker, to help her return home. But the social worker had already developed a relationship in which confrontation with death had been forthright. It was, therefore, easy for the patient to drop the denial and to accept death, once again.

DIAGNOSIS OF DENIAL

The diagnosis of first-order denial is usually simple. A sick patient has few, if any, complaints; he shows unjustified optimism or even indifference. He seems unable or unwilling to draw inferences about self-evident facts of illness.

Anyone faced with threats to survival and self-esteem is apt to call upon strategies of denial and nullification. He may say or do things that the rest of the world considers unrealistic and inappropriate. However, dogmatic classification of different types of denial is not useful, because some forms of denial exist only in the observer's mind.

ⵊⵊ

*Denial is so closely affiliated with
one's values and self-image that
whenever illness threatens to be a
humiliating as well as an extended
and incapacitating experience, denial
may be expected to ensue.*

ⵊⵊ

Denial, like its opposite, affirmation, is grounded in biological, social, and psychological processes. Like any so-called ego function, denying entails perception, performance, symbolic forms, and interpersonal transactions. People who are abruptly exposed to external danger may freeze, close off, go dead, and then, with unnatural deliberation and calm, take steps to escape and master the threat. These are emergency situations, calling for concentration of all available energy and skills for the task. They are not instances of denial because the realistic danger is recognized and responded to appropriately and effectively. The threat is perceived; it is not negated, nor is it transformed into a more congenial reality. The ensuing behavior fits the predicament and is not incongruous. Lifton described psychological "closure" among Hiroshima survivors.* Concentration camp survivors are also said

*See—in Chapter 2—the previous selection "Nuclear Age," by Lifton and Olson—ED.

to undergo chronic deadening of perceptions and emotions, as a result of their experiences. Some patients facing terminal illness may find themselves depersonalized, unable to share in the life that streams around them. Although these are examples of psychic nullification, they are not strategies that serve denial. The distinctive quality of denying and denial is that it occurs only in relation to certain people, not to all, and has the primary purpose of protecting a significant relationship.

Denial may be a personality trait of chronic optimists, or of people who are fond of "pseudo-reminiscences" that glamorize their past. Certain investigators (Rosen & Bibring, 1966) suggest that people on the "white collar" level are less likely to deny than those who are "blue collar" or "no collar." In other words, people with more to lose, with fewer resources, might deny more. This is an oversimplification because it puts the principal distinction on the basis of socioeconomic status; a better test would be the need for preserving self-esteem and significant relationships.

The dynamic interpretation of denying and denial recognizes that the investigator himself can produce denial. Articulate, educated, and prosperous patients may not be so threatened by serious illness. Their lives might not be subject to such drastic changes. More important, perhaps, is the attitude of their doctor. If he is responsive and sympathetic, he can encourage valid communication, or shut it off. The range of denial may be a monitor of any relationship. Alienation was first described among industrial workers, cut off from sources of creation and disposition. Now, however, alienation has become a favorite word, signifying disenchantment with what one has or can attain. Denial is so closely affiliated with one's values and self-image that whenever illness threatens to be a humiliating as well as an extended and incapacitating experience, denial may be expected to ensue.

Glaser and Strauss (1968) found that dying patients have either closed or open awareness of their plight. The degree of openness is not absolute. From time to time, there is selective closure and receptiveness. Often enough to be considered typical is the finding that first-order denial takes place mostly among people who are recently afflicted, and much less among the chronically ill, unless surrounding circumstances are just too much to bear. Some dying patients deny more to their earlier visitors, much less to people who remain in frequent contact. Doubt, despair, and equivocation can generate denial at any stage. The presuppositions of the observer may, indeed, prompt him to decide that denial is strong, but closer inquiry may disclose that it is the observer who has been alienated and closed off.

CASE 11   A middle-aged woman with severe syringomyelia seemed to be pleased when informed of her husband's death. Her behavior contrasted with the deep concern she had felt during his chronic and fatal illness, carcinoma of the lung.

A consultant interviewed the patient, because it was feared that her "denial" might be the prelude of a serious depression. He discovered, however, that she did grieve for her husband, for their disrupted home, for her own invalidism. Her reaction of pleasure after his death was neither a sign of denial nor was it inappropriate. She was glad he died, because now she would not cause him additional worry when, as was inevitable, her neurological condition deteriorated. She knew about her own future. Had he lived long enough to become an invalid, she also knew that her daughters could not have left home, and might have compromised their own future.

Some professionals cannot understand that death may be both appropriate and acceptable as a solution for life's problems. Young people, insofar as they do not utterly repudiate the aged, may not believe that old people can calmly look upon death as the conclusion of a script written long ago. Therapists with "never say die" enthusiasm may diagnose depression and denial when there is no evidence of either.

The diagnosis of denial is usually decided because the reality testing used by the examiner has been violated. The preliminary process called denying, as well as its constructive dimension, is seldom heeded. The diagnosis of denial, therefore, is determined by whatever the patient and the examiner, investigator, or judge *deem to be certain.* If there is discrepancy, the weight of judgment pushes away from candid realization that, for some people, the disposition to die is more acceptable than the threat of abandonment, humiliation, loneliness.

REFERENCES

Fenichel, Otto. *The Psychoanalytic Theory of Neurosis.* New York: W. W. Norton and Co., 1945.

Freud, Anna. *The Ego and the Mechanisms of Defence.* (Translated by C. Baines). London: Hogarth Press, 1948.

Glaser, Barney G., and Strauss, Anselm L. *Time for Dying.* Chicago: Aldine Publishing Co., 1968.

Lewin, B. *The Psychoanalysis of Elation.* New York: W. W. Norton and Co., 1950.

Rosen, J., and Bibring, G. Psychological Reactions of Hospitalized Male Patients to a Heart Attack: Age and Social-Class Differences. *Psychosomatic Medicine,* 1966, *28,* 808–821.

Weisman, Avery D., and Hackett, Thomas P. Denial as a Social Act. In S. Levin and R. Kahana (Eds.), *Psychodynamic Studies on Aging: Creativity, Reminiscing, and Dying.* New York: International Universities Press, 1967.

·8·

DEATH
AND DIGNITY

Is it true that the most ignominious event, the ultimate indignity that can happen to a person is to have his life taken from him, and that dying is often a "degradation ceremony"? We know that over-burdened and harried personnel in gyroscopic institutions sometimes fail to find time or energy for the moments of civility that could impart dignity to the patient; and the dying person himself may oscillate between moments of rebellion, terror, and despair and moments of courage, resolve, and dignity. Always, as Hinton says, "the aim is to make dying a little easier." Or, to put it another way, the aim is, in a desperate and dire situation, to salvage a little something; in this case, a little dignity.

It doesn't take much imagination to see some of the ways in which the advent of recent technological advances have affected those aspects of death related to legality, ethics, and civility (dignity). In organ transplantation: when can an organ legally and morally be removed? In kidney dialysis: who shall be given dialysis when the number of needful people exceeds the number of available machines? With heart pacemakers and intravenous feedings: how long should a comatose terminal person be

470

kept alive? And should these issues be decided only by physicians, or should family members, lay groups, or legislators also be a part of the decision-making process? And what about the dying person himself (who may be weak, confused, frightened, or constricted by pain or unconsciousness): what should his voice be in his own death? Should he be permitted to die without his consent or, conversely, should he be forced to stay alive against his express wishes?

The seven selections in this final chapter might be viewed as a series that treats the topics of dying with dignity and the search for an "appropriate death." The Richards selection introduces dignity and dying with a description of how the ordinary man approaches death, oscillating between acceptance and rebellion with moments of great dignity and courage, and presages the idea of an appropriate death by suggesting that death can be a positive experience. Richards also touches on euthanasia as a means of preserving identity and dignity.

Preserving identity and dignity to the dying is basic to the arguments advanced in the Fletcher and Matthews selections. Fletcher is concerned with legal considerations relating to the prolongation of life. Oftentimes lawyers and doctors seem to be on the outs, even adversaries, but attorney Fletcher makes a strong case for increased emphasis on a meaningful doctor-patient relationship.

In general, doctors and churchmen in England have taken, compared to their counterparts in the United States, a leadership role in the current discussion relating to euthanasia (as they have regarding legislation relating to suicide). The selection by Reverend Matthews presents a rather cogent argument, based on church morality, for voluntary euthanasia. All this reminds us of some of the selections in Chapter 4 (and the comments thereto) relating to the modern complexities of death and of the subtle, personal, often idiosyncratic elements in a particular person's dying and death. The editor's purpose in displaying these selections is not so much an attempt to persuade the reader as it is to acquaint him with the complexities of the basic issues of who and what should determine whether life be prolonged or terminated, and to provide some background materials as a basis for further reflection.

Every once in a while, some gifted student of human nature enunciates an especially felicitous and powerful concept: Freud's ideas of dreams as wish fulfillment, Kohler's concept of insight, Jung's archetypes, Maslow's peak experiences, or Murray's need achievement and projective techniques. Weisman's concept of an "appropriate death" would seem to belong in such company. It is illuminating, elevating, just right, and eminently humanitarian. In essence, the basic notion—resting on the realistic observation that some deaths *are* better than others (just as some lives are better than others)—is that individuals who are in fact dying should, as much as possible, be helped to a better death. Weisman has defined an appropriate death as "one in which there is reduction of conflict, compatability with the ego ideal, continuity of significant relationships, and consummation of prevailing wishes. In short, an appropriate death is one which a person might choose for himself had he an option. It is not merely conclusive; it is consummatory." It is probably safe to say that dying with dignity is integral to the concept of an appropriate death.

The selection by Weisman defines and describes an appropriate death—the consummatory end that one would wish for oneself if it were possible to do so—and contrasts it with an "appropriated death," that is suicide. It is probably not unreasonable to say that the goal of every person (physician, nurse, relative, or friend) who interacts with a dying individual should be to help that individual achieve a more appropriate death. It is an idea worth mastering.

In this light the Trombley selection can be seen as a fascinating description of how one person attempted to negotiate an appropriate death for himself. It is an extraordinary "death document" written during the last few months in the life of a young psychiatrist dying of leukemia. In interesting ways it touches some of the same themes—but is dramatically different in its style—as the death poem that constitutes the epilogue to this volume. Diaries and journals of persons dying of natural causes (over time) contrast sharply with that other kind of death document, the suicide note (see E. S. Shneidman, "Suicide Notes Reconsidered," *Psychiatry,* November, 1973, Vol. 36, pp. 379-394).

The contemporary American hospital is probably the best place for care if one is severely ill or badly injured, but perhaps the worst place to be if one is dying. The human being gets lost in the treatment of the disease and, as we have seen, the social system of the hospital often works against closeness and appropriate psychological care as the person moves closer to actually dying. Saunders's selection can be seen as illustrating how death can be both institutionalized and, at the same time, appropriate. She is the medical director of a hospice near London and, as I have seen, has a fervent vendetta against unnecessary pain and needless indignity often associated with death. She directs an institution pointed toward helping the terminal people entrusted to its care achieve a better death.

But it is possible to take the position that no death is appropriate; that it comes too soon or too late and that it is always intrusive and corroding. In the last selection Simone de Beauvoir describes the difficult death of her mother, a death painful for the mother and immensely complicated for the daughter. She puzzles as to why her mother's death shook her so deeply. The sentence with which de Beauvoir concludes her book (and this selection) openly brands death as *the enemy.* In it she speaks the language of her life-long friend, Jean Paul Sartre and of other existential philosophers whose focus of concern were the topics of death and despair. She says: "All men must die: but for every man his death is an accident and, even if he knows it and consents to it, an unjustifiable violation."

All these selections are part of the current scene of changes in our approach to the dying person, with special emphasis on the desirability of ensuring that the terminal person *lives* until he dies. They are all part of the oxymoronic climate of our century: the massive destruction of our fellow humans and the concomitant movement toward the more humanitarian treatment of the dying individual, where the latter is, in turn, an integral part of the many current humanistic movements that one sees in various sectors of our society. Is it possible that these two seemingly polarized potentialities—our capability for wreaking global death and our concern with the individual's dying—are integrally related to one another, perhaps one as the reaction or antidote to the other?

Death and Cancer

Victor Richards
Victor Richards is Chief of Surgery at the Children's Hospital in San Francisco and Clinical Professor of Surgery at both the University of California School of Medicine and the Stanford University School of Medicine. In this selection taken from his book *Cancer, the Wayward Cell*, Dr. Richards, speaking with the insight of a modern physician and the wisdom of an ancient priest, discusses the attitudes and behaviors of dying patients.

From *Cancer, the Wayward Cell: Its Origins, Nature and Treatment* by Victor Richards, University of California Press, 1972. Reprinted by permission of the Regents of the University of California.

*"The beauty of failure
is the only lasting beauty.
Who does not understand failure
is lost."*

—Jean Cocteau

In the world of medicine where all efforts are dedicated to success—the overcoming of illness, the restoration of the sick to a healthy life—the admission of failure may seem absurd. Failure? An insult, almost, to doctors and patients alike. Even if it is at times accepted as unavoidable, failure is always acknowledged as unfortunate. But if one examines the meaning of failure more closely one may come to quite different conclusions.

Where there is failure there has also been effort. Without effort failure would make no sense. Effort leads to success and to failure, and indeed many successes are failures in disguise. They do not leave the successful man with a feeling of fullness, of completeness, but with a feeling of emptiness and sometimes of fear. Success, to be complete, must satisfy the beholder. Paradoxically, failure may, and at times does, satisfy the person who has failed, because it brings with itself the realization of the attempt, a particular quality of fulfillment.

We fail only because and after we have tried. We reach the destination of failure not because we are inert or powerless, but for just the opposite

reasons. It is often because we have looked in all directions and tried all
avenues available to us. We are not powerless: our power finds limits within
and without. After many a failure, the best of us, and the best in each of us,
rises again. But there comes a time when we have to confront the ultimate
failure, our death and the death of others. If we know how to transform this
apparent failure into an accomplishment, we shall have defeated death
itself, at least to the limits of our individual capacities. How does one defeat
death? How does one prove stronger than annihilation?

↑↑↑

*We fail only because and after we have
tried. We reach the destination of failure
not because we are inert or powerless,
but for just the opposite reasons.*

↑↑↑

Perhaps if we understand what death really is we shall also find the
answer to our other question, how to defeat death: for understanding alters
our point of view and therefore allows attitudes which were unknown to us,
or appeared impossible. Although we may see death as a clear termination
of life, a definite break with living, an irreversible event which happens
once and only once, it may be denied to be that simple. For one does not
actually die once, never to return again. Like life, death is a continuing
process, as the process of aging and dying of our body cells demonstrates.
From the time of birth one grows into death at a slow but steady pace: this
growing into death encompasses psychological and spiritual as well as
physical changes. The physical changes, viewed as the natural process of
growth, are not necessarily painful. The discovery of one's separateness
from others, of pain, of sickness, even of joy and happiness are often in-
communicable and increase our sense of being alone. The fear of being
alone contains the germ of our death, the ultimate separation.

Some people go through the changes and small deaths of their lives with
a completely natural acceptance. Few or no questions are asked. People like
these are steeped in life and its vicissitudes so thoroughly that, like healthy
children, they remain largely untouched. They have an innocence which
protects them all through their years and the suffering common to all does
not find them rebellious.

A woman who was told by her doctor that her cancer was probably incurable reacted in a way which exemplifies this fundamental trust in life, and the acceptance of the end of life. She said that it was all very interesting, that she was looking forward to this new experience, that since it was unavoidable she was determined to enjoy it in the sense of embarking on an unknown and therefore fascinating voyage. She would welcome drugs or sedatives only when the pain became too difficult to bear, and she hoped she would be conscious of all that lay ahead of her, including her own death. This woman was not trying to impress her doctor, she was not pretending to be superior to fate, for she actually maintained her attitude quite naturally until her death. There was an innate grandeur in her faith in herself which carried her through the ordeal exactly as she had foreseen.

Not everyone is capable of instinctive faith in all the processes of life, including death. The extreme neurotic attitude toward life and death, which we all share at times, confuses death and life, takes one for the other, and searches for death where it is not, and for life where it is not either. Fear dominates, not the natural fear of frightful realities, but a fear detached from actual happenings, free-floating and always ready to invade the psychic life. For the neurotic "what is called death . . . mainly because it is dark and unknown, is a new life trying to break into consciousness; what he calls life because it is familiar is but a dying pattern he tries to keep alive" (Hillman, 1964). He clings to the past, to habitual reactions, out of fear of what has never been experienced. The small deaths of his universe do not find him ready and accepting, but fill him with apprehension and resistance. Facing real death may thus prove extremely difficult for him and his confusion may be extreme. He may desire death, he may feel an impulse to suicide: but this is entirely different from the true facing of death: he runs to death out of his need for annihilation, out of his fears, whereas, for facing the death which comes to him, at its own time and place, he would need presence of mind and body; it is a conscious confrontation which is required of him, and of which he is incapable, for his very need is to flee and disappear.

Midway between the attitude of total acceptance and that of total refusal lies the attitude of the ordinary man, who is neither completely at ease with life and death, nor entirely in rebellion. The ordinary man oscillates between yes and no, and he will do the same if he is faced with death from an incurable illness. This ordinary man is depicted to perfection by Pirandello in his play *The Man With The Flower in His Mouth*. The man has an epithelioma: "Death passed my way. It planted this flower in my mouth and said to me: 'Keep it, friend, I'll be back in eight or ten months'." An ordinary man (in the play he does not even have a name, he is just "the man"), the sick hero oscillates between cheerful sarcasm, amused acceptance, and terror. He struggles for peace through his imagination. "I never let my imagination rest, even for a moment. I use it to cling continually to the lives of others. . . . If you only knew how well it works! I see somebody's house and I live in it. I feel a part of it. . . ." But later he says: "In fact I do it because I want to share everyone else's troubles, be able to judge life as silly and vain. If you can make yourself feel that way, then it won't matter if you have to come to the end of it." He has now oscillated to the no. But the yes comes back to him. He remembers the sensuous joys of life: "These wonderful apricots are in season now. . . . How do you eat them? With the skin on, don't you? You break them in half, you squeeze them in your fingers slowly. . . . Like a pair of juicy lips. . . . Ah, delicious!" Then he returns to resentful rage: "We all feel this terrible thirst for life, though we have no idea what it consists of. But it's there, there, like an ache in our throats that can never be satisfied. . . . Life, by God, the mere thought of losing it—especially when you know it's a matter of days. . . . ."

The ordinary man's death, which is the death that most of us will encounter, is described at length by Thomas Bell (1961). His book is the record of his last year. Bell, a not very successful writer as he admits himself, has a malignant tumor near his liver and his pancreas. He knows that he will die. After an exploratory operation his surgeon has decided that the excision of the tumor is impossible. The X-ray treatments Bell receives are ineffectual, the drugs he takes have no power. What is his reaction? He is sometimes frightened and discouraged, disgusted at the sight of his body invaded by the tumor, sad for himself and his wife, puzzled by the mystery of fate, but above all courageous and dignified. His book opens with the words: "I said to myself: 'I'll make a journal of it, a book; put down all these thoughts and fears as they come and so get rid of them. Once they're written out in words they won't be confined inside my skull, making trouble.'" Not everyone is a writer, but everyone may decide to face his own thoughts and fears. All through the book one witnesses the author's love of life, which both sustains and saddens him. ("My curiosity is insatiable, my pleasure in reading undiminished. . . . I like, as I always have, privacy and solitude, they are as necessary to me as air. . . . My appetite is excellent and my pleasure in food has never been greater.")

According to Weisman and Hackett (1961) when we are near death a new world opens up to our perception. While "the fear of dying is the sense of impending dissolution or disintegration of all familiar ways of thought and action," while "the world normally at one with our perceptions suddenly becomes alien, disjointed, and runs along without us," while "few patients save the truly predilected, approach death without despair," it is also "frequently clear that in the terminal phase the sharp antithesis of living and dying gradually become modulated into a dampened harmonic line," and that "for the majority of dying patients, it is likely that there is neither complete acceptance nor total repudiation of the imminence of death."

The fear and rebellion experienced at the coming of one's own death is admittedly stronger in young people who have not yet lived full lives, whose hopes, expectations, and responsibilities are threatened beyond their endurance, whose sense of an unjust fate cannot easily be dismissed. Fortunately "during the decades from fifteen to forty years, there is a relatively low . . . toll of deaths, largely due to fatal accidents and a few cancers" (Hinton, 1967). However, for the young, there is no comfort in statistics. One's life is unique and precious. To younger people the sense of failure from an imminent death cannot be anything but acute. Yet there must be some way to prove stronger than one's fate. When Cocteau writes that the "beauty of failure is the only lasting beauty" doesn't he offer us the solution? In other words everything eventually deserts us, and at a time that we have not chosen; but the power to face our bankruptcy remains our privilege: in so doing we penetrate it and master it, we transmute it through imagination, understanding, and the will to stay in control. The beauty and grandeur of such mastery is exemplified at its most sublime in the death of Christ, in the death of Socrates.

Failure, the success in reverse, can be the success of the ordinary men, who, like Bell and many others, feel "a kind of despairing, dragged-by-the-hand unwillingness," and also, "for no obvious reason . . . smile in the darkness." It is not easy to "smile in the darkness" if one has no previous experience of what that darkness is. In Francis Bacon's words "Man fears death as the child fears the dark," and truly the child in us will always fear the dark until he has gone through it once and for all, willingly and thoroughly. What is this darkness? Is it not the unknown in us, the unresolved, the intricacies and mysteries of an inner life not totally adult, and does not this darkness take its most vivid and its most valid symbol in death, the last question, the perfect unknown? But the exploration of our night can bring strength and a peaceful acceptance of life and of death. In the effort at understanding oneself and one's fears, the frightening bugbear, death, appears in a much gentler light. Death may remain the image of all the unattainables. However, these unattainables, these unreachables, these failures, can become a simple question mark, troubling, but incapable of destroying one any longer.

Hope, "the thing with feathers," in Emily Dickinson's words, almost always "perches in the soul," regardless of our nearness to death, regardless of the mortal quality of our illness, regardless of how small a material hope we harbor. For hope is a quality of being, rather than a rational expectation. And in that sense hope can and must be implanted in the person who is fatally ill.

The quantity and the quality of care that a dying patient receives are powerful adjuvants to the growth of hope, of openness to whatever future may be his. This case is dependent upon the kind of persons physicians are—or nurses, psychiatrists, social workers, family, and friends—all of those who are in contact with the patient in the terminal stage of his illness. Certain qualities are demanded. A profound sense of right judgments. A subtle and supple mind. No preconceived or unchangeable opinions. A willingness to meet the patients on their own terms. No moralistic or religious zeal on the part of the "believing" doctor, nurse, or relative. No skepticism or hardened professional "scientism" from the unbelievers. The first thing to remember about dying patients is that it is *their* death.

Some patients do not want to know of their impending death. Many studies indicate that this wish is rare. Yet in the words of Dr. Paul R. Rhoads "honesty should often be tempered with optimistic uncertainty" (Ross, 1965). He illustrates the necessity of this attitude: two patients present the same type of cancer at the same time: both have a retroperitoneal lymphosarcoma of about the same size in the same site; they receive the same X-ray treatment. One dies within three months, the other lives an active life for nine years. The future is unpredictable, even in some apparently desperate cases, and optimism and hope can be maintained in many instances, perhaps even when they do not seem warranted by the facts known to the physician, or by his experience.

Dr. Alvarez writes (1965): "I doubt if a physician who has examined an old man and found an inoperable cancer of the prostate gland need always tell about it. Especially when the man has high blood pressure and heart disease or has had some minor strokes, it may be that he will die of one of these before the cancer kills him, and then it may be best to let him live in mental peace."

A reasonable and perceptive openness to the improbable does not mean dishonesty. However, when patients indicate that they desire to know that they may die in the near future, there is little doubt that they must be told the truth. It is a great comfort to some people to be given the time and opportunity to put their affairs in order, to arrange material details with their families, to explore their thoughts, to deepen and enjoy their relationships. Yet even in those who wish to confront their own death, fears still exist, and they should be encouraged to speak freely about themselves, and about everything and anything that troubles them. "Many a dying man," writes Dr. Alvarez (1952), "would like to discuss the problems that are in his mind, but he would like to do this dispassionately, much as if it were someone else whose troubles were being talked about."

Dr. John Hinton has explored many aspects of the act of dying, many attitudes toward death, and a number of ways to make the end of a life more peaceful and more comfortable, mentally and physically (Hinton, 1967). He points out that if a patient receives all the relief from pain to which he is entitled, with the help of drugs and surgery (surgery in such instances is purely palliative and entirely justified on this basis as it allows the sick person to live his remaining days in less discomfort), he will be offered the first and indispensable condition for a painless and peaceful death.

"A painless, peaceful death," are the words used in the dictionary to define euthanasia, which is at other times vividly described as "mercy-killing." In August, 1967, a young man killed his mother who was dying of leukemia. "She reportedly had begged him to kill her, and even as he was arrested, his mother's sister embraced him saying, 'God bless you'" (Kinsolving, 1967). One can easily understand the pity that husbands, wives, children, parents feel for a loved person who is going to die, who is suffering without much hope, or without any hope at all. One can understand the pity that the doctor feels for a patient to whom he can no longer offer anything but a "painless, peaceful death." But one cannot help but be overwhelmed with the immense problems and responsibilities that euthanasia would present, even to those who have no religious convictions against the taking of a life and even to those who would never kill in any other circumstance. For if euthanasia were to be considered acceptable in cases of terminal cancer, why should it not be acceptable as well in other painful illnesses which are not leading to death? In an editorial in *The Lancet*

(Anon., 1961), we read that "in his recent study, Exton-Smith found that unrelievable enduring pain and misery is worst not, as the public suppose, among patients dying of cancer whose pain, if present, he found controllable and relatively short, but in the victims of locomotor disorders not essentially lethal. If 'euthanasia' is granted to the first class, can it be long denied to the second?"

Euthanasia is a "painless, peaceful death," and also "a means of producing it." Must this means be of necessity killing? Rarely can an easy and happy death be produced by killing, for, despite the hope of relief that the promise of death does bring, death by killing carries violence within itself. What if the patient who desired to die reconsidered at the last minute and nobody but himself was aware of his reconsideration? If euthanasia were ever to be legalized, would not the anguish of making such a decision add an insufferable weight to the already difficult task of facing an involuntary death? The task, by adding a new stress to the stress already existing, would make the act of deciding almost impossible.

Is it desirable to prolong life when death is very near? A number of means to prolong life artificially do not add to the quality of life of a very sick person.

But there are alternatives to the stark conception of euthanasia as "mercy-killing." A painless, peaceful death can be given to people in the terminal stage of cancer. In a letter to the editor of *The Lancet* (1961), Cicely Saunders writes: "We are now always able to control pain in terminal cancer . . . and only very rarely indeed do we have to make (patients) continually asleep in doing so." And in a later editorial in the same medical journal (1961) one reads: "If euthanasia . . . were put on a par with, say, safe childbirth; if the known means to make death comfortable were applied by individual and collective effort with intelligence and energy, could not all but a few deaths be made at least easy?"

An important consideration is, is it desirable to prolong life when death is very near? A number of means to prolong life artificially do not add to the quality of life of a very sick person. According to one observer, J. W. Reid (1964), perhaps "the patient . . . lies in bed surrounded by standards from which dangle bottles of various solutions with tubing running to arms fixed to boards projecting on either side of the bed as though he were nailed to a cross. A nurse stands at one side, and the intern on the other side is injecting a new drug that has successfully prolonged life in a small series (of patients) for a few weeks and (the clincher) as long as a year in one authenticated case! The wife stands uncertainly in the doorway wanting to be with her husband in these last hours but diffident about pushing her way through the busy traffic around the bed." The author goes on to say: "Is not all this activity to keep alive a dying man more often merely an educated cruelty?"

His opinion is echoed by many physicians. The prolongation of life often does more harm than good in the pursuit of a peaceful death. The quality of a human life, which at that stage is synonymous with physical comfort and mental peace, must be the only consideration.

Together with the problem of prolonging or not prolonging life, doctors face that of the free use of powerful drugs to relieve pain as completely as possible. Heroin and morphine are addictive drugs, but what is the importance of addiction at a stage of life when death is so near? The answer seems obvious. However, Dr. John Hinton expresses the opinion that "there is too much error on the side of caution." He believes that "given in adequate and frequent enough doses to begin with, so that the patient is confident that the pain is controllable, the need to increase the dose of morphia or heroin and the undue dependence of the patient on the drug do not often constitute a great problem in dying patients" (Hinton, 1967). This inducement of confidence in the patient seems extremely important, for if he knows from the very beginning that his physical pain will be controlled, his fear of future suffering will be greatly alleviated. The anticipation of pain is as difficult to bear as the pain itself, and more frightening. The certainty that one's doctor is able to control both of these by his skill in the handling of the drugs available, is deeply comforting to the dying patient. Such practices can result in true euthanasia, a means to a painless, peaceful death.

Finally, mental suffering often accompanies physical pain in terminal cancer. Sometimes psychiatric intervention is indispensable, perhaps more often than is the common practice. Its object is, as expressed by Weisman and Hackett (1961), "to help the dying patient preserve his identity and dignity as a unique individual, despite the disease, or, in some cases, because of it." They introduce the concept of "appropriate death." It is "an aspect of euthanasia—death without suffering—for patients whose death is imminent . . . the conventional concept of euthanasia as the hastening of the death of the incurably ill patients is the antithesis of the appropriate attitude towards death which psychiatric intervention advocates. In conventional euthanasia the patient's personality is ignored; in the proposal of therapeutic dissociation of the patient from the disease, the personality in its unique dignity is enhanced." Nonpsychiatrists express similar ideas when, like Dr. Cicely Saunders, they say (1961): "We try, and we believe very often with success, to enable our patients to remain themselves throughout their illness, to find their own key to the situation and to use it. They make of it (consciously or unconsciously) not just a long defeat of living but a positive achievement of dying."

All religions and most philosophies have recognized death as a challenge, as a beginning. In the words of Plato, "Those who tackle philosophy aright are simply and solely practicing dying, practicing death, all the time, but nobody sees it." One does not have to be religious, or a philosopher, to confront death in a manly way. One has only to be human, to realize that the acceptance of everything which is our lot is under the control of our intellect and of our sensibility. Everything which happens to us is ours if we make it so. It is within our power of understanding. This is where hope enters. It is when one may hear what W. H. Auden calls the "imaginary song":

You, alone, o imaginary song
Are unable to say an existence is wrong

Our existence before death is worth living to the fullest. All of us, within limits, can measure up to the last "failure." Jean Cocteau says that who does not understand failure is lost: he is lost to the hope and to the deepening of experience that failure offers. In the elation of success, when we ride the crest of the wave, our sense of power blinds us. Success is intoxicating, and the intoxication is authentic, as are all our experiences. But success is not the whole. In the hollow of the wave, in failure and in the approach of death, we can experience a humble power, and the knowledge of peace. Physicians and families care best for the dying patient by helping to make death an inevitable but positive experience, from which none of us is spared.

REFERENCES

Alvarez, W. C. Care of the Dying. *Journal of the American Medical Association,* 1952, *150,* 89–91.

Anon. Euthanasia. *Lancet,* 1961, *1* (12 Aug.), 351–354.

Bell, Thomas. *In the Midst of Life.* New York: Atheneum, 1961.

Hillman, James. *Suicide and the Soul.* New York: Harper and Row, 1964.

Hinton, John. *Dying.* London: Penguin Books, 1967.

Kinsolving, Lester. Some Thoughts on Mercy Killing. *San Francisco Chronicle,* Aug. 26, 1967.

Reid, J. W. On the Road to the River. *Canadian Medical Association Journal,* 1964, *91,* 911–913.

Ross, W. S. *The Climate is Hope.* New York: Prentice-Hall, 1965.

Saunders, Cicely. Letter to the Editor. *Lancet,* 1961, *2* (2 Sept.), 548–549.

Weisman, Avery D., and Hackett, Thomas P. Predilection to Death. *Psychosomatic Medicine,* 1961, *23,* 232–256.

Prolonging Life:
Some Legal Considerations

George P. Fletcher

George P. Fletcher is a faculty member of the School of Law at the University of Washington. In this selection taken from the book *Euthanasia and the Right to Death,* Professor Fletcher discusses the possible legal consequences of a physician's refusal to artificially prolong life and concludes that custom, not law, should dictate the physician's choice in this instance.

1   New medical techniques for prolonging life force both the legal and medical professions to re-examine their traditional attitudes towards life and death. New problems emerge from the following recurrent situation: a comatose patient shows no signs of brain activity; according to the best medical judgment, he has an infinitesimal chance of

recovery; yet he can be sustained by a mechanical respirator. How long should his physician so keep him alive? And in making his decision, how much weight should the physician give to the wishes and resources of the family, and to the prospect that his time might be profitably used in caring for patients with a better chance of recovery?

According to one line of thought, the physician's leeway in caring for terminal patients is limited indeed. He may turn off the respirator, but only at the risk of prosecution and conviction for murder. The insensitive logic of the law of homicide, disregarding as it does the context of the purpose of the physician's effort, would prompt some to equate the physician's turning off the respirator with a hired gunman's killing in cold blood. The acts of both result in death; the actors intend that death should follow; and in neither case is the killing provoked, excused, or justified. Thus like the gunman, the physician is guilty of murder.

The approach of equating the physician's turning off a mechanical respirator with the gunman's killing for hire is, to say the least, askew with reality. It totally misses the demands of the medical mission. It means that physicians must use modern devices for sustaining life with trepidation; they must proceed haltingly, unsure of the legal consequences of discontinuing therapy. It is of little solace to the medical practitioner that institutional facts check the cold rigor of the common law. True, his decisions in the operating room are minimally visible; not even the patient's family need learn whether death came "naturally" or upon the disruption of therapy. And even if it should become known to the family and the community that the physician's decision shortened the lifespan of the patient, it is unlikely that the physician should suffer. Common law courts have never convicted a medical practitioner either for shortening the life of a suffering, terminal patient or for refusing to render life-sustaining aid. Yet men of goodwill wish to proceed not by predictions of what will befall them but by perceiving and conforming to their legal and moral obligations.

The apparent rigidity of the common law of homicide has evoked demands for reform. The proposals for vesting physicians with greater flexibility in caring for terminal patients are of two strands. The first is a movement towards instituting voluntary euthanasia, which would permit the medically supervised killing of patients who consent to death. These proposals warrant continued discussion and criticism, but they apply only in cases of patients still conscious and able to consent to their own demise. Separate problems adhere to the cases of doomed, unconscious patients who may be kept alive by mechanical means. In the latter area, the movement for reform has stimulated the pursuit of a definition of death that would permit physicians to do what they will with the bodies of hopeless, "legally dead" patients. In France and Sweden, as well as in the United States, proponents of reform have urged the cessation of brain activity—as evidenced by a flat electroencephalograph (EEG) reading—as the criterion of death. Setting the moment of legal death prior to the stilling of the heart is critical to those pressing for greater legal flexibility in transplanting vital organs from doomed patients to those with greater hopes of recovery. Waiting until the heart fails makes transplanting difficult, if not impossible. At stake in the pursuit of a legal definition of death is the prospect of a vast increase in the supply of kidneys and, some day, of livers, hearts, and ovaries for the purpose of transplanting. The reliance on the concept of death, however, is a verbal detour. The reformers are concerned about two practical decisions: (1) when can a physician legally discontinue aid to a patient with an infinitesimal chance of recovery; and (2) when can a physician legally remove organs from a terminal patient. To resolve these problems, one need not construct a concept of legal death. Concern for the moment of death presupposes: (1) that both of these decisions should depend on the same criteria; and (2) that the controlling criteria should be medical facts, rather than the host of criteria relating to the patient's family condition and to the importance of the physician's time and of the machinery used in sustaining life.

Rather than promote either the movement for voluntary euthanasia or the search for a new definition of death, this essay proposes a third approach to the legal situation. We can furnish practising physicians at least some flexibility in the operating room by invoking a more sensitive interpretation of the law as it now stands. To loosen the legal vice of the law of homicide, we need only take a closer look at its pinions. We need to question each of the steps leading to the view that the physician's turning off a respirator or a kidney machine is an act subjecting him to tort and criminal liability for homicide.

There are only a few points at which the structure can give. Consider the applicable elements of common law murder: (1) an act resulting in death, (2) an intent to inflict death, (3) malice aforethought, (4) absence of defences. Beginning at the end of the list, one is hard pressed to justify or excuse the killing by invoking a recognized defence. If the common law courts were more amenable to a general defence of necessity in homicide cases, one could argue that if another patient had a superior likelihood of recovery using the machine, the attending physician would be warranted in removing a patient from the machine who was then dependent upon it for his life. A defence of this sort could serve as a welcome guide to those concerned about the legal limits of allocating the use of kidney machines. The appropriate foothold for the defence would be a physician's common law prerogative to abort a foetus when necessary to save the life of the mother. Yet that defence is premised on the judgment that the life of the mother represents a more worthy interest than that of the unborn child; when it comes to a choice between the two, the mother has a superior right to live. One is advisedly wary of the analogical claim that the patient with the greater likelihood of recovery has a superior right to live. We have lived too long with the notion that all human beings have an equal claim to life.

If the prospects of a defence are questionable, forays on the issues of intent and malice seem hopeless. The aim of the physician's behavior may not be to kill, yet he knows that death is certain to follow if he interrupts therapy to free the respirator for another patient. And knowledge that death is certain to follow is enough to say, at least according to the dictionary of the law, that he "intends" death to result from his conduct. Also, it is too late in the evolution of the common law to make the concept of malice mean what it purports to mean, namely ill-will, base motives, and the like. Surely, the man on the street would not say that a physician is malicious in breaking off his care of a fated patient. Indeed, in the interest of saving the family from financial ruin or directing his efforts more profitably, it might be the humane thing to do. Yet the common law long ago betrayed the ordinary English background of its rule that a man must kill "maliciously" to be guilty of murder. The rigors of distinguishing good motives from bad and the elusiveness of motive as an object of prosecutorial proof gave way nearly four centuries ago to the concept of implied malice as a tool for drawing important distinctions in the law of homicide.

It appears that there is only one stage in the structure that might readily yield under analysis. That is the initial claim that the turning off of a mechanical respirator is an act resulting in death. The alternative would be to regard the flipping of the switch as an omission, a forbearance—a classification that would lead to a wholly different track of legal analysis. It seems novel to suggest that flipping a switch should count as an omission or forbearance to act. For like the act of the gunman in pulling a trigger, flipping a switch represents an exertion of the will. It is bodily movement, and for many, that would be enough to say that the behavior constitutes an act, not an omission. Yet as I shall argue in this essay, the turning off of a mechanical respirator should be classified as omission. It should be

regarded on a par with the passivity of that infamous passer-by who glee-
fully watches a stranded child drown in a swimming pool. As we shall see,
this view of the problem has vast implications for advising physicians of
their legal leeway in rendering therapy to terminal patients.

ʃʃʃ

*The question is posed: Is the
physician's discontinuing aid to a
terminal patient an act or omission?*

ʃʃʃ

Much of what follows is an exercise in conceptual analysis. It is an effort
to devise a test for determining which of two competitive schemes—that for
acts or that for omissions—should apply in analysing a given question of
responsibility for the death of another. It is significant inquiry, if only to
add a word to the discussion of the ponderous legal quandaries of physicians who care for terminal patients. The problem is also of wider significance for the theory of tort and criminal liability. The area of liability for
omissions bristles with moral, analytic, and institutional puzzles. In the
course of this inquiry, we shall confront some of those problems; others
we shall catalogue in passing.

2   The question is posed: Is the physician's discontinuing aid to a terminal
patient an act or omission? To be sure, the choice of legal track does not
yield radically different results. For some omissions, physicians are liable
in much the same way as they are for unpermitted operations and negligent
treatment. One need only consider the following turn of events. Dr Brown
is the family doctor of the Smith family and has been for several years. Tim
Smith falls ill with pneumonia. Brown sees him once or twice at the family
home and administers the necessary therapy. One evening, upon receiving
a telephone call from the Smith family that Tim is in critical condition,
Dr Brown decides that he should prefer to remain at his bridge game than
to visit the sick child. Brown fails to render aid to the child; it is clear that
Brown would be liable criminally and civilly if death should ensue. That
he has merely omitted to act, rather than asserted himself intentionally to
end life, is immaterial in assessing his criminal and civil liability. Of course,

the doctor would not be under an obligation to respond to the call of a stranger who said that he needed help. But there is a difference between a stranger and someone who has placed himself in the care of a physician. The factor of reliance and reasonable expectation that the doctor will render aid means that the doctor is legally obligated to do so. His failure to do so is then tantamount to an intentional infliction of harm. As his motive, be it for good or ill, is irrelevant in analysing his liability for assertive killing, his motive is also irrelevant in analysing his liability for omitting to render aid when he is obligated to do so.

Thus, it makes no difference whether a doctor omits to render aid because he prefers to continue playing bridge, or if he does so in the hope that the patient's misery will come quickly to a natural end. A doctor may be criminally and civilly liable either for intentionally taking life or for omitting to act and thus permitting death to occur. However, the sources of these two legal proscriptions are different. And this difference in the source of the law may provide the key for the analysis of the doctor's liability in failing to prolong life in the case discussed at the outset of this essay. That a doctor may not actively kill is an application of the general principle that no man may actively kill a fellow human being. In contrast, the principle that a doctor may not omit to render aid to a patient justifiably relying upon him is a function of the special relationship that exists between doctor and patient. Thus, in analysing the doctor's legal duty to his patient, one must take into consideration whether the question involved is an act or an omission. If it is an act, the relationship between the doctor and patient is irrelevant. If it is an omission, the relationship is all-controlling.

With these points in mind, we may turn to an analysis of specific aspects of the medical decision not to prolong life. The first problem is to isolate the relevant medical activity. The recurrent pattern includes: stopping cardiac resuscitation, turning off a respirator, a pacemaker, or a kidney machine, and removing the tubes and devices used with these life-sustaining machines. The initial decision of classification determines the subsequent legal analysis of the case. If turning off the respirator is an "act" under the law, then it is unequivocally forbidden: it is on a par with injecting air into the patient's veins. If, on the other hand, it is classified as an "omission," the analysis proceeds more flexibly. Whether it would be forbidden as an omission would depend on the demands imposed by the relationship between doctor and patient.

There are gaps in the law; and we are confronted with one of them. There is simply no way of focusing the legal authorities so as to determine whether the process of turning off the respirator is an act or an omission. That turning off the respirator takes physical movement need not be controlling. There might be "acts" without physical movement, as, for example, if one should sit motionless in the driver's seat as one's car heads towards an intended victim. Surely that would be an act causing death; it would be murder regardless of the relationship between the victim and his assassin. Similarly, there might be cases of omissions involving physical exertion, perhaps even the effort required to turn off the respirator. The problem is not whether there is or there is not physical movement; there must be another test.

That other test, I should propose, is whether on all the facts we should be inclined to speak of the activity as one that causes harm or one merely that permits harm to occur. The usage of the verbs "causing" and "permitting" corresponds to the distinction in the clear cases between acts and omissions. If a doctor injects air into the veins of a suffering patient, he causes harm. On the other hand, if the doctor fails to stop on the highway to aid a stranger injured in a motor-car accident, he surely permits harm to occur, and he might be morally blameworthy for that; but as the verb "cause" is ordinarily used, his failing to stop is not the cause of the harm.

As native speakers of English, we are equipped with linguistic sensitivity for the distinction between causing harm and permitting harm to occur. That sensitivity reflects a common-sense perception of reality; and we should employ it in classifying the hard cases arising in discussions of the prolongation of life. Is turning off the respirator an instance of causing death or permitting death to occur? If the patient is beyond recovery and on the verge of death, one balks at saying that the activity causes death. It is far more natural to speak of the case as one of permitting death to occur. It is significant that we are inclined to refer to the respirator as a means for prolonging life; we would not speak of insulin shots for a diabetic in the same way. The use of the term "prolongation of life" builds on the same perception of reality that prompts us to say that turning off the respirator is an activity permitting death to occur, rather than causing death. And that basic perception is that using the respirator interferes artificially in the pattern of events. Of course, the perception of the natural and of the artificial is a function of time and culture. What may seem artificial today, may be a matter of course in ten years. Nonetheless, one *does* perceive many uses of the respirator today as artificial prolongations of life. And that perception of artificiality should be enough to determine the legal classification of the case. Because we are prompted to refer to the activity of turning off the respirator as activity permitting death to occur, rather than causing death, we may classify the case as an omission, rather than as an act.

To clarify our approach, we might consider the following possible case. A pedestrian D. notices that a nearby car, parked with apparently inadequate brakes, is about to roll downhill. P.'s house is parked directly in its path. D. rushes to the front of the car and with effort manages to arrest its movement for a few minutes. Though he feels able to hold back the car for several more minutes (time enough perhaps to give warning of the danger), he decides that he has had enough; and he steps to one side, knowing full well that the car will roll squarely into P.'s front-yard. That is precisely what it does. What are P.'s rights against D.? Again, the problem is whether the defendant's behavior should be treated as an act or as an omission. If it is act, he is liable for trespass against P.'s property. If it is an omission, the law of trespass is inapplicable; and the problem devolves into a search for a relationship between P. and D. that would impose on D. the duty to prevent this form of damage to P.'s property. Initially, one is inclined to regard D.'s behavior as an act bringing on harm. Like the physician's turning off a respirator, his stepping aside represents physical exertion. Yet, as in the physician's case, we are led to the opposite result by asking whether in the circumstances D. caused the harm or merely permitted it to occur. Surely, a newspaper account would employ the latter description; D. let the car go, he permitted it to roll on, but he is no more a causal factor than if he had not initially intervened to halt its forward motion. We deny D.'s causal contribution for reasons akin to those in the physician's case. In both instances, other factors are sufficient in themselves to bring on the harmful result. As the car's brakes were inadequate to hold it on the hill, so the patient's hopeless condition brought on his death. With sufficient causal factors present, we can imagine the harm's occurring without the physician's or the pedestrian's contribution. And thus we are inclined to think of the behavior of each as something less than a causal force.

One might agree that, as a matter of common sense, we can distinguish between causing harm and permitting harm to occur and yet balk at referring to the way people ordinarily describe phenomena in order to solve hard problems of legal policy. After all, what if people happen to describe things differently? Would that mean that we would have to devise different answers to the same legal problems? To vindicate a resort to common-sense notions and linguistic usage as a touchstone for separating acts from omissions, we must clarify the interlacing of these three planes of the problem: (1) the distinction between acts and omissions, (2) the ordinary usage of the terms "causing" and "permitting," and (3) resorting in cases of omissions, but not in cases of acts, to the relationship between the agent and his victim in setting the scope of the agent's duties. The ultimate claim is that perceiving an activity as one permitting rather than causing harm is a sufficient condition for classifying it as an omission. Admittedly, the path of demonstration is roundabout. We turn first to the proposition that the relationship between the parties is an indispensable factor in the just evaluation of liability for permitting harm; and second to the conclusion that, to permit recourse to the relationship of the parties, cases of permitting harm should be classified as legal omissions. The former proposition is one of policy and fairness; the latter is one of the demands of the legal tradition. To make the policy claim, we need a clear understanding of the function of causal judgments in legal analysis. It is only then that we may perceive why the relationship of the parties is critical when the actor does not cause, but merely permits, harm to occur.

In the ascription of tort and criminal liability, causal judgments function to isolate from the mass of society those individuals whose liability may be left to turn on an examination of personal fault. Those who have caused harm are, in this sense, candidates for liability. They possess a minimal connection with the harm that has occurred. From this class of candidates for liability, the apt rules of law function to determine who should be held liable and who should be excused from liability.

The one area of the law where one has difficulty in isolating candidates for liability is the area of omissions. When others have stood by and permitted harm to occur, we either have too many candidates for liability or we have none at all. A helpless old woman succumbs to starvation. Many people knew of her condition and did nothing: the postman, her hired nurse, her daughter, the bill collector, the telephone operator—each of them allowed her to die. Could we say, on analogy to causing death, that permitting the death to occur should serve as the criterion for selecting these people as candidates for liability? If we say that all of them are candidates for liability, then the burden falls to the criteria of fault to decide which of them, if any, should be liable for wrongful death and criminal homicide. The problem is whether the criteria of fault are sufficiently sensitive to resolve the question of liability. What kinds of questions should we ask in assessing fault? Did each voluntarily omit to render aid? Did any of them face a particular hazard in doing so? Were any of them in a particularly favorable position to avert the risk of death? If these are the questions we must ask in assessing fault and affixing liability, we are at a loss to discriminate among the candidates for liability. Each acted voluntarily with knowledge of the peril; none faced personal hazard in offering assistance; and their capacities to avert the risk were equal. Thus the criteria of fault are useless (at least in the type of case sketched here) for discriminating among the candidates.

Affixing liability fairly in cases of omission requires a more sensitive filtering mechanism prior to the application of the traditional criteria of personal fault. The concept of permitting harm sweeps too wide; and the criteria of personal fault tend to be of little avail in narrowing the field. Thus one can understand the role of the relationship between the parties as a touchstone of liability. Legal systems, both common law and continental, have resorted to the relationship between the parties as a device for narrowing the field to those individuals whose liability may be left to depend on personal fault. According to the conventional rules, the old woman's nurse and daughter are candidates potentially liable for permitting death to occur. Liability would rest on personal fault, primarily on the voluntariness of each in omitting to render aid. Thus the conventional rules as to when one has a duty to render aid fulfill the same function as the causal inquiry in its domain: these rules, like the predication of causation, isolate individuals whose behavior is then scrutinized for the marks of negligent and intentional wrongdoing.

By demonstrating the parallel between the causal concept in cases of acts and the relationship between the parties in cases of omissions, we have come a long way in support of our thesis. We have shown that in cases of permitting harm to occur, one is required to resort to the relationship between the parties in order fairly to select those parties whose liability should turn on criteria of personal fault. In the absence of a causal judgment, with its attendant assignment of differentiated responsibility for the risk of harm, one can proceed only by asking: Is this the kind of relationship—for example, parent-child, doctor-patient—in which one person ought to help another? And on grounds ranging from common decency to contract, one derives individual duties to render aid when needed.

One step of the argument remains: the conclusion that cases of permitting harm are instances of omissions, not of acts. This is a step that turns not so much on policy and analysis, as on acceptance of the received premises of the law of homicide. One of these premises is that acting intentionally to cause death is unconditionally prohibited: the relationship between the defendant and his victim is irrelevant. One may resort to the relationship between the parties only in cases of omissions indirectly resulting in harm.[1] With these two choices and no others, the logic of classification is ineluctable. Cases of permitting harm, where one must have recourse to the relationship between the parties, cannot be classified as cases of acts: to do so would preclude excusing the harm on the ground that the relationship between the parties did not require its avoidance. Thus, to permit recourse to relationship of the parties, one must treat cases of permitting harm as cases of omissions.

To complete our inquiry, we need attend to an asymmetry in the analysis of causing and permitting. As Professors Hart and Honore have shown, some omissions may be the causes of harm.[2] And thus, the category of causing harm includes some cases of omitting, as well as all cases of acting, to bring on harm. Suppose, for example, that an epileptic regularly takes pills to avert a seizure. Yet on one occasion he omits to take the pills in the hope that he is no longer required to do so. He has a seizure. The cause of his seizure is clear: he omitted to take the prescribed pill. In the same way, a physician failing to give a diabetic patient a routine shot of insulin would be the cause of harm that might ensue. The taking of the pill and the giving of the shot are the expected state of affairs. They represent normality, and their omission, abnormality. Because we anticipate the opposite, the omission explains what went wrong, why our expectations were not realized. In contrast, if pills to avert epileptic seizures had just been devised, we would not say, as to someone who have never taken the pills, that his failure to do so had brought on his attack. In that case, our expectations would be different, the omission to take pills would not represent an abnormality, and the anticipated omission would not be a satisfying causal explanation of the attack.[3]

A doctor's failure to give his diabetic patient an insulin shot is a case warranting some attention. By contemporary standards, insulin shots, unlike mechanical respirators, do not interfere artificially in the course of nature; because the use of insulin is standard medical practice, we would not describe its effect as one of prolonging life. We would not say that withholding the shot permits death; it is a case of an omission causing harm.

---

[1]For example, Rex v. Smith, 2 Car. and p. 448, 172 E.R. 203 (Gloucester Assizes, 1826). The analysis of criminality of D., for failing to care for an idiot brother, turns on whether keeping the brother locked up was an act or an omission. Finding the latter, the court held that the defendant bore no duty to aid his brother and directed an acquittal.

[2]H. L. A. Hart and A. M. Honore, *Causation in the Law* (1957), pp. 35–6.

[3]The relationship between expectations and causation is developed more fully in Hart and Honore, op cit., Chap. 2.

With the prohibition against causing death, one should not have to refer to the doctor-patient relationship to determine the criminality of the doctor's omission. Yet, in fact, common law courts would ground a conviction for omitting to give the shot on the doctor's duty to render aid to his patient—a duty derived from the doctor-patient relationship. Thus we encounter an apparent inconsistency: a case of causing in which one resorts to the relationship of the parties to determine criminality. We can reconcile the case with our thesis by noting that cases of omissions causing harm, possess the criteria—regularity of performance and reliance—that give rise to duties of care. The doctor is clearly under a duty to provide his patient with an insulin shot if the situation demands it. And the duty is so clear, precisely because one expects an average doctor in the 1960s to use insulin when necessary; this is the same expectation that prompts us to say that his failure to give the shot would be the cause of his patient's death.

That an omission can on occasion be the cause of harm prompts us, to some extent, to reformulate our thesis. We cannot say that causing harm may serve as the criterion for an act, as opposed to an omission, because some instances of causation are omissions. But we may claim with undiminished force that permitting harm to occur should be sufficient for classification as an omission. Upon analysis, we find that our thesis for distinguishing acts from omissions survives only in part; it works for some omissions, but not for all. Yet, so far as the stimulus of this investigation is concerned—the problem of physicians' permitting death to come to their terminal patients—the thesis continues to hold: permitting a patient to die is a case in which one appropriately refers to the relationship of the parties to set the scope of the physician's legal duty to his patient; in this sense it functions as an omission in legal analysis.

3   By permitting recourse to the doctor-patient relationship in fixing the scope of the doctor's duties to his patient, we have at least fashioned the concepts of the common law to respond more sensitively to the problems of the day. We have circumvented the extravagant legal conclusion that a physician's turning off a kidney machine or a respirator is tantamount to murder. Yet one critical inquiry remains. How does shunting the analysis into the track of legal omissions actually affect the physician's flexibility in the operating room? We say that his duties are determined by his relationship with his patient; specifically, it is the consensual aspect of the relationship that is supposed to control the leeway of the physician. Yet there is some question as to where the control actually resides.

To take a clear case, let us suppose that prior to the onset of a terminal illness, the patient demands that his physician do everything to keep him alive and breathing as long as possible. And the physician responds, "Even if you have a flat EEG reading and there is no chance of recovery?" "Yes," the patient replies. If the doctor agrees to this bizarre demand, he becomes obligated to keep the respirator going indefinitely. Happily, cases of this type do not occur in day-to-day medical practice. In the average case, the patient has not given a thought to the problem; and his physician is not likely to alert him to it. The problem then is whether there is an implicit understanding between physician and patient as to how the physician should proceed in the last stages of a terminal illness. But would there be an implicit understanding about what the physician should do if the patient is in a coma and dependent on a mechanical respirator? This is not the kind of eventuality the average man anticipates or expects. And if he did, his would be expectations based on the customary practices of the time. If he had heard about a number of cases in which patients had been sustained for long periods of time on respirators, he might (at least prior to going into the coma) expect that he would be similarly sustained.

Thus, the analysis leads us along the following path. The doctor's duty to prolong life is a function of his relationship with his patient; and in the typical case, that relationship devolves into the patient's expectations of the treatment he will receive. Those expectations, in turn, are a function of the practices prevailing in the community at the time; and practices in the use of respirators to prolong life are no more and no less than what doctors actually do in the time and place. Thus, we have come full circle. We began the inquiry by asking: Is it legally permissible for doctors to turn off respirators used to prolong the life of doomed patients? And the answer after our tortuous journey is simply: It all depends on what doctors customarily do. The law is sometimes no more precise than that.

The conclusion of our circular journey is that doctors are in a position to fashion their own law to deal with cases of prolongation of life. By establishing customary standards, they may determine the expectations of their patients and thus regulate the understanding and the relationship between doctor and patient. And by regulating that relationship, they may control their legal obligations to render aid to doomed patients.

Thus the medical profession confronts the challenge of developing humane and sensitive customary standards for guiding decisions to prolong the lives of terminal patients. This is not a challenge that the profession may shirk. For the the doctor's legal duties to render aid derive from his relationship with the patient. That relationship, along with the expectations implicit in it, is the responsibility of the individual doctor and the individual patient. With respect to problems not commonly discussed by the doctor with his patient, particularly the problems of prolonging life, the responsibility for the patient's expectations lies with the medical profession as a whole.

Voluntary Euthanasia:
The Ethical Aspect

W. R. Matthews

W. R. Matthews was Dean of St. Paul's in London from 1934 to 1967. In this selection, the Very Reverend Matthews makes a case for *voluntary* euthanasia, based on what he describes as the Christian ethical "doctrine of the sacredness of the human personality."

From *Euthanasia and the Right to Death* edited by A. B. Downing, pp. 25-29. Copyright © 1970 by Nash Publishing Co. Reprinted by permission.

The proposal to legalize, under stringent conditions, voluntary euthanasia, has called forth much criticism from Christians. We ought not to be surprised at this, because the sacredness of human life and personality is a fundamental tenet of the Christian faith. Some of its earliest battles against paganism were fought against customs which presupposed that human lives could rightly be disposed of according to the convenience or pleasure of the State, or of some other human institution, such as the family. From the first the Church stood against the exposure of unwanted babies and against gladiatorial shows, in which human lives were sacrificed for the amusement of the populace. The racial theories and practices of the Nazis remind us that this emphasis on the sacredness of human personality is needed today, and I should like to make it quite clear that I have no sympathy whatever with any design either to breed or to destroy human beings for some purpose of the State. I hold firmly the doctrine of the sacredness of human personality.

When a Christian first hears of the proposal to legalize voluntary euthanasia he naturally thinks that it is a dangerous one, because it may weaken, or even seem to contradict, the principle of the sacredness of human personality. That was my own primary reaction and, therefore, I wish to treat opponents of voluntary euthanasia with respect and to recognize that they have a case. I have come, however, to believe that they are mistaken, and I will try to state briefly the reasons which have caused me to change my mind.

ɪɪ

> *It is contended that the endurance of suffering may be a means of grace and no Christian would deny this, but I would urge that, in the case of a man whose existence is a continuous drugged dream, this cannot be alleged.*

ɪɪ

It seems plain to me that the principle of the sacredness of human personality cannot be stretched to cover the case of those whom the proposed legislation has in mind. We have to present to ourselves the condition of a man who is incurably ill and destined to a period of agonized suffering, relieved only by the administration of narcotic drugs. The situation here, in many instances, is that a disintegration of the personality occurs. Nothing could be more distressing than to observe the gradual degeneration of a fine and firm character into something which we hardly recognize as our friend, as the result of physical causes and of the means adopted to assuage intolerable pain. It is contended that the endurance of suffering may be a means of grace and no Christian would deny this, but I would urge that, in the case of a man whose existence is a continuous drugged dream, this cannot be alleged.

Though we must readily agree that endurance of suffering in the right spirit may be a means of grace for the deepening of the spiritual life, we are bound to hold that, in itself, suffering is evil. If it were not so, how could it be a duty to relieve it as far as we are able? We should all revolt against a person who complacently regarded the suffering of someone else as "a blessing in disguise" and refused to do anything about it on those grounds. It seems to be an incontrovertible proposition that, when we are confronted with suffering which is wholly destructive in its consequences and, so far as we can see, could have no beneficial result, there is a prima facie duty to bring it to an end.

We sometimes hear it said that voluntary euthanasia is an attempt to interfere with the providential order of the world and to cut short the allocated span of life. It seems to be assumed by those who argue in this way that God has assigned to each one a definite number of days—"the term of his natural life"—and that to take any measure to reduce this number must in all circumstances be wrong. But we must observe that this argument would cut both ways and would equally condemn any attempt to lengthen the term. All medical treatment, which after all is an interference with the natural processes, would on this assumption be wrong, and many of us who are alive now because doctors have saved our lives have in effect no right to continue to exist in this world. Surely this view of the providential order is not the true one. Worked out to its logical conclusion it would lead to intolerable absurdities and even to the doctrine that every human effort to lengthen life or improve its condition is to be reprobated as contrary to the will of God.

No one is really prepared to act on this assumption. I suggest that a truer view of the providential order would be as follows: The Creator has given man reason, freedom, and conscience and has left him with the possibility of ordering his own life within limits. He is to do the best he can with the material presented to him, and that means that it is the will of God that we should use our reason and conscience and our power to choose when we are faced with evils that have a remedy. My view of Providence then leads me to suppose that we are required by our belief in God to give the most earnest consideration to the proposal to legalize voluntary euthanasia. We are not at liberty to dismiss it on some preconceived prejudice.

The less reflective critics of voluntary euthanasia allege that it would be legalized murder, or suicide, or both. But surely before we fling these ugly words about we should be careful to inquire what we mean by them.

Legally, since the Suicide Act of 1961* (passed without any opposition), it is no longer a criminal offence for any person to commit suicide or to

---

*Rev. Matthews is referring to the 1961 Act passed in England.—ED.

attempt to do so, although it remains an offence, punishable by heavy penalties, to assist a suicide. Morally the act of the suicide may be wrong because he takes his own life solely on his own judgment. It may be that he does so in a mood of despair or remorse and thus evades the responsibility of doing what he can to repair the wrong or improve the situation. He may fling away his life when there is still the possibility of service and when there are still duties to be done. The proposals for voluntary euthanasia, as advocated by the contributors to this volume,** have nothing in common with this kind of suicide. The choice of the individual concerned—a person faced with hopeless and useless suffering—is submitted to the objective judgment of doctors, and his decision can only be carried out with their assistance.

Murder consists in the taking of the life of another person with deliberate intention, "with malice aforethought." Very few people are prepared to take the command "Thou shalt not kill" as universally applicable and admitting no exceptions. If we did so, we should all have to be vegetarians. But supposing the command to apply only to human life, we can all imagine circumstances in which it would be a duty to kill. For example, if an innocent person is being murderously assaulted and there is no other way of defending him, we ought to try to kill the assailant. The suggestion that voluntary euthanasia—under the conditions considered by the contributors to this volume—is murder, seems to me absurd. The life which is abbreviated is one which the patient ardently wishes to resign; there is no malice in the hearts of those who co-operate, but rather love and compassion; the community is not deprived of any valuable service. None of the conditions which constitute the sin of murder are present in voluntary euthanasia as envisaged in this volume.

Something must be said in reply to those who deprecate the raising of these questions and would prefer to leave things as they are. "Why not leave it to the doctor?" they cry, imagining—I do not know with what justification—that doctors often take measures to shorten the suffering of the hopelessly ill.

This attitude appears to me to be really immoral, because it is an excuse for shuffling off responsibility. By what right do we place this terrible burden on the individual doctor? We have to remember that, as the law stands at present, if he does not do all he can to preserve the tortured life up to the

---

**The volume referred to is, of course, the book from which this selection is taken: A. B. Downing (Ed.), Euthanasia and the Right to Death (Los Angeles: Nash Publishing Company, 1970). The subtitle of that book is "A Case for Voluntary Euthanasia."—ED.

last possible gasp, he renders himself liable to grave penalties—even perhaps to the charge of murder. Is this a position in which one's conscience
can be easy? The answer must be, no. There is no honorable way of dealing with the question except by making up our minds whether or not
voluntary euthanasia under proper safeguards is ethically justifiable and,
if we decide that it is, embodying that conclusion in the law. Moreover, if
the legitimacy of properly safeguarded euthanasia at the request of a patient
is accepted, every suffer *in extremis* and in severe pain has a right to be able
to choose it. It is unjust that he should have to depend upon the views of the
individual doctor who happens to attend him.

I have met the argument that we can never be certain that any illness is
incurable; that "while there is life there is hope." It is of course true that
we hear of remarkable recoveries which confound the prognosis of the
physician. I do not disregard the potentialities of "spiritual healing," nor
would I exclude even the possibility of miracle, but I do not see how anyone
who has had any experience of visiting the sick can question the proposition
that there are cases where nothing but a miracle could restore the patient
or stave off his dissolution within a brief period, and where nothing but
useless agony can be anticipated. We cannot regulate our conduct at all
unless we assume that it must be guided by the knowledge that we have.
We take for granted that known causes will be followed by known effects
in the overwhelming majority of cases. Any other assumption would strike
at the roots of sanity.

The advance of medical science has changed the conditions of human life.
It is true that the ultimate principles of Christian morals do not change. The
root of all Christian morality is the injunction to love God and our neighbor;
as St. Paul says, "love is the fulfilling of the law." But though the fundamental principles do not change, their application may differ as the needs of
the time require. Rules which were once valid and useful may become obsolete and even an obstacle to the true "fulfilling of the law." We must be-
ware lest, in holding fast to "the letter," we betray "the spirit." In my
belief it is the vocation of the Christian to be alert to see where the law of
love points to "new duties."

The great master principle of love and its child, compassion, should
impel us to support measures which would make voluntary euthanasia
lawful and which, as stated by the Euthanasia Society, "would permit an
adult person of sound mind, whose life is ending with much suffering, to
choose between an easy death and a hard one, and to obtain medical aid in
implementing that choice."

Appropriate and Appropriated Death

Avery D. Weisman

Avery D. Weisman has contributed much to our understanding of death and dying. One of his most felicitous contributions to the field of thanatology is the concept of an "appropriate death"—a consummatory end that each person would seek for himself were he able to do so. In this paper from his book *On Dying and Denying,* Dr. Weisman contrasts appropriate death with appropriated death (suicide) and discusses how the dying may be helped toward achieving a more appropriate death.

From *On Dying and Denying: A Psychiatric Study of Terminality* by Avery D. Weisman. Copyright © 1972 by Behavioral Publications, Inc., New York. Reprinted by permission.

Every idea about death is a version of life. Concepts of heaven and hell, damnation and redemption, resolution of suffering, and rewards for deeds, good and ill, are simply extensions of what is already here. To look far into the future is largely an unrevealing pastime. Those events which we glimpse in the distant future are contemporary occasions, seen through the wrong end of a telescope. Even with thorough knowledge of someone's habits, thoughts, and style of life, we cannot accurately predict how and when he will come to the end of his life. Nor can we do this for ourselves. Like living, dying cannot be reduced to a small package of maxims. To tell another person what he ought to do, think, or be is an affront at any time; but to do this when he nears the end of life is sanctimonious cruelty.

We need not be very perceptive to realize that the unceasing destruction afflicting mankind supports the belief that death is senseless, unfair, painful, and tragic. Wars and calamities of nature somehow change our image of death, even giving it a bitter meaning. Where individual death is concerned, however, few of us would ever be prepared to die, if we did not die until we chose. Human beings struggle, suffer, falter, and ask for more. But when the margin between life and death blurs, as in many illnesses, people are then willing to slip quietly into oblivion. Indeed, were it possible for a few people in every generation to live on forever, we would soon cease thinking of them as members of the human race. This elite group might even be feared, like some monstrosity who could not die. Although in the flush of health, we may want to live on, and spontaneously assume that this is possible, the gift of immortality, were it available, might turn out to be a curse.

Appropriate death is a form of purposeful death, but not every instance of purposeful death is an appropriate death. To be willing to die does not mean that someone is able to die, or that his death would be appropriate. Death may be appropriate, but not acceptable; acceptable, but not appropriate. Obviously, appropriate death for one person might be unsuitable for another. Finally, what might seem appropriate from the outside, might be utterly meaningless to the dying person himself. Conversely, deaths that seem unacceptable to an outsider, might be desirable from the inner viewpoint of the patient.

APPROPRIATED DEATH

Appropriate death has a superficial resemblance to rational suicide, i.e., self-elected death compatible with the ego ideal. In olden times, suicide was an option that ensured honor for certain steadfast people. Many famous men took their own life, instead of surrendering their principles or compromising integrity. A legendary contrast in two manners of suicide is that of Seneca who chose death by his own hand, as opposed to his pupil, Nero, who had to be forced into suicide.

Actually, suicides of great men are often misinterpreted as great and rational deeds, worthy of the man. But we may forget that a great man may be subject to deep depressions and fully capable of destroying himself without the exoneration of "good reasons." The school-book jingle that "Lives of great men all remind us/We can make our lives sublime . . ." hides another fact, that the deaths of great men also show how mortal and fallible they can be. Who has the audacity to approve or disapprove of how anyone chooses to die, unless by his death, he nullifies whatever potential being alive holds? We can readily conjure up events that might justify self-destruction, but there are also circumstances in which murder could be condoned. An act of destruction might resolve conflict and relieve suffering, but for whom—the victim or the executioner?

It can be argued that to deprive man of his right to terminate life is an abridgement of his freedom. Yet, few suicides, rescued after an attempt, complain about their freedom, though they might regret being saved. The reasons that people assign to a suicide may be "good," but not the correct reasons. A man who is suicidal at 3 a.m. may find the idea unthinkable at 9 a.m., even though his reasons remain the same. One part of his personality decrees death for every other part. In a sense, suicide is an external agency that victimizes; the option to destroy oneself is not an expression of freedom, but one of despair. We lament a suicide; arguments for its freedom and rationality are only sophistries. Suffering of any origin is deplorable; any of us might choose to die before being completely tyrannized by disease or despotism. Few of us can predict with unerring certainty what we would do if. . . . Suicide must be construed as an emergency exit, not the main approach to a style of life. The suicide, for his own private reasons and intentionality, appropriates death for himself; he does not seek appropriate conditions in which to die. His death usually negates his ego ideal, and in other respects, as well, may be the antithesis of the conditions and circumstances for an appropriate death.

If we believe that death is bad, and dying people, by a magical contagion, are tainted, then appropriate deaths are never possible. By discouraging therapeutic intercessions, therefore, we may contribute deep alienation, hopelessness, and loneliness.

It is conceivable that at the very end of life, people can undergo changes in outlook, so that the meaning of having existed acquires a special significance. Appropriate death does not require complete knowledge about the dying person; few of us could satisfy these preconditions, even about ourselves! Appropriate death does require that we understand the contemporaneous experience that we call dying-in-the-here-and-now. The Greek word Kairos, an auspicious moment that leads to a decisive change, can also be applied to the event called dying. It is not an idealized image of death, nor does it delete the painful implications of dying to and from a number of things. The here-and-now significance of dying is very concrete, and should not be confused with the imaginary then-and-there of a "promised land."

The dying person can, at best, only foresee a wisp of future time. Hence, the now-and-here has a pungency that draws upon every level and period of his existence. Like some memento, it is a unit of reality that may encompass a lifetime.

CONDITIONS OF AN APPROPRIATE DEATH

Someone who dies an appropriate death must be helped in the following ways: He should be relatively pain-free, his suffering reduced, and emotional and social impoverishments kept to a minimum. Within the limits of disability, he should operate on as high and effective a level as possible, even though only tokens of former fulfillments can be offered. He should also recognize and resolve residual conflicts, and satisfy whatever remaining wishes are consistent with his present plight and with his ego ideal. Finally, among his choices, he should be able to yield control to others in whom he has confidence. He also has the option of seeking or relinquishing significant key people.

Obviously, these conditions of an appropriate death are like the highest aspirations of mankind! Few people are ever fortunate enough to realize these goals. Consequently, it may seem most unlikely that people about to die could reach or even care about appropriate death, if the requirements are so unrealistic. On the other hand, our preconception that death can *never* be appropriate may be a self-fulfilling idea. If we believe that death is bad, and dying people, by a magical contagion, are tainted, then appropriate deaths are never possible. By discouraging therapeutic intercessions, therefore, we may contribute deep alienation, hopelessness, and loneliness.

Given a measure of consciousness, control and competence to work with, we can encourage appropriate death, or at least a purposeful death. Patients can, for example, be protected from needless procedures that only dehumanize and demean, without offering suitable compensation. We can, moreover, ask people how much consciousness is desirable. Some patients prefer solitude toward the end in order to collect their thoughts. Others, more gregarious, need family and friends. As life ebbs away, some patients want to doze, while others prefer to be alert, and to simulate the regular periods of sleep and wakefulness that healthy people enjoy.

If we refuse to think of appropriate death as a quixotic vision beyond reach, we will protect the patient's autonomy and personal dignity. Much, of course, depends upon the concern of the key participants. Although most people tremble at the notion of dying, it is wholly practical that they can offer a substantial contribution to the mutual task. An appropriate death, in brief, is a death that someone might choose for himself—had he a choice. The central idea, of course, is that to foster an appropriate death, one must realize that death is not an ironic choice without an option, but a way of living as long as possible. Our task is therefore to separate death and its prejudices from each other.

A Psychiatrist's Response to a Life-Threatening Illness

Lauren E. Trombley

Lauren E. Trombley, a young psychiatrist, died some eight months after he discovered that he was suffering from leukemia. The poignant, personal document reproduced here is Dr. Trombley's account of his psychological journey to death written during the last two months of his life.

From *Life-Threatening Behavior*, Vol. 2, No. 1, 1972. Reprinted by permission.

The idea of this essay was conceived in November of 1966 but lay fallow until May of the following year because of my inability to delineate clearly both the objective and content of this paper. The passage of time has, of itself, provided some jelling of the ideas and content which, for a time, were so amorphous and jumbled in my mind.

My reasons for writing this essay are to objectify and clarify my own feelings regarding my illness, to help crystallize my perspective on matters of living and dying, and to inform others in a subjective way about the psychological processes that take place in a person who has a life-threatening disease. This does not mean that such information is not available, although it is difficult to find in the psychiatric literature. One would have to look in works of fiction for the most part and, I suppose, in some essays of a philosophical nature by nonmedical authors to find the same kind of information but, of course, couched in much different terms. The problems encompassed by the therapist's efforts to understand himself in relation to his life-threatening disease, his shifting relationships to his family, his patients, and his colleagues as he is grappling with his problem have not been explored in any systematic way. I have not yet found any enlightenment as to why people in our profession do not write about this.

A narration of the chronological events pertaining to my predicament is in order to keep the reader properly oriented. In November 1966, I discovered that I had acute myelogenous leukemia.* This discovery was quite by accident and did not occur because of any perception of anything seriously amiss. I had noticed one evening that I had a number of petechiae.** The following day I saw a physician who was a friend, and he recommended, after examining me and finding nothing unusual, that some blood tests be performed. This led to the ultimate diagnosis by bone marrow examination of the true picture. The next day the hematologist who had subsequently examined me and examined the slides of blood and bone marrow very reluctantly told me that I had this disease.

My initial reactions are difficult to describe and still more difficult to recall accurately. However, I do remember feeling that somehow the doctor's remarks could not be directed to me but must be about some other person. Of course, I shook off that feeling very soon during this conversation, and the full realization of the import of this diagnosis struck me. I was steeped in a pervasive sense of deep and bitter disappointment. I thought that I had been maliciously cheated out of the realization of all the hopes and aims that I had accrued during my professional career. I was in the third year of my psychiatric residency and on the brink of fully developing a professional identity. Further, and more important, I was also on the threshold of developing a true sense of personal maturity and personal identity. I felt now that this would all be denied me and that I would never live to realize the fruit of the struggles in which I had been engaged for so long a time. I immediately went to see my department chief and discovered that he had already been informed. He was most kind and gracious and extremely helpful in setting my skewed perspective back on the right track. For that matter, from that moment onward I never wanted for good counsel and enormous equanimity and maturity from my supervisors and teachers, without whom I doubt I could have rallied as well as I did.

The next subjective feeling I can clearly identify is that I was increasingly apprehensive following the diagnosis about my inevitable decreasing body

---

*Dr. Trombley died on July 18, 1967.—ED.

**Small spots on a body surface, such as the skin or a mucous membrane, caused by minute hemorrhages.—ED.

507

efficiency and thus very likely my decreasing efficiency and interest in my work. This engendered some little guilt over my anticipating not being able to do the job I had been doing. Indeed, because of the drugs it was necessary to take for the illness and not really because of the illness itself, the capability of my usual performance was sharply curtailed. Luckily when I expressed such feelings of guilt over not pulling my weight in the organization, this was immediately squelched by my teachers who were able to assuage my unnecessarily hypertrophied superego, which has since become of a much more manageable size. Nonetheless, I did have pangs of remorse when I finally had to stop seeing long-term patients because my physical symptoms interfered too much with appointments. Surprisingly, I did not feel consciously angry or frightened by the knowledge that I had a life-threatening illness.

I was gravely disappointed and terribly annoyed that this thing inside my body would interfere with my life. But at no time did I really feel, as one might put it, "angered at the gods" for having such sport with me. Nor did I find that I used denial as a defense to any extent early in the course of the illness, as I did later on when it appeared that some of the chemotherapeutic measures were having considerably good effect and I began to feel that I could go on interminably from drug to drug and not die of my disease. Instead my attention was directed away from my illness in its early phases by some very practical matters that might be called "setting my affairs in order." I was so busy with this that it served quite well to focus on an aspect of dying that is not connected with the disease process itself and thus considerably decreased my own anxiety. There was an enormous mobilization of energy to get things accomplished in this regard by both me and my wife. There were a number of changes we needed to make in our lives in order to fulfill sooner than we had anticipated some of the expectations we had about how we would live. Although a great many things actually transpired I shall mention only two or three here as examples. We first moved from a small rented apartment that was adequate for our needs at the time to a larger house and we purchased additional furniture. Because I was deeply interested in music and particularly in composing, we borrowed a grand piano from friends who were extremely gracious in allowing us to use it while they were living in the area and did not find as much use for it as they had in the past. My wife undertook practically all of the details of this move herself and also redecorated one of the three bedrooms we had in the home so that I might have a private study and library. When we got all these things accomplished, we took stock of the situation and came to the realization that

it had not really required a serious illness to do these things because we had
not overextended ourselves in any financial sense and we could have done
all this before I got sick if we had really set our minds to it. Sometimes it
takes a crisis in an individual's life to get him to do the things that he could
well have done to change his life for the better. We had, in effect, denied
ourselves some of the comfort of a real home and space in which to work for
no valid practical reason.

My parents expressed shock, grief, and disbelief over the situation. They
worried about such things as how one gets such an illness or, perhaps more
cogently, why one *should* get such an illness, reflecting, I suppose, a very
common fantasy that such a thing must be some kind of a punishment—just
or unjust—visited upon the victim.

When it came to the question of informing my three young children
(by a previous marriage) about my illness, I was met with the question based
on the precept "How could you do this to them just before Christmas?" I
explained that it was far better for the children to understand precisely
what it was that was going on, rather than permit them to develop their own
fantasies about it which could very easily be far worse than the truth. The
fact that it was close to Christmas was quite beside the point. As a matter of
fact, the holiday gave me an opportunity to fly to my former home state and
visit with both my parents and the children and to clarify personally some
of the confusion I was sure existed about the nature of this disease. Indeed,
there were a number of fantasies, doubts, and fears that very much needed
to be dispelled. The children were prepared to some extent for a not-very-
well father who had an illness that might easily take his life in a short period
of time. One fantasy they all had (unexpressed except through probing) was,
"Is this thing contagious? Will I get it if I am close to you?" As soon as this
was corrected the children found themselves able to be much closer to me
than they had been when we first met at the airport. As it turned out later
nearly all of the children with whom I had therapeutic contact had this same
fantasy.

Some of my colleagues may very well have had similar fantasies. If they
did, I have not discovered it but can only surmise it because there have been
practically no contacts at all with some of the people with whom I worked
since the inception of my illness. There has been some speculation on my
part (reinforced to some extent by conversations with supervisors) that some
of the people with whom I have had fairly close contact in the past found it
almost impossible to deal with me and my illness because of their own fears
and fantasies concerning death. One almost amusing idea came to light

through one of my supervisors, namely, that some of my colleagues might very well be wishing that I would drop dead and get it over with rather than continue to torment them as I was. For others there was a heightened awareness of a close relationship that had never been verbalized in the past. This occurred with two or three of my fellow residents, and certainly we were all the better for it. Not only was there some clarification of feelings and a chance to discuss them openly between us, but also this produced a closer relationship.

At all times I tried to make it clear that I in no way wanted to avoid open discussion of my illness. I did not want to play any games of pretending that I was better than I was (although I am prone to do so), nor did I want to avoid responding to questions about how I was from day to day under the assumption that to be reminded of my illness might hurt me. On the contrary, I felt somehow annoyed if I was not asked how things were going with me because I wanted to share with others feelings about my illness. One of my friends and teachers commented that one of the things that bothered him most was the destruction of his fantasies of omnipotence by the knowledge of my illness. In other words, there was nothing he could do to change the situation, although he wanted to very much. I imagine that many of my fellow residents felt the same way, and they responded to this in a very constructive manner. They were discussing this one day among themselves, and one of them suggested they donate blood, which most certainly I would eventually need, as a means of doing something positive and relieving the terrible feeling that there was nothing that could be done. This was, I think, of enormous help to them and, of course, to me too. This concrete measure proved to be so popular with all of my acquaintances in the Department of Psychiatry that the Blood Bank was soon swamped with individuals wishing to donate blood in my behalf.

All this took place in the first few weeks of my illness. During this time, I was also increasingly apprehensive about my ability to continue the program. I was vastly reassured when the acting department chief asked me, "What is it that the residency can do for you?" I was also repeatedly assured by my division chief that I should assume only the work that I felt really capable of doing efficiently. He would rather, he said, that I did less than I had been doing and do a good job of that, than try to put in a full day and have to drag around looking rather dreary, reminding other people that I was sick. This made good sense to me so I was able to stay home part of the time after I started to feel less well without feeling guilty about it. I have been enormously buoyed up by the generous support of the staff, and

I hope they know how deeply grateful I am to them. At this point I was feeling very dismal about my prospects for any longevity, and I was very glad to get all the support that I did. I did not enter the hospital but continued working and began a program of medication as an outpatient. This was a very important step because otherwise I might have been compelled to concentrate almost exclusively on the internal workings of my disabled body and would not have been able to continue working. As it turned out, this was one of the most important features of the total adaptation to this disease, because everybody made me feel that I was not giving up, despite the reduction in the time I actually spent at work.

ↆↆ

People wrongly assume that a sick person should be "protected" from strong, and particularly negative, feelings. The truth is that there is probably no more crucial time in a person's life when he needs to know what's going on with those who are important to him.

ↆↆ

The relationship between me and my wife was also exceedingly important at this time. At first, of course, she responded with remorse, sympathy, and total understanding. As time progressed and it appeared that I was evincing some durability and I was pretty much my old self despite the shadow I lived under, she was able to express some of the deeper feelings concerning me and my illness which were not really seen by her as separate entities. Since then we have been able to share feelings, more openly than ever before, never to the detriment of either of us. People wrongly assume that a sick person should be "protected" from strong, and particularly negative, feelings. The truth is that there is probably no more crucial time in a person's life when he needs to know what's going on with those who are important to him.

Some special problems arose in the therapeutic relationship with child patients. On occasion, I would be absent either because I did not feel well or because it was necessary for me to be hospitalized briefly for some special treatment or because some complication had developed. The children were apprised of the reason for my absence without elaboration, and they rarely would press for information beyond what was given to them. One child in particular, a 10-year-old boy with a borderline psychosis, continued his relationship to me with little allusion to my impairment resulting, for example, in my not going outside with him to play games, realizing that I had some limitations because I did not feel well. Although he did not ask for any further explanation, it evolved later on when he was transferred to another therapist that he understood (how I am still not clear) that I had a serious illness and that the transfer was necessary because of this. He was not able to express (or else I could not permit him to express) his feelings regarding this during the time that we had our relationship. The reason given for transferring him to another therapist was my needing to reduce my schedule because I was going to be more involved with teaching and could not continue with some patients. This, in fact, was true, but it did not offer the real underlying explanation for the reduction in my therapy time with patients.

This illustrated for me two things about working with children: (*a*) they are extraordinarily perceptive and will pick up difficulties in a nonverbal way that the therapist is struggling with even though he may be trying to hide them; and (*b*) even borderline children are quite adaptable and will readily accept the limitations of the therapist, providing he is quite clear about them. It is rare that the child will press to see whether or not the therapist is indeed as limited as he indicates. There were occasions in the treatment of the two borderline children I was seeing when they sought to understand whether or not I was strong enough to be able to control them. I handled this in several ways, one being to indicate to them that if things were going to continue to be as upsetting as they were, probably we should terminate the hour and continue again next time. Or more frequently, and usually at least as effectively, I would indicate to the child that I was not up to wrestling with him or having to assume control over him and I would have to depend upon his own ability to conform to the limits I had set without my needing to restrain him physically. Somewhat to my surprise this was often readily accepted by the child who would comment, "OK, I'll stop," and the rest of the hour would be much more manageable for both of us. Eventually, every therapist experiences, somewhat to his astonishment, the ability of even very sick patients to protect the therapist under certain circumstances.

On a number of occasions I have found it necessary either to change or cancel an appointment with the mother of a certain patient who was being seen in the clinic. This particular patient had a great deal of difficulty in expressing any overt anger or hostility. It was a constructive experience for both of us to be able to get this patient to see that I was perfectly capable (sick or not) of tolerating her annoyance with my not being present at an expected time and that I would still see her and not hate her for having such negative feelings about me, although I could not help the fact that I could not meet with her at that specific time. Here, perhaps, is one of the few times the countertransference needs of the therapist were beneficial to the patient. In other words, because of the guilt I felt in not being able to meet with the patient because I was under the weather, I really needed her to be angry with me in an open and direct way. By getting her to understand that I would be much relieved in knowing precisely what her feelings were, she was able to tell me, still in a tentative way, that she was angry. This marked, I believe, a significant turning point for this patient who is probably one of the most inhibited women in her affective life that I have dealt with.

In the several months since the inception of my illness I became increasingly aware of a new sensitivity that had gradually but progressively developed in my interpersonal relationships, both with patients and with all my acquaintances. The sensitivity of which I speak is rather elusive insofar as a clear definition is concerned, but perhaps I can resort to describing it in terms of its effect. One thing I noticed most pointedly was that I was very much more tolerant of the vagaries and inconsistencies of other people's attitudes and behavior than I had ever been before. Perhaps "tolerant" is not a very good word. It might be better to use the word "understanding," because many times I have found myself perceiving very quickly what lay beneath a particular person's attitude or affect which did not seem altogether appropriate to the situation. Thus I found myself much more at ease with people whom I had found difficult to tolerate in the past. Some people commented that they found it easy to be with me because I openly invited questions about my illness.

This heightened awareness of affect in others also extended to myself, and I found that my own feelings were much more accessible to my conscious recognition than they had been in the past. I also found that all of my senses seemed more acute, though I believe that really I simply paid more attention to what was going on around me and, in a way, I found myself hungering for every sensory experience that I could absorb. In many ways the world seemed to offer more beauty, and there was a heightened awareness of sounds and sights, which in the past I may have only casually observed or simply not have paid much attention to at all. This kind of experience was by no means unique to me. It has, for example, been quite accurately described by Hans Zinnser in his autobiography, *As I Remember Him*. But aside from the sensory and affective sensitivity that I had seemed to acquire, there appeared to me to be a culmination of all the learning experience that I had in my professional career which, in a compressed space of time, became the foundation for practically a new way of life. Another way to put this is that there was quite suddenly an integration of all the values and understanding I had of human experience into some kind of cohesive whole which, although difficult to describe, made extremely good sense to me.

This brings me to a question that I had earlier put aside: What happened to all the anger and depression that should have occurred after the news of my illness? I think I know. It would seem that the struggles I had with myself had not been in vain, and it was fortunate that I was where I was at the time all this happened, since I had a great deal of psychological help available to me. At any rate, it would appear that the peace I made with myself during my illness, and the maturing ability that I was developing to cope with life crises like this one, arose from several dynamic factors. One was the increasing capacity to sublimate the rage and aggression engendered by the impotency I felt regarding this invasion from within. Instead of striking blindly outwardly or, probably more likely, addressing the anger inward and thus becoming depressed, I became intensely involved in musical composition and composed practically like a madman for the first several weeks of my illness, completing one lengthy work and two smaller ones which represented in that space of time more output in this field of art than I had ever been able to accomplish in the past. This outlet proved so effective that it was very seldom that I was conscious of any feelings of despair or depression. Indeed, I suspect that when they began to reach consciousness I would begin furiously (and I use the word quite deliberately) to become creatively involved, and thus dispel the unpleasant affect. One other possibility as to my rather benign attitude was the simple reversal of affect, though I doubt that played as large a part as sublimation. Certain instruments lend themselves to this kind of alteration in the discharge of affect better than others. For example, the percussion instruments, which in a sense include the piano, are really excellent ways to deal with the aggressive energy present in everyone. But it is revealing to cite the ways I thought of working with music in these past few months. I would attack the piano, I would literally hammer out a new piece. I think that further illustrations are not necessary because it is obvious now how music and I served each other in this regard now that I am able to look at this in retrospect.

Certainly there are rewarding aspects of facing a life-threatening illness. I have learned much about the alterations in my own internal psychological processes, and the subtle metamorphosis in interpersonal relationships that have occurred and are still occurring. I wish that other people in my position would also write subjectively about this. Perhaps this paper may encourage it.

By way of completing this little essay I might comment that the Eastern or Oriental view of the life cycle of constant renewal and death as not being clear endings or beginnings to anything has been extremely useful to me. In a way I have, at least intellectually, accepted and I hope that I can wholeheartedly embrace the idea that the death of any individual is really no more nor less than a punctuation mark in the endlessly fascinating conversation amongst all living things.

St. Christopher's Hospice

Cicely Saunders

Dr. Cicely Saunders, Medical Director of St. Christopher's Hospice near London, has waged a life-long war against the needless pain and indignity which so often surround death. This selection, which is excerpted from her annual report of St. Christopher's, reviews some of the ways in which a contemporary institution is developing programs for helping terminally ill patients achieve a decent and "appropriate" death.

From St. Christopher's Hospice *Annual Report 1971-72.* Reprinted by permission.

WHAT IS A HOSPICE?

In one sense, St. Christopher's was founded when a patient left us the first gift of all, back in 1948, but in a deeper one, it belongs to a tradition stretching back to the hospices of the Middle Ages which welcomed the pilgrims who arrived hungry, tired, and sore as they crossed Europe on the way to the various sites of pilgrimage. The word continued to be used in France and was extended to hospices for the elderly, the incurable and for foundlings (enfants trouvés). Mother Mary Aidenhead then took up the title when she founded the Irish Sisters of Charity in the middle of the last century, although the Hospice at Harold's Cross, Dublin, was only dedicated especially to the care of dying patients 67 years ago. Her foundation has long extended to several hospices, mainly concerned with the care of the dying and the long-term sick. St. Joseph's Hospice, Hackney, was founded in 1905, but before it opened its doors the Sisters were visiting the sick in their homes, thus foreshadowing the domiciliary work we have now started at St. Christopher's over the past three years.

The other tradition from which St. Christopher's springs is that of the mediaeval hospital. Apart from the hospices which followed the pilgrim routes and which were primarily for hospitality, there came to be others, located in towns, "for the sick and poor" who were literally dying in the streets through cold and malnutrition, and who were picked up from the gutters and brought in for care and treatment. It was when these began to be staffed by professional physicians and surgeons that they took the name "hospital." The rich were nursed and died at home, although at times they made arrangements to spend their old age in a hospital, praying and preparing their souls for death; a hospital would often have a special wing for such patients with private rooms and many amenities. Poor patients, on the other hand, arrived *in extremis* because they had nowhere else to go. Medical treatment was still limited, and the chief comfort they could be offered was a religious consolation; they could contemplate the crucifix—"He suffered as I suffer now."

So the work originates back in time with the stopping places for pilgrims, and extends through the French hospices and above all through the work of the Irish Sisters of Charity, to the present day. All the groups we have mentioned are gathered within our walls: the elderly residents in the Drapers' Wing; the Playgroup members—not foundlings but the children of staff—who come and cheer us all by their noisy play; those who need longer-term nursing than can be carried out in an ordinary hospital, and who make their home with us and give us all so much in friendship and life; and the very ill to whom we can give a great deal of treatment, often unexpected remission or even cure, but always, we hope, something of real comfort. The staff is, no doubt, more numerous than the monks of the hospice in the St. Bernard Pass, but I think that the way they involve themselves so deeply in the lives and problems of the patients and their families, the way they stay with us and bring their own families and friends to see us, and the way in which students come and come again combine to give us something of the busy, many-sided life of the mediaeval pilgrimage and its resting places.

The life of St. Christopher's is illustrated by the variety of announcements on the notice board. There is a diagram of the way the Hospice finances have gone during these five years, with the mounting expenses (mainly consisting of the payments for salaries and wages of staff) met partly by monies from the regional board and the teaching hospitals and fully supplemented by the many good gifts we receive. There are frequent announcements of the birth of a baby to an ex-staff member, often set alongside the list of the anniversaries of patients who died during the same week a year ago. There is the chapel diary and notices of social and more serious meetings, and sometimes extras such as one never-to-be-forgotten notice, "As you know, the goldfish pond needs restocking . . ." Small things are very important. . . .

THE WORKING OF ST. CHRISTOPHER'S

People often ask us about the waiting list and are concerned at the number of applications they feel we must have to refuse. The situation has changed surprisingly little over the five years since we opened, and numbers have remained fairly constant. We have about 1,500 enquiries a year. Some 500 of these are about patients for whom St. Christopher's care has not been designed. We are often able to make suggestions about other organisations who may be able to help them. Sometimes we have heard that the chance to talk on the telephone has been all that was needed to help people to sort out their problems.

We help approximately two-thirds of the roughly 1,000 patient enquirers which remain. Most of those at home are visited before admission, and it is rare that we fail to admit a patient who is in distress which cannot be helped at home. Some of those who are never admitted include people who, having been given assurance that St. Christopher's will help if the time comes, remain well cared for in their own homes. One of the local family doctors has repeatedly said that he puts his patients on our list as a sort of insurance because he has found that the fact that the family are aware that St. Christopher's is in the background often means that admission will not be necessary.

People often say, "How can you work at St. Christopher's Hospice? It must be so depressing." This is just not true.

The number of people we have been able to help has been increasing. During the first full year (1968) we admitted 380 patients, and during 1971 we admitted 489; during 1972, 519; and during 1973, 579.

The first voice on the telephone answering an enquiry from a member of family or the first person seen at the Hospice is of great importance. The stewards and everyone at reception are the first people who are met as the hosts at St. Christopher's. The many jobs that they and the maintenance staff do around the Hospice in keeping everything as a good gift should be kept is important, but their availability to meet any members of families, visitors, or any other enquirer who comes in is rightly put first by them. We have always tried to make it possible for each patient to see a doctor every day. . . .

All analgesics for patients with malignant pain should be given regularly, usually 4 hourly. The aim is to titrate the level of analgesia against the patient's pain, gradually increasing the dose until the patient is pain-free. At this stage the dose of analgesic will be given before the effect of the previous one has worn off and therefore before the patient may think it necessary. It is thus possible to erase the memory and fear of pain.

Since the opening of St. Christopher's Hospice considerable interest has been stimulated among nursing staff about the care of the dying and those with chronic pain, and we find that trained staff want to come and work with us to further their experience in this type of nursing. Obviously these trained nurses are not going to stay indefinitely, and therefore it means that we always have a need for this type of staff. One interesting fact has emerged and that is that there is an obvious place here for the young, who show a great interest and an amazing capacity for understanding the needs of our patients. Again, they do not stay longer than about a year as they either marry or move on.

The fact that we have a playroom for the children of the staff has played an enormous part in maintaining a continuity of staffing. This enables a married person, trained or untrained, who has a desire to come back to nursing or care for people, to return to a field of nursing where she has a tremendous amount to give and also finds satisfaction.

There have been times when in order to keep the wards running as they should we have been extended as far as we are able, but help has always come just when we were getting desperate. We have not employed agency nurses—the gaps that occur at holiday periods have been filled by volunteers or by the students and others who do much of their learning by working. . . .

People often say, "How can you work at St. Christopher's Hospice? It must be so depressing." This is just not true. It is a very happy place, but, of course, it has its moments of tension, its moments of distress; but amongst all this there is also joy and fulfilment. The work is hard and heavy, both physically and emotionally, but also very satisfying. Over the past five years the demands on the nursing staff have increased. When we started we based our ratio of staff on a 1–1 basis over 24 hours, but that has now been increased to 1.25–1 over 24 hours on a year-round basis. I think the fact that 14 nurses have been with us for over five years and another 12 nurses for over four years emphasizes that there are people who really do want to nurse and that this type of nursing is rewarding. . . .

519

Referrals come to the staff medical social worker from the doctors, ward and clinic sisters, other staff, from patients themselves and their families, or from the social worker who arranges the admission. Numbers remain steady, at around 90 a year, with proportionately more men than women. Many contacts are necessarily short, and help when needed must be given immediately. Needs vary and are often practical—fares for visiting relatives can be heavy—advice over sorting personal and legal affairs is often needed, and a few patients and residents have been helped to have a holiday. But help is not only of a material kind. As with all the staff, the social worker's job is to listen, support, and counsel.

The social worker also organises the Family Service Project, a study of the effects of bereavement, which is directed by Dr. Murray Parkes, and was started in May, 1970. The purpose is to identify and offer help to any recently bereaved families or friends who may prove unlikely to be able to cope unaided with their grief and the stresses of life caused by their loss. Staff and volunteers visit to assess the need and to offer support, and if more specialized help is indicated, this can be arranged.

The work involved in keeping the records and arranging visits is cumulative. Out of approximately 750 records reviewed since the project started, 118 people have been visited or offered help, and once contact has been established by a visitor, it may continue over several months or occasionally years. . . .

It is good to know that we still have 26 volunteers who came to us soon after the Hospice opened, and although many volunteers have had to leave us during the past five years, we have been able to maintain a steady flow of new helpers, and our numbers stay at around 100 to 110.

We use voluntary help in every department of the Hospice, and this has now been extended to making the curtains and assembling the library for the new teaching and residential block. A team of volunteers also help to get the news letters distributed three or four times a year. . . .

TEACHING

During the year, we have been watching with interest developments on the second site and the rapid rise of the teaching and residential unit down the road. Even more important, though less spectacular, has been the steady growth in the amount of teaching undertaken in the Hospice itself. More time has been spent over in-service training for new members of the staff and voluntary workers. We have had in all 2,383 visitors either for a day or for an afternoon visit. This number includes doctors, nurses, social workers, priests, and students of all sorts. There have been over 100 residential visitors—people who have lived and worked with us and who have been able to learn from the patients and their families the problems of long-term illness and ways of coping.

All the members of the Hospice staff are involved in one way or another with the teaching. As the program develops it will still be based on experience in the wards. Nothing else can take the place of such experience. . . .

CLINICAL STUDIES AND RESEARCH

Our Department of Clinical Studies is gradually extending its work. The evaluation of analgesic (pain relieving) drugs continues, and one of the ward staff nurses has now joined the team as nurse observer. This is enabling us to look at well-established drugs and their use while patients are fully relieved and comfortable and to plan the treatment that suits them best. At the same time a number of other symptoms and their treatment are being considered. This is a long-term project which will eventually be fully reported in the medical press.

A marathon task is undertaken by the recorder (one of the doctors on our council) in making precis of the notes of all the patients who have been in the Hospice. This enables us to keep records on a punch card system and to review the many facets of our work year by year. It gives valuable information on the demands for our care as well as our success in giving it, and the statistics compiled from these records have been used by the groups who are planning to enter this field.

Some people with cancer spend most of their illness in hospital, some are cared for at home, and others spend part of their time at home and part in hospital. Each pattern of care has advantages and disadvantages for the patient and for the family. We have been trying to assess these by visiting the surviving spouses of people who have died of cancer in two London boroughs and asking them for their opinion about each phase of the illness. Our analysis to date indicates that although patients are often sent into hospital because of painful symptoms, those who die at home will have more pain than those who die in hospital. From the relative's point of view nursing someone at home is often a time of severe stress, but there is reason to believe that, in the long term, people who have been able to care for someone in this way may find themselves coping with life rather better after bereavement than those who have never had the opportunity to do so.

This study is also enabling us to discover the comments, criticisms, and general attitudes of family members towards various aspects of the care provided by St. Christopher's Hospice. These comments are of particular value in helping us to improve our standards of care. . . .

TWO STORIES

Mr. P. was 52 and a proof reader for a national newspaper. He came to us from a teaching hospital with an unsolved problem of pain, unhappy and breathless.

He quickly settled to our regime of drugs, and pain was never a problem again. Mr. P. used the ten weeks he was with us to sort out his thoughts on life and faith, and he found his own way into peace. He was quiet and self-contained, but he enjoyed meeting students and visitors and he made good friends in the ward.

After Christmas I took him some copies of a photograph I had taken of him at one of our parties. I wanted to give it to him, he wanted to pay for it. We ended by each accepting something from the other. As we were discussing this I held my hand out. At this he held both his, palms upwards, next to mine and said, "That's what life is about, four hands held out together." After that we could discuss anything. Once I asked him what he thought about heaven. "If you believe in Him there's just no question," he said promptly. Pressed to go further he added, "It's not as if I could think of Him —like a breathing person—it's the same when you are going on a holiday— you don't know what it will be like when you get there, you just hope it will be nice."

Mr. P. became weary before he died, and though he was somewhat confused for a day or two, this quickly disappeared, and he was very peaceful till he died in his sleep one morning without a sign of distress, not even a sigh. I will never forget the picture of the hands he gave us. I cannot think of a better symbol for our aims for St. Christopher's.

Mr. A., a bricklayer of 61, came to the ward after Mr. P. left us. He had been visited at home for 15 weeks before his admission. He was not very keen to let anyone into his flat, where he lived alone, protecting his independence even from his daughter. Throughout the weeks of his stay in St. Christopher's we had to help him maintain his fight for independence. Short of breath as he was, he would stump up and down the stairs to the garden or the Pilgrim Room, pausing to look very critically at the progress of the Play Group Wing building on the way. He made many friends and established himself as escort and guide to a blind patient in his bay. His relationships with the other patients were often colourful but always kind. Bed was definitely not on his schedule, and he sat out beside it till his last day surrounded by the *Daily Mirror*, well spread out, ashtrays with endless cigarette ends and ash everywhere.

On his last day he was still in charge, dictating what he would let us give him and very much himself. In the evening he checked that Sister had his sons' phone numbers correctly. When the night nurses came on he said, "I may give you trouble tonight." He died quietly in his sleep early next morning.

Epilogue to *A Very Easy Death*

Simone de Beauvoir
Simone de Beauvoir is an internationally famous author, best known, perhaps, for her three books *The Mandarins, The Second Sex,* and *Coming of Age.* The title of her book *A Very Easy Death*—from which this selection is taken—appears to be sardonic inasmuch as the book is a description of the difficult, tortuous death of her mother. In the final passages of the book, reproduced here, de Beauvoir reviews her feelings about her mother's death, sees death in a new form, and reaches a shattering conclusion.

Why did my mother's death shake me so deeply? Since the time I left home I had felt little in the way of emotional impulse towards her. When she lost my father the intensity and the simplicity of her sorrow moved me, and so did her care for others —"Think of yourself," she said to me, supposing that I was holding back my tears so as not to make her suffering worse. A year later her mother's dying was a painful reminder of her husband's: on the day of the funeral a nervous breakdown compelled her to stay in bed. I spent the night beside her: forgetting my disgust for this marriage-bed in which I had been born and in which my father had died, I watched her sleeping; at fifty-five, with her eyes closed and her face calm, she was still beautiful; I wondered that the strength of her feelings should have overcome her will. Generally speaking I thought of her with no particular feeling. Yet in my sleep (although my father only made very rare and then insignificant appearances) she often played a most important part: she blended with Sartre, and we were happy together. And then the dream would turn into a nightmare: why was I living with her once more? How had I come to be in her power again? So our former relationship lived on in me in its double aspect—a subjection that I loved and hated. It revived with all its strength when Maman's accident, her illness and her death shattered the routine that then governed our contacts. Time vanishes behind those who leave this world, and the older I get the more my past years draw together. The "Maman darling" of the days when I was ten can no longer be told from the inimical woman who oppressed my adolescence; I wept for them both when I wept for my old mother. I thought I had made up my mind about our failure and accepted it; but its sadness comes back to my heart. There are photographs of both of us, taken at about the same time: I am eighteen, she is nearly forty. Today I could almost be her mother and the grandmother of that sad-eyed girl. I am so sorry for them—for me because I am so young and I understand nothing; for her because her future is closed and she has never understood anything. But I would not know how to advise them. It was not in my power to wipe out the unhappiness in her childhood that condemned Maman to make me unhappy and to suffer in her turn from having done so. For if she embittered several years of my life, I certainly paid her back though I did not set out to do so. She was intensely anxious about my soul. As far as this world was concerned, she was pleased at my successes, but she was hurt by the scandal that I aroused among the people she knew. It was not pleasant for her to hear a cousin state, "Simone is the family's disgrace."

The changes in Maman during her illness made my sorrow all the greater. As I have already said, she was a woman of a strong and eager temperament, and because of her renunciations she had grown confused and difficult. Confined to her bed, she decided to live for herself; and yet at the same time she retained an unvarying care for others—from her conflicts there arose a harmony. My father and his social character coincided exactly: his class and he spoke through his mouth with one identical voice. His last words, "You began to earn your living very young, Simone: your sister cost me a great deal of money," were not of a kind to encourage tears. My mother was awkwardly laced into a spiritualistic ideology; but she had an animal passion for life which was the source of her courage and which, once she was conscious of the weight of her body, brought her towards truth. She got rid of the ready-made notions that hid her sincere and lovable side. It was then that I felt the warmth of an affection that had often been distorted by jealousy and that she expressed so badly. In her papers I have found touching evidence of it. She had put aside two letters, the one written by a Jesuit and the other by a friend; they both assured her that one day I should come back to God. She had copied out a passage from Chamson in which he says in effect, "If, when I was twenty, I had met an older, highly-regarded man who had talked to me about Nietszche and Gide and freedom, I should have broken with home." The file was completed by an article cut out of a paper—*Jean-Paul Sartre has saved a soul.* In this Rémy Roure said—quite untruthfully, by the way—that after *Bariona* had been acted at Stalag XII D an atheistical doctor was converted. I know very well what she wanted from these pieces—it was to be reassured about me; but she would never have felt the need if she had not been intensely anxious as to my salvation. "Of course I should like to go to Heaven: but not all alone, not without my daughters," she wrote to a young nun.

ᚱᚱ

*"He is certainly of an age to die."
The sadness of the old; their banishment: most of them do not think that this age has yet come for them.*

ᚱᚱᚱ

Sometimes, though very rarely, it happens that love, friendship or comradely feeling overcomes the loneliness of death: in spite of appearances, even when I was holding Maman's hand, I was not with her—I was lying to her. Because she had always been deceived, gulled, I found this ultimate deception revolting. I was making myself an accomplice of that fate which was so misusing her. Yet at the same time in every cell of my body I joined in her refusal, in her rebellion: and it was also because of that that her defeat overwhelmed me. Although I was not with Maman when she died, and although I had been with three people when they were actually dying, it was when I was at her bedside that I saw Death, the Death of the dance of death, with its bantering grin, the Death of fireside tales that knocks on the door, a scythe in its hand, the Death that comes from elsewhere, strange and inhuman: it had the very face of Maman when she showed her gums in a wide smile of unknowingness.

"He is certainly of an age to die." The sadness of the old; their banishment: most of them do not think that this age has yet come for them. I too made use of this cliché, and that when I was referring to my mother. I did not understand that one might sincerely weep for a relative, a grandfather aged seventy and more. If I met a woman of fifty overcome with sadness because she had just lost her mother, I thought her neurotic: we are all mortal; at eighty you are quite old enough to be one of the dead . . .

But it is not true. You do not die from being born, nor from having lived, nor from old age. You die from *something*. The knowledge that because of her age my mother's life must soon come to an end did not lessen the horrible surprise: she had sarcoma. Cancer, thrombosis, pneumonia: it is as violent and unforeseen as an engine stopping in the middle of the sky. My mother encouraged one to be optimistic when, crippled with arthritis and dying, she asserted the infinite value of each instant; but her vain tenaciousness also ripped and tore the reassuring curtain of everyday triviality. There is no such thing as a natural death: nothing that happens to a man is ever natural, since his presence calls the world into question. All men must die: but for every man his death is an accident and, even if he knows it and consents to it, an unjustifiable violation.

POETIC

EPILOGUE

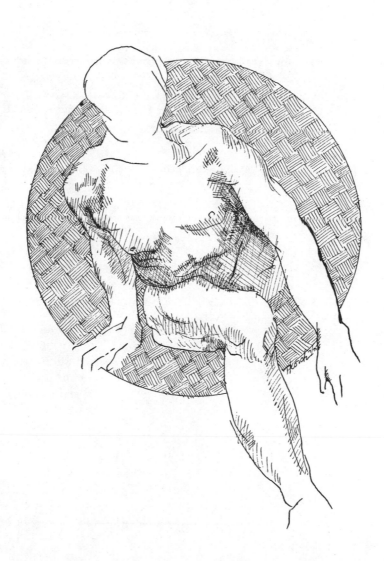

POETIC EPILOGUE

This selection—a poem about a person's own
impending death—can legitimately be thought of as a
"personal document" in the sense that Gordon
Allport, the famed psychologist, called diaries, letters,
and journals personal documents. (See *The Use of
Personal Documents in Psychological Science.* New
York: SSRC, 1942.) Apart from the poetry of death,
other examples of death-oriented personal documents
are, of course, suicide notes, and "death journals,"
(as they might be called), accounts written in the
context of the author's actually dying. Recent
examples of this latter genre would include "Notes
of a Dying Professor," *Pennsylvania Gazette,* March,
1972; Betty Harker, "Cancer and Communication
Problems: A Personal Experience," *Psychiatry in
Medicine,* Volume 3, 1972; and Lauren Trombley,
"A Psychiatrist's Response to a Life-Threatening
Illness," (included as a selection in this volume).
In each of these, the writer expresses his or her
feelings and experiences in the last few months of
life. There are many poems about death. The reader
interested in this fascinating but lugubrious topic
may wish to peruse Corliss Lamont's edited book
Man Answers Death: An Anthology of Poetry, which

contains 302 poems from the early Greeks and Romans to contemporary times.

Perhaps almost every person thinks in some artistic or romantic way about his or her death, but only a very few of us are able to put organized thoughts on paper in moving poetry. Ted Rosenthal was very lucky that he could. He was very unlucky that he was dying of leukemia. Like some other potentially great young poetic voices (he died in 1972 when he was 34), he had just begun to speak his mind. The threat of death seemed to catalyze his talents. He was able to communicate to us all what the essence of the pain of dying is like. (There is a remarkable film of Ted Rosenthal which is available from Eccentric Circle Cinema Workshop of Evanston, Illinois.) His book of poetry (like the film) is called, poignantly, *How Could I Not Be Among You?* The lines that comprise this Epilogue represent a portion of the first stanza of that work, plus the nine concluding stanzas.

How Could I Not Be Among You?

Ted Rosenthal

My name is Ted Rosenthal.
I am 31.
I live in Berkeley where I have
Lived for the last 10 years.
I was born and raised in New York City.
So I am 31.
I lived well into my thirties.
I can always say that. . . .

Though you may find me picking flowers
Or washing my body in a river, or kicking rocks,
Don't think my eyes don't hold yours.

529

Poetic
Epilogue

And look hard upon them
and drop tears as long as you stay before me
Because I live as a man who knows death
and I speak the only truth
to those who will listen.

Never yield a minute to despair, sloth, fantasy.
I say to you, you will face pain in your life
You may lose your limbs, bleed to death
Shriek for hours on into weeks in unimaginable agony.
It is not aimed at anyone
but it will come your way.
The wind sweeps over everyone.

You will feel so all alone, abandoned,
come to see that life is brief.
And you will cry, "No, it cannot be so,"
but nothing will avail you.
I tell you never to yearn for the past.
Speak certain knowledge.
Your childhood is worthless.
Seek not ritual. There is no escape in Christmas.
Santa Claus will not ease your pain.
No fantasy will soothe you.

You must bare your heart and expect nothing in return.
You must respond totally to nature.
You must return to your simple self.
I do not fool you. There lies no other path.
I have not forsaken you, but I cannot be among you all.
You are not alone
so long as you love your own true simple selves.
Your natural hair, your skin, your graceful bodies,
your knowing eyes and your tears and tongues.

I stand before you all aching with truth
Trembling with desire to make you know.
Eat, sleep, and be serious about life.
To be serious is to be simple;

to be simple is to love.
Don't wait another minute, make tracks, go home.
Admit you have some place to return to.
The bugs are crawling over the earth, the sun shining over everyone.
The rains are pounding, the winds driving.
The breeze is gentle and the grass burns.
The earth is dusty. Go ankle deep in mud.

Get tickled by the tall cattails.
Kick crazily into the burrs and prickles.
Rub your back against the bark, and go ahead, peel it.
Adore the sun.
O people, you are dying! Live while you can.
What can I say?
The blackbirds blow the bush.
Get glass in your feet if you must, but take off the shoes.
O heed me. There is pain all over!
There is continual suffering, puking and coughing.
Don't wait on it. It is stalking you.
Tear ass up the mountainside, duck into the mist.

Roll among the wet daisies. Blow out your lungs
among the dead dandelion fields.
But don't delay, time is not on your side.
Soon you will be crying for the hurt, make speed.
Splash in the Ocean,
leap in the snow.
Come on everybody! Love your neighbor
Love your mother, love your lover,
love the man who just stands there staring.
But first, that's alright, go ahead and cry.
Cry, cry, cry your heart out.
It's love. It's your only path.

O people, I am so sorry.
Nothing can be hid.
It's a circle in the round.
It's group theater,
no wings, no backstage, no leading act.

531

O, I am weeping, but it's stage center for all of us.
Hide in the weeds but come out naked.
Dance in the sand while lightning bands all around us.

Step lightly, we're walking home now.
The clouds take every shape.
We climb up the boulders; there is no plateau.
We cross the stream and walk up the slope.
See, the hawk is diving.
The plain stretches out ahead,
then the hills, the valleys, the meadows.
Keep moving people. How could I not be among you?

NAME INDEX

SUBJECT INDEX

Abandonment, 276, 373-75, 445, 468, 530

Absence, 373, 391

Acceptance: as stage in dying process, 295, 445; as general theme among college students, 415; as aspect of act of denying, 455-56; complications of, 297; fluctuations in, 477; interplay with denial, 447; of death, 475, 479, 483; re appropriate death, 503; re emotions, 294

Accidents, 139, 158, 160, 247, 250-51

Affectlessness, 68, 108

Afterlife, 3-7, 10-11, 58-62, 63-67. See also Immortality; Rebirth; Resurrection

Aggression. See Hostility

Agnosticism, 4, 61

Alienation, 69, 111-12, 116, 427, 467, 505

Ambivalence, 2, 276, 443

Anger: and family, 293-94, 296, 300, 351; as stage in dying process, 445, 514; in psychotherapy, 303, 355, 513; in survivors, 302, 338, 351; of dying person toward relatives, 317

Animism, 403-6

Anxiety: in children, 399; re death, 107, 109, 370, 424, 428; re pain and fear, 445; of parents over child's death, 425

Appropriate death, 447, 471-72, 483, 502-6, 516

Appropriated death, 472, 502-6

Atomic bomb, 69, 99-109, 325. See also Nuclear destruction

Attempts to circumvent death, 19-20, 21-29

Attitudes toward death, 77-82, 366-67, 371, 410-17, 423-29

Autopsy, 198-99, 222, 300. See also Psychological autopsy

Bargaining, 445-46

Bereavement: and effects on physical health, 336-38, 340, 442; and mental illness, 341-43; and families, 322-23, 357, 520-21; as adaptational strategy, 424; as aspect of dying, 332; initial impact of, 361-62; death following bereavement, 335; typical reactions to, 344

"Bet situation," 34

542

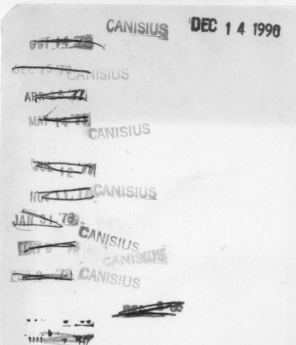